Christian Dimpker

Extended Notation

Christian Dimpker

Extended Notation

The depiction of the unconventional

LIT

This treatise was composed at the Interdisciplinary Centre for Computer Music Research with financial support from the University of Plymouth. http://christiandimpker.de

Bibliographic information published by the Deutsche Nationalbibliothek
The Deutsche Nationalbibliothek lists this publication in the Deutsche Nationalbibliografie; detailed bibliographic data are available in the Internet at http://dnb.d-nb.de.

ISBN 978-3-643-90302-0

A catalogue record for this book is available from the British Library

©LIT VERLAG GmbH & Co. KG Wien,   LIT VERLAG Dr. W. Hopf
Zweigniederlassung Zürich 2013   Berlin 2013
Klosbachstr. 107   Fresnostr. 2
CH-8032 Zürich   D-48159 Münster
Tel. +41 (0) 44-251 75 05   Tel. +49 (0) 2 51-62 03 20
Fax +41 (0) 44-251 75 06   Fax +49 (0) 2 51-23 19 72
E-Mail: zuerich@lit-verlag.ch   E-Mail: lit@lit-verlag.de
http://www.lit-verlag.ch   http://www.lit-verlag.de

Distribution:
In Germany: LIT Verlag Fresnostr. 2, D-48159 Münster
Tel. +49 (0) 2 51-620 32 22, Fax +49 (0) 2 51-922 60 99, E-mail: vertrieb@lit-verlag.de

In Austria: Medienlogistik Pichler-ÖBZ, e-mail: mlo@medien-logistik.at
In Switzerland: B + M Buch- und Medienvertrieb, e-mail: order@buch-medien.ch
In the UK: Global Book Marketing, e-mail: mo@centralbooks.com
In North America: International Specialized Book Services, e-mail: orders@isbs.com
e-books are available at www.litwebshop.de

Contents overview

Table of contents

XI

XV

INTRODUCTION

The origin of this treatise lies within a piece I composed in January 2010 called »Tatsachen in zwei Sätzen«[1] for violin alone. In this work, I utilised a large number of extended instrumental playing techniques. However, the employment of uncommon ways of sound production caused a lot of difficulties. This was because for most of the playing techniques applied in the piece a conventional method of notation had not been established. Hence when wanting to make use of such techniques, one is forced to develop one's own methods or select existing unconventional methods that serve one's needs and explain these sufficiently whilst the interpreters are then confronted with the task of comprehending the new notations before they can start rehearsing. In the course of the year, I further extensively studied the extended playing techniques of woodwinds, the piano, percussion instruments and string instruments during the composition process of a piece called »Entgleisungen«[2] for flute, B♭ clarinet, piano, percussion, violin and violincello as well as a work called »Zu vier Händen – Interventionen für Konzertflügel«[3] for piano and assistance. The examination of the technical instrumental possibilities and methods of their notation resulted in the desire to develop a coherent system of depiction for the unconventional means of instrumental sound production. I thought that such a system would, firstly, simplify the composition process because one would no longer be forced to either develop methods of notation before actually starting with a composition or *ad hoc* invent such methods during the writing of a piece. Secondly, if adopted by other composers, it could not only facilitate their composition process, but also the performance of extended playing techniques because the instrumentalists could become used to these methods of notation. Prior to these works, I had also made initial attempts to utilise electroacoustic elements, such as effects units, in combination with notated acoustic instruments and produced various electroacoustic works for fixed media. When I started to focus completely on notation, I became interested in developing methods of notation that enable the employment of electroacoustic means of sound production, transformation and modulation in a score. But the notation of these processes led to even more difficulties because there are fewer examples of notation and nearly no conventions at all. Additionally, the field of electroacoustic music is – despite having, in contrast to instrumental music, a rather short tradition – vast.

In this work, a coherent and consistent notation system for most of the unconventional elements in music, including extended instrumental playing techniques of the common orchestral instruments and electroacoustic music, is developed with regard to string instruments, wind instruments, percussion instruments, plucked instruments, keyboard instruments and vocal techniques as well as sound synthesis, audio processing and sound recording. In order to fulfil this task, a set of criteria is defined. It may be used to judge previous methods of notation. On the basis of such analyses, new methods that completely agree with the postulations are then designed. The criteria used within this work have evolved during my practice as a composer when studying and developing notation systems for extended playing techniques and electroacoustic music. However, they might not be accepted by all other composers. This is because by implementing them, some methods of notation – that might be regarded as a useful way of depicting unconventional musical elements – are rejected. After defining the criteria, it is, therefore, explained why they are considered to be important, shown which methods of notation are rejected by employing them as well as which methods of notation agree with the premises and hence may be utilised for the development of a coherent system that depicts the unconventional. Nevertheless, it needs to be noted that even though there are good reasons for

---

[1] Facts in two movements.

[2] Derailments.

[3] For four hands – Interventions for grand piano.

postulating these criteria, they remain subjective, and anyone who cannot accept them might not be satisfied with the results of this work. In such a case, other methods may, however, be derived from the presented suggestions and this work be used to study unconventional instrumental playing techniques and the elements of electroacoustic music.

The methods of notation are supposed to be **1. as exact as possible** and **2. as simple as possible**. Moreover, they may **3. not be contradictory to traditional notation, but should instead extend and be closely related to it**. Finally, in order to guarantee that the additions are legitimate and not contradictory, they need to be – as *Dahlhaus* declares – **compatible with, and distinct from, all other signs of the system**[4].

1. The criteria of exactness: it is related to the fundamental function of notation systems, as defined by *Wittgenstein* in the »Tractatus logico-philosophicus«[5]. In this work, *Wittgenstein* equates the natural sciences with musical notations: "[a] gramophone record, the musical idea, the written notes, and the sound-waves, all stand to one another in the same internal relation of depicting that holds between language and the world. They are all constructed according to a common logical pattern"[6]. Generally, all sonic events can be regarded as facts. This is because the production of a sound can be repeated and observed. When the parameters are the same, the experiment will always lead to the same result. However, there are better and worse pictures of facts: "[a] picture agrees with reality or fails to agree; it is correct or incorrect, true or false. (...) The agreement or disagreement of its sense with reality constitutes its truth or falsity"[7]. With regard to music, pictures that agree with reality can be described as exact notations whilst pictures that fail to agree with reality are inexact or approximate. When being in possession of an exact picture of a musical fact, it is possible to re-use it with the certainty that it will always result in the desired sound. Therefore, the criteria of exactness is postulated here. It aims at creating correct depictions of musical facts and developing notation systems that are as clear as the depiction of a tone produced by an acoustic instrument. The verification of this criterion is reliant on conducting several experiments. This means that a method of notation that tries to depict a particular fact is examined by making various performers realise it and hence produce the notated sound. When the results equal each other, a particular method may be described as exact. However, such an observation requires a large number of performers and huge effort. This is why a sufficient number of experiments could not be conducted during the making of this work. But nevertheless, it could be investigated which parameters the production of a particular sound involves and if they are adequately represented in the depiction. The more parameters a particular method of notation describes, the more exact it is. Another limitation to the criterion of exactness is the factor of interpretation, which leads to the creation of versions of the same piece. When interpreting a piece, the performers bring the work into existence by means of artistic expression. This may lead to an uncertainty between the picture of and the realised sonic events. Another reason for the uncertainty between the depiction and the realisation is the human factor of inaccurate performance, e. g. slight deviations between the requested and the actual tempo. However, the liberty of interpretation is always dependent on the exactness of the underlying notation system. The less exact it is, the more will the versions differ from each other and vice versa. Further, inaccuracy is only a small factor when working with highly-trained performers. But

---

[4] Carl Dahlhaus: Notenschrift heute [Notation today]. In: Ernst Thomas (ed.): Notation Neuer Musik [Notation of New Music]. Darmstädter Beiträge zur Neuen Musik IX [Darmstadt's contributions to New Music IX]. Mainz 1965, pp. 9-34, here: pp. 15f.

[5] Cf. Ludwig Wittgenstein: Tractatus logico-philosophicus. Translation by D. F. Pears and B. F. McGuinness. Reprinted with corrections. London et al. 1972, pp. 7-49 [odd pages in English].

[6] Ibid., p. 39.

[7] Ibid., pp. 17 and 19.

nevertheless, it needs to be admitted that the factors of interpretation and inaccuracy limit the exactness of a notation system.

When determining that the developments are supposed to be as exact as possible, two inexact methods of notation called **qualitative notation** and **approximate notation** need to be excluded. To give an example, *Pousseur* makes use of qualitative notation in »Caractères 1a, 1b«[8]. The metre is, in this work, supposed to be derived from numbers, "which appear either in place of normal tempo indications (...) or above the chronometric subdivision in question"[9]. They are "not to be regarded in a strict quantitive sense"[10], but "are symbols for the concrete values of an approximated, progressive scale (...). All these values must be felt as units, whose relations are of a qualitative nature"[11]. By introducing such a method of notation, the performer is liberated from the determination of a strict metre. Further, *Gubaidulina's* »Dots, lines and zigzag«[12] makes use of approximate notation. She does, for instance, not use traditional rests, but six unspecified replacements – 1. ᵕ 2. ᵛᵛ 3. ᵛᵛᵛ 4. ∧ 5. ⌢ 6. ⌐[13] – that need to be interpreted by the instrumentalists. Moreover, two playing techniques are notated in an approximate way: the *glissando* on the piano's bass strings and the pitch bending[14] of the clarinet:

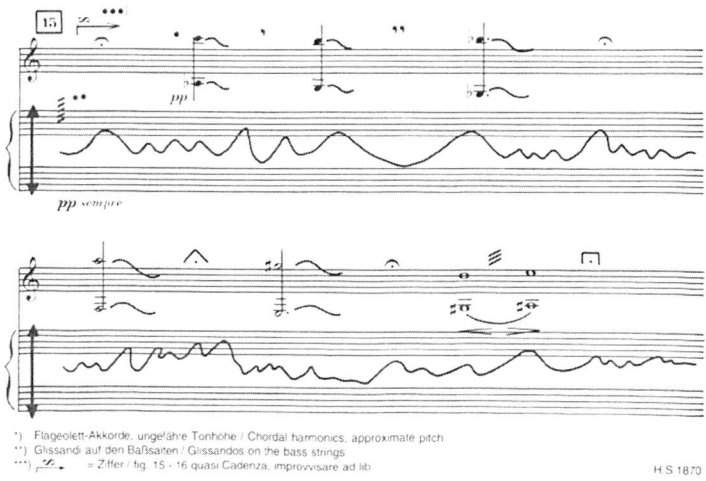

*) Flageolett-Akkorde, ungefähre Tonhöhe / Chordal harmonics, approximate pitch
**) Glissandi auf den Baßsaiten / Glissandos on the bass strings
***) ⌐ = Ziffer / fig. 15 - 16 quasi Cadenza, improvvisare ad lib   H.S 1870

Fig. 1 Gubaidulina, Dots, p. 6.

As can be seen in Figure 1, the range of the bass strings is indicated by a two-headed arrow whilst the *glissando* action is depicted by means of a line that approximately describes the motion the pianist is supposed to perform. Simultaneously, the clarinettist produces harmonics. *Gubaidulina* determines that the pitch of the harmonics is approximate whilst the pitch bending technique is depicted similarly to the *glissando* on the bass strings by a line. However, when postulating exactness, qualitative and approximate notation need to be exclu-

---

8 Henri Pousseur: Caractères 1a, 1b. Piano solo. Vienna 1962.

9 Ibid., no page named [foreword].

10 Ibid., no page named [foreword].

11 Ibid., no page named [foreword].

12 Sofia Gubaidulina: Dots, lines and zigzag. For bass clarinet and piano. Hamburg 1995.

13 Cf. ibid., p. 2.

14 On the clarinet the pitch can be adjusted via changes in lip tension or embouchure and/or opening and closing tone holes. This technique is referred to as pitch bending (cf. Chapter »2. 4 Pitch bending – the extended *glissando*«).

3

ded because – as is apparent from the examples – in both methods the parameters are only approximately indicated[15].

2. The criterion of simplicity: it is related to the introduction of new methods of notation. As mentioned, it is necessary to explain these to performers who are supposed to realise a particular work. Their task is to comprehend the explanation, presumably learn uncommon playing techniques and their notation as well as – after having done so – to rehearse the piece. In order to facilitate the performance, it is therefore reasonable to construct the notation system – which depicts the unconventional elements – in the simplest possible way. However, it needs to be noted that the method of depiction can only be as simple as the sonic material it is trying to depict. When the production of a sound is very complicated because it involves many parameters or complex actions, the method of notation needs to adapt. This criterion can also be verified by conducting experiments. Any experiment, i. e. realisation, helps examine the practicability and hence simplicity of the developments.

3. The criterion of close relation to traditional notation: the postulation of simplicity is linked to the third criterion. This is because the depiction of unconventional sonic events is easier to understand when they are constructed with regard to the common method of notation because instrumentalists are used to traditional notation. By contrast, the introduction of a fundamentally different notation system would cause the performers a great deal of additional work and might lead to rejection or irritation. This might have been the reason why, for example, the reform attempts *Klavarscribo* or *Equitone*, have not been established[16]. Moreover, since the traditional system is, and will be, utilised to depict the conventional elements of music and there is, further, no need to replace it – because the common elements of notated music can be adequately depicted by this system – additional elements can only be introduced when they do not interfere with the conventional elements. When doing so, the unconventional may be combined with the conventional and the interpreters' effort far be reduced. In order to fulfil the third criterion, two main elements of traditional notation, in any case, need to be retained. These are, respectively, traditional durations or the time axis and the instantaneous comprehension. The latter rests upon learnable directions – e. g. *sul ponticello* – symbols – e. g. for the *Bartók pizzicato* – diagrams or schemes (see below). When these can be read and understood in a quick manner, the performer may simultaneously read and play or the recipient read and listen, respectively.

The postulation of the premises 1 and 3 leads to the exclusion of two methods called **graphic notation** and **descriptive notation**. In the lexicon graphic notation is characterised as the final stage of a random and approximate method of notation, which does not indicate any musical relations. Moreover, *Goebels* defines musical graphics as pure drawings without verbal comment or constricting semantic determination of signs. He further adds that graphic notation does not make use of an obligatory sign system[17]. However, most works that make use of graphic notation imply a relation between the utilised signs and the realisation. An example of such a method of notation is *Brown's* »December 1952«[18], which is presented in Figure 2. In the foreword *Brown* explains how the score is supposed to be read: "[t]he composition may be performed in any direction from any point in the defined space for any length of time (...). [T]he thickness of the event indicates the relative intensity and/or (where

---

[15] Cf. Erhard Karkoschka: Notation in New Music. A critical guide to interpretation and realisation. Translation by Ruth Koenig. 1st published in German 1966. New York and Washington 1972, p. 3.

[16] Cf. ibid., pp. 11-15.

[17] Franzpeter Goebels: Gestalt und Gestaltung musikalischer Grafik [Shape and design of musical graphics. In: Melos. Zeitschrift für Neue Musik [Journal for New Music]. Mainz 1972, pp. 23-34, here: p. 23.

[18] Earle Brown: December 1952. For one or more instruments and/or sound-producing media. In: Earle Brown: Folio and 4 systems. New York 1961, no page named.

applicable instrumentally) clusters". Hence even though the interpretation of the score is arbitrary, the drawings have semantic content. In other works of the same kind, as *Logothetis'* »Styx«[19] or *Moran's* »Four visions«[20], the employed signs are, for instance, related to articulations, the dynamic level or the tempo. Generally, what graphic notations have in common is that the interpreter needs to become a composer when performing them[21]. This is because these notations are very inexact and indeterminate. Hence graphic notation can be understood as ambiguous notation[22] and a provocation to improvisation[23]. In most cases, the traditional time axis is, further, non-existent while composers that make use of graphic notation aim rather at replacing traditional notation than at extending it.

Fig. 2 Brown, December 1952, no page named.

[19] Anestis Logothetis: Styx. Composition for any combination of instruments. Cologne 1972.

[20] Robert Moran: Four visions. For flute, harp and string quartet. London 1974.

[21] Cf. Györgi Ligeti: Neue Notation – Kommunikationsmittel oder Selbstzweck? [New notation – medium of communication or self purpose?]. In: Ernst Thomas (ed.): Notation Neuer Musik [Notation of New Music]. Darmstädter Beiträge zur Neuen Musik IX [Darmstadt's contributions to New Music IX]. Mainz 1965, pp. 35-50, here: p. 40.

[22] Cf. Dahlhaus, Notation, p. 30.

[23] Roman Haubenstock-Ramati: Notation – Material und Form [Notation – material and form]. In: Ernst Thomas (ed.): Notation Neuer Musik [Notation of New Music]. Darmstädter Beiträge zur Neuen Musik IX [Darmstadt's contributions to New Music IX]. Mainz 1965, pp. 51-54, here: p. 52.

Further, descriptive notation completely abandons the utilisation of a notation system. The action that leads to a sonic result is, in such a case, depicted by writing it down in the traditional manner[24]. An example of such a method of notation is *König's* electroacoustic composition »Essay«[25]. It mainly consists of technical instructions presented in the form of a book. The sonic material, its transformation and the organisation of the events in time are exactly described in the work. However, the score lacks the time axis and the instantaneous comprehension of traditional notation. Thus graphic notation does not fulfil the second and third criteria because it may be described as approximate, the time axis is often not retained, and it generally aims rather at replacing traditional notation instead of extending it. Further, descriptive notation does not retain the time axis and instantaneous comprehension. Hence it is opposed to the third criterion.

The exclusion of approximate, qualitative, graphic and descriptive notation leaves four main methods of notation that agree with the postulated criteria. They are called **action notation, symbolic notation, diagrammatic notation** and **schematic notation**. The first three methods are commonly used in traditional notation. As mentioned, instantaneous comprehension inter alia rests on learnable directions. When these directions do not indicate the resultant sound, but the action leading to it, action notation is utilised. The instruction *sul ponticello* – (bowing) close to the bridge – does not, for instance, describe the sound itself, which consists of higher partials and implies an increase of bowing noise, but tells the string player what kind of action he needs to perform in order to produce it[26]. However, in order to retain instantaneous comprehension, the length of the directions needs to be limited to a small number of words. Further, the closer they are related to traditional notation, the better do these directions fulfil the third criterion. Moreover, symbolic notation makes use of symbols that depict the performance of particular actions. The symbol for the *Bartók pizzicato* (↻), for instance, requests to pluck the string vertically and make it rebound off the fingerboard, producing a percussive effect that complements the fingered tone. Theoretically, any sonic event might be depicted by symbolic notation. However, in order to fulfil the criterion of simplicity, the performers should not be forced to learn a huge number of new symbols while the process of learning new symbols could be facilitated when they are related to the action they are supposed to depict instead of being an abstract representation of it. Furthermore, traditional notation itself may be regarded as a musical diagram because it is a two-dimensional geometric symbolic representation of sonic events[27]: the (horizontal) x-axis represents time in a geometric symbolic way by utilising sequences of note values or rests, respectively, whilst the (vertical) y-axis represents the pitch or frequency (in tempered notation) by means of the factor $^{12}\sqrt{2}$ and with the help of accidental symbols. However, the traditional musical diagram can be modified in order to notate parameters other than pitch. As long as the time axis is retained extended, or other forms of diagrams, may be used to depict any kind of parameter in accordance with the third criterion. The fourth method of notation, which implies the utilisation of schemes in order to depict a sonic event, has not been commonly used in traditional notation. However, many examples of schematic notation can, for instance, be found in

---

[24] Cf. Karkoschka, Notation, p. 3.

[25] Gottfried Michael König: Essay. Composition for electronic sounds. Vienna 1960.

[26] Cf. Karkoschka, Notation, p. 3.

[27] Diagrams are, as *Brasseur* explains, abstract graphic portrayals of the subject matter they represent. This definition includes any visual formatting device that does not display quantitative data, has simple shapes and is connected by lines, arrows or other visual links. The characteristics of a good diagram were, according to him, elegance, clarity, ease, pattern, simplicity and validity. Moreover, these kinds of visuals are very good at showing actions, processes, events or ideas (cf. Lee Brasseur: Visualizing technical information. A cultural critique. New York 2003, p. 71). In fact, a musical diagram may resemble a scatter plot or line chart whilst one of the coordinates is normally time.

Kagel's »Staatstheater«[28]. As can be seen in Figure 3, *Kagel* makes use of a simple schematic drawing in order to explain that the performer is supposed to open a hollow sphere. This process is then depicted in time by means of traditional durations[29].

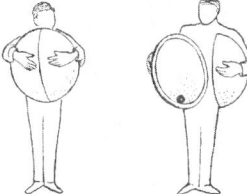

Fig. 3 Kagel, Staatstheater, p. 3 [Repertoire].

Further, schematic notation has, in the form of circuit plans, often been used to notate the disposal of instruments, microphones and loudspeakers in a concert (cf. »Part II: Electroacoustic music – 1. 4. 2 The harmonizer« and »2. 2 Spatialisation« for examples of these). Generally, such schematic notations need to be as exact and simple as possible in order to fulfil the first and second criteria. Additionally, when schemes become part of a score, they have to be – as in the example – depicted by means of a traditional timeline in order to comply with the third criterion. Finally, it needs to be noted that the developments presented in this work are regarded as suggestions that aim at fulfilling the defined criteria. They do not claim to be a universal method of notation, but can instead rather be understood as an initial approach towards the coherent depiction of the unconventional that may be further elaborated, adapted to the needs of the composer who makes use of them or be inspired by the analyses of the techniques.

---

[28] Kagel, Mauricio: Staatstheater. Scenic composition. London 1971.
[29] Cf. ibid., p. 3 [Repertoire].

PART I: EXTENDED INSTRUMENTAL PLAYING TECHNIQUES

The first part of the work presents the development of a coherent and consistent notation system for the unconventional elements in instrumental sound production. This field is divided into chapters on string instruments, wind instruments, percussion instruments, plucked instruments, keyboard instruments and vocal techniques. All extended playing techniques are, in the following chapters, explained with regard to these categories. Moreover, previous approaches towards their notation are analysed concerning their agreement with the criteria defined in the introduction. As a reminder, these criteria are exactness, simplicity and not to be contradictory to traditional notation, but to extend and be closely related to it. Subsequently, suggestions for the notation are presented. They are supposed to fulfil the criteria in the best possible way. As mentioned in the introduction, in notated instrumental music problems evolve when a conventional method of depiction has not been established for a particular playing technique. As is apparent, there are conventions for notating certain elements, such as tones, most harmonics or *glissandi*. However, other elements, such as microtones, are ambiguous since despite having been widely used in contemporary compositions, no definite method of depiction has up to now been established. Again other aspects of instrumental music, such as the instrumental production of most noises, can quite clearly be determined as unconventional due to that either these sounds have been used seldom or their method of notation varies strongly from composer to composer. Whether a conventional method of depiction exists for a particular playing technique can be determined by comparing the methods utilised by the essential composers and referring to the handbooks that grapple with instrumentation. The main references for this part of the work are *Sevsay's* »Handbuch der Instrumentationspraxis«[1] and *Stone's* »Music notation in the twentieth century«[2]. *Sevsay's* work has, despite its impact and importance, unfortunately not yet been translated. Hopefully, an English version will be available soon. When no adequate other examples for the notation of a particular effect may be presented, the suggested method of notation needs to be developed without a previous discussion. However, such cases are generally rare.

1. THE TECHNIQUES OF STRING INSTRUMENTS

String instruments are considered here to be a homogeneous group[3]. The extended playing techniques demonstrated in this chapter only vary slightly from instrument to instrument. Therefore, most methods of depiction can easily be transferred from, for instance, a violin to a contrabass and are explained here in a general way. In the case of a particular playing technique being limited to some of the four instruments, it is outlined which string instruments can be used to perform the technique. In order to limit the extent of the work, this chapter solely focuses on the violin, viola, violincello and contrabass. All historic string instruments, such as the rebab, the viola de braccio or the lira de gamba, are disregarded here. The harp and guitar are discussed in the chapter on plucked instruments. In the case of string instruments, the notation of the *vibrato* and trill, stops, clusters (cf. Chapter »5. 6. 1 Clusters«), the basic *pizzicato* and *Bartók pizzicato,* the basic *glissando*, the common bowing positions and techniques, the application of mutes, the production of harmonics and the *scordatura* (previous to, or simultaneous with, playing) are regarded here as conventional[4]. Their notation can be adopted from the essential handbooks on instrumentation whilst most composers use the

---

1 Ertuğrul Sevsay: Handbuch der Instrumentationspraxis [Handbook of instrumentation practice]. Kassel et al. 2005.

2 Kurt Stone: Music notation in the twentieth century. New York and London 1980

3 Cf. Sevsay, Handbuch, p. 27.

4 Cf. ibid., pp. 27-86.

method of depiction that can be found there. Whereas, the main unconventional elements of sound production presented in this chapter are extended *pizzicato* techniques, extended *glissando* techniques, extended bowing techniques, extended playing positions on the string, playing exceptional spots, extended stopping techniques, percussive effects and preparing the instrument. Concerning the dynamic level of these articulations, indications are – as far as possible – presented when the execution of the action is, in terms of the loudness, limited. As mentioned, the notation of microtones is ambiguous. This is because although microtones have been used frequently in the 20th century, no main method of depiction has been established. In most cases accidentals, derived from the traditional accidentals, are employed. Normally, these symbols are not opposed to the criteria postulated in the introduction. Therefore, and because it is quite unlikely that a general method of notation will be established in the near future, an extensive discussion of microtones is dismissed here. Nevertheless, a suggestion for the notation of microtonal frequencies is presented in »Part II: Electroacoustic music – 1. 1. 1 Periodic wave generators and their envelopes«.

1. 1 Extended *pizzicato* techniques and their notation

Besides the basic *pizzicato* and the *Bartók pizzicato*, there are a number of extended plucking techniques that are more or less notated in a standardised manner. One of them is the performance of a **pizzicato with the left hand**. This technique is either notated by using a plus sign (+)[5] whilst sometimes the addition left or left hand (abbreviated L. H. or LH) is given[6] or – as employed by *Kagel* in »Streichquartett I/II«[7] – by giving the direction *LH: pizz.*[8]. Apparently, the *pizzicato* with the left hand is a variation of the basic *pizzicato*, which is conventionally requested by means of a direction. When depicting it by means of a plus sign, a new symbol is introduced in order to merely request the utilisation of the left hand instead of the right. However, it would be simpler to only present a variation of the original method of notation. Therefore, it is preferred here to depict the *pizzicato* with the left hand similarly to the original articulation, rather than by introducing a new symbol. Hence it is suggested employing the direction *LH: pizz.* or the Italian variants *mano sinistra: pizz.* or *pizz. (mano sinistra)*, abbreviated *m. s.*, in order to notate it. When doing so, this technique is depicted in close relation to traditional notation.

Another simple augmentation of the basic *pizzicato* articulation is achieved by involving the fingernail when plucking the string. This technique is usually requested by means of a fingernail symbol. *Lachenmann*, in »Staub«[9], makes use of such a symbol to depict the **fingernail *pizzicato***:

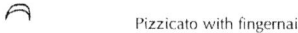 Pizzicato with fingernail

Fig. 1 Lachenmann, Staub, no page named [foreword].

Alternatively, the fingernail symbol may be drawn the other way round[10]. However, since it is not as common as, for instance, the symbolic representation of the *Bartók pizzicato* and may also be utilised in combination with other articulations that involve the fingernails, it should be complemented by the direction *pizzicato*. Moreover, a **pizzicato tremolo** may also

---

[5] Cf. Sevsay, Handbuch, p. 63 and Stone, Notation, p. 313.

[6] Cf. Heinz Holliger: Duo II. For violin and violincello. Mainz et al. 2005, p. 11 or Beat Furrer: Spur. For string quartet and piano. Kassel 1998, no page named [foreword].

[7] Mauricio Kagel: Streichquartett I/II. London 1974.

[8] Cf. ibid., p. 12.

[9] Helmut Lachenmann: Staub. For orchestra. Wiesbaden et al. 1997.

[10] Stone, Notation, p. 313.

be requested. It can be depicted by combining the common *pizzicato* and *tremolo* notation while additionally mentioning the fingers the instrumentalist is supposed to utilise in the same way as on the piano[11], e. g. 1, 2 or 1, 2, 3[12]. Furthermore, it is in some compositions required to pluck the string with a pick instead of with the fingers. *Holliger*, in »Duo II«, requests this **plectrum *pizzicato*** by giving the direction *pizzicato* and presenting a drawing of the plectrum:

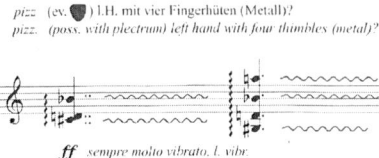

Fig. 2 Holliger, Duo II, p. 11.

The displayed method of notation is related to the depiction of the fingernail *pizzicato*, may easily be comprehended and is often employed. Therefore, it is recommended here being used for the plectrum *pizzicato*. A variant is to hold the violin or viola like a mandolin when plucking it with the plectrum, which is normally requested by the direction *pizzicato al mandolino*[13]. However, when items other than a plectrum are utilised for the performance of a *pizzicato*, no conventional method of notation has been established. The most common item that is used aside from a pick is the screw or nut of the bow. As can be seen in Figure 3, *Cervetti*, in »Zinctum«[14], requests such a **bow-screw *pizzicato*** by giving the direction *pizzicato* with the nut in a footnote[15].

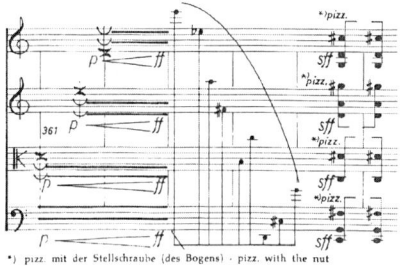

Fig. 3 Cervetti, Zinctum, p. 13.

Moreover, *Lachenmann*, in »Toccatina«[16], depicts a technique referred to as the bow-screw *pizzicato* by means of note heads shaped similarly to the symbolic representation of the *Bartók pizzicato*. However, he explains that the articulation is not performed in the same way as a *pizzicato*, but the player is supposed to hit the fingerboard and string[17]. Therefore, this way of producing sound is discussed in Chapter »1. 3. 2 Extended *battuto* and *tratto* techniques and their notation«. When requesting a *pizzicato* that is performed with the screw of the bow, a method of notation similar to the one employed by *Cervetti* may be used as it fulfils the

---

[11] Cf. Sevsay, Handbuch, p. 65.

[12] 0 = thumb, 1 = index finger, 2 = middle finger, 3 = ring finger, 4 = little finger.

[13] Cf. Sevsay, Handbuch, p. 65.

[14] Sergio Cervetti: Zinctum. For string quartet. Celle 1969.

[15] As is apparent from Figure 3, two or three tones are supposed to be plucked simultaneously by each player. However, since such an action is impossible to be performed, presumably an *arpeggio* symbol is missing.

[16] Helmut Lachenmann: Toccatina. Study for violin alone. Wiesbaden et al. 2006.

[17] Cf. ibid., no page named [Appendix].

requirements of simplicity and exactness. However, in order to achieve a greater degree of instantaneous comprehension, it may be more appropriate to notate the direction (bow-)screw *pizzicato/pizzicato della vite*, over the the note instead of in a footnote or to depict the screw of the bow by a symbol:

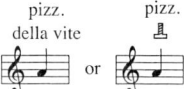

Fig. 4 The bow-screw *pizzicato*.

If any other item, e. g. a nail file, pencil or metal rod, is supposed to be used for the production of a *pizzicato*[18] and hence a so-called **pizzicato with items** is employed, its notation can be achieved similarly to the method of depiction displayed in Figures 2 and 4 (also cf. Figure 8). However, it needs to be noted that a graphic depiction of the item contains, in most cases, a greater degree of instantaneous comprehension.

Further, there is a *pizzicato* variant that may be referred to as the **lateral *Bartók pizzicato***. In this case, the player is supposed to pull the lowest string to the side instead of upwards. When doing so, the string bounces back on the fingerboard and may even hit its adjacent string. The articulation sounds best on violincellos and contrabasses[19]. *Sevsay* suggests that this technique should be depicted by means of a previously defined symbol or verbal explanation, but does not mention any examples. As this articulation is closely related to the more common *Bartók pizzicato*, it can, however, easily be depicted by means of a variation of the symbol used for its notation (↔) and common note heads that determine which string is supposed to be plucked (the C-string in the case of the violincello and the E-string in the case of the contrabass). Moreover, *Sevsay* mentions another technique called the pinch-*pizzicato*, which refers to the string being plucked by two fingers. However, because the sound-wise result is not very different from the common way of performing a *pizzicato*, this technique is neglected here and regarded rather as a means of expression. Further, three other techniques that are related to performing the *pizzicato* articulation – *pizzicato* behind the bridge, *pizzicato* in the pegbox and the buzz-*pizzicato* – are discussed in Chapters »1. 4 Extended playing positions on the strings«, »1. 5 Playing exceptional spots« and »1. 6 Extended stopping techniques«.

1. 2 Extended *glissando* techniques

The basic *glissando* (notation: *gliss.* and a line) is regarded here as to include *pizzicato glissandi*, chordal *glissandi*, harmonic *glissandi*, microtonal *glissandi* etc.[20] whilst the unconventional *glissando* techniques are considered here to be the performance of a **harmonic-*glissando* without bowing** and the **bow-*glissando***.

1. 2. 1 The harmonic-*glissando* **with bowing and its notation**

Lachenmann, in »Pression«[21], makes excessive use of the harmonic-*glissando* without bowing. He explains that the cellist is supposed to use the tips of his fingers to slide – quasi *flageolet* – up and down on the string. In order to depict this motion, *Lachenmann* utilises a »bridge clef«. This special clef is in his compositions employed "when not the pitch but the

---

[18] Cf. Sevsay, Handbuch, p. 66.

[19] Ibid., p. 66.

[20] Cf. ibid., pp. 59f.

[21] Helmut Lachenmann: Pression. For one cellist. Cologne 1972.

place on the surface of the instrument (...) is indicated"[22]. The motion the player is required to perform is – as is apparent from Figure 5 – represented by a line. Moreover, the traditional timeline is replaced by division lines whilst a "division line represents a quarter-note value"[23]. In the example, the cellist plays on the bridge (for this technique cf. Chapter »1. 4 Extended playing positions on the strings«) and simultaneously moves the tip of one finger, after the duration of a minim and two triplet quavers, initially on string I [I. Saite] up and down. When bowing on the bridge, stopping does not modify the sound production by the bow. Therefore, two distinct sounds can be perceived, the bowing noise and the sliding noise. When the player is supposed to slide on more than one string, additional lines are utilised. In the end of the example, the cellist is supposed to slide on string I and II.

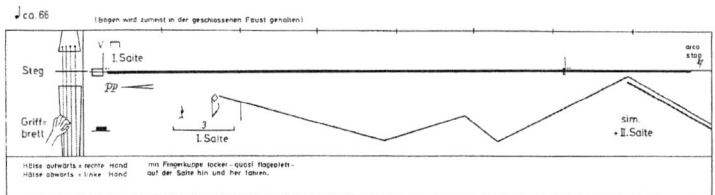

Fig. 5 Lachenmann, Pression, p. 2.

However, *Lachenmann's* approach does not comply with the first and third premise: both the duration and the length of the *glissando* are only depicted in an approximate way whilst the traditional timeline is dismissed. The action *Lachenmann* requests is, however, simply a *glissando* that involves harmonic fingering and is performed without using the bow. Hence it can be depicted in the same way as, for instance, a common harmonic-*glissando* when determining that the player is, in this case, not supposed to bow. Because the exact duration could then be notated by means of common note heads (as it is partially done in »Pression«) and the length of the *glissando* be determined more accurately by means of pitch-based notation, the articulation may be requested in a more exact and even simpler manner as well as in closer relation to traditional notation. Therefore, the harmonic-*glissando* without bowing is suggested here being requested by means of pitch-based notation. As is apparent from Figure 6, diamond-shaped note heads are used for the depiction of the motion (also cf. Chapter »1. 6. 2 Exact muting stops and their notation«). This is because these note heads are also used for the notation of artificial harmonics and certain natural harmonics. The direction *senza arco* (which is related to the direction *arco* that requests normal bowing) determines that the bow is not utilised. Hence when performing this articulation only the scratching noise that is produced by the fingers sliding on the strings can be heard. Moreover, in this work, the *glissando* – in order to achieve a greater clarity and enable the depiction of *glissando* motions that do not involve changes in pitch (see below) – is requested by means of an arrow and not in the traditional manner. Alternatively, the common method of depiction may be restored. In Figure 6, a cellist is supposed to perform a continuous harmonic-*glissando* without bowing. The starting point is the »h/B3« on the A-string. For the duration of a dotted crotchet the player is required to perform a motion to »c²/C5«, followed by a motion to »eb¹/Eb4«, which is performed for the duration of a crotchet. Subsequently, a motion to »f²/F5« is executed for the duration of a crotchet. When this position is reached, the player starts sliding on the A- and D-string simultaneously: from »b¹ – f²/Bb4 – F5« to »g¹ – d²/G4 – D5« for the duration of a quaver and finally to »c#² – ab²/C#5 – Ab5« for the duration of another quaver. The demisemiquaver is applied pro forma since the sound production actually ends at this point.

---

[22] Lachenmann, Toccatina, no page named [appendix].

[23] Lachenmann, Pression, p. 1.

12

Fig. 6 The harmonic-*glissando* without bowing.

This articulation can only be performed with a very low dynamic level. Moreover, it needs to be noted that the interval of the »harmonic chords« is constantly a fifth. Especially when more than two fingers are involved, this interval (or, in the case of the contrabass, a fourth) should be chosen in order to facilitate the performance of this articulation. A variant of this articulation is to perform the motion directly on the fingerboard and hence in between the strings. In this case, the player is supposed to **scratch the fingerboard**. This technique is notated here in the same way as the harmonic-*glissando* without bowing. However, in order to outline that the action is supposed to be executed directly on the fingerboard, the additional direction *il tasto* (the fingerboard) is given. Hence the notes depict in this context fingerboard positions. As can be seen in Figure 7, the cellist is supposed to place three fingers in between all four strings (*tra A, D, G e C*) and execute a single motion from the position »a♭ – e♭^{1} – b^1 – f^2/A♭3 – E♭4 – B♭4 – F5« to »h – f♯^{1} – c♯^{2} – a♭^{2}/B3 – F♯4 – C♯5 – A♭5« for the duration of a crotchet (the demisemiquaver is again applied pro forma). This articulation may be performed with a higher dynamic level than the harmonic-*glissando*.

Fig. 7 Scratching over the fingerboard.

Another variant is to perform a **harmonic-*glissando* with items**, e. g. a sponge, bottleneck, pencil etc. These items can be depicted in the same way as they are in the case of the *pizzicato* with items and hence by means of a drawing. In the example presented in Figure 8, the cellist is supposed to use the rough side of a sponge in order to slide on all four strings. The dynamic level of such an articulation is normally low, but varies from item to item. Moreover, when using, for instance, a bottleneck, simultaneous bowing or plucking the string would lead to a clearly perceivable *glissando* sound while the notes then depict the pitch that is produced. In this case, the direction *senza arco* needs to be replaced by the direction *arco* or the direction *pizzicato* and – if appropriate – common note heads with small circles above them should be used.

Fig. 8 The harmonic-*glissando* with a sponge.

1. 2. 2 The bow-*glissando*

The extended *glissando* articulations displayed in the previous chapter are related to a bowing technique that may be referred to as bow-*glissando*, elliptic bowing or the rotating bow. When this technique is applied, the player is supposed to move the bow not only from the left to the right or right to the left (here designated as horizontal), but also up and down/away from and towards the body (here designated as vertical). This technique has been employed in various compositions and is, in most cases, limited to the three common bowing positions. Further, more seldom utilisations of the bow-*glissando* are to make the player slide the bow on the fingerboard or to solely request a vertical shift, which does not involve any horizontal motion.

1. 2. 2. 1 Previous methods of notation

In *Dittrich's* »Streichquartett III«[24] all four strings move the bow simultaneously from *sul tasto* to *ordinario* for the duration of a dotted semiquaver and back to *sul tasto* for the duration of another dotted semiquaver. This vertical motion is notated by connecting the bowing position with arrows:

Fig. 9 Dittrich, Streichquartett III, p. 85.

Moreover, *Haubenstock-Ramati*, in »Séquences«[25], uses a similar method of depiction in order to make a violinist constantly change the bowing between the indicated areas[26]. In the example presented in Figure 10, the player at first repetitively moves the bow between the positions *sul tasto* and *ordinario*. Then he is supposed to play only on the *ordinario* position, before moving the bow from *sul tasto* to *ordinario* to *sul ponticello* to *ordinario* etc.

---

[24] Paul-Heinz Dittrich: Streichquartett III. Nacht-Musik. Wiesbaden et al. 1995.

[25] Roman Haubenstock-Ramati: Séquences. Music for violin and orchestra. London 1961.

[26] Cf. Howard Risatti: New music vocabulary. A guide to notational signs for contemporary music. Chicago and London 1975, p. 78.

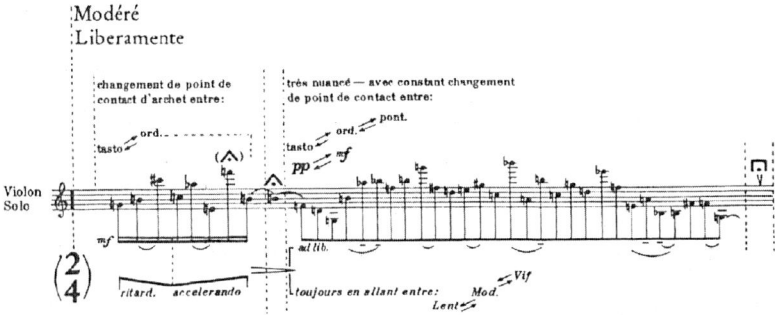

Fig. 10 Haubenstock-Ramati, Séquences, p. 27.

Further, *Lachenmann*, in »Gran torso«[27], makes augmented use of the vertical bowing motion. He depicts this articulation by again employing a bridge clef. Additionally, he introduces drawings that request various complex motions, such as an irregular motion in the form of an »eight«, an irregular circular motion, an oblique motion or a vertical motion[28]. In the example presented in Figure 11, a violinist is supposed to perform a bow-*glissando* in between the *sul ponticello* [Steg] position and a fingered chord. The action starts on the G-string (III) and is then translocated to the D-string (II). Two drawings are additionally employed. The first one requests an irregular circular motion and the second one an irregular motion in the form of an eight[29]. The plus sign expresses that "the indicated direction does not annul the previous motion, but increases it"[30]. When these drawings occur, the motion seems to involve all four strings.

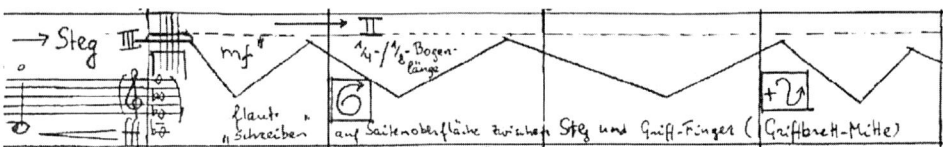

Fig. 11 Lachenmann, Torso, p. 3.

Lachenmann explains that normally the "shifts of the bow on the surface of the string are oblique, that is, they always contain an upbow or downbow motion"[31] whilst "[v]ertical shifts of the bow at an angle of 90° to the usual horizontal motion occur only where an arrow pointed upwards or downwards is drawn into the first note tail of (..) a passage"[32]:

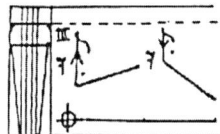

Fig. 12 Lachenmann, Torso, no page named [foreword].

---

[27] Helmut Lachenmann: Gran torso. Music for string quartet. Wiesbaden 1972.

[28] Cf. ibid., no page named [foreword].

[29] Cf. ibid., no page named [foreword].

[30] Ibid., no page named [foreword].

[31] Ibid., no page named [foreword].

[32] Ibid., no page named [foreword].

Further, *Dittrich*, in his »Streichquartett III«, also employs presumably a solely vertical motion[33] by introducing a special note head that requests to wipe over the string with the bow[34]. The articulation is always performed simultaneously by all four instruments on string IV while the extent of the motion is not determined[35]:

Fig. 13 Dittrich, Streichquartett III, p. 34.

1. 2. 2. 2 Discussion

Dittrich's approach (cf. Figure 9) may be described as simple and exact. However, it does not comply with the third criterion: the gradual change of the bowing position is regarded here as a *glissando* because the bow travels on the string in a similar way as the fingers, for instance, in the case of the harmonic-*glissando* do. Therefore, it is preferred to depict a change in the bowing position by means of requesting a *glissando* between these. When doing so, the technique is requested in close relation to traditional notation. The same applies to *Hauben-stock-Ramati's* method of notating a continuous switch between two common bowing positions (cf. Figure 10). Actually, this action may be referred to as a trill-*glissando* because the bow is repetitively moved between the positions *sul tasto* and *ordinario*. Hence it could be notated by combining the method of notation for trills and *glissandi*. Further, his approach towards the depiction of such a trill-*glissando* between all three common bowing positions may be described as containing redundant elements. This is because there is no need to mention that the bow passes the ordinary bowing position when travelling from *sul tasto* to *sul ponticello* and the other way round. Additionally, both methods need to be augmented when the bow is supposed to travel further down the fingerboard. *Lachenmann* depicts such an extended bow-glissando by means of the bridge clef (cf. Figure 11). However, since the motions, as mentioned, resemble a harmonic-*glissando*, it may, in this case, also be stated that there is no need for introducing a special clef in order to notate them. Instead, they can be depicted in the same way as the harmonic-*glissando* with items (cf. Figure 8) and hence by means of the pitch-based notation system. Further, with regard to the vertical shifts that do not involve any horizontal motion, another method of notation needs to be developed. This is

---

[33] *Dittrich* does not clearly outline if this motion is complemented by horizontal bowing. But since the articulation only occurs in combination with a low dynamic level (cf. Dittrich, Streichquartett III, pp. 34f.), it is assumed here that solely vertical bowing is supposed to be performed.

[34] Dittrich, Streichquartett III, p. 2.

[35] Cf. ibid., pp. 34f.

because *Lachenmann's* method of adding symbols to the note tail (cf. Figure 12) might lead to confusion when semibreves are employed and *Dittrich's* approach towards the notation of such a wiping (cf. Figure 13) is inexact because he does not outline whether the articulation involves horizontal bowing or not and the extent of the bow-*glissando* is not determined.

1. 2. 2. 3 Suggestion for the notation of the bow-*glissando*

Thus vertical motions of the bow are depicted here by means of the *glissando* notation. In order to outline that the bow (and not the hand) travels on the string, the additional direction *glissando d'arco* is given. In the example presented in Figure 14, the method of notation for the bow-*glissando* on the common bowing positions is displayed. A violinist is supposed here to bow a »c¹/C4« whilst moving the bow from *sul ponticello* to *sul tasto* for the duration of a dotted crotchet and to *ordinario* for the duration of a quaver. After a crotchet rest, a trill-*glissando* between *sul tasto* and *sul ponticello* is performed for the duration of a minim. During this second bow-*glissando*, the player fingers a »g¹/G4«. In the case of combining the trill-*glissando* of the bow with a normal trill(-*glissando*), an additional trill(-*glissando*) symbol would have to be used and placed below the one for the bow.

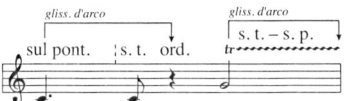

Fig. 14 The bow-*glissando* on the common positions.

Moreover, when the bow is supposed to leave the common bowing positions and slide on the fingerboard, an additional notation system needs to be used. This second system is placed above the one that depicts the stops. As can be seen in Figure 15, the violinist is supposed to finger the same tones as in the previous example, but this time moves the bow from *sul ponticello* to the position »a¹/A4« on the fingerboard for the duration of a dotted crotchet and subsequently performs a trill-*glissando* with »h¹/B4« (double sharp) for the duration of a quaver. After a crotchet rest, the player starts bowing the D-string on position »a¹/A4« and hence close to the fingered »g¹/G4«. The bow is then moved to the normal position for the duration of a dotted crotchet, which is subsequently bowed for the duration of a quaver.

Fig. 15 The extended bow-*glissando*.

Diamond-shaped note heads are employed here because the bow is – as in the case of the harmonic fingering – attached to the string, but does not depress it. It needs to be noted that the further the bow travels down the fingerboard, the more difficult it becomes for the player to bow one string only. This inexactness of performance might result in additional strings being bowed (especially when fingering tones on the middle strings). Further, when, for instance, two strings are supposed to be bowed simultaneously, two notes need to be employed. In the case of their interval being a fifth (or, in the case of the contrabass, a fourth), the bow is aligned at right angles to the string. When changing this interval, the alignment of the bow is altered. Such an alteration may also be performed during the performance of the bow-*glissando*. Further, when sliding onto the fingerboard, it is possible to make the player bow more than two strings at the same time. Additionally, the introduced method of notation may be used to request the player to bow on a lower position than the tone he fingers, i. e. closer to the pegbox[36]. Alternatively, the additional notation system could also be used to depict the duration of the bow-*glissandi* on the common bowing positions independently (cf. Figure 6 in the chapter on plucked instruments).

A variant of this motion is, as mentioned, to perform a vertical shift without any horizontal motion. Its notation is achieved here by simply giving the additional direction *non tratto*. When doing so, it needs to be noted that the dynamic level is – except for when exaggerated bow pressure is applied (cf. Chapter »1. 3. 1 Exaggerated bow pressure«) – always relatively low. The articulation can be reversed by either giving the direction *tratto* or *arco*. Further, vertical motions can also be executed by means of the hand itself or any kind of item. In such a case, the player needs to place down the bow. The method of notation introduced in the previous chapter (cf. Figure 8) may then be employed for the right hand. Further, it is theoretically possible to notate any kind of complex vertical bowing motion on the string by means of a second notation system. However, because one would have to constantly determine the string to which the depicted position is related, the appearance of the score would become confusing. Therefore, it is suggested here employing a variant of depiction, which enables the notation of switching strings during a vertical shift. In this method the strings upon which the bow is not placed are bracketed whilst a tetrad of fifths (or fourths) is the home position. As can be seen in the example presented in Figure 16, a violinist is supposed to attach his fingers to all strings on position »a♭ – e♭¹ – b¹ – f²/A♭3 – E♭4 – B♭4 – F5« (for a detailed explanation of such muting techniques see Chapter »1. 6 Extended stopping techniques«) for the duration of a semibreve. Simultaneously, a bow-*glissando* is performed: in the beginning solely vertical bowing is applied since the direction *non tratto* is given. The motion starts on the fingerboard. Because the two highest notes of the additional notation system are bracketed, the player applies the bow to the G- and D-string on position »g¹ – d²/G4 – D5«. By passing the A-string, the bow is then moved down to »a²/A5« on the E-string for the duration of a crotchet. Hence the violinist needs to switch strings during the shift and performs a kind of oblique motion. Subsequently, the bow is moved to position »e³/E6« on the same string for the duration of another crotchet. When this position is reached, horizontal bowing (*tratto*; down-bow) complements the vertical shift, and the dynamic level is suddenly increased from *piano pianissimo* to *mezzopiano*. The bow is then moved to position »a¹ – e♭²/A4 – E♭5« on the A- and D-string. Whilst moving the bow down, the player needs to additionally turn his wrist since the interval is reduced to a tritone. Subsequently, the violinist performs a motion to the common *sul tasto* position (up-bow).

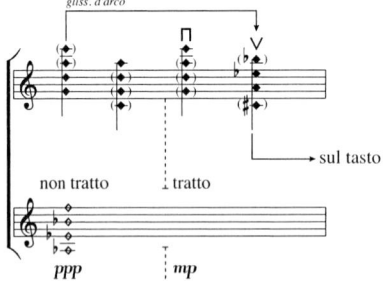

Fig. 16 Complex motions during the extended bow-*glissando*.

---

36 Cf. Gardner Read: Contemporary instrumental techniques New York and London 1976, p. 210.

When the bow-*glissando* is performed on the common bowing positions, it is not possible to make the player turn his wrist since the alignment on the strings is not depicted. Moreover, when bowing one of the two outer strings in the area of the body, the player might be forced to additionally bow the body (cf. Chapter »1. 5. 4 Bowing the body of the instrument«). Further, the bow-*glissando* may also be performed in combination with bowing techniques, such as *tremolo*, *col legno battuto*, *col legno tratto*, *gettato* etc. whilst the paradigm for the performance of complex motions on the string may be used to depict all complex variants of the harmonic-*glissando* without bowing. Further, solely vertical *glissandi* may, for example, be performed with the wood of the bow, the screw (*glissando della vite*) or items in combination with a left-hand *pizzicato*.

Finally, there is an uncommon variant of the bow-*glissando* that can only be performed on the violincello and the contrabass. When requested, the player is supposed to place the bow in the space between fingerboard and body (*dietro il tasto*) and scratch the back of the finger-board either with the hair or the wood of the bow. Such a vertical shift does normally not involve any horizontal motion. When employing this articulation, it may be useful to present an image of the action:

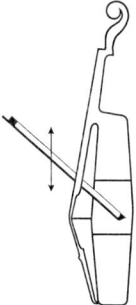

Fig. 17 Placing the bow between fingerboard and body.

In Figure 17, it can be seen that a cellist is supposed to attach the wood of the bow to the back of the fingerboard and move it up and down. This **bow-*glissando* dietro il tasto** is depicted here by a notation system similar to *Lachenmann*'s bridge clef. A special method of depiction needs to be used because the motion cannot be related to pitch. It consists of two components, a traditional timeline and a representation of the length of the fingerboard's back. The timeline is employed in order to establish a stronger relation to traditional notation whilst arrows depict what kind of motion the player is supposed to perform.

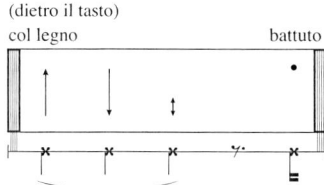

Fig. 18 The bow-*glissando dietro il tasto*.

As is apparent from Figure 18, the cellist initially moves the bow up (here: towards the peg-box) for the duration of a crotchet and then back down for the duration of another crotchet. Subsequently, a two-headed arrow is employed. It requests the execution of a similar motion to the one previously defined as trill-*glissando*. Since all articulations are connected by a *legato* slur, they need to be performed in a continuous way and hence without releasing the bow. The dynamic level of these actions is always low. After a dotted quaver rest, the player is finally required to perform a *col legno battuto*. The point that is supposed to be hit with the bow's wood is depicted by a dot (also cf. Chapter »3. 2. 6 Playing the snares«).

1. 3 Extended bowing techniques

Besides the basic bowing techniques, such as *legato, portato, staccato, gettato, tremolo* etc., as well as the basic *col legno battuto* and *tratto*, there are a number of extended techniques that are deprived of a conventional method of notation. These are the **exaggerated bow pressure**, **extended *battuto* and *tratto* techniques**, the articulations *saltando*, *balzando* and *toccato* and the **rolling bow**.

1. 3. 1 Exaggerated bow pressure

The technique of applying exaggerated bow pressure is often employed. When requested, the player is supposed to increase the string tension, e. g. by means of the right thumb[37], and/or apply more pressure to the string as usual. The resulting sound may be described as rough and scratchy[38], a dry rattling[39] or noisy and grating[40].

1. 3. 1. 1 Previous methods of notation

The articulation is notated in many different ways. One is to employ a special note head, as utilised by *Ferneyhough* in »Incipits«:

Exaggerated bow pressure with slow movement of bow over string: a noisy, grating sound with little specific pitch content. Finger the pitches specified.

Fig. 19 Ferneyhough, Incipits, no page named [foreword].

Further, *Dittrich* makes in his »Streichquartett III« use of two different note heads that depict two degrees of bow pressure, high [starker] and extremely high bow pressure [mit überstarkem Bogendruck]:

starker Bogendruck, gepreßt

mit überstarkem Bogendruck

Fig. 20 Dittrich, Streichquartett III, p. 3.

Another method is to complement the note by a symbol. For instance, *Crumb*, in »Echoes of time and the river«[41], makes use of a symbol that resembles the depiction of a *vibrato*. As is apparent from Figure 21, a gradual decrease of the bow pressure is depicted by a direction and changing the shape of the line (see the four lowest notation systems).

---

[37] Sevsay, Handbuch, p. 82.

[38] Ibid., p. 82.

[39] Lachenmann, Torso, no page named [foreword].

[40] Brian Ferneyhough: Incipits. Solo viola, percussion and six instruments. London et al. 2002, no page named [foreword].

[41] George Crumb: Echoes of time and the river. Four processionals for orchestra. New York 1986.

molto vibr. sempre
gliss.
fff intense!
molto vibr sempre
Violin II
Viola
gradually go to normal bowing
Apply great pressure to bow while moving it very slowly!
(normal bow position)
molto

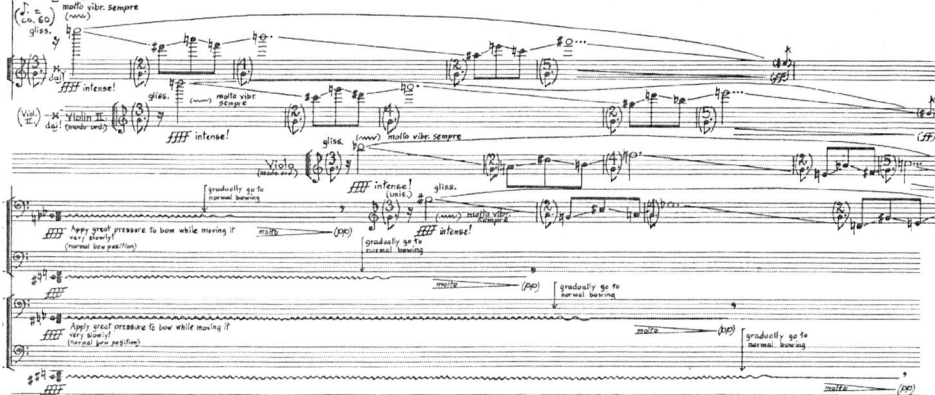

Fig. 21 Crumb, Echoes, p. 12.

Moreover, *Lachenmann*, in »Staub«, notates the technique in a similar manner. Here the symbol may be clearly differentiated from a *vibrato*, but no degrees of pressure are determined:

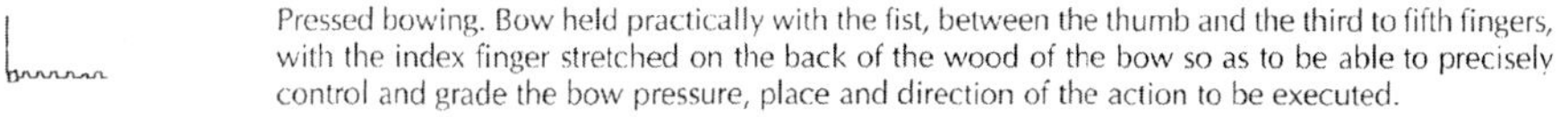

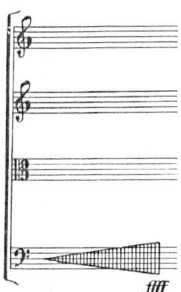

Pressed bowing. Bow held practically with the fist, between the thumb and the third to fifth fingers, with the index finger stretched on the back of the wood of the bow so as to be able to precisely control and grade the bow pressure, place and direction of the action to be executed.

Fig. 22 Lachenmann, Staub, no page named [foreword].

Further, *Henze*, in his »4th string quartet«[42], utilises no note heads, but a symbol that replaces the note:

Fig. 23 Henze, 4th string quartet, p. 7.

Finally, some composers place symbols over the note that is supposed to be bowed with exaggerated pressure. Most commonly, they are derived from the common up-bow and down-bow symbol. Examples for this can, for instance, be found in *Holliger's* »Vier Lieder ohne Worte«[43] or *Kagel's* »Streichquartett I/II«[44] and »Match«[45]:

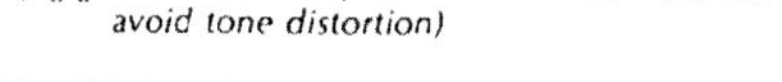

excessive pressure of the bow (do not avoid tone distortion)

Fig. 24 Kagel, Match, p. 4.

---

[42] Hans Werner Henze: 4th string quartet. Mainz 1976.

[43] Cf. Heinz Holliger: Vier Lieder ohne Worte. Mainz 1987, p. 15.

[44] Cf. Kagel, Streichquartett I/II, p. 2.

[45] Mauricio Kagel: Match. For three players. London 1967.

1.3.1.2 Discussion

Concerning the first approach of depicting exaggerated bow pressure by means of special note heads, it may be said that *Dittrich's* method (cf. Figure 20) may be preferred from the one by *Ferneyhough* (cf. Figure 19) since it is more exact with regard to notating different degrees of bow pressure. However, it may generally be difficult to request the transition between two degrees of pressure or sounds that already require special note heads, such as harmonics, in combination with exaggerated bow pressure when employing such a method of notation. Moreover, each of the three note heads cannot be used in the case of notating minims or semibreves. Further, when compared, *Lachenmann's* method of complementing the note by a symbol (cf. Figure 22) may be preferred from the one by *Crumb* (cf. Figure 21). This is because *Crumb's* method makes use of a symbol that is normally employed to request *vibrati*. Hence such an addition can, as mentioned, not be regarded as legitimate since it is not distinct from another sign of the system even though an unrelated action is depicted. In order to guarantee consistency, only similar articulations should be depicted by similar symbols and all signs used in a distinctive way. However, despite being preferred from *Crumb's* method, *Lachenmann's* approach lacks exactness when concerned with the notation of different pressure degrees as well as with the depiction of the action's exact duration. Further, the extension of *Lachenmann's* method by more than one pressure degree – as it is kind of applied by *Henze* (cf. Figure 23) – would still remain inexact because the duration of the action was not clearly indicated. Additionally, *Henze's* approach barely enables the depiction of the fingering. A more exact variant of notation would place a symbol over the note and depict the fingered pitch rather than replacing or complementing the note head. In the case of requesting exaggerated bow pressure by a means of a symbol, a simple method would be quickly identifiable as a depiction of the articulation it requests. Since the symbol displayed in Figure 24 is stronger related to applying pressure to the bow, it is preferred here from the ones introduced by *Lachenmann* and *Henze*. However, it would have to be further extended when depicting more than one pressure degree (e. g. by means of an additional up-bow or down-bow symbol) whilst the transition between pressure degrees could then be depicted by utilising *de-/crescendo* symbols. Nevertheless, the extended up-bow or down-bow symbol would, due to its relation to bowing techniques, always refer to string instruments. Hence when requesting increased pressure in any other context another sign would have to be introduced and, by doing so, the number of symbols be increased. Therefore, a general symbol for the increase of pressure – which may also be utilised when requesting similar actions on other instruments[46] – is in the following chapter introduced.

1.3.1.3 Suggestion for the notation of exaggerated bow pressure

Two degrees of bow pressure – 1. Increased pressure and 2. Highest possible pressure – are used here and, as is apparent from Figure 25, depicted by two similar symbols. A low pressure could analogously be depicted by means of two white arrows.

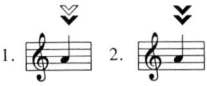

Fig. 25 The pressure degrees.

---

[46] The increase of bow pressure is the only unconventional articulation the symbol is used for in this work. However, pressure degrees may, for instance in the case of producing multiphonics on woodwinds, be employed in order to request an increased lip tension or blowing pressure.

In Figure 26, the player is supposed to bow a semibreve »a¹/A4« and, while doing so, increase the bow pressure from »increased pressure« to »highest possible pressure« for the duration of a crotchet . Subsequently, the bow pressure is decreased to the ordinary level – which is requested by the direction *arco* – for the duration of a minim. For the rest of the note's duration, common bow pressure is applied.

Fig. 26 The *de-/crescendo* of pressure degrees.

The dynamic level is always high when applying exaggerated bow pressure. Furthermore, this technique may complement the bow-*glissando*[47], including the solely vertical variant (cf. Chapter »1. 2. 2 The bow-*glissando*«).

1. 3. 2 Extended *battuto* and *tratto* techniques and their notation

There are a number of ways to extend the normal *col legno battuto* and *tratto*. In the case of the former, the hit on the strings may also be performed by applying the bow's wood and hair simultaneously (notation: 1/2 *legno battuto* or *mezzo legno battuto*)[48] or only the bow's hair (notation: *col arco battuto*)[49]. Similarly, the latter technique may also simultaneously involve the bow's wood and hair (notation: *1/2 legno tratto* or *mezzo legno tratto*)[50]. Since these three articulations derive from, and are strongly related to, the common *col legno battuto* and *tratto*, they can be notated in the same way: by employing the displayed directions.

However, there are some extended *battuto* articulations that need to be examined more thoroughly. One is to hit the string (and fingerboard) with the screw of the bow. The most common way of applying such a ***battuto* with the screw** can – as in the case of the bow-screw *pizzicato* (cf. Figure 4) and in accordance with all other *battuto* techniques – be requested by the direction *colla vite battuto* or a symbolic representation of the screw (and the direction *battuto*):

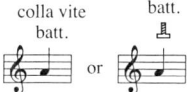

Fig. 27 *Battuto* with the screw.

However, the displayed method of depiction needs to be further augmented when the hit is supposed to be performed on the fingerboard. This articulation is applied by *Lachenmann* in »Toccatina«. As can be seen in Figure 28, a violinist is, during the performance of such actions on the fingerboard, supposed to constantly mute the E-, A- and G-string as well as to finger the first node of the fifth partial on the D-string (cf. Chapter »1. 6. 2 Exact muting stops and their notation«). Moreover, *Lachenmann* makes use of squared note heads to depict the position on the fingerboard where the screw hits the string and, if needed, a second transposed notation system. As mentioned, he additionally employs a technique designated by him as screw *pizzicato*, which is depicted by means of note heads that resemble the shape of a *Bartók*

---

[47] As, for instance, requested in Helmut Lachenmann: „.... zwei Gefühle ...", Musik mit Leonardo. For speakers and ensemble. Wiesbaden et al. 2002, pp. 1f., 7, 9-12 etc.

[48] Cf. Kagel, Match, p. 3.

[49] Cf. Lachenmann, Torso, no page named [foreword].

[50] Cf. Brian Ferneyhough: Third string quartet. London et al. 1988, p. 3.

pizzicato symbol and refer to the position where the player mutes the strings with the left hand. However, this action may rather be regarded as a *battuto* since the screw of the bow is used to knock on the fingerboard and, when doing so, slightly touches the string before the fingerboard is hit[51/52].

Dämpfgriff nicht zu locker, damit die Tonhöhen der „Schrauben-Pizzicati" hörbar sind
Muting stop, not too loose, firm enough to enable the pitch of the "screw pizzicati" to be heard

Fig. 28 Lachenmann, Toccatina, p. 3.

As shown in Chapter »1. 2. 2 The bow-*glissando*«, bowing on the fingerboard is, in this work, depicted by means of an additional notation system and diamond-shaped note heads. Diamond-shaped note heads are used because the string is not depressed. This is also the case when playing a *battuto* with the screw on the fingerboard. Moreover, since the screw *pizzicato* was defined here as rather being a *battuto*, and the hit on the fingerboard is related to the harmonic-*glissando il tasto* (cf. Chapter »1. 2. 1 The harmonic-*glissando* without bowing and its notation«), there is no need to introduce a special note head and refer to the muting stop when hitting the fingerboard. In order to notate the described articulations in a uniform manner, *Lachenmann's* approach needs to be slightly altered: in Figure 29, the first »bar« of the example presented in the previous figure, is adapted to the manner the bow-*glissando* was notated in Figure 15. Hence the exact duration of the muting action is given and diamond-shaped note heads are used instead of squared ones while *battuto* on the fingerboard is uniformly depicted by means of an additional notation system and the direction *battuto*. Further, the symbol for the screw *pizzicato* is replaced by two connected note heads and the direction *il tasto* (which requests – as in the case of the harmonic-*glissando il tasto* – to play the fingerboard itself).

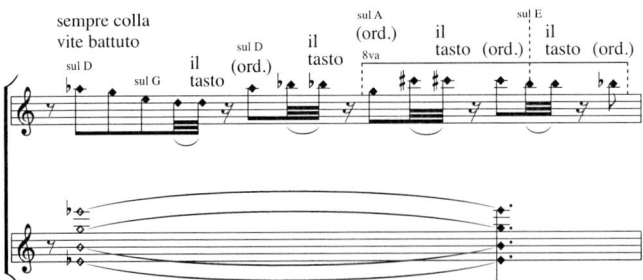

Fig. 29 *Battuto* with the screw on the fingerboard.

---

[51] Lachenmann, Toccatina, no page named [appendix].

[52] The English translation of the appendix is, in this case, confusing because it is explained that the "screw of the bow knocks on the fingerboard and touches the string at the same time" even though these actions are in the original German version clearly indicated as being successive.

In the example, the player is required to constantly hit the string (or fingerboard) with the bow's screw (*sempre colla vita battuto* or, alternatively, a symbol for the screw and the direction *sempre battuto*) and four times slightly touches the string before the fingerboard is hit. In order to restore the original articulation, the direction *ordinario* is given. The direction is employed in brackets because it does not refer to the ordinary bowing position, but the *battuto* on the string. This method of notation may also be applied in the case of any other right hand articulation on the fingerboard – e. g. ordinary bowing, *pizzicato* or *col legno battuto* – and may additionally be employed in the case of the left-hand *pizzicato* (cf. Chapter »1. 1 Extended *pizzicato* techniques and their notation«).

Another articulation is to utilise items other than the bow to hit the strings. This **battuto with items** is inter alia employed by *Kagel* in »Streichquartett I/II«. As can be seen in Figure 30, a cellist is supposed to hit the string close to the bridge with a knitting needle [mit Stricknadel am Steg geschlagen]. Additionally to giving the direction *battuto sul ponticello*, *Kagel* makes use of a triangular symbol that represents the needle.

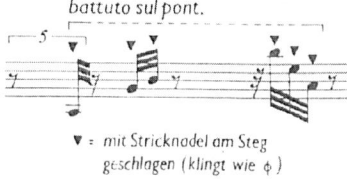

Fig. 30 Kagel, Streichquartett I/II, p. 12.

As is apparent, *Kagel's* method of notation complies with the method employed for the depiction of the *pizzicato* with items. However, since the symbol *Kagel* utilises in Figure 27 is commonly used for the plectrum *pizzicato* (cf. Figure 2), another symbol – which is more strongly related to the actual shape of a knitting needle – should be chosen.

Finally, it is also possible to produce tones by fingering the strings without bowing. When doing so, the finger needs to strongly hit the string and push it against the fingerboard[53]. This articulation is also sometimes referred to as tapping. *Sevsay* suggests that it should be notated by means of a circled plus sign:

Fig. 31 Sevsay, Handbuch, p. 81.

However, since this action resembles the ordinary *battuto* articulation and can be compared to the performance of a left-hand *pizzicato*, it is rather regarded here as a **left-hand battuto** than a special manner of sound production. Therefore, it is suggested notating it, according to the left-hand *pizzicato*, as an extended *battuto* articulation by the direction *battuto (mano sinistra),* abbreviated *batt. (m. s.).* Since the string is depressed and the fingered pitch evolves, a common note head needs to be employed:

Fig. 32 Left-hand *battuto*.

---

[53] Sevsay, Handbuch, p. 81.

Two or more fingers may, in the case of this technique, also be involved as well as variations, such as a trill, trill-*glissando* or *vibrato* without bowing, be performed. In the case of requesting trills or *vibrati*, it might be useful to additionally explain that the action is performed *senza arco*[54]. Further, another extended *battuto* technique, referred to as strokes on the string, is discussed in Chapter »1. 7 Percussive effects«. This is because it is strongly related to a percussive technique designated as stop attack or dead stroke.

1. 3. 3 The *saltando*, *balzando* and *toccato* and its notation

There are a further three more articulations that may be regarded as variations of the common *col arco/legno gettato* and *col arco/legno battuto*. *Lachenmann* makes use of these and defines them adequately. **Saltando**: "[d]ense shake of the bow after striking the string. (...) It is particularly important to avoid muddying the envisaged (...) pitches by accidental horizontal motions of the bow during the shake"[55]. **Balzando**: "A gentle »bouncing« of the bow on the string by its own weight. This produces a very gradual accelerando of the bouncing sound"[56]. Both actions may be performed *col arco* and *col legno*. *Lachenmann* further utilises two different methods for their notation: in »Klangschatten – mein Saitenspiel«[57] a special note (and the addition *legno saltando*) is used for the depiction of the *col legno saltando*[58], but none of the other techniques are applied[59], whereas in »Gran torso« the articulations are notated by giving the directions *saltando*, *legno saltando* and *arco balzando* (whilst the *legno balzando* does not occur)[60]. Further, in the case of the balzando articulation, *Lachenmann* differentiates between a bowed and an unbowed performance: "[i]n this performance technique, a vertical arrow in the note tail (..) signifies that an up- or down-bow motion should be avoided"[61]. However, since the described techniques may, as mentioned, be regarded as variations of the *col arco/legno gettato* and *col arco/legno battuto* and these articulations are conventionally depicted by means of directions, the introduction of special notes would mean to give up a close relation to traditional notation. Moreover, it would result in a more complex notation system. Hence in order to notate these articulations in a uniform manner, they are requested here by means of directions:

col arco   col legno   col arco   col legno
salt.   salt.   balz.   balz.

Fig. 33 The *saltando* and *balzando* techniques.

Furthermore, concerning the *balzando*, the unbowed performance of this technique is regarded here as the standard variant. In order to request a bowed performance, the direction *gettato* may be used in combination with a low dynamic level, which then requests not to throw the bow, but merely requires the combination of the *balzando* bouncing with an up- or down-bow motion. As a reminder, the *gettato* may generally be only performed with a high dynamic level. However, a soft variant of this technique may also be executed[62]. In such a

---

[54] Cf. ibid., p. 81.

[55] Lachenmann, Torso, no page named [foreword].

[56] Ibid., no page named [foreword].

[57] Helmut Lachenmann: Klangschatten – mein Saitenspiel. For 48 strings and 3 grand pianos. Cologne 1978.

[58] Cf. ibid., p. 19.

[59] Cf. ibid., no page named [foreword].

[60] Cf. Lachenmann, Torso, no page named [foreword], pp. 1 and 4f.

[61] Ibid., no page named [foreword].

[62] Cf. Sevsay, Handbuch, p. 41.

case, the bow rather bounces on the string instead of being thrown. The lower the dynamic level, the less forceful is the initial attack. A variant of notation would be to introduce a special direction for the soft *gettato* analogously to the differentiation between the *saltando* (which can be regarded as an unbowed *gettato*) and *balzando* (which can be regarded as an unbowed soft *gettato*). The *saltando*, analogously, cannot be performed with a very low dynamic level and the *balzando* not with a very high dynamic level whilst higher dynamic levels are generally produced by using the wood of the bow. Moreover, it needs to be noted that the *saltando* may be kept going: "[t]he phase of the most rapid bouncing up and down is prevented from dying out when the bow is tossed upwards again and again by a minimal and highly sensitive push in a down-bow motion – nothing more than a minute horizontal frictional resistance. The dense final phase of the rapid bouncing then perpetuates itself in this manner without interruption ad infinitum"[63]. Its notation can be achieved by simply utilising longer durations and *ad libitum* the direction *perpetuo*, meaning that the action is performed in a perpetual way. Additionally, all motions may be performed vertically and on the fingerboard.

The third variation, here designated as **toccato**, can only be performed *col legno*. A sound effect is achieved when the previously struck string is still vibrating. The technique is most effective on the cello and contrabass. *Lachenmann*, in »Klangschatten – mein Saitenspiel«, makes use of this technique only in combination with contrabasses: "[a]fter the left hand has jerked the string sharply, place the bow stick very gently on the string. The vibrating string should thus clatter loudly upon contact with the wood of the bow. In order to have the rattling sound last as long as the given duration, the contact of the bow stick with the vibrating string must be brought about very cautiously"[64]. He depicts the *legno toccato* [legno berühren] by means of a special note tail, which is complemented by a sign resembling a »Z«:

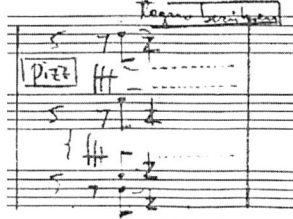

Fig. 34 Lachenmann, Klangschatten, p. 35.

However, the *col legno toccato* is – as are the *saltando* and *balzando* articulations – strongly related to traditional bowing techniques. Therefore, it is suggested here not depicting it by means of a special symbol, but requesting it by means of a direction. The point of attachment may be either determined by means of the three common bowing positions or – in the case of attaching the bow on the fingerboard – in the same way as the bow-*glissando* and hence by means of an additional notation system and diamond-shaped note heads (cf. Chapter »1. 2. 2 The bow-*glissando*«). In the example presented in Figure 35, the *toccato* articulation is depicted. A contrabassist initially plays a *pizzicato sul tasto* on the open E-string with the dynamic level *fortissimo*. After the duration of a quaver, he subsequently performs a *col legno toccato* on the same position. Moreover, the *legato* slur underlines that the string lingers on when the player starts touching it with the wood of the bow. The dynamic level of the *col legno toccato* is always dependent on the dynamic level of the preceding articulation and cannot be varied.

---

[63] Lachenmann, Torso, no page named [foreword].
[64] Lachenmann, Klangschatten, no page named [foreword].

sul tasto
pizz.   col legno toccato

Fig. 35 The *col legno toccato*.

Additionally, it is also possible to execute a ***col legno toccato* with the screw** (*colla vite toccato*) or **with items**. A method of notation for these actions can be derived from the previous examples (cf. Figure 4 for the screw *pizzicato* and Figure 27 for the *battuto* with the screw, Chapter »1. 1 Extended *pizzicato* techniques and their notation« for the *pizzicato* with items and the previous chapter for the *battuto* with items). Further, another *toccato* articulation, referred to as the buzz-*pizzicato*, is discussed in Chapter »1. 6. 2 Exact muting stops and their notation«. This is because it is strongly related to the depiction of muting stops.

1. 3. 4 The rolling bow and its notation

The technique designated as the rolling bow is rarely used in compositions. When requested, the bow is attached to the string normally, but "the wood of the bow pressed into the hair of the bow (...). As a result of the rolling motion of the pressed wood of the bow, the combined friction of the bow hair, the string and the wood of the bow produces a dryly crackling grinding" [65].

In »Arco« [66] *Lehmann* employs this technique, but only gives a verbal explanation and explains that this and other articulations "can be distributed freely" [67]. Moreover, *Lachenmann* gives the verbal explanation: press the wood into the hair (slow rolling motion) – grinding [Stange ins Bogenhaar gedrückt (langsame Rollbewegung) – knirschend] and uses a zigzag line that replaces the note head in order to depict the action:

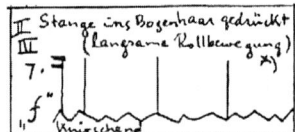

Fig. 36 Lachenmann, Torso, p. 2.

Apparently, *Lehmann's* approach is very approximate and, therefore, does not meet the requirement of exactness. Further, the complementation or replacement of a note by a symbol, such as the one introduced by *Lachenmann*, leads – as mentioned – to inexactness. This is because the duration of the action is not clearly indicated. Even though note tails are used in the example, minims and semibreves could not be depicted. Therefore, it is suggested here placing such a symbolic representation of the rolling bow over the note rather than replacing or complementing the note head. Nevertheless, the symbol seems to be adequate since the motion is related to the performance of a *vibrato*, which is notated by a waved line. Moreover, the strings that are involved in the this articulation need to be depicted. As is apparent from Figure 36, *Lachenmann*, therefore, makes use of Roman numerals. However, the strings could also be notated by means of a pitch-based system and hence in closer relation to traditional

---

[65] Lachenmann, Torso, no page named [foreword].

[66] Hans Ulrich Lehmann: Arco. For violin. In: Eckart Schloifer (ed.): Pro musica nova. Studies for playing contemporary music. For violin. Wiesbaden 1986, pp. 27-31.

[67] Ibid., p. 27.

notation. Such a method is suggested here. As the influence of stops is negligible, the position of the bow is depicted by notating the open strings. In Figure 37, a contrabassist is supposed to attach the bow to the A- and E-string and perform a rolling bow articulation, which results in a grinding with the dynamic level *mezzoforte* and the duration of a semibreve. The optional direction *rotolato* (rolled) is additionally employed in order to emphasise what kind of motion the player is supposed to execute.

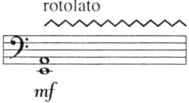

Fig. 37 The rolling bow.

Moreover, it may be requested to let the strings vibrate after the action (*lasciar vibrare*) or to execute an irregular rolling motion (*irregolare*) while speed levels may also be introduced. Further, the rolling bow may be performed on the fingerboard, behind the bridge or on the body (cf., for instance, Figure 29 for the notation of playing on the fingerboard, Chapter »1. 4. 4 Playing behind the bridge« for playing behind the bridge and Chapter »1. 5. 4 Bowing the body of the instrument« for the rolling bow articulation on the body). Finally, left-hand *pizzicati* or *battuti* may complement the articulation. They would then have to be depicted in a distinct notation system.

1. 4 Extended playing positions on the strings

This chapter focuses on uncommon bowing positions and stops on the strings, including the **highest possible tone, fingering in between fingerboard and bridge, bowing on the bridge, playing behind the bridge/on the tailpiece** and **fingering behind the bridge**. Because it is often employed as an extended *glissando* technique, bowing on the fingerboard has been introduced in Chapter »1. 2. 2 The bow-*glissando*«. Moreover, it is also discussed in Chapter »1. 3. 2 Extended *battuto* and *tratto* techniques and their notation«.

1. 4. 1 The highest possible tone and its notation

In New Music the ordinary range of string instruments is often exceeded. *Sevsay* mentions that composers, for instance, notate a (written) »c⁴/C7« or even »c♯⁴/C♯7« for the contrabass. Moreover, the highest possible tone is often also requested[68]. In such a case, *Sevsay* suggests the following method of notation:

Fig. 38 Sevsay, Handbuch, p. 30.

This depiction of the highest possible tone may be described as nearly conventional. There are only slight differences between the methods composers employ: For instance, *Szalonek*, in »Concertino«[69], also makes use of triangular note heads pointing upwards to notate this articulation. However, he clearly indicates on which string the highest possible tone is supposed to be fingered:

---

[68] Cf. Sevsay, Handbuch, p. 30.
[69] Witold Szalonek: Concertino. For flute and chamber orchestra. Warsaw 1965.

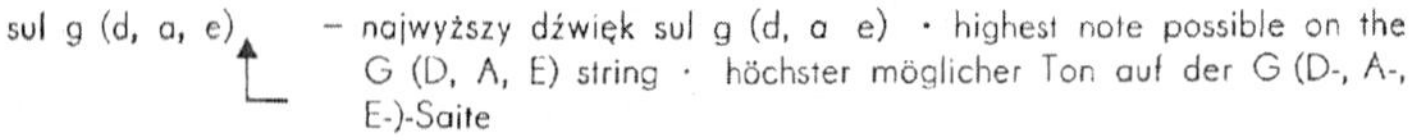

sul g (d, a, e)   – najwyższy dźwięk sul g (d, a e) · highest note possible on the
G (D, A, E) string · höchster möglicher Ton auf der G (D-, A-,
E-)-Saite

Fig. 39 Szalonek, Concertino, p. 4.

Further, *Cervetti*, in »Zinctum«, depicts the string upon which the highest possible tone is fingered by means of the notation system[70]:

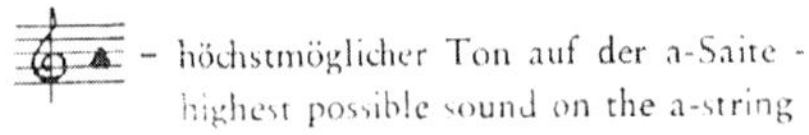

– höchstmöglicher Ton auf der a-Saite -
highest possible sound on the a-string

Fig. 40 Cervetti, Zinctum, no page named [appendix].

Since *Szalonek's* and *Cervetti's* methods imply a determination of the string, they are more exact and enable the production of more tones than *Sevsay's* method. However, there is no need to dismiss the traditional notation system – as is the case in *Szalonek's* approach – and *Cervetti's* method could be specified by exactly depicting the note's duration. Moreover, with regard to the notation of the string, it may be said that both alternatives are simple and exact. Consequently, *Sevsay's* method could be simply complemented by a determination of the string in order to be as exact as the other ones. For these reasons, two suggestions for the notation of the highest possible tone (on the A-string of a violin) are presented in Figure 41. The second method may be used preferably in the case of requesting the player to switch strings in fast succession.

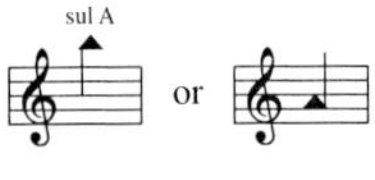

sul A

or

Fig. 41 The highest possible tone.

Further, the highest possible harmonic may also be requested. It can vary according to the technical capability of the player[71] and consequently be notated in the same way as the highest possible tone:

sul A

or

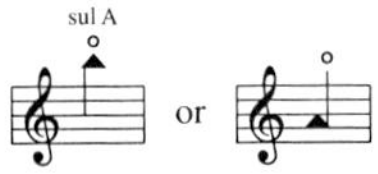

Fig. 42 The highest possible harmonic.

1. 4. 2 Fingering in between fingerboard and bridge and its notation

When the left hand leaves the fingerboard and moves into the space between the fingerboard and bridge, the method of notation needs to be augmented. This is because the sounds that evolve no longer have a definite pitch, and the position on the string may not be determined by means of pitch-based notation. When fingering in between fingerboard and bridge, squeaky sounds are produced.

In »Firebird«[72] *Pröve* utilises this playing technique. As can be seen in Figure 43, the fingers slide from the fingerboard into the space between the bridge and fingerboard [Zwischen Steg u. Griffbrett]. At this point, an additional notation system is introduced. This system, which is referred to as the string clef system here, no longer depicts the pitch, but the position

---

[70] This example may refer to a violin or viola.

[71] Sevsay, Handbuch, p. 80.

[72] Bernfried Pröve: Firebird. For violin alone. Celle 1993.

of the fingers on a particular string (string I of a violin in the example) by means of note heads derived from the notation of the highest possible tone. In the example, the finger constantly slides up and down the E-string for the duration of five semiquaver quintuplets, eight demi-semiquavers and seven semiquaver septuplets. Moreover, it seems as if three positions are depicted. The violinist plays the *glissando* in between the fingerboard and bridge in the order of the lowest position, middle position, lowest position, middle position, lowest position, highest position, middle position etc.

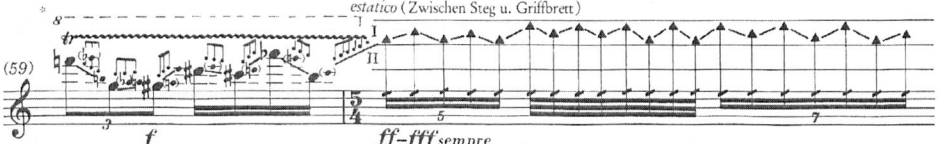

Fig. 43 Pröve, Firebird, p. 7.

Concerning the agreement with the requirements, *Pröve's* approach may be described as closely related to traditional notation and simple. This is because the note heads he employs are derived from the (nearly) conventional way of notating the highest possible tone and the notation system he uses may be easily comprehended. However, his approach lacks exactness because it is unclear how many fingering positions there are in between fingerboard and bridge. Moreover, an additional grid would have to be introduced in order to clearly depict these positions. But at the same time, the introduction of a grid – and hence the addition of lines – would complicate the string clef system. Therefore, *Pröve's* approach towards the notation of the articulation is augmented here by defining exact positions and depicting these by means of a slightly varying string clef system and accidentals. The system employed here consists of five lines and replaces the traditional system instead of being placed over it. Each spacing in between the lines refers to one of the four strings. For each string instrument four distinct stops are determined: position 1 can be described as the closest to the fingerboard. It is depicted by the accidental »♭«. The next position is located further to the bridge and is required when no accidental is employed. These positions may be fingered when bowing *ordinario* or *sul ponticello*. Moreover, positions 3 and 4 can be only fingered when bowing *sul ponticello*. They are depicted by the accidentals »♯« and »𝄪« whilst position 4 (double sharp) is located closer to the bridge. In the example presented in Figure 44, the string clef system of a violin is displayed. The positions are depicted in the order of position 1 on the G-string, position 2 on the D-string, position 3 on the A-string and position 4 on the E-string.

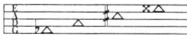

Fig. 44 Fingering in between fingerboard and bridge.

Concerning the positions, there is no distinction made between the string instruments in order to retain uniformity. This means that even though it might be possible to produce more sounds on a contrabass by fingering more than four positions, it is neglected in order to enable the application of the same method of notation for all four string instruments. However, when a five-stringed contrabass is used, an additional string needs to be introduced to the string clef system (also cf. Figure 4 in the chapter on plucked instruments). Further, all common bowing techniques, such as *legato*, *tremolo*, *gettato*, *battuto* etc., as well as all normal fingering techniques, such as *vibrato*, the trill, *glissando* etc., can be employed when playing in between the fingerboard and bridge.

1. 4. 3 Bowing on the bridge

When bowing on the bridge, a whirring sound with indefinite pitch evolves[73]. This articulation is employed by various composers. When requested, the player is normally supposed to additionally mute the strings in order to keep them from vibrating[74].

1. 4. 3. 1 Previous methods of notation

Despite the articulation having been used frequently, no definite method of notation has yet been established. *Sevsay* suggests employing either a traditional notation system or a string clef system, a special symbol (which resembles the shape of the bridge) added to the note tail and x-shaped note heads:

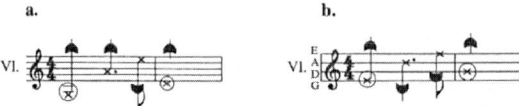

Fig. 45 Sevsay, Handbuch, p. 58.

This method of notation resembles the one utilised by *Lachenmann* in »Mouvement (– vor der Erstarrung)«[75]. In this piece he makes use of a note head shaped like a semicircle (depicting the bridge) and a black square to request this playing technique. However, *Lachenmann* does not determine the strings the player is supposed to bow. As can be seen in Figure 46, a circled plus sign further complements the depiction of this playing technique. It is employed in order to emphasise that the strings are muted when bowing on the bridge.

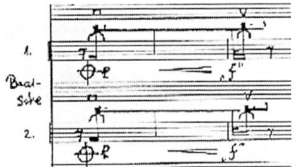

Fig. 46 Lachenmann, Mouvement, p. 1.

Furthermore, as already displayed in Figure 5, *Lachenmann*, in »Pression«, also makes use of a bridge clef to depict the articulation. As a reminder, the traditional timeline is replaced by division lines whilst each line represents a crotchet[76]. In order to determine that the player is supposed to bow the A-string, *Lachenmann* gives the verbal explanation string I [I. Saite]:

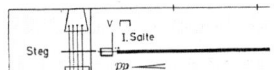

Fig. 47 Lachenmann, Pression, p. 2.

Moreover, *Holliger* requests the articulation by means of a special note head shaped like a bridge, but does not clearly indicate which strings are supposed to be bowed:

---

[73] Sevsay, Handbuch, p. 58.

[74] Cf. Lachenmann, Staub, no page named [foreword].

[75] Helmut Lachenmann: Mouvement (– vor der Erstarrung). For ensemble. Wiesbaden 1985.

[76] Cf. Lachenmann, Pression, p. 1.

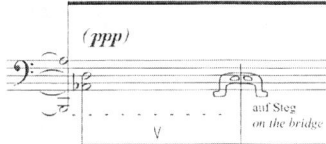

Fig. 48 Holliger, Duo II, p. 21.

Another method of notation is employed by *Dittrich* in his »Streichquartett III«. As can be seen in Figure 49, playing directly on the bridge [direkt auf dem Steg spielen] is requested by a squared note head and a special tail. The string is, in the piece, depicted by means of the traditional system[77].

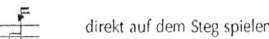
direkt auf dem Steg spielen

Fig. 49 Dittrich, Streichquartett III, p. 2.

1. 4. 3. 2 Discussion

Sevsay's approaches towards the notation of playing on the bridge (cf. Figure 45) may both be described as complying with the requirements. They are simple, exact and closely related to traditional notation. However, as is apparent from the example, it might be confusing to add a symbol to the note tail when semibreves or additional *tremolo* symbols are employed. Therefore, it is preferred here to solely use a special note head to request the articulation. Moreover, in order to achieve a uniform method of notation for all playing positions on the string that produce an indefinite pitch, the string clef system is favoured from the traditional system. Concerning *Lachenmann's* first method of notation (cf. Figure 46) it may be said that it is not able to depict minims and semibreves. Additionally, the utilised strings could be only depicted by means of directions. Moreover, his second approach (cf. Figure 47) is not closely related to traditional notation. Further, the bowed string(s) may generally be depicted in a simpler manner by means of the string clef rather than by the bridge clef system. *Holliger's* approach (cf. Figure 48) may be judged similarly because it does not enable the depiction of minims and semibreves. Additionally, the determination of the strings by means of the notation system becomes complicated when using such a complex note head. In opposition, *Dittrich's* approach (cf. Figure 49) – which resembles the one by *Sevsay* – agrees with the postulated requirements since it is simple, exact and closely related to traditional notation. However, when the squared note head already clearly requests the articulation, there is no need for utilising a symbol added to the note tail, which might, as mentioned, cause confusion. In order to ensure that the note head distinctly depicts the playing technique, it needs to be distinct from all other note heads of the system. Further, in order to retain uniformity, the string clef system is, as mentioned, in this context preferred from the traditional system.

1. 4. 3. 3 Suggestion for the notation of bowing on the bridge

Hence it is in the following chapter suggested employing the string clef system and a special note head in order to depict the technique of bowing on the bridge. The note head employed for the depiction of this playing technique is derived from the one employed by *Lachenmann* in »Pression« and *Dittrich* in his »Streichquartett III«. This is because it is a commonly applied note head and kind of symbolises a middle stage between fingering in between fingerboard and bridge (which is, as is apparent from Figure 44, depicted by triangular note

---

[77] Cf. Dittrich, Streichquartett III, pp. 58f.

heads pointing upwards) and fingering behind the bridge (which is, as shown in the following chapter, requested by triangular note heads pointing downwards). In Figure 50, the suggested method of notation for playing behind the bridge is presented. In the example, a violinist is supposed to initially bow the D- and G-string on the bridge for the duration of a minim and subsequently play a succession of quavers on the A-, G-, D- and E-string. These quavers are played *staccato*. Other common playing techniques can also be employed when bowing on the bridge. However, it needs to be noted that it becomes difficult to bow exactly on the bridge when, for instance, a *gettato* is requested. Moreover, a *col legno battuto* would solely result in the wood of the bow hitting the wood of the bridge.

Fig. 50 Bowing on the bridge.

Muting the strings when bowing on the bridge is regarded here as the common way of executing this playing technique. Therefore, an additional symbol, as applied by *Lachenmann* in »Mouvement (– vor der Erstarrung)« (cf. Figure 46), is not utilised. Moreover, when the open strings are supposed to sound during, or at some point of the articulation, the direction *lasciar vibrare* may be given. The impact of fingering tones whilst bowing on the bridge is negligible. However, it is possible to bow with one half of the hair on the bridge and with the other half on a very extreme *sul ponticello* position. When doing so, tones mix with the indefinite whirring sound. This articulation may be depicted by means of traditional notation and squared note heads in combination with common note heads. Two note heads are applied here because two articulations/sounds mix. A variant of notation is to depict the additional bowing position by means of a direction. This fourth position could be designated as *il ponticello*. In Figure 51, the open A-string of a violin is bowed in this manner. Stops could, as usual, be requested by transposing the common note head.

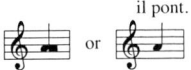

Fig. 51 Bowing on the bridge and *sul ponticello* simultaneously.

1. 4. 4 Playing behind the bridge

When playing behind the bridge, squeaky sounds with indefinite pitch evolve[78]. Despite being one of the most important playing techniques in New Music[79], no conventional method of notation has yet been established.

1. 4. 4. 1 Previous methods of notation

Sevsay suggests notating the articulation of playing behind the bridge similarly to bowing on the bridge and hence by means of a symbol added to the note tail and x-shaped note heads:

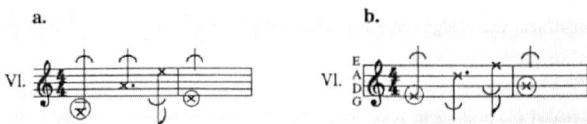

Fig. 52 Sevsay, Handbuch, p. 58.

---

[78] Sevsay, Handbuch, p. 58.

[79] Samuel Adler: The study of orchestration. 3rd edition. New York and London 2002, p. 49.

A similar method of depiction is employed by Crumb in »Echoes of time and the river«. He makes use of a traditional notation system and employs x-shaped note heads to request the articulation:

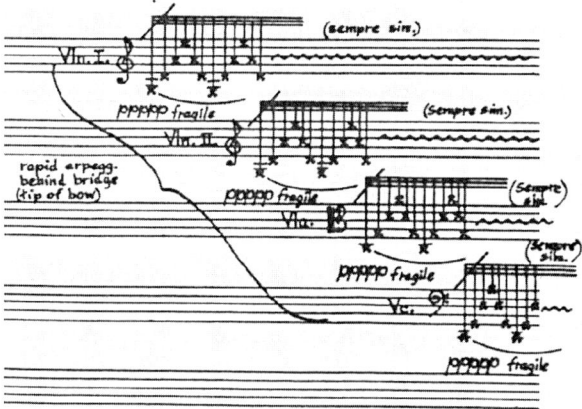

Fig. 53 Crumb, Echoes, p. 9.

The same method is applied by *Maderna* in »Widmung«[80]. In the example presented in Figure 54, a violinist is supposed to pluck the G- and D-string of a violin behind the bridge.

Fig. 54 Maderna, Widmung, p. 6.

Moreover, in »Threnody«[81] *Penderecki* utilises the symbol *Sevsay* adds to the note tail in order to replace the note head:

zwischen Steg und Saitenhalter spielen
   play between bridge and tailpiece

Fig. 55 Penderecki, Threnody, p. 3.

Another note head is applied by *Lachenmann* in »Klangschatten – mein Saitenspiel«. The strings are, in this case, depicted by means of Roman numerals:

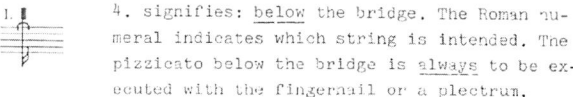

4. signifies: below the bridge. The Roman numeral indicates which string is intended. The pizzicato below the bridge is always to be executed with the fingernail or a plectrum.

Fig. 56 Lachenmann, Klangschatten, no page named [foreword].

Further, in »Pression« *Lachenmann* again makes use of the bridge clef in order to notate a vertical motion of the bow behind the bridge:

[80] Bruno Maderna: Widmung. For violin alone. Milan 1976.
[81] Krzysztof Penderecki: Threnody. To the victims of Hiroshima. For 52 strings. London et al. 1961.

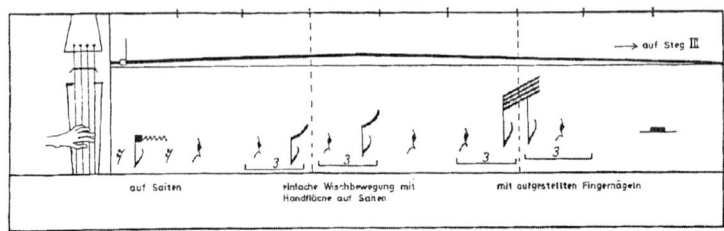

Fig. 57 Lachenmann, Pression, p. 6.

1. 4. 4. 2 Discussion

The methods of notation employed for playing behind the bridge resemble the ones applied for bowing on the bridge and may be judged similarly: hence with regard to *Sevsay's* methods (cf. Figure 52), it is preferred to request the technique by means of the note head instead of by adding a symbol to the note tail as well as to utilise the string clef instead of the traditional system. The note head may be x-shaped, as in the case of *Crumb's* and *Maderna's* approach (cf. Figures 53 and 54), but should rather not look like the symbols employed by *Penderecki* and *Lachenmann* (cf. Figures 55 and 56). This is because x-shaped note heads may be used to depict any duration, whereas minims and semibreves could not be notated by means of the other two symbols. As in the case of bowing on the bridge, the string clef system is also preferred here from the bridge clef system. A vertical motion (cf. Figure 57) may, as shown in the following chapter, be depicted similarly to the bow-*glissando* (see Chapter »1. 2. 2 The bow-*glissando*«).

1. 4. 4. 3 Suggestion for the notation of playing behind the bridge

The note head utilised to depict the articulation of playing behind the bridge is derived from the one employed by *Crumb* and *Maderna*. This is because it is a commonly applied note head and often used to request playing behind the bridge. Further, since the bowing position has an impact on the resulting sound when playing behind the bridge, the method of notation needs to be further augmented. With respect to the three traditional bowing positions, three positions are defined for the area behind the bridge. They are also requested by means of directions and strongly related to the common positions: *sul ponticello* also requests to bow close to the bridge. However, in this case, on the other side of the bridge. The next position is designated as *ordinario* and located in the middle of the string length (from the bridge to the tailpiece). Moreover, the position that corresponds to *sul tasto* is called *sulla cordiera* (on the tailpiece) and requests to bow close to the tailpiece. This position is located on the fabric covering of the strings and as close to the tailpiece as possible. When bowing *sulla cordiera*, the tailpiece starts vibrating and a hum complements the squeak. As can be seen in Figure 58, a violinist is supposed to initially bow the D- and G-string *sulla cordiera* behind the bridge for the duration of a minim and subsequently play a succession of quavers on the A-, G-, D- and E-string. The first two quavers are bowed *sul ponticello* and the last two ones on the position *ordinario*.

sulla cordiera   sul pont.   ord.

Fig. 58 Playing behind the bridge.

36

When playing behind the bridge, all common and extended playing techniques (except for the *Bartók* pizzicato) may be performed. Moreover, the introduction of the positions enables, as mentioned, the depiction of a bow-*glissando*. It can be notated in the same way as the one displayed in Figure 14. Furthermore, it is also possible to bow the fine-tuners themselves. When doing so, the tailpiece vibrates and an additional hum sound evolves. This playing position is suggested here being requested by the string clef system, x-shaped note heads and the direction *sugli tiracantini* (on the fine-tuners).

1. 4. 5 Fingering behind the bridge and its notation

Another special articulation is to attach the finger to the strings whilst playing behind the bridge. This playing technique resembles the fingering in between fingerboard and bridge. The sounds that evolve may be described as »transposed« squeaks. When this articulation is requested on the violincello or contrabass, it might be more comfortable for the player to sit down. Since there is a lack of previous adequate approaches towards the notation of this technique, the method of depiction is developed here in accordance with the related fingering in between fingerboard and bridge[82] (cf. »1. 4. 2 Fingering in between fingerboard and bridge and its notation«) and the bowing positions defined in the previous chapter: fingering behind the bridge is suggested being requested by means of the string clef system and triangular note heads pointing downwards. The fingering positions correspond to the stops between fingerboard and bridge: position 1 can be described as the closest to the bridge. It is depicted by the accidental »♭«. The next position is located further to the tailpiece and is required when no accidental is employed. These positions may be fingered when bowing *ordinario* or *sulla cordiera*. Moreover, position 3 and 4 can be only fingered when bowing *sulla cordiera*. They are depicted by the accidentals »♯« and »x« whilst position 4 (double sharp) is located closer to the tailpiece. In the example presented in Figure 59, the four fingering positions are displayed by taking the example of a violin. They are fingered in the order of position 1 on the G-string, position 2 on the D-string, position 3 on the A-string and position 4 on the E-string.

Fig. 59 Fingering behind the bridge.

As in the case of the related fingering in between fingerboard and bridge, there is no distinction made between the string instruments in order to retain uniformity. This means that even though it might be possible to produce more sounds on a contrabass by fingering more than four positions, it is neglected in order to enable the application of the same method of notation for all four string instruments. Further, all common bowing techniques, such as *legato*, *tremolo*, *gettato*, *battuto* etc. as well as all normal fingering techniques, such as *vibrato*, the trill, *glissando* etc. can be employed when playing behind the bridge.

1. 5 Playing exceptional spots

Besides the strings, all other parts of the violin, such as the **tailpiece** itself, the **side of the bridge**, as well as the **tuning pegs**, **pegbox** and **scroll** may be bowed. Further, the **body of the instrument** may also be bowed.

---

[82] Even though the area in between the fingerboard and bridge is slightly longer than the area behind the bridge.

1.5.1 Bowing the tailpiece

When bowing the tailpiece, a rushing evolves. *Lachenmann* describes it as a "veiled, almost eerie (..) sound". Moreover, similarly to bowing the fine-tuners, the tailpiece vibrates when bowing it with a higher dynamic level.

1.5.1.1 Previous methods of notation

There have been several attempts to notate this articulation. For instance, in »Duo II« *Holliger* makes use of this technique and, as can be seen in Figure 60, depicts it by presenting a drawing of the tailpiece and bow. However, the duration of the articulation is only determined approximately.

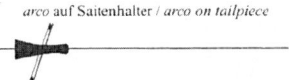

Fig. 60 Holliger, Duo II, p. 20.

Moreover, *Lachenmann* requests to bow the tailpiece in »Klangschatten – mein Saitenspiel« by means of a squared note head and a black triangle added to the note tail or, in the case of a *col legno tratto* on the tailpiece, by means of a squared note head and an additional white triangle:

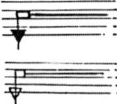

Fig. 61 Lachenmann, Klangschatten, no page named [foreword].

However, in »Gran torso« *Lachenmann* makes use of the bridge clef and squared note heads in order to depict this articulation:

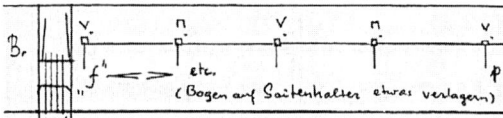

Fig. 62 Lachenmann, Torso, p. 11.

1.5.1.2 Discussion

When comparing the displayed approaches, it may be said that *Holliger's* method (cf. Figure 60) can be described as the simplest because the player can instantly understand what kind of action he is supposed to perform. However, the method of depiction is at the same time inexact since the duration is only determined approximately. Moreover, *Lachenmann's* first approach (cf. Figure 61) requires the player to learn the meaning of an unrelated symbol. As mentioned before, it might also be problematic to add a symbol to the note tail. Further, *Lachenmann's* second method of notation (cf. Figure 62) resembles the one by *Holliger* because a drawing of the tailpiece is also employed here. However, it may be described as more exact because the point of contact between the bow and the tailpiece is depicted and the duration clearly determined. Hence a method of notation that complies with all criteria would be as simple as *Holliger's* approach, but describe the point of contact and the duration in an exact manner.

1. 5. 1. 3 Suggestion for the notation of bowing the tailpiece

In order to depict the articulation of bowing the tailpiece in a simple and exact way, a hybrid of the described methods is suggested. However, the method of depiction used here employs x-shaped note heads and a single lined notation system with no clef instead of squared note heads and a bridge clef. This is because x-shaped note heads are normally utilised for the notation of noisy sounds (cf., for instance, the chapter on percussion instruments). Further, the drawing of the tailpiece is – with regard to the notation of the other exceptional spots discussed in the following chapters and in order to achieve an even greater degree of instantaneous comprehension – presented as a part of the whole instrument and the bow symbol complemented by an arrow, which determines the spot that is bowed. As can be seen in Figure 63, a cellist is supposed to bow the tailpiece at the point designated by the arrow for the duration of a semibreve. When requesting this articulation, it needs to be noted that the dynamic level may become quite high (because the tailpiece vibrates) and the basic bowing techniques, such as *arco, tremolo, gettato, col legno tratto* (low dynamic level), *col arco battuto* etc. may be employed. Additionally, the rolling bow technique (cf. Chapter »1. 3. 4 The rolling bow and its notation«) may be utilised when bowing the tailpiece. A similar extension of this technique is discussed in Chapter »1. 5. 4 Bowing the body of the instrument«. The paradigm presented there may be easily transferred to bowing the tailpiece.

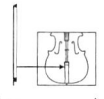

Fig. 63 Bowing the tailpiece.

Moreover, the bow may be moved vertically on the tailpiece. This motion can be either executed with or without horizontal bowing. The notation of this technique is suggested here being achieved similarly to the bow-*glissando* on the strings (see Chapter »1. 2. 2 The bow-*glissando*« for a detailed explanation). In Figure 64, a vertical and horizontal motion in combination is displayed. The cellist is, in the example, again supposed to start bowing close to the fine-tuners. However, this time the bow is during the bowing motion moved towards the endpin (*glissando d'arco*). The latter position is reached after a dotted minim (up-bow). The player is then supposed to bow this position for the duration of a crotchet (down-bow). A solely vertical motion would, in this case, also be requested by the direction *non tratto*.

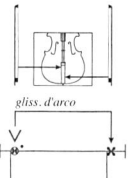

Fig. 64 Bow-*glissando* on the tailpiece.

1. 5. 2 Bowing the side of the bridge

Bowing the side of a cello's or contrabass's bridge results in a "clear toneless bowing sound" [83]. However, when bowing close to the slit of the bridge, squeaky "whistling tones can

---

[83] Lachenmann, Mouvement, no page named [foreword].

occur"[84]. Since the bridges of violins and violas are smaller, only squeaky sounds can be produced on them.

1.5.2.1 Previous methods of notation

Holliger, in »Duo II«, makes use of this technique. As can be seen in Figure 65, the note head is replaced by a drawing of the bridge and bow in order to request this articulation. In the example, a cello's bridge is played. *Holliger* indicates whether the sound should be squeaky or toneless by means of directions. Further, when requesting squeaky sounds, the note head is placed higher than when requesting toneless sounds.

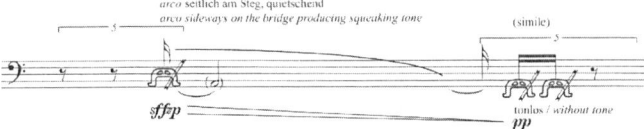

Fig. 65 Holliger, Duo II, p. 20.

Moreover, *Lachenmann* depicts this articulation in two ways. As can be seen in Figure 66, in »Mouvement (– vor der Erstarrung)« an abstracted bridge clef is utilised in combination with a white squared note head. This method of notation resembles the one that requests the player to bow on the bridge (cf. Figure 46) or behind the bridge (cf. Figure 56). When applied, the player is always supposed to produce a toneless sound. The squeaky whistling is not requested[85].

Fig. 66 Lachenmann, Mouvement, no page named [foreword].

Further, *Lachenmann*, in »Pression«, makes use of another method, which also enables the depiction of a vertical motion. The notation system he employs may be described as a »side of the bridge clef«. In the example presented in Figure 67, a cellist is supposed to perform a *col legno battuto* on the lowest point of the bridge [legno-Schlag auf Stegfuß] and subsequently bow the side of the bridge [arco unter den Saiten auf Stegwand].

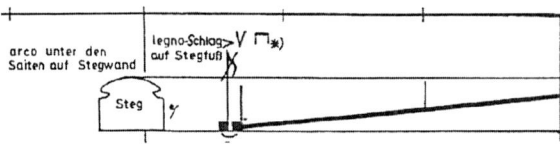

Fig. 67 Lachenmann, Pression, p. 4.

1.5.2.2 Discussion

Holliger's approach (cf. Figure 65) agrees with the requirement of simplicity and is closely related to traditional notation. This is because it can easily be comprehended what kind of action is supposed to be executed and the traditional clef is employed. However, it is confusing to depict the bowing on the side of the bridge, which result in sounds with indefinite pitch, by means of a bass clef whilst it is – as is apparent from the example – impossible to

---

[84] Ibid., no page named [foreword].

[85] Cf. ibid., no page named [foreword].

depict minims or semibreves when using these kinds of note heads. Therefore, he employs an additional traditional note head, which makes the appearance of the score even more confusing because it is normally related to playing on the strings. Further, *Lachenmann's* first method of depiction (cf. Figure 66) is similar to the one employed by *Holliger*. But since the clef is abstracted and the note head unrelated to the requested articulation, it may be stated that it is less comprehensive. This is because it requires the player – as in the case of *Lachenmann's* method of notation employed to request bowing the tailpiece (cf. Figure 61) – to learn the meaning of an unrelated symbolic representation before being able to perform the articulation in an *ad hoc* situation. However, with regard to the point of contact between the bow and the bridge, *Lachenmann's* second method of notation (cf. Figure 67) can be described as more exact than *Holliger's* approach. However, he does not employ the traditional way of requesting the *col legno battuto* and ordinary bowing, determines the duration only approximately and depicts the vertical motion by means of a special clef unless it may be notated similarly to the bow-*glissando* (cf. the previous chapter).

1. 5. 2. 3 Suggestion for the notation of bowing the side of the bridge

The method of notation suggested here is an elaboration of *Holliger's* approach and *Lachenmann's* second approach. The drawing, which is used to request the articulation, is a combination of the ones applied by the two composers. By employing such a hybrid, the articulation may be depicted in a simple way and with the greatest possible degree of instantaneous comprehension. Moreover, in order to determine the duration in a more exact way, x-shaped note heads complement the drawing. In the example presented in Figure 68, a cellist is required to perform various actions on the side of the bridge. Initially, he is supposed to execute a semiquaver *col legno battuto* on the lowest point of the bridge. Subsequently, the slit of the bridge is bowed for the duration of a minim. When doing so, a squeaky sound is produced. The player is then supposed to perform a bow-*glissando* (*glissando d'arco*), starting from the position slightly above the slit and ending on the highest point of the bridge. The *glissando* is executed for the duration of a crotchet and the highest point subsequently bowed for the duration of a dotted quaver.

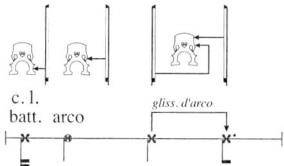

Fig. 68 Bowing the side of the bridge.

The maximum dynamic level of this articulation depends on which part of the bridge is bowed and which bowing technique is applied. A *col legno battuto* may be performed in a loud manner whilst the whistling sound may even reach the highest dynamic level. However, the *col legno tratto* or ordinary bowing of the other spots can only be executed with a low dynamic level. In the case of the *col legno battuto*, the highest dynamic levels cannot be used in order to protect the *bow* and bridge. Further, the player may execute a *tremolo* motion and apply the rolling bow technique on the side of the bridge (cf. Chapter »1. 3. 4 The rolling bow and its notation« as well as Chapter »1. 5. 4 Bowing the body of the instrument« for the extended rolling bow). Further, a similar method of notation may be used in order to request bowing on the top or side of the mute[86]. In such a case, the drawing of the bridge would have to be simply augmented by a graphic depiction of the mute.

1. 5. 3 Playing the tuning pegs, pegbox and scroll

When bowing the tuning pegs, pegbox and scroll, slightly varying noisy sounds are produced. Additionally, it is possible to bow the strings on the nut and play *pizzicato* in the pegbox.

1. 5. 3. 1 Previous methods of notation

Lachenmann requests to bow the scroll or tuning pegs by means of the bridge clef. In »Toccatina« he employs the full clef and gives additional directions in order to clarify which part is bowed:

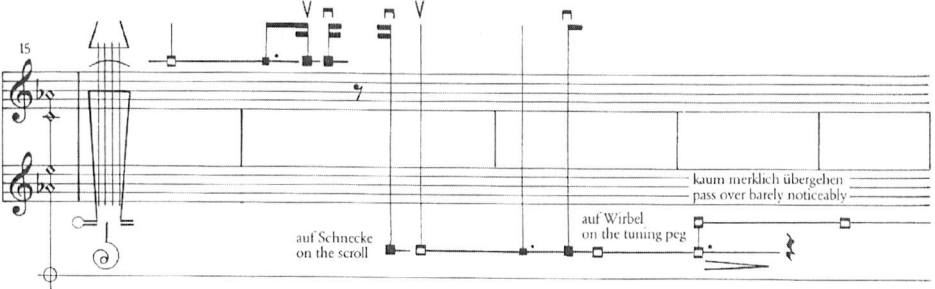

Fig. 69 Lachenmann, Toccatina, p. 5.

Moreover, in »Staub« *Lachenmann* solely uses a detail of the full clef in order to request bowing the scroll and gives additional directions as to how the articulation should be performed:

 Toneless bowing on the scroll. Draw the bow somewhat obliquely on the scroll. Remove the instrument from the chin if necessary so as to gain a better overall view of the action and to prevent the bow from slipping away.

Fig. 70 Lachenmann, Staub, no page named [foreword].

Further, in »Mouvement (– vor der Erstarrung)« the player is only supposed to bow on the tuning pegs and may decide by himself which peg is actually played:

 There are also bowing actions on the tuning pegs for the violas and celli. The performer should choose one of the two right-hand pegs on the side of the neck which is at a proper angle to the bow so that the bow does not slide off. The bow should not be pressed, but drawn quickly and loosely. The violas can eventually be held on the knees.

Fig. 71 Lachenmann, Mouvement, no page named [foreword].

Cervetti, in »Zinctum«, makes use of a special note head shaped like the pegbox and a single lined notation system with no clef in order to request bowing in between the pegs and fingerboard[87]. Since the dynamic level he employs is very high, it can be assumed that not the pegbox itself, but the strings on the nut are supposed to be bowed:

---

[86] Cf. Read, Contemporary, p. 212.

[87] Cf. Cervetti, Zinctum, no page named [appendix].

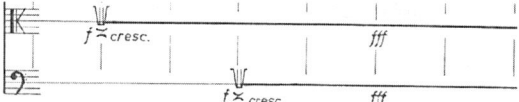

Fig. 72 Cervetti, Zinctum, p. 2.

Additionally, in »Klangschatten – mein Saitenspiel« *Lachenmann* requests to pluck the strings inside the pegbox in combination with a *pizzicato* behind the bridge. In the example presented in Figure 73, a cellist is supposed to pluck the D-string in the pegbox (grace note) and subsequently behind the bridge.

12. only for celli. This combination of a
pizzicato in the pegbox (left hand, fingernail) with a pizzicato below the bridge right
hand) must be prepared ahead of time. The second pizz. should follow the first as rapidly
as possible, but neither one should cover up
the other.

Fig. 73 Lachenmann, Klangschatten, no page named [foreword].

1. 5. 3. 2 Discussion

The articulations that involve bowing the tuning pegs and scroll resemble bowing the tailpiece. As shown in Chapter »1. 5. 1 Bowing the tailpiece«, a method of notation that presents a drawing of the bow and the part that is supposed to be played, is simpler and contains a greater degree of instantaneous comprehension than the depiction by means of the bridge clef commonly utilised by *Lachenmann* (cf. Figures 69-71). Therefore, a method similar to the one presented in Figure 63 is preferred here. It may also be utilised in order to request the player to bow the pegbox when no strings are involved. Likewise, playing the strings on the nut or inside the pegbox may be compared to playing special string positions. As shown in Chapter »1. 4 Extended playing positions on the strings«, methods of notation that make use of a distinct note head in order to request bowing an uncommon position on the string, agree with the requirements. *Cervetti* indeed employs a distinct note head (cf. Figure 72). However, his approach may be described as inexact since the duration is only determined approximately, the symbol he employs could not be used to depict minims and semibreves, and he does not indicate which strings are supposed to be bowed. However, the bowed strings could be depicted in a simple manner by using a special note head in combination with the string clef system. This method is also simpler than *Lachenmann*'s depiction of the pegbox *pizzicato* (cf. Figure 73). In order to determine a uniform and clear method notation for all special string positions, the string clef system is chosen here as the preferred method of depiction. A distinct note head can then be used to request plucking the string inside the pegbox as well as bowing on the nut.

1. 5. 3. 3 Suggestion for the notation of playing the tuning pegs, pegbox and scroll

Hence the method of notation suggested for bowing the tuning pegs, pegbox and scroll makes use of x-shaped note heads, a single lined notation system with no clef as well as a drawing of the instrument and bow. As can be seen in Figure 74, the player is initially requested to bow the scroll for the duration of a minim and subsequently play on the designated tuning peg. Since a *legato* slur is used, these two positions are played with a single stroke. The player is then supposed to bow the pegbox for the duration of another crotchet. Additionally, a *tremolo* motion could be effectively performed on these parts of the instrument. However, tt needs to be noted that all articulations can only be executed with a low dynamic level.

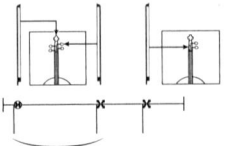

Fig. 74 Bowing the tuning pegs, pegbox and scroll.

When any other spot of a string instrument, such as the tail spike, the back of the finger-board or the rib, is supposed to bowed, the action can be depicted in the same manner and hence by means of x-shaped note heads, a single lined notation system with no clef and pre-senting a drawing of the particular spot (also cf. Figure 92). Further, the notation of bowing the nut and plucking the strings in the pegbox is achieved by means of the string clef system. Since the two playing positions are very close to each other and limited to the performance of two distinct articulations (*arco* on the nut and *pizzicato* in the pegbox), they can both be nota-ted by means of the same note head and an additional direction. Because each position only occurs with its respective articulation, they may clearly be distinguished and hence the addi-tion be described as legitimate. As can be seen in Figure 75, the note head used to depict the actions on the nut/in the pegbox is spherical. In the example, a contrabassist is initially sup-posed to pluck the D-string in the pegbox. Subsequently, he is required to bow the E-string for the duration of a minim (down-bow), then play all four strings for the duration of a dotted crotchet (up-bow) and finally pluck the A-string.

Fig. 75 Bowing the nut and *pizzicato* in the pegbox.

In the case of the *pizzicato*, only the middle strings vibrate when being plucked. The dyna-mic level of this articulation is low. Further, it needs to be noted that only the two outer strings may be bowed distinctly and otherwise all four (or five) strings have be to bowed at the same time. Moreover, as in the case of bowing on the bridge, the simultaneous muting of the strings is regarded here as the common way of performing this articulation (cf. Chapter »1. 4. 3 Bowing on the bridge«). When the open strings are supposed to sound during or at some point of the articulation, the direction *lasciar vibrare* may be given. Alternatively, any other distinct note head may be utilised.

1. 5. 4 Bowing the body of the instrument

Finally, it is also possible to bow the body of the instrument. In this case, either the edges of the body, the F-holes, the ribs or the back of the body are played. This action resembles bow-ing the scroll, pegbox or tuning pegs. The produced noise can be described as "a weak, rather breathy sound"[88] and varies slightly according to which part of the body is played.

1. 5. 4. 1 Previous methods of notation

Lachenmann, in »Klangschatten – mein Saitenspiel«, makes use of this technique. As can be seen in Figure 76, the letter »C« (as in corpus) is added to the note tail in order to request the

---

[88] Lachenmann, Klangschatten, no page named [foreword].

articulation whilst "the performer should bow where it is more comfortable and where the volume of the desired toneless effect is relatively strong"[89].

Fig. 76 Lachenmann, Klangschatten, p. 39.

Moreover, in »Pression« *Lachenmann* utilises a special system to request this articulation and gives additional directions concerning the performance, e. g. let the tip of the bow (hair) fall on the body without pressure [Bogen (Haar) an der Spitze ohne Druck auf Corpus fallen lassen] or start on the right F-hole → to the left F-hole [auf rechtem F-Loch beginnend → zum linken F-Loch]:

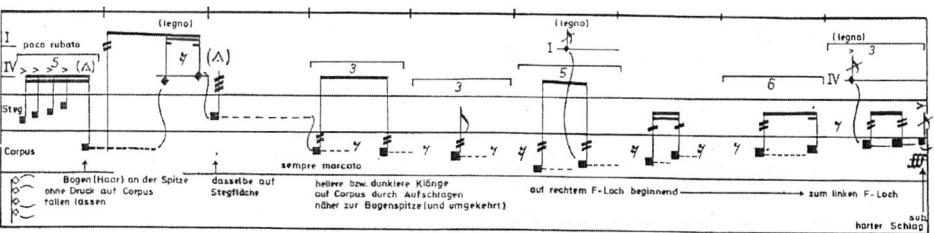

Fig. 77 Lachenmann, Pression, p. 5.

Further, in »..., den 24. xii. 1931«[90] *Kagel* requests a rolling bow articulation (cf. Chapter »1. 3. 4 The rolling bow and its notation«) on the body of all four string instruments by means of x-shaped not heads, a single lined notation system (with a drum clef) and an arrow added to the note tail:

---

[89] Ibid., no page named [foreword].

[90] Mauricio Kagel: ..., den 24. xii. 1931. Garbled messages for baritone and instruments. Frankfurt/M. et al. 1995.

45

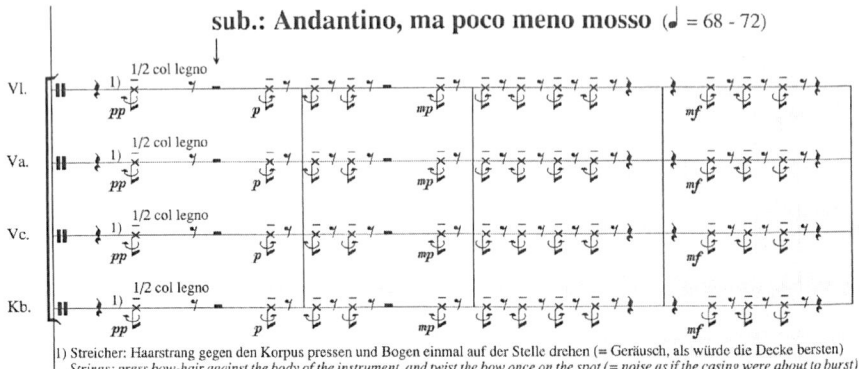

sub.: Andantino, ma poco meno mosso (♩ = 68 - 72)

1) Streicher: Haarstrang gegen den Korpus pressen und Bogen einmal auf der Stelle drehen (= Geräusch, als würde die Decke bersten)
Strings: press bow-hair against the body of the instrument, and twist the bow once on the spot (= noise as if the casing were about to burst)

Fig. 78 Kagel, 1931, p. 4.

1. 5. 4. 2 Discussion

Lachenmann's first method of notation (cf. Figure 76) may be described as imprecise and hence does not agree with the second requirement. This is because he does not determine which part of the body should be bowed. However, the depiction of the body by means of the special system *Lachenmann* employs in »Pression« (cf. Figure 77) is more exact even though the spot that is supposed to be played is not always exactly defined. Moreover, when comparing his directions with the notation of bowing parts of the body by means of a drawing (cf. Figures 63 and 74), the graphic depiction of the bowed spots contains a greater degree of instantaneous comprehension and may be described as simpler. Further, *Kagel's* method of notation (cf. Figure 78) is closely related to traditional notation since x-shaped note heads are, as mentioned, commonly applied to depict noisy sounds. However, it might be confusing to add a symbol to the note tail when semibreves are supposed to be depicted. Therefore, it is preferred here to notate the rolling bow by means of a symbol placed over the note. Further, in order to depict this articulation in a uniform manner, and because it resembles – as mentioned – a *vibrato* motion, the symbol introduced in Figure 37 should also be utilised here. Moreover, *Kagel* does not determine the spot upon which the motion is performed. With regard to this matter, his method of notation may, therefore, be described as inexact.

1. 5. 4. 3 Suggestion for the notation of bowing the body of the instrument.

The method of notation suggested here is related to the way bowing on the tailpiece, the tuning pegs, the pegbox or scroll is depicted. Hence it makes use of x-shaped note heads, a single lined notation system with no clef as well as a drawing of the body and bow. In the example presented in Figure 79, a cellist is supposed to initially bow the front edge of the c-rib at the designated point for the duration of a crotchet (down-bow). Subsequently, the F-hole is bowed for the duration of a dotted quaver (up-bow). After a quaver rest, the player is then supposed to perform a rolling bow articulation (*rotolato*) on the back of the instrument for the duration of a semiquaver. This request may result in a single motion. Opposed to *Kagel's* approach, the rolling direction is not indicated since the sound-wise difference is negligible. After another quaver rest, the back edge of the shoulder is then bowed for the duration of a crotchet (up-bow).

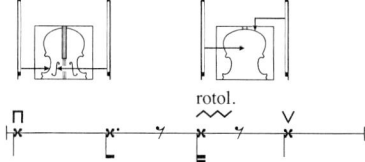

Fig. 79 Bowing the body of the instrument.

It needs to be noted that when bowing the F-hole, whistle sounds may additionally occur. Further, several other bowing techniques, such as *col arco battuto, gettato, saltando, balzando* or *tremolo* may be performed on the body. Additionally, the bow may be moved vertically on the edges or the back of the instrument (cf. Figure 64 for an example of how such a *glissando d'arco* on the instrument may be notated). However, *col legno* techniques should not be employed when bowing on the body since they might damage the instrument. Further, the dynamic level is always very low when bowing on the body.

1. 6 Extended stopping techniques

There are two special fingering techniques explained in this chapter. One is to finger **half harmonic stops** and the other one to perform **exact muting stops**. The buzz-*pizzicato* is also discussed in this chapter.

1. 6. 1 Half harmonic stops and their notation

When half harmonics are requested, the applied finger pressure is higher than when stopping harmonics and lower than in the case of fingering normal tones[91]. Moreover, *Lachenmann* explains that it is "important not to produce any harmonics here; the result should be a veiled, almost immaterial and hardly perceptible coloring of the dominating string sound produced by the stopped note" [92].

This stopping technique is normally notated by means of employing a special note head, which is derived from the conventional way of depicting harmonics. For instance, *Pröve* employs this method in »Firebird«. As can be seen in Figure 80, the note head commonly used for the notation of half harmonics is half white and half black.

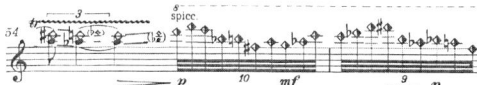

Fig. 80 Pröve, Firebird, p. 7.

However, a slightly varying method is utilised by *Kagel* in his »Streichquartett I/II«. Here an additional white and black diamond-shaped note head complements the conventional harmonic notation in order to request half harmonic pressure [1/2 Flageolettdruck] (as well as a circle to request the original harmonic fingering):

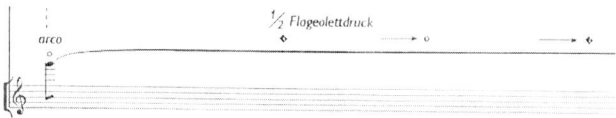

Fig. 81 Kagel, Streichquartett I/II, p. 31.

---

[91] Cf. Holliger, Lieder, p 16.

[92] Lachenmann, Torso, no page named [foreword].

When comparing the two methods of notation, it may be stated that both agree with the postulated requirements. However, *Pröve's* approach has a disadvantage since crotchets and minims would be confused with each other. Therefore, *Kagel's* method of using a white and black note head as a symbol that is placed over the note is preferred here. When employing this method, it needs to be noted that half harmonic stops are not limited to the nodes and hence the natural harmonics, but may be executed on all fingerboard positions. Here the suggested method of notation makes use of diamond-shaped note heads to depict the stopping position and a complementary white and black diamond-shaped symbol placed above the note in order to request the articulation. Diamond-shaped note heads are employed since the fingering of half harmonic stops is rather a variation of fingering harmonics than normal tones. They are used for all fingering positions (and hence no common note head with a small circle above it is complemented by the half harmonic symbol). As can be seen in Figure 82, a violist is supposed to play a sequence of half harmonic stops, starting with a minim »e¹/E4«, followed by the four semiquavers »g/G3«, »h¹/B4«, »e/E3, »b¹/B♭4« and ending with a crotchet »h/B3«. The transition from half harmonic pressure to harmonic pressure, and vice versa, could be requested by using two notes of the same pitch (one for the half harmonic and one for the harmonic stops) and connecting them by means of a *legato* slur.

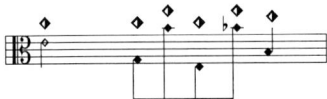

Fig. 82 Half harmonic stops.

1. 6. 2 Exact muting stops and their notation

The strings may be bowed and at the same time muted, which smothers the oscillation. When bowing *arco*, a rough whistle sound with indefinite pitch is produced. This sound varies when the position of the fingers is changed. When a *col legno battuto* or a *battuto* with the screw (for the latter cf. Chapter »1. 3. 2 Extended *battuto* and *tratto* techniques and their notation«) is performed, a subtle pitch, which varies according to the muting position as well as the (vertical) point of impact, can be perceived. However, the changes in pitch are stronger when altering the bow position than when changing the stopping position.

Muting the strings may be requested by means of a muting sign, as suggested by *Stone* in his handbook on music notation:

Cello

Fig. 83 Stone, Notation, p. 312.

The fingering position is depicted here by means of common note heads. However, it may – as in *Lachenmann's* »Toccatina« – be alternatively notated by means of diamond-shaped note heads:

Fig. 84 Lachenmann, Toccatina, p. 2.

As mentioned, diamond-shaped note heads are used as the conventional method of notation for harmonics. They are utilised by *Lachenmann* for the depiction of muting stops because the pressure that is applied to the string is similar to when fingering harmonics. When the finger touches the string on one of its nodes, a particular partial is produced. However, when the string is fingered on an off-node position with the same pressure, it is muted. Due to these techniques close relationship, it is preferred here to depict muting stops by means of diamond-shaped note heads instead of common ones. The muting sign may complement the notation of this articulation, but does not have to be employed. This is because all the necessary information is already given by explaining that the string is fingered in the same way as harmonics are fingered, but on an off-node position. Further, as opposed to *Lachenmann's* method of notation, it is suggested here depicting the duration of the muting stop in the traditional way. When utilising this stopping technique, all common and extended playing techniques may be applied.

Additionally, this technique may be further extended by attaching the fingernail, instead of the tip of the finger, to the string. When doing so, the string may either be bowed or plucked. In the case of the *pizzicato*, this articulation is referred to as a one variant of the **buzz-*pizzicato***. There are three ways of creating it: 1. By slightly touching the lingering string with the right hand's fingernail after a *pizzicato*. 2. By slightly touching the lingering string with the left hand's fingertip after a *pizzicato*. 3. By slightly touching the string with the left hand's fingernail during the performance of a *pizzicato*. In the case of variants 1 and 2, a *pizzicato*-sound is followed by a buzzing whilst in the case of variant 3, a *pizzicato*-sound and buzzing blend[93]. *Sevsay* suggests a symbol resembling the one representing a *Bartók pizzicato* (⊖) for the notation of variant 1 and explains that, in the case of the other two variants, a predefined symbol or verbal explanation should be used[94]. Moreover, in »Enjambements«[95] *Cerha* makes use of variant 3 and combines a symbol he uses to request the common *pizzicato* articulation with the letter »N« (as in the German *Nagel* or nail) in order to depict it:

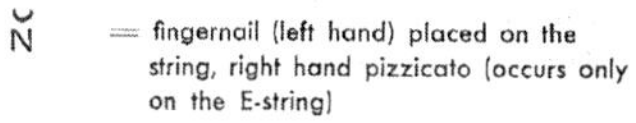

N̆   = fingernail (left hand) placed on the
     string, right hand pizzicato (occurs only
     on the E-string)

Fig. 85 Cerha, Enjambements, no page named [foreword].

Concerning the method of notation presented by *Sevsay*, it can be said that despite being valid with regard to the requirements, it might be irritating to employ the pictured symbol for an articulation that is not related to a *Bartók pizzicato*. As shown above, there is another *pizzicato* articulation (which is in Chapter »1. 1 Extended *pizzicato* techniques and their notation« referred to as the lateral *Bartók pizzicato*) that rather deserves to be requested by means of this symbol. Moreover, *Cerha's* method of notation violates the third requirement since the traditionally utilised method of depicting the *pizzicato* is replaced by a sign shaped like a fingernail symbol (cf. Figure 1). However, it would generally be valid to request the buzz-*pizzicato* by means of a symbol. But such a method would have to be complemented by a depiction of the fingering position. Since none of these examples can adequately be utilised for the depiction of all buzz-*pizzicato* variants, another method needs to be developed. As mentioned, there are three variants of this technique. In the case of the first one, the right hand touches the string and, in the case of the second and third one, the left hand performs this action. The first variant is strongly related to the *col legno toccato* (cf. Figure 35). However, here the string is not touched with the bow's wood, but the right hand's fingernail. Nevertheless, it may be notated by giving the direction *toccato* and employing an additional fingernail symbol. More-

---

[93] Sevsay, Handbuch, p. 64.
[94] Cf. ibid., p. 64.
[95] Friedrich Cerha: Enjambement. [For flute, violin, percussion, trumpet, trombone and double-bass]. Vienna 1963.

over, the method of notation suggested for the second and third variant is related to the *col legno toccato* on the fingerboard. This is because, in the case of these buzz-*pizzicati*, the player acts similarly to when touching the string with the bow's wood on the fingerboard. However, since only the left hand is involved in this action, no additional notation system needs to be employed. Therefore, this articulation can be notated by means of diamond-shaped note heads complemented by the direction *toccato* and – if necessary – a fingernail symbol. The first and second variant of the buzz-*pizzicato* consists of two distinct actions and is, therefore, notated by means of two note heads. In Figure 89, the actions are performed on the D-string of a violin, and all three variants of the buzz-*pizzicato* are displayed: 1. The instrumentalist plays a demisemiquaver *pizzicato sul tasto* »f¹/F4« and subsequently touches the string with the right hand's fingernail on the *sul tasto* position for the duration of a semiquaver. The *legato* slur underlines that the finger is not released, but the player constantly stops the same tone and additionally touches the string after a demisemiquaver. 2. The player performs a *pizzicato* »f¹/F4« and subsequently touches the string with the left hand's fingernail on position »g¹/G4« for the duration of a semiquaver. The *legato* slur emphasises that the »f¹/F4« is again constantly fingered and the string is additionally touched after a demisemiquaver. 3. The player performs a *pizzicato*. At the same time, he stops an »f¹/F4« and touches the string with the left hand's fingernail on position »g¹/G4«. The direction *pizzicato e toccato* is used – instead of merely depicting a fingernail muting stop that is plucked – in order to outline that a fingernail *pizzicato* is not supposed to be executed, but a fingernail *toccato*.

Fig. 86 The three variants of the buzz-*pizzicato*.

1. 7 Percussive effects

Percussive effects can be either produced **on the body** of the instrument (including other parts, such as the tuning pegs) or **on the strings**. When requested, the player is supposed to hit the designated spot with knuckles, the flat of the hand or single fingers.

1. 7. 1 Strokes on the body and their notation

When hitting the body of the instrument, a "mellow, hollow"[96] sound is produced. It varies according to which spot of the body is struck and which part of the hand is used for the performance of the percussive effect. This articulation is often requested by means of x-shaped note heads, a single lined notation system with no clef and an additional direction[97]. An example of such a method of notation can, as is apparent from Figure 87, be found in *Kagel's* »Match«.

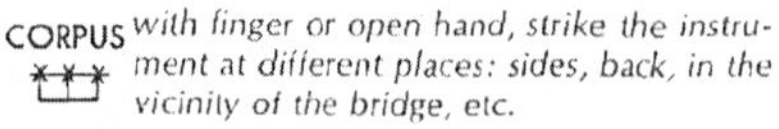

CORPUS *with finger or open hand, strike the instru-*
ment at different places: sides, back, in the
vicinity of the bridge, etc.

Fig. 87 Kagel, Match, p. 5.

Another method is utilised by *Szalonek* in »Concertino«. He requests such a percussive effect by means of an x-shaped note head and a note tail shaped like the body of a string instrument:

---

[96] Crumb, Echoes, p. 17.

[97] Cf. Cerha, Enjambements, p. D₂ or Crumb, Echoes, p. 17.

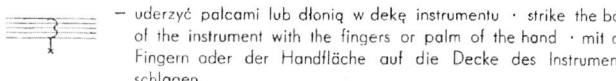

— uderzyć palcami lub dłonią w dekę instrumentu · strike the body of the instrument with the fingers or palm of the hand · mit den Fingern oder der Handfläche auf die Decke des Instrumentes schlagen

Fig. 88 Szalonek, Concertino, p. 4.

However, these two methods may be described as imprecise since neither the exact point of impact nor the part of the hand which performs the strike is precisely determined. Further, *Szalonek's* method does apparently not enable the utilisation of all possible durations. In order to fulfil the postulated requirement of exactness, the methods of notation need to be further elaborated. This elaboration is, as *Kagel's* approach, based on the utilisation of x-shaped note heads and a single lined notation system with no clef. This is because sounds with indefinite pitch are, as mentioned, commonly notated in this way. Moreover, since the action of hitting the body resembles the action of bowing the body (see Chapter »1. 5. 4 Bowing the body of the instrument« for further details), it may be notated in the same way. Hence a drawing of the instrument's body, which enables the determination of the point of impact, is combined here with a drawing of the player's hand. This sound producer may be employed in various ways. Knuckles, the side of the fist, the palm, single fingers and finger tips (with or without involving the fingernails) may be used to strike the body. In Figure 89, the drawings utilised to request a stroke with 1. the knuckles and 2. the side of the fist are presented.

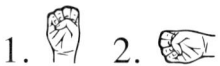

Fig. 89 The knuckles and the side of the fist.

Moreover, another drawing needs to be applied in order to determine whether the instrument should be struck with the palm, single fingers or the finger tips. As can be seen in Figure 90, the part of the hand that is supposed to be utilised is always coloured black. The drawings are in this example presented in the order of a stroke with 1. the palm, 2. the index, middle and ring finger, 3. the tip of the thumb, index and middle finger and 4. the tip and fingernail of the index finger[98]. The fingernail is depicted by means of a symbol derived from *Lachenmann's* fingernail symbol (cf. Figure 1).

Fig. 90 Parts of the hand.

The exact spot that is supposed to be struck is indicated by a black dot placed on the drawing of the instrument. In the example presented in Figure 91, six different strokes are performed on various parts of a contrabass. They are executed in the order of 1. with the knuckles on the right upper front, 2. with the side of the fist on the left upper front, 3. with the palm on the right lower back, 4. with the index, middle and ring finger on the right lower front, 5. with the tip of the thumb, index and middle finger on the right lower front, 6. with the tip and fingernail of the index finger on the left upper back (out of the player's perspective). All actions are separated by quaver rests.

---

[98] The drawings from Figures 92f. were created with the help of the *Hand Sign* font by *Sam Wang*.

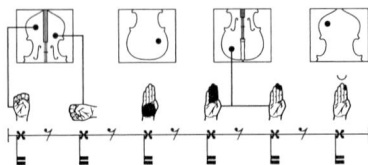

Fig. 91 Strokes on the body.

When single fingers are supposed to be used in fast succession, the order can be additionally depicted as on the piano, e. g. 4, 3, 1, 4, 0, 5 (also cf. the *pizzicato tremolo* in Chapter »1. 1 Extended *pizzicato* techniques and their notation«). Further, complex rubbing motions can also be executed on the body (cf. Chapter »3. 2. 4 Rubbing and bowing motions«) and other parts of the instrument, such as the tailpiece, bridge, scroll, pegbox or tuning pegs, may also be struck. These actions may be requested by employing a drawing of the respective part (cf. Chapters »1. 5. 1 Bowing the tailpiece«, »1. 5. 2 Bowing the side of the bridge« and »1. 5. 3 Playing the tuning pegs, pegbox and scroll«). Additionally, the side of the body may be struck. This part of the string instrument may be depicted by means a drawing similar to the one presented in Figure 17 (or by means of a variation of such a drawing when depicting a violin or viola):

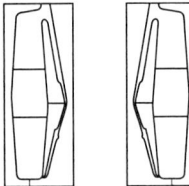

Fig. 92 The right and left side of a violincello.

Moreover, muting the strings during the execution of the strokes is regarded here as the common way of applying the articulation (except for when the player is supposed to simultaneously hit the instrument with both hands). When the open strings are supposed to sound during or after the articulation (including after the two-handed hit), the direction *lasciar vibrare* may be given. In order to prevent the instrument from being damaged, the dynamic level, and hence the applied force, needs to be low. Therefore, it is also not possible to scratch the instrument's body with the fingernails or, as mentioned, bow or hit it *col legno*.

1. 7. 2 Strokes on the strings and their notation

When the strings are struck sharply with the hand and simultaneously muted, only the percussive sound of the stroke may be perceived. This kind of attack is principally a hybrid of an extended technique of percussion instruments – referred to as the stop attack or dead stroke – and a *battuto* on the fingerboard/with the left hand (cf. Figures 29 and 32). Due to the strong relation of this technique to these articulations, a discussion of previous methods of notation is dismissed here, but instead a suggestion presented which complies with the methods of notation for the described techniques: as it is shown in Chapter »3. 4. 3 The stop attack and its notation«, dead strokes may be depicted by utilising a symbol of the beater and a muting sign (⊕). Because the stop attack on percussion instruments and the strokes on the strings strongly resemble each other, the method of notation may be transferred from percussion to string instruments. The beater here is the hand. However, in the case of string instruments, the point of impact on the string needs to be determined differently. As shown above, all actions on the fingerboard – which do not imply that the string is completely depressed on the fingerboard –

are depicted by means of diamond-shaped note heads. This method of notation can also be applied to the strokes on the strings because the strings are, in this case, not depressed either. Further, when strokes on the ordinary playing positions are supposed to be executed, common note heads that depict the string (by taking the example of the violin, by means of the pitches »e²/E5«, »a¹/A4«, »d¹/D4« and/or »g/G3«) need to be employed and the additional direction *sul tasto*, *ordinario* or *sul ponticello* be given. This is because an action of this kind resembles the performance of any kind of bowing motion on the ordinary playing positions with open strings. Additionally, it should be outlined which hand is used to execute the stroke. In Figure 93, a violinist is supposed to perform a stop attack on the position »f¹ – c² – g² – d³/F4 – C5 – G5 – D6«, using the index, middle, ring and little finger of his left hand (*mano sinistra*). The second hit is executed on the same position, but now with the palm. Subsequently, all strings are hit with the right hand's (*mano destra*) knuckles on the *sul tasto* position and finally on the *sul ponticello* position.

Fig. 93 Stop attack with the hand.

Sounds with a higher dynamic level than in the case of the strokes on the body may be produced when executing stop attacks with the hand on the strings. However, the fingernails cannot be employed and only the right hand's knuckles and side of the fist may be comfortably utilised for the execution of such strokes. But when previously placing down the bow, the player may apparently also use all other parts of the hand. Another percussive effect is produced by **striking the fingerboard** between the strings with single fingers. This articulation can be requested in the same way as the action of scratching the fingerboard and hence by the additional direction *il tasto* and diamond-shaped note heads (cf. Figure 7). Since the fingerboard is more resistant than the body, higher dynamic levels may, in this case, be produced.

Furthermore, in the case of executing dead strokes with the hand, it does not make a difference whether the strings are additionally muted with the other hand or not because they do not vibrate subsequently to the stroke. However, when using a beater or the wood of the bow, the strings linger after the attack. Therefore, the notation becomes more complex. As it is shown in the chapter on percussion instruments, beaters are normally depicted by means of symbols. When using the bow as a beater, no symbol, but the direction *col legno battuto* is conventionally employed. A stop attack can also be performed with the wood of the bow when it remains firmly in contact with the string after the attack. Eight different types of dead stroke articulations may be performed: a stroke on the ordinary bowing positions with 1. open strings, 2. depressed strings, 3. muted strings, 4. harmonic fingering and a stroke on a fingerboard position with 1. open strings, 2. depressed strings, 3. muted strings, 4. harmonic fingering. In order to notate these attacks, the paradigms presented in Chapter »1. 6. 2 Exact muting stops and their notation« (for the depiction of strokes with muted strings) and Figure 29 (for the depiction of the »bowing« on the fingerboard) need to be employed. In the example presented in Figure 94, the eight types of stop attacks, executed with the wood of the bow, are displayed in the order of a stroke on the position *ordinario* 1. with open G-string, 2. whilst depressing the string on position »a/A3«, 3. whilst muting the string on position »a/A3«, 4. whilst fingering the second partial and, further, a stroke on the fingerboard position »f¹/F4«

1. with open G-string, 2. whilst depressing the string on position »a/A3«, 3. whilst muting the string on position »a/A3«, 4. whilst fingering the second partial.

Fig. 94 Stop attack with the wood of the bow.

In the case of utilising a beater, the direction *col legno battuto* may be simply replaced by the beater symbol. Furthermore, the strings may also be struck in the same way as the common *col legno battuto* is performed with the hand or a beater. In such a case, it also makes a difference whether the strings are open, depressed, muted or a harmonic fingering is used. Such an attack may be notated by replacing the direction *col legno battuto* with the beater symbol and not employing the muting sign. Hence the paradigms used for the depiction of the conventional and extended *col legno battuto* on the fingerboard (cf. Chapter »1. 3. 2 Extended *battuto* and *tratto* techniques and their notation«) need to be simply transferred to the usage of a beater. Moreover, various other attacks, such as normal strokes, *pizzicati*, harmonic-*glissandi* etc. may be executed by means of beaters. However, because these playing techniques are primarily used on the harp, they are discussed in Chapter »4. 4. 3 The utilisation of beaters and its notation«.

1. 8 Preparing the instrument and its notation

There are numerous ways of preparing string instruments. It is, on the one hand, barely possible to list them all and subsequently develop a coherent method of depiction whilst, on the other hand, it is also not necessary to do so since most preparations are executed previously to a performance and may be simply described in the foreword to a work. However, when preparations are supposed to be performed during a concert, they become in some sense an extended playing technique. Because there are manifold ways to manipulate the instrument, only a few examples can be presented here.

An extended utilisation of the bow – designated as »curved bow« or »loosen the bow« – is employed by *Holliger* in »Duo II«. In order to request it, he gives the following explanation: "Bow stick below and hairs above the violin: evenly over four strings"[99]. Subsequently, the player is required to bow all four strings simultaneously. Further, in the same piece *Holliger* also makes the player attach a length of string to the G-string of a violin. This time the explanation is complemented by a sketch:

Faden (mit viel Kolophonium) an 4. Saite (ganz am Steg) befestigt. Zwischen Daumen und Zeigefinger hindurchziehen: quasi "Tambour à corde".
Tonhöhe durch Glissandi parallel unterstützen. *Attach a length of string (with plenty of resin) to the 4ᵗʰ string (right to the bridge). Pull through between thumb and index finger: quasi "tambour à corde" (= lions roar). Simultaneously support pitch through glissandi.*

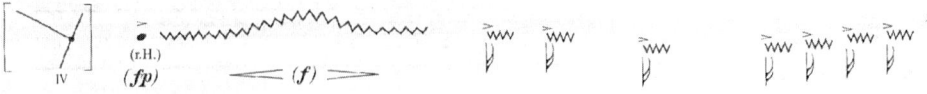

Fig. 95 Holliger, Duo II, p. 13.

---

[99] Holliger, Duo II, p. 13.

Various examples of preparations can also be found in *Kagel's* »Streichquartett I/II«. All requisites and materials he utilises are listed in the foreword of the work. As can be seen in Figure 96, one example of a preparation is to place a knitting needle (made of metal) [Stricknadel (aus Metall)] in between the strings. The needle is supposed to be attached on the string position 10[100]. *Kagel* explains this preparation by means of a sketch:

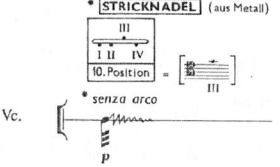

Fig. 96 Kagel, Streichquartett, p. 1.

Further, *Kagel* also makes a cellist attach sticky tape [Klebefilm] to the ordinary bowing position on all four strings. He again depicts this action by means of a sketch:

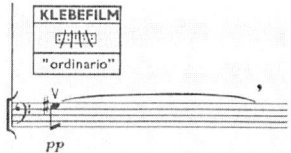

Fig. 97 Kagel, Streichquartett I/II, p. 20.

As is apparent from these examples, the simplest way of explaining the preparations that are supposed to be carried out is to use a sketch. When the sketch is not clear enough, it may be complemented by an explanation (cf. Figure 95). Hence a simpler method of depiction for *Holliger's* so-called »curved bow« would be to present an additional drawing of the preparation's outcome. When disregarding this example, all presented approaches towards the depiction of preparations comply with the postulated requirements. They are exact, simple and may be used to augment the traditional notation system. Therefore, it is suggested here presenting any preparation that is supposed to take place during the course of a piece by means of a sketch and – if necessary – an additional explanation. Nevertheless, preparations may – as is apparent from Figure 95 – lead to the introduction of new playing techniques that should then be notated in accordance with all other techniques presented in this work.

1. 9 Other extended playing techniques and their notation

There are a few more rare playing techniques that are discussed separately here. One is to **hold the bow under the strings** and perform simple playing techniques, such as *col arco* or *col legno battuto/tratto*. This action may be either performed in between fingerboard and bridge or behind the bridge. When the bow is held in this way, the two outer strings may be played simultaneously, but the middle strings cannot be played at all.

Lachenmann, in »Gran torso«, makes use of this articulation. A cellist is supposed here to place the bow under the strings [Bogen unter den Saiten] in between fingerboard and bridge. Subsequently, he is required to perform a *col legno battuto* on the muted A-string. The posi-

---

[100]*Kagel* depicts a »g¹/G4« in the example and states that this is the 10. position on the G-string (III) of a violincello. However, position no. 10 on the G-string would be depicted by an »f/F3«. Therefore, it is assumed that the 10. position on the A-string (I) is depicted and the wrong numeral used.

tion of the bow is explained by means of a sketch. Additionally, a squared note head and a note tail complemented by an arrow pointing upwards is utilised to depict the *battuto*:

Fig. 98 Lachenmann, Torso, p. 14.

Since this articulation is very uncommon, it does make sense to notate it by presenting a sketch and giving an additional explanation. However, because the technique is at the same time closely related to ordinary playing techniques, there is no need to utilise a special note head and tail. Therefore, it is suggested here introducing this articulation by means of a sketch similar to the one presented by *Lachenmann* and an explanation, such as *arco sotto la corda* (bow underneath the string), but then notate the playing action in the normal way. In the case of playing in between fingerboard and bridge, the notes may, further, be complemented by indicating that the action takes place underneath particular strings. In the case of the violin-cello, the directions *sotto A e C*, *sotto A* or *sotto C* could be employed. As can be seen in Figure 99, a cellist is supposed to initially bow the A- and C-string *sul ponticello* whilst stop-ping the chord »D – c¹/D2 – C4« for the duration of a minim. After a dotted quaver rest, a *col legno battuto sul tasto* is performed on the C-string whilst fingering a »d/D3«. Finally, the player is requested to execute a *col legno tratto sul tasto* on the A- and C-string while stop-ping the chord »E – c¹/E2 – C4« for the duration of a crotchet. The utilisation of the bow in the normal way is then requested by the direction *arco sulla corda*.

Fig. 99 Playing under the strings in between fingerboard and bridge.

Playing under the strings behind the bridge may be notated similarly. The action of placing the bow underneath the string should again be explained by means of a sketch. Subsequently, the suggested method of notation for playing behind the bridge – and hence x-shaped note heads and the string clef system – may be employed (cf. Chapter »1. 4. 4 Playing behind the bridge«). The indication *sotto A e C* etc. is replaced here by simply leaving the spaces that normally represent the middle strings blank. In Figure 100, the player is at first supposed to bow the A- and C-string *sul ponticello* for the duration of a minim. After a dotted quaver rest, a *col legno battuto sulla cordiera* is then performed on the C-string. Finally, the player is requested to execute a *col legno tratto sulla cordiera* on the A- and C-string. Afterwards, the bow is supposed to be utilised in the normal way.

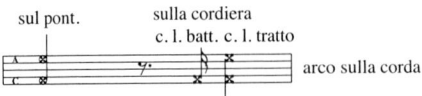

Fig. 100 Playing under the strings behind the bridge.

When bowing under the strings behind the bridge, it is possible to further transform the sound by attaching the fingers to the string. This technique may also be notated by transferring the paradigm presented in Chapter »1. 4. 5 Fingering behind the bridge and its notation«. Generally, bowing underneath the strings may be executed with all possible dynamic levels. However, the *col legno battuto* may only be performed with a low dynamic level.

Another extraordinary articulation is to **scratch on the fabric covering of the strings** with the fingernail. *Holliger* requests this action in »Duo II« by means of a fingernail symbol, an additional explanation, a wavy line and *de-/crescendo* symbols:

Fig. 101 Holliger, Duo II, p. 20.

However, this method of notation is, as obvious, very imprecise since exact durations are not determined. Further, because he makes use of a long explanation, the degree of instantaneous comprehension is very low. For these reasons, a further elaborated method of notation is suggested here. It involves – as in the case of executing strokes on the body – a drawing of the sound producer (cf. Figure 91). However, this time the hand is not used for the performance of a stroke, but to scratch on the string, which is expressed by an additional direction. Since the positioning of the finger is similar to when bowing *sulla cordiera* behind the bridge, x-shaped note heads and the string clef system may be employed to depict this articulation. As can be seen in Figure 102, a violinist is supposed to scratch on the string winding of the D-string with the tip of his index finger whilst involving the fingernail for the duration of a semibreve. The dynamic level of this articulation is always very low.

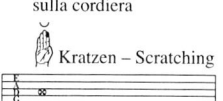

Fig. 102 Scratching *sulla cordiera*.

Finally, *Kagel* requests a cellist to **blow into one of the F-holes** of his instrument by means of a symbol that represents the holes and the following explanation: "BLOWING: Raise the cello and blow into one of the sound-holes in such a way that a highly resonant sound results. Meanwhile, move the instrument slightly, thereby producing continual changes of timbre" [101]:

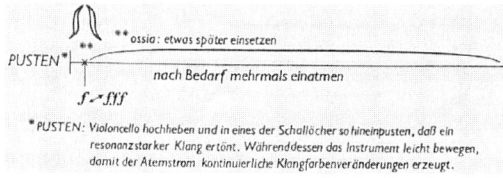

Fig. 103 Kagel, Streichquartett I/II, p. 32.

However, *Kagel's* method of notation is quite unclear and imprecise. This is because the symbol he employs does not clearly depict the action that is supposed to be performed, an additional long explanation is necessary, and it is not indicated when the so-called changes in timbre are supposed to be performed. Further, the action of blowing into the instrument resembles other articulations that are executed on the body. As shown in Chapters »1. 5. 4

---

[101] Kagel, Streichquartett I/II, p. 32.

Bowing the body of the instrument« and »1. 7. 1 Strokes on the body and their notation«, the preferred method of notation for such effects is to present a drawing of the instrument and the sound producer. Nevertheless, the notation of the duration by means of x-shaped note heads and a single lined notation system with no clef is adequate since the produced sound has an indefinite pitch. Therefore, the method of notation suggested here makes use of x-shaped note heads, a single lined notation system with no clef as well as drawings of the instrument and sound producer. As can be seen in Figure 104, the exact point of »embouchure« is indicated by arrows while the motion up and down the F-hole is, in reference to the bow-*glissando* on the body, designated as a *glissando della bocca* (mouth *glissando*). In the example, a cellist is supposed to start blowing the lowest point of the F-hole and then gradually change the point of embouchure for the duration of a minim until the highest point is reached. Subsequently, the mouth is again moved downwards for the duration of a crotchet. Then the player blows the lowest point of the F-hole for the duration of another crotchet.

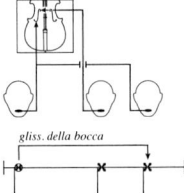

Fig. 104 Blowing into the instrument.

In order to clearly outline what kind of action the player is supposed to execute, it may be useful to present an additional short explanation such as »blowing into the F-hole«, at the first occurrence of this articulation. Moreover, the dynamic level requested by *Kagel (forte* and *forte fortissimo)* is impossible to be produced by blowing into the sound-holes. On the contrary, the loudness of this articulation is actually always low.

Furthermore, any other rare extended playing technique, which has not been taken into consideration here, should be depicted in accordance with the methods of notation suggested in the previous chapters. Additionally, some of the playing techniques discussed in the chapter on plucked instruments may also be applied on string instruments (cf., for instance, Chapter »4. 1 Extended *pizzicato, tremolo* and trill techniques and their notation« or Chapter »4. 4. 5 Strumming and its notation«). They are not discussed here because they are primarily plucked instruments' techniques.

2. THE TECHNIQUES OF WIND INSTRUMENTS

There are two groups of wind instruments: woodwinds and brass instruments. Woodwinds are, inter alia due to their distinct sound character and timbre, considered to be a heterogeneous group, which includes flutes, oboes, bassoons, clarinets and saxophones. However, brass instruments may be regarded as a rather homogeneous group. Horns, trumpets, trombones and tubas belong to this family of instruments[1]. Despite their different character, many extended playing techniques may, however, be produced on both – woodwinds and brass instruments – in the same manner. Therefore, this chapter is not divided into two parts or single instruments, but solely grouped by unconventional extended playing techniques. In the beginning of each chapter, it is indicated if a special technique may not be executed on a particular instrument. Moreover, this chapter mainly focuses on the most common wind instruments, including the flutes, oboes, the bassoon, the clarinets, the F horn, C trumpet, tenor trombone and the bass tubas. When employing rather uncommon instruments, such as the recorder, double bassoon, flügelhorn, cornet, bass trombone or contrabass tuba, the methods of notation may, in most cases, simply be transferred because the more common instruments resemble these. With regard to wind instruments, the notation of the basic *vibrato* and the basic trill (including double trills), the basic (fingered) *glissando*, the common playing techniques (including single-, double- and triple-tonguing), extended ranges, harmonics (including double harmonics) and circular breathing as well as clusters (also cf. Chapter »5. 6. 1 Clusters«) and multiphonics are regarded here as conventional[2]. Their notation can be adopted from the essential handbooks on instrumentation whilst most composers use the method of depiction that can be found there. In the case of the *vibrato*, it needs to be noted that, for instance, on the bassoon three types may be produced: the diaphragm vibrato, the lip vibrato and the so-called *smorzato*[3]. The latter articulation may be described as an oscillating change of, firstly, the volume and, secondly, the timbre without altering the pitch[4]. It is thus strictly speaking not a *vibrato*, but nevertheless normally referred to as a *vibrato* variant[5] and discussed in the following chapter. All other *vibrato* variants may be notated by means of the *vibrato* symbol and giving an additional direction, such as *vibrato di diaframma* (diaphragm *vibrato*) or *vibrato di labbro* (lip *vibrato*). Further, fingering charts for multiphonics and microtones on the woodwinds are presented in *Levine and Mitropoulos-Bott*[6/7] for the flutes, in *Peter Veale et al.*[8] for the oboes, in *Rehfeldt*[9] for the clarinets and in *Krassnitzer*[10] for the German B♭ clarinet, in *Gallois*[11] for the bassoon as well as in *Weiss and Netti*[12] or *Kientzy*[13] for the saxophones. When applying these techniques, one will have to simply use the charts

---

[1] Sevsay, Handbuch, pp. 90, 94 and 107.

[2] Cf. Sevsay, Handbuch, pp. 134-148 as well as the handbooks mentioned below.

[3] Pascal Gallois. The techniques of bassoon playing. Kassel et al. 2009, p. 59.

[4] Peter Veale et al.: The techniques of oboe playing. Kassel et al. 1994, p. 137.

[5] Carin Levine and Christina Mitropoulos-Bott: The techniques of flute playing. Kassel et al. 2002, p. 33.

[6] Ibid.

[7] Carin Levine and Christina Mitropoulos-Bott: The techniques of flute playing II. Piccolo, alto and bass flute. Kassel et al. 2004.

[8] Veale, Oboe.

[9] Phillip Rehfeldt: New directions for clarinet. Los Angeles and London 1977.

[10] Gerhard Krassnitzer: Multiphonics für Klarinette mit deutschem System und andere erweiterte Spieltechniken [Multiphonics for clarinets with German system and other contemporary playing techniques]. Aachen 2002.

[11] Gallois, Bassoon.

[12] Marcus Weiss and Giorgio Netti: The techniques of saxophone playing. Kassel et al. 2010.

[13] Daniel Kientzy: Les sons multiples aux saxophones [Multiphonics on saxophones]. For sopranino, soprano, alto, tenor and baritone saxophones. Paris 1982.

presented within these works in a uniform way. When no such book is yet available for a particular instrument, multiphonics may only be used in an approximate way by indicating the fundamental upon which the chord is supposed to be produced. Alternatively, charts may be created in cooperation with players. Moreover, the described handbooks are, in this chapter, used as the main references concerning the execution of extended playing techniques. As already explained in the introduction to the chapter on string instruments, microtones are not specifically discussed in this work. However, a suggestion for the notation of microtonal frequencies is presented in »Part II: Electroacoustic music – 1. 1. 1 Periodic wave generators and their envelopes«. Further, the main unconventional elements of sound production discussed in this chapter are extended *vibrato*, *tremolo* and trill techniques, extended tongue and embouchure techniques, the pitch bending articulation, extended winding techniques, preparing the instrument, whistle techniques, muting, percussive effects and resonance effects. Concerning the dynamic level of these articulations, indications are – as far as possible – presented when the execution of the action is in terms of the loudness limited.

2. 1 Extended *vibrato*, *tremolo* and trill techniques and their notation

The *smorzato* articulation has been introduced in the previous chapter. As mentioned, it implies an oscillating change of the amplitude and timbre. Therefore, the *smorzato* may be described as a *tremolo* (amplitude modulation) and overtone *vibrato* (frequency modulation) hybrid. This effect can be executed on the woodwinds. On the saxophone it can, for instance, be produced in two ways, with movements in the jaw or diaphragm accents[14] (please also confer Chapter »2. 5. 3 The air and tone technique« for diaphragm accents), on the bassoon by strong pressure of the jaw and lips on the reed[15] or on the flute by a fast upward and downward movements of the upper and lower lips[16].

Bartolozzi suggests notating this effect by means of a special note head[17]. The one he employs is spherical and always white. Additionally, he indicates that there is no fixed rhythm [rhythmisch frei]:

Fig. 1 Bartolozzi, Klänge, p. 27.

Moreover, *Ferneyhough*, in »Mnemosyne«[18], makes use of waved lines, as utilised for the *vibrato* notation, a *tremolo* symbol and the direction *smorzato aperiodico* in order to request an irregular *smorzato*. Moreover, he utilises spatial notation to emphasise the aperiodic character of the articulation:

Fig. 2 Ferneyhough, Mnemosyne, p. 1.

---

[14] Weiss and Netti, Saxophone, p. 151.

[15] Gallois, Bassoon, p. 51.

[16] Levine and Mitropoulos-Bott, Flute, p. 33.

[17] Cf. Bruno Bartolozzi: Neue Klänge für Holzblasinstrumente [New sounds for woodwinds]. Mainz 1971, pp. 26f., 70f. and 76.

[18] Brian Ferneyhough: Mnemosyne. Bass flute and pre-recorded tape. London et al. 1996.

When compared, *Ferneyhough's* method of notation is preferred here. This is because *Bartolozzi's* approach is confusing as he employs single notes for an articulation that is continuous and depicts a rhythm whilst determining that there is no such thing. Further, *Ferneyhough's* method of notation may be described as simpler and closer related to traditional notation. Since the effect has been defined as partially being an overtone *vibrato*, it may be depicted by means of the symbol normally used for the notation of *vibrati*. This method of depiction may easily be comprehended since the symbol and direction are well known. As displayed, *Ferneyhough* additionally employs a *tremolo* symbol. However, despite the depiction of the *smorzato* by means of a *vibrato* and *tremolo* symbol is exact and correct, instantaneous comprehension is compromised. A variant of notation would be to employ solely the *tremolo* symbol and the direction *smorzato*. But since the effect is – as mentioned in the foreword – normally referred to as a *vibrato* variant, waved lines are preferred here. Further, with regard to *Ferneyhough's* depiction of an aperiodic *smorzato* by means of spatial notation, it may be stated that the method seems to distort the clear appearance of the score. A simpler, but admittedly less exact, method would request an aperiodic *smorzato* solely by the direction *smorzato aperiodico* or *smorzato irregolare*. When doing so, it is at the player's discretion to determine the irregular character of the *smorzato*. This method is preferred here from the one by *Ferneyhough* in order to enable the depiction of this articulation in a simple manner. Optionally, the rhythm could, however, be notated by means of splitting longer note values in a number of shorter ones, e. g. a minim into four quavers (cf. Figure 5). Hence the suggested method of notation for the *smorzato* makes use of the *vibrato* symbol and the direction *smorzato*. As can be seen in Figure 3, the player is supposed to perform a *smorzato* on the »c♯/C♯3« for the duration of a minim, followed by a *smorzato irregolare* on the »e/E3«, which is executed for the duration of another minim. In the case of the saxophone, the addition *di mascellare* (jaw) or *di diaframma* (diaphragm) could also be utilised (see above).

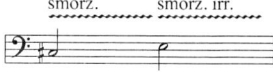

Fig. 3 The *smorzato*.

Further, the so-called extended *tremoli* and trills need to be discussed here because there is an unconventional variant of these techniques. This articulation may be referred to as **bisbigliando**, but is also known as unison *tremolo*, enharmonic trill or timbre trill. If requested, the player is supposed to quickly switch between two or more fingerings of the same pitch. This technique may be executed on all wind instruments with keys or valves, and on the trombone only a slow *bisbigliando* is possible[19]. Moreover, the *bisbigliando* may not be executed on every pitch. However, it is outlined in the handbooks mentioned above if two or more fingerings of the same pitch exist. When performing this articulation, actually neither a *tremolo* nor a real trill is performed because simply the timbre is changing. Hence this effect strongly resembles the *smorzato* articulation.

There are various methods of notation for this technique. One is to complement the common trill notation by the direction timbre trill [Klangfarbentriller] or *bisbigliando*. An example of such a method of notation – employed by *Pagh-Paan* in »Dreisam-Nore« – is presented by *Levine and Mitropoulos-Bott*[20]:

---

[19] Sevsay, Handbuch, p. 147.

[20] Please note that in Younghi Pagh-Paan: Dreisam-Nore. For flute alone. Munich et al. 1980, p. 1 the direction *Klangfarbentriller* is replaced by a chart of the fingerings the flautist is supposed to trill with. However, this example is not displayed here because a similar method is presented in Figure 5.

Fig. 4 Levine and Mitropoulos-Bott, Flute, p. 42.

A variation of this method is suggested by *Sevsay*. He also employs the trill symbol, but determines that this articulation is performed without changing the pitch by utilising an additional note head in brackets. Further, he suggests two other methods of notation. Both make use of a determination of the fingerings the player is supposed to utilise for the timbre trill. As is apparent from Figure 5, he is required to switch between two fingerings whilst each one lasts for the duration of a quaver. The actual switch is, in the example, requested either by letters, index numbers or note heads that represent one of the two fingerings.

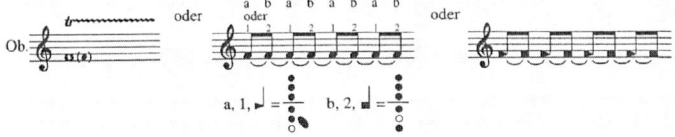

Fig. 5 Sevsay, Handbuch, p. 147.

Finally, *Gallois* suggests depicting the articulation by means of waved lines and the direction *bisbigliando*:

Fig. 6 Gallois, Bassoon, p. 65.

In order to discuss the previous approaches and suggest a method of notation that agrees with the postulated requirements, one needs to determine what kind of sound is produced when the *bisbigliando* technique is applied: the articulation is very similar to the previously described *smorzato* unless only the frequency is modulated, not the amplitude (as in the case of a *tremolo*). However, the actual performance of the articulation resembles playing trill keys. Further, the timbre is not changed in a gliding way (as in the case of an overtone *vibrato*), but abruptly (as in the case of an enharmonic trill). Thus the *bisbigliando* may be described rather as an enharmonic trill than an overtone *vibrato* and is apparently not related to the *tremolo*. Nevertheless, an overtone *vibrato* and the *bisbigliando* articulation resemble each other strongly when the latter is performed in a fast manner because in both cases only the timbre changes. Therefore, the effect is defined here as an enharmonic trill, but also the definition of this articulation as an overtone *vibrato* is regarded as valid. As displayed, *Pagh-Paan* depicts an enharmonic trill. Her method may be described as simple, exact and closely related to traditional notation. However, it would have to be extended when wanting to determine fingerings. As is apparent from the first example of Figure 5, the enharmonic trill may, moreover, be notated with a greater degree of instantaneous comprehension, which is, in this case, achieved by depicting the timbral switch by means of an additional note head. A related variant of notation would be to request the *bisbigliando* by means of an additional natural sign, which is preferred here because additional note heads are – as is apparent from Chapter »2. 9 Percussive effects« – also used for the notation of key clicks and a combination of this effect with an enharmonic trill would cause an unclear appearance of the score. Further, it may be stated that *Sevsay* determines the fingerings and rhythm of the trill in the other two examples in a simple manner. However, the second example may be preferred over the third one. This is because – if, for instance, more than two fingerings of the same pitch were requested – the utilisation of several note heads could cause confusion. Moreover, both methods seem to depict a continuous tone even though a *legato* quaver rhythm is actually requested because the fingering repetitively switches after the duration of a quaver. Finally, an additional trill symbol should, in any case, be used in order to notate the articulation in a uniform manner. Furthermore, *Gallois'* depiction of the *bisbigliando* as an overtone *vibrato* complies with the criteria apart from the fact that he does not make use of exact durations. Thus the suggested method of notation for the *bisbigliando* either makes use of a trill symbol and the natural sign or a *vibrato* symbol and the direction *bisbigliando*. The *bisbigliando* effect is, in Figure 7, employed on a B♭ clarinet[21]. In the first example, the player is supposed to perform an enharmonic trill on the (written) »b/B♭3«. The fingerings are, in this case, determined by the clarinettist. By contrast, in the second example three fingerings are determined between which he is supposed to constantly switch. Additionally, the order of the timbres could be determined by giving a direction, such as 1., 2., 1., 3., 2., 3. (*da capo*). The other two examples depict the same events. However, in this case, the *bisbigliando* is notated as an overtone *vibrato*. The rhythm is undetermined here, but could be depicted by using a number of smaller note values connected by a *legato* slur or directions, such as *irregolare* or *aperiodico*.

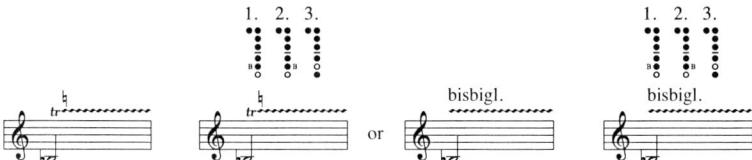

Fig. 7 The *bisbigliando* effect.

Apparently, the fingering chart needs to be altered for other woodwinds or brass instruments whilst on the trombone the slide positions – which the player is supposed to use in order to produce the same pitch – could be determined by giving a direction, e. g. 3 & 5.

Furthermore, it needs to be noted that the **conventional** *tremolo* on woodwinds "is the alternation between two tones, whereby the ambitus is larger than a major second"[22]. Hence actually an augmented trill between two tones rather than a *tremolo* is performed. This is because the term *tremolo* solely describes the modulation of the amplitude. A more correct method would notate this technique similarly to a trill while describing the exact ambitus either by means of a direction (e. g. »g – e♭2/G3 – E♭5«) or using two notes with an interval larger than a major second (cf. Figure 14 in the chapter on plucked instruments). However, the depiction of this articulation by means of the *tremolo* symbol and two notes has been established and will presumably be maintained in the case of wind instruments. Further, there is another variant of this technique that is designated by *Sevsay* as the **broken unison** *tremolo*. It can be produced on woodwinds and brass instruments with valves. When requested, the player is supposed to repeatedly depress and release the same key(s) or valve(s). On brass instruments the articulation is supposed to be performed by means of two fingers that alternately depress a particular valve[23]. Hence actually an extended trill between the pitch pro-

---

[21] Cf. Krassnitzer, Klarinette, pp. 28 and 161: German designations of the keys (B=B♭) are used, and the second fingering is depicted wrongly in the book.

[22] Levine and Mitropoulos-Bott, Flute, p. 42.

[23] Sevsay, Handbuch, pp. 147f.

duced by a particular fingering and the pitch that evolves when the fingered key/s or valve/s is/are released is executed. Therefore, this technique may be depicted similarly to the conventional *tremolo* (or trill when the ambitus is a major second second or smaller).

2. 2 Extended tongue techniques

There are various effects that may be produced by means of the tongue. The most important one is designated as **flutter-tonguing**. Moreover, *pizzicato* effects may be produced and two techniques normally referred to as **slap tongue** and **tongue ram** be employed.

2. 2. 1 The flutter tongue and its notation

Flutter-tonguing is a very popular playing technique, which has been utilised by many composers and may be produced on all wind instruments, but works best on flutes, clarinets, saxophones and brass instruments[24]. It is discussed here because there are two types of flutter tongue. This technique may be either applied by rolling the tip of tongue on the alveolar ridge[25] – which is in the International Phonetic Alphabet (IPA) (see Chapter »6. 2 Extended tongue techniques and their notation« for a chart) designated with the sign [r] – or rolling the back of the tongue at the uvular[26] – which is in the IPA designated with the sign [R][27].

Normally, this technique is notated by giving the direction *Flatt.* or *Flz.* – derived from the German *Flatterzunge* – or the direction *frull.* – derived from the Italian *frullato* – and an additional *tremolo* symbol added to the note tail. This method of notation can, for instance, be found in *Kelemen's* »Changeant«[28] and is presented in Figure 8. There it is not determined which type of flutter tongue the players are supposed to apply.

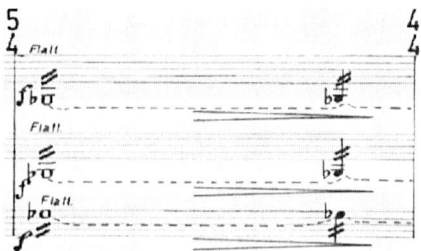

Fig. 8 Kelemen, Changeant, p. 44.

However, some composers differentiate between the two flutter tongue types: in »Segmenti«[29] *Serocki* requests a normal variant (presumably the [R]-flutter tongue) simply by

---

[24] Sevsay, Handbuch, p. 138.

[25] Cf. Gallois, Bassoon, p. 23.

[26] In Levine and Mitropoulos-Bott, Flute, p. 12 the two types of flutter-tonguing are described. However, they explain wrongly that the uvular variant is produced at the glottis. As is apparent from the International Phonetic Alphabet (revised to 2005), such an articulation is impossible.

[27] Cf. Bernd Pompino-Marschall: Einführung in die Phonetik [Introduction to phonetics]. 2nd revised and extended edition. Berlin and New York 2003, p. 185 and the International Phonetic Alphabet (revised to 2005).

[28] Milko Kelemen: Changeant. For violincello and orchestra. Frankfurt/M. et al. 1969.

[29] Kazimierz Serocki: Segmenti. For chamber orchestra. Celle 1962.

means of *tremolo* bars and (presumably) the [r]-flutter tongue[30] by an additional »(r)« placed above these:

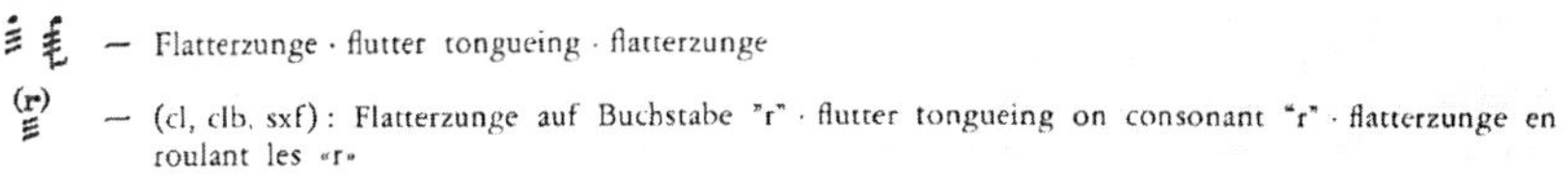

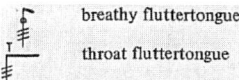

— Flatterzunge · flutter tongueing · flatterzunge

— (cl, clb, sxf): Flatterzunge auf Buchstabe "r" · flutter tongueing on consonant "r" · flatterzunge en roulant les »r«

Fig. 9 Serocki, Segmenti, p. 4.

Further, *Berio* requests a so-called breathy and a throat flutter tongue in »Gesti«[31]. The breathy [r]-variant is depicted by a *tremolo* symbol and a circle added to the note tail whilst the [R]-flutter tongue is requested by writing a »T« over the note:

breathy fluttertongue

throat fluttertongue

Fig. 10 Berio, Gesti, p. 3.

The common method of notation for flutter-tonguing (cf. Figure 8) may be described as accurate. This is mainly because it can be regarded as nearly conventional and simple. When flutter-tonguing, the player produces a kind of *tremolo*[32] and hence modulates the amplitude. However, flutter-tonguing may not simply be requested by means of the *tremolo* symbol since there is – as shown in the previous chapter – another articulation conventionally depicted by means of it. Unless the conventional *tremolo* always occurs in combination with two note heads – and hence is distinct from the depiction of the flutter tongue – the utilisation of a *tremolo* symbol and only one note head to request the flutter tongue might cause confusion. An alternative of notation could be to depict this articulation by means of solely giving the direction *frullato* since it already adequately requests the performance of the flutter tongue. Therefore, *Serocki's* and *Berio's* methods of depiction for the flutter tongue itself here are suggested not being employed. Concerning the notation of the two flutter tongue types, it may be stated that *Serocki's* approach may be preferred over the one by *Berio*. This is because *Berio* introduces two more or less unrelated symbols in order to distinguish the two types. Hence his approach cannot easily be comprehended and, therefore, does not comply with the requirement of simplicity. A more comprehensible symbol is introduced by *Serocki*. However, he does not clearly indicate which method requests which type of flutter tongue. Thus in order to enable the clear and simple depiction of the augmented flutter tongue, another method of notation needs to be developed: since both types may easily be described by means of the IPA, the previously introduced phonetic symbols are utilised here for their depiction. Hence it is suggested depicting the »normal« [r]-flutter tongue by means of the direction *frullato* [r] or [r]-*Flatterzunge* and the [R]-flutter tongue by the direction *frullato* [R] or [R]-*Flatterzunge*. Alternatively, the more common [r]-variant could be requested by solely giving the direction *frullato/Flatterzunge* or the flutter tongue types not be distinguished and hence the exact performance be left to the player's discretion. When the flutter tongue types are not distinguished, the notation of this technique is actually facilitated. This is because both flutter tongue types cannot be produced in every register of every wind instrument. For instance, on

---

[30] As is apparent from Figure 9, he does not clearly indicate whether the »r« is rolled at the alveolar ridge or the uvular. However, since *Serocki* was born in Poland and the [r] – but not the [R] – is a common phoneme in the polish language, this assumption is made here (with regard to that he mentions the consonant »r«).

[31] Luciano Berio: Gesti. For alto recorder. London 1970.

[32] Weiss and Netti, Saxophone, p. 150.

the B♭ clarinet the [r]-flutter tongue may only be used up to the (written) »g²/G5«[33] whilst on the oboe normally the [R]-flutter tongue is utilised since the [r]-flutter tongue may disturb the reed[34]. Therefore, one needs to be aware of the instrument's characteristic when notating both flutter tongue variants. Additionally, the flutter tongue may be performed in an irregular manner. As can be seen in Figure 11, *Xenakis,* in »Linaia – Agon«[35], requests the performance of such an articulation by means of the direction *flatterzunge irrégulier.*

Fig. 11 Xenakis, Linaia, p. 13.

Since this method of notation complies with all criteria, the irregular variant can be depicted by either giving this or the direction *frullato* ([r] or [R]) *irregolare.*

2. 2. 2 The *pizzicato* effect and its notation

A *pizzicato* effect can on wind instruments be produced in two ways: firstly, by modifying the normal articulation of the tongue. This is achieved by placing the tongue firmly on the roof of the mouth and then, supported by a strong air stream, explosively throwing it to the bottom. Secondly, the same effect may be produced by the lips. In this case, the lips are first pressed tightly together and then explosively ripped apart by a strong jet of air[36]. The first technique produces a rather dry and the second technique a rather wet sound. The *pizzicato* technique may be employed on all wind instruments. However, on the bassoon (and due to the similar embouchure also on the oboe) the lip *pizzicato* is preferably used[37].

In most cases, composers do not notate two different *pizzicato* types, but simply request the performance of a *pizzicato*. In »Linaia – Agon« *Xenakis* simply gives a horn blower, trombonist and tuba player the direction *pizzicato*, but does not explain whether this effect is produced by means of the tongue or lips:

Fig. 12 Xenakis, Linaia, p. 3.

---

33 Krassnitzer, Klarinette, p. 21.

34 Veale, Oboe, p. 130.

35 Iannis Xenakis: Linaia – Agon. For horn, trombone and tuba. Paris 1972.

36 Levine and Mitropoulos-Bott, Flute, p. 25.

37 Gallois, Bassoon, p. 47.

Further, *Michael*, in »Invocationes«[38], makes use of a note head shaped like an accent in order to request inter alia the tongue *pizzicato*[39]:

Fig. 13 Michael, Invocationes, p. 6.

The *pizzicato* effect on wind instruments is apparently different from the original articulation on string instruments since no strings are plucked. Nevertheless, the character of both sounds is similar and the characterisation of this technique as a *pizzicato* has been established. Therefore, it can be regarded as valid to request the articulation by means of the direction *pizzicato*, as executed by *Xenakis*. Moreover, it may be stated that this method of notation is simple and closely related to traditional notation. However, in order to enable the differentiation of the two *pizzicato* types, one would have to further augment it. Opposed to *Xenakis'* approach, *Michael's* method of notation is not closely related to traditional notation since he introduces a new symbol for a technique that may also be notated in a conventional manner. Therefore, it does not agree with the postulated requirements. *Xenakis'* approach is, therefore, adopted here and suggested as the method of notation for the *pizzicato* effect on wind instruments. It could be augmented further by describing the utilised *pizzicato* technique by means of the IPA. This is because both articulations are augmented clicks. The tongue *pizzicato* can actually be described by the phoneme [!], and the lip *pizzicato* may be described by the sign [⊙]. Therefore, the two types may be requested by the directions *pizzicato* [!] and *pizzicato* [⊙] (see Chapter »6. 2 Extended tongue techniques and their notation« for the IPA chart). However, the manner of performance may also be determined by the player. In such a case, it is sufficient to use *Xenakis'* method of notation.

2. 2. 3 The slap tongue

The two tongue techniques slap tongue and tongue ram produce similar sounds and are often confused with each other. Both techniques may be performed on all wind instruments, but on flutes only with trumpet embouchure[40] (cf. Chapter »2. 3. 1 The trumpet embouchure«). This chapter focuses on the slap tongue whilst the tongue ram effect is explained in the following chapter. For example, on the saxophone the slap tongue is executed by pressing the tongue against the reed and almost immediately pulling it off. The slap tongue can be performed *staccato*, but may also be the attack of a longer tone. This technique can be compared to the *Bartók pizzicato* of the strings because the character of both sounds is similar[41]. *Krassnitzer* and *Weiss and Netti* define three different types of slaps: **1. The *secco* slap**. Only the slap portion, the percussive part of the sound is audible since the player does not blow into the instrument. The pitch is only a shadow. This type of slap can only be performed *staccato*. **2. The standard slap**. It has a clear pitch and the typical noise component of the slap tongue. It can be performed *staccato* or as the attack of a sustained tone. **3. The open slap**. At the moment of

---

[38] Frank Michael: Invocationes. For flute alone. Berlin and Wiesbaden 1979.

[39] As is apparent from the foreword, *Michael* actually requests two different articulations by means of this symbol, the tongue *pizzicato* and a technique resembling the articulation which is in Chapter »2. 7 Whistle techniques« referred to as the jet whistle.

[40] Levine and Mitropoulos-Bott, Flute, p. 28.

[41] Cf. Weiss and Netti, Saxophone, p. 142.

the attack, the jaw is dropped, producing a strong, percussive sound. This articulation is only possible *staccato* since the embouchure is opened[42].

2. 2. 3. 1 Previous methods of notation

Holliger, in »Three pieces«[43], requests a *secco* slap by means of an additional symbol added to the note tail. This method of notation is presented in Figure 14. Other slap tongue variants are not employed in this work.

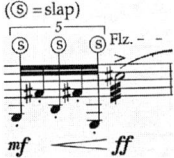 quasi ‚slap‘, tonguing only, no blowing! sempre leggero
quasi ‚slap‘, nur Zungenstösse, nicht blasen! sempre leggero
quasi ‚slap‘, coups de langue seulement, sans souffler! sempre leggero

Fig. 14 Holliger, Pieces, p. 5.

Moreover, in »Schattenklänge«[44] *Kagel* requests the slap tongue by means of a circled »s« placed above the note. However, he does not explain which type of slap tongue the player is supposed to execute:

Fig. 15 Kagel, Schattenklänge, p. 3.

Further, *Weiss and Netti* present an example by *Birkenkötter*. In his »Tripelkonzert« for saxophone, percussion, piano (soli) and orchestra the slap tongue is requested by means of the symbol normally used for the depiction of the *Bartók pizzicato*. However, from the example it cannot be determined which type of slap tongue is requested.

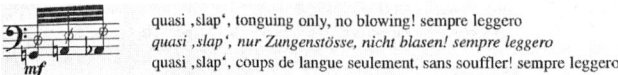

Fig. 16 Weiss and Netti, Saxophone, p. 146.

2. 2. 3. 2 Discussion

Kagel's method of notation (cf. Figure 15) is preferred here over *Holliger's* one (cf. Figure 14). This is because the addition of symbols to the note tail might lead to confusion when semibreves or additional *tremolo* symbols are depicted. Unless such a long duration would not be requested in combination with the *secco* or open slap, it is – with regard to the necessary depiction of the standard slap – preferred here to place the symbol above the note. Although *Holliger's* symbol could also be utilised in this way, *Kagel's* symbolic notation is favoured here because it contains a greater degree of instantaneous comprehension. This is because it can easily be identified as a depiction of the slap tongue technique. Further, the symbol employed by *Birkenkötter* (cf. Figure 16) is likewise very simple and clear because the slap tongue technique produces, as mentioned, sounds that resemble the *Bartók pizzicato*. Moreo-

---

[42] Cf. Krassnitzer, Klarinette, p. 22 and Weiss and Netti, Saxophone, p. 143.

[43] Heinz Holliger: Three pieces. For bassoon solo. Mainz 2002.

[44] Mauricio Kagel: Schattenklänge. Three pieces for bass clarinet. Frankfurt/M. et al. 1997.

ver, by introducing this approach a stronger coherence would be achieved since two similar articulations would be notated in the same manner and the *pizzicato* effect is also notated by means of the method derived from string instruments (cf. Chapter »2. 2. 2 The *pizzicato* effect and its notation«). However, none of the three methods of notation enables the depiction of the three slap tongue types. Thus the method of notation needs to be augmented further.

2. 2. 3. 3 Suggestion for the notation of the slap tongue

Hence the *Bartók pizzicato* symbol is suggested being used for the depiction of the slap tongue articulation. When employing it, the standard slap is supposed to be executed. The *secco* and the open slap can be requested by means of the additional directions *secco* and (*bocca*) *aperta* (open mouth). As is apparent from Figure 17, the player is at first supposed to perform a *secco* semiquaver slap »c¹/C4«. It is followed by a sustained standard slap »d¹/D4« that is the attack of a sustained tone. After a dotted crotchet rest, the player is then required to perform an open semiquaver slap »f¹/F4«. *Staccato* dots are, in the example, not employed because there is only one way of executing the *secco* and open slap, and the *staccato* performance is already adequately expressed by using small note values.

Fig. 17 The slap tongue articulation.

The dynamic level of this articulation is limited. For instance, on the saxophone the *secco* slap can be played with the dynamic level *pianissimo* to *mezzoforte*, the standard slap with the dynamic level *piano* to *forte fortissimo* and the open slap with the dynamic level *mezzoforte* to *forte fortissimo*[45].

2. 2. 4 The tongue ram

The tongue ram is a forceful, explosive effect. For instance, on flutes the tongue is propelled into the embouchure hole with a strong thrust of air and then stopped or already stopped on the roof of the mouth, respectively[46]. However, on the saxophone the tongue »rams« against the reed or, with an embouchure without mouthpiece, is propelled directly into the open, upper end of the saxophone tube[47]. The same technique of hitting the reed with the tongue is by *Gallois* designated as a flap[48] and by *Veale* confused with the slap tongue[49]. Additionally, the articulation is sometimes also referred to as a tongue stop[50] and may in a similar manner be performed on all wind instruments. When performing a tongue ram on, for instance, the flutes (as mentioned, only in combination with trumpet embouchure), the produced tone sounds a major seventh lower than the fingered tone on the concert and alto flute, a minor ninth lower on the piccolo and a minor seventh lower on the bass flute[51]. The tongue ram may only be performed *staccato* since it results in the flow of air being blocked.

---

[45] Weiss and Netti, Saxophone, pp. 142f.

[46] Levine and Mitropoulos-Bott, Flute, p. 28.

[47] Weiss and Netti, Saxophone, p. 148.

[48] Cf. Gallois, Bassoon, p. 45.

[49] Cf. Veale, Oboe, p. 143.

[50] Sevsay, Handbuch, p. 151.

[51] Levine and Mitropoulos-Bott, Flute II, p. 21.

2. 2. 4. 1 Previous methods of notation

In »Sen I«[52] *Hosokawa* notates the tongue ram articulation on the concert flute similarly to the way artificial harmonics on string instruments are depicted. However, in this case, the diamond-shaped note head depicts the fingering and the common note head the pitch that is produced when employing this articulation (a major seventh lower than the fingered tone):

 = Tongue-ram. To produce tongue-ram, one must violently close the hole of the mouthpiece with the tongue without breathing any air out. The air, which is thus forced into the bore of the flute by the tongue, produces a note of identifiable pitch sounding a major seventh below the fundamental frequency of the fingering which one employs.

Fig. 18 Hosokawa, Sen I, p. 4.

Further, many composers confuse the slap tongue and tongue ram effect with each other. For instance, *Lachenmann*, in »Allegro sostenuto«[53], designates the tongue ram on the clarinet as slap tones and notates these by means of a special note head shaped like a triangle:

 Slap tones correspond to the "tongue ram" on the flute: in conjunction with a thrust of air from the diaphragm, the tongue flicks towards the front between the lips, thus abruptly blocking the flow of air. The result is a hard, percussive click whose pitch is determined by the fingering on the clarinet.

Fig. 19 Lachenmann, Allegro, no page named [foreword].

Moreover, *Braun*, in »Tuba Tabu«[54], depicts the tongue ram effect by means of a note head shaped like an accent and additionally describing the sound the player produces when performing this articulation as »ft«[55]:

Fig. 20 Braun, Tuba, p. 4.

2. 2. 4. 2 Discussion

Hosokawa's approach of depicting the tongue ram as a reversed artificial harmonic (cf. Figure 18) can be described as exact since the fingered and resulting pitch is notated. However, opposed to the notation of artificial harmonics, it is not necessary to depict two tones, but sufficient to notate the fingering because the resulting pitch is immanent to the employed tongue ram technique. Moreover, since the tongue ram technique involves different transpositions and is – depending on the instrument – performed in slightly varying ways, the resulting pitch would have to be determined for each wind instrument. This would in turn lead to the introduction of a complex method of notation for a technique, which could simply be depicted by giving a direction. Further, *Lachenmann's* method (cf. Figure 19) may be described as simple. When the note head is distinct from all other note heads used for the depiction of extended playing techniques of wind instrument, his method of notation may be utilised. Moreover, even though the accent note head (cf. Figure 20) could not be used when semibreves were requested, it may still be described as valid. This is because the tongue ram articulation can only be performed *staccato* and hence longer note values are normally not

---

[52] Toshio Hosokawa: Sen I. For flute. Mainz et al. 1993.

[53] Helmut Lachenmann: Allegro sostenuto. For clarinet, bass clarinet in B♭, violincello and piano. Wiesbaden et al. 2003.

[54] Gerhard Braun: Tuba - Tabu. For tuba solo. Bad Schwalbach 2004.

[55] Also cf. Veale, Oboe, p. 143.

employed. However, despite that it may be stated that *Lachenmann's* and *Braun's* methods agree with the postulated requirements, they are rejected here. This is because the slap tongue and tongue ram articulations are related to each other since similar sounds are produced. Thus in order to coherently depict these two playing techniques, a method resembling the one for the slap tongue is preferred here to be developed.

2. 2. 4. 3 Suggestion for the notation of the tongue ram

The symbol suggested for the notation of the tongue ram technique is derived from the one utilised for the depiction of the slap tongue (cf. Figure 17). As can be seen in Figure 21, the articulation is requested by means of a completely black *Bartók pizzicato* symbol, referring to the closure of the embouchure hole/reed/tube etc.

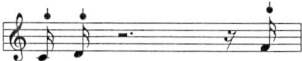

Fig. 21 The tongue ram effect.

The tongue ram effect can be performed with a dynamic level ranging from approximately *pianissimo* to *mezzopiano*[56]. Moreover, when executed without reed (oboe) or without mouthpiece (saxophone), the dynamic level can even be raised up to *mezzoforte* or *forte*[57] (see Chapter »2. 6. 1 Detaching the headjoint/mouthpiece/reed/bocal and its notation« for the notation of playing without mouthpiece).

2. 3 Extended embouchure techniques

In order to transform the sound of wind instruments, the embouchure may be changed. One special technique, which is normally employed on flutes, is referred to as **trumpet embouchure**. Additionally, flutes may be played with **closed embouchure**. Another technique, which can be applied on instruments with reeds, is the **teeth embouchure**. Finally, the **recorder embouchure** may be requested on all wind instruments, but the flute.

2. 3. 1 The trumpet embouchure

The technique designated as trumpet embouchure or *alla tromba* is normally executed on flutes. However, it can also be performed on the other woodwinds when playing without mouthpiece (clarinet and saxophone) or without reed (oboe, bassoon) as well as on flutes without the headjoint. A method of notation for removing the reed, mouthpiece or headjoint is presented in Chapter »2. 6. 1 Detaching the headjoint/mouthpiece/reed/bocal and its notation« whilst this chapter solely focuses on the notation of the trumpet embouchure articulation. When requested on woodwinds other than flutes, the notation for removing the reed, or the mouthpiece, needs to precede the depiction of the trumpet embouchure. For example, in the case of the flute, a tone is created *alla tromba* through a combination of lip tension, air pressure and resonating spaces. The lips need to be pressed tightly together and forced to vibrate through a strong exhaling pressure. The production of a specific pitch is determined by the lip tension and the shape of the mouth. Hence several tones and *glissandi* may be performed without changing the fingering position[58]. Further, when employing this technique tones may

---

[56] Cf. Gallois, Bassoon, p. 45, Veale, Oboe, p. 143 and Weiss and Netti, Saxophone, p. 149.

[57] Veale, Oboe, p. 143 and Weiss and Netti, Saxophone, p. 149.

[58] Levine and Mitropoulos-Bott, Flute, p. 18.

also be produced by inhaling air. When doing so, the pitch is lower than the fingered tone[59]. Moreover, when playing *alla tromba* without mouthpiece, the resulting pitch is higher than the fingered tone since the tube is shortened by the length of the mouthpiece.

2. 3. 1. 1 Previous methods of notation

The notation for this articulation has not yet been standardised. *Levine and Mitropoulos-Bott* recommend simply giving the direction trumpet embouchure[60] (or alternatively *alla tromba*). Moreover, *Holliger*, in »Sonate (in)solit(air)e«[61], makes use of an enclosed note head and an enclosed »T« in order to request the trumpet embouchure. He further differentiates between trumpet embouchure while exhaling (an arrow pointing downwards added to the note tail), trumpet embouchure while inhaling (an arrow pointing upwards added to the note tail) and trumpet embouchure with less lip tension, which results in a pitch one octave or a minor seventh lower than the fingered tone (no enclosed note head, but instead the resulting pitch in brackets):

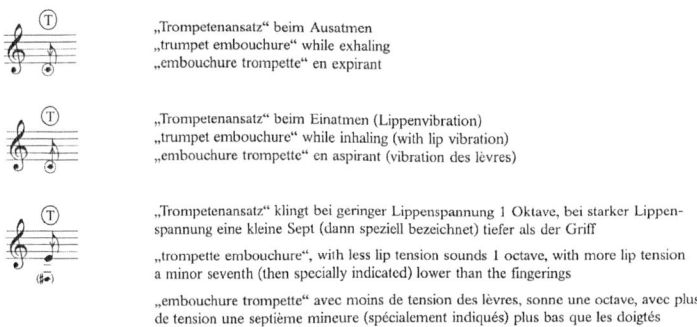

„Trompetenansatz" beim Ausatmen
„trumpet embouchure" while exhaling
„embouchure trompette" en expirant

„Trompetenansatz" beim Einatmen (Lippenvibration)
„trumpet embouchure" while inhaling (with lip vibration)
„embouchure trompette" en aspirant (vibration des lèvres)

„Trompetenansatz" klingt bei geringer Lippenspannung 1 Oktave, bei starker Lippen-spannung eine kleine Sept (dann speziell bezeichnet) tiefer als der Griff

„trompette embouchure", with less lip tension sounds 1 octave, with more lip tension a minor seventh (then specially indicated) lower than the fingerings

„embouchure trompette" avec moins de tension des lèvres, sonne une octave, avec plus de tension une septième mineure (spécialement indiqués) plus bas que les doigtés

Fig. 22 Holliger, Sonate, p. 4.

2. 3. 1. 2 Discussion

The utilisation of a woodwind in the same manner as a brass instrument may be compared to the utilisation of a violin or viola in the same manner as a mandolin. The latter is traditionally requested by the direction *al mandolino* (cf. Chapter »1. 1 Extended *pizzicato* techniques and their notation«). Thus the direction *alla tromba* would request the trumpet embouchure in close relation to traditional notation. This direction may at the same time be described as simple and is clearer than *Holliger's* enclosure of the note (cf. Figure 22). Moreover, the depiction of the pitch the player is supposed to produce by means of changing the lip tension and/or inhaling needs to be determined. *Holliger's* method of notation is able to depict whether the player is inhaling or exhaling. However, the addition of symbols to the note tail leads, as mentioned, to confusion when semibreves or additional *tremolo* symbols are depicted. Alternatively, the arrows could be placed over the note. But nevertheless, it would still not be obvious if the depicted tone is related to the fingered/resulting pitch or if the fingered pitch equals the resulting pitch. Hence it is clearer to notate both, the fingered and the resulting pitch, as executed by *Holliger* in terms of the trumpet embouchure with less lip tension (which results in a lower tone). However, firstly, the production of tones with trumpet embou-chure is very complex since it is dependent on the skills of the player as well as the instrument that is employed (whilst, for instance, the instruments without mouthpiece are transposed up),

[59] Cf. Veale, Oboe, p. 137.
[60] Levine and Mitropoulos-Bott, Flute, p. 18.
[61] Heinz Holliger: Sonate (in)solit(air)e. For flute solo. Mainz et al. 1998.

and, secondly, there has not been an adequate amount of research conducted concerning this articulation. Thus it cannot be determined exactly which tones can be produced on a single fingering position, and the resulting sounds need to be determined approximately, which can only be executed by introducing an extended method of notation.

2. 3. 1. 3 Suggestion for the notation of the trumpet embouchure

Hence the trumpet embouchure is requested by giving the direction *alla tromba*. Further, the depiction of the pitch the player is supposed to produce is not depicted by means of the traditional notation system, but by means of relative values and an additional system. This is because when the resulting pitch cannot be determined exactly, it is clearer to notate it by means of a value that represents the degree of transposition than by notating wrong or approximate pitches. Here the traditional system depicts the fingered tone and the additional system the transposition in time. The x-axis of the transposition system represents, as usual, the duration and the y-axis the degree of the transposition. There are six levels for upward and six levels for downward transpositions. The middle axis (0) represents the kind of trumpet embouchure articulation that produces the most natural tone (and hence the fingered tone on the flute and, in the case of instruments without a mouthpiece, a pitch that is higher than the fingered tone). Moreover, the dots (◇◆) depict the degree of transposition in time. This system enables the depiction of any kind of transposition executed by changing the lip tension and/or inhaling as well as *glissandi*. The act of in- or exhaling is, in combination with this system, not notated specifically since the player will automatically inhale if it is necessary to produce a certain pitch (however, also cf. Chapter »2. 5. 3 The air and tone technique« for a distinct notation of inhaled winding). Rests are used in this system since no additional sound is produced (which would be suggested by notes), but the fingered sound transformed. As is apparent from Figure 23, initially four crotchets »f¹/F4« are supposed to be played *alla tromba*. However, each crotchet is transposed in a different manner: the first one is transposed down by 2/6 levels, the second one transposed up by 4/6 levels, the third one transposed up by 2/6 levels and the last one transposed as far down as possible. Subsequently, the instrumentalist plays a semibreve »f¹/F4«. This sound is transformed in a gliding way and hence a *glissando* executed. It starts on the most natural tone, which is then gradually transposed down to level 3/6 for the duration of a minim and subsequently transposed up to level 2/6 for the duration of a crotchet. This pitch then remains constant for another crotchet. Black and white note heads are utilised here in order to clearly outline which note is related to which degree of transposition.

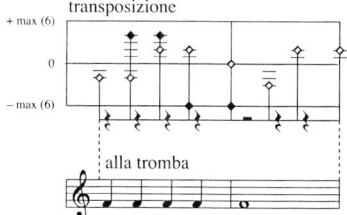

Fig. 23 The trumpet embouchure and the transposition system.

Because the pitch is modified by actually changing the lip tension and shape of the mouth, the pitch bending technique is applied (cf. Chapter »2. 4 Pitch bending – the extended *glissando*«). A transposition system only needs to be applied when the resulting pitch ≠ 0. When solely the most natural tone is supposed to be produced, it is sufficient to give the direction *alla tromba*. In the case of playing without mouthpiece, the system can be regarded as a

73

transposing notation system. Alternatively, the transposition system may be changed to more or less than 12 + 1 levels (please also cf. Figure 29 for an alternative method of notation). Further, the dynamic level of this articulation is limited. It can, for instance, on the saxophone only be executed with the dynamic level *pianissimo* to approximately *forte*[62].

2. 3. 2 The closed embouchure and its notation

The closed embouchure is a variation of the trumpet embouchure and may be executed solely on flutes. When requesting this rare technique, the player is supposed to cover the whole mouthpiece with his lips. *Holliger* depicts the closed embouchure similarly to the trumpet embouchure by means of an enclosed note head:

Fig. 24 Holliger, Sonate, p. 4.

This playing technique may be compared with the clarinet (or saxophone) embouchure since in both cases the embouchure hole is sealed with the lips. Admittedly, the relation between playing *alla tromba* and the original trumpet embouchure is stronger than the one between playing *al clarinetto* and the original clarinet embouchure, but it is still sufficient in order to describe the closed embouchure. Since such a direction is, as shown before by taking the example of the trumpet embouchure and playing *al mandolino*, strongly related to traditional notation and clearer than *Holliger's* method of employing an enclosed note head, as well as because it enables the uniform depiction of the different embouchure techniques, this method of notation is suggested being utilised in order to depict the closed embouchure. Hence the technique may simply be requested by giving the direction *al clarinetto* (or alternatively *al sassofono*).

2. 3. 3 Teeth embouchure

Teeth tones may be produced by slightly touching the reed of certain woodwinds with the lower incisors[63]. The result is that high tones of harmonic character are created[64]. The timbral quality of these sharp and shrill notes deviates considerably from common tones[65]. However, pitches and the exact intonation of the teeth tones cannot be predicted exactly since it is determined by the performer and materials. Moreover, by moving the teeth forward and backward on the mouthpiece *glissandi* occur[66].

2. 3. 3. 1 Previous methods of notation

The teeth embouchure is notated in various ways. *Dittrich*, in »– the – m –«[67], requests it by giving the direction with teeth [mit den Zähnen] and crossing out the note head. Since no additional explanation is provided by him, the depicted pitch presumably refers to the fingered tone:

---

[62] Weiss and Netti, Saxophone, p. 147.

[63] Cf. Krassnitzer, Klarinette, p. 26.

[64] Weiss and Netti, Saxophone, p. 164.

[65] Veale, Oboe, p. 63.

[66] Weiss and Netti, Saxophone, pp. 164f.

[67] Paul-Heinz Dittrich: – the – m –. For bassoon solo and live-electronics based on an epigram by e. e. cummings. In: Dieter Hähnchen (ed.): Zeitgenössische Musik für Fagott solo [Contemporary music for bassoon alone]. Leipzig 1986, pp. 19-33.

Fig. 25 Dittrich, – the – m –, p. 25a.

Another approach is employed by *Serocki* in »Swinging music«[68]. He depicts the teeth embouchure by means of note heads shaped like a triangle pointing downwards and determines the produced pitch in an approximate way:

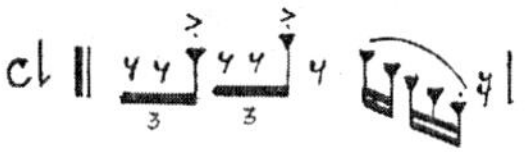

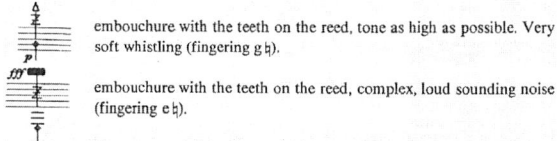

Fig. 26 Serocki, Swinging, p. 12.

Moreover, *Lachenmann*, in »Dal niente (Interieur III)«[69], notates this articulation by means of a note head shaped like a »Z« (as in the German *Zähne*, meaning teeth). As is apparent from Figure 27, the pitch is not determined when this articulation is employed.

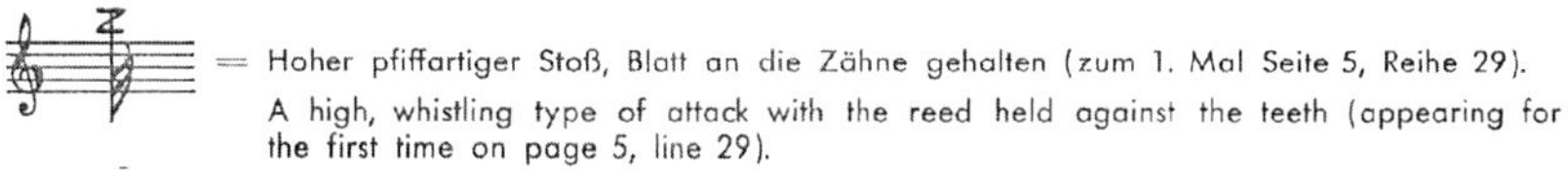

= Hoher pfiffartiger Stoß, Blatt an die Zähne gehalten (zum 1. Mal Seite 5, Reihe 29).

A high, whistling type of attack with the reed held against the teeth (appearing for the first time on page 5, line 29).

Fig. 27 Lachenmann, Niente, no page named [foreword].

Finally, *Holliger*, in »Pneuma«[70], adds a »Z« to the note tail, determines which tone is fingered and differentiates between two types of teeth tones, the highest possible tone produced with a low dynamic level and a loud sounding noise:

embouchure with the teeth on the reed, tone as high as possible. Very soft whistling (fingering g♮).

embouchure with the teeth on the reed, complex, loud sounding noise (fingering e♮).

Fig. 28 Holliger, Pneuma, p. 6.

2. 3. 3. 2 Discussion

Dittrich's method of notation (cf. Figure 25) is simple, but may also be described as containing redundant elements. This is because the teeth embouchure is requested by means of a direction and a crossed out note head, although utilising one of the two methods would be sufficient. Further, since techniques that resemble changing the embouchure on woodwinds are normally requested by means of directions, e. g. the determination of the manner the bow is used by directions such as *arco sul ponticello* or *col legno tratto sul tasto*, and the other embouchure techniques have also been notated in this way, the method of depicting the teeth tone by means of a special note head – as employed by *Serocki* (cf. Figure 26) and *Lachenmann* (cf. Figure 27) – as well as the method of requesting the teeth tone by means of a »Z« added to the note tail – as employed by *Holliger* (cf. Figure 28) – is rejected here in favour of giving the direction with teeth or *con denti* – as employed by *Dittrich*. Concerning the

[68] Kazimierz Serocki: Swinging music. For clarinet, trombone, cello (or double bass), and piano. Celle 1971.

[69] Helmut Lachenmann: Dal niente (Interieur III). For a solo clarinet-player. Cologne 1974.

[70] Heinz Holliger: Pneuma. For wind, percussion, organ and radios. Mainz 1972.

notation of the produced pitch, it may be stated that *Dittrich* requests only one type of teeth tone and disregards the teeth tone variations. Moreover, *Serocki's* approach is very approximate. This is because the fingered tone is not depicted and the resulting sound is only determined in a very inexact manner. Apparently, *Lachenmann's* method is even less exact since neither the fingered tone nor the resulting pitch is depicted, whilst *Holliger's* approach is the most exact one. However, in the case of requesting the player to produce the highest possible tone, it is not necessary to employ two note heads. As shown in Chapter »1. 4. 1 The highest possible tone and its notation«, the note head used to depict the string may at the same time request the production of the highest possible tone when it is shaped like a triangle pointing upwards. Since the string upon which the highest possible tone is produced is an equivalent to the fingering upon which the highest possible tone is produced, it would be sufficient to only employ a single note head shaped like a triangle pointing upwards in order to depict the fingered tone and the production of the highest possible pitch at the same time. Further, a loud sounding noise cannot be requested when the player is supposed to play *con denti*. This is because only high tones of harmonic character may, as mentioned, be created. Therefore, a method of notation that complies with the depiction of the highest possible pitch used in this work needs to be introduced in order to request a variation of pitches and *glissandi*.

2. 3. 3. 3 Suggestion for the notation of the teeth embouchure

The teeth embouchure is requested by giving the direction *con denti*. In order to request the production of the most natural teeth tone/middle pitch, the highest possible tone as well as *glissandi* between these two pitches, one could simply employ common note heads (for the most natural teeth tone), triangular note heads pointing upwards (for the highest possible tone) and the common *glissando* notation. Additionally, triangular note heads pointing downwards could be employed in order to request the lowest possible tone. Such a method of notation is presented in Figure 29. Here the player is at first supposed to produce the most natural teeth tone/middle pitch on the fingering position »f¹/F4« for the duration of a crotchet. Subsequently, a *glissando* from the lowest possible teeth tone to the highest possible teeth tone is performed for the duration of a crotchet on the same fingering position. The highest possible tone is then played for the duration of another crotchet and followed by the most natural tone/middle pitch, executed again on the same fingering position for the duration of a crotchet.

Fig. 29 The teeth embouchure.

As mentioned above, in this work the *glissando* – in order to achieve a greater clarity and enable the depiction of *glissando* motions that do not involve changes in pitch – is requested by means of an arrow and not in the traditional manner. Alternatively, the common method of depiction may be restored. However, this might cause confusion because the notes are not transposed. Further, when more than three different pitches are supposed to be requested, a transposition system similar to the one employed in Figure 23 can be utilised (and likewise the transposition system be replaced by the method of depiction introduced here when only the described three pitches are supposed to be produced by means of trumpet embouchure). As teeth tones require a change of embouchure, *legato* articulations between teeth and common tones, as well as rapid passages between these two, are not possible. Similarly problematic are large intervals and fast tempos[71]. The dynamic level of this articulation ranges, for

---

[71] Veale, Oboe, p. 63.

instance, on the saxophone from approximately *pianissimo* to *forte fortissimo*. However, it cannot always be controlled precisely. Further, teeth tones may be combined with flutter-tonguing[72] (cf. Chapter »2. 2. 1 The flutter tongue and its notation«).

2. 3. 4 The recorder embouchure and its notation

The recorder embouchure is a technique, which is barely utilised. It may be requested on all wind instruments except for the flutes. *Lachenmann* describes this embouchure as an articulation "where the player must blow onto the mouthpiece from the shortest distance possible, similarly to playing a recorder"[73]. He notates this articulation by means of diamond-shaped note heads and additionally indicating to wind the mouthpiece from a distance [aus der Entfernung aufs Mundstück geblasen]:

Fig. 30 Lachenmann, Allegro, p. 11.

However, similarly to the trumpet embouchure, this technique may be requested in closer relation to traditional notation by simply giving the direction *al flauto dolce* (in the manner of a recorder). By introducing this method of notation, a uniform depiction of the trumpet, teeth and recorder embouchure is achieved. The dynamic level of this articulation is limited. As is apparent from Figure 30, *Lachenmann*, for example, requests a maximum dynamic level that is louder than *piano*, but not as loud as *forte* since »[f]orte markings in quotation marks (...) do not indicate the objective resulting volume, but (»subjective«) intensity of the effort during the execution"[74].

2. 4 Pitch bending – the extended *glissando*

The term pitch bending or bend tone describes a special *glissando* technique[75]. It is executed via changes in lip tension (all brass instruments) or embouchure (all woodwinds) and/or opening and closing tone holes[76] (only woodwinds and, for instance, in a limited manner on the piccolo, alto and bass flute)[77]. The extent of the *glissando* is dependent on the instrument. For instance, on the B♭ clarinet pitch bending may be performed by means of opening and closing the keys over the range (of the written) »g/G3« to »g¹/G4« and from »d²/D5« upwards. These *glissandi* can additionally be reinforced above about »d²/D5« by means of the embouchure. Further, on this instrument the pitch can only be raised slightly, but lowered by several semitones[78]. Moreover, on the flute the embouchure *glissando* may also be executed by turning the instrument inward (to produce a descending *glissando*) and outward (to produce an ascending

---

[72] Cf. Weiss and Netti, Saxophone, p. 165 and Serocki, Swinging, no page named [foreword].

[73] Lachenmann, Allegro, no page named [foreword].

[74] Ibid., no page named [foreword].

[75] Sevsay, Handbuch, p. 141.

[76] Cf. Jer-Ming Chen et al.: Pitch bending and *glissandi* on the clarinet. Roles of the vocal tract and partial tone hole closure. In: Journal of the Acoustic Society of America, vol. 126(3). No city named 2009, pp. 1511-1520, here: p. 1511.

[77] Levine and Mitropoulos-Bott, Flute II, p. 37.

[78] Chen, Pitch, p. 1511.

glissando)[79]. Generally, the possible extent of these *glissandi* also depends on the tone that is fingered. Hence when requesting this technique, one needs to study the capacities of the instrument and could discuss the technique with the performers.

2. 4. 1 Previous methods of notation

Most composers notate the pitch bending articulation in an approximate way. In »Changeant« *Kelemen*, for instance, depicts this type of *glissando* on a trumpet by means of a line that describes how the player is supposed to bend the tone:

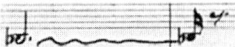

Fig. 31 Kelemen, Changeant, p. 29.

Moreover, *Ferneyhough* utilises a similar method in »Incipits«. Here the *glissando* on a piccolo is designated as lip *glissando* and a grace note employed to mark the endpoint of the articulation:

Fig. 32 Ferneyhough, Incipits, p. 19.

Foss, in »Echoi«[80], also makes use of a similar technique. However, in this case, the lines depict a *glissando* of exactly a quarter tone:

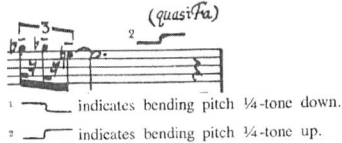

¹ ⌐⌐ indicates bending pitch ¼-tone down.

² ⌐⌐ indicates bending pitch ¼-tone up.

Fig. 33 Foss, Echoi, p. 28.

Further, *Köszeghy*, in »Mortualium, (coins for Charon)«[81] requests a *glissando*, which is performed by solely turning the flute [nur durch Drehen der Flöte]:

Fig. 34 Köszeghy, Mortualium, p. 5.

For this particular technique *Dick* suggests five different embouchure angles[82]: normal angle [Normaler Winkel], turned slightly outwards [leicht nach außen gedreht], turned slightly inwards [leicht nach innen gedreht], as far as possible turned outwards [so weit als möglich

---

[79] Levine and Mitropoulos-Bott, Flute, p. 46.

[80] Lukas Foss: Echoi. For four soloists. Clarinet, cello, percussion, and piano. New York and Mainz 1964.

[81] Pèter Köszeghy: Mortualium (coins for Charon). For ensemble. No city named [Berlin] 2008.

[82] Cf. Robert Dick: Neuer Klang durch neue Technik [Tone development through extended techniques]. Frankfurt/M. 1992, p. 8.

nach außen gedreht] and as far as possible turned inwards [so weit als möglich nach innen gedreht]:

U— Normaler Winkel   C — so weit als möglich nach außen gedreht

Ʊ— leicht nach außen gedreht   ⊃ — so weit als möglich nach innen gedreht

⟍⟍— leicht nach innen gedreht

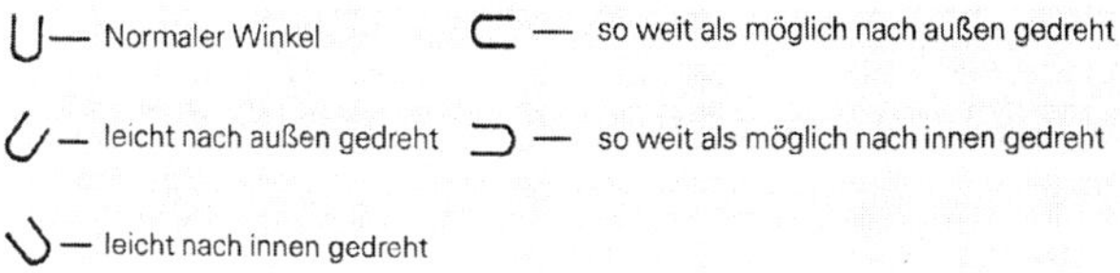

Fig. 35 Dick, Klang, p. 8.

2. 4. 2 Discussion

As mentioned, the pitch bending articulation may be performed in many different ways and varies from fingering to fingering. One method of notation would be to determine the extent of the tone bend for every instrument/pitch and subsequently notate the bending in the same manner as a *glissando* with microtones (whilst giving the additional direction pitch bending). However, it is very difficult to apply this exact method of notation because one would have to constantly refer to lists that describe the pitch bending range. Moreover, there has not been an adequate amount of research conducted concerning this technique and hence such lists simply do not yet exist for each instrument and pitch bending technique. Therefore, when wanting to exploit the full potential of the tone bend and depict it in a uniform way for all wind instruments, it is necessary to request this articulation in an approximate way. An approach towards the approximate notation of pitch bending has already been introduced in Figure 23. It is referred to as the transposition system. When comparing this notation system with the methods employed by Kelemen (cf. Figure 31) and Ferneyhough (cf. Figure 32), it may be stated that the latter two are less exact since both do not determine degrees of pitch bending, and Kelemen does not depict the bendings' exact duration. Further, Foss' method (cf. Figure 33) is similar to the one employed by Ferneyhough whilst the lines enable the depiction of two degrees of pitch bending (a quarter tone up and down). However, more than these two degrees could not be depicted by means of this method. Concerning the two methods of depiction introduced for the special pitch bending technique of flutes, it may be said that *Köszeghy's* approach (cf. Figure 34) could be used for the notation of this special technique if all bending ranges were known whilst *Dick's* suggestion (cf. Figure 35) can be regarded as a valid approach towards this particular bending technique and would enable the depiction of bending degrees if the resulting pitch is not known. However, both methods could not be employed for all bending techniques and the introduction of a special method of notation for each bending technique would result in a more complex notation system than the introduction of a single method for all of them. Therefore, it is preferred here to utilise the transposition system in order to request the pitch bending articulation and leave the exact performance to the player's discretion. Alternatively, the transposition system could be limited to only one technique by giving additional directions, e. g. only embouchure, opening and closing tone holes or turning the flute.

2. 4. 3 Suggestion for the notation of pitch bending

Hence the method of notation suggested being employed for all kinds of pitch bending techniques is the transposition system. It may be employed in the same manner as in Figure 23. Since the direction *alla tromba* (or the like) is not given, it is obvious that the respective instrument is, in this case, played with ordinary embouchure. As described above, the traditional system depicts the fingered tone and the additional system the transposition in time. In Figure 36, the pitch bending articulation is notated by taking the example of a B♭ clarinet. As mentioned, on this instrument the pitch can only be raised slightly, but lowered by several semitones. Therefore, four levels for upward and eight levels for downward transpositions are utilised whilst the middle axis (0) represents the unbent tone. Moreover, the white dots (◇) depict the degree of transposition in time. In the example, a clarinettist continuously bends the semibreve »c2/C5«. This tone is transposed up to the degree 3/4 for the duration of a crotchet, subsequently transposed down to the degree 4/8 for the duration of minim and then again transposed up to the degree 1/4 for the duration of a crotchet.

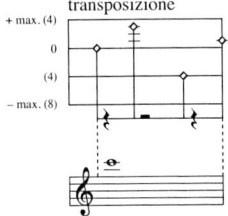

Fig. 36 Pitch bending on the B♭ clarinet.

2. 5 Extended winding techniques

Brasses and woodwinds may be utilised in an extended manner by employing special winding techniques. The articulations explained in this chapter are the **singing and playing technique**, the **speaking and playing technique**, the **air and tone technique** and the effect referred to as **vocalisation**.

2. 5. 1 The playing and singing technique and its notation

It is possible to sing within the respective vocal range while playing any of wind instruments. The movement of the voice is independent of playing the instrument. Female voices approximately range from »a/A3« to »d2/D5« (a limited mezzo-soprano voice) and male voices from »A/A2« to »d1/D4« (a limited baritone voice)[83].

The most common form of depiction is to notate the two produced tones in two systems, with the system on top representing the instrument[84]. An example of this (nearly) conventional method can be found in *Michael's* »Epigramme«[85]. The voice [Stimme] is notated here in the lower system:

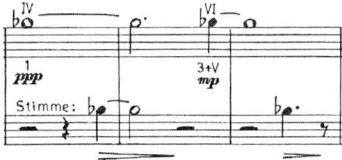

Fig. 37 Michael, Epigramme, p. 6.

Less frequently, both actions are notated in one system. In such a case, the note that is supposed to be sung is normally diamond-shaped or squared[86]. However, since the former method can be regarded as the most common form of notation and may be described as exact as well as simple, it is suggested here depicting the articulation in this manner. Further, as in normal voice notation, it may be determined which words the player sings. Therefore,

[83] Cf. Weiss and Netti, Saxophone, pp. 178f.
[84] Levine and Mitropoulos-Bott, Flute, p. 20.
[85] Frank Michael: Epigramme. For trombone alone. Berlin 1982.
[86] Levine and Mitropoulos-Bott, Flute, p. 20.

Michael's method of notation needs to be extended. An example of such an augmentation can be found in *Hosokawa's* »Sen I«. Here the player is supposed to sing the vowel »u« whilst playing on the flute:

Fig. 38 Hosokawa, Sen I, p. 9.

However, it needs to be noted that when utilising written vowels (or consonants) in a score, they should be notated in a universal way. This is because, for instance, an English-speaking performer could interpret the letter differently from a French-speaking performer. Hence in order to level language differences and guarantee the correct pronunciation, it is suggested here always referring to the International Phonetic Alphabet when depicting text. The utilised phonemes may be either placed below or on top of the additional voice system (cf. the IPA chart in Chapter »6. 2 Extended tongue techniques and their notation« and Chapter »6. 3. 2 The singing and speaking modes«). The dynamic level of this articulation ranges, for instance, on the oboe and bassoon from *pianissimo* to *mezzoforte*[87]. Moreover, in order to achieve a balanced dynamic between instrument and voice, one must sing slightly louder than he plays. If this balance of presence is not achieved, the result has the effect of a rough coloration[88]. It also needs to be noted that, for instance, on flutes a low tone can be sung and a higher tone be played as well as vice versa[89], whereas on the oboe the vocal pitches should be close to those played[90]. Further, the displayed method of notation can be used to depict the so-called humming while playing[91]. In order to request it, a nasal phoneme, e. g. [m], should be employed for the singing voice. Additionally, this technique may be combined with teeth embouchure[92] (cf. Chapter »2. 3. 3 Teeth embouchure«).

2. 5. 2 The speaking and playing technique and its notation

A popular technique, especially on flutes, is to make the player speak words or text sequences over the hole or directly into the flute. Here the resonance relationship of the instrument comes into play because the fingered pitch colours the resulting sound[93]. This articulation can be performed on woodwinds with or without the headjoint/mouthpiece/reed/bocal (cf. Chapter »2. 6. 1 Detaching the headjoint/mouthpiece/reed/bocal and its notation«) and on all brass instruments.

Crumb, in »Echoes of time and the river«, makes use of speaking and playing. He notates it by giving the direction whisper through brass instruments and x-shaped note heads placed on the middle line of a five lined notation system with no clef:

[87] Gallois, Bassoon, p. 27 and Veale, Oboe, p. 147.

[88] Weiss and Netti, Saxophone, p. 179.

[89] Levine and Mitropoulos-Bott, Flute, p. 20.

[90] Veale, Oboe, p. 147.

[91] Cf. Stone, Notation, p. 188.

[92] Weiss and Netti, Saxophone, p. 165.

[93] Levine and Mitropoulos-Bott, Flute, p. 37.

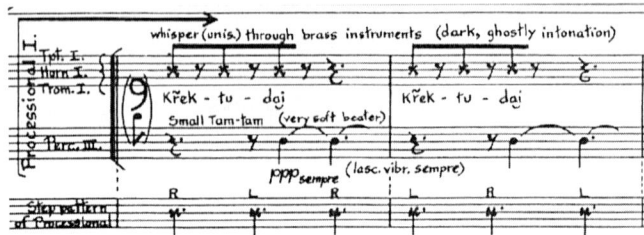

Fig. 39 Crumb, Echoes, p. 18.

Moreover, *Sotelo*, in »Del aura al suspirar«[94], makes use of two notation systems to depict the articulation[95]. The upper one represents the fingering whilst the lower one depicts the phonemes the player is supposed to speak by means of triangular note heads:

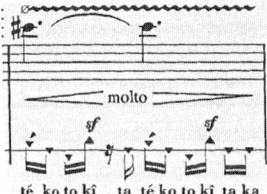

Fig. 40 Sotelo, Aura, p. 13.

When compared, *Sotelo's* approach may be preferred over the one by *Crumb*. This is because the latter neglects the influence of the fingering on the resulting sound. However, as it is shown in Chapter »6. 3. 2 The singing and speaking modes«, in this work speaking is suggested being requested by means of x-shaped note heads in a single lined notation system with no clef. Therefore, this method of notation is also used in the case of wind instruments. Moreover, the notation of the dynamic level between the two systems seems to suggest that the pitch is not only fingered, but also ordinary winding applied. The suggested method of notation is, therefore, a variation of *Sotelo's* approach. Analogous to the singing and playing technique, the system that determines the pitch is suggested here being placed on top and the system that determines the voice on the bottom. In order to outline that no common winding is employed, the dynamic level of the pitches is designated as »Ø«. Again, all phonemes should be notated with reference to the IPA (see Chapter »6. 2 Extended tongue techniques and their notation« for a chart). As is apparent from Figure 41, the player is supposed to speak the phonemes [tɛ], [kɔ], [tɔ] and [kɪ] into the instrument. Each has the duration of a crotchet. At the same time, he is supposed to finger an »f¹/F4« for the duration of a minim, the two quavers »h¹/B4« and »e¹/E4« as well as a crotchet »g¹/G4«.

Fig. 41 Speaking and playing.

---

94 Mauricio Sotelo: Del aura al suspirar. For contrabass flute (or alto flute) and sound carrier. Vienna 2001.

95 Also cf. Levine and Mitropoulos-Bott, Flute II, pp. 28f.

This articulation may on the flute also be performed *al clarinetto*[96] (cf. Chapter »2. 3. 2 The closed embouchure and its notation«). Moreover, »flutter-tonguing« can be combined with speaking and playing[97]. However, here the direction *frullato* does not need to be employed, but simply the phonemes [r] and [R] be depicted. This is because no tones are – as in the case of real flutter-tonguing – produced (cf. Chapter »2. 2. 1 The flutter tongue and its notation«). Further, in the case of all wind instruments, only the fingering influences the sound, and no overblown tones may be produced. Hence the notation of a tone that is produced by over-blowing a natural tone would mean to provide false information because the text is not coloured by the higher (overblown) tone, but the lower (natural) tone. Therefore, it is, for instance, on the horn in F sufficient to notate the (written) pitches »c/C3« to »F♯/F♯2« because they describe all possible fingerings (with the second natural »c/C3« the normal range of the F horn begins whilst each of the six possible fingerings lowers it by a semitone). Special tongue effects, such as the smacking noise or kissing sound[98], respectively, can also be depicted by means of the International Phonetic Alphabet. They are in the chart referred to as clicks.

Additionally, a hybrid of singing/playing and speaking/playing may be performed by making the player **whistle into the embouchure hole**[99]. This articulation is especially effective on flutes. In order to depict it, the methods of notation for singing/playing and speaking/playing need to be combined: the upper system would again represent the fingered pitch of the resonating instrument while the dynamic level of the pitches would have to be determined as »∅«. Moreover, the lower system would be used to depict the whistled pitches. The method of notation for whistling presented in Chapter »6. 5 Whistling and its notation« can be employed in this case.

2. 5. 3 The air and tone technique

The air and tone articulation or air sound is created when an amount of air is mixed with the normal tone[100]. Actually, this articulation is a variation of the technique designated as speaking and playing. However, normally only fricatives (cf. the IPA chart in Chapter »6. 2 Extended tongue techniques and their notation«) are articulated in order to produce the air sound. *Weiss and Netti*, for instance, (presumably) suggest the fricatives [s], [ʃ], [χ] and [ɦ][101] for the transition from bright to dark air sounds. Another difference to speaking and playing is that the sound is not just coloured, but the pitch may be clearly perceived. The air and tone technique can be employed on all wind instruments.

2. 5. 3. 1 Previous methods of notation

There are various examples for the notation of air sounds. In »Pneuma« *Holliger*, for instance, differentiates between three types of air and tone articulations as well as the (toneless) spea-king and playing technique. Additionally, he requests the player to exhale or inhale by means of arrows added to the note tail:

---

[96] Cf. Holliger, Sonate, p. 4.

[97] Cf. Lachenmann, Staub, no page named [foreword].

[98] Cf. Lachenmann, Niente, no page named [foreword] or Holliger, Pieces, p. 5.

[99] Cf. Holliger, Sonate, p. 7.

[100] Levine and Mitropoulos-Bott, Flute, p. 35.

[101] In Weiss and Netti, Saxophone, p. 157 they actually designate the phonemes as »s«, »sh«, »hr« and »hro«. These sounds were transferred to phonetic spelling.

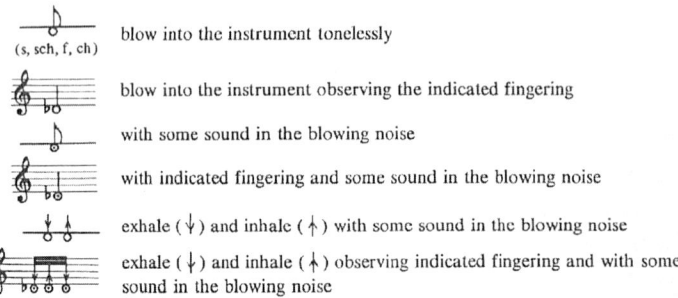

blow into the instrument tonelessly

blow into the instrument observing the indicated fingering

with some sound in the blowing noise

with indicated fingering and some sound in the blowing noise

exhale (↓) and inhale (↑) with some sound in the blowing noise

exhale (↓) and inhale (↑) observing indicated fingering and with some sound in the blowing noise

Fig. 42 Holliger, Pneuma, p. 6.

Moreover, in »Schattenklänge« *Kagel* requests two air sounds, very breathy and half breathy. He depicts the former one by means of a white diamond-shaped note head and the latter one by a black and white diamond-shaped note head placed over the system:

Fig. 43 Kagel, Schattenklänge, p. 2.

Finally, *Katzer*, in »Dialog imaginär«[102], requests a transition from air [Luft] to tone [Ton] whilst the air sound is depicted by means of a diamond-shaped note head:

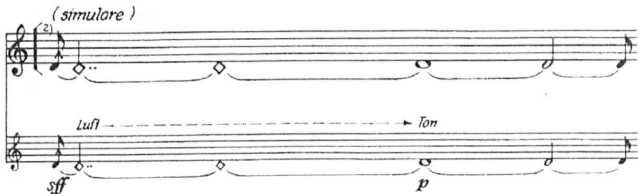

Fig. 44 Katzer, Dialog, p. 1.

2.5.3.2 Discussion

As mentioned, the air and tone articulation is a variant of the speaking and playing technique. Since a method of notation has been suggested for the latter, the displayed approaches need to be compared to it. As is apparent, none of the previous attempts (cf. Figures 42 to 44) is as exact as the method presented in Figure 41 concerning the notation of the actual air sounds and the ratio between the dynamic levels of air and tone. This is mainly because in none of the examples is it specifically determined which air sound the player is supposed to produce. Admittedly, *Holliger* depicts phonemes (in Figure 42, for instance, »s«, »sch«, »f« and »ch«), but, firstly, does not make use of the International Phonetic Alphabet and, secondly, only employs these when the player is supposed to blow tonelessly. Further, *Holliger's* approach is more complex because he introduces various methods of notation in order to depict different

---

[102]Georg Katzer: Dialog imaginär. For flute and tape. In: Werner Tast (ed.): Zeitgenössische Musik für Flöte solo [Contemporary music for flute alone]. Leipzig 1987, piece no. 8.

ratios or a voiced/unvoiced articulation, whilst the suggestion from the air and speaking technique could depict more than the ratios utilised by *Holliger* and all kinds of voiced/unvoiced
fricatives by simply determining the dynamic level of the air sound and the tone as well as the
utilised phoneme. Concerning the depiction of in- and exhaling, it may be stated that arrows
cannot be added to the note tail when semibreves or additional *tremolo* symbols are applied.
Therefore, it is preferred here to place these over the note. Moreover, it is sufficient to solely
request the action of inhaling since fricatives are normally pronounced whilst exhaling. Furthermore, *Kagel* only determines two ratios, very breathy and half breathy (cf. Figure 43),
whilst *Katzer's* method is solely able to basically depict the speaking and playing technique,
the air and tone technique as well as the transition from one to the other. Additionally, his
method suggests that the fricative itself has a definite pitch (cf. Figure 44). Finally, since the
approach of using two notation system is – as shown in Figure 45 – able to describe the transition from air sounds to normal tones, as well as many different ratios and air sounds, it is preferred here over *Holliger's*, *Kagel's* and *Katzer's* methods.

2. 5. 3. 3 Suggestion for the notation of the air and tone technique

The method of notation suggested for the air and tone technique is derived from the one introduced for the speaking and playing technique. Hence the upper system represents the fingered
pitch and the lower system the air sounds or phonemes the player articulates. As mentioned,
the ratio between the air and tone is depicted by means of the dynamic level assigned to each
system. When the dynamic level for the pitches drops to »∅«, the speaking and playing technique is performed[103]. As can be seen in Figure 45, the player is supposed to articulate the
fricatives [s], [ʃ], [χ] and [h]. Each phoneme has the duration of a crotchet whilst the dynamic
level is increased from *piano pianissimo* to *mezzoforte* for the duration of a minim and then
decreased to quadruple *piano* for the duration of a crotchet. The third fricative [χ] is supposed
to be produced whilst inhaling. Opposed to *Holliger's* method of notation, the arrow requesting it is pointing downwards. This is because the jet whistle technique (where the player
exhales) is notated by an arrow that points upwards (cf. Chapter »2. 7. 2 The jet whistle«). As
in Figure 41, the player is supposed to finger an »f¹/F4« for the duration of a minim, the two
quavers »h¹/B4« and »e¹/E4« and a »g¹/G4«. However, this time the pitch can be perceived
clearly since the dynamic level is constantly *mezzoforte*. Moreover, the last note has the duration of a semibreve and a crotchet. The transition from air and tone to the production of only
tones is achieved by reducing the dynamic level of the phonemes and stopping the production
of phonemes with the beginning of the second bar. Further, a transition from speaking and
playing to the air and tone technique could be depicted by making the player articulate a fricative and increasing the dynamic level of the upper system from »∅« to any other dynamic
level. Moreover, a transition to playing and singing could be depicted by replacing the single
lined notation system by a pitch-based notation system.

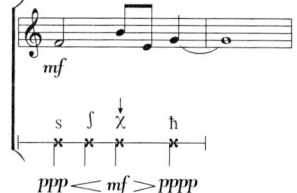

Fig. 45 Air and tone.

---

[103]In Levine and Mitropoulos-Bott, Flute, p. 36 the articulation of fricatives without winding is designated as
    aeolian sounds. However, in fact this action is a variant of the speaking and playing technique.

The maximum dynamic level of the air sound is always dependent on the fricative employed to produce it. Generally, only low dynamic levels are possible in the case of unvoiced phonemes and higher dynamic levels in the case of voiced phonemes. Moreover, the *alla tromba* embouchure (cf. Chapter »2. 3. 1 The trumpet embouchure«) can be combined with air tones. However, in this case, exact pitches are not produced[104]. Further, when the air is sucked in and not exhaled, the timbre and pitch is dependent on the instrument. For instance, on the bassoon sounds that strongly resemble that of a French horn may be created after removing the reed[105] whilst on the oboe sucking noises do not have a precisely determinable pitch[106] (also cf. Chapter »2. 3. 1 The trumpet embouchure« for »automatic« inhaled winding). Moreover, the articulation may vary according to the phoneme that is pronounced when inhaling. The phonemes that are closely related to the normal breathing action are the bilabial [ɸ] or the glottal [h]. The latter phoneme can also be employed to depict the so-called diaphragm accents[107]. Additionally, air sounds may also be performed *al clarinetto* and with a kind of *al flauto dolce* embouchure[108] (cf. Chapters »2. 3. 2 The closed embouchure and its notation« and »2. 3. 4 The recorder embouchure and its notation«).

2. 5. 4 Vocalisation and its notation

Vocalisation refers to the technique of changing a tone's timbre by altering the resonance of the mouth cavity. In order to do so, vowels are formed with the mouth whilst simultaneously playing held notes[109]. However, these vowels are not articulated, but simply determine the position of the tongue and lips. In the case of bright vowels, such as [i] or [a], a bright sound is produced by favouring high overtones, whereas in the case of dark vowels, such as [y], [o] or [ʊ], the sound will be darker because low overtones are favoured[110]. The vocalisation technique may be described as a variation of the speaking and playing articulation. However, in this case, the vowels colour the produced pitch. The articulation may be performed on all wind instruments.

Gallois suggests notating vocalisation by writing vowels over the note that depicts the fingered pitch. As is apparent from Figure 46, he does not make use of the IPA.

*) deutsch/English: U, français: OU

Fig. 46 Gallois, Bassoon, p. 22.

If the vowels were depicted by means of phonemes derived from the International Phonetic Alphabet, *Gallois'* approach could be described as adequate since it is exact and simple. However, in order to achieve a uniform method of notation for the singing and playing, speaking and playing as well as the air and tone technique, another approach is introduced here. It is a

---

[104]Veale, Oboe, p. 137.

[105]Gallois, Bassoon, p. 50.

[106]Veale, Oboe, p. 146.

[107]Cf. Helmut Lachenmann: temA. For flute, voice (mezzo-soprano) and violincello. Cologne 1971, no page named [foreword], Pagh-Paan, Dreisam-Nore, no page named [p. 1] or Takashi Matsuoka: Pietà. For flute alone. Tokyo 1989, p. 4.

[108]Cf. Lachenmann, Staub, no page named [foreword].

[109]Veale, Oboe, p. 146.

[110]Cf. Weiss and Netti, Saxophone, pp. 21f.

variant of the method displayed in Figure 41. In this case, the pitch may, however, be perceived clearly, and the vowel is only formed with the mouth. In order to outline that the vowels are not pronounced, their dynamic level is designated as »∅«. In the example presented in Figure 47, the player is during normal winding supposed to form each of the vowels [i], [a], [y] and [ʊ] for the duration of a crotchet.

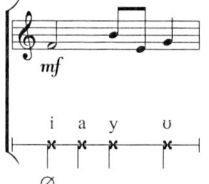

Fig. 47 Vocalisation.

2. 6 Preparing the instrument

This chapter focuses on two main ways of modifying wind instruments, **detaching the headjoint/mouthpiece/reed/bocal** and **constructional modifications**.

2. 6. 1 Detaching the headjoint/mouthpiece/reed/bocal and its notation

The most common way of preparing wind instruments is to detach the headjoint (flutes) mouthpiece (clarinets, saxophone and brass instruments), reed or bocal (oboes, bassoons). As mentioned above, the resulting pitch is higher when the mouthpiece is removed. This is also valid when removing the headjoint or read.

Detaching the headjoint/mouthpiece/reed/bocal is normally requested by giving a direction. An example of such a method of notation – as employed by *Heyn* in »Buon natale, fratello Fritz« – is presented by *Weiss and Netti*:

Fig. 48 Weiss and Netti, Saxophone, p. 149.

Moreover, *Leidel*, in »Drei Aperçus«[111] for instance, requests a bassoonist to remove the reed in a similar manner[112]. The detachment or re-attachment of the headjoint/mouthpiece/reed/bocal can be compared to the attachment and removal of a mute on string instruments. Since this articulation is also normally requested by means of a direction (*con/senza sordino*), *Heyn's* and *Leidel's* method may be described as being closely related to traditional notation. Additionally, the employment of short directions may be regarded as simple. Therefore, it is suggested here requesting the detachment and re-attachment of the headjoint/mouthpiece/reed/bocal by means of the direction without/with the headjoint/mouthpiece/reed/bocal or *senza/con testata* (flutes), *imboccatura* (clarinets and saxophones), *bocchino* (brass instru-

---

[111]Wolf-G. Leidel: Drei Aperçus. For bassoon. In: Dieter Hähnchen (ed.): Zeitgenössische Musik für Fagott solo [Contemporary music for bassoon alone]. Leipzig 1986, p. 54a.

[112]Ibid., p. 54a.

ments), *ancia* or *aletta* (oboes, bassoons). As explained above, the articulation *alla tromba* is on clarinets, saxophones, oboes and bassoons always executed *senza imboccatura/ancia*. When detaching the mouthpiece and playing in this way, the pitch, as mentioned, can still be depicted as if the mouthpiece was not detached because the system may, in such a case, be regarded as a transposed notation system. Additionally, the removal of other parts, such as the *oboe d'amore's* crook, may be depicted analogously and hence by directions. Further, other embouchures, such as *al clarinetto* or *al flauto dolce* (cf. Chapter »2. 3 Extended embouchure techniques«), and effects, such as the *pizzicato*, slap tongue and flutter tongue (cf. Chapter »2. 2 Extended tongue techniques«), may be employed in combination with the described preparations. When the mouthpiece of clarinets and saxophones is detached, it may be useful to additionally determine which type of embouchure the player is supposed to apply. This is because the embouchure hole is, in such a case, very different from the original one.

Additionally, it is possible to only **play on the headjoint/mouthpiece** of wind instruments. *Szalonek* requests this articulation in »Concertino«. The flute player is there supposed to detach the headjoint of the flute and play on it. He determines that three different tones can be produced. These tones are notated by means of x-shaped note heads:

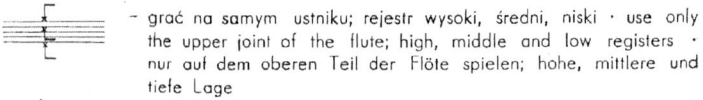

Fig. 49 Szalonek, Concertino, p. 3.

However, it would be clearer to request the utilisation of only the headjoint or mouthpiece analogous to the way the other embouchure techniques are notated because it is related to these. In order to do so, the simple direction on the headjoint/mouthpiece or *sulla testata/imboccatura/bocchino* is suggested here being employed. Further, since x-shaped note heads are, in this work, utilised for the depiction of key clicks (cf. Chapter »2. 9. 1 Key/valve clicks«), another method of notation for the resulting pitch needs to be introduced. One method would be to determine which tones may be produced by blowing on the headjoint/mouthpiece. However, if the resulting pitch is not known, another method has to be applied. Since this is the case here, an augmented approach is adopted: the suggested method refers to the three registers that may be produced on headjoints of flutes, as determined by *Szalonek*, and the method of notation for the teeth embouchure displayed in Figure 29. When playing *sulla testata/imboccatura/bocchino*, a single lined notation system with no clef is used. In Figure 50 three tones are depicted by this system: the most natural tone by means of common note heads, the highest possible tone by triangular note heads pointing upwards and the lowest possible tone by triangular note heads pointing downwards. In the example, a flautist is supposed to produce the most natural tone on the headjoint for the duration of a crotchet and then play the highest possible tone for the duration of a minim. Subsequently, the lowest possible tone is supposed to be produced for the duration of a crotchet. In order to depict more than three tones, the single lined notation system could be augmented further by means of additional lines.

Fig. 50 Playing on the headjoint of a flute.

2. 6. 2 Constructional modifications and their notation

There have been various attempts at combining parts of different instruments with each other – e. g. taping a double reed to a brass instrument – utilising additional joints, valves or mouthpieces – e. g. trumpets with two mouthpieces and/or six to seven valves[113]. Moreover, *Holliger*, in »Siebengesang«[114], requests the player to use a bare staple instead of the oboe's reed[115]. Simpler modifications can be executed by removing the lower joint, bell etc. of a woodwind instrument or the slide of a trombone[116]. As in the case of string instruments, there are numerous ways of preparing wind instruments. Similarly, it is also, on the one hand, barely possible to list them all and subsequently develop a coherent method of depiction whilst, on the other hand, it is also not necessary to do so since most preparations are executed previously to a performance and may simply be described in the foreword to a work. When preparations are supposed to be executed during a performance, they are here suggested being always notated by means of a sketch. This is because it is the simplest way of depicting these. When the sketch is not clear enough, it may be complemented by an explanation (cf. Chapter »1. 8 Preparing the instrument and its notation«). Nevertheless, preparations may, as mentioned, lead to the introduction of new playing techniques that should then be notated in accordance with all other techniques presented in this work.

2. 7 Whistle techniques

Whistle techniques are primarily used on flutes[117]. There are two types of whistle sounds: **whistle tones** and an articulation designated as **jet whistle**.

2. 7. 1 Whistle tones and their notation

Whistle tones are lightly fluctuating tones in the very high register based on the harmonic series[118]. These sounds can, for instance, on the concert flute be produced by using the fingerings of the lowest register (»h/B3« or »c¹/C4« to »e♭²/E♭5«) as well as those for the highest register (from »d³/D6« on). This is because the middle register is produced by overblowing to the second partial. When whistle tones are requested, the player needs to turn the flute slightly outward and blow across the embouchure hole with almost no lip tension. The air stream is then weak, but remains constant[119].

Whistle tones are most commonly notated by depicting the fundamental by means of a diamond-shaped note head and the produced harmonic by a normal note head. For instance, in »Sonate (in)solit(air)e« *Holliger* requests whistle tones in this manner:

Fig. 51 Holliger, Sonate, p. 13.

Other similar examples can be found in *Levine and Mitropoulos-Bott*[120]. This method of notation also resembles the one conventionally employed for the depiction of certain harmonics on string instruments. Diamond-shaped note heads are, in this context, used to outline

---

[113]Sevsay, Handbuch, p. 153.

[114]Heinz Holliger: Siebengesang. For oboe, orchestra, singing voices and loudspeaker. Mainz 1969.

[115]Ibid., p. 53.

[116]Sevsay, Handbuch, p. 151.

[117]Cf. Sevsay, Handbuch, p. 143.

[118]Levine and Mitropoulos-Bott, Flute, p. 15.

[119]Cf. Levine and Mitropoulos-Bott, Flute, pp. 15f., 65-67 and 68-70.

[120]Levine and Mitropoulos-Bott, Flute, pp. 16f. and Levine and Mitropoulos-Bott, Flute II, p. 14.

that a particular position on the string needs to be lightly fingered in order to create a harmonic[121/122]. As mentioned, in the case of the whistle tones, the player needs to produce a weak air stream with low lip tension in order to create harmonics. Hence lightly fingered harmonics on string instruments and whistle tones on flutes resemble each other. Therefore, it may be stated that the method of notation utilised by *Holliger* is related to traditional notation. Further, it can be described as simple and exact despite the durations of the fingered and the whistle tones do not match (the quavers would have to be replaced by crotchets with a black note head). Thus *Holliger's* method of notation is suggested here being employed for the notation of whistle tones. It is distinct from the depiction of common harmonics since these are requested by means of two common note heads (for the fingered tone and the harmonic) and a small circle on top of the upper tone. The dynamic level of whistle tones is always low. Further, this technique can also be employed *al clarinetto*[123] (cf. Chapter »2. 3. 2 The closed embouchure and its notation«). As mentioned, whistle tones are primarily a flute technique. However, when the reed is removed on the oboe or the reed and crook on the oboe d'amore and the cor anglais (cf. Chapter »2. 6. 1 Detaching the headjoint/mouthpiece/reed/bocal and its notation«) and the closed embouchure is applied, similar sounds may be created by inhaling. Moreover, whistle tones may also be produced by clasping the lips around the aperture of the cor anglais' crook (without reed)[124].

2. 7. 2 The jet whistle

A jet whistle is a short, forceful and loud attack of air. It may only be created on flutes. When requested, the embouchure hole of the flute is completely covered with the lips (and hence the *al clarinetto* embouchure employed) while exhaled air is forced into the flute with a strong air impulse. The lower the pitch that is fingered, the richer frequencies are produced. The jet whistle conjures up associations with the starting of a jet plane and includes a *glissando*-like rise in pitch[125].

2. 7. 2. 1 Previous methods of notation

There are many different approaches towards the notation of the jet whistle. Most of them try to depict the energetic quality of the attack. For instance, *Lachenmann*, in »„... zwei Gefühle ...", Musik mit Leonardo«, makes use of a bent line that replaces the note head whilst a common note in brackets determines the fingering:

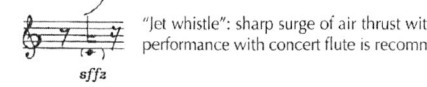
"Jet whistle": sharp surge of air thrust with arched mouth cavity, virtually an "overtone whistle". The performance with concert flute is recommended. The note in brackets indicates the desired fingering.

Fig. 52 Lachenmann, Gefühle, no page named [foreword].

As can be seen in Figure 53, *Holliger*, in »Sonate (in)solit(air)e«, makes use of an additional arrow to depict the articulation (which is followed by a tongue ram). As explained above,

---

[121]Sevsay, Handbuch, p. 70.

[122]Even though the produced harmonic, in this case, does not need to be depicted since it cannot be varied on string instruments.

[123]Cf. Levine and Mitropoulos-Bott, Flute, p. 17 and Salvatore Sciarrino: All'aure in una lontanza. For G flute (or C flute or bass flute). In: Salvatore Sciarrino: L'opera per flauto. Milan 1990, pp. 3-6.

[124]Veale, Oboe, p. 138.

[125]Cf. Levine and Mitropoulos-Bott, Flute, p. 17.

the note head is circled in order to outline that the player is supposed to perform this articulation *al clarinetto*.

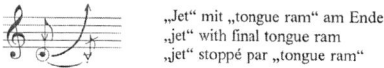
„Jet" mit „tongue ram" am Ende
„jet" with final tongue ram
„jet" stoppé par „tongue ram"

Fig. 53 Holliger, Sonate, p. 4.

Moreover, another method is utilised by *Lachenmann* in »Staub«. In this piece he makes use of an oval note head and a common note head in brackets for the depiction of the jet whistle:

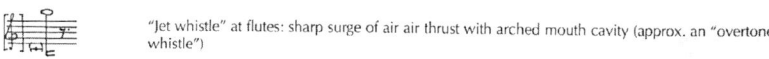
"Jet whistle" at flutes: sharp surge of air air thrust with arched mouth cavity (approx. an "overtone whistle")

Fig. 54 Lachenmann, Staub, no page named [foreword].

2. 7. 2. 2 Discussion

In order to notate the jet whistle articulation in a comprehensive way, it is preferred here to utilise a method of depiction that displays the forceful nature of the air attack. Therefore, *Lachenmann's* first method (cf. Figure 52) and *Holliger's* method (cf. Figure 53) are favoured from the approach of depicting the action by means of an oval note head (cf. Figure 54). However, as shown above, the action of inhaling and exhaling is normally depicted by means of arrows. Since the jet whistle is in the first place an air attack, *Holliger's* method of utilising an additional arrow does make sense. Moreover, since the overtones are emphasised and a kind of ascending *glissando* is elementary to the articulation, the arrow should point upwards. Therefore, it is preferred here to utilise an additional arrow instead of a bent line. Furthermore, since there is no necessity for employing two note heads, it is preferred to solely depict the fingered pitch. As shown in Chapter »2. 3. 2 The closed embouchure and its notation«, the embouchure necessary for the air attack is, moreover, in this work depicted by means of the direction *al clarinetto*.

2. 7. 2. 3 Suggestion for the notation of the jet whistle

Hence the jet whistle technique is suggested being notated by means of employing a normal note head that depicts the fingered pitch, an additional arrow pointing upwards and giving the direction *al clarinetto*. As can be seen in Figure 55, the player is supposed to finger a »c¹/C4« and perform the jet whistle articulation for the duration of a quaver.

al clarinetto

Fig. 55 The jet whistle.

Further, a subsequent tongue ram could be depicted by an additional note connected by means of a *legato* slur and the method presented in Chapter »2. 2. 4 The tongue ram«.

2. 8 Muting

The application of mutes is not very effective on woodwinds, but a very popular technique on brass instruments[126]. Mutes can be either employed in the common way by inserting them

---

[126]Sevsay, Handbuch, p. 142.

previously to a passage and removing them afterwards or be applied and removed repetitively in a fast manner during the sound production in order to produce **the wah-wah effect**.

2. 8. 1 The application of mutes

On woodwinds normally a piece of cloth or a handkerchief is loosely inserted in the sound hole at the end of the instrument. Another possibility is to cover the opening with a suitable item, such as a mute made of cork. However, in both cases, only certain tones are influenced by the muting. Moreover, when playing on the mouthpiece of a clarinet or saxophone (cf. Figure 50), it can be muted by means of putting the hand over the opening. Further, the horn player can achieve a muting effect by hand stopping, i. e. pushing the hand tightly into the bell. However, this action raises the pitch. The player compensates this effect by fingering a semitone lower. The commercial horn mute corrects the alteration in pitch that would be caused by hand muffling. For the tubas, there is only one mute available whilst a large collection of mutes exists for the trumpets and trombones, such as the straight mute, the cup mute, the whispa mute, the solotone mute, the bucket mute and the harmon or wah-wah mute. Harmon mutes are manufactured with and without stem. The stem can be adjusted to produce a variety of timbres. There are three positions: stem in, half stem and stem out. Additionally, these instruments can be muted by means of a plunger, a hat or derby, by putting the hand over or in the bell, inserting cloth/a handkerchief in the bell or playing into the stand. It is also possible to insert other items into the bell, e. g. paper, fur or a small basket (please refer for further details to *Adler*[127], *Rehfeldt*[128] or *Sevsay*[129]).

2. 8. 1. 1 Previous methods of notation

The action of employing a mute is, as on string instruments, normally requested by means of giving the direction with/without mute or *con/senza sordino*. *Halffter*, in »Lineas y puntos«[130] for instance, employs such a method of notation for the horn section:

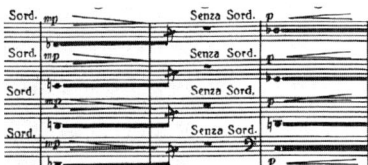

Fig. 56 Halffter, Lineas, p. 7.

Moreover, in order to outline which mute the player is supposed to utilise, *Kelemen*, in »Changeant«, gives an additional description of the type in brackets (cup mute):

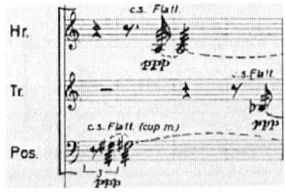

Fig. 57 Kelemen, Changeant, p. 29.

---

[127]Adler, Orchestration, pp. 308-311.
[128]Rehfeldt, Directions, pp. 72-74.
[129]Sevsay, Handbuch, pp. 142-144.
[130]Cristobal Halffter: Lineas y puntos. For 20 instruments, 2 loudspeakers and tape. London 1967.

Further, *Ligeti* makes use of the same method. In »Apparitions«[131] he requests a trombonist to use cardboard as a mute by giving the direction with mute (cardboard) [mit Dämpfer (Karton)]:

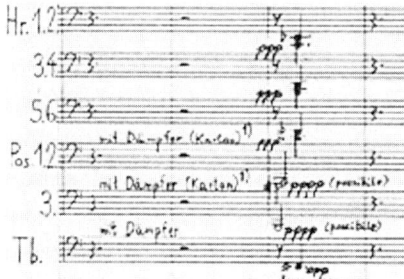

Fig. 58 Ligeti, Apparitions, p. 2.

However, *Kagel*, in »Atem«[132], requests the application of mutes by means of symbols and numbers, indicating which type of mute is utilised:

Mutes: The indications regarding mutes (▢, ▢, ▢, ▢) apply first and foremost to brass instruments*. The performer will need as many different mutes as there are numbers. The same number always means the same mute (▢ = mute A, ▢ = mute B, etc.).

Fig. 59 Kagel, Atem, p. 4 [foreword].

Finally, *Holliger*, in »Siebengesang«, requests to mute the horn only as far as to make it sound a quarter tone higher[133]. This effect is requested by means of the plus sign and microtonal symbols:

Fig. 60 Holliger, Siebengesang, p. 58.

2. 8. 1. 2 Discussion

As is apparent from the examples, the application of a mute is commonly requested by means of giving a direction. Moreover, since the same method of notation is also conventionally employed in the case of string instruments, it may be described as being closely related to traditional notation. With regard to the utilisation of different mutes, they may be either depicted by means of writing these mutes down (cf. Figures 57 and 58) or by a symbol and numbers (cf. Figure 59). In the case of the former method, the direction in brackets needs to be short in order to retain instantaneous comprehension. When the application of a special mute requires additional information, it should be provided in the foreword to the work. To give an example, *Ligeti*, in »Aventures«, employs a "vase with a relatively small opening (short, narrow, neck)"[134] as a mute. This information is part of the score. However, in such a case, the

---

[131]György Ligeti: Apparitions. For orchestra. 2nd revised edition. Vienna 1971.

[132]Mauricio Kagel: Atem. For a wind instrumentalist. London 1976.

[133]Cf. Holliger, Siebengesang, p. 58.

[134]György Ligeti: Aventures. For three singers and seven instrumentalists. Frankfurt/M. et al. 1964, p. 7 [appendix].

description of the vase should be presented in the foreword and the actual application be rather requested by means of the direction *con sordino* (vase). Concerning the depiction of the mute type by means of a symbol and numbers, it may be stated that it is simpler to request a particular mute by means of a description than by a number since the former method does not require previously learning the meaning of the numbers. Therefore, it is preferred here to utilise the method of notation employed by *Kelemen* and *Ligeti* in order to request the normal mutes. However, when uncommon mutes – such as the vase – are employed, the utilisation of a symbol for the item could contain a greater degree of instantaneous comprehension than requesting it by means of a direction. Further, when microtonal frequencies are supposed to be produced (cf. Figure 60), this action can be requested clearly by means of microtonal symbols (cf. »Part II: Electroacoustic music – 1. 1. 1 Periodic wave generators and their envelopes« for a suggestion of such symbols). However, in order to depict the application of the mute in accordance with traditional notation, the plus symbol would have to be replaced by the direction *con sordino* (hand) or *(mano)*.

2. 8. 1. 3 Suggestion for the notation of the application of mutes

Hence the attachment and removal of mutes is requested by giving the direction *con/senza sordino* whilst the description of the mute type may be given in brackets. In the case of the tuba or if only one mute type is used, it is apparently sufficient not to specify what kind of mute the player is supposed to employ. When utilising the harmon mute with stem, the additional direction in, half and out (*dentro, 1/2* or *mezzo* and *fuori*) needs to be given. Further, the utilisation of special mutes, such as the plunger, hat, hand, cloth, a handkerchief and even the note stand, can also be requested in this manner. However, as mentioned, for such uncommon mutes a symbol could, alternatively, be introduced.

2. 8. 2 The wah-wah effect

The wah-wah effect (cf. for further details »Part II: Electroacoustic music – 2. 3. 1 High-pass, low-pass, band-pass and band-reject filters«) is on brass instruments produced by adjusting the harmon mute with the hand in order to open or close the bell. In the case of the stem being adjusted to the stem out position, the sound is thin but sharp and, in the case of being adjusted to the stem in position, the sound is clear and resembles the miaow of a cat[135]. When transitions between these two positions are requested simultaneous with normal playing, the wah-wah effect is produced. Additionally, a similar effect can be created by slowly inserting and removing other mutes or slowly opening and closing the bell when hand muffling.

2. 8. 2. 1 Previous methods of notation

Normally, the wah-wah effect is notated by utilising the two symbols »o« (open) and »+« (closed). An example of this method can be found in *Serocki's* »Segmenti«. He uses the two designated symbols in order to make a horn player open and close the bell of his instrument. Moreover, a waved line is employed in order to outline that there is a transition between the two states:

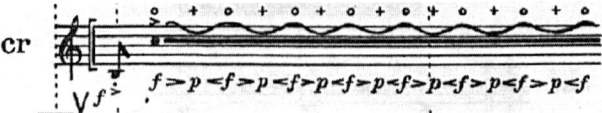

Fig. 61 Serocki, Segmenti, p. 8.

---

[135]Sevsay, Handbuch, p. 143.

Lachenmann further augments this method by introducing exact durations. This is executed by utilising the two symbols as note heads. Additionally, he makes use of a *legato* slur, which requests soft transitions between »o« and »+« [weiche Übergänge zwischen »o« und »+«]:

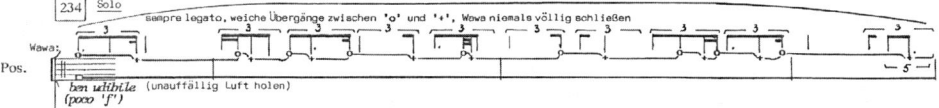

Fig. 62 Lachenmann, Gefühle, p. 47.

2. 8. 2. 2 Discussion

The plus and circle symbols are conventionally employed for the depiction of the wah-wah effect. However, as is apparent from Figure 61, *Serocki's* method of notation is not able to depict the duration of the transition between the open and closed stage, whereas *Lachenmann's* method exactly determines at which point in time the bell is open and closed (cf. Figure 62). Further, the utilisation of an additional *legato* slur even enables the notation of different manners of transition. Therefore, his augmented method is more exact and hence preferred over the one utilised by *Serocki*. The only limitation of this method is that neither minims nor semibreves may be employed, but the largest duration is a crotchet. However, since the employed symbols are conventional, they should not be replaced, and because the transition is normally performed in a fast manner, this limitation will not cause fundamental problems.

2. 8. 2. 3 Suggestion for the notation of the wah-wah effect

Hence it is suggested here notating the wah-wah effect by means of the symbols »o« and »+« whilst the duration of the transition between these two states is depicted by using the symbols as note heads. These note heads may be used in a single lined notation system similar to the one employed by *Lachenmann*. Moreover, articulation symbols, such as the *legato* slur or *staccato* dots, can be used to determine the character of the transition between the two states whilst the mute used to create the effect needs to be described (also cf., for instance, Figure 32 in the chapter on vocal techniques). As the plus sign is used here as a note head, it does not conflict with the method of notation introduced in »Part II: Electroacoustic music – 3. 2. 1 Basic elements (monophonic recordings)«. An alternative method of notation would be to employ the two states in a »transposition« system (cf. Figure 23) because notes, as mentioned, suggest that additional sound is produced. However, the original sound is, in this case, actually transformed.

2. 9 Percussive effects

There are two kinds of percussive effects that may be produced on wind instruments, **key/valve clicks** or **strokes on the body**.

2. 9. 1 Key/valve clicks

Key/valve clicks can either be executed in addition to the sounding note or as a percussive effect without any winding. In the case of the latter, the fingered pitches colour the clicks. This articulation may be utilised on all wind instruments with keys or valves.

2.9.1.1 Previous methods of notation

Most commonly, this articulation is notated by means of the traditional notation system and x-shaped note heads[136]. An example of such a method of notation can be found in *Saariaho's* »Laconisme de l'aile«[137]. She depicts pure key clicks by means of x-shaped note heads and additional key clicks by means of a crossed out note:

Fig. 63 Saariaho, Laconisme, p. 4.

However, *Lachenmann*, in »Staub«, for instance, makes use of a special note head in order to request key clicks on flutes and clarinets:

     Flutes and clarinets: key noise with prescribed fingering

Fig. 64 Lachenmann, Staub, no page named [foreword].

Moreover, in »Dal niente (Interieur III)« he makes use of a symbol resembling the displayed note head. Whenever it is placed under the notes, key clicks are required to complement the tone production (whilst diamond-shaped notes depict a *presto*-movement in *pianissimo*)[138]:

stems above the notes).

≈ Klappengeräusch laut, Tonhöhen möglichst noch durchscheinen lassen.
  Loud key-noises, the pitch nevertheless audible.

Fig. 65 Lachenmann, Niente, no page named [foreword].

Further, in order to enable the depiction of diverging dynamic levels for the tone production and the clicks, *Gaber*, in »Voce II«[139], employs two dynamic levels that are applied simultaneously:

When two dynamics are indicated; i.e., $\frac{p}{f}$, the one below refers to the clicking of the keys.

Fig. 66 Gaber, Voce II, no page named [foreword].

2.9.1.2 Discussion

Because x-shaped note heads are most commonly used for the depiction of key clicks as well as for percussive effects (cf., for instance, Chapter »1.7 Percussive effects«), *Saariaho's* method of notation (cf. Figure 63) is preferred here over the ones by *Lachenmann* (cf. Figures 64 and 65). Further, *Lachenmann's* first approach would have to be augmented in order to enable the depiction of key clicks that complement tones whilst the second approach could not be employed for the notation of the solely percussive clicks. Moreover, since the percussive clicks and the tone production may be regarded as two distinct sonic events, *Saariaho's* method of notation also needs to be elaborated slightly in terms of the notation of the tone and click. In order to depict these sounds as two events, two note heads instead of one combined

---

[136]Cf. Levine and Mitropoulos-Bott, Flute, pp. 26f., Stone, Notation, pp. 192f. and Weiss and Netti, Saxophone, pp. 177f.

[137]Kaija Saariaho: Laconisme de l'aile. For flute solo with optional electronics. No city and year named [Helsinki 2002].

[138]Cf. Lachenmann, Niente, no page named [foreword].

[139]Harley Gaber: Voce II. Female voice, alto flute, and percussion. Cincinnati 1967.

(crossed out) head would have to be utilised. Further, concerning *Gaber's* method of employing simultaneous dynamic levels, it may be stated that it is useful to depict the dynamic levels of the two sonic events distinctly. This is because divergent dynamic levels may be employed.

2. 9. 1. 3 Suggestion for the notation of key/valve clicks

Key/valve clicks are suggested here being notated by means of the traditional notation system and x-shaped note heads. When key clicks are used as a complementary effect, two note heads and dynamic levels are employed whilst the purely percussive effect is depicted by utilising only x-shaped note heads. As can be seen in Figure 67, a woodwind player is supposed to perform a chromatic semiquaver anabasis from »c¹/C4« to »g¹/G4« and a subsequent katabasis to »h/B3«. In the case of the anabasis, the tone (*mezzopiano*) is complemented by key clicks (*pianissimo*) whilst the katabasis consists of coloured key clicks only.

Fig. 67 Key clicks.

The dynamic level of the clicks is limited. For instance, on the saxophone, the upper limit is *piano*[140] or on the oboe *mezzopiano*[141] (and hence the dynamic level requested by *Gaber* in Figure 66 could not be reached). Further, when executing the purely percussive effect on valve instruments, apparently only the valve positions need to be depicted. As mentioned, they can, for example, on the F horn be depicted by means of the (written) pitches »c/C3« to »F#/F#2« (with the second natural »c/C3« the normal range of the F horn begins whilst each of the six possible fingerings lowers it by a semitone). When playing sustained tones, the percussive effect normally only complements the attack. In such a case, the duration of the x-shaped note heads needs to differ from the duration of the tone. However, key clicks may also sound through a sustained note. In order to do so, a free »helping finger« performs the percussive attack. However, this finger must not influence the sound of the tone in any way[142]. This effect can be notated similarly to the enharmonic trill by presenting two fingering charts (cf. Chapter »2. 1 Extended *vibrato*, *tremolo* and trill techniques and their notation«). On the basis of such charts it may be depicted which key is used for the percussive effect and that it is released and depressed in a repetitive manner. Additionally, the percussive clicks may on flutes be performed in combination with a covered embouchure hole. In the case of the concert flute, this results in a coloration that sounds a major seventh lower[143]. As shown in Chapter »2. 3. 2 The closed embouchure and its notation«, this kind of embouchure may be requested by giving the direction *al clarinetto*.

2. 9. 2 Strokes on the body

When strokes on the body are requested, the player is normally supposed to hit the mouthpiece (brass instruments) or bell of the instrument with the palm of the hand or his fingers. Moreover, the barrel of certain wind instruments may be struck after removing the mouthpiece. In the case of such strokes, the fingerings may colour and modify the sound that

---

[140]Weiss and Netti, Saxophone, p. 176.
[141]Veale, Oboe, p. 139.
[142]Cf. Levine and Mitropoulos-Bott, Flute, p. 26.
[143]Ibid., p. 27.

evolves[144]. Additionally, strokes may, especially on brass instruments, be performed on other parts of the body and also be executed by means of items, e. g. mutes or mallets.

2.9.2.1 Previous methods of notation

Concerning the percussive effects, there are various approaches of notation. In »Aventures« *Ligeti* makes use of a single lined notation system with no clef and x-shaped note heads. He further advises the player to perform a short, sharp blow with the hand on the mouthpiece [mit der Hand kurz und kräftig auf das Mundstück schlagen]:

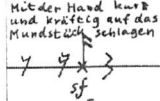

Fig. 68 Ligeti, Aventures, p. 6.

Moreover, *Lachenmann*, in »NUN«[145], makes use of a special note head and a bracketed traditional clef in order to depict the strokes and the additional fingerings, which colour the produced sound:

Klarinetten: Schlag auf die obere Öffnung des Instruments bei abgenommenem Mundstück und Birne mit flachgestreckter Handinnenfläche auf die Öffnung schlagen. Die vorgeschriebenen Griffe dienen der Helligkeitsabstufung.

Clarinets: Attack on the upper opening of the instrument with the mouthpiece and tuning socket removed. Use the flat of the stretched hand to strike against the opening. The prescribed fingerings serve to grade the brightness.

Kl., T. 84ff.   Cl., mm. 84ff.

Hörner, Trompeten, Tuben: Schlag aufs Mundstück mit flach gestreckter Hand-Innenfläche (bei Hörnern und Trompeten: vorgeschriebene Ventilstellung beachten).
Der Gefahr, daß sich hierbei ein Mundstück festklemmt, kann dadurch begegnet werden, daß letzteres mit feinem Seidenpapier umspannt und so ins Instrument eingesetzt wird.

Horns, trumpets, tubas: Attack on mouthpiece with the flat of the stretched hand. (Horns and trumpets must pay attention to the prescribed valve position).
One can avoid the danger of getting a mouthpiece stuck too tightly by wrapping tissue paper around the mouthpiece before placing it into the instrument.

Hn./Trp./Tb., T. 78f.   Hn./Trp./Tb., mm. 78f.

Fig. 69 Lachenmann, NUN, p. V.

Further, *Alsina*, in »Consecuenza«[146], requests a single hit or roll with the mute (whilst *Alsina* refers to the roll as a trill). As can be seen in Figure 70, single strokes are notated by a line added to the note tail and rolls by means of zigzag line that replaces the note head. These notes are utilised in combination with a single lined notation system[147].

---

[144]Cf. Rehfeldt, Directions, p. 75.
[145]Helmut Lachenmann: NUN. Music for flute, trombone, male voices and orchestra. Wiesbaden 2002.
[146]Carlos Roqué Alsina: Consecuenza. Trombone solo. Berlin and Wiesbaden 1969.
[147]Cf. ibid., p. 2.

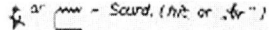

Fig. 70 Alsina, Consecuenza, p. 7.

2. 9. 2. 2 Discussion

Strokes on the bodies of wind instruments can be compared to strokes on the bodies of string instruments. As shown in Chapter »1. 7. 1 Strokes on the body and their notation«, these can be notated by means of a drawing of the instrument's body, which enables the determination of the point of impact, in combination with a drawing of the player's hand. When compared to the methods of notation by *Ligeti* (cf. Figure 68), *Lachenmann* (cf. Figure 69) and *Alsina* (cf. Figure 70), it may be stated that all of these contain a lesser degree of instantaneous comprehension. Further, all methods would have to be augmented in order to enable the depiction of strokes on other parts of the body than the ones they request. Nevertheless, *Ligeti's* method of utilising a single lined notation system with no clef and x-shaped note heads can be described as being closely related to traditional notation in terms of the depiction of the pitchless strokes. This is because strokes with indefinite pitch are commonly notated by x-shaped note heads (cf. the chapter on percussion instruments). However, his approach needs to be complemented by a depiction of the fingering when the bell, mouthpiece or open barrel of the wind instrument is hit. These articulations resemble the speaking and playing technique since in both cases a sound with indefinite pitch is coloured by the fingering. As is apparent from Chapter »2. 5. 2 The speaking and playing technique and its notation«, the technique is notated by means of two notation systems. The fingering is depicted by a common notation system and normal note heads whilst the spoken words are notated by means of a single lined notation system with no clef. Further, the dynamic level of the pitches is designated as »∅« in order to outline that no common winding is employed. Since the speaking and playing technique and the strokes on the mouthpiece, bell or barrel are strongly related, they could be depicted in the same manner. This approach is preferred here over the one introduced by *Lachenmann* because there is no need to employ special note heads when the percussive action is depicted by an additional notation system and a greater coherence is achieved when using a method similar to the one for speaking and playing. Further, *Alsina's* method of replacing the note by a symbol leads, as mentioned, to inexactness. This is because minims or semibreves could not be depicted. Moreover, since a conventional method of notation for rolls already exists (in the form of the *tremolo* symbol)[148], there is no need to introduce a new method for a similar action.

2. 9. 2. 3 Suggestion for the notation of strokes on the body

Two notation systems are employed here: one that depicts the fingering and one that depicts the stroke. Analogous to the speaking and playing technique, the system that determines the pitch is placed on top and the system that determines the strokes on the bottom. As mentioned, the dynamic level of the pitches is designated as »∅« whilst the point of impact and the sound producer is notated by means of a drawing. When the sound producer is the hand, the method of depiction introduced in the chapter on string instruments (Figures 89f.) may be utilised. When a standard mute is used to execute a stroke, a drawing similar to the one employed by *Kagel* in »Atem« (cf. Figure 59) can be used whilst the utilisation of mallets (and special agents of attack) is explained in the chapter on percussion instruments. Further, the removal of the mouthpiece, bell etc. is discussed in Chapter »2. 6 Preparing the instrument«. Percussive effects are displayed here by taking the example of a trumpet. The player is in Figure 71 supposed to initially perform four semiquaver strokes on the mouthpiece with the

---

[148]Cf. Sevsay, Handbuch, p. 207.

index, middle and ring finger whilst fingering a »c¹/C4«. After a crotchet rest, he is then required to hit the bell once with the palm and finger an »a/A3«. Subsequent to a dotted quaver rest, the trumpeter executes four semiquaver strokes with the knuckles on the spot designated by the dot. In the case of these hits, the fingered pitch does not influence the sound and hence does not need to be determined.

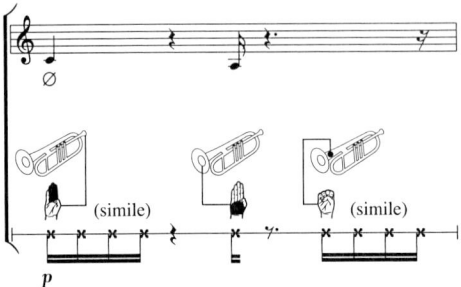

Fig. 71 Strokes on the body of a trumpet.

When strokes on the bell or barrel of woodwinds are performed, the player can apparently only finger the pitches with one of his hands. Nevertheless, the tones may be depicted in the usual way when it is clear which hand is used for the strokes and with which hand the incomplete fingering is executed. This could be outlined by giving an additional direction, such as left/right hand (*mano sinistra/destra*), or alternatively presenting a fingering chart. When executing strokes on parts of the instrument other than the mouthpiece or barrel, only a single lined notation system apparently needs to be employed. Further, it needs to be noted that the strokes have to be performed cautiously in order to retain the instrument[149]. Hence the dynamic level always needs to be low.

2. 10 Resonance effects

Another popular effect is to direct the bell of a wind instrument towards the strings of a grand piano with depressed pedal, a timpano or other percussion instruments. When the wind instrument is then played, sympathetic vibrations are produced. Additionally, it is possible to further modify the sound by moving the bell over the surface of the instrument. However, certain wind instruments, such as the bass clarinet, saxophone, bassoon, tuba etc., are not perfectly suitable for the performance of such effects (but nevertheless sometimes used to produce them). This is because their bell cannot be directed comfortably towards the resonating instrument[150].

2. 10. 1 Previous methods of notation

Gubaidulina, in »Dots, lines and zigzag«, makes use of resonance effects. She requests these by means of a simple explanation in the foreword to the work: "[a]t the beginning the clarinettist sits at the piano instead of the pianist, and depresses the right pedal"[151]. When the clarinettist starts playing, the strings of the piano vibrate. Moreover, *Lachenmann*, in »„... zwei Gefühle ...", Musik mit Leonardo«, notates a similar action in the same manner. However, he gives the directions in the score and not the foreword. In the piece a tubist is supposed to walk

---

[149]Cf. ibid., p. 152.

[150]Cf. ibid., p. 152.

[151]Gubaidulina, Dots, p. 2.

to the grand piano [geht zum Flügel] and play into the grand piano [spielt in den Flügel] (which means that he will have to bend over before he starts playing):

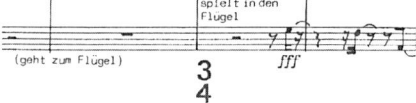

Fig. 72 Lachenmann, Gefühle, p. 43.

Further, in *Szalonek's* »Piernikiana«[152] a tubist is placed behind a piano with depressed pedal and a tam-tam. When he starts playing, sympathetic vibrations are produced on both instruments. The disposal of the instruments is, as can be seen in Figure 73, depicted by a sketch. A similar drawing is then used to make the tubist move his instrument towards the piano or tam-tam[153].

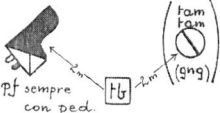

Fig. 73 Szalonek, Piernikiana, p. 2.

Moreover, the action of moving a clarinet's bell over the surface of the piano's bass strings is utilised by *Foss* in »Echoi«. He employs arrows in order to depict the motions the player is supposed to perform:

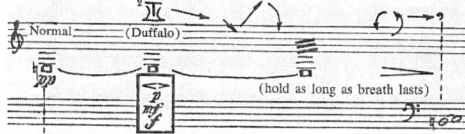

Fig. 74 Foss, Echoi, p. 29.

2. 10. 2 Discussion

Resonance effects as well as the actions of walking and directing the bell towards the instrument may be notated adequately by means of directions (cf. the example by *Gubaidulina* and Figure 72). These directions can even be longer and hence contain a low degree of instantaneous comprehension. This is because when requested in the course of the piece, the player anyway needs time to prepare the articulation, i. e. to walk to the instrument, before being able to perform it. Alternatively, the positioning of the player can be depicted by means of a sketch (cf. Figure 73). Such a sketch could describe the disposal of the instrument in an exact way and even be used to determine the path the player is supposed to walk. Additionally, even the walk itself may be notated and used as the sonic material of a work. Further, the movement of the instrument's bell modifies the resonance effect. Therefore, it may be desirable to depict it. However, *Foss* notates this action in a very approximate manner (cf. Figure 74). As shown below, a more exact method could utilise a drawing of the instrument's body in order to depict the bell's motion.

---

[152]Witold Szalonek: Piernikiana. For tube solo. Kraków and Munich 1978.
[153]Cf. ibid., pp. 1 and 4.

2. 10. 3 Suggestion for the notation of resonance effects

The suggested method of notation for the resonance effect makes either use of a direction or a sketch, which explains the positioning of the instrumentalist and the paths they are supposed to walk. Additionally, the distance between the bell and the resonating instrument may be determined. The direction or sketch may be presented in the foreword of the work or be a part of the score. An example of a sketch is displayed in Figure 73. Further, the movement of the bell is notated here by presenting a drawing of the instrument's body, dashed lines and arrows that depict the motion. Dashed lines are used in order to outline that the instrument itself is not touched, but the bell merely moved over it. Since no sound is produced by this movement, but the resonating sound modified, no common notes are utilised for the depiction of the motion's duration. Instead, a time related starting point and endpoint (◇) is used to notate the action's duration by means of an additional single lined notation system with no clef placed below the original system. In Figure 75, the action of moving an instrument's bell over a piano's bass strings is displayed. Initially, the player moves the bell from the left to the right for the duration of a crotchet, then remains on this position for another crotchet and subsequently performs a spiral motion for the duration of a minim. Simultaneously, a semibreve »c¹/C4« is played (also cf. Chapter »3. 2. 4 Rubbing and bowing motions« for more complex motions and Figure 25 in the chapter on keyboard instruments for the complete illustration of the grand piano's body).

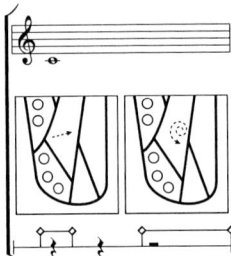

Fig. 75 Resonance effects on the grand piano.

2. 11 Other extended playing techniques and their notation

There are a couple of rare playing techniques that are explained here separately. One of these is normally referred to as **subtone** and only introduced briefly in this chapter because a conventional method of notation has already been established. The subtone technique refers to the airy, breathy way of playing lower tones. Subtones are overtone-weak and quiet sounds. This effect can be produced on clarinets and saxophones. It is normally notated by means of the lowest dynamic level and the additional direction subtone. In the case of the saxophone, it is difficult to play very quiet in the lower register. Therefore, the articulation is, in such a case, realised with the dynamic level *pianissimo*. Transitions between normal and subtone playing are difficult and cannot always be smoothly executed[154]. Moreover, similar sounds can be produced on the bassoon. *Gallois* designates these as **velvet sounds** and explains that these extremely soft sounds resemble the sound colour produced by brass instruments played with mutes. He further suggests notating them by giving the direction velvet mode[155]. However, velvet sounds could alternatively be requested in the same way as subtones and hence by giving the direction velvet sound/tone.

---

[154]Cf. Weiss and Netti, Saxophone, pp. 161f.

[155]Gallois, Bassoon, pp. 25f.

Further, wind players are occasionally requested to produce the highest possible and some-times even the lowest possible tone[156]. This is because the usual range of some instruments may be extended. However, the lowest possible tone is clearly defined for all wind instru-ments and hence does not need to be specifically requested. A method of notation for the **highest possible tone** has been presented in Chapter »2. 3. 3 Teeth embouchure« and »1. 4. 1 The highest possible tone and its notation«. These paradigms may be transferred easily. Ano-ther extended technique is the **half valve** technique. It may be executed on all brass instru-ments with valves. When requested, the valves are only supposed to be depressed halfway. The result is a transposition upwards and a modification of the timbre. The articulation is nor-mally notated by means of diamond-shaped notes that replace the common notes[157]. Since these are, in the case of wind instruments, only suggested being utilised for the depiction of the woodwinds' whistle tones (cf. Chapter »2. 7 Whistle techniques«), and the pitch is raised similarly to playing harmonics, they may also be employed for the notation of the brass instruments' half valve technique. Because the utilisation of a diamond-shaped note head already adequately requests this technique, only the fingered tone, but not the resulting pitch needs to be depicted. As mentioned, the system can then be regarded as transposing. Moreo-ver, transitions between normal and the half valve articulation can be executed smoothly.

Further, *Lachenmann*, in »Mouvement (– vor der Erstarrung)«, requests so-called **breath accents**. Flute and trumpet players are in this piece supposed to move the instrument before the mouth and release a steam of air on the blow hole at the appropriate moment. He depicts this effect by means of a special note head:

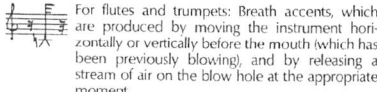 For flutes and trumpets: Breath accents, which are produced by moving the instrument hori-zontally or vertically before the mouth (which has been previously blowing), and by releasing a stream of air on the blow hole at the appropriate moment.

Fig. 76 Lachenmann, Mouvement, no page named [foreword].

The articulation described by *Lachenmann* as breath accents resembles the jet whistle tech-nique. This is because in both cases the sound is created by a strong air attack. However, in the case of breath accents, the embouchure may be described as *al flauto dolce* (cf. Chapter »2. 3. 4 The recorder embouchure and its notation«), and the instrument is moved. Neverthe-less, due to the similarity of the two techniques, and because the breath attack articulation is only rarely utilised, it is suggested here notating it in the same manner as the jet whistle instead of by introducing a completely new method. Therefore, breath attacks on flutes are depicted by means of giving the direction *al flauto dolce* and utilising the same arrow that requests the jet whistle. An additional symbol, which depicts the motion of the instrument, is not used here in order to preserve a clear appearance of the score. In Figure 77, the player is supposed to perform a breath attack whilst fingering the tone »c¹/C4«.

al flauto dolce

Fig. 77 Breath accents.

[156]Cf. Erwin Koch-Raphael: Spuren. Tenor trombone solo with optional percussion. Berlin and Wiesbaden 1980, no page named [appendix] and Krzysztof Penderecki: Capriccio. For oboe and 11 strings. Celle and Kraków 1968, p. 15.

[157]Stone, Notation, p. 199 and Sevsay, Handbuch, p. 148.

Further, some composers direct the player to reverse the instrument and **blow into the bell**[158]. In such a case, the player is supposed to finger the keys/valves conversely. Apparently, this action cannot be performed on large wind instruments. As this technique can be regarded as a rare extended embouchure, it is suggested here requesting it similarly and hence by means of a direction, such as *all'incontrario* (back to front). This articulation may also be performed after removing parts of the instrument or modifying it (cf. Chapter »2. 6 Preparing the instrument«). Additionally, woodwind players are also sometimes required to blow through the tone holes[159]. Since this is a very uncommon action, it should, however, be explained by means of a sketch (cf. Figure 104 in the chapter on string instruments) and determining the embouchure.

Another rare articulation is to either **move the bell of the instrument** up and down or from the left to the right. When the instrument is moved up prior to the winding, a fanfare is played, whereas when the motions are performed during normal winding, a kind of *Doppler* effect is produced[160]. The former action is normally requested by means of the direction bells up. However, when the extent and duration of such motions is supposed to be notated in an exact manner, an additional single lined notation system may be employed. It can be used to depict the extent in degrees and the duration by means of the timeline. Since the action of performing complex motions with the bell is similar to executing motions of the bell over the surface of an instrument, it may, alternatively, be notated in the same way as in Chapter »2. 10 Resonance effects«. However, in this case, the reference instrument is missing. Therefore, the maximum radius of the movement is displayed and the motion drawn into it. Dashed lines are employed here because no instrument is depicted in this case, and hence the method of notation can be clearly distinguished from the method used to depict rubbing motions on percussion instruments (cf. Chapter »3. 2. 4 Rubbing and bowing motions«) and resonance effects (cf. Chapter »2. 10 Resonance effects«). As can be seen in Figure 78, the radius is depicted by a circle, which also contains the home position of the bell. In the example, a clarinettist is supposed to perform the motions. Since the clarinet is normally held inclined, the ordinary position is not in the middle of the radius. Initially, the player moves the bell from the home position to the right for the duration of a crotchet, then remains on this position for another crotchet and subsequently performs a spiral motion for the duration of a minim. During these motions, a (written) semibreve »c¹/C4« is played.

Fig. 78 Moving the bell.

[158]Read, Contemporary, p. 147.
[159]Sevsay, Handbuch, p. 151.
[160]Ibid., pp. 152f.

3. THE TECHNIQUES OF PERCUSSION INSTRUMENTS

There are four groups of percussion instruments: idiophones, membranophones, chordo-phones and aerophones. When producing sound on idiophones, the whole body of the instru-ment is caused to vibrate. Idiophones may have a definite pitch (e. g. mallet instruments, tubu-lar bells, cymbales antiques), indefinite pitch (e. g. cymbals, tam-tams, triangles) or a slightly perceptible pitch (e. g. temple blocks, wood blocks). Membranophones are either single-headed (e. g. timpani, bongos, timbales) or two-headed (e. g. snare drums, bass drums) while the membrane is stretched over a soundbox. These types of drums may also produce sounds with definite pitch (e. g. timpani, rototoms), indefinite pitch (e. g. snare drums, bass drums) or slightly perceptible pitch (e. g. tom-toms, bongos). Further, when producing sound on chordo-phones, strings are caused to vibrate. All string, plucked and keyboard instruments are referred to as chordophones. Besides these, there is only one instrument that is considered to be a percussion instrument: the cimbalon. On aerophones tones are produced by causing an air column to vibrate. All wind instruments are part of this group whilst some aerophones are regarded as percussion instruments (e. g. slide whistles, wind machines, vehicle horns)[1]. As is apparent, there is a huge variety of percussion instruments. However, the aim of this chapter is not to focus on every single instrument, but to discuss unconventional extended playing techniques of percussion instruments in a general manner. Therefore, it is structured by play-ing techniques and not grouped by instruments. Most of the examined techniques may be applied on idiophones and/or membranophones. With regard to percussion instruments, the notation of rolls, the *vibrato* (which is, for instance, on cymbales antiques produced by waving the hand over the instrument subsequently to the attack or on clash cymbals by sha-king these after the attack)[2], trills, clusters (on mallet instruments; also cf. Chapter »5. 6. 1 Clusters«), the basic *glissando* (which is, for instance, on timpani produced by means of the pedal), normal attacks (e. g. striking, shaking or activating the instrument), the production of harmonics (e. g. on the vibraphone) and other basic articulations, such as turning the motor of a vibraphone on/off or changing the speed of the fan, are regarded here as conventional ele-ments[3]. Their notation can be adopted from the essential handbooks on instrumentation whilst most composers use the method of depiction that can be found there. Moreover, the determi-nation of the standard agents of attack, i. e. which mallet the percussionist is supposed to use, and their basic utilisation, i. e. how many mallets he holds in his hands, is not discussed here. A virtually conventional approach towards the notation of these parameters can be found in *Adler*[4], *Sevsay*[5] or *Stone*[6] whilst the explanation by *Sevsay* is the most complete one and, therefore, recommended here. The cimbalon is also not discussed here. However, some of the extended playing techniques explained in the chapter on plucked and keyboard instruments, such as percussive effects, *pizzicato* on the neck or playing on the strings of a piano, may easily be transferred to this instrument. Further, an approach towards the notation of whistles is presented in Chapter »2. 6. 1 Detaching the head joint/mouthpiece/reed/bocal and its nota-tion«. Whereas, the main unconventional elements discussed in this chapter are the extension of the percussive apparatus, extended modes of attack, »pitch« bending – the extended *glis-sando*, muting and preparing the instrument. As the number of percussion instruments is vast, indications concerning the limitation of the dynamic level may, in most cases, not be pre-sented.

---

[1] Sevsay, Handbuch, pp. 157, 171 and 202f.

[2] Ibid., pp. 180f.

[3] Cf. ibid., pp. 159-207.

[4] Adler, Orchestration, pp. 434f.

[5] Sevsay, Handbuch, pp. 214-216.

[6] Stone, Notation, pp. 210-213.

3. 1 The extension of the percussive apparatus

The percussive apparatus can be either extended by **introducing special agents of attack** or **percussion instruments**. There are various examples for the two varieties.

3. 1. 1 Introducing special agents of attack and its notation

Theoretically, any kind of item a percussionist is able to hold in his hands can be used as a mallet. Therefore, the number of special agents of attack is vast. Examples of such items can, for instance, be found in *Lachenmann's* »Staub«. There he makes use of a cardboard tube in order to produce sound on a tam-tam. The utilisation of this kind of mallet is requested by giving the direction cardboard tube [Papprohr][7]. Moreover, *Szalonek*, in »Concertino«, utilises inter alia a tuning fork to strike a rubber plate and subsequently touch an instrument with it[8]. The tuning fork is notated by means of a symbol:

Fig. 1 Szalonek, Concertino, p. 3.

Further, *Kagel*, in »Dressur«[9], makes use of a carpet beater, which is also introduced by means of a symbol:

1 *carpet beater* made of basket -work

Fig. 2 Kagel, Dressur, no page named [foreword].

As mentioned in the previous chapter, there is a general method of notation for the standard agents of attack. In this method the mallets the percussionist is supposed to employ are depicted by means of symbols. In order to comply with the conventional manner of depicting agents of attack, special mallets should be notated in the same fashion. Therefore, *Szalonek's* and *Kagel's* approach is preferred over the one by *Lachenmann*. Hence any special agent of attack is suggested here being introduced by means of a symbol. The more this symbol resembles the shape of the mallet, the greater the instantaneous comprehension and simpler the method of notation (the utilisation of the hand as an agent of attack is discussed in Chapter »3. 2. 1 The extended utilisation of the agents of attack«). However, since there is a vast number of special agents of attack, symbols for all possible mallets can apparently not be presented here. Even percussion instruments are sometimes utilised as mallets. In »Anagrama«[10] *Kagel*, for instance, uses claves, güiros, maracas or triangles to strike percussion instruments[11]. However, these instruments are not introduced by symbols, but directions. In order to depict the mallets in the same manner as the standard and other extended agents of attack, symbols would have to be employed. Examples for graphic representations of percussion

---

7   Cf. Lachenmann, Staub, p. 85.
8   Cf. Szalonek, Concertino, p. 3.
9   Mauricio Kagel: Dressur. Drum trio for wood instruments. Frankfurt/M. et al. 1983.
10 Mauricio Kagel: Anagrama. For four solo singers, speaking choir and chamber ensemble. London 1965.
11 Cf. Kagel, Anagrama, pp. 7 and 23.

instruments can, for example, be found in *Sevsay*[12], *Stone*[13], *Kagel's* »Match«[14] and »L'art bruit«[15] or *Stockhausen's* »Kontakte«[16].

3. 1. 2 Introducing special percussion instruments and its notation

As in the case of the special agents of attack, any non-instrumental item that can be struck, shaken or used to produce any kind of sound, extends the percussive apparatus. Therefore, a coherent method of notation for all possible augmentations cannot be presented here. However, an approach towards the notation of special sound producers is presented in »Part II: Electroacoustic music – 3. 3. 2 Non-instrumental sound sources«. As can be seen there, two groups of non-instrumental sounds are discussed, reproducible and extractable sounds. All reproducible sounds may also be regarded as percussive effects since the sound producers may be utilised in the same way as percussion instruments. Further, percussive sounds that can be created on other orchestral instruments are discussed separately in the chapter on the respective instrument.

3. 2 Extended modes of attack

In this chapter **the extended utilisation of the agents of attack, extended striking techniques,** the problem of **determining the point of impact** as well as **rubbing and bowing motions** and **the sound production without agents of attack** is discussed. Moreover, **playing the snares** of a drum is specifically examined. This is because a number of special techniques may be employed when playing a snare drum in this way.

3. 2. 1 The extended utilisation of the agents of attack

The agents of attack are used in an augmented manner when a strike is executed with the handle of the beater, a percussion instrument is struck with the entire length of a stick, one of the ends of the the beater is used to touch an instrument at right angles as well as when the agent's point of contact differs from the normal one or is shifted during the execution of several strokes.

3. 2. 1. 1 Previous methods of notation

The utilisation of the handle is requested in various works. Most composers depict this way of striking the instrument by means of a reversed mallet symbol. In »Musik für Klavier und Schlaginstrumente«[17] *Redel*, for example, requires the player to strike with the wood handle of the respective beater [mit dem Holzende des jeweiligen Schlegels] by utilising this method of notation:

♩ ♩ ♩ = mit dem Holzende des jeweiligen Schlegels

Fig. 3 Redel, Musik, p. 2.

---

[12] Sevsay, Handbuch, pp. 212f.

[13] Stone, Notation, pp. 206-210.

[14] Kagel, Match, pp. 2f.

[15] Mauricio Kagel: L'art bruit. Solo for two. Frankfurt/M. et al. 1998, pp. If.

[16] Karlheinz Stockhausen: Kontakte. For electronic sounds, piano and percussion. London 1966, pp. 3-6.

[17] Martin Redel: Musik für Klavier und Schlaginstrumente. Berlin and Wiesbaden 1970.

However, sometimes, for instance, the direction with handle [mit Stiel][18] or with wood handle [mit Holzstiel][19] is given. Moreover, *Penderecki*, in »Dimensions of time and silence«, requests this articulation by marking the handle end of the drumstick:

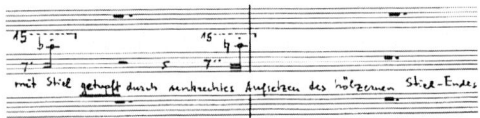

strike the instrument with
the handle end of the
drumstick

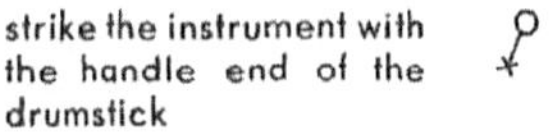

Fig. 4 Penderecki, Dimensions, p. 4.

Further, *Varèse*, in »Offrandes«[20], makes the player "strike the head of drum with entire length of stick"[21] by giving this direction in a footnote[22] whilst the action of touching an instrument at right angles is requested by *Lachenmann* in »Accanto«[23]. He depicts it by means of the direction dapped with the handle by attaching the wooden handle end perpendicularly [mit Stiel getupft durch senkrechtes Aufsetzen des hölzernen Stiel-Endes]:

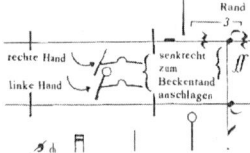

Fig. 5 Lachenmann, Accanto, p. 2.

Moreover, *Kagel*, in »Match«, requests this articulation by means of a symbol for the mallet, an arrow pointing downwards and the additional direction with handle vertical on the cup [mit Stiel vertikal auf Kuppe]:

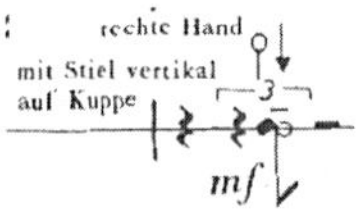

Fig. 6 Kagel, Match, p. 23.

In the same piece he makes the player also hit the edge of two cymbals with the middle point of the agent's handle. This action is depicted by means of a drawing and the additional direction attack perpendicular to the cymbal's edge [senkrecht zum Beckenrand anschlagen]:

Fig. 7 Kagel, Match, p. 23.

Finally, *Lachenmann*, in »Accanto«, requests the percussionist to shift the point of contact between a stick and a xylorimba during the execution of several strokes. This action is reques-

---

[18] Cf. Kelemen, Changeant, p. 56.

[19] Cf. Stockhausen, Kontakte, p. 18.

[20] Edgard Varèse: Offrandes. For soprano and chamber orchestra. New York 1927.

[21] Varèse, Offrandes, p. 31.

[22] Cf. ibid., p. 31.

[23] Helmut Lachenmann: Accanto. Music for a clarinetist with orchestra. Wiesbaden 1984.

ted by means of the direction shift the stick's point of contact to the handle [Anschlagstelle des Stockes zum Schaft verlagern] and notes that underline the agent's motion:

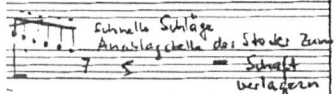

Fig. 8 Lachenmann, Accanto, p. 18.

3. 2. 1. 2 Discussion

As mentioned, the agent of attack is conventionally depicted by means of a symbol. Hence this symbol needs to be also employed when a mallet or stick is utilised in an extended manner. When requesting any of the augmented techniques, the articulations may be either notated by altering the symbol or giving an additional direction. However, an additional direction needs to be limited to a few words in order to guarantee instantaneous comprehension. Therefore, the direction by *Varèse* (strike the head of drum with entire length of the stick) and the direction by *Lachenmann* (dapped with the handle by attaching the wooden handle end perpendicularly) cannot be used to request augmented actions. Further, since simple drawings contain a greater degree of instantaneous comprehension, and hence facilitate the comprehension of the requested technique, this method of depiction is preferred here over giving an additional direction. Thus it is, concerning the utilisation of the agent's handle, favoured to depict the action by means of an extended beater symbol, and it is not suggested giving the direction with handle or with handle end. Moreover, with regard to the displayed methods of notation, it may be stated that *Redel's* method (cf. Figure 3) is simpler and clearer than the one by *Penderecki* (cf. Figure 4). This is because the former approach refers to the way the player holds the mallet or stick. Moreover, when the normal utilisation of the mallet is depicted by a drawing in which the tip of the agent is on top and the handle end on the bottom, it is consequent to depict the utilisation of the agent in a reversed manner by a drawing in which the handle end is on top and the tip on the bottom. Furthermore, since *Varèse's* direction does – as mentioned – not comply with the requirement of enabling instantaneous comprehension, an alternative method of notation needs to be developed in order to depict the action of striking the instrument with the entire length of the agent. Such a method is presented in the following chapter. Concerning the performance of a perpendicular hit, it may be stated that *Kagel's* approach (cf. Figure 6) does not agree with the suggested method of notation for the reversed utilisation of the mallet. If it was transferred to his approach, the arrow would have to point upwards (in order to request the execution of a vertical stroke by means of the agent's handle). But this would in turn cause confusion because the percussionists normally moves the mallet downwards when performing such a stroke. Alternatively, an arrow could be used to depict the point of contact on the agent instead of the motion the player is supposed to perform. With regard to the augmented determination or shift of the agent's point of contact, the depiction by means of a simple drawing (cf. Figure 7) is also preferred here over notating the action by means of a direction (cf. Figure 8). However, it is not necessary that this image contains a graphic depiction of the agent and the percussion instrument when only the agent is used in an augmented manner (cf. Chapter »3. 2. 3 The point of impact« for the augmented determination of the point of impact, such as striking the edge of a cymbal). Therefore, it is preferred here not to notate the described articulations in reference to the instrument, but solely by means of a depiction of the mallet. As can be seen in the following chapter, the exact determination of the point of contact and shifts may be notated by means of arrows.

3. 2. 1. 3 Suggestion for the notation of the extended utilisation of the agents of attack

All augmented utilisations of the agents of attack are depicted by means of a symbol for the mallet the percussionist employs. The beater utilised in the example is a wooden headed drumstick[24]. All strokes are depicted by means of x-shaped note heads and a single lined notation system with no clef. This is because the hits are executed here on a percussion instrument with indefinite pitch, which is notated in this manner in order to distinguish these kinds of instruments from the ones with definite pitch. Alternatively, a drum clef system and x-shaped note heads could be employed to enable the simultaneous depiction of strokes on several instruments by means of a single system. In Figure 9, eight distinct articulations are depicted in the order of 1. a normal stroke which implies the determination of the agent of attack (conventional method of notation), 2. a stroke with the handle, 3. a stroke with the entire length of the beater, 4. a stroke which involves touching the instrument at right angles with the stick's tip, 5. a stroke which involves touching the instrument at right angles with the stick's handle end, 6. a stroke where the agent's point of contact is determined as the middle of the stick length and 7. six semiquaver strokes where the agent's point of contact is shifted from the tip to the handle (depending on the percussion instrument, articulation six and seven need to be complemented by a depiction of the point of impact on the instrument). As can be seen in the example, the point of contact is determined by an additional arrow when it differs from the normal utilisation of the beater. This is the case in articulation four to seven. However, this method cannot be applied to articulation three since the agent's point of contact is not a single point, but the whole surface of the stick. Therefore, a curly bracket is utilised. Moreover, the shift of the stick's point of contact is notated by an arrow as used for the depiction of all *glissando* actions in this work. However, since the shift only resembles a *glissando* – because the stick does not actually slide – the additional direction *glissando* is dismissed. Alternatively, the exact point of contact for every stroke could be determined. Further, the arrows that depict the point of contact could alternatively point in the direction of the motion. However, this might – as mentioned – cause confusion with regard to articulation four and five. Another rare extended utilisation of the agents of attack is 8. to hit two beaters against each other (clap). This articulation is depicted here by crossing two beater symbols.

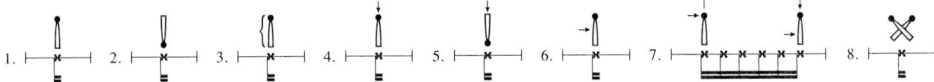

Fig. 9 The normal attack and the extended utilisation of the beater.

The displayed methods of notation can also be transferred to any special agent of attack. However, when the hand is used to attack the instrument, another method of notation needs to be employed. This is because the articulations that may be performed by means of the hand are more complex than the actions that may be executed by means of a mallet or stick. The utilisation of the hand as an agent of attack has already been discussed in Chapter »1. 7. 1 Strokes on the body and their notation« by taking the example of string instruments. Since the action of striking the body of, for instance, a cello resembles the action of striking any kind of percussion instrument, the method of notation introduced in this chapter may be transferred. Therefore, the drawings presented in the chapter on string instruments (Figures 89f.) here serve as a paradigm for the utilisation of the hand as an agent of attack and an extensive discussion of the execution of this playing technique on percussion instruments is dismissed. Moreover, when the player is supposed to clap his hands, two hand symbols should be crossed.

---

[24] Cf. Sevsay, Handbuch, p. 214.

3. 2. 2 Extended striking techniques

Most extended striking techniques are related to the augmented bowing techniques *saltando*, *balzando* and *gettato* discussed in Chapter »1. 3. 3 The *saltando*, *balzando* and *toccato* and its notation«. When applied on percussion instruments, the utilisation of the beater resembles the *col legno* performance of these techniques. Moreover, the conventional bowing technique designated as *gettato* may also be executed by means of mallets or sticks.

3. 2. 2. 1 Previous methods of notation

The four »bowing techniques« are only seldom applied. However, for instance, *Lachenmann*, in »NUN«, makes use of an action designated by him as *saltando glissando*. As in the case of the *saltando* on string instruments, the beater shakes after the striking. Further, this articulation is combined with a shifting of the point of contact between the head of the beater and the proximity to the shaft. *Lachenmann* requests the action by means of the direction trill/mordent [Praller] and a line which depicts the *glissando*:

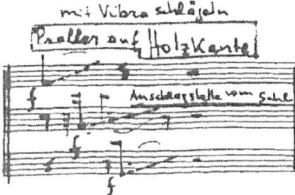

Fig. 10 Lachenmann, NUN, p. VIII.

Moreover, *Kagel*, in »Anagrama«, requests a *toccato* articulation on a gong by means of the direction touch the gong with no attack [ohne Anschlag den Gong berühren], diamond-shaped note heads and a zigzag line. Since the gong still vibrates from the previous attack when it is touched, a sizzle effect[25] is produced:

Fig. 11 Kagel, Anagrama, p. 23.

3. 2. 2. 2 Discussion

With regard to the striking techniques related to the four bowing techniques *saltando*, *balzando*, *toccato* and *gettato*, it may be stated that there is no necessity to introduce a method different from the one employed for string instruments in order to request these. Thus these articulations may, in the case of percussion instruments, be depicted by means of additional directions. When doing so, the articulations are coherently depicted and the method closely related to traditional notation. Therefore, the approaches by *Lachenmann* (cf. Figure 10) and *Kagel* (cf. Figure 11) are dismissed here in favour of the methods introduced in the chapter on string instruments and the conventional manner of depicting the *gettato* articulation. Moreover, the action referred to as *saltando glissando* by *Lachenmann* needs to be labelled differently. As shown in the respective section in the chapter on string instruments, the direction *saltando* refers to a dense shake without any horizontal motion. As *Lachenmann* wants the player to shift the point of contact during the *saltando* stroke, the additional direction *glis-*

---

[25] A similar sound effect also occurs in the case of the buzz-*pizzicato* because the lingering string is touched with the fingernail or fingertip (cf. Chapter »1. 6. 2 Exact muting stops and their notation«).

111

sando and a line is employed. However, this performance of a *saltando* may be rather described as a *gettato* articulation. This is because the *gettato* is basically a *saltando* that involves a horizontal bowing motion. When transferred to beater attacks, the player shifts the point of contact from the proximity to the shaft to the head of the beater (when executing a normal stroke) or the other way round (when executing a stroke with the handle) by »throwing« the agent of attack. Further, concerning *Kagel's* method of notation it may be said that diamond-shaped note heads are, in the case of the *col legno toccato* on string instruments, only employed in order to determine the exact point of attachment on the fingerboard of a string instrument. However, since this point needs to be determined in another way in the case of percussion instruments (see Chapter »3. 2. 3 The point of impact«), the utilisation of these note heads in combination with the *toccato* articulation would lead to confusion. Moreover, there is no need to utilise an additional zigzag line when the articulation is already clearly depicted by means of the direction *toccato*.

3. 2. 2. 3 Suggestion for the notation of extended striking techniques

Hence the extended striking techniques are suggested being notated by means of the additional directions *saltando*, *balzando*, *toccato* or *gettato*. These directions may complement the method of depiction for the agents of attack presented in Figure 9. The *gettato* may be regarded as a variant of the extended attack, which involves a shifting of the point of contact (cf. attack no. 7). However, in this case, only one stroke is performed. It implies a dense shake of the beater on the percussion instrument and a simultaneous shifting of the point of contact.

3. 2. 3 The point of impact

Any spot of a percussion instrument may be struck in order to produce sound. Besides the normal attacks, for instance, the middle or edge of the surface, as well as the rim or shell of membranophones, may be hit. Further, it is possible to gradually shift the point of impact and to simultaneously strike different spots on the same instrument with a single or more beaters. Moreover, the back of certain idiophones and items or beaters lying on the instrument can be struck.

3. 2. 3. 1 Previous methods of notation

In the case of membranophones, most composers differentiate between five (normal attack on the head, middle, edge, rim and shell) or fewer points of impact. In »Intégrales«[26] *Varèse*, for instance, requests the player to either hit the head [membrane], rim [rebord] or shell [caisse] of the instrument by giving the additional direction M, R or C[27]. Moreover, *Zimmermann*, in »Canto di speranza«[28], utilises two symbols in order to request strokes in the middle or at the edge of the skin:

In the middle of the skin ○

At the edge of the skin, close to the frame ∪

Fig. 12 Zimmermann, Canto, no page named [foreword].

However, *Sevsay* suggests depicting the point of impact by means of using different note heads in combination with a drum clef[29]. Further, *Lachenmann*, in »Staub«, utilises squared

---

[26] Edgard Varèse: Intégrales. For small orchestra and percussion. No city named 1926.

[27] Cf. ibid., p. 1.

[28] Bernd Alois Zimmermann: Canto di speranza. Mainz 1958.

[29] Cf. Sevsay, Handbuch, p. 160.

note heads to depict shell attacks on timpani and differentiates between higher and lower sounds. Therefore, the notes are employed in a five lined notation system with no clef while the higher the sounds are, the higher is the position of the note in the system:

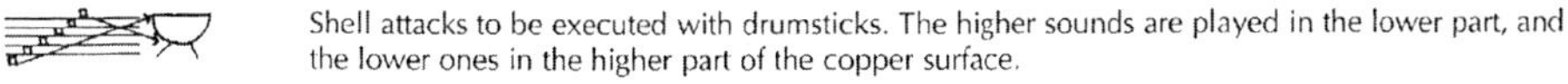

Shell attacks to be executed with drumsticks. The higher sounds are played in the lower part, and the lower ones in the higher part of the copper surface.

Fig. 13 Lachenmann, Staub, no page named [foreword].

Another method of notation is employed by *Kotoński* in »A battere«[30]. He makes use of a graphic depiction in order to determine the point of impact on the instrument:

 — indicates the kind of beater, its position in relation to the instrument and the place on the instrument (in this case on the cymbal) where the strokes fall · das Symbol zeigt Schlegelart und Schlegelposition beim Schlag (hier für Becken) und die gewünschte Anschlagstelle · wskazuje rodzaj pałeczki i jej położenie względem instrumentu oraz miejsce na instrumencie (w tym wypadku na talerzu), na które padają uderzenia

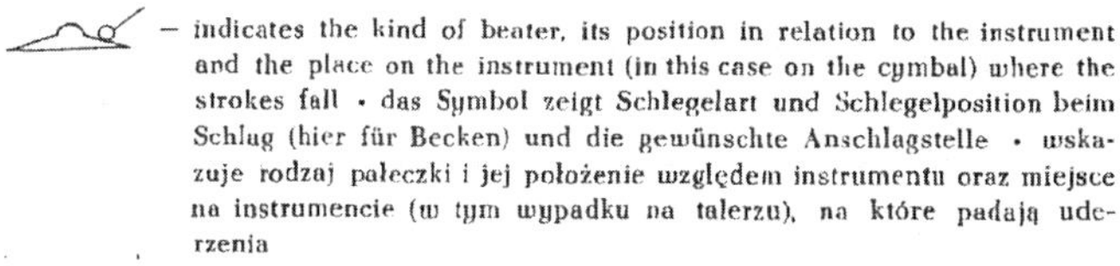

Fig. 14 Kotoński, Battere, p. 3.

Moreover, *Redel*, in »Rounds«[31], requests a gradual shifting of the point of impact from the edge [Rand] to the middle [Mitte] by means of the letters »R« and »M« as well as an arrow:

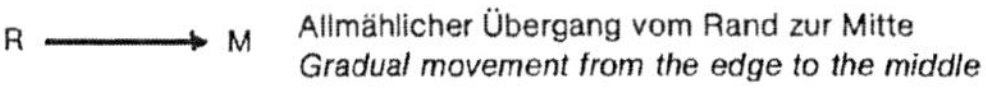

R ⟶ M   Allmählicher Übergang vom Rand zur Mitte
Gradual movement from the edge to the middle

Fig. 15 Redel, Rounds, no page named [appendix].

Furthermore, *Kagel*, in »Sonant (1960/....)«[32], request a (non-specified) rim shot either by means of the direction RS or a symbol:

RS or ⏀   rimshot

Fig. 16 Kagel, Sonant, p. 22 [explanation of symbols].

Kagel, in »L'art bruit«, also makes the player strike a Chinese cymbal from underneath. This action is requested by means of a graphic depiction:

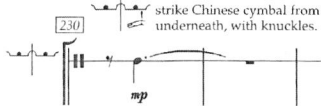

strike Chinese cymbal from underneath, with knuckles.

Fig. 17 Kagel, Bruit, p. 11a.

Finally, *Penderecki*, in »Fluorescences«[33], requests a hit on a drumstick lying on the surface of a percussion instrument by means of a variation of the symbol he employs to depict the drumstick:

[30] Włodozmierz Kotoński: A battere. For percussion, guitar, harpsichord, viola and violincello. Celle 1963.

[31] Martin Redel: Rounds. For percussion solo. Berlin and Wiesbaden 1979.

[32] Mauricio Kagel: Sonant (1969/....). For guitar, harp, double bass and membranophones. Frankfurt/M. et al. 1964.

[33] Krzysztof Penderecki: Fluorescences. For orchestra. Celle 1962.

$\nearrow^{\bullet}$ = Schlag auf die Mitte eines auf die Schlagfläche gelegten Schlegels mit einem zweiten · With one drumstick strike the other drumstick, after having laid it on the striking surface of the instrument · Frapper le milieu d'une baguette posée sur la peau avec une autre baguette

Fig. 18 Penderecki, Fluorescences, p. 3.

3. 2. 3. 2 Discussion

When only a very limited number of points on a percussion instrument are supposed to be struck, the methods of notation utilised by *Varèse* and *Zimmermann* (for the latter cf. Figure 12) are sufficient. However, when the percussionist is supposed to quickly switch instruments, it is clearer to make use of *Sevsay's* method and hence depict the point of impact by means of the note head itself and a drum clef system instead of by placing letters or symbols above the notes. This is because attacking one or the other instrument could simply be requested by placing the note head on another line. An example of this method of notation is given in the following chapter. However, very complex attacks could not be depicted in this manner since the introduction of numerous new directions, symbols or note heads would not comply with the requirement of simplicity. For instance, the six points *Lachenmann* makes the player strike (cf. Figure 13) could not be depicted in a simple way by means of directions. However, *Lachenmann's* method of introducing special note heads for shell attacks and a notation system derived from pitch-based notation would also become confusing if it was utilised for the notation of all points of impact on all sorts of percussion instruments. Many different variants of this system would have to be introduced in order to depict the point of impact on percussion instruments of different shape and size, which would also in turn lead to a very complex method of notation. Further, the graphic depiction of the point that is supposed to be struck can be described as simple. Additionally, it contains a high degree of instantaneous comprehension. However, in order to display more than one dimension, the graphic depiction of the instrument's side, as utilised by *Kotoński* (cf. Figure 14), would have to be replaced by a top view of the instrument. Such a method of notation could also be used to display a gradual shift of the point of impact, e. g. from the edge to the middle (cf. Figure 15) as well as more complex shiftings and rim shots (cf. Figure 16) and – if slightly modified – shell attacks in a simpler manner than by using letters, arrows and/or symbols as well as a distinct notation system and special note heads. However, concerning the notation of hits on a cymbal from underneath (cf. Figure 17), a variant of depiction would have to be introduced in order to clearly distinguish the front and back of the cymbal. Moreover, as in the case of *Kotoński's* approach, the side view would have to be replaced by a »top« view. Further, concerning the method of notation for hits on a beater or item lying on the surface of a drum (cf. Figure 18), it may be said that *Penderecki's* approach could lead to confusion. This is because when employing a graphic depiction of the drum's surface in order to notate the point of impact and different beater symbols in order to notate the manner of attack, a variation of the beater symbol would suggest rather employing another extended attack instead of striking a »modified« drum surface. Therefore, a simpler and clearer method would include the beater or item in the graphic depiction of the instrument.

3. 2. 3. 3 Suggestion for the notation of the point of impact

As mentioned, a limited number of points on percussion instruments can be depicted by means of employing different note heads. When using these in combination with a drum clef system, each line or (additionally) each spacing between the lines refers to a particular instrument. As the common attack (on instruments with indefinite pitch) is requested by means of x-shaped note heads, these note heads could, in such a case, also be used to depict the common attack whilst, for example, triangular note heads pointing upwards could be used to request attacks on the edge, spherical note heads to notate hits on the rim (only membrano-phones), triangular note heads pointing downwards to depict strokes on the shell and squared note heads could be employed to make the player strike the midpoint of the instrument/the dome. When employing instruments with definite pitch, the drum clef system would have to be replaced by a pitch-based notation system and the x-shaped note head by a common one whilst the other note heads could be used in the same manner.

However, in the case of more complex attacks, the point of impact on percussion instru-ments is suggested here being notated by means of a graphic depiction of the instrument. This method can be employed for the notation of complex hits on the surface of membranophones, many idiophones or special percussion instruments. In the example presented in Figure 19, the player is supposed to perform six semiquaver strokes on a bass drum, which are followed by a semibreve roll. The beater is again a wooden headed drumstick and the roll executed with two sticks. The first three hits are normal attacks on a point close to the edge, on the rim and on the edge. The next two hits are performed with the entire length of the stick and the last semiquaver stroke is executed with the stick's tip. It hits the middle of the drum at right angles. Finally, the roll involves a complex gradual shifting of the point of impact in the direc-tion of the arrow. In order to facilitate the performance, the graphic depiction of the surface and hits is always regarded here as being the percussionist's perspective (also cf. Figure 9).

Gr. Trommel – Bass drum

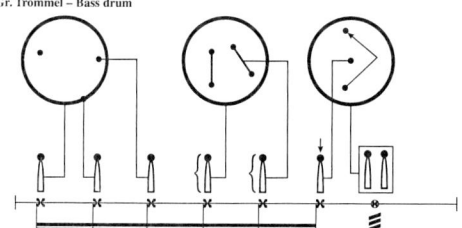

Fig. 19 Complex attacks on a bass drum.

Such graphic depictions may be either employed in a uniform size or correspond to the actual size of the utilised instruments, e. g. when utilising several different membranophones. The former method is apparently less exact, but enables a simpler handling of the illustrations. Moreover, a similar method of notation can also be employed for mallet instruments in order to depict gradual changes of location and varying points of impact on the bars. When doing so, it is sufficient to solely present drawings of the bars that are actually struck. The depicted size of the bars may remain the same as long as only single tones are played because the percussionist should be able to transfer the notated point of impact to any of the bars, consi-dering their actual size. However, when requesting chords, the higher tone's bar needs to be smaller than the lower tone's bar or, alternatively, be complemented by an additional depic-tion of the pitch in order to clearly outline which point of impact is related to which tone. Fur-ther, when notating the point of impact on güiros, slit gongs, cowbells etc., different graphic depictions apparently need to be utilised.

Shell attacks can be notated by means of a graphic depiction of this part of the instrument. In Figure 20, the method of notation for these attacks is presented by taking the example of a timpano. Six semiquaver strokes are performed on its body. All six hits are normal attacks. The first five strokes are executed on various points of the shell. Subsequently, the percus-sionist is supposed to hit the metal frame of the timpano. Further, in »Accanto« *Lachenmann*, for instance, requests the player to hit the tuning screw of a timpano[34]. In order to notate such

---

[34] Cf. Lachenmann, Accanto, p. 12.

an action, the graphic depiction of the kettledrum would have to be more detailed and contain this part of the instrument (also cf. Chapter »1. 5 Playing exceptional spots« and all chapters on percussive effects).

Pauke – Timpano

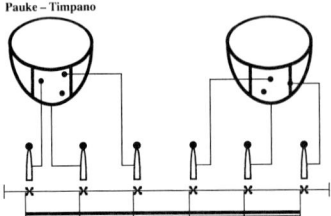

Fig. 20 Hitting the shell of a timpano.

Strokes from underneath are notated here similarly to strokes on the front. However, it is outlined that the back is supposed to be hit because the instrument is coloured black (and the dots, therefore, white). Hence in Figure 21, the first three strokes are executed on the front and the last three strokes on the back of a cymbal.

Becken – Cymbal

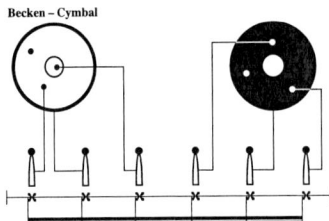

Fig. 21 Strokes on the front and back of a cymbal.

Moreover, hits on beaters or items lying on the surface of the instrument are notated here by extending the drawing of the percussion instrument. In the example presented in Figure 22, a stroke on a drumstick lying on the surface of an instrument is depicted. However, the placement of any kind of item on the surface may be notated by replacing the drumstick with another distinct symbol, e. g. for a comb, spoon, book etc.

Fig. 22 Striking a drumstick lying on the surface of an instrument.

Further, simultaneous hits on different spots of the same instrument are depicted here by means of the conventional method of notation for the utilisation of the mallets and determining which mallet is used to strike which spot on the head (which is especially important when using two or more different mallets):

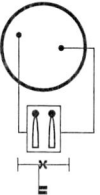

Fig. 23 Striking different spots simultaneously.

Additionally, rim shots may be performed in various ways. In Figure 24, six different variants are displayed. The first stroke is executed with the entire length of the stick. However, other than in Figure 19, the stick only hits two distinct points. This is depicted by connecting these by means of a dashed line. Further, rim shots which involve a shifting of the point of impact – as requested by *Lachenmann* in »Accanto«[35] – can be depicted by combining the method of notation for the rim shot (two dots and a dashed line) and the gradual shifting (two dots and an arrow). In the example, the player is after the first hit supposed to perform four semiquaver rim shots which involve a shifting in the direction of the player. Subsequently, a (one-handed) crotchet roll, which involves a shifting in the other direction, is executed. Other variants of the rim shot are to hit a drumstick lying on the head and rim, to place the tip of the beater on the head and strike the rim with the shaft or to place the tip of a drumstick on the head and subsequently hit its shaft with another beater[36]. These three attacks follow the shifting. The first variant may be notated in the same way as the action of striking a drumstick lying on the surface of an instrument (cf. Figure 22). However, the other two variants require other methods of notation. As can be seen in Figure 24, the player is, subsequently to the hit on the drumstick lying on the head and rim, requested to touch the surface with the stick's head (*toccato*) and then hit the rim with the shaft (*ordinario*, while another variant would be to employ the direction *battuto*). Since the *toccato* action does not end before the rim is struck, two »transposed« notes are used to depict the actions (cf. Chapter »3. 2. 2 Extended striking techniques« for the *toccato* articulation). Finally, the last variant of the rim shot is again notated similarly to a hit on a drumstick lying on the head. However, this time only the head of the beater is lying on the surface, which is depicted by the additional arrow. The player is then supposed to hit the shaft of the stick.

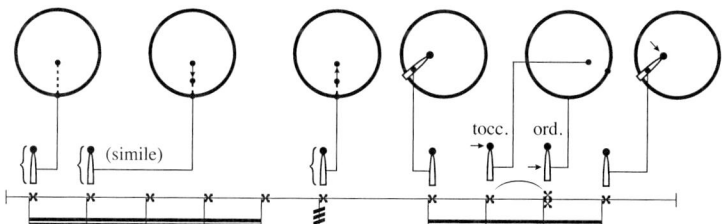

Fig. 24 Six rim shot variants.

3. 2. 4 Rubbing and bowing motions

Besides the normal and extended attacks, rubbing and bowing motions can be executed on percussion instruments. Rubbing motions can be performed on all membranophones and many idiophones, even the bars of mallet instruments or their resonators may be scraped in

---

[35] Cf. Lachenmann, Accanto, p. 37.

[36] Sevsay, Handbuch, p. 193.

order to produce different sounds. They range from simple to very complex motions that may, in the case of the membranophones, involve the head and/or rim. Moreover, bowing motions are especially effective on certain idiophones, such as cymbals, tam-tams or the bars of mallet instruments. They are normally executed by means of a common bow, but, for instance, drumsticks or threaded wooden/metal rods can also be utilised.

3. 2. 4. 1 Previous methods of notation

Some composers do not specify which spot on the instrument is supposed to be rubbed, but merely request the player to perform a rubbing motion. For instance, *Nono*, in »Composizione per orchestra nr. 2«[37], makes use of two directions, rubbed [*strisciando*] and rubbed circularly [*strisciando circolarmente*][38]. Moreover, *Lachenmann*, in »Mouvement (– vor der Erstarrung)«, depicts the action of scraping the bars of a xylorimba by means of a special note head and a *tremolo* symbol:

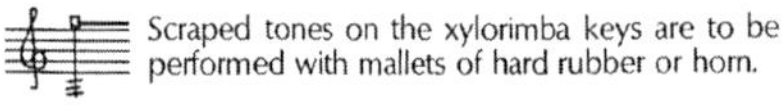

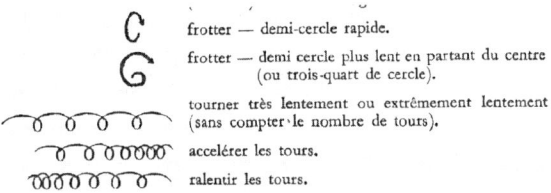

Fig. 25 Lachenmann, Mouvement, no page named [foreword].

However, *Eloy*, in »Equivalences«[39], utilises five different symbols in order to depict a rubbing – rapid semicircle [frotter – demi-cercle rapide], a rubbing – semicircle, slower after the half (or three-fourths of the circle) [frotter – demi-cercle plus lent en partant du centre (ou trois-quart de cercle)], a rotation in a very slow or extremely slow manner [tourner très lentement ou extrêmement lentement], an accelerated rotation [accélérer les tours] and a decelerated rotation [ralentir les tours]:

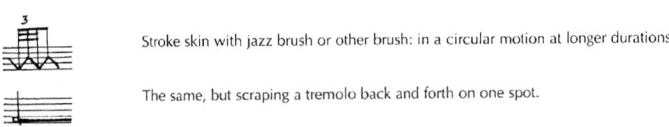

Fig. 26 Eloy, Equivalences, no page named [foreword].

Further, in »Staub« *Lachenmann* differentiates between two rubbing motions, performed on the surface of percussion instruments. As can be seen in Figure 27, he utilises a zigzag line as a note head in order to request a circular motion and a special note head to depict a back and forth scraping.

Stroke skin with jazz brush or other brush: in a circular motion at longer durations.

The same, but scraping a tremolo back and forth on one spot.

Fig. 27 Lachenmann, Staub, no page named [foreword].

In »NUN« *Lachenmann* also employs very complex scraping motions, executed with two drumsticks. The lower stick is always placed on the head and optionally makes circles on the skin whilst the upper stick scrapes the lower stick either in circles or from the shaft to the

---

[37] Luigi Nono: Composizione per orchestra nr. 2. Diario polacco '58. Mainz 1959.

[38] Cf. ibid., p. 3.

[39] Jean-Claude Eloy: Equivalences. For 18 instrumentalists. Paris 1965.

head. As can be seen in Figure 28, *Lachenmann* depicts these actions by, firstly, presenting a drawing of the instrument and the two sticks and, secondly, special note heads. Moreover, a fast *tremolo* action is notated by a waved line and the shifting from the shaft [Schaft] to the tip [Spitze] by means of a common notation system with no clef, which represents the length of the beater.

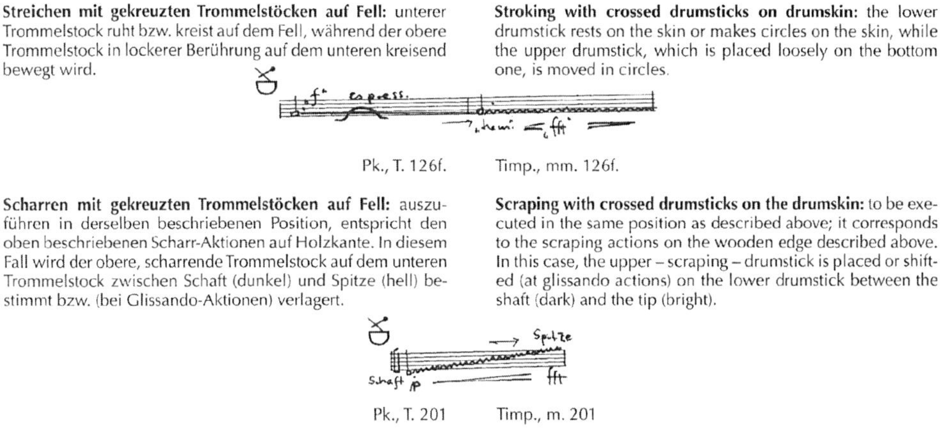

Streichen mit gekreuzten Trommelstöcken auf Fell: unterer Trommelstock ruht bzw. kreist auf dem Fell, während der obere Trommelstock in lockerer Berührung auf dem unteren kreisend bewegt wird.

Stroking with crossed drumsticks on drumskin: the lower drumstick rests on the skin or makes circles on the skin, while the upper drumstick, which is placed loosely on the bottom one, is moved in circles.

Pk., T. 126f.   Timp., mm. 126f.

Scharren mit gekreuzten Trommelstöcken auf Fell: auszuführen in derselben beschriebenen Position, entspricht den oben beschriebenen Scharr-Aktionen auf Holzkante. In diesem Fall wird der obere, scharrende Trommelstock auf dem unteren Trommelstock zwischen Schaft (dunkel) und Spitze (hell) bestimmt bzw. (bei Glissando-Aktionen) verlagert.

Scraping with crossed drumsticks on the drumskin: to be executed in the same position as described above; it corresponds to the scraping actions on the wooden edge described above. In this case, the upper – scraping – drumstick is placed or shifted (at glissando actions) on the lower drumstick between the shaft (dark) and the tip (bright).

Pk., T. 201   Timp., m. 201

Fig. 28 Lachenmann, NUN, p. IX.

Further, *Stockhausen*, in »Mikrophonie I«[40], utilises a special notation system in order to depict scraping motions on the surface of a tam-tam. The x-axis of this system represents, as usual, the time and the y-axis the length of the instrument. This enables the depiction of up- and downward motions. The thicker the line, the higher the dynamic level. As can be seen in Figure 29, transitions from low/high to high/low dynamic levels (*crescendi* and *decrescendi*) are also requested.

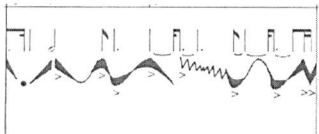

Fig. 29 Stockhausen, Mikrophonie I, Moment "TUTTI forte".

A complex motion on the head and rim is utilised by *Lachenmann* in »Accanto«. As can be seen in Figure 30, he makes the percussionist stroke the rim and head (of a tom-tom) with a rough drumstick while he is supposed to simultaneously shift the point of contact from the tip to the shaft [mit rauhem Trommelstock gleichzeitig über Fell und Rand streichen, dabei Berührstelle von der Spitze zum Schaft verlagern]. This direction is complemented by a note head, which depicts the motion from the tip to the shaft (also cf. Figure 28).

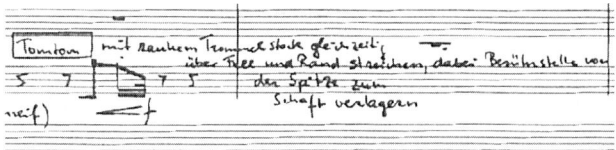

Fig. 30 Lachenmann, Accanto, p. 13.

---

[40] Karlheinz Stockhausen: Mikrophonie I. For tamtam, 2 microphones, 2 filters and controller. London 1964.

Moreover, *Szalonek*, in »Concertino«, requests rubbing motions on the rim by means of a special symbol, which is connected to the note head. As is apparent from Figure 31, he does not specify what kind of motion the player is supposed to perform.

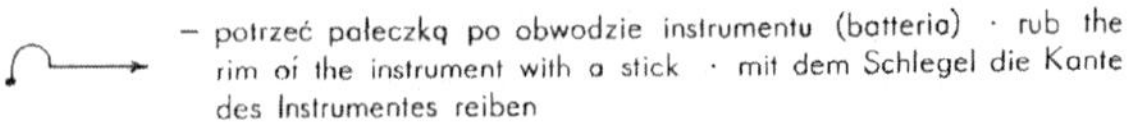

Fig. 31 Szalonek, Concertino, p. 4.

Further, *Halffter*, in »Fibonaciana«, requests bowing motions by means of a symbol that replaces the note and the direction *con arco*. In the example presented in Figure 32, the player is supposed to bow a suspended cymbal.

Fig. 32 Halffter, Fibonaciana, p. 24.

Moreover, *Lachenmann*, in »Air«[41], requests the same action by means of a special note head and the direction *arco*:

Fig. 33 Lachenmann, Air, p. 47.

3. 2. 4. 2 Discussion

In the case of requesting an unspecified rubbing motion, it is sufficient – as *Nono* does – solely to give the direction rubbed or *strisciando*. Since the scraping motions executable on mallet instruments are very limited, they can be notated in this way. This method of notation is preferred here over the one introduced by *Lachenmann* (cf. Figure 25) because it is simpler to request the rubbing motion by means of a distinct direction than by a special note head. However, another method of notation needs to be introduced when more complex motions are supposed to be performed. This is because such motions could not be depicted in a simple manner by means of directions. As the determination of the point of impact is closely related to the depiction of scraping motions, the method of notation introduced in Chapter »3. 2. 3 The point of impact« may be transferred to the notation of complex rubbing motions. Howe-ver, in such a case, the dot would have to be replaced by a distinct drawing, which displays the direction and extent of the motion. When compared to *Eloy's* symbolic method of depic-tion (cf. Figure 26) or *Lachenmann's* method of notating each motion by means of a special note head (cf. Figure 27), it may be stated that it is clearer and simpler to draw the motion on the surface of the instrument than to introduce a symbol or note head for any distinct motion. Further, the graphic depiction is capable of notating various complex motions in a simple manner whilst the two latter ones become more complex if further extended. As shown in the following chapter, it is also simpler to notate the complex motions with two drumsticks requested by *Lachenmann* (cf. Figure 28) by means of a drawing than by special note heads and an extended notation system. This is because a drawing contains a greater degree of instantaneous comprehension. Further, such a graphic depiction enables the notation of more complex motions than *Stockhausen's* method (cf. Figure 29) because not only up- and down-ward motions may be depicted, but also – due to the additional axis – for instance, motions

---

[41] Helmut Lachenmann: Air. Music for large orchestra and percussion-solo. Revised edition. Wiesbaden et al. 1994.

from the right to the left. Moreover, *Lachenmann's* method of requesting a shifting of the point of contact whilst rubbing on the head and rim (cf. Figure 30) only contains a low degree of instantaneous comprehension. As in the case of the other approaches, it would be simpler and clearer to depict the motion by means of drawing. Finally, *Szalonek's* approach towards the notation of rubbing the rim (cf. Figure 31) can only be employed when an unspecified rubbing motion on the rim was supposed to be performed. Any further determination concerning the direction or extent of the motion could not be depicted by a symbol of this kind. Additionally, an unspecified rubbing motion could be requested in a clearer manner by giving a direction, such as *strisciando* (rim). Furthermore, all bowing motions on percussion instruments resemble the action of bowing the body or other parts of string instruments (cf. Chapter »1. 5 Playing exceptional spots«). Therefore, the method of notation introduced in the chapter on string instruments may be transferred when concerned with the depiction of rubbing motions on the rim or bowing motions on idiophones. This method of notation also resembles the one introduced for the determination of the point of contact and is preferred over *Halffter's* approach (cf. Figure 32) because it enables the depiction of any duration and is more exact with regard to the determination of the point of contact between the bow and instrument. Further, it is also clearer and simpler than *Lachenmann's* method of utilising a special note head and the direction *arco* (cf. Figure 33). However, an unspecified bowing motion could be depicted by means of this direction and a common note head.

3. 2. 4. 3 Suggestion for the notation of rubbing and bowing motions

Because the variation of the scraping motion on mallet instruments is limited, the method of depiction suggested here is to request it by means of the direction rubbed or *strisciando* and an optional *tremolo* symbol, which complements the pitch-based notation system (see below for an alternative method). This method could also be employed when an unspecified rubbing motion was supposed to be depicted on other percussion instruments. Moreover, the direction *strisciando* (rim) can be used to request an unspecified rubbing motion on the rim and the direction *arco* to request an unspecified bowing motion.

However, more complex motions are displayed here in a graphic way. As can be seen in Figure 34, singular motions are notated by means of a line complemented by an arrow, which is drawn onto the surface of a drum. In the example, the percussionist is initially supposed to execute a semicircle rubbing motion for the duration of a dotted crotchet. This action is followed by a semicircle motion in the opposite direction. However, the speed of this motion is not constant. This is because two distinct notes are employed. The first one depicts the duration of the first half of the motion (a quaver) whilst the second one depicts the duration of the second half of the motion (a crotchet). As these motions are supposed to be connected, a *legato* slur is used.

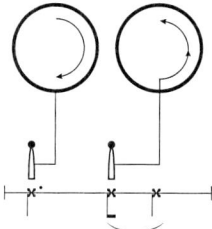

Fig. 34 Singular rubbing motions.

Moreover, an acceleration or deceleration of singular motions can also be requested by utilising additional agogic designations, such as *accelerando* or *ritardando*. However, it needs to be clearly outlined that these directions are not related to the overall tempo of the piece, but only the motion on the skin. Additionally, the motions could also be complemented by the direction *irregolare* in order to make the player execute these in an irregular manner. With regard to the dynamic level of rubbing motions, it needs to be noted that the tempo and dynamic level are partially related. This is because very low dynamic level may barely be achieved in combination with a very fast performance speed.

Further, repetitive motions are notated here by means of a line and a two-headed arrow. These kinds of motions are always complemented by a speed level designated as tempo, which is divided into six degrees. This index is necessary for the control of the performance speed because repetitive actions do – as opposed to singular actions – not have a fixed endpoint. Alternatively, more or less speed levels may be used. As is apparent from Figure 35, the percussionist is supposed to perform three repetitive actions whilst each one lasts for the duration of a semibreve. The first complex motion is executed with the minimum speed level 1/6, whereas during the second motion, the speed level is increased from 2/6 to 5/6. The last articulation is similar to the action designated by *Lachenmann* as a *tremolo* back and forth (cf. Figure 27). Hence it is supposed to be performed virtually on a single spot. The speed level is now at its maximum.

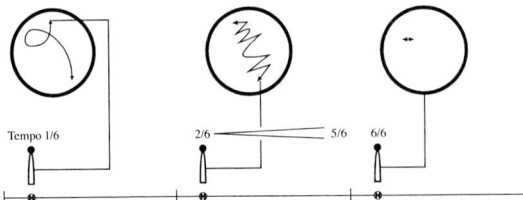

Fig. 35 Repetitive rubbing motions.

The starting point of the repetitive motion is determined by the line connecting the beater and the graphic depiction of the motion. When any other point than the ones where the direction of the motion is reversed is supposed to be determined as the starting point, an additional arrow – which determines the running direction of the initial motion – should be employed. This arrow needs to have a different shape in order to distinguish it from the other arrows. Further, the tempo index could be used as a complementation of the simple scraping motions on mallet instruments. Moreover, the arrow utilised to depict the *tremolo* motion – or an extended variant – could alternatively be employed for the notation of such a motion on mallet instruments when combined with a depiction of the instrument or single bars.

Further, the execution of singular or repetitive rubbing motions on the resonators of mallet instruments can be depicted by presenting a drawing of the instruments, including its resonators, in combination with a pitch-based notation system (because the pitch is slightly perceptible)[42]. This method of notation is presented in Figure 36 by taking the example of a vibraphone. The player is supposed here to initially perform a repetitive rubbing motion with tempo 4/6 on the resonator tube »f/F3« for the duration of a minim. After a crotchet rest, a singular *glissando*-motion from »a/A3« to »a²/A5« is executed on the resonators. The sound production actually ends when the »a²/A5« is reached and hence the demisemiquaver is applied pro forma. Moreover, strokes could be depicted by employing a dot instead of an arrow (cf. the previous chapter).

---

[42] Cf. Sevsay, Handbuch, p. 168.

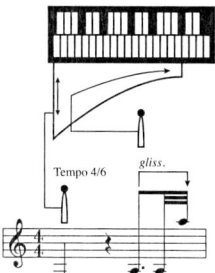

Fig. 36 Rubbing motions on the resonators of a vibraphone.

As mentioned, int this work the *glissando* – in order to achieve a greater clarity and to enable the depiction of sliding motions that do not imply a gliding change of pitch – is requested by means of an arrow and not in the traditional manner. Alternatively, the common method of depiction may be restored.

Furthermore, there are repetitive rubbing motions that do not involve a reversal of the running direction. They are referred to here as »circular« motions. These kinds of articulations are also requested by means of two arrows. However, such motions may also be singular. In such cases, only a single arrow is employed. Four examples are presented in Figure 37. The first three »circular« motions are repetitive. In the case of the last example, only one arrow is utilised. Hence a singular motion – which has the same starting point and endpoint – is requested. An additional arrow with another shape is, in this case, employed in order to clearly depict the running direction of the motion.

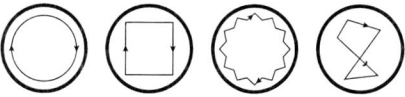

Fig. 37 »Circular« rubbing motions.

Moreover, *Lachenmann's* complex motions with two drumsticks (cf. Figure 28) are presented in Figure 38. In the example, the player is supposed to perform three different articulations whilst each one lasts for the duration of a semibreve: 1. The tip of one drumstick is lying on the surface of the instrument and moved repetitively in circles. Simultaneously, the player uses another beater to execute a repetitive circular motion on the first stick. As is apparent from the figure, the point of contact is the middle of the handle length. However, due to the character of the motion, it constantly varies and is, therefore, actually only depicted approximately. The described motion is supposed to be performed with tempo 1/6. This tempo is also supposed to be applied to the motion of the first drumstick. In order to retain a clear appearance of the score, the determination of a second speed index for this beater is dismissed. Thus both actions are always performed here with the same tempo. 2. The percussionist is supposed to perform a repetitive scraping motion on a drumstick lying on the skin of the drum (the shaft is black and the arrow white in order to enable a clearer depiction). During this action, the tempo is increased from 2/6 to 5/6. 3. The player is required to repetitively move a drumstick lying on the surface of the percussion instrument from the left to the right (while the initial running direction is not determined). Simultaneously, another beater is again used to execute a repetitive circular motion on the first stick. The speed level is now at its maximum.

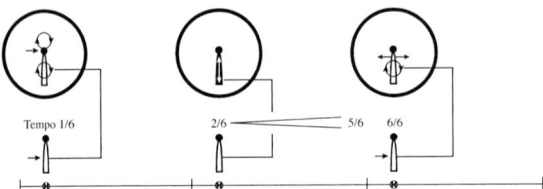

Fig. 38 Complex motions with two beaters.

Further, rubbing motions that involve the rim can be depicted in a similar manner as motions on the head. In the example presented in Figure 39, three motions are executed. Each one again lasts for the duration of a semibreve. The first motion is performed with the entire length of the stick and (as a rim shot) simultaneously on the head and rim. Because the tip of the stick is during the motion moved away from the rim, the point of contact (between the stick and rim) is shifted from the head to the shaft (cf. Figure 30). A dashed line is utilised here since there are only two points of contact (cf. Figure 24). The second motion is a singular motion on the rim, executed with the middle of the handle. Subsequently, the percussionist is supposed to perform a repetitive circular motion on the rim. The speed level is 6/6. As is apparent from the example, scraping motions on the rim are also notated by means of a line and a single-/two-headed arrow while the line and arrow is white.

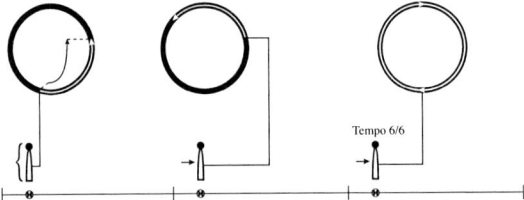

Fig. 39 Rubbing motions that involve the rim.

Further, the specified bowing of percussion instruments is requested by means of a symbol for the bow and an arrow, which determines the spot that is bowed. In the example, the percussionist is supposed to bow the edge of a cymbal for the duration of a semibreve and then let it vibrate (*lasciar vibrare*). After a semibreve rest, the player is required to bow the cymbal with a drumstick. As the stick is shorter, two note heads are utilised (whilst the player decides whether to perform an up- and down-bow or down- and up-bow motion).

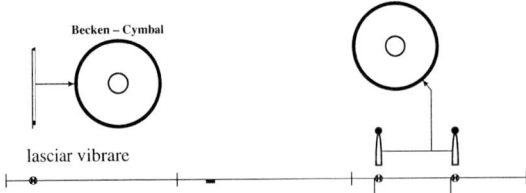

Fig. 40 Bowing percussion instruments.

Moreover, when percussion instruments are bowed, additional up- and down-bow symbols may be employed, the type of bow be determined (e. g. contrabass bow), a so-called *glissando d'arco* be performed (cf. Chapter »1. 2. 2 The bow-*glissando*« and Figure 64 in the chapter on string instruments) as well as conventional and unconventional bowing techniques be requested. Further, when the bars of a mallet instrument, such as a vibraphone, are supposed to be bowed, it is sufficient to solely give the direction *arco* or *con/col arco* and depict the produced pitch. This is because the point of contact between the bow and a single bar cannot be significantly varied (also cf. Chapter »4. 4. 2 The utilisation of a bow and its notation«).

3. 2. 5 Articulations without agents of attack

On many percussion instruments sound may be produced without actually attacking these by means of beaters: cymbals may be swung in the air after the attack or smaller instruments be rubbed against each other. When previously prepared, it is – as shown below – also possible to produce sound, for example, on bongos by spinning or pushing these. Moreover, the percussionist is sometimes asked to drop items, such as rice or marbles, into or on percussion instruments.

3. 2. 5. 1 Previous methods of notation

Lachenmann, in »NUN«, requests to strike and subsequently swing a Chinese cymbal by means of squared note heads, a line derived from the notation of *glissandi*, accents in brackets and the additional direction swing rhythmically [rhythmisch schwenken]:

Chinesisches Becken, durch die Luft geschwenkt: Becken wird an der wulstigen Kuppe gepackt, in die Höhe gehalten und nach dem Schlag mit äußerst eckigen Bewegungen um das Handgelenk gedreht („geschwenkt"), sodaß eine Art ruckartig rythmisierter „Hall-Schwankung" erzeugt wird.

Chinese cymbal swung in the air: the cymbals are grabbed by the bulge at the center, held in the air and, after they've been struck, are turned around the wrist ("swung") with extremely angular motions so as to produce a kind of jerkily rhythmic "echo variation."

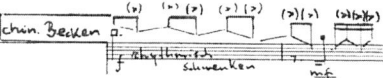

Fig. 41 Lachenmann, NUN, p. X.

Further, *Kagel*, in »L'art bruit«, requests the player to rub two sand blocks against each other by means of adding an arrow to the note tail and giving the direction rub slowly:

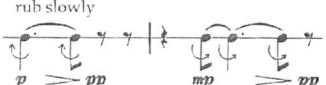

Fig. 42 Kagel, Bruit, p. 10a.

Moreover, in »Match« he requests the percussionist to hold two clash cymbals perpendicular to each other and turn these in opposite directions [beide Handbecken senkrecht aneinander halten und in entgegesetzter Richtung drehen]. As can be seen in Figure 43, *Kagel* presents a drawing of the action, as well as an explanation, and notates it by means of two note heads, arrows added to their note tails and circles above and below the notes.

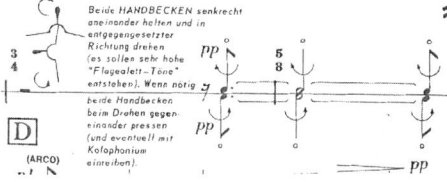

Fig. 43 Kagel, Match, p. 8.

In »Kontakte« *Stockhausen* makes use of a prepared instrument. A concert bongo is in this piece turned upside down and filled "with a few beans that roll around on the membrane when the bongo is shaken (as in a rattle)"[43]. The player is then either supposed to spin the bongo or to push it. The spinning action is – as is apparent from Figure 44 – depicted by a waved line whilst the push is requested by means of a note head without note tail and an accent. Additionally, *Stockhausen* gives the additional direction spin slowly, push [langsam drehen, anstoßen] and utilises the agogic designation *accelerando*.

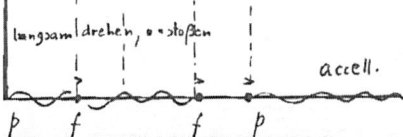

Fig. 44 Stockhausen, Kontakte, p. 5.

Finally, *Kagel* in »L'art bruit« makes a percussionist empty rice – which was previously filled into a dobachi[44] – into another dobachi. This action is, as is apparent from Figure 45, requested by means of a graphic depiction of the rice, which complements the common note, and an explanation.

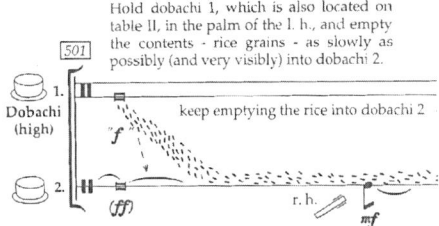

Fig. 45 Kagel, Bruit, p. 30a.

3. 2. 5. 2 Discussion

Because the articulations that are executed without agents of attack are uncommon and only rarely used, it is especially vital to depict these in the simplest and most comprehensible way. As shown in Chapter »1. 8 Preparing the instrument and its notation«, the simplest method of notation makes use of a sketch that sufficiently explains the articulation or – according to the actions described in this chapter – preparation. Moreover, when the sketch is not clear enough, it may be complemented by an explanation. Therefore, *Lachenmann's* method of notating the swinging of cymbals by means of a line derived from the *glissando* notation (cf. Figure 41) or circular stroking (cf. Figure 27) lacks simplicity. It would be more comprehensible to present a sketch of the action than to use a method of notation, which normally requests sliding/stroking motions. However, the direction he gives could be used as an additional explanation of the articulation. The same may be said about *Kagel's* approach towards the notation of rubbing two sand blocks against each other (cf. Figure 42) since it would also be simpler to request the articulation by means of a graphic depiction. Moreover, it might, as mentioned, be confusing to add a symbol to the note tail when semibreves are supposed to be depicted. In opposition, *Kagel's* notation of the spinning motion performed with two cymbals (cf. Figure 43) is comprehensible and simple. However, in order to depict repetitive circular motions in a uniform manner, the arrow used to describe the character of the spinning motion (which is repetitive and circular) would have to be replaced by the method of notation presented in Figure 37. Additionally, a speed level would have to be introduced as well as the note

---

[43] Stockhausen, Kontakte, p. V.

[44] Japanese temple gong.

heads, arrows and circles be replaced with x-shaped notes. Further, *Stockhausen's* method of notating the spinning motion or pushes (cf. Figure 44) also lacks simplicity because the action is not depicted in a comprehensible manner. However, the directions he gives could be used as an additional explanation of a sketch, which depicts the action. By contrast, *Kagel's* approach towards the notation of emptying rice in an instrument (cf. Figure 45) is simple and comprehensible. However, instead of complementing the notes with a graphic depiction of the rice, a sketch of the action should be used in order to gain an even greater degree of simplicity and instantaneous comprehension.

3. 2. 5. 3 Suggestion for the notation of articulations without agents of attack

All suggested methods of notation depict the action the percussionist is supposed to perform in a graphic way. In Figure 46, two notation systems are utilised. The lower one (left hand) requests two hits on a Chinese cymbal and the system on top (right hand) depicts the swinging motion. After both hits, it is required to let the cymbal further vibrate (*lasciar vibrare*). The first attack and the swinging action start simultaneously, whereas the second swinging action starts right after the strike. Moreover, in the case of the first swinging motion, the player is supposed to move his wrist in a quaver rhythm and in the case of the second motion, in a semiquaver rhythm (cf. Figure 41). Since the action is repetitive, a single note and a speed level could, alternatively, be used in order to notate the swinging (cf. Figure 35).

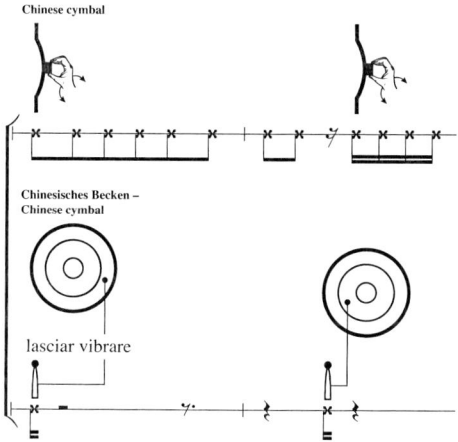

Fig. 46 Striking and swinging a Chinese cymbal.

Further, in Figure 47, three special rubbing motions are depicted by taking the example of two Chinese cymbals. In the case of the first action, the percussionist is virtually supposed to use Chinese cymbal I as a beater and perform a repetitive circular motion on Chinese cymbal II. This action is for the duration of a minim executed with tempo 3/6. Subsequently, the percussionist is required to repetitively rub both cymbals against each other (or in other words to execute a repetitive circular motion with cymbal I on cymbal II whilst performing a repetitive circular motion with cymbal II on cymbal I). This action lasts for the duration of a dotted crotchet and is performed with speed level 5/6. Finally, the player is supposed to execute a singular rubbing motion with cymbal I on cymbal II and subsequently let them vibrate.

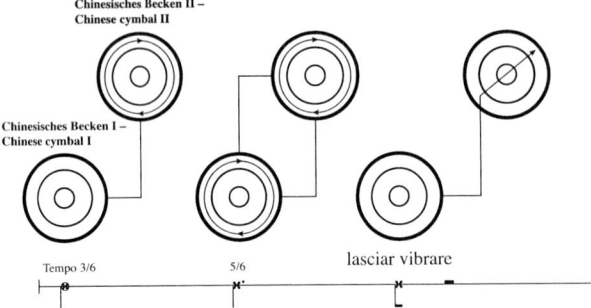

Fig. 47 Special rubbing motions.

Further, in Figure 48, the action requested by *Kagel* in »Match« is notated here in a similar manner as in Figure 43. However, in this case, the arrows uniformly request the performance of a repetitive circular motion in opposite directions. Both motions are performed with the speed level 2/6 and last for the duration of a semibreve. Only one notation system and a single note are employed here for the right and left hand because their actions are (similarly to rubbing two cymbals against each other) connected. If one hand was supposed to stop spinning, a new sketch would have to be presented in order to show which of the two cymbals is spinning and which one is stopped.

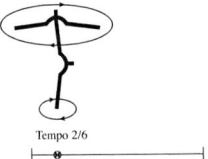

Fig. 48 Special circular motions.

The spinning motion of a concert bongo filled with beans (for the modification of percussion instruments cf. Chapter »3. 5 Preparing the instrument and its notation«) may be depicted similarly. As can be seen in Figure 49, the percussionist is initially supposed to repetitively turn the bongo clockwise with tempo 3/6 for the duration of a minim, then execute a single push away from his body and go on with the spinning. However, this time the bongo is spun counter-clockwise with tempo 5/6 for the duration of a dotted crotchet. Subsequently, the player is required to repetitively push the bongo back and forth with speed level 4/6 for the duration of a quaver and finally perform repetitive pushes up and down with the same tempo for the duration of a dotted crotchet. In the case of the last pushes, the beans jump up and down on the skin and the percussionist might have to be advised to close the opening hole with the hand, with cardboard etc.

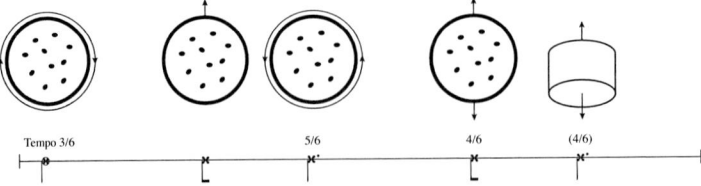

Fig. 49 Spinning and shaking a concert bongo.

128

Finally, the emptying of rice into an instrument or, for instance, letting a marble drop on the head of a timpano can be depicted by means of presenting a sketch of the action the player is supposed to perform. Such graphic depictions are presented in Figure 50. Additionally, the distance between the dropped item(s) and the percussion instrument may be determined (e. g. very high – high – medium height – low – very low or 3 m – 2 m – 1 m – 50 cm – 25 cm) and transitions between two heights be notated in the case of continuous actions (cf. Figure 39 in »Part II: Electroacoustic music – 3. 3. 2 Non-instrumental sound sources« for the notation of such transitions).

Fig. 50 Dropping items into/on instruments.

3. 2. 6 Playing the snares

When turned upside down, the snares of a drum may be played *alla chitarra* (guitar-style): they can be plucked (*pizzicato* – the snares only vibrate when playing with snares off), plucked vertically in order to make them rebound on the head (*Bartók pizzicato* – it can be executed when playing with snares on/off) and the snares be strummed (as in the case of the *pizzicato*, the snares only vibrate when playing with snares off). Further, the percussionist may also use his hand, as well as any kind of beater or item, to slide over the snares/over the head and snares simultaneously.

3. 2. 6. 1 Previous methods of notation

In »..., den 24. xii. 1931« *Kagel* requests the percussionist to pluck the snares by means of a symbol resembling the one utilised for the depiction of the *Bartók pizzicato* and the direction pluck. Additionally, a zigzag line is employed to depict the subsequent vibration (the snare drum is played with snares off)[45]:

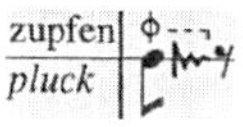

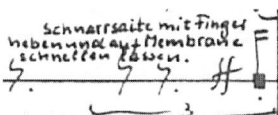

Fig. 51 Kagel, 1931, p. 91.

A *Bartók pizzicato* is also requested by *Holliger* in »Pneuma«. He depicts it by means of a squared note head and giving the direction lift the snare with the finger and make it rebound on the membrane [Schnarrsaite mit Finger heben und auf Membrane schnellen lassen]:

Fig. 52 Holliger, Pneuma, p. 37.

Further, in »L'art bruit« *Kagel* requests to strum the snares by means of the common *arpeggio* symbol and five »transposed« notes. As is apparent from Figure 53, the snares are supposed to vibrate. Hence the articulation is executed with snares off.

---

[45] Cf. Kagel, 1931, p. 90.

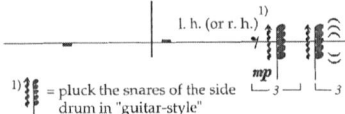

¹⁾ ♪ = pluck the snares of the side
drum in "guitar-style"

Fig. 53 Kagel, Bruit, p. 6a.

In the same piece he makes the percussionist also slide along the strings with his finger-nails. As can be seen in Figure 54, this action is depicted by means of five diamond-shaped and common note heads used in combination. In this case, a two lined notation system with drum clef is used. The upper line depicts the actions of the right hand whilst the lower line depicts the left hand's actions[46].

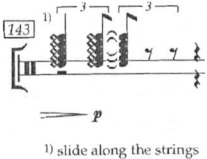

¹⁾ slide along the strings
with fingernails

Fig. 54 Kagel, Bruit, p. 7a.

3. 2. 6. 2 Discussion

As most of the actions that may be performed on the snares are strongly related to conventional articulations of string or plucked instruments, they can be notated in the same way as the original articulations. By doing so, these sonic events are depicted in close relation to traditional notation as well as in a comprehensible and simple manner. However, this means that *Kagel's* method of notation for the *pizzicato* (cf. Figure 51) as well as *Holliger's* approach towards the notation of the *Bartók pizzicato* (cf. Figure 52) cannot be employed. *Kagel* depicts the normal plucking of the string in the way the *Bartók pizzicato* should be notated, although the direction *pizzicato* would adequately request it. Further, he makes use of a zigzag line to depict the subsequent vibration, which is traditionally depicted by the direction *lasciar vibrare* or simply by means of the duration. Moreover, *Holliger* makes use of a long direction in order to depict an event, which could in compliance with the requirements be simply depicted by means of the *Bartók pizzicato* symbol. Furthermore, *Kagel* depicts the strumming of the snares by means of an *arpeggio* symbol (cf. Figure 53). However, the action of strumming strings is – as shown in Chapter »4. 4. 5 Strumming and its notation« – different from performing an *arpeggio*. Therefore, another method of notation needs to be employed in order to prevent the player from confusing the two articulations. Since the articulation is primarily a guitar technique, it is discussed below. As can be seen there, the action of strumming is depicted by means of an arrow pointing up- (upbeat) or downwards (downbeat). Moreover, x-shaped note heads should rather be utilised than common and diamond-shaped ones because plucking the snares produces sounds with indefinite pitch. Further, with regard to the determination of how many strings are plucked, it needs to be noted that the number of snares may vary from instrument to instrument. Therefore, this parameter can only be depicted approximately. When compared, the introduction of a notation system with several lines that represents the strings of the snare drum is preferred here over *Kagel's* method. This is because such a notation system would depict the (single) snares in a clearer way. However, since the sound-wise difference between plucking one snare or another is small, and it is barely possible to pluck only one snare at a time, it is sufficient to utilise the notation system in order to depict a

---

[46] Cf. Kagel, Bruit, p. 5a.

reduced number (as in *Kagel's* »L'art bruit«) instead of ten to fifteen snares (which is, in most cases, the actual number of strings of a common snare drum). Concerning the notation of sliding motions on the string, the traditional manner of notating these cannot be employed. This is because they are on string instruments notated by means of a pitch-based notation system and the common *glissando* notation, but on a snare drum the pitch-based system cannot be utilised in order to depict the position on the string. However, this action resembles the articulation designated as the bow-*glissando dietro il tasto* (cf. Figures 17 and 18 in the chapter on string instruments) as well as the performance of a rubbing motion on the skin. When requesting solely motions on the snares, it is sufficient to use a similar system as the one employed for the bow-*glissando* behind the fingerboard because only motions up and down would have to be depicted. However, when more complex motions are required, the method of notation introduced for the rubbing motions would have to be utilised. In comparison to *Kagel's* approach towards the notation of a *glissando* on the snares (cf. Figure 54), these two methods are more exact since they permit the notation of various different motions, whereas *Kagel's* method is only able to depict a single kind of motion.

3. 2. 6. 3 Suggestion for the notation of playing the snares

As is apparent from Figure 55, a common notation system with no clef is employed here to depict any of the conventional articulations executed on the snares. The system depicts the extent of the strings while any of the line represents, as far as possible, a single snare in the case of the *pizzicato*, or shows if 1/5, 2/5, 3/5, 4/5 or all strings are strummed. It may be moreover defined if the lowest line/highest line represents the left/right outer string (from the player's perspective). In the example, the percussionist is supposed to always let the strings vibrate (*sempre lasciar vibrare*). Initially, he is required to play a sequence of six semiquaver *pizzicati*, starting and ending with the same outer string. These actions are performed *senza corde* (with snares off). After a crotchet rest, two *Bartók pizzicati* are executed *con corde* (with snares on). The first *pizzicato* is executed on the middle snares and the second one on the outermost snares. After another crotchet rest, the strings are strummed. The first strumming (upbeat) involves all strings, whereas the second one (downbeat) is only executed on 3/5 of the strings. Further, the two actions designated as *senza* and *con corde* could be notated as distinct sonic events by utilising (five) notes in combination with the respective direction. Generally, the dynamic level is always low when playing on the snares.

Fig. 55 Playing on the snares.

When requesting rubbing or sliding motions that involve the snares, the notation system changes. As is apparent from Figure 56, two different methods can be used to depict these motions. The first variant consists of two components, a traditional timeline and a representation of the length of the snares whilst the arrows depict what kind of motion the player is supposed to perform. They are related to the duration, determined by the notes. In the example, a brush is used[47], and the snares are on. An arrow pointing upwards requests that the beater is moved away from the body and an arrow pointing downwards that the motion is executed in the direction of the player's body. The first two singular crotchet motions are executed *sulle*

---

[47] Cf. Sevsay, Handbuch, p. 215.

corde (on the strings) while the third repetitive crotchet motion and the final singular semiquaver motion are executed *sulle corde e sulla pelle* (on the strings and the head). The *legato* slur is used to depict that the first three motions are connected. Further, when a more complex motion on the head and the snares is supposed to be performed, another method of notation needs to be employed. In the second example, the player executes a singular motion with a brush for the duration of a semibreve. During this motion, the strings are crossed two times.

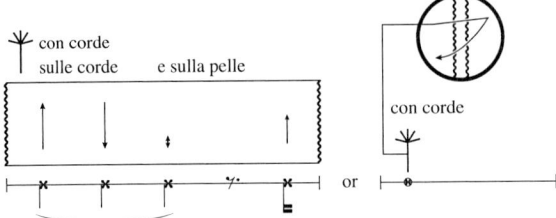

Fig. 56 Motions on the snares and head.

3.3 »Pitch« bending – the extended *glissando*

As mentioned in the chapter on wind instruments, the term pitch bending or bend tone describes a special *glissando* technique. On membranophones the »pitch« may be raised by controlled hand or elbow pressure on the drum head[48] whilst on gongs and tam-tams the same effect is created by lowering these instruments after or during the attack into a tub of water – which lowers their »pitch« – or removing them from the water tub – which raises their »pitch«[49/50]. Further, on the vibraphone the pitch may be bent by placing a mallet on the nodal point of a bar after the attack and sliding towards the middle. This produces a decrease in pitch.

3.3.1 Previous methods of notation

Stone suggests notating the »pitch« bending technique on membranophones by means of note heads placed in between two lines, indicating whether the attack produces a low or high sound:

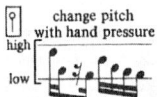

Fig. 57 Stone, Notation, p. 223.

Moreover, *Cage* – the discoverer of the water gong effect – in »First construction (in metal)«[51] depicts the pitch bending articulation by means of an arrow pointing downwards or upwards and the direction lower (gong into water) or raise. As is apparent from Figure 58, the percussionist is supposed to play rolls whilst lowering or raising the instrument.

---

[48] Cf. Stone, Notation, p. 223.
[49] Cf. Sevsay, Handbuch, p. 162.
[50] As mentioned, most membranophones and all tam-tams have an indefinite pitch.
[51] John Cage: First construction (in metal). Percussion sextet with assistant. New York 1962.

Fig. 58 Cage, First construction, p. 5.

Further, in »Mundus canis ("A dog's world")«[52] *Crumb* requests the percussionist to lower a tam-tam into a water tub by means of »transposed« notes and the common *glissando* notation. Three different »pitches« are employed. The highest note requests the player to hold the tam-tam above water, the middle note (on the line) depicts that the tam-tam is half-submerged and the lowest note that the tam-tam is fully submerged[53]. Simultaneous to the »pitch« bending, the percussionist is supposed to play a roll, which is (wrongly) depicted by means of the trill symbol[54]:

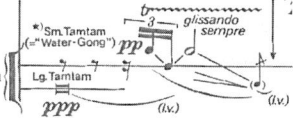

Fig. 59 Crumb, Mundus, p. 8.

3. 3. 2 Discussion

In Chapter »2. 4 Pitch bending – the extended *glissando*« a method of notation for the pitch bending technique that complies with the postulated criteria has been presented. This method may be transferred to percussion instruments in order to depict the »pitch« bending on percussion instruments with definite and even indefinite pitch. When doing so, the technique is depicted in a uniform way. The method of notation resembles *Stone's* approach towards the notation of the »pitch« bending on membranophones (cf. Figure 57). However, the pitch bending system for wind instruments complements the normal notation system, whereas *Stone's* system replaces it. Since it is necessary to have two systems in the case of wind instruments (one that depicts the fingered tone and one that presents the transposition in time), the method of notation for the »pitch« bending on membranophones should also consist of two systems (one that depicts the attack and one that depicts the »transposition« in time). The introduction of a distinct timeline for the »transposition« would, in the case of percussion instruments, also enable notating the sound production and its transformation independently from each other. With regard to *Cage's* method of notation (cf. Figure 58), it may additionally be said that it is inexact because only one bending level – no pitch bending (instrument above the water) plus the maximum pitch bending (fully submerged) – as well as the transition from one to the other level (lower and raise) may be depicted. Further, his approach is confusing because he requests the lowering by means of an arrow pointing upwards (despite the pitch is lowered) and vice versa. Further, *Crumb's* method (cf. Figure 59) may be described as a variation of *Stone's* approach. It permits the notation of two bending levels – no pitch bending (instrument above water) plus the medium pitch bending (half-submerged) and the maximum pitch bending (fully submerged). Unless the method could be extended further in order to depict more than two levels, it is – as mentioned – preferred here to notate the articulation by means of a distinct system.

---

[52] George Crumb: Mundus canis ("A dog's world"). Guitar and percussion. New York et al. 2000.

[53] Cf. Crumb, Mundus, p. 8.

[54] Cf. Sevsay, Handbuch, p. 207.

3. 3. 3 Suggestion for the notation of »pitch« bending

Hence the suggested method of notation makes use of an additional notation system, referred to as the »transposition« system. The x-axis of the »transposition« system represents, as usual, the duration and the y-axis the degree of the »transposition«. Moreover, the white dots (◇) depict the degree of the »transposition« in time. In Figure 60, the »pitch« of a membranophone is bent. There are four levels for upward transpositions whilst the lowest axis (0) depicts the unbent sound. In the example, the percussionist is supposed to perform a (one-handed) roll on the head of a membranophone and constantly shift the point of impact for the duration of a semibreve (cf. Chapter »3. 2. 3 The point of impact«). Simultaneously, the player is required to use the other hand or elbow to raise the »pitch« of the instrument. Initially, it is raised to level 3/4 for the duration of a crotchet, then lowered to the original unbent sound for the duration of a minim and finally raised to level 1/4 for the duration of a crotchet.

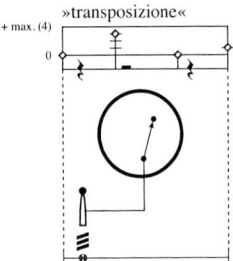

Fig. 60 »Pitch« bending and shifting the point of impact.

Alternatively, more or less than four levels may be employed. Further, the reversed transposition system (e. g. from 0 to –4) may be utilised for the notation of the water gong effect and the pitch bending on the vibraphone. However, in the case of the gong and vibraphone, the lower system depicts the pitch, the indication *transposizione* therefore does not need to be put in quotation marks and two dots could – in the case of the vibraphone – be used in order to depict a simultaneous pitch bending on two bars. Moreover, it needs to be noted that the further the tam-tam or gong is lowered, the higher the point of impact needs to be.

3. 4 Muting

This chapter focuses on the **application of mutes** as well as the **hand muffling**. Moreover, because they may be described as extended muting techniques, the **stop attack** and the **wah-wah effect** on percussion instruments are also discussed.

3. 4. 1 The application of mutes and its notation

The application of mutes depends on the instrument that is supposed to be muffled. For instance, tam-tams may be muted by placing these on cloth or holding the instrument between the knees. Moreover, membranophones may be muted by placing cloth or other items on the head. The application of mutes has been extensively discussed in Chapter »2. 8. 1 The application of mutes« by taking the example of wind instruments and can be regarded as nearly conventional. Therefore, another discussion of this topic is dismissed here. When wishing to employ mutes on percussion instruments, the paradigm presented in the chapter on wind instruments may be transferred to percussion instruments. Hence the application of mutes is suggested here being notated by means of the direction with/without mute or *con/senza sordino* whilst the description of the mute – e. g. on cloth, between knees or cloth – may be given in brackets. Further, in the case of playing on the snares, the plucking of muted strings (*senza corde*) is very ineffective and, therefore, here not discussed. A variant would be to pluck the snares *con corde* (cf. Chapter »3. 2. 6 Playing the snares«).

3. 4. 2 Hand muffling and its notation

Hand muffling is discussed in its own chapter because this muting technique may be used in a more complex way as the techniques described in the previous chapter. The instrument may be either muted prior to/simultaneous with or subsequent to the attack. When employed in the same way as the other mutes and hence slightly prior to/simultaneous with the attack, hand muffling may be notated by means of the direction with/without mute (hand) or *con/senza sordino* (*mano*). However, when requested subsequent to the attack, the muting is often depicted by means of a diamond-shaped note head or a muting sign[55]. The latter variant is, for instance, employed by *Lachenmann* in »NUN«. As is apparent from Figure 61, the muting sign is used in order to clearly outline that the instrument is muted at a given moment.

Dämpfzeichen: Angeschlagenen Klang präzis zum angezeigten Zeitpunkt wegdämpfen. **Mute signs:** mute the sound precisely at the given moment.

Fig. 61 Lachenmann, NUN, p. VII.

Further, some composers employ x-shaped note heads instead of diamond-shaped ones. For instance, *Foss* in »Echoi« makes use of this method. In the example presented in Figure 62, a vibraphone player is supposed to mute one bar after another.

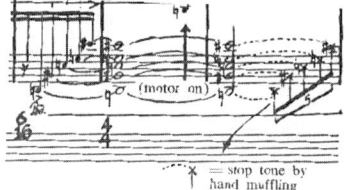

Fig. 62 Foss, Echoi, p. 18.

However, it needs to be noted that there is not always a necessity to specifically outline that an instrument is muted, but this information may, in some cases, be regarded as redundant. This is because the duration of the subsequent vibration can be depicted sufficiently by the note's duration when playing *non lasciar vibrare*. For example, when the player is supposed to hit a cymbal with a high dynamic level and the sound that is produced has the duration of a crotchet, the cymbal needs to be muted after a crotchet because otherwise the sound would last longer than depicted. However, the depiction of the muting could become necessary when previously giving the direction *sempre lasciar vibrare*. This is because, in such a case, only the duration of the attack needs to be depicted, and all sounds last as long as they naturally last when not muted. If one would want one of the sounds to last shorter, either the direction *non lasciar vibrare* needs to be utilised, the duration of the sound be notated and, subsequently, the direction *sempre lasciar vibrare* again be employed or the muting simply be specifically requested by means of a sign or special note head. With regard to the approaches towards the notation of the muting, it may be said that diamond-shaped note heads are normally employed for the notation of harmonics. They are also used for the depiction of muting stops on string and plucked instruments because the pressure that is applied to the string is

---

[55] Ibid., p. 208.

135

similar to when fingering harmonics. In both cases, the notes are used to determine the fingering (cf. Chapter »1. 6. 2 Exact muting stops and their notation«). However, on percussions instruments no fingerings are employed, but only the point of impact may be determined. Moreover, in the case of hand muffling, it is not necessary to determine the point of impact. Therefore, it would be confusing to employ diamond-shaped note heads in order to request the muting of a percussion instrument. Further, x-shaped note heads cannot be used for the depiction of the hand muffling because they are, in this work, constantly employed to notate sounds with indefinite pitch and hence could not be used in order to depict the muting of these instruments. Therefore, it is preferred here to request the muting by means of the muting sign.

In Figure 63, the player is supposed to let the instrument vibrate. Hence all produced sounds either linger on until they naturally decay or need to be muted. Initially, the player strikes the tones »f^1/F4« and »a^1/A4«. These bars are muted after they have vibrated for the duration of a crotchet (in total). In this case, only the muting sign needs to be employed because it distinctly requests that the whole instrument is muted simultaneously. After a crotchet rest, the instrument is struck again. However, this time a chord is played and each bar muted at a different point in time. Each of the produced tones here lasts a semiquaver longer than the adjacent lower tone. In order to notate this, the muting sign is used in combination with a depiction of the bar that is supposed to be muted. It needs to be noted that the action of muffling an instrument is different from touching a vibrating instrument with a beater or item. This is because this articulation is utilised to produce the sizzle effect and hence the instrument is not muted, but played (cf. Chapter »3. 2. 2 Extended striking techniques« for the notation of this technique).

Fig. 63 Hand muffling (*lasciar vibrare*).

When playing *non lasciar vibrare*, the muting can be notated by means of the note's duration. As is apparent from Figure 64, each of the tones produced by the percussionist lasts again a semiquaver longer than the adjacent lower tone. This is depicted by simply determining each tone's duration.

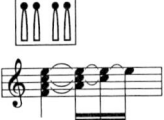

Fig. 64 Hand muffling (*non lasciar vibrare*).

3. 4. 3 The stop attack and its notation

Another special muting articulation, referred to as the stop attack or dead stroke, is often performed on percussion instruments. When requested, the beater does not bounce back, but remains firmly in contact with the surface after the attack[56]. Hence the instrument is attacked and simultaneously muted. The result is that the instrument vibrates shorter than it would if the beater was released after the attack. Stop attacks are often used. For example, *Lachen-*

---

[56] Cf. ibid., p. 209.

mann in »NUN« employs this articulation. He requests dead strokes by means of *staccato* dots:

Notenköpfe mit Staccato-Punkten bedeuten Stop-Schläge.   **Note heads with staccato dots** signify stop attacks.

Fig. 65 Lachenmann, NUN, p. VII.

However, because the stop attack is, as mentioned, a stroke that involves a simultaneous muting with the beater itself, the method of notation should take this into account. Further, concerning *Lachenmann's* method it may additionally be said that it could be employed in the case of playing on most membranophones. But on instruments that vibrate longer than these, a *staccato* can also be produced by muting the instrument with the hand before the next attack. Thus the utilisation of the *staccato* dot could become ambiguous. Therefore, the suggested method of notation requests this articulation by means of the beater symbol – which depicts the normal attack – and a muting sign in combination. In Figure 66, the bars of a mallet instrument are attacked in this way. Initially, the player executes a dead stroke on the »f/F3«. After a crotchet rest, four beaters are used simultaneously. The sticks in the left hand execute a dead stroke and the sticks in the right hand a normal attack. Hence the beaters only remain firmly on the bars »f/F3« and »a/A3«. When this sequence is played *lasciar vibrare*, the other tones linger on after the stop attack, and when playing *non lasciar vibrare*, all bars are additionally muted with the hand after the duration of a semiquaver (cf. the previous chapter).

Fig. 66 The stop attack.

3. 4. 4 The wah-wah effect and its notation

The wah-wah effect (cf. for further details »Part II: Electroacoustic music – 2. 3. 1 High-pass, low-pass, band-pass and band-reject filters«) can on small percussion instruments, such as sleigh bells or maracas, be produced by slowly opening and closing the hand while shaking these repetitively. Moreover, a kind of wah-wah effect also occurs when gradually opening or closing two hi-hat cymbals. For instance, *Kagel* in »Fürst Igor, Strawinsky«[57] requests a wah-wah effect on sleigh bells by means of a diamond-shaped note head (which depicts the muting) and the direction wow-wow-effect[58]. Moreover, the player is supposed to execute a roll and hence repetitively shake the bells:

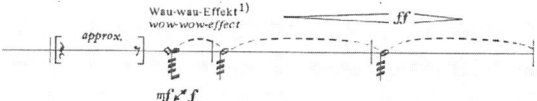

1) Rollschelle(n) in der freien Hand halten (◊ =dämpfen) und durch langsames Öffnen und Schliessen der Hand während des Tremolierens die Klangfarbe verändern.
Hold sleigh bell(s) in free hand (◊ =damp) and change timbre by opening and closing the hand slowly while performing tremolo.

Fig. 67 Kagel, Fürst, p. 11.

---

[57] Mauricio Kagel: Fürst Igor, Strawinsky. For bass voice and instruments. Frankfurt/M. et al. 1988.

[58] The wah-wah effect is, in this work, wrongly referred to as the *Wau-wau-Effekt* or wow-wow-effect.

Moreover, *Stone* suggests utilising an additional notation system placed above the original system in order to depict the gradual opening and closing of a hi-hat. The x-axis of this system depicts, as usual, the time, and the y-axis the degree of opening. No distinct timeline is introduced for this system, but the x-axis of the additional system related to the lower notation system. As can be seen in Figure 68, either a graphic depiction of the open and closed hi-hat or the symbols »o« (open) and »+« (closed) are employed.

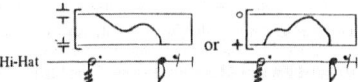

Fig. 68 Stone, Notation, p. 223.

The notation of the wah-wah effect has been extensively discussed in Chapter »2. 8. 2 The wah-wah effect«. As mentioned there, the two symbols »o« and »+« are conventionally employed for the notation of the wah-wah effect while in the suggested method of notation these symbols are used as note heads to exactly notate the transitions between these two states. In order to request the effect in a uniform way, this method needs to be transferred to percussion instrument. Moreover, this approach towards the notation of the wah-wah effect may be described as more exact than the method suggested by *Kagel*. This is because the actual performance of the effect is in »Fürst Igor, Strawinsky« at the player's discretion. Concerning *Stone's* method of notation, the introduction of a distinct timeline for the effect is preferred here. This is because depicting the wah-wah effect in relation to the original system complicates notating the sound production and the effect independently from each other. However, *Stone's* approach admittedly enables (similarly to the »transposition« system displayed in Figure 60) the depiction of different opening degrees. Hence when wanting to request more than two states (e. g. an open, half-closed and closed hi-hat), the method of notation suggested in the chapter on wind instruments needs to be extended further. Therefore, it is suggested here notating the wah-wah effect by means of the symbols »o« and »+« whilst the duration of the transition between these two states is depicted by using the symbols as note heads. Moreover, an additional state »(+)« (half-closed) is introduced for the hi-hat. Articulation symbols, such as *legato* slurs or *staccato* dots, can additionally be used to determine the character of the transitions. In the example presented in Figure 69, a percussionist is supposed to play a semibreve roll on a hi-hat. The transitions between opening and closing may be described as follows: open to closed (quaver – *legato*), to half-closed (semiquaver – *staccato*), to open (quaver – normal articulation), to open, closed, open (quavers – *legato*), to half-closed (quaver – normal articulation), to closed, open and half-closed (semiquavers – *staccato*). In the same way – but without the additional state »(+)« – can the wah-wah effect on small percussion instruments be notated.

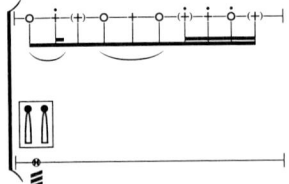

Fig. 69 The wah-wah effect on a hi-hat.

As mentioned in the chapter on wind instruments, an alternative method of notation would be to employ the two to three states in a »transposition« system (cf. Figure 60) because notes suggest that sound is produced and the original sound is, in this case, actually transformed.

3. 5 Preparing the instrument and its notation

There are various examples of preparations: as mentioned above, *Stockhausen* in »Kontakte«, for instance, requests the percussionist to fill a bongo with beans. Moreover, he makes in the same piece use of three tom-toms with plywood glued on in place of the membrane[59]. Further, *Kagel* in »Anagrama« requests to fix three castanets to a board[60] or *Lachenmann* in »NUN« to attach a bongo drum to a timpano[61]. As in the case of the string and wind instruments, there are numerous ways of preparing percussion instruments. Similarly, it is also, on the one hand, barely possible to list them all and subsequently develop a coherent method of depiction whilst, on the other hand, it is also not necessary to do so since most preparations are executed previously to a performance and may simply be described in the foreword to a work. Further, when preparations are supposed to be executed during a performance, they are suggested here always being notated by means of a sketch. This is because it is the simplest way of depicting these. When the sketch is not clear enough, it may be complemented by an explanation (cf. Chapters »1. 8 Preparing the instrument and its notation« and »2. 6. 2 Constructional modifications and their notation«). Nevertheless, preparations may lead to the introduction of new playing techniques that should then be notated in accordance with all other techniques presented in this work.

---

[59] Cf. Stockhausen, Kontakte, pp. III and V.
[60] Cf. Kagel, Anagrama, no page named [foreword].
[61] Cf. Lachenmann, NUN, p. IX.

4. THE TECHNIQUES OF PLUCKED INSTRUMENTS

There are two big groups of plucked instruments, plucked chordophones and plucked idiophones. When producing sound on chordophones, strings are plucked whilst, in the case of idiophones (e. g. jew's harps, kalimbas, marimbulas), an elastic body is plucked. The chapter on plucked instruments, however, only discusses the extended playing techniques of the two most important plucked chordophones, the harp and the guitar. This is because plucked idiophones are only rarely used in Western art music and comprise only a very limited number of unconventional extended playing techniques[1]. Moreover, the notation of these techniques may easily be derived from the methods of notation presented in the previous chapters (for instance, because on the kalimba the wah-wah effect may be produced, the paradigm presented in Chapter »2. 8. 2 The wah-wah effect« or Chapter »3. 4. 4 The wah-wah effect and its notation« may be employed when utilising this instrument). Further, electric guitars and basses are in this chapter not specifically discussed. However, most playing techniques may simply be transferred to these instruments. The utilisation of the so-called whammy, *vibrato* or *tremolo* arm/bar on the electric guitar – which actually produces a *vibrato* – may, moreover, be depicted in the conventional manner and hence by means of the method normally employed to notate the *vibrato* and an addition, such as lever *vibrato* or *vibrato della leva*. The effects that may be utilised to modulate or transform the sound of the electric instrument and the control of the output level are discussed in »Part II: Electroacoustic music – 1. Sound synthesis« and »2. Audio processing«. Despite the harp and guitar being heterogeneous instruments, many extended playing techniques may be produced on both instruments in the same manner. Therefore, this chapter is not divided into two parts, but solely grouped by unconventional extended playing techniques. In the beginning of each chapter, it is indicated if a special technique may only be produced on one of these instruments. Moreover, all techniques of the guitar may be employed on steel-string acoustic guitars and classical guitars. When an unconventional extended playing technique of string instruments may also be employed on plucked instruments, another discussion of this technique is dismissed in the following chapters and merely the already suggested method of notation presented. With regard to plucked instruments, the notation of the *vibrato* (guitar) and trill, stops, clusters (cf. Chapter »5. 6. 1 Clusters«), the basic *pizzicato*, the *Bartók pizzicato* (guitar), the basic *glissando* (playing adjacent strings in a fast manner in the case of the harp and sliding on the fretboard in the case of the guitar), the common modes of attack, the production of harmonics and the *scordatura* (previous to, or simultaneous with, playing and including the utilisation of a capo tasto) are regarded here as conventional[2]. Their notation can be adopted from the essential handbooks on instrumentation whilst most composers use the method of depiction that can be found there. Whereas, the main unconventional elements of sound production presented in this chapter are extended *pizzicato*, *tremolo* and trill techniques, common and extended playing positions on the string, extended *glissando* techniques, extended modes of attack, playing exceptional spots, muting, extended stopping techniques, percussive effects and preparing the instrument. Concerning the dynamic level of these articulations, indications are – as far as possible – presented when the execution of the action is, in terms of the loudness, limited. Microtones on the guitar can be produced by means of microtonal *vibrati* or the *scordatura*. Another variant is the bending technique, which is discussed in Chapter »4. 3. 2 The pitch bending technique and its notation«. On the harp microtones may be created by means of the *scordatura* or adjusting the pedal in between two positions[3]. The latter variant is discussed in Chapter

---

[1] Cf. Sevsay, Handbuch, pp. 187 and 217.

[2] Cf. ibid., pp. 217-248.

[3] Cf. ibid., pp. 241f. and 247f.

»4. 3. 6 The pedal-*glissando*« (cf. the introduction to the chapter on string instruments for the notation of microtones).

4. 1 Extended *pizzicato*, *tremolo* and trill techniques and their notation

In the case of the guitar, the direction *pizzicato* normally requests to mute the strings, while the direction *pizzicato effleuré* requires the player to touch the string lightly with the left hand[4]. However, this method of notation is opposed to the conventional method of depiction for the *pizzicato* and the muting on all other instruments as well as the notation of the extended playing technique discussed in Chapter »1. 6. 2 Exact muting stops and their notation«. As the traditional utilisation of these directions causes a great deal of confusion, they are dismissed here. However, when handling these directions in this way, it is absolutely necessary to explain the violation of the convention when the direction *pizzicato* or exact muting stops first occurs in a musical work. Alternatively, the conventional method of depiction for the muting may be employed only on the guitar, the normal plucking of the string be requested by the direction *modo ordinario* and the direction *pizzicato effleuré* be complemented by the method used for the depiction of exact muting stops (cf. Chapter »4. 7. 1 Exact muting stops and their notation«).

Further, all extended *pizzicato* techniques discussed in Chapter »1. 1 Extended *pizzicato* techniques and their notation« may be transferred to either the harp or the guitar: however, the ***pizzicato* with the left hand** only needs to specifically be requested in the case of the guitar because the utilisation of the left hand is depicted on the harp by means of the two notation systems. As shown, the execution of the left-hand *pizzicato* on string instruments can be requested by means of the direction *pizzicato* (*mano sinistra*). This method of notation is, therefore, also suggested for the guitar. Further, the fingernail *pizzicato* is normally depicted by means of an additional fingernail symbol whilst the utilisation of a pick instead of the fingers is, in most cases, requested by employing a drawing of the plectrum and giving the direction *pizzicato* (cf. Figures 1 and 2 in the chapter on string instruments). Therefore, it is also suggested notating the **fingernail** and **plectrum *pizzicato*** in this way.

Moreover, the bow-screw *pizzicato* is seldom used on the harp and guitar. However, for instance, on the harp a **tuning key *pizzicato*** is sometimes requested. Due to its similarity, the method of notation introduced for the bow-screw *pizzicato* in the chapter on string instruments (Figure 4) can be employed. Hence the action of plucking the string with the tuning key may – as is apparent from Figure 1 – be either requested by means of the direction *pizzicato della chiave* (key *pizzicato*) or the direction *pizzicato* and a symbol for the screw. Any other ***pizzicato* with items** may be requested in the same way and hence either by means of a direction or a symbolic representation of the item. However, it needs to be noted that a graphic depiction of the item contains, in most cases, a greater degree of instantaneous comprehension.

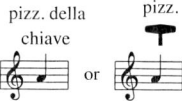

Fig. 1 The tuning key *pizzicato*.

Further, the **lateral *Bartók pizzicato*** may also be produced on the guitar and harp. In the case of the guitar, the player pulls the low E-string to the side instead of upwards. When doing so, the string bounces back on the fretboard and may even hit adjacent strings. In the case of

---

[4] Ibid., p. 247.

the harp, this kind of *pizzicato* is normally executed on the lower strings[5]. It can be depicted by means of a variation of the symbol used for the *Bartók pizzicato* (⊖) and a common note head that determines which string is supposed to be plucked. However, the harpist is sometimes required to pull two adjacent strings in opposite directions and let them bounce against each other[6]. In such a case, the method of notation can be extended in order to depict the action adequately. As is apparent from the example presented in Figure 2, the player is supposed to play a lateral *Bartók pizzicato* »D/D2« with the right hand and a lateral *Bartók pizzicato* »C/C2« with the left hand. Because the line of the lower *pizzicato* is pointing to the right, the harpist is supposed to pull these two adjacent strings in opposite directions. As a result, the strings bounce against each other and a buzzing sound evolves.

Fig. 2 The lateral *Bartók pizzicato* on two adjacent strings.

Moreover, such a buzzing may also be produced when plucking single or several strings in a very loud manner[7] or executing a loud *glissando*[8]. Further, the so-called extended *tremolo* and trill need to be discussed here because there is an unconventional variant of these techniques. This articulation may be referred to as **bisbigliando**, but is also known as unison *tremolo*, enharmonic or timbre trill. If requested on plucked instruments, the player is supposed to repetitively produce the same pitch on two different strings in a rapid succession. As shown in Chapter »2. 1 Extended *vibrato, tremolo* and trill techniques and their notation«, the *bisbigliando* may be either defined as an enharmonic trill or overtone *vibrato*. Therefore, it is – as is apparent from Figure 3 – depicted by means of a trill symbol and the natural sign or a *vibrato* symbol and the direction *bisbigliando*. When executing this articulation on a harp, two adjacent strings need to be tuned to the same pitch. In the example, an enharmonic trill or overtone *vibrato* »c♯1/C♯4« is played. Hence the adjacent D-string needs to be previously tuned to »d♭1/D♭4«. Additionally, the pitch of the second string could be depicted in brackets.

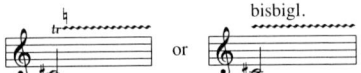

Fig. 3 The *bisbigliando* effect.

When the harpist/guitarist is supposed to repetitively pluck a single string, a *tremolo* may simply be notated. Moreover, the pinch-*pizzicato* refers, as mentioned, to the string being plucked by two fingers. However, because the sound-wise result is not very different from the common way of performing a *pizzicato*, this technique is neglected here and rather regarded as a means of expression. Further, three other techniques that are related to performing the trill or *pizzicato* – the extended trill with items, *pizzicato* on the neck/in the headstock and the buzz-*pizzicato* – are discussed in Chapters »4. 4. 3 The utilisation of beaters and its notation«, »4. 5 Playing exceptional spots« and »4. 7. 1 Exact muting stops and their notation«.

---

5 Cf., for instance, Kelemen, Changeant, p. 8.
6 Cf. Mauricio Kagel: Heterophonie. For orchestra. Frankfurt/M. et al. 1969, p. 14.
7 Cf. Kagel, Anagrama, p. 32.
8 Cf. Luciano Berio: Sequenza II. For harp alone. London 1965, no page named [foreword].

4. 2 Common and extended playing positions on the strings and their notation

The **common playing positions** are discussed here because – especially on the guitar – they are not clearly defined. *Lachenmann*, in »Salut für Caudwell«, for instance, differentiates between four positions: at the bridge, almost on the bridge, the ordinary position and *tasto*[9]. As these positions resemble the playing positions on string instruments, they may be notated in the same manner and hence by means of the directions *sul ponticello, ordinario* and *sul tasto*. The additional position designated by *Lachenmann* as almost on the bridge may analogously be referred to as *quasi sul ponticello*, abbreviated *quasi s. p.* Concerning the common playing positions on the harp, most composers distinguish three or less positions: close to the soundboard or *sulla tavola*, on the midpoint of the string or *ordinario* and close to the neck or *sulla mensola*[10]. Moreover, it might be desirable to request additional positions on the lower strings, such as *quasi sulla tavola* or *quasi sulla mensola*.

Further, on the guitar the technique of **fingering in between fingerboard and saddle** may be employed. When the left hand leaves the fretboard and slides into the space between fingerboard and saddle, the method of notation needs to be augmented. This is because the sounds that evolve do not have a definite pitch. As shown in Chapter »1. 4. 2 Fingering in between fingerboard and bridge and its notation«, this articulation may be depicted by means of a string clef system and triangular note heads pointing upwards. However, it needs to be extended in order to depict six instead of four strings. The system employed here consists of five lines and replaces the traditional system. Each spacing in between the lines and the space above the highest and below the lowest line refers to one of the six strings. For the guitar four distinct stops are also determined: position 1 can be described as the closest to the fretboard. It is depicted by the accidental »♭« and can be fingered when playing *ordinario, quasi sul ponticello* or *sul ponticello*. The next two positions are located closer to the saddle. Position 2 is requested when no accidental is employed whilst position 3 is depicted by the accidental »♯«. These positions may be fingered when bowing *quasi sul ponticello* or *sul ponticello*. Moreover, position 4 can only be fingered when playing *sul ponticello*. It is notated by the accidental »𝄪« and is the closest to the saddle. In the example presented in Figure 4, the string clef system is displayed. The described positions are depicted in the order of position 1 on the low E-string, position 2 on the D-string, position 3 on the H/B-string and position 4 on the high E-string.

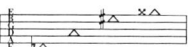

Fig. 4 Fingering in between fretboard and saddle.

Concerning this technique, there is – apart from considering the additional playing position *quasi sul ponticello* – no distinction made between string instruments and the guitar in order to retain uniformity. This means that even though it might be possible to produce more sounds on a guitar than on a violin by fingering more than four positions, it is neglected here in order to enable the application of the same method of notation for strings and the guitar. Moreover, in order to produce similar sounds as on string instruments, the guitar needs to be bowed (cf. Chapter »4. 4. 2 The utilisation of a bow and its notation«). Otherwise, varying muted plucking noises are produced.

Another special guitar technique is to finger the string on a fret instead of in between two frets. The result is that the tone is slightly muted and an additional buzzing sound evolves.

---

[9] Cf. Helmut Lachenmann: Salut für Caudwell. For two guitarists. Wiesbaden 1985, no page named [foreword].

[10] Cf. Kagel, Sonant, pp. 20f. [explanation of symbols], Kelemen, Changeant, p. 4 or Karlheinz Stockhausen: Kontra-punkte. For ten instruments. London 1953, p. 1.

Kagel, in »Sonant (1960/....)«, depicts the **fingering on the fret** by means of notating a »B«[11] (as in the German *Bund*, meaning fret). Another variant was to introduce a special symbol. As the fingering of special positions on the strings is, in this work however, uniformly depicted by means of special note heads (cf. Chapter »1. 4 Extended playing positions on the strings«), such a method of notation is favoured here. The note head used to notate playing on the fret is suggested being x-shaped. This is because, in this case, the pitch is augmented by a noise component, and x-shaped note heads are normally used to depict such sounds. When utilising these note heads in combination with a pitch-based notation system, it is, however, described that the noise is complemented by a definite pitch (also cf., for example, Chapter »3. 9. 1 Key/ valve clicks«). Thus fingering the first fret of the lower E-string would, for instance, be requested by notating a (written) »f/F3« and utilising an x-shaped note head. Further, the articulation of **bowing on the saddle** is not discussed here because this technique is primarily applied on string instruments (bowing on the bridge). However, in the case of using a bow to play the strings of a guitar, it may also be requested to bow on the saddle of a guitar. In such a case, the method of notation suggested in Chapter »1. 4. 3 Bowing on the bridge« – which implies requesting this technique by means of the string clef system and squared note heads – may be employed. Further, on some guitar models the action of **playing behind the saddle** may be executed[12]. As shown in Chapter »1. 4. 4 Playing behind the bridge«, this articulation may be requested by means of the string clef system and x-shaped note heads.

Additionally, a technique often employed as an extended *glissando* on string instruments can also be performed on the guitar. This technique is referred to here as **playing on the fretboard**. For instance, *Lachenmann*, in »Salut für Caudwell«, requests the guitarist to pluck directly at the stopping finger[13]. As shown in Chapter »1. 2. 2 The bow-*glissando*«, an action of this kind may be depicted by means of an additional notation system placed above the one that depicts the stops while the playing position on the fretboard is notated by diamond-shaped note heads. In the example presented in Figure 5, the player is supposed to finger a (written) »c1/C4« for the duration of a semibreve. The string is plucked here on the fretboard position »c♯1/C♯4« and hence close to the stopping finger. As the action of plucking is only of short duration, it is depicted by a semiquaver (also cf. Chapter »4. 3. 1. The progressive modification of the point of plucking«). This method of notation may also be applied in the case of the left-hand *pizzicato* and any other right hand articulation on the fingerboard, e. g. bowing (cf. Chapter »4. 1 Extended *pizzicato*, *tremolo* and trill techniques and their notation« and »4. 4. 2 The utilisation of a bow and its notation«).

Fig. 5 Playing on the fretboard.

4. 3 Extended *glissando* techniques

Various extended *glissando* techniques may be executed on plucked instruments. One is the **progressive modification of the point of plucking**. Moreover, the **pitch bending technique** may also be performed on both instruments whilst the **vertical *glissando* with/without**

---

[11] Cf. Kagel, Sonant, p. 19 [appendix].
[12] Cf. Sevsay, Handbuch, p. 248.
[13] Cf. Lachenmann, Salut, no page named [foreword].

plucking is a harp technique. However, it resembles the technique referred to as the **harmonic-*glissando* without plucking** on the guitar. Further, because the methods of notation for the **basic *glissando* techniques on the harp** suggested by *Stone*[14] and *Sevsay*[15] are confusing, they need to be discussed here. Finally, on the harp a special *glissando* technique, referred to as the **pedal-*glissando***, may be executed.

4. 3. 1 The progressive modification of the point of plucking and its notation

The modification of the point of plucking on plucked instruments resembles the technique referred to as the bow-*glissando* on string instruments (cf. Chapter »1. 2. 2 The bow-*glissando*«). As shown there, changing the point of bowing may be requested by means of the common *glissando* notation and the additional direction *glissando d'arco*. This method of notation may be transferred to plucked instruments. However, since the string is played with the hands, the direction *glissando del mano* (*glissando* with the hand) needs to be employed. Despite the progressive modification of the point of plucking it is not, in the strict sense, a *glissando* because the fingers do not slide over, but simply move on the string. However, it may be notated in the same way as the bow-*glissando* because both techniques strongly resemble each other. The technique is, in Figure 6, depicted by taking the example of the guitar. As shown above, four different playing positions – *sul tasto, ordinario, quasi sul ponticello* and *sul ponticello* – are determined for this instrument. In the example, the guitarist is supposed to play two (written) *tremolo pizzicati* »c¹/C4« and »c♯¹/C♯4« for the duration of a minim. During these, the point of plucking is constantly modified. In order to depict the duration of these »*glissandi*«, an additional notation system is used. By means of this system it is requested that the point of plucking is changed from the initial position to *sul tasto* for the duration of a dotted crotchet. Subsequently, the hand is moved to the position *sul ponticello* for the duration of a quaver. During the plucking of the »c♯¹/C♯4«, the hand moves to the position *ordinario* for the duration of a quaver, then to *quasi sul ponticello* for the duration of another quaver and remains on this position until the end of the *tremolo pizzicato*.

Fig. 6 The progressive modification of the point of plucking on the guitar.

The additional system here used is in treble clef because it would also be employed when playing on the fretboard (cf. Figure 15 in the chapter on string instruments). In such a case, the position on the fretboard would – as in Figure 5 – be depicted by means of diamond-shaped note heads whilst the *glissando* notation and the direction *glissando del mano* would request to progressively move the hand on the fretboard.

On the harp the »hand-*glissando*« can be notated by means of an additional single lined notation system with no clef and the plucking positions determined in the previous chapter. However, it cannot adequately be executed on the highest strings. Moreover, an additional notation system may alternatively be dismissed when depicting motions between the common plucking positions (cf. Figure 14 in the chapter on string instruments). There is no need to utilise more than the 3 to 5 playing positions on the harp because the sound-wise difference is

---

[14] Cf. Stone, Notation, pp. 236-239.
[15] Cf. Sevsay, Handbuch, pp. 224-230.

negligible. Nevertheless, in the case of combining certain articulations, such as the extended *battuto* with exact muting stops (cf. Chapters »4. 4. 4 Extended *battuto* techniques and their notation« and »4. 7. 1 Exact muting stops and their notation«), it may be desirable to request the playing positions in a more exact way because various different sounds could then be produced. As it is shown in Chapter »4. 3. 3 The vertical *glissando* with/without plucking«, the string can, for instance, also be divided by means of its nodal points (and muting stops). Hence the playing position may be determined by the pitch-based notation system. However, this would lead to confusion in the case of the harp because, for example, the playing position *ordinario* and the first partial (octave) are both located on the midpoint of the string, whereas, in the case of the guitar and string instruments, the normal playing positions are located in between the fretboard/fingerboard and bridge and the nodal points (and muting stops) on the fretboard/fingerboard. When the right hand/bow is supposed to slide on the fingerboard an additional notation system is, therefore, used. Moreover, the transfer of this method of notation to the harp could lead to an unclear appearance of the score and confusion since one or two additional pitch-based notation system would have to be introduced. Therefore, it is suggested here only using the described 3 to 5 directions in order to determine the playing positions.

4. 3. 2 The pitch bending technique and its notation

The pitch bending technique may on the harp be executed in two ways, either by inserting the wooden part of the tuning key between two strings, pluck one of them and twist the key in order to raise the pitch slightly[16] or by pressing the string prior to, simultaneous with or after the plucking[17]. On the guitar the pitch may be raised by pulling the string to the side prior to, simultaneous with or after plucking it[18]. As shown in Chapter »2. 4 Pitch bending – the extended *glissando*« and »3. 3 »Pitch« bending – the extended glissando«, the technique is, in this work, depicted by means of an additional notation system, referred to as the transposition system. Another discussion of this technique is, therefore, dismissed here. The x-axis of the transposition system represents, as usual, the duration and the y-axis the degree of the transposition. Moreover, the white dots (◊) depict the degree of the transposition in time.

The pitch bending technique is, in Figure 7, notated by taking the example of the harp. In this case, the two pitch bending techniques need to be distinguished. The first technique is referred to as *transposizione della chiave* (transposition by the key) and the second as *transposizione del mano* (transposition by the hand). There are four levels for upward transpositions whilst the lowest axis (0) depicts the unbent sound. In the example, the harpist plucks the string twice and bends the first tone »c^1/C4« with the key and the second tone »d^1/D4« with the hand. The first tone is raised to level 3/4 for the duration of a dotted crotchet. After a quaver rest, the player plucks the second tone. Because it is already supposed to be transposed to level 4/4 in the beginning, the already bent string is, in this case, plucked. The pitch is then lowered to level 1/4 for the duration of a minim.

Fig. 7 Pitch bending on the harp.

[16] Stone, Notation, p. 229.

[17] Cf. Sevsay, Handbuch, p. 242.

[18] Cf. ibid., p. 247.

The pitch bending technique may be depicted similarly on the guitar. However, in this case, no distinction between different bending techniques needs to be made. Moreover, bending *vibrati* can be performed on the guitar and harp. On the guitar it is executed by moving the bent string quickly up and down, whereas on the harp the player pushes and releases the string in fast succession[19]. In such cases, the *vibrato* symbol may complement the dots in the transposition system.

4.3.3 The vertical *glissando* with/without plucking

Vertical motions on the strings of a harp can be executed with the fingers/hand, the fingernails or items, such as the tuning key or a brush. These slides may be performed as distinct articulations or in combination with a *pizzicato* played by the other hand. When only a sliding motion is executed, whistling sounds are produced, and when the plucking and vertical *glissando* are employed in combination, harmonics evolve in the case of sliding over or resting on the nodes[20].

4.3.3.1 Previous methods of notation

Most composers notate the vertical *glissando* in an approximate way. In »Changeant« *Kelemen* depicts the string upon which the motion is performed in brackets and replaces the note head with an arrow in order to request a vertical *glissando* up- or downwards:

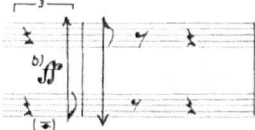

Fig. 8 Kelemen, Changeant, p. 46.

Sevsay and *Stone* suggest a similar method of notation with the difference that they distinguish between slow and fast vertical slides. Fast slides are notated by means of two lines that complement the note head and an arrow head pointing up- or downwards whilst slow slides are notated by means of two lines and an additional oblique arrow pointing up- or downwards. Additionally, a Pan-pipe symbol, which depicts the produced sound, is employed. This approach is presented in Figure 9. Further, when the slides are supposed to be executed with the fingernails, a fingernail symbol is utilised[21].

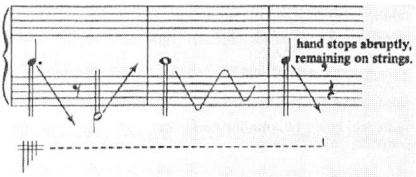

Fig. 9 Stone, Notation, p. 255.

Moreover, *Kagel*, in »Anagrama«, depicts the extent of the *glissando* by means of the regular playing positions *près des chevilles* (here referred to as *sulla mensola*) and *près de la table* (here referred to as *sulla tavola*). As is apparent from Figure 10, the vertical *glissando*

---

[19] For the latter cf. Sevsay, Handbuch, p. 236.
[20] Cf. Stone, Notation, pp. 251-256.
[21] Cf. Sevsay, Handbuch, pp. 230-232 and Stone, Notation, pp. 253-256.

itself is requested by means of additional arrows and the direction string *glissando* with plectrum or tuning key [Saitenglissando mit Plectrum oder Harfenschlüssel].

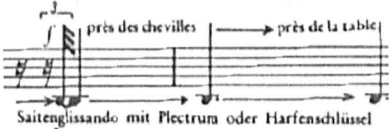

Fig. 10 Kagel, Anagrama, p. 9.

Further, *Holliger*, in »Partita (II)«[22], employs a vertical *glissando* with plucking. The harpist is supposed here to slide on the string with the tuning key or a metal stick and pluck the string with the left hand. As is apparent from Figure 11, he makes use of the conventional harmonic notation for the harp – including the actual pitch (always »c2/C5«) that is produced in this way – in order to depict this articulation. In the beginning of the example, the harpist is supposed to produce harmonics. Subsequently, the player is required to move the key/stick along the string[23], thereby passing the same nodes. The vertical motion on the string is notated by means of treble clef system.

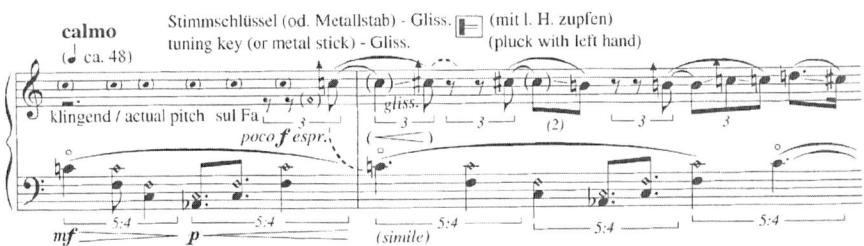

Fig. 11 Holliger, Partita (II), p. 20.

4. 3. 3. 2 Discussion

As is apparent, *Kelemen's* approach towards the notation of the vertical *glissando* (cf. Figure 8) is very inexact. This is because he neither defines the starting point nor the endpoint of the motion, but merely determines the direction of the *glissando*. By contrast, the method suggested by *Stone* (cf. Figure 9) is more exact because two speed levels – slow and fast – are determined. These levels resemble the tempo index introduced in Chapter »3. 2. 4 Rubbing and bowing motions«. It is utilised in the case of repetitive rubbing motions on percussion instruments because they do not have a fixed endpoint. However, when the starting point and endpoint may be determined, it is more exact and simpler to do so instead of depicting a speed level. The performance speed may then be derived from the duration of the action and the extent of the motion. One approach towards the determination of the vertical motion's extent is presented by *Kagel*. As can be seen in Figure 10, he depicts it by means of the regular playing positions. The more playing positions are introduced, the more exact can the extent of the motion be described. However, the most exact method of notation is utilised by *Holliger* who makes use of harmonic notation (cf. Figure 11). As a reminder, the second to fifth partial are often requested on the harp. The partials are produced by touching the respective node on the string. For the second partial the string is touched in the middle, for the third partial it is touched after 1/3, for the fourth partial after 1/4 and for the fifth partial after 1/5 of the string length (always starting from the neck). The second partial is requested by notating a circle

---

[22] Heinz Holliger: Partita (II). For harp. Mainz 2004.

[23] Cf. ibid., p. 20.

over the plucked note itself and the other partials are depicted in the same way as on string instruments[24]:

Fig. 12 Sevsay, Handbuch, p. 238.

Thus four different positions may be determined by means of harmonic notation and *glissandi* between these positions be performed. As is apparent from Figure 11, *Holliger* also requests vertical motions beyond the nodal points. However, the method of notation he employs is confusing because it suggests fingering a certain nodal point, but the resulting pitch is actually different from the pitch that evolves when fingering this node. Therefore, it would be clearer to depict the attachment of an item or finger on the nodes simply by means of a common note (which determines the string that is subject to the sliding motion) and a circle above it or an additional diamond-shaped note head (which determines the node that is touched) and any motion beyond the nodes also by means of diamond-shaped note heads. As shown in Chapter »1. 2. 1 The harmonic-*glissando* without bowing and its notation«, diamond-shaped note heads may be used to depict any fingering position on a particular string. As harp strings behave in the same way as the strings of, for instance, a violin, the method of notation introduced in this chapter may be transferred to this plucked instrument. However, it needs to be noted that the fingering positions, in the case of the harp, apparently cannot be defined by means of a fingerboard. Nevertheless, the player may on the harp easily determine the nodal points by hearing (because a certain harmonic is produced) whilst all other positions can be determined with regard to the normal behaviour of strings (in the case of minor seconds, the string is touched after 1/10 of the string length and, in the case of major seconds, after 1/9 of the string length etc.). When attaching the fingers beyond the nodal points, no harmonics are produced, but the string is actually muted. However, when attaching an item, such as a bottleneck or the harp's tuning key, to off-node positions, the pitch depicted by the diamond-shaped note head is produced. Additionally, the string upon which the *glissando* is executed may not be determined in the same way as on string instruments (e. g. *sul E, A, D, G*), but simply be depicted by a common note. The described approach may also be used to depict motions on the strings that have not been plucked. Since no harmonics evolve, all positions on the string should be notated by means of diamond-shaped note heads (e. g. the middle point of the string »c¹/C4« by a diamond-shaped note head on position »c²/C5«).

4. 3. 3. 3 Suggestion for the notation of the vertical *glissando* with/without plucking

Hence vertical *glissandi* are notated similarly to the harmonic-*glissando* without bowing on string instruments. Apparently, such motions on the harp may preferably be executed on the lower strings and cannot be performed on the highest strings. When requesting a vertical *glissando*, the fingers may, for instance, slide from the minor second position (which requests that the string is touched after 1/10 of the string length and hence, in the case of the longest string (150 cm), after 15 cm, starting from the neck) down to the quadruple octave position (which requests that the string is touched after 15/16 of the string length and hence, in the case of the longest string, after approximately 141 cm).

In Figure 13, all vertical motions are executed on the »c¹/C4« string. It is in the beginning plucked and vibrates – due to playing *non lasciar vibrare* – for the duration of a minim (for the subsequent muting of plucked strings cf. Chapter »4. 6 Muting and its notation«). During

---

[24] Cf. Sevsay, Handbuch, pp. 237f.

this time, a *glissando* with the tuning key is executed, starting on the second partial (octave). The key is then moved to position »g¹/G4« (third partial) for the duration of a quaver, to »c♯³/C♯6« for the duration of another quaver and finally to »f¹/F4« (fourth partial) also for the duration of a quaver. The next motion can be described in the same way. However, this time the string is not plucked (*non pizzicato*). Therefore, the harmonic notation for the second partial is replaced by a diamond-shaped note head on position »c²/C5«. When the string is not plucked, no sound is produced when the key rests. Therefore, the *glissando* ends when the »e¹/E4« is reached and a demisemiquaver is applied pro forma. Alternatively, the vertical *glissando* may also be depicted by means of two systems (one for the plucking/basic string and one for the *glissando* with the key).

Fig. 13 The vertical *glissando* with/without plucking.

As it is always requested by means of harmonic notation, the vertical *glissando* can be distinguished from the basic *glissando* on the harp. Further, the dynamic level of the vertical *glissando* without plucking is low when executed with the hand or fingers, but may be increased by using the fingernails or items (cf., for instance, Chapter »4. 1 Extended *pizzicato*, *tremolo* and trill techniques and their notation« for the depiction of the fingernails and items). Moreover, it can also be executed on more than one string simultaneously and/or with both hands. When the player is supposed to slide on a cluster of strings, the harmonic cluster notation presented in Figure 26 may be utilised. In the case of utilising both hands to perform a vertical *glissando* without plucking, the method of depiction from Figure 13 needs to simply be employed for the left and right hand. As mentioned, in this work the *glissando* – in order to achieve a greater clarity and to enable the depiction of sliding motions that do not imply a gliding change of pitch – is requested by means of an arrow and not in the traditional manner. Alternatively, the common method of depiction may be restored.

4. 3. 4 The harmonic-*glissando* without plucking and its notation

As mentioned in the previous chapter, diamond-shaped note heads may be used to depict the position of a finger or item on a string in the case of the *harmonic*-glissando on string instruments. As the guitar and all string instruments strongly resemble each other concerning this articulation, it may be notated in the same way as suggested in Chapter »1. 2. 1 The harmonic-*glissando* without bowing and its notation«. The string(s) upon which the slide is executed may also be determined by means of directions (*sul e, B, G, D, A, E*), but the direction *senza arco* needs to, in the case of the guitar, be replaced by the direction *non pizzicato*. Moreover, the guitarist may also be requested to scratch over the fretboard by giving the direction *il tasto* as well as to execute a harmonic-*glissando* with the fingernails or items (cf. Figures 1 and 6 to 8 in the chapter on string instruments). The dynamic level may – in comparison to string instruments – become slightly higher when sliding over the strings of an acoustic guitar or the fretboard of a classical/acoustic guitar. When the performance of a harmonic-*glissando* is supposed to be executed with the right hand or both hands, this method of notation can likewise be used (cf. also Chapter »1. 2. 2 The bow-*glissando*«). Further, especially the execution of a harmonic-*glissando* with a bottleneck is employed very often on the guitar while the bottleneck can be depicted by means of a symbol or direction (cf. Figure 8 in the chapter on string instruments).

4. 3. 5 *Glissando* variants on the harp and their notation

The basic *glissando* on the harp is strictly speaking not a *glissando* because this technique does actually not imply a gliding change of pitch, but gliding from one string to another. However, in this work, the term *glissando* is utilised to describe all sorts of gliding motions and, therefore, also employed for horizontal gliding motions on the strings of a harp. Further, *Sevsay* presents various basic *glissando* techniques and methods of notation. In order to clarify these, the most important ones are discussed here and methods suggested that comply with the notation of the basic *glissando* on the other instruments.

The normal *glissando* is in the compendium referred to as *flux éoliens*. When executing this technique *sulla tavola*, the *glissando* technique is called *flux hautboïstique*. Moreover, a *glissando* with the fingernails is referred to as *flux en grêle* and a *glissando* with the nails *sulla tavola* as *xyloflux*. These techniques may be depicted by means of the common *glissando* notation and – dependent on the articulation – an additional fingernail symbol (cf. inter alia Figure 1 in the chapter on string instruments) and the direction *sulla tavola*. Another technique, designated as *bruissement éoliens*, refers to a tetrad *glissando*. *Sevsay* suggests a special method of notation, which inter alia implies the lowest and highest tone of the chord and oblique arrows. However, since it is sufficient to employ the standard *glissando* notation and depict all tones of the chord in the beginning and at the end of the *glissando*, another method does not have to be employed. Further, a very rapid *glissando* is referred to as *accords en jet* and also depicted in a special manner. However, when the starting point, endpoint and the duration of the *glissando* is given, the harpist knows how fast the *glissando* is supposed to be executed. Therefore, the standard *glissando* notation can also be applied in this case. Further, the term *trémolo éolien* refers to a repetitive *glissando* executed in between two tones. *Sevsay* suggests notating this technique by depicting the two tones and utilising a *tremolo* symbol[25]. However, a *glissando* of that kind is in Chapter »1. 2. 2 The bow-*glissando*« defined as a trill-*glissando*. This is because a repetitive gliding switch between two tones is executed instead of a *tremolo*, which would signify that the amplitude is modulated. Therefore, the method of notation for the so-called *trémolo éoliens* makes use of the *glissando* notation in combination with the common way of depicting a trill. As in Figure 14, an augmented trill – which exceeds the normal trill intervals – is requested, the two tones »g – e♭2/G3 – E♭5« are notated and additionally written in brackets. Hence the player is, in the example, requested to perform a repetitive *glissando* motion from »g/G3« to »e♭2/E♭5«.

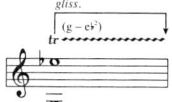

Fig. 14 The *trémolo éoliens* or trill-*glissando*.

Finally, *Sevsay* even suggests a special method of depiction for a sequence of *glissandi*. The technique designated as ascending/descending eolian chords refers to playing the first *glissando* with one finger, the second *glissando* with another finger et cetera[26]. However, this technique may also be depicted in the conventional manner by notating a *glissando* from, for instance, a very low tone to a low tone, then a *glissando* from a high tone to a higher tone etc.

---

[25] Cf. ibid., pp. 224-229.
[26] Cf. ibid., pp. 229f.

The order of the fingers can be depicted as on the piano, e. g. 1, 2, 3 etc. However, the impact of determining the fingers is quite low. Alternatively, the graphic depiction of the hand introduced in the chapter on string instruments (Figure 90) could be employed in order to request the utilisation of particular parts of the hand when executing a *glissando* (cf., for instance, Figure 29 in the chapter on keyboard instruments).

4. 3. 6 The pedal-*glissando*

The pedal-*glissando* is a harp technique. It is normally performed simultaneous with, or subsequent to, plucking a string. When the pedal position is changed, the pitch may – dependent on the previous position – be raised and/or lowered. Moreover, when adjusting the pedal in between two positions, microtones are produced. Additionally, a trill-*glissando* may also be played with the pedals, and the alteration of the pedal position may solely be used as an effect. In such a case, the string is not plucked. However, it needs to be noted that this effect is controversial because some harpists contend that it is damaging to the mechanism. As a reminder, the left foot controls the D-, C- and H/B-pedal and the right foot the E-, F-, G- and A-pedal. Two adjacent pedals may only be moved simultaneously when the starting point and endpoint of the motion is equal, e. g. »F♯ – G♯« to »F – G«[27].

4. 3. 6. 1 Previous methods of notation

There are mainly two different ways to notate this articulation. One is to depict the pedal-*glissando* underneath the harp's notation systems. This method is employed by *Berio* in »Sequenza II«. As is apparent from Figure 15, the harpist is supposed to change the position of the F-pedal from »F« to »F♯«, then to »F♭« and back to »F«. Simultaneously, a normal *glissando* from »a/A3« to »G/G2« (the system is in bass clef) is played with the left hand for the duration of a quaver and a rapid repetitive sequence, which inter alia involves the »f¹/F4« (the system is in treble clef), is played with the right hand.

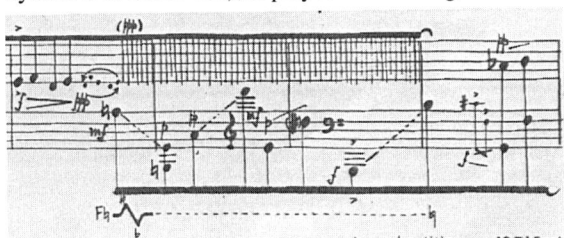

Fig. 15 Berio, Sequenza II, p. 1.

In »Sonant (1960/....)« *Kagel* notates this articulation similarly. Changing the pedal position (which is, in this case, referred to as a *portato*) is requested by means of an arrow and a trill-*glissando* by a waved line:

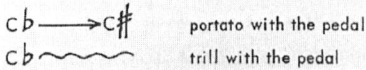

Fig. 16 Kagel, Sonant, p. 21.

The other method of notation is to give the direction pedal-*glissando* and depict the extent of the *glissando* by means of transposed notes. *Holliger*, in »Partita (II)«, makes use of this method. As can be seen in Figure 17, the harpist is supposed to execute a pedal-*glissando*

---

[27] Cf. Sevsay, Handbuch, pp. 218f., 232f., 239 and 241 and Stone, Notation, pp. 242f.

from »D/D2« to »D♯/D♯2« for the duration of a semiquaver, then back to »D/D2« for the duration of a quaver and finally to »D♭/D♭2« for the duration of a semiquaver.

Fig. 17 Holliger, Partita (II), p. 24.

Moreover, both methods can also be used in combination and *glissandi* to microtones be depicted by means of microtonal accidentals[28].

4. 3. 6. 2 Discussion

When depicting the pedal-*glissando* in the same manner a change in the pedal positions is requested, the articulation may easily be comprehended by the harpist. However, *Berio* notates the pedal positions by means of a diagram[29] and the pedal-*glissando* by characters, accidentals and a line (cf. Figure 15), which leads to confusion. However, the method of depiction could easily be simplified by notating both – a change in the pedal positions and the pedal-*glissando* – similarly. Hence when wanting to depict the pedal-*glissando* by means of characters, accidentals and a line, the pedal position as well should be notated in this way, e. g. »D, C♯, B/B♭ ‖ E, F♯, G, A♭«. Moreover, in »Sequenza II« the duration of the pedal-*glissandi* is only determined approximately. A greater degree of exactness could be gained by depicting the duration either by means of the harp's notation system or introducing a distinct timeline for the pedal. Further, because in this work any kind of *glissando* is depicted by means of arrows, and there is no need to further emphasise that the pedal is lifted or lowered when giving directions, such as »F«, »F♯« and »F♭«, *Kagel's* method of depicting the pedal-*glissando* (cf. Figure 16) is preferred over *Berio's* approach. Hence it is favoured here to use an arrow instead of *Berio's* line. However, it might be helpful to outline that a pedal-*glissando* is performed by giving a direction, such as pedal-*glissando* or *glissando del pedale*. Moreover, concerning the trill-*glissando* with the pedal, it may be stated that *Kagel's* approach needs to be extended in order to depict the trill in the conventional and a more exact manner. Thus a trill and *glissando* symbols, which depicts the extent of the trill-*glissando*, should instead be used.

Furthermore, *Holliger's* method of notation (cf. Figure 17) may easily be comprehended when only one string is involved in the *glissando*. However, it becomes confusing when several strings are plucked and only some of them are involved in the *glissando*. Moreover, it cannot be employed when – as, for instance, in Figure 15 – a basic *glissando* is used in combination with a pedal-*glissando*. Because the harpist is used to the depiction of the pedal position by means of diagrams, symbols or characters and accidentals, it is also simpler to depict the pedal-*glissando* in this fashion.

4. 3. 6. 3 Suggestion for the notation of the pedal-*glissando*

The pedal-*glissando* is notated here by means of characters, accidentals, arrows and giving the direction *glissando del pedale*. Further, an additional timeline is introduced in order to depict the duration of the pedal-*glissando* independently from the harp's notation system. As is apparent from Figure 18, the player is initially supposed to execute a *glissando* upwards,

---

[28] Cf. Sevsay, Handbuch, pp. 232f.
[29] Cf. Berio, Sequenza II, p. 1.

starting from »a/A3« and pluck the chord »G – c – d/G2 – C3 – D3«. Both the *glissando* and the *pizzicato* last for the duration of a minim. Simultaneously, the harpist is requested to move the D- and C-pedal from »D – C« to »D♯ – C♯« for the duration of a quaver, then back to »D – C« for the duration of a semiquaver, to »D♭ – C♭« for the duration of another semiquaver, subsequently to »D – C« for the duration of a quaver and finally to »D♯ – C♯« for the duration of another quaver. Additionally, the right foot executes a trill-*glissando* »A – A♭«, which ends on the »A♭«. The resulting pedal positions are then depicted in brackets. After the pedal-*glissando* has ended, the harpist plays a »b¹/B♭4« and the chord »G – c♯ – d♯«/G2 – C♯3 – D♯3«.

Fig. 18 The pedal-*glissando*.

There is no need to use a timeline for the trill-*glissando* because it lasts as long as the normal *glissando*. When wanting to depict the duration of two pedal-*glissandi* independently from the harp's notation system, they can be either notated by means of the same timeline or two independent ones. Further, when the pedal is supposed to be adjusted between two positions, a microtonal symbol requesting a quarter tone above/below the middle position »♮« can be employed (or a quarter tone below the bottom position »♯« and a quarter tone above the top position »♭«, respectively). As mentioned above, microtonal symbols are, in this work however, not discussed, but a suggestion for the notation of microtonal frequencies presented in »Part II: Electroacoustic music – 1. 1. 1 Periodic wave generators and their envelopes«. Pedals can also be constantly adjusted to such a half depressed position, but, in such a case, the foot that adjusts the pedal needs to hold it when playing the respective microtone and cannot simultaneously set other pedals[30]. Additionally, a so-called rattling effect is obtained by half depressing the pedal[31]. Further, the production of pedal »noise« can be requested similarly to the pedal-*glissando*. When the pedals are moved vigorously and the strings are not plucked, the strings anyway start to vibrate. In the case of using this effect, the additional direction *lasciar vibrare* should complement the pedal-*glissando*. The dynamic level of the pedal »noise« is always very low.

4. 4 Extended modes of attack

One extended mode of attack explained in this chapter can be described as touching the string after the attack. It is referred to as the ***toccato***. There are a further two main extended modes of attack with items. One involves the **utilisation of a bow** and the other one the **utilisation**

---

[30] Cf. Sevsay, Handbuch, p. 239.
[31] Lachenmann, Gefühle, no page named [foreword].

of beaters. The latter is principally an extended harp technique. Additionally, so-called **extended** *battuto* **techniques** may be executed. These articulations are mainly related to the guitar,
but may in some cases also be employed on the harp. Further, **strumming** is a guitar technique that needs to be discussed here because there is no conventional method of notation for
this articulation.

4. 4. 1 The *toccato* and its notation

The *toccato* articulation has been extensively discussed in Chapter »1. 3. 3 The *saltando*,
balzando and *toccato* and its notation«. As shown there, it can be notated by simply giving the
direction *toccato*, depicting the string that is touched by a common note head and determining
the playing position. On the harp this action may, for instance, be executed by means of the
tuning key (*colla chiave toccato*), and on the guitar it may additionally be performed on the
fretboard. In the case of the latter, the method of notation presented in Figure 5 needs to be
combined with the direction *toccato*. Further, any item or beater can be used for this technique
(cf. Chapter »4. 1 Extended *pizzicato*, *tremolo* and trill techniques and their notation« for the
depiction of the tuning key and other items as well as Chapter »4. 4. 3 The utilisation of
beaters and its notation« for the depiction of beaters). When the string has been played and
still vibrates, a sound effect occurs. Moreover, another *toccato* articulation, referred to as the
buzz-*pizzicato*, is discussed in Chapter »4. 7. 1 Exact muting stops and their notation«
because it is related to the depiction of muting stops.

4. 4. 2 The utilisation of a bow and its notation

The utilisation of a bow on the harp and guitar is strongly related to the common usage of the
bow on string instruments and hence can be depicted in a similar manner. Therefore, the conventional method of notation used to request the utilisation of the bow on strings may be
transferred to the harp and guitar: the direction *arco* or *con/col arco* should be used when the
player is required to bow the strings of these instruments, the produced tone should be depicted and the playing position be notated. Moreover, when plucked instruments are bowed, the
type of bow may be determined (e. g. contrabass bow), a so-called *glissando d'arco* be performed (cf. Chapter »1. 2. 2 The bow-*glissando*«), all parts of the instrument be bowed (cf.
Chapter »1. 5 Playing exceptional spots«) as well as other conventional and unconventional
bowing techniques be requested. In such cases, the conventional methods of notation or the
ones presented in the chapter on string instruments, may easily be transferred. However, it
needs to be noted that, in the case of the harp, the bow needs to be tilted when bowing the
strings, so that no other string is touched[32]. Therefore, the manoeuvrability of the bow is limited.

4. 4. 3 The utilisation of beaters and its notation

Beaters are primarily used on the harp, but may also be utilised to strike the strings of the
guitar or string instruments. As is apparent from the chapter on percussion instruments, beaters are always depicted by means of symbols. Further, the standard utilisation of beaters on
the harp is strongly related to striking mallet instruments and, therefore, can be depicted by
means of the conventional method of notation employed for these instruments. Hence when
beating the strings of a harp or executing *glissandi*, a beater symbol can be used in combination with a depiction of the strings that are struck or involved in the *glissando*. Additionally,
the playing position needs to be described. Moreover, most extended harp techniques and
several extended beaters attacks, such as plucking the string with a beater, modifying the

---

[32] Cf. Holliger, Partita (II), p. 16.

point of impact, executing a vertical *glissando* with/without plucking, striking with the handle of a beater or entire length of a stick, rubbing motions with beaters as well as the stop attack, can be performed on the harp. They may be depicted by using the paradigms presented in Figures 1 (extended *pizzicato*), 6 (modification of the point of plucking) and 13 (vertical *glissando*) in combination with a beater symbol as well as by transferring the methods from Figures 9 (common and extended attacks), 34, 35 (rubbing motions) and 66 (stop attack) in the chapter on percussion instruments. Moreover, strokes on the bodies of plucked instruments are discussed in Chapter »4. 8 Percussive effects and their notation«. Further, most of these attacks may be employed on the guitar and string instruments. However, the articulation referred to as the basic *glissando* on the harp is on the guitar and strings referred to as strumming and discussed in the following chapter while the vertical *glissando* is on these instruments described as a harmonic-*glissando* without plucking/bowing (cf. Chapters »4. 3. 4 The harmonic-*glissando* without plucking and its notation« and »1. 2. 1 The harmonic-*glissando* without bowing and its notation«).

Another extended technique – which is primarily employed on the harp, but may also be transferred to the guitar or string instruments – is to insert an item (e. g. a tuning key, plectrum, metal stick, pencil or nail) in between two strings and repetitively hit these. *Sevsay* describes this kind of action as a *tremolo* and suggests notating it in this way[33]. However, it is not actually the amplitude that is modulated (as in the case of a *tremolo*) since a rapid alteration between two tones is executed (as in the case of a trill). Nevertheless, this **extended trill with items** cannot be depicted by means of a trill symbol because trills are normally plucked on the harp as well as on the guitar and string instruments executed with the left hand. Hence the utilisation of a trill symbol would in this context lead to ambiguity. Instead, the articulation is rather regarded as a rare extended beater technique. In order to notate it in a simple manner, a sketch of the action is employed here. This is because it is, as mentioned, the most comprehensible and simplest method of depiction.

As can be seen in Figure 19, the player is supposed to perform an extended trill *sulla tavola* with a tuning key, and then a plectrum, in between the strings »c¹/C4« and »d¹/D4«. These actions are notated by means of two notes that depict the tones, a description of the playing position, the symbol for the tuning key/plectrum (cf. Chapter »4. 1 Extended *pizzicato*, *tremolo* and trill techniques and their notation«) and a sketch of the action. Each trill lasts for the duration of a minim.

Fig. 19 The extended trill with items.

When transferring this articulation to the guitar or string instruments, fingerings may additionally be employed and only four to six strings need to be depicted (e. g. on the guitar by the indications e, H/B, G, D, A, E). Further, the playing position may on all instruments be modified during the extended trill with items or when playing with beaters (cf. Chapter »4. 3. 1 The progressive modification of the point of plucking and its notation«).

4. 4. 4 Extended *battuto* techniques and their notation

Extended *battuto* techniques have been discussed in Chapter »1. 3. 2 Extended *battuto* and *tratto* techniques and their notation«. As shown there, *battuto* articulations that involve the

---

[33] Cf. Sevsay, Handbuch, p. 244.

screw of the bow or items may be depicted by means of a direction for or presenting a symbol of the item and giving the additional direction *battuto*. Such a **battuto with the screw/with items** may be transferred to the harp and guitar. As these techniques may be used in a similar manner on plucked instruments, they can be notated in the same way. The position on the string can, in the case of the harp, be depicted by means of the common playing positions and be modified. In the case of the guitar, it may be notated by means of the common playing positions and the method employed for playing on the fretboard (cf. Chapter »5. 3. 1 The progressive modification of the point of plucking and its notation«). Further, it is possible on the guitar to produce tones by fingering the strings without plucking. When doing so, the finger needs to hit the string with force and push it against the fretboard. As shown, this articulation is regarded as a **left-hand** *battuto* and can be depicted by giving the direction *battuto* (*mano sinistra*) as well as notating the produced tone (also cf. Figures 29 and 32 in the chapter on string instruments for the *battuto* on the fingerboard and the left-hand *battuto*).

4. 4. 5 Strumming and its notation

Strumming is a standard guitar technique, which may also be employed on string instruments especially on the violin or viola when playing *al mandolino* with a plectrum (cf. Chapter »1. 1 Extended *pizzicato* techniques and their notation«). As mentioned, this technique resembles the *glissando* on the harp. However, in the case of the guitar and strings, it cannot be notated in this way because the common *glissando* is executed with the left hand on these instruments.

Most composers notate the articulation by means of a symbol derived from the notation of *arpeggi*. This is because the articulation is strongly related to strumming. In »Salut für Caudwell« *Lachenmann,* for instance, depicts a downbeat by means of an arrow pointing downwards and an upbeat by means of an arrow pointing upwards placed over the notation system[34] (whilst the triangular note heads request that a plectrum is used)[35]:

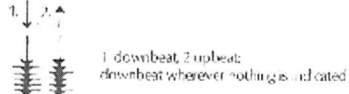

Fig. 20 Lachenmann, Salut, no page named [foreword].

Further, *Kagel,* in »Heterophonie«, places such an arrow in front of the chord[36] and *Crumb,* in »Mundus canis ("A dog's world")«[37], uses the *arpeggio* symbol in order to request strumming. However, the latter method of notation is confusing because it suggests that an *arpeggio* and strumming is the same articulation. By contrast, when playing *arpeggi*, the string is plucked and, in the case of the strumming, the hand glides over the string. Therefore, *Lachenmann's* and *Kagel's* methods are preferred here over the one by *Crumb.* When compared, *Kagel's* method of notation is closer related to traditional notation because it is employed in the same way as the *arpeggio* symbol and, therefore, favoured. Further, the action of strumming does not only resemble the *arpeggio*, but also the up- and down-bow motion on string instruments. However, the notation of this action by means of up- and down-bow symbols should not be employed because this could lead to confusion when using this technique on strings. As can be seen in Figure 21, the player is supposed to strum the (written) chord

---

[34] *Lachenmann* refers to a downbeat as a motion from the highest to the lowest string and to an upbeat as a motion from the lowest to the highest strings.

[35] Cf. Lachenmann, Salut, no page named [foreword].

[36] Cf. Kagel, Heterophonie, p. IX.

[37] Cf. Crumb, Mundus, p. 5.

»c¹ – g¹ – d²/C4 – G4 – D5« twice (upbeat, downbeat) with the hand and hence in the normal way. Subsequently, the same chord is strummed twice (downbeat, upbeat) with a plectrum (cf. Chapter »4. 1 Extended *pizzicato*, *tremolo* and trill techniques and their notation« for the notation of the plectrum).

Fig. 21 Strumming.

4. 5 Playing exceptional spots and its notation

Two exceptional spots may be played on plucked instruments. In the case of the harp, the player may pluck the strings **on the neck** above the tuning pins and, in the case of the guitar, **inside the headstock**. All other techniques are related to the utilisation of a bow: on the harp the body and other parts, such as the tuning pins or pedal, and on the guitar the body and parts, such as the tuning pegs, nut or headstock, may be bowed. The methods of notation for these actions may be derived from the paradigms presented in Chapter »1. 5 Playing exceptional spots« (also cf. Chapter »4. 4. 2 The utilisation of a bow and its notation«).

The action of plucking the strings on the neck is strongly related to plucking string instruments inside the pegbox. As shown in Chapter »1. 5. 3 Playing the tuning pegs, pegbox and scroll«, the latter articulation is notated by means of the string clef system and spherical note heads. However, even though the two techniques resemble each other, the method of notation cannot be transferred in its full extent. This is because the string clef system cannot be employed on the harp. Nevertheless, plucking on the neck may, in this case, simply be requested by means of spherical note heads and a pitch-based notation system that determines the string that is plucked. When requesting this technique, it needs to be taken into account that the pedal position does not have an impact on the produced sound. Therefore, all accidentals can be dismissed[38]. A suggestion for the notation of this technique is presented in Figure 22. As can be seen there, the harpist is supposed to pluck the strings in the order of »d/D3«, »G/G2«, »A/A2« and »e/E3« on the neck. The dynamic level of this articulation is always low[39].

Fig. 22 *Pizzicato* on the neck.

Plucking inside the headstock of a guitar is likewise strongly related to the technique of plucking inside the pegbox of string instruments. However, in this case, the string clef system may be employed. Therefore, the articulation may on the guitar be requested by means of spherical note heads in combination with this notation system (cf. Figure 4 as well as Figure 75 in the chapter on string instruments). As in the case of the harp, the dynamic level of the articulation is always low.

4. 6 Muting and its notation

This chapter mainly focuses on the muting of the harp. This is because the execution of exact muting stops is regarded here as the common way of muting the guitar and subsequent muffling does not need to be requested specifically. With regard to the harp, the muting position

---

[38] Cf. Sevsay, Handbuch, p. 243.

[39] Cf. ibid., p. 243.

also has an impact on the produced sound. However, this technique is discussed in Chapter »4. 7. 1 Exact muting stops and their notation«. Moreover, when all strings of a harp (or guitar) are supposed to be muted, the instrument can be prepared, e. g. by inserting a strip of paper between the strings. Such actions are discussed in Chapter »4. 9 Preparing the instrument and its notation«. Besides these preparations, there is one muting variant on the harp and guitar. It may be described as muting the string with the palm whilst simultaneously plucking it with the same hand. This constant muffling resembles the **application of mutes**. As shown in Chapters »2. 8. 1 The application of mutes« and »3. 4. 2 Hand muffling and its notation«, it can be notated by giving the direction with/without mute (hand) or *con/senza sordino (mano)*. When playing in this way, the dynamic level is always low.

Further, the **hand muffling** of the harp strongly resembles the execution of this technique on mallet instruments. As this muting technique has been extensively discussed in Chapter »3. 4 Muting«, another discussion is dismissed here, but the methods of notation transferred to the harp. There are – according to *Sevsay* – mainly three subsequent muting techniques on the harp. The first technique is defined by him as the normal muting and refers to the muting of tones according to their duration[40]. This is valid for playing *non lasciar vibrare* because the tones are then supposed to be muted according to the depicted duration and no specific muting symbol is necessary. However, when playing *lasciar vibrare*, hand muffling needs to be specifically requested. As can be seen in Figure 23, only the muting sign may be employed when it distinctly requests that all tones played by one hand are muted simultaneously. However, when the tones are supposed to be muted in a sequence, the muting sign needs to be used in combination with a depiction of the string that is muted (cf. Figures 63 and 64 in the chapter on percussion instruments).

Fig. 23 The normal muting.

Further, *Sevsay* refers to a second muting technique as isolated tones or *sons isolés*. It implies that one tone is plucked and muted exactly when the next tone is played[41]. When playing *non lasciar vibrare*, this technique may simply be requested by notating a sequence of tones and – optionally – *staccato* dots. However, when playing *lasciar vibrare*, another method of notation needs to be used. As is apparent from Figure 24, the harpist is supposed to pluck an »f¹/F4« and mute it exactly when the next tone »g¹/G4« is played. Because such an action cannot be depicted by means of a single notation system, two systems are employed.

Fig. 24 Isolated tones (*lasciar vibrare*).

The third technique is called *sons etouffés*, damped tones. However, it merely refers to a subsequent muting that is requested by means of the muting sign. Therefore, it does not differ

---

[40] Cf. ibid., p. 233.
[41] Ibid., p. 233.

from the normal muting when playing *lasciar vibrare*. *Sevsay* further describes variants of the *sons etouffés*, e. g. muting only some of the strings that have been previously plucked, muting a set of pitches or muting in a sequential manner[42]. All of these variants may be depicted by means of the paradigm presented in Figure 23.

4.7 Extended stopping techniques

There is one extended stopping technique that may be employed on the guitar and harp. It is referred to as **exact muting stops**. The chapter on this articulation implies the description of the buzz-*pizzicato*. Additionally, on the guitar **half harmonic stops** may be executed and *barré* **stops** be requested.

4.7.1 Exact muting stops and their notation

As mentioned in Chapter »1. 6. 2 Exact muting stops and their notation«, diamond-shaped note heads are commonly used to depict harmonics. They can also be utilised for the depiction of muting stops because the pressure that is applied to the string is similar to when fingering harmonics. When the string is fingered on an off-node position with the same pressure, it is muted. Due to the similar nature of the guitar and string instruments, the method of notation suggested in the chapter on string instruments can easily be transferred to this kind of plucked instrument. Moreover, the same is valid for the harp. However, in the case of this instrument, only a very limited number of muting stops may be executed on the highest strings. The method of notation for off-node positions may be derived from the method of depiction for harmonics with diamond-shaped note heads (cf. Figure 12). When requesting muting stops on the harp, the player needs to simply be advised to finger an off-node position. As can be seen in Figure 25, the harpist is supposed to play four quavers »d/D3«, »G/G2«, »A/A2« and »e/E3«. When plucking these tones, the string is at the same time touched at an off-node position (here constantly a tritone, starting from the neck).

Fig. 25 Exact muting stops on the harp.

When the strings of a harp are muted close to the soundboard, the produced sound is referred to as xylophonic tones or *sons xylophoniques*. Moreover, when muting stops are executed approximately in the middle of the string length (beyond the nodal point) and plucked *sulla tavola*, they are referred to as xylophonic sounds *a la guitarra*[43]. This technique may further be extended by using the whole hand, the tuning key or foreign objects, such as a threaded rod or a long wooden stick instead of the fingers. When doing so, a larger range of strings may simultaneously be muted. These extended muting stops may be notated in the same way as the basic muting stops. However, an additional direction, such as with the tuning key or *con/col chiave*, or a symbol for the foreign object should additionally be employed when using items and not the hand (cf. Chapters »4. 1 Extended *pizzicato*, *tremolo* and trill techniques and their notation« and »4. 4. 4 Extended *battuto* techniques and their notation«). Moreover, when a set of pitches or a cluster, respectively, is supposed to be muted, a special method of notation needs to be employed. This is because the utilisation of common notes in combination with diamond-shaped note heads would lead to an unclear appearance of the score. Such an **exact cluster muting stop** is requested here by means of a squared cluster

---

[42] Cf. ibid., pp. 234f.
[43] Cf. ibid., pp. 235f.

note (cf. Chapters »5. 6. 1 Clusters« and »5. 6. 3 Exact muting stops/harmonics and their notation« for a detailed explanation of this technique) – which depicts the muted strings – and a cluster of diamond-shaped note heads. In Figure 26, the player is required to mute the cluster »A/A2« to »h/B3« on the tritone position »e♭/E♭3« to »f¹/F4« (only the lowest and highest tone of these clusters is notated exactly) for the duration of a minim. In this case, he uses a threaded rod to mute the strings. This item is depicted here by means of a symbol. Alternatively, it could be notated by means of a direction. During the muting, the harpist plays four quavers »d/D3«, »G/G2«, »A/A2« and »h/B3«. The »G/G2« is, in this case, not muted. In order to facilitate the notation of cluster muting stops (or harmonics), the muting position should be the same for each string. Otherwise, the appearance of the score could become unclear. Moreover, the harpist may also mute single strings or chords with items. This action can be depicted by means of the method displayed in the previous figure and an additional symbol for the item. When it becomes unclear – because too many strings are involved – the notation for the cluster muting should be employed. Further, when muting strings with items, an additional buzzing sound may occur.

Fig. 26 Cluster muting with a threaded rod.

Furthermore, the **buzz-*pizzicato*** is executed on both – the harp and guitar – in the same way as on string instruments. Therefore, the method of notation presented in the chapter on string instruments (Figure 86) may be transferred to plucked instruments. As mentioned in the section on the buzz-*pizzicato*, there are three variants of producing it: 1. By slightly touching the lingering string with the fingernail after a *pizzicato*. 2. By slightly touching the lingering string with the fingertip after a *pizzicato*. 3. By slightly touching the string with the fingernail during the performance of a *pizzicato*. In the case of variants 1 and 2, a *pizzicato*-sound is followed by a buzzing whilst, in the case of variant 3, a *pizzicato*-sound and buzzing blend. In Figure 27, the method of notation suggested in the chapter on string instruments is transferred to the harp. The *toccato* action may – in the case of variant 1 – be notated in the same way as the common *toccato* (cf. Chapter »4. 4. 1 The *toccato*«) and – in the case of variants 2 and 3 – by means of the *toccato* and harmonic notation. All actions are performed on the »f¹/F4«-string. In the example, all three variants of the buzz-*pizzicato* are displayed: 1. The player performs a demisemiquaver *pizzicato sulla tavola* »f¹/F4« and subsequently touches the string with the fingernail on the *sulla tavola* position for the duration of a semiquaver. The *legato* slur underlines that the string is not previously muted, but the tone still lingers when the string is touched after a demisemiquaver (the *legato* slur apparently only needs to be employed on the harp when playing *non lasciar vibrare*). 2. The player performs a *pizzicato* »f¹/F4« and subsequently touches the string with the fingertip on the position »g¹/G4« for the duration of a semiquaver. The *legato* slur emphasises that again the »f¹/F4« still lingers and the string is additionally touched after a demisemiquaver. 3. The player performs a *pizzicato* and simultaneously touches the string with the fingernail on the position »g¹/G4«. The direction *pizzicato e toccato* is used – instead of merely depicting a fingernail muting stop that is plucked – in order to outline that it is not a fingernail *pizzicato* that is supposed to be executed.

161

Fig. 27 The buzz-*pizzicato* on the harp.

4. 7. 2 Half harmonic stops and their notation

Half harmonic stops are a guitar technique. As on string instruments, the applied finger pressure is higher than when stopping harmonics and lower than when fingering normal tones. However, when executing half harmonic stops on the guitar, the string hits the frets when plucked and an additional buzzing sound evolves. The technique is most effective on the lower strings. Because the half harmonic articulation on the guitar is strongly related to the performance of this technique on string instruments, it may be notated in the same way as in Chapter »1. 6. 1 Half harmonic stops and their notation«. Hence the employed method of notation makes use of diamond-shaped note heads to depict the stopping position and a complementary white and black diamond-shaped symbol placed above the note in order to request the stopping technique. As mentioned, diamond-shaped note heads are employed since the fingering of half harmonic stops is rather a variation of fingering harmonics than normal tones.

4. 7. 3 *Barré* stops and their notation

Barré stops are a guitar technique. They can be defined as using the index finger to simultaneously depress all strings on the same fretboard position. This technique is discussed here because *Lachenmann*, in »Salut für Caudwell«, employs a special method of depiction in order to notate these stops. As can be seen in Figure 28, he makes use of diamond-shaped note heads (to depict harmonic fingering) and notates only the highest and lowest tone of the stop in order to request the *barré* stop.

 Barré stops (which predominate in this piece) are generally notated with vertical connecting beams due to their pitch restriction on the first and sixth strings; this applies even if not all of the six strings are played.

Fig. 28 Lachenmann, Salut, no page named [foreword].

Further, *Lachenmann* introduces an additional system that is used to describe which string is in combination with the constantly fingered *barré* stop plucked[44]. However, the utilisation of two systems complicates the notation of normally fingered tones/harmonics/muting stops because they could sufficiently be depicted by utilising only one notation system. Further, there is no need to alter the conventional method of notation for stops when requesting this special fingering technique. However, it could be helpful to additionally depict the *barré* chord when the player is supposed to constantly finger it whilst only plucking, for instance, single strings. The fingered chord could, in such a case, be notated in brackets above the normal notation system.

4. 8 Percussive effects and their notation

Percussive effects may be produced on the body (or other parts) of the harp and guitar as well as on their strings. In the case of the harp, the hands or items may be used to strike the neck, shoulder, column, pillar, soundboard etc. of the instrument. However, it needs to be noted that sharp-edged items should not be utilised[45]. As shown in Chapter »1. 7. 1 Strokes on the body

---

[44] Cf. Lachenmann, Salut, pp. 1ff.
[45] Cf. Sevsay, Handbuch, p. 244.

and their notation«, hits on the body of an instrument may be depicted by means of a drawing of the instrument's body – which enables the determination of the point of impact – in combination with a drawing of the player's hand. When items are supposed to be used, another symbol replaces the drawing of the hand (cf., for instance, Chapter »3. 1. 1 Introducing special agents of attack and its notation«). In Figure 29, various **strokes on the body** of a harp are requested. They are executed in the order of with the knuckles on the column – with the side of the fist on the soundboard – with the palm on the shoulder – with the index, middle and ring finger on the crown – with the tip of the thumb, index and middle finger on the soundboard – with the tip and fingernail of the index finger on the soundbox. All actions are separated by quaver rests (also cf. Figures 89 to 91 in the chapter on string instruments) and performed with the left hand. When the right hand is supposed to be used, a mirror inverted drawing of the harp should be used. However, in this case, it needs to be considered that the upper part of the instrument's body is resting against the right shoulder.

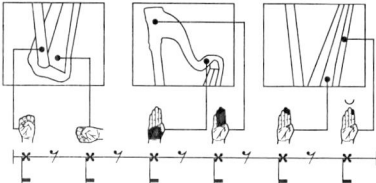

Fig. 29 Strokes on the body of a harp.

Further, a special striking technique may be executed on the harp. It is referred to as *sons timbaliques* (timpanic tones). When requested, one finger of the right hand dabs the resonating area of the soundboard whilst the left hand plucks the string[46]. In order to depict timpanic tones, two notation systems need to be used: one that depicts the plucked string and one that depicts the dabbing of the resonating area. Because this spot varies according to the string that is plucked and needs to be determined in a very exact way, a drawing of the instrument cannot be used in this case. *Varèse*, in »Amériques«[47], notates this action by means of an additional enclosed »T« placed above the note[48]. Another simple variant was to give the direction *son timbalique* or *suono timpanico*, employ a drawing of the hand and depict the percussive effect – as usual – by means of x-shaped note heads in a single lined notation system with no clef:

Fig. 30 *Sons timbaliques.*

Additionally, *Sevsay* mentions the rare **anvil effect**. It is produced when the tip of the tuning key is used to stroke the brass plate, which is located over the tuning pins[49]. This arti-

---

[46] Ibid., p. 245.

[47] Edgard Varèse: Amériques. Performance edition prepared form the original manuscript by Chou Wen-chung. San Giuliano Milanese 1997.

[48] Varèse, Amériques, p. 1.

[49] Sevsay, Handbuch, p. 245.

culation resembles two techniques: the bow-*glissando dietro il tasto* and simple rubbing motions, as employed on the strings of a snare drum (cf. Chapter »1. 2. 2 The bow-*glissando*« and »3. 2. 6 Playing the snares«). In order to depict the anvil effect in accordance with these techniques, a special notation system, which consists of two components – a traditional time-line and a representation of the length of the brass plate – may be employed. Additionally, a sketch might have to be used in order to outline what the player needs to do in order to produce the desired sound (cf. Figures 17 and 18 in the chapter on string instruments). The tuning key should, in this case, be depicted by means of a symbol and the utilisation of its tip be requested by an additional little arrow (cf. Figure 1 as well as Figure 9 in the chapter on percussion instruments).

As mentioned in Chapter »1. 7. 2 Strokes on the strings and their notation«, **strokes on the strings** may be described as stop attacks executed with the hand. Because this technique is on string, percussion and plucked instruments executed in a similar manner, it can be notated in the same way and hence by utilising a symbol of the hand, a muting sign ($\oplus$) and determining the playing position (cf. Figure 93 in the chapter on string instruments). Further, in the case of the guitar, dead strokes on the fretboard may be requested. When executing dead strokes with the hand, it does not make a difference whether the strings are additionally muted with the other hand or not because they do not vibrate subsequently to the stroke. However, when using a beater or the wood of a bow, the strings linger after the attack. Therefore, the method of notation may be augmented in order to make the player additionally execute exact muting stops (or apply a mute on the harp), which keep the strings from vibrating. Moreover, in the case of the guitar, the string may also simultaneously be depressed and strokes on the fret-board be requested. These articulations may depicted in the same way as in the chapter on string instruments (Figure 94 – also cf. Chapters »4. 4. 3 The utilisation of beaters and its notation«, »4. 6 Muting and its notation« and »4. 7. 1 Exact muting stops and their notation«). Finally, stop attacks with the right hand's palm are a popular technique on acoustic guitars. They are often used to mute a previously plucked string. In order to depict this, the plucked tone and the stop attack would have to be connected by means of a *legato slur*.

4. 9 Preparing the instrument and its notation

Plucked instruments can, for instance, be prepared by means of the preparations applied to string instruments, such as placing a knitting needle between the strings or muting a number of or all strings with adhesive tape. Further, *Varèse*, in »Amériques«, for instance, requests the player to mute the harp by inserting a strip of paper at the upper extremity of the string[50]. Other preparations may involve cloth or foam rubber[51]. As in the case of the other instruments, there are numerous ways of preparing plucked instruments. Similarly it is also, on the one hand, barely possible to list them all and subsequently develop a coherent method of depiction whilst, on the other hand, it is also not necessary to do so since most preparations are executed previously to a performance and may simply be described in the foreword to a work. Further, when preparations are supposed to be executed during a performance, they are here suggested being always notated by means of a sketch. This is because it is the simplest way of depicting these. Such a sketch should include the determination of the strings that are prepared, e. g. when only a certain range is muted with adhesive tape. When the sketch is not clear enough, it may be complemented by an explanation (cf. Chapters »1. 8 Preparing the instrument and its notation« and »2. 6. 2 Constructional modifications and their notation«). Nevertheless, preparations may lead to the introduction of new playing techniques that should then be notated in accordance with all other techniques presented in this work.

---

[50] Varèse, Amériques, p. 13.
[51] Cf. Sevsay, Handbuch, p. 147.

5. THE TECHNIQUES OF KEYBOARD INSTRUMENTS

The chapter on keyboard instruments solely focuses on the grand piano. All other keyboard instruments, such as the upright piano, organ, harpsichord or celesta, are not discussed specifically here in order to limit the extent of the work. Nevertheless, many augmented techniques that may be employed on the piano can easily be transferred to the other keyboard instruments. In the case of the grand piano, there are two main playing positions: at the keys and inside the piano. The pianist himself may play inside the piano from the keyboard position when the lid is open or removed. Additionally, an assistant located at the rear end of the instrument can also play inside the piano while the pianist is playing at the keys. As many extended techniques that may be executed on the strings of a piano strongly resemble the techniques of the harp (and other plucked or string instruments), the methods of notation presented in the previous chapters may often simply be transferred. In such cases, a detailed discussion of the technique is dismissed and merely the already suggested method of notation presented. It needs to be further noted that – according to *Sevsay* – playing inside the instrument may be only performed on pianos, not on the harpsichord and celesta. *Sevsay* explains that the sensitivity of the harpsichord does not permit any playing inside the instrument and it is not possible to reach the interior of a celesta[1]. However, for instance, *Essl*, in »Sequitur XII«[2], makes a performer play inside a harpsichord and execute several extended articulations, such as vertical *glissandi* on the strings, *pizzicati* on the strings as well as the production of harmonics by touching the strings[3]. Hence when employing them in a careful way, the utilisation of such techniques should be possible on the harpsichord. With regard to the grand piano, the notation of the trill, the common articulations (*legato, staccato* etc.), the ordinary utilisation of the three pedals and the (rare) *scordatura* are regarded here as conventional[4]. Their notation can be adopted from the essential handbooks on instrumentation whilst most composers use the method of depiction that can be found there (also cf. the introduction to the chapter on string instruments for the notation of microtones). Whereas, the main unconventional elements of sound production presented in this chapter are extended *pizzicato* techniques, common and extended playing positions on the strings, the common and extended *glissando*, extended modes of attack, muting, extended stopping techniques, pedal effects, percussive effects and preparing the instrument. Concerning the dynamic level of these articulations, indications are – as far as possible – presented when the execution of the action is, in terms of the loudness, limited.

5. 1 Extended *pizzicato* techniques

All *pizzicato* techniques on the piano are extended techniques. The pianist may play a ***pizzicato* on the keys** as well as the pianist or assistant perform a ***pizzicato* on the strings**.

5. 1. 1 The *pizzicato* on the keys and its notation

The *pizzicato* on the keys is a very rare technique. When employed, the pianist is supposed to pull and pluck the key upwards instead of depressing it. The result is a subtle click with indefinite pitch. Apparently, the articulation can only be executed on the white keys. In »Guero«[5] *Lachenmann* introduces this technique. As obvious from Figure 1, he requests it by means of

---

[1] Cf. Sevsay, Handbuch, pp. 268f.
[2] Karlheinz Essl: Sequitur XII. For harpsichord and live-electronics. No city named 2009.
[3] Cf. Essl, Sequitur XII, no page named [foreword].
[4] Cf. Sevsay, Handbuch, pp. 253f. and 266.
[5] Helmut Lachenmann: Guero. For piano. Wiesbaden 1972.

a diamond-shaped note. Moreover, te key that is supposed to be plucked is determined in an approximate manner[6].

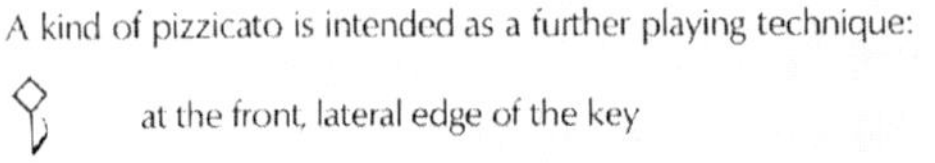

A kind of pizzicato is intended as a further playing technique:

 at the front, lateral edge of the key

Fig. 1 Lachenmann, Guero, no page named [foreword].

However, the note head *Lachenmann* utilises is normally used for the notation of harmonics or related techniques. Further, there is no need to determine the key that is plucked in an approximate manner when it can be done in an exact way by means of the pitch-based notation system (although the sound-wise difference between plucking one key or another is admittedly very small). Moreover, because the key *pizzicato* is related to the key/valve clicks on wind instruments – which are requested by means of x-shaped note heads in a pitch-based notation system (cf. Chapter »2. 9. 1 Key/valve clicks«) – as well as the normal *pizzicato* articulation, it is suggested here depicting the articulation by means of x-shaped note heads, the traditional notation system and the direction *pizzicato*. Furthermore, *Lachenmann* also requires the pianist to pluck the tuning pegs[7]. However, this technique is discussed in the chapter on percussive effects.

5. 1. 2 The *pizzicato* on the strings and its notation

Concerning the *pizzicato* on the strings, there are a couple of conditions that need to be taken into account. From the pianist's position all strings may be plucked between the tuning pins and the felt strip. However, some of the middle range strings located adjacent to the cross-beam that separates the bass strings from the middle range strings cannot be plucked behind the hammers and dampers because they are completely covered by the bass strings. Since the shape of the metal frame and the number of strings covered by the bass strings is dependent on the model, it is necessary to consider this when requesting the string *pizzicato*: *Vaes* presents a listing of 17 piano models that inter alia describes between which intervals the cross-beams are located[8]. A similar listing can also be found in the »Appendix«. It presents the data by *Vaes* as well as of several more *Bechstein, Bösendorfer, Boston, Steinway, Wendt & Lung* and *Yamaha* models. The *Vaes* listing does not take into account which strings may not be plucked behind the hammers and dampers. But it is shown in the appendix that 2-3 completely covered strings cannot, on several *Steinway* and *Bechstein* models and even less on the *Bösendorfer* models, be plucked, but the assistant is able to bend forward in order to reach the strings that are partially covered by the bass strings, and the pianist can also play these. Therefore, it can be assumed that normally, at the most, three strings adjacent to the bass strings cannot be plucked. As is apparent from the appendix, the bass strings' number may, however, also differ. When utilising techniques that are executed on the strings, it would, therefore, be helpful to refer to the appendix of this work and suggest models upon which these articulations may be performed. Further, the lowest strings of a grand piano consist of a single wire, whereas the strings in the middle range consist of two and the highest strings of three wires. When requesting the player to pluck a string, which is made of two or three wires, the player might wonder whether he should pluck only one of the wires or two/three simultaneously. However, because considering these circumstances would lead to a very complex method of

---

[6] Cf. ibid., p. 2.

[7] Cf. ibid., no page named [foreword].

[8] Cf. Luk Vaes: Extended piano techniques. In theory, history and performance practice. No city named 2009, pp. 1032-1048.

notation and is also dependent on the utilised piano model, this aspect is regarded here as a means of interpretation.

The notation of the *pizzicato* on the strings may be regarded as nearly conventional. As any plucking of strings, it is, in most cases, requested by means of the direction *pizzicato*[9]. However, some composers use a special note head in combination with this direction[10]. Further, when the pianist himself is supposed to pluck the string (or perform other actions on these), the instructions are often boxed in order to distinguish them from playing at the keys:

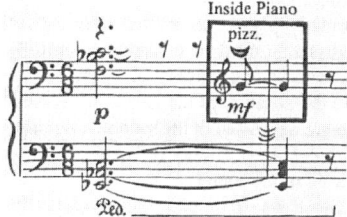

Fig. 2 Stone, Notation, p. 263.

Additionally, *Lachenmann*, in »Guero«, distinguishes between two playing positions for the pianist: on the strings between the tuning pegs and the felt strip as well as in the normal (upper) area of the strings, close to the dampers. The first variant is requested by means of a special note head and the second one by means of a common note head[11].

Concerning the variants of notation, it may be stated that the *pizzicato* on the strings of a *piano* resembles the *pizzicato* on the strings of a harp. It should, therefore, be notated in the same manner and hence simply by means of giving the direction *pizzicato*. However, because some of the techniques that may be performed on the strings by the pianist resemble techniques that may be performed on the keys (e. g. the *glissando*), it needs to be indicated whether the articulation is executed on the keys or strings. Therefore, the approach of using a box is suggested here being employed whenever the pianist himself executes actions on the strings. An alternative method of notation was to notate these by means of a distinct notation system or give a short explanation if the pianist is supposed to consistently play inside the pianos. In the case of the assistant, no boxes need to be utilised because a player standing at the rear of the piano may only perform articulations inside the piano. These actions are suggested here being notated by means of a distinct notation system. Further, concerning the playing positions, the first position (between the tuning pegs and the felt strip) resembles the *pizzicato* inside the pegbox of string instruments as well as the *pizzicato* on the neck of a harp. As shown in Chapters »1. 5. 3 Playing the tuning pegs, pegbox and scroll« and »4. 5 Playing exceptional spots and its notation«, this action is depicted by means of spherical note heads, the additional direction *pizzicato* and – on string instruments – by a string clef system. The same method of notation is also suggested here being employed when requesting *pizzicati* »in the pegbox/on the neck« of a piano. However, the normal pitch-based notation system needs to be employed in order to distinguish the strings. Only the pianist himself may pluck the string on this position. Further, he may only play a *pizzicato* at the dampers because the music rest (and score) might otherwise compromise the articulation. However, the assistant may

---

[9] Cf., for instance, George Crumb: Ancient voices of children. Soprano, boy soprano, oboe, mandolin, harp, electric piano, percussion. New York et al. 1970, p. 3, Kagel, Anagrama, p. 36 or John Cage: Music of changes II. New York 1961, p. 2.

[10] Cf. Lachenmann, Air, p. 19 or Karlheinz Stockhausen: Klavierstück XII. Examen von Donnerstag aus Licht. As a piano solo. Kürten 1983, p. V.

[11] Lachenmann, Guero, no page named [foreword].

pluck the string on all positions except for in between the tuning strips and felt strip (cf. the following chapter for the determination of the playing positions).

As is apparent from Figure 2, it is, moreover, possible to execute some of the extended *pizzicato* techniques explained in Chapter »4. 1 Extended *pizzicato*, *tremolo* and trill techniques and their notation«, such as the **fingernail** and **plectrum** *pizzicato* or the *pizzicato* **with items**. In the case of these techniques, the methods of notation may simply be transferred from plucked instruments to the piano because the described articulations are strongly related. Hence the fingernail *pizzicato* can be depicted by means of an additional fingernail symbol whilst the utilisation of a plectrum may be requested by employing a drawing of the plectrum and giving the direction *pizzicato*. Any other *pizzicato* with items may be notated by giving a direction or presenting a symbol of the item. Further, another technique that is related to performing a *pizzicato* – the buzz-*pizzicato* – is discussed in Chapter »5. 6. 3 Exact muting stops/harmonics and their notation«.

5. 2 Common playing positions on the strings and their notation

As shown in Chapter »4. 2 Common and extended playing positions on the strings and their notation«, three main playing positions on the strings of a harp are normally requested. As the shape of the harp and the piano (frame) resemble each other, similar playing positions are also suggested here being employed. These playing positions are depicted in the traditional manner and hence by directions: close to the damper or *sul smorzatore*, on the midpoint of the string or *ordinario* and close to the bridge or *sul ponticello*. It needs to be noted that the lowest strings of a grand piano may be longer than those of a harp. Therefore, it may – especially in the case of long pianos – even be more desirable to request additional playing positions, such as *quasi sul smorzatore* or *quasi sul ponticello*. The pianist normally plays *sul smorzatore* because, as mentioned, the music rest might compromise articulations, such as *pizzicati ordinario*, whilst the assistant may reach any of these playing positions. However, he might not be able to reach the playing position *sul smorzatore* (or *quasi sul smorzatore*) on the bass strings of concert grand pianos, such as the *Bechstein D 282* or *Steinway D-274*, from the rear position. Further, all playing positions may only be plucked on strings that are not covered by the bass strings whilst the partially covered strings may, in any case, be played *sul smorzatore* (cf. the »Appendix«). In the case of utilising pianos with additional crossbeams that connect the basic braces (e. g. the *Steinway B* or *D* type[12]), the player may simply pluck the string a little further to the dampers or bridge when, for instance, the midpoint of the string is covered by the beam. Concerning the position *sul smorzatore* it needs to be noted that no dampers are applied on grand pianos either from »f♯3/F♯6«, »g3/G6« or »g♯3/G♯6« on[13]. However, the position is also designated here as »close to the dampers« for the highest strings.

5. 3 The *glissando*

There are four types of *glissandi* on the piano, the common **glissando on the keys**, the **glissando on the strings**, **the progressive modification of the point of plucking** as well as the **vertical** *glissando* **on the strings with/without plucking**. They are all unconventional articulations because there is no common method of notation for any of these techniques.

---

12 Cf. Vaes, Extended, pp. 1042f.
13 Cf. Vaes, Extended, pp. 1032-1048.

5. 3. 1 The *glissando* on the keys

Even though the *glissando* on the keys is an old technique, it is still depicted in varying ways. The most common variant is a diatonic *glissando* on the white keys[14]. However, it may also be performed on the black keys or as a chromatic *glissando* on the white and black keys. The technique is sometimes also referred to as an *arpeggio*. However, since the fingers slide over the keys in the case of the *glissando*, it is different from an *arpeggio*.

5. 3. 1. 1 Previous methods of notation

Henze, in »Sinfonia N. 6«[15], makes use of a key *glissando* (referred to as *quasi arpeggio*). In this piece the *glissando* is always executed by rolling the palm on the keys. As can be seen in Figure 3, the key *glissando* is notated by using several note heads with a similar shape that indicate whether the right or left hand is rolled on the black or white keys from the top to the bottom or the other way round in a slow or fast manner. The pitch is, as is apparent from the score, only determined in an approximate way[16].

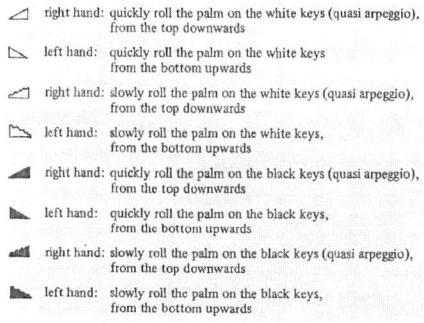

Fig. 3 Henze, Sinfonia N. 6, p. 7.

Moreover, *Kagel*, in »Norden«[17], from the cycle »Die Stücke der Windrose« makes use of a chromatic key *glissando*. It is depicted by means of a variation of the *arpeggio* symbol and several transposed note heads:

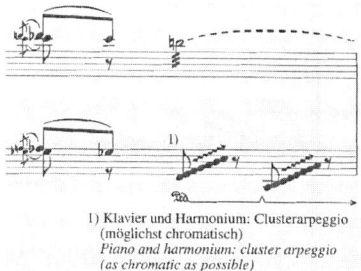

Fig. 4 Kagel, Norden, p. 85.

Another more conventional method is to depict all tones that are part of the *glissando* and give the direction *glissando*. This method of depiction has, for instance, already been applied

---

[14] Cf. Sevsay, Handbuch, p. 257.
[15] Hans Werner Henze: Sinfonia N. 6. For two chamber orchestras. Mainz 1970.
[16] Cf. ibid., p. 129.
[17] Mauricio Kagel: Die Stücke der Windrose. Norden. For salon orchestra. Frankfurt/M. et al. 1996.

by *Brahms* in his »Hungarian dances«[18]. In the example presented in Figure 5, diatonic double *glissandi* are supposed to be performed.

Fig. 5 Brahms, Hungarian, p. 28.

5. 3. 1. 2 Discussion

Generally, it needs to be acknowledged that there is a conventional method of notation for the *glissando*, which should only be altered when there is a sufficient reason. Otherwise, the previously defined criteria would be violated. As mentioned above, in this work the *glissando* – in order to achieve a greater clarity and to enable the depiction of sliding motions that do not imply a gliding change of pitch – is notated in a slightly varying way. This method (or the conventional one) could basically be used to depict the *glissandi* requested by *Henze* (cf. Figure 3) or *Kagel* (cf. Figure 4). Further, the approach by *Henze* is very complex and would even have to be extended in order to enable the notation of other *glissandi* than the ones he makes use of. Moreover, *Kagel's* method would also have to be augmented and is related rather to the *arpeggio* than the *glissando* notation. The only sufficient reason for altering the *glissando* notation is that there are three types of *glissandi* on the keys, and it could not clearly be comprehended whether a diatonic *glissando* on the black/white keys or a chromatic *glissando* is requested when only the lowest and highest tone of the *glissando* is given. Nevertheless, since the diatonic *glissando* on the white keys is the most common one and it can be distinguished from the diatonic *glissando* on the black keys when the highest and lowest tone are notated, the conventional method of notation or the extended variant employed in this work, respectively, may be used to request it. However, another method needs to be used for the chromatic *glissando*. It may be derived from *Brahms'* method (cf. Figure 5) because this way of depicting the *glissando* is simple, exact and, apparently, strongly related to traditional notation. However, it is not necessary to depict each tone's duration, but merely the overall duration of the *glissando*. This method could even be used to notate a more complex *glissando* gesture, which, for instance, starts solely on the white keys, is then executed on the white and black keys and ends on the black keys.

5. 3. 1. 3 Suggestion for the notation of the *glissando* on the keys

The diatonic *glissando* on the white/black keys is notated here in the same way as all (pitch) *glissandi* in this work and hence by depicting the starting point and endpoint of the *glissando* and connecting these by an arrow. Moreover, any chromatic or more complex *glissando* is suggested being notated by determining the starting point and endpoint as well as notating each key the player slides over in brackets. In the example presented in Figure 6, four different *glissandi* are performed. The first one is a diatonic *glissando* on the white keys. The *glis-*

---

[18] Johannes Brahms: Hungarian dances I and II. For piano four hands. Mainz and Leipzig no year named [ca. 1920].

sando starts on the »d¹/D4« and ends on the »a²/A5«. After the duration of a dotted crotchet, the »a²/A5« is reached and depressed for a demisemiquaver. The second *glissando* is diatonic and executed on the black keys. It starts on the »c♯¹/C♯4« and ends on the »a♭²/A♭5«. The third one is a chromatic *glissando* from »a/A3« to »a¹/A4«, whereas the fourth *glissando* starts on the white keys (»a/A3« to »d¹/D4«), is then executed on the white and black keys (»e♭¹/E♭4« to »g¹/G4«) and ends on the black keys (»a♭¹/A♭4« to »e♭²/E♭5«). Moreover, any kind of double *glissando* or *glissando* executed with both hands (travelling in the same or opposite direction) may be notated in this manner. Alternatively, the common *glissando* notation may, in the case of the key *glissando*, also be restored.

Fig. 6 The diatonic and chromatic key *glissando*.

Furthermore, the so-called additive/subtractive cluster *glissando* is discussed in Chapter »5. 6. 1 Clusters« because it is strongly related to the notation of clusters while the *glissando* without depressing the keys is regarded as a percussive effect and, therefore, discussed in Chapter »5. 8 Percussive effects and their notation«.

5. 3. 2 The *glissando* on the strings and its notation

The *glissando* on the strings of a piano strongly resembles the common *glissando* of a harp and may, therefore, be notated in the same manner. As mentioned above, when the pianist performs a *glissando*, the action needs to be either boxed or depicted by means of a distinct notation system. When the assistant performs a *glissando*, a distinct notation system needs to be employed. However, it needs to be considered that – depending on the framework of the piano model – certain *glissandi* may be executed on one model, but are impossible on the other. In his »Klavierstück XIII«[19] *Stockhausen*, therefore, mentions that the "***glissandi* on the strings** were tried out on a *Steinway B* model grand piano. With differently constructed pianos one may to have to interrupt some *glissandi* at a metal brace and quickly continue on the other side"[20]. Other composers determine four[21] or five[22] registers for the piano and depict all actions on the strings in an approximate way. *Kagel* further mentions that these "registers are defined by the framework of the grand piano. Divergences from the given ranges are, of course, to be decided upon if the framework is laid out differently"[23]. However, since listings of the framework of various piano models are available (cf. the »Appendix«), it is possible to depict *glissandi* in an exact manner and suggest models upon which these actions may be performed. An alternative was (in the case of the unavailability of such piano models) to permit that the *glissandi* with differently constructed pianos may – as in *Stockhausen's* »Klavierstück XIII« – be interrupted. Additional crossbeams that connect the basic braces do not cause a problem for the *glissando* on the strings because the player might, in such a case, vary the vertical position on the string at his discretion. All *glissandi* on the strings are chromatic.

---

[19] Karlheinz Stockhausen: Luzifers Traum oder Klavierstück XIII. As a piano solo. Kürten 1982.

[20] Ibid., p. VII.

[21] Cf. Mauricio Kagel: Transición II. For piano, percussion and two magnetic tapes. London 1963, pp. 10 and 9A or Cristobal Halffter: Noche pasiva del sentido (San Juan de la Cruz). For soprano, percussion and electronics. London 1973, no page named [foreword].

[22] Cf. Witold Szalonek: Proporzioni II. For flute, violincello and grand piano (or harp). Kraków 1971, no page named [foreword].

[23] Kagel, Transición II, p. 10.

Therefore, no special method of notation needs to be introduced, but the common *glissando* notation may be used.

5. 3. 3 The progressive modification of the point of plucking and its notation

The technique of modifying the point of plucking can be executed in the same manner on the strings of a piano and the harp. Hence the method of notation suggested in Chapter »4. 3. 1 The progressive modification of the point of plucking and its notation« can be transferred to the piano. As shown there, the articulation may be depicted by means of the common *glissando* notation, giving the direction *glissando del mano* (*glissando* with the hand), the playing positions determined for the instrument and an optional additional (single lined) notation system. However, in the case of the piano, additional crossbeams that connect the basic braces may compromise the performance of unrestricted modifications of the point of plucking. However, the beam between the first and second basic brace may on some models be detached, e. g. on the *Steinway D-274* the crossbeam that is located over the strings »F – c#²/ F2 – C#5«. Moreover, the articulation may preferably be executed by the assistant because the music rest (and score) restrict the pianist, the modification of the point of plucking can only be executed on the uncovered strings (cf. the »Appendix« for additional crossbeams and concerning the uncovered strings) and it may not be possible to reach any position on the bass strings. Therefore, it is suggested here permitting that the modification of the point of plucking may – as in the case of *Stockhausen's* horizontal string *glissando* – be interrupted in the case of additional crossbeams and should preferably be executed with both hands by the assistant on the uncovered strings. As shown above, 3 to 5 playing positions (*sul smorzatore, quasi sul smorzatore, ordinario, sul ponticello* and *quasi sul ponticello*) can be employed, whereas on long piano models only the positions *ordinario* to *sul ponticello* may presumably be reached on the bass strings. Further, this technique cannot adequately be executed on the highest strings.

5. 3. 4 The vertical *glissando* on the strings with/without playing and its notation

The vertical *glissando* on the strings of a piano is, apparently, strongly related to the vertical *glissando* on the harp. Hence it may be notated in the same manner and be executed by means of the fingers/hand, the fingernails or items, such as brushes, threaded rods or plectrums. However, there are differences that need to be acknowledged: as in the case of the progressive modification of the point of plucking, additional crossbeams that connect the basic braces do not permit the performance of unrestricted vertical *glissandi*, the articulation may only be adequately executed from the assistant's position and on the strings that are not covered by the bass strings (cf. the »Appendix«). Moreover, the assistant may not be able to reach any position on the bass strings. The length of a piano string reaches from the short or long bridge (at the assistant's position) to the felt strip (at the pianist's position). However, the assistant may only slide up to the dampers. As in the case of the harp, the vertical *glissando* may preferably be executed on the lower strings and cannot be executed on the highest strings.

As shown in Chapter »4. 3. 3 The vertical *glissando* with/without plucking«, the position on the string is depicted by means of the common harmonic notation whilst starting from the neck. Because the shape of the neck and the rear end of the frame correlate, and it is easier for an assistant standing at the rear of a piano to execute vertical sliding motions (as well as to stop harmonics), it is reasonable to use a method of depiction that is, firstly, related to the harmonic notation of the harp and, secondly, corresponds to the assistant's perspective. In order to execute the sliding motions in an exact manner, the assistant may have to mark the nodes with chalk[24]. Moreover, it is suggested here permitting that the vertical *glissando* may – as in the case of the modification of the point of plucking – be interrupted in the case of additional crossbeams and should preferably be executed with both hands. Additionally, it is assumed that the player may only slide up to 1/2 of the string length on the bass strings of concert grand pianos and 4/5 of the string length on the other uncovered strings, including all bass strings on short models. The point at 4/5 of the string length corresponds to the *sul smorzatore* position. The most unlimited vertical motions may be executed on short models without additional crossbeams, such as the *Boston GP-156, -163 (PE)* and *-178*, the *Steinway O-180* and *S-155* as well as the *Yamaha C3*. However, such models are rather rare. When it is unsure whether the articulation may perfectly be executed, an alternative option could be presented. Sliding motions on the partially covered strings are not recommended here being employed because it is hard to predict whether they may be executed or not on the piano models available for performance. Further, it needs to be taken into account that the number of uncovered bass or middle range strings varies from model to model. To give an example, the highest bass strings on one model could be covered middle range strings on another model. Likewise, the highest of the uncovered middle range strings on one model could be partially covered middle range strings on another model. Hence the number of strings that need to be considered as partially covered may be higher than the actual number of the model used in a performance and is dependent on the suggested models.

The notation of this technique can be achieved in the same way as in the chapter plucked on instruments (Figure 13). When the assistant performs a vertical *glissando* on the strings, he may also either pluck the strings or execute the motion without any *pizzicato*. As this technique is the most common articulation when playing on the strings, it will be treated in the same way as on the harp. Thus when the player is supposed to execute a vertical *glissando* without plucking, the direction *non pizzicato* is suggested here being employed. Additionally, the assistant may slide on strings that are played by the pianist. As in the case of simultaneously plucking the string, a harmonic *glissando* evolves when sliding over the nodes.

Fig. 7 The vertical *glissando* with/without plucking.

In Figure 7, an assistant is supposed to execute two motions on the »c¹/C4«-string. It is in the beginning plucked and vibrates – due to playing *non lasciar vibrare* – for the duration of a minim (for the subsequent muting of plucked strings cf. Chapter »5. 5 Muting and its notation«). During this time, a *glissando* with the finger is executed, starting on the second partial (octave; notated in the same way as on the harp). The finger is then moved to the »g¹/G4« (third partial) for the duration of a quaver, to position »c♯³/C♯6« for the duration of another quaver and finally to »f¹/F4« (fourth partial) also for the duration of a quaver. The next motion can be described in the same way. However, this time the string is not plucked (*non pizzicato*) and the player employs the fingernail. Moreover, the harmonic notation for the second partial is replaced by means of a diamond-shaped note head on position »c²/C5«. When the string is not plucked, no sound is produced when the finger rests. Therefore, the

---

[24] Cf. Sevsay, Handbuch, p. 263.

glissando ends when the »e¹/E4« is reached and a demisemiquaver is applied pro forma. This transferred *glissando* motion may only be executed without any problems on the *Bechstein C 234* and *D 282* or similar models. However, on the other models listed in the appendix (disregarding those examined by *Vaes*), the »c¹/C4« string is partially covered by the bass strings and/or an additional crossbeam is located in this area of the strings. Alternatively, the vertical *glissando* may also be depicted by means of two systems (one for the plucking/basic string and one for the *glissando*).

The dynamic level is low when executing a vertical *glissando* without playing, but may be increased by using items (for the depiction of items cf. Chapter »5. 1. 2 The *pizzicato* on the strings and its notation«). The dynamic level of such vertical slides should be limited when using items that could harm the material of the string. However, in »Sinfonia N. 6« *Henze*, for instance, requests to stroke the strings of a piano with the highest dynamic level using a brush with natural bristles and with the dynamic level *forte* using an iron brush[25]. Moreover, *Holliger* in »Partita«[26] requests a vertical *glissando* with the dynamic level *forte* using a plectrum, and *Szalonek* in »Proporzioni II« makes use of a vertical *glissando* using a threaded rod. The highest dynamic level is, in this case however, *pianissimo*[27]. Further, cluster slides may be notated by means of utilising the paradigm presented in Figure 17.

5. 4 Extended modes of attack

Most extended modes of attack involve the interior of the piano. As in the case of the harp, a *toccato* – which refers to the string being touched after the attack – may be performed. Further, the **utilisation of beaters** is another extended mode of attack while on the piano **extended** *battuto* **techniques** may also be executed.

5. 4. 1 The *toccato* and its notation

The *toccato* technique may be employed in the same way as on the harp. Hence it can be notated similarly when utilised on the piano strings. As shown in Chapter »4. 4. 1 The *toccato* and its notation«, the articulation is simply requested by giving the direction *toccato*, depicting the string that is touched by common note heads and determining the playing position. Any item or beater can be used for this technique (cf. Chapter »5. 1. 2 The *pizzicato* on the strings and its notation« for the depiction of items and Chapter »5. 4. 2 The utilisation of beaters and its notation« for the depiction of beaters). When the string has been played and still vibrates, a sound effect occurs. Moreover, another *toccato* articulation, referred to as the buzz-*pizzicato*, is discussed in Chapter »5. 6. 3 Exact muting stops/harmonics and their notation« because it is related to the depiction of muting stops.

5. 4. 2 The utilisation of beaters and its notation

The utilisation of beaters on the strings of a piano strongly resembles the utilisation of beaters on the harp. Therefore, it may be requested in the same way. As mentioned in Chapter »4. 4. 3 The utilisation of beaters and its notation«, beaters may on the harp be employed in the same way as on mallet instruments. Hence when beating the strings of a piano or executing *glissandi* with an agent of attack, a beater symbol can be used in combination with a depiction of the strings that are struck or involved in the *glissando*. Additionally, the playing position needs to be described. Moreover, most extended piano techniques and several extended beater attacks, such as plucking the string with the beater (especially on the single wired strings),

---

[25] Cf. Henze, Sinfonia N. 6, pp. 68 and 126.

[26] Cf. Heinz Holliger: Partita. For piano. Mainz et al. 2003, p. 25.

[27] Cf. Szalonek, Proporzioni II, p. 1.

modifying the point of impact, executing a vertical *glissando* with/without plucking, striking with the handle of a beater or entire length of a stick, rubbing motions with beaters on the body as well as the stop attack can be performed. They may be depicted by adding a beater symbol to the paradigms presented in Figures 1 (extended *pizzicato*), 6 (modification of the point of plucking) and 13 (vertical *glissando*) in the chapter on plucked instruments. Moreover, the methods of notation presented in Figures 9 (common and extended attacks), 34, 35 (rubbing motions) and 66 (stop attack) in the chapter on percussion instruments can also be transferred to the piano. Moreover, strokes on the body and frame of the instrument are discussed in Chapter »5. 8 Percussive effects and their notation«.

Another extended harp technique is referred to as the **extended trill with items** and described by inserting an item in between two strings and repetitively hitting these. It may, in the case of the piano, preferably be executed between the single wired strings from the assistant's position, but when using a thin item, such as a plectrum, also on the other uncovered strings by the pianist or assistant. The number of low bass strings that are single wired varies depending on the piano model. However, as is apparent from the *Vaes* listing, at least eight bass strings (»$_2$A – $_1$E/A0 – E1«) are, on the examined pianos, single wired whilst ten models actually have eight single wired strings. Moreover, three models have nine single wired strings (up to »$_1$F/F1«), three models ten single wired strings (up to »$_1$F♯/F♯1«) and one model eleven single wired strings (up to »$_1$G/G1«)[28]. Hence the extended trill with items may be preferably executed between the eight lowest strings. The method of notation for the harp may, in this case, also be transferred to the piano, which means that a sketch of the action should be employed and the two strings that are played be depicted (cf. Figure 19 in the chapter on plucked instruments). Further, the playing position may on the piano be modified during the extended trill with items (cf. Chapter »5. 3. 3 The progressive modification of the point of plucking«).

5. 4. 3 Extended battuto techniques and their notation

As shown in Chapter »4. 4. 4 Extended *battuto* techniques and their notation«, the *battuto* with items is, in the case of the harp, suggested being depicted by giving the direction *battuto*, employing common note heads in a pitch-based notation system as well presenting a symbol of the item or requesting it by means of a direction. The position on the string is depicted by means of the common playing positions and can be modified (see above). As this technique may be employed in a similar manner on the strings of a piano, it may be notated in the same way.

5. 5 Muting and its notation

The muting of piano strings works in the same way as on the harp whilst the muting position also has an impact on the produced sound. However, this technique is discussed in Chapter »5. 6. 3 Exact muting stops/harmonics and their notation«. Moreover, when all strings of a piano are supposed to be muted, the instrument can be prepared, e. g. by attaching adhesive tape to the strings. Such actions are discussed in Chapter »5. 9 Preparing the instrument and its notation«. Besides these preparations, there is one muting variant on the piano. It may be described as muting the string with the palm whilst simultaneously plucking it with the same hand. This technique may preferably be executed by the assistant. This constant muffling resembles the **application of mutes**. It can be notated in the same way as on plucked instruments and hence by giving the direction with/without mute (hand) or *con/senza sordino*

---

[28] Cf. Vaes, Extended, pp. 1032-1048.

(*mano*). However, the impact of this muting technique is only extensive in the case of released dampers. When playing in this way, the dynamic level is always low.

Further, **hand muffling** may also be executed in the same way as on the harp when playing on the strings of a piano: in the case of the assistant playing *non lasciar vibrare* and the damper pedal (or, in certain cases, the *sostenuto* pedal) being depressed or playing on undamped strings, the tones are muted according to the depicted duration. However, when the assistant is playing *lasciar vibrare* and the dampers are released, the hand muffling needs to be notated specifically. In such a case, the muting sign ($\oplus$) is used. The muting sign may solely be employed in order to request that all tones played by one hand are muted simultaneously. However, when the tones are supposed to be muted in a sequence, the muting sign needs to be used in combination with a depiction of the string that is muted (cf. Figures 23f. in the chapter on plucked instruments as well as Figures 63f. in the chapter on percussion instruments).

5. 6 Extended stopping techniques

There are three extended stopping techniques on the piano. The first one – **clusters** – is discussed here with regard to playing at the keys. Moreover, another augmented articulation, which may be regarded as nearly conventional, is referred to as **depressing the keys silently**. Further, the third technique – **exact muting stops/harmonics** – may only be executed on the strings of the piano. The chapter on this articulation implies the description of the buzz-*pizzicato*.

5. 6. 1 Clusters

Clusters are discussed specifically because they can be produced in different ways on the keyboard of a piano: either by depressing the white, black (diatonic clusters) or the black and white keys (chromatic cluster). Moreover, the keys may also be depressed or released in a sequence. These two techniques are referred to here as the additive and subtractive cluster *glissando*. This is because, in the case of the additive cluster *glissando,* the pianist performs a *glissando* motion on the keys, but does not release the keys after depressing them while, in the case of the subtractive cluster *glissando*, a previously depressed cluster is successively released.

5. 6. 1. 1 Previous methods of notation

There are various ways of notating clusters. In »Vestiges«[29] *Cowell*, for instance, simply connects the highest and lowest tone of the cluster by a line and requests the two variants of diatonic clusters by placing either the accidental flat (cluster on the white keys) or sharp (cluster on the black keys) above the notes:

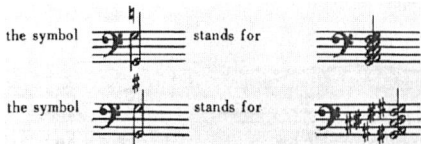

Fig. 8 Cowell, Vestiges, p. 3.

Moreover, when no additional accidental is used, the pianist is supposed to perform a chromatic cluster. *Cowell* uses two variants of notation for these kinds of clusters:

---

[29] Henry Cowell: Vestiges. In: Henry Cowell: The piano music of Henry Cowell. Volume two. New York and London 1982, pp. 3-6.

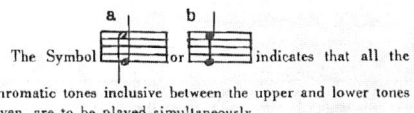

The Symbol ⬚ or ⬚ indicates that all the Chromatic tones inclusive between the upper and lower tones given, are to be played simultaneously.

Fig. 9 Cowell, Vestiges, p. 3.

Sevsay and *Stone* also suggest using this approach. However, they recommend additionally depicting the highest and lowest tone of the diatonic cluster on the black keys (as well as of the chromatic cluster if the highest or lowest tone is a black key) by means of common accidentals (placed in front of the cluster note)[30]. Moreover, Cage in »In the name of the Holocaust«[31] employs the two variants of diatonic clusters. They are requested by means of a squared cluster note and – as in the case of *Cowell's* approach – placing accidentals above or beneath the note. In Figure 10, Cage requests two diatonic crotchet clusters in combination. They range from presumably »F♯/F♯2« to »a♯/A♯3« or »c♯¹/C♯4« on the black keys and an undetermined low pitch (presumably »₁E/E1« or »₁F/F1«) to »A/A2« on the white keys (the lower system is in bass clef).

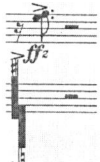

Fig. 10 Cage, Holocaust, p. 29.

Further, the subtractive cluster *glissando* is utilised by *Kagel* in »Anagrama«. As is apparent from Figure 11, a chromatic cluster ranging from »C/C2« to »B/B♭2« is released to »B/B♭2« for the duration of a dotted quaver. Subsequently, another cluster is released in a successive manner. Moreover, *Kagel* in »Heterophonie« notates additive cluster *glissandi* similarly: by flipping the shape of the note head vertically[32].

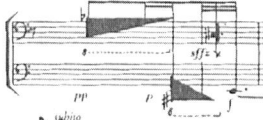

Fig. 11 Kagel, Anagrama, p. 6.

5. 6. 1. 2 Discussion

When employing the approach by *Cowell* (cf. Figures 8f.), the three variants of clusters may be depicted in a simple and exact manner. However, it becomes even more exact and comprehensible when accidentals are placed in front of the highest/lowest tone if needed. Moreover, *Cowell's* method is more exact than the one used by *Cage* because, as is apparent from Figure 10, *Cage* does not determine the outer boundaries of the cluster in an exact manner. However, concerning the shape of the notes involved in cluster chords, *Cage's* approach is preferred. This is because cluster chords are, for instance, in the case of string instruments,

---

[30] Cf. Sevsay, Handbuch, pp. 255f. and Stone, Notation, p. 259.

[31] John Cage: In the name of the Holocaust. Music for the dance by Merce Cunningham. In: John Cage: Prepared piano music. Volume 1. 1940-47. New York et al. 1960, pp. 25-29.

[32] Cf. Kagel, Heterophonie, p. IX.

most commonly notated by means of squared cluster notes[33] and there is no need to introduce another method of notation for the piano. Consequently, microtonal clusters may be requested by placing a microtonal symbol above or beneath the note and determining the outer boundaries of the chord. On the piano they can be produced by previously retuning it, but they are more common in compositions that involve large string and/or wind ensembles. Concerning *Kagel's* approach towards the notation of the subtractive and additive cluster *glissandi*, it may be said that this method clearly determines what kind of action the pianist is supposed to perform. However, it could be augmented by depicting the cluster chord in the described manner. Moreover, since the pianist, as mentioned, executes a *glissando* motion on the keys, it is preferred here to request this articulation in the same way as all other *glissando* articulations. Thus, in the case of the subtractive cluster *glissando*, the starting point (a cluster) and endpoint (a single tone) of the *glissando* would have to be determined and be connected by an arrow. This method could also be employed in the case of the additive cluster *glissando* as well as when the action starts/ends on a cluster or normal chord.

5. 6. 1. 3 Suggestion for the notation of clusters

Hence clusters are suggested being notated by means of squared cluster notes and placing accidentals above or beneath the note (diatonic clusters) or not placing any accidental above or beneath the note (chromatic clusters) as well as by determining the highest/lowest note of the chord. In Figure 12, the pianist is supposed to execute four clusters in the order of a diatonic cluster »a – c²/A3 – C5« on the white keys, a diatonic cluster »eb¹ – f#²/Eb4 – F#5« on the black keys, a chromatic cluster »a – c²/A3 – C5« as well as two diatonic clusters »eb¹ – f#²/Eb4 – F#5« (on the black keys) and »a – c²/A3 – C5« (on the white keys) simultaneously. The duration of each cluster chord is a crotchet. When minims or semibreves are supposed to be utilised, the cluster note needs to be white.

Fig. 12 Diatonic and chromatic clusters.

When playing clusters on the strings of the piano – for instance, by hitting the string with a long item (cf. Chapter »5. 4. 3 Extended battuto techniques and their notation«) – they are always chromatic. Hence the method of notation without any additional accidentals can be employed[34].

Further, additive/subtractive cluster *glissandi* are depicted here by means of the *glissando* notation used in this work. As is apparent from Figure 13, the player is supposed to execute three *glissandi* of this kind. Initially, he is required to play a subtractive cluster *glissando* from the diatonic cluster »a – h²/A3 – B5« to »h²/B5« for the duration of a crotchet. The endpoint of the *glissando* is then further depressed for the duration of a quaver. Subsequently, the pianist is supposed to execute an additive cluster glissando from »a/A3« to the chromatic cluster »a – h²/A3 – B5«. Hence the additive *glissando* itself is also chromatic. Finally, he plays an additive cluster *glissando* from the diatonic cluster »ab – b¹/Ab3 – Bb4« to the diatonic cluster »ab – ab²/Ab3 – Ab5«. Moreover, the endpoint and starting point of the *glissando* may also be a normal chord while the conventional *glissando* notation could (with difficulties) alternatively be restored.

---

[33] Cf. Sevsay, Handbuch, pp. 84f.

[34] This method of notation can also be used when only one type of cluster may be produced and even when this cluster is not chromatic (which may be the case on the harp).

Fig. 13 Additive and subtractive *glissandi*.

5. 6. 2 Depressing the keys silently and its notation

The technique of depressing the keys silently was discovered by *Schönberg*. He used the so-called piano *flageolet* in his song »Am Strande«[35] for the first time[36]. By means of this articulation harmonics can be produced. They occur when lower tones than the silently depressed ones are played: when, for instance, a semiquaver »c/C3« is played and simultaneously its first three overtones »c¹/C4«, »g¹/G4« and »c²/C5« are depressed silently for the duration of a semibreve, only these overtones linger after releasing the »c/C3«. The notation of this technique may be regarded as nearly conventional. Most composers depict this technique in the same way as *Schönberg* in »Drei Klavierstücke«[37] and hence by means of diamond-shaped notes:

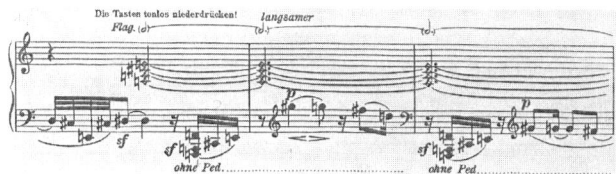

Fig. 14 Schoenberg, Drei Klavierstücke, p. 3.

This method of notation tallies with the conventional notation of harmonics because diamond-shaped notes are, for example, also used for the notation of artificial harmonics and certain natural harmonics on string instruments. However, it is not necessary to explain that this playing technique results in harmonics being produced. This is because when the pianist follows the instructions, it is the automatic result. Therefore, *Schönberg's* additional direction *Flageolett* and the note in brackets do not have to be employed.

Further, cluster chords may also be depressed silently. In »„... zwei Gefühle ...“, Musik mit Leonardo« *Lachenmann* requests this technique by connecting the lowest and highest tone of the »harmonic« cluster by means of a single line[38], whereas *Holliger* in »Elis«[39] connects the notes by two lines[40]. However, in order to depict silently depressed cluster chords in accordance with normal cluster chords, a »harmonic« cluster note – which consists of a number of transposed diamond-shaped notes – is suggested here being used. Diatonic clusters can then be requested by means of accidentals placed above or beneath the note and chromatic clusters by employing no additional accidental above or beneath the note (cf. the previous chapter). As can be seen in Figure 15, the pianist is supposed to depress four »harmonic« clusters in the order of a diatonic cluster »a – c²/A3 – C5« on the white keys, a diatonic cluster »e♭¹ – f♯²/

---

[35] Arnold Schönberg; Two songs for voice and piano. I. Gedenken. II. Am Strande. Los Angeles 1966.

[36] Peter Roggenkamp: Schriftbild und Interpretation in neuer Klaviermusik [Type face and interpretation in new piano music]. Vienna 1996, p. 22.

[37] Arnold Schönberg: Drei Klavierstücke [Three piano pieces]. Los Angeles 1910.

[38] Cf. Helmut Lachenmann, Gefühle, no page named [foreword].

[39] Heinz Holliger: Elis. Three nocturnal pieces for piano. Mainz 1964.

[40] Cf. ibid., p. 4.

Eb4 – F#5« on the black keys, a chromatic cluster »a – c²/A3 – C5« as well as the two diatonic clusters »eb¹ – f#²/Eb4 – F#5« (on the black keys) and »a – c²/A3 – C5« (on the white keys) simultaneously.

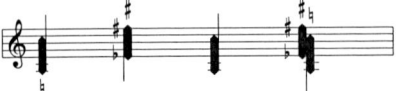

Fig. 15 Silently depressed diatonic and chromatic clusters.

Moreover, additive and subtractive *glissandi* may also be played »silently«. In order to depict this articulation, for instance, the notes in Figure 13 need to simply be replaced by diamond-shaped notes and clusters.

5. 6. 3 Exact muting stops/harmonics and their notation

Exact muting stops may on the strings of a piano be executed in the same way as on the harp. They are performed by fingering an off-node position with the same pressure as harmonics. When the string is then played (at the keyboard, *pizzicato* etc.), a muted tone can be perceived. This technique may preferably be executed by the assistant. Due to the similar nature of the harp and the piano, the method of notation employed for plucked instruments is transferred to the piano. Hence exact muting stops are requested by utilising diamond-shaped notes that depict an off-node position, starting from the assistant's position (cf. Chapter »5. 3. 4 The vertical *glissando* on the strings with/without playing and its notation«). As mentioned, on the strings of a piano muting stops up to approximately 4/5 of the string length on the uncovered strings of all models may normally be fingered, whereas only 1/2 of the string length may be reached on the bass strings of concert grand pianos. Additional crossbeams that connect the basic braces do not have a big impact on the technique because the player may reach positions underneath or behind these crossbeams. However, this technique may, in its full extent, only be performed on the uncovered strings (cf. the »Appendix«). Moreover, only a very limited number of muting stops may be played on the highest strings. When fingering the nodes and the string is played, harmonics evolve. They can be depicted by means of the conventional method of notation for harmonics. However, in this case, it needs to be taken into account that, for instance, the fifth node of the sixth partial (double octave and fifth) cannot be fingered, the second partial is notated in the same way as on the harp and only a very limited number of harmonics may be produced on the highest strings.

In Figure 16, the pianist is supposed to play on the keyboard while the assistant simultaneously fingers muting stops or harmonics. The mutual impact of the pianist's and assistant's actions is expressed by the additional two-headed arrow between the notation systems. The pianist plays four crotchets »c¹/C4«. However, each time another sound is produced because the assistant fingers the position »g¹/G4« (third partial), the second partial (octave; notated in the same way as on the harp), mutes the string on position »f#¹/F#4« and finally fingers the position »f¹/F4« (fourth partial) on the »c¹/C4«-string (also cf. the vertical *glissando* in Figure 7 as well as Figure 25 in the chapter on plucked instruments). In order to facilitate the performance, the assistant may, as mentioned, have to mark the nodes with chalk.

Fig. 16 Exact muting stops/harmonics and playing on the keyboard.

Muting stops or harmonics may also be executed by means of items. As mentioned in Chapter »5. 4. 3 Extended battuto techniques and their notation«, the utilisation of items is either requested by a direction or by presenting a symbol for the item. Thus the notation of muting stops or harmonics executed with items may be achieved by depicting the position on the string and the item that is used. In the case of stopping clusters with a long item, the method of notation for exact muting stops/harmonics needs to be augmented to cluster chords. Hence either a normal cluster chord with a small circle above it (for certain harmonic clusters) or a normal cluster chord in combination with a »harmonic« cluster chord (which, as mentioned, consists of a number of transposed diamond-shaped notes, as used for the notation of exact muting stops) needs to be employed.

In Figure 17, **exact cluster muting stops/harmonic clusters** are requested. They are both executed by means of a threaded rod on the (chromatic) string cluster »$c^1 - c^2/C4 - C5$« for the duration of a minim. The assistant is, in the example, supposed to attach the item on the tritone position and the first node. The muting position needs to be the same for each string. Otherwise, the appearance of the score would become unclear. When the pianist simultaneously plays all or a number of the strings involved in the muted/harmonic cluster, at first muted tones and then the second partial of these tones can be perceived. Additionally, a clanking noise or buzzing evolves because the string/s repetitively hit/s the rod when the pianist plays one or more tones of the muted/harmonic cluster. This effect apparently varies according to the material of the utilised item. Further, it may be useful to give the direction *non battuto* in order to prevent the assistant from hitting the strings.

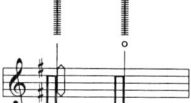

Fig. 17 Exact cluster muting stops/harmonic clusters.

Moreover, when moving an item, such as the threaded rod, vertically on the strings, the method of notation for the vertical *glissando* (cf. Chapter »5. 3. 3 The vertical *glissando* on the strings with/without playing and its notation«) needs to be extended by the method used for the depiction of exact cluster muting stops/harmonic clusters (while harmonic clusters only need to be employed in the case of the pianist or assistant simultaneously playing one of the tones involved in the cluster).

Further, the **buzz-*pizzicato*** is executed in the same way as on plucked and string instruments. Therefore, the method of notation presented in the chapter on plucked instruments (Figure 27) or chapter the string instruments (Figure 86) may be transferred to the piano. As mentioned, the buzz-*pizzicato* may be produced in three ways: 1. By slightly touching the lingering string with the fingernail after a pizzicato/the respective key is played. 2. By slightly touching the lingering string with the fingertip after a *pizzicato*/the respective key is played. 3. By slightly touching the string with the fingernail during the performance of a *pizzicato*/whilst the respective key is played. In the case of variants 1 and 2, a *pizzicato*-sound is followed by a buzzing, whereas, in the case of variant 3, a *pizzicato*-sound and buzzing blend. The method of notation can be derived from the described figures (and Figure 16 in the case of variant 3).

5. 6. 4 »Half harmonic« stops and their notation

As mentioned in Chapter »4. 7. 2 Half harmonic stops and their notation«, half harmonic stops are a string instrument and guitar technique, which cannot be employed on the harp. However, it may be used on the piano since the pressure applied to the string may – in comparison to exact muting stops/harmonics – be increased. The result is that the string bends a little. When, for instance, the pianist plays a string that is muted with increased pressure, the sound produced by the hammers hitting the string and a hardly perceptible colouring can be heard. Since this technique is strongly related to the performance of half harmonic stops on string instruments and the guitar – because the pressure is on these instruments, in comparison to the normal harmonic fingering, also increased – it can be notated by transferring the paradigm presented in Chapter »1. 6. 1 Half harmonic stops and their notation«. Hence a normal note head that depicts the involved string, a diamond-shaped note that determines the muting position and a complementary white and black diamond-shaped symbol placed above the note can be used to request this articulation (cf. the previous chapter as well as Figure 82 in the chapter on string instruments). Additionally, clusters may also be muted in this way and hence the paradigm presented in Figure 17 (exact cluster muting stop) be complemented by the described symbol. In the case of applying these »half harmonic« stops on nodes, diamond-shaped notes should always be employed to depict the position on the string because no harmonics are produced, but the string is – due to the increased pressure – muted.

5. 7 Pedal effects

There are two pedal effects. One is referred to as **extended pedal changes** while the other can be described as **pedal strokes**.

5. 7. 1 Extended pedal changes

The gradual change of the damper pedal position resembles the pedal-*glissando* on the harp (cf. Chapter »4. 3. 6 The pedal-*glissando*«). However, on the piano the change of the pedal position does not result in raising or lowering the pitch, but a gradual release or depression of the dampers. Additionally, the pedal may constantly be »half« depressed[41]. *Stockhausen* explains that, in this case, the right pedal is depressed "just so far down that the duration of the attack and a soft continuation of the note are audible after releasing the key"[42]. This means that the pedal is depressed halfway for notes in the middle register, one-third for the low register, two-thirds for the high register and completely for the highest register[43] (whilst no dampers are, as mentioned, applied on grand pianos either from »f$\sharp^3$/F$\sharp$6«, »g^3/G6« or »g$\sharp^3$/ G$\sharp$6« on).

5. 7. 1. 1 Previous methods of notation

In most cases, a gradual depression or release of the damper pedal is requested by means of the conventional pedal symbol and an additional line. Moreover, a gradual change to the »half« pedal position is depicted by adding the direction 1/2. *Kagel* in »Passé composé«[44], for instance, makes use of this method of notation. Rapid releases and re-depressions are in this piece also requested by means of the additional line. In the example presented in Figure 18, the pianist is supposed to depress the pedal, release and re-depress it quickly, then release the pedal quickly and change to the »half« pedal, release the pedal quickly and change to the completely depressed pedal, release and re-depress the pedal quickly etc. The duration of each action is depicted in relation to the piano's notation system.

---

[41] Cf. Sevsay, Handbuch, p. 264.
[42] Karlheinz Stockhausen: Klavierstück VI. London 1965, no page named [foreword].
[43] Ibid., no page named [foreword].
[44] Mauricio Kagel: Passé composé. Frankfurt/M. et al. 1996.

Fig. 18 Kagel, Passé, p. 26.

However, *Stockhausen* in »Klavierstück VI«, for instance, does not make use of the conventional method of notation for the depression of the pedal, but requests to use the damper pedal by means of the letter »P« whilst the pedal position is related to the vertical position of an additional line. In Figure 19, the pedal is initially »half« depressed, then gradually released and again »half« depressed. Shortly (i. e. a quaver »grace rest«) after attacking the »C/C2« the pedal position is changed to completely depressed and then quickly to »half« depressed. Subsequently, the pedal is gradually released, after a rest again »half« depressed and released. This action is followed by a quick change between the completely depressed pedal and the »half« pedal etc.

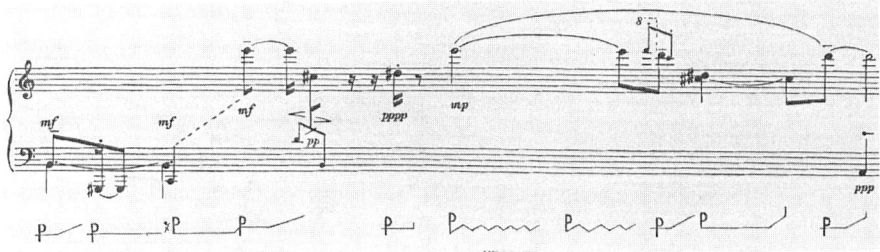

Fig. 19 Stockhausen, Klavierstück VI, p. 25.

Moreover, *Sevsay* suggests making use of the conventional symbol for depressing the pedal whilst the pedal position is, in this case, also related to the vertical position of an additional line. Further, a dotted line is used whenever the position is changed gradually. Additionally, bracketed notes may be used to depict the duration of the change:

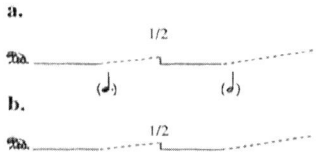

Fig. 20 Sevsay, Handbuch, p. 264.

5. 7. 1. 2 Discussion

The normal depression of the pedal is conventionally depicted by means of the pedal symbol whilst the normal release is depicted by means of a star or a vertical line[45]. These methods of notation should, therefore, also be employed in the case of a gradual depression or release of

---

[45] Sevsay, Handbuch, p. 254.

the pedal. Hence concerning this matter, *Kagel's* method of notation (cf. Figure 18) can be preferred from *Stockhausen's* approach (cf. Figure 19). However, it is clearer to depict any gradual change to one of the three pedal positions by means of the vertical position of the additional line. Therefore, *Stockhausen's* and *Sevsay's* method (cf. Figure 20) may be preferred in this matter. When comparing these two approaches, *Sevsay* suggests a clearer method because the pedal position is not only depicted by means of the line, but (as in the case of *Kagel's* approach) also determined by means of the direction 1/2 and the pedal symbol. However, there is no need to employ a dotted line and the actual release of the pedal should, as mentioned, be either requested by means of a star or vertical line. Moreover, when wishing to depict the duration of the gradual change in an exact way, a distinct timeline for the pedal is suggested here being used instead of the bracketed notes (cf. Figure 18 in the chapter on plucked instruments).

5. 7. 1. 3 Suggestion for the notation of extended pedal changes

Hence extended pedal changes are suggested being notated by combining the methods of notation by *Kagel*, *Stockhausen* and *Sevsay* while it is preferred to request the release of the pedal by means of a star. This is because when requesting a long depression of the pedal (without gradual changes), an additional line would otherwise have to complement the notation system constantly[46] and the star is – despite being rarely used in contemporary works[47] – the more traditional method of notation. Further, a quick release and re-depression may be depicted in a clearer manner when additionally using a star[48].

In Figure 21, two alternative methods for the depiction of pedal position changes are presented. In the case of the first method, the changes are displayed by means of the piano's notation system: the pianist plays four crotchets »c¹/C4«. The pedal is, in the beginning, depressed, but from this point on gradually released for the duration of a crotchet to the »half« pedal position. The pedal position is then changed back to the completely depressed pedal for the duration of another crotchet and, before the fourth note is played, quickly released and re-depressed. Finally, the pedal is gradually released for the duration of a crotchet. When depicting the pedal changes by means of a distinct timeline, more complex actions may be notated: the pianist again plays four crotchets »c¹/C4«. In the beginning of the second example, the pedal is »half« depressed (this symbol may also be used to request a constant utilisation of the »half« pedal position). Subsequently, the pedal position is in turns changed from completely depressed to »half« depressed in a semiquaver rhythm. After this »trill-*glissando*«, the pedal remains depressed »halfway« for the duration of a dotted quaver, is then released for the duration of a semiquaver and gradually depressed for the duration of a crotchet.

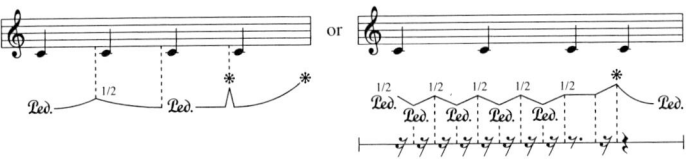

Fig. 21 Gradual pedal changes.

Further, in the case of requesting the »half« pedal, the pianist needs to determine how far the pedal is depressed. Even though *Stockhausen* has clearly explained the execution of this technique, it is still at the pianist's discretion how far the pedal is depressed when, for exam-

---

[46] Cf. Kagel, Passé, p. 11.

[47] Cf. Sevsay, Handbuch, p. 254.

[48] Cf. ibid., p. 264.

ple, notes in the low and middle register are simultaneously played. Another option was to introduce more pedal positions, e. g. 1/3, 1/2 and 2/3. Further, the production of pedal »noise« may be requested in the same way as gradual pedal changes. When the pedals are moved vigorously and the strings are not played, they start to vibrate anyway. The dynamic level of the pedal noise is always very low.

5. 7. 2 Pedal strokes

When requesting pedal strokes, the pianist is supposed to hit the pedal box with the pedal itself, which results in a popping sound. This action may be executed in combination with depressing or releasing the pedal. In the case of hitting the pedal box, the strings are caused to vibrate when the pedal is not released after the violent depression. Moreover, pedal strokes may complement the articulation of silently depressing the keys (cf. Chapter »5. 6. 2 Depressing the keys silently and its notation«). However, when the pedal is violently depressed and a number of keys at the same time silently depressed, it needs to subsequently be released in order to produce the desired effect[49].

5. 7. 2. 1 Previous methods of notation

There are a number of approaches towards the notation of pedal strokes. *Delás* in »Outremer clair et foncé«[50], for instance, depicts this articulation by means of a special arrow pointing downwards, a (modern) pedal symbol and an additional dynamic level:

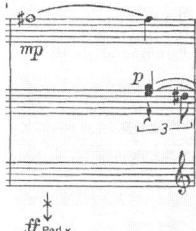

Fig. 22 Delás, Outremer, p. 31.

Another method is suggested by *Sevsay*. He recommends depicting pedal strokes by means of additional x-shaped note heads in a single lined notation system with no clef:

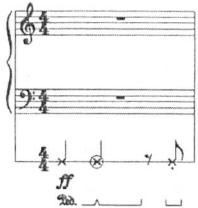

Fig. 23 Sevsay, Handbuch, p. 265.

Moreover, *Stone* suggests using diamond-shaped notes instead of x-shaped ones in a single lined notation system[51].

---

[49] Cf. ibid., p. 264.

[50] José Luis Delás: Outremer clair et foncé. In: Alfons Kontarsky (ed.): Pro musica nova. Studies for playing avant-garde music. For piano. Cologne 1972, pp. 30-33.

[51] Cf. Stone, Notation, p. 271.

5.7.2.2 Discussion

In this work percussive effects, such as strokes on the body of an instrument, are depicted by means of a symbol for the sound producer, a sketch of the instrument and x-shaped note heads in a single lined notation system with no clef (cf. Chapter »1.7.1 Strokes on the body and their notation«). However, in the case of pedal strokes, the action itself is already adequately described by means of the symbol for depressing or releasing the pedal. This symbol merely needs to be complemented by a note, symbol or direction that requests to additionally hit the pedal box when using the pedal. Since x-shaped note heads are normally used to depict percussive effects, they could also be utilised in this case. However, another additional notation system could cause an unclear appearance of the score when used in combination with gradual pedal changes (cf. Figure 21). But if x-shaped note heads were used in the system that depicts the duration of the gradual pedal changes, both articulations could simultaneously be employed without causing confusion. Therefore, requesting pedal strokes by means of x-shaped note heads (cf. Figure 23) is preferred here over utilising an additional symbol (cf. Figure 22). Moreover, *Stone's* diamond-shaped notes should not be used for the notation of pedal strokes because they are, in this work, only utilised to request harmonics or related articulations (cf., for instance, Chapter »5.6.3 Exact muting stops/harmonics and their notation«).

5.7.2.3 Suggestion for the notation of pedal strokes

Hence pedal strokes are suggested being notated by means of x-shaped note heads in a single lined notation system with no clef. In Figure 24, the pedal changes from the previous example are augmented by making the player strike the pedal box when depressing the pedal completely for the first, third and fourth time as well as when releasing the pedal. The dynamic level of the first three strokes is *forte* and of the last one *piano*.

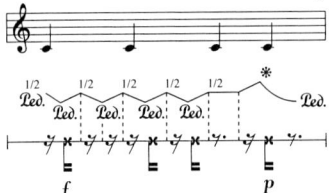

Fig. 24 Pedal changes and strokes.

5.8 Percussive effects and their notation

Percussive effects may be produced on the piano's body (or other parts) as well as on its strings. The hand or items may be used to strike the frame, soundboard, lid etc. of the instrument. As shown in Chapter »1.7.1 Strokes on the body and their notation«, strokes on the body of an instrument may be depicted by means of a drawing of the instrument's body – which enables the determination of the point of impact – in combination with a drawing of the player's hand. When items are supposed to be used, a symbol replaces the drawing of the hand (cf., for instance, Chapter »3.1.1 Introducing special agents of attack and its notation«). Therefore, **strokes on the body** of a piano can be notated similarly and hence by means of a drawing, such as the one presented in Figure 25. However, as in the case of the other instruments, only a section should be displayed in the score. Moreover, the drawing is related here to the assistant's position because strokes on the body may preferably be executed by this player. When the pianist is supposed to perform such actions, the drawing may be flipped horizontally in order to adapt it to his perspective. In the case of using a piano with more than three crossbeams, the sketch needs to be either changed or the player be advised to transfer the strokes to a different model at his own discretion. Apparently, it is impossible to predict the exact shape of the frame or length of the piano. Therefore, the drawing is always approximate and only able to exactly depict the material (frame, crossbeams = metal, soundboard = wood) or part (crossbeam, frame, soundboard) and approximate position that is hit. Further, strokes on the lid can be requested by presenting a drawing of the lid. Strokes from underneath can be notated similarly to strokes on the front whilst it may be outlined that the bottom side is supposed to be hit by colouring the drawing black (cf. Figure 21 in the chapter on percussion instruments).

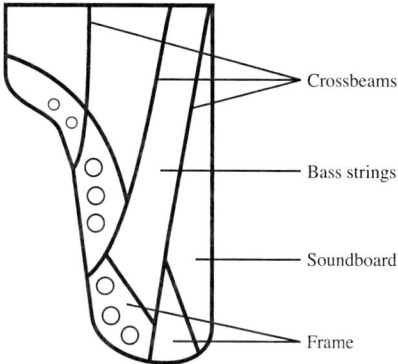

Crossbeams

Bass strings

Soundboard

Frame

Fig. 25 The interior of a grand piano.

Moreover, the pianist may be requested to strike the keyboard lid or the wooden strip at the edge of the keyboard. In this case, another drawing needs to be employed. In Figure 26, such strokes are performed. They are executed in the order of – with the knuckles on the left wooden strip – with the side of the fist on the lid (middle) – with the palm on the lid (right side) – with the index, middle and ring finger on the lid (left to the middle) – with the tip of the thumb, index and middle finger as well as with the tip and fingernail of the index finger on the lid (left side). All actions are separated by quaver rests (also cf. Figures 89 to 91 in the chapter on string instruments). When single fingers are supposed to be used in fast succession, the order can, as mentioned, additionally be depicted as on the piano, e. g. 4, 3, 1, 4, 0, 5.

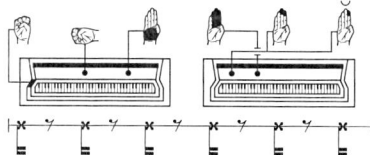

Fig. 26 Strokes on the keyboard lid and wooden strip.

Further, another percussive effect may be produced by **slamming the keyboard lid**. *Cage* has often used this effect. For instance, in »Music of Changes III«[52] it is notated by means of an additional single lined notation system. A normal note head and the direction slam keyboard lid request to close the lid violently whilst a bracketed diamond-shaped note and the direction open depict the opening:

---

[52] John Cage: Music of changes III. For piano. New York et al. 1961.

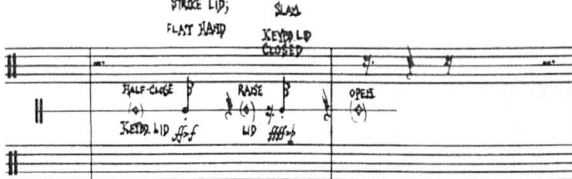

Fig. 27 Cage, Changes III, p. 62.

However, as mentioned, percussive effects are, in this work, always notated by means of x-shaped note heads. Whereas, common note heads are normally related to sounds with definite pitch and diamond-shaped notes to actions that resemble the production of harmonics. Additionally, the simplest way of depicting articulations like this is to present a sketch of the action. Therefore, it is suggested here using x-shaped note heads in a single lined notation system with no clef in combination with a drawing that distinctly requests to slam or open the lid. Such a drawing is presented in Figure 28. As can be seen there, the pianist is supposed to slam the keyboard lid with the dynamic level *fortissimo*, then open it after a crotchet rest with the dynamic level *pianissimo* and slam it again after a quaver rest. When the lid is supposed to be opened without producing any sound at all, no x-shaped note heads are employed here, but the player simply advised when to open the lid again. Hence the lid is, in the example, subsequently opened again after a crotchet rest without producing any sound. Alternatively, x-shaped note heads and the dynamic level »∅« may, in such a case, be used.

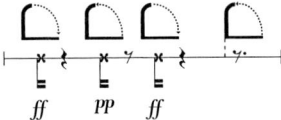

Fig. 28 Slamming and opening the keyboard lid.

As mentioned in Chapter »1. 7. 2 Strokes on the strings and their notation«, **strokes on the strings** may be described as stop attacks executed with the hand. As this technique is on string, percussion, plucked and keyboard instruments executed in a similar manner, it can be notated by means of the paradigm presented in this chapter and hence by utilising a symbol of the hand, a muting sign (⊕) and determining the playing position (cf. Figure 93 in the chapter on string instruments). When executing dead strokes with the hand, it does not make a difference whether the strings are additionally muted with the other hand or not because they do not vibrate subsequently to the stroke. However when using, for instance, a beater or the wood of a bow, the strings linger after the attack. Therefore, the method of notation may be augmented in order to make the player additionally finger harmonics or mute the strings (cf. Figure 94 in the chapter on string instruments, Chapters »5. 4. 2 The utilisation of beaters and its notation«, »5. 5 Muting and its notation« and »5. 6. 3 Exact muting stops/harmonics and their notation«).

Further, it is possible to play a *glissando* **without depressing the keys**[53]. When doing so, only the subtle noise that evolves when the fingers slide over the keys can be perceived. This articulation is strongly related to the normal key *glissando* and the key *pizzicato*. Therefore, it is suggested here depicting it in the same way as the common key *glissando* while replacing the common with x-shaped note heads (cf. Figure 6). The dynamic level of this articulation is always low, but may be increased by using the fingernails or items, such as a plectrum or pen-

---

[53] Cf. Lachenmann, Guero, pp. 1-5.

cil (cf., for instance, Chapter »5. 1. 2 The *pizzicato* on the strings and its notation« for the notation of items). The exact determination of the fingers (and fingernails) the pianist is supposed to employ can be achieved by using a hand symbols, such as the ones presented in Figure 26.

In Figure 29, the pianist is required to perform four different *glissandi*. The first one is a diatonic *glissando* on the white keys executed with the index and middle finger whilst involving the fingernails. The *glissando* starts on the »d¹/D4« and ends on the »a²/A5«. The sound production ends when the last note is reached and the demisemiquaver is therefore applied pro forma. The second *glissando* is diatonic and executed on the black keys with a plectrum. It starts on the »c♯¹/C♯4« and ends on the »a♭²/A♭5«. The third one is a chromatic *glissando* with the index and middle finger from »a/A3« to »a¹/A4« while the fourth *glissando* starts on the white keys (»a/A3« to »d¹/D4«), is then executed on the white and black keys (»e♭¹/E♭4« to »g¹/G4«) and ends on the black keys (»a♭¹/A♭4« to »e♭²/E♭5«). In this case, the player makes use of the index, middle and ring finger whilst involving the fingernails. Moreover, *glissandi* executed with both hands (travelling the same or opposite direction) may also be notated in this manner. Alternatively, the common *glissando* notation may be restored.

Fig. 29 The diatonic and chromatic *glissando* without depressing the keys.

Finally, another extended percussive effect is the **glissando on the tuning pins**[54]. When executing this kind of *glissando*, the pitch of the strings that are connected to the pins the player slides over is slightly perceptible. This effect can be increased by depressing the damper pedal. The technique is related to rubbing motions on the resonators of mallet instruments because, in the case of both, a percussive effect is complemented by a slightly perceptible *glissando* of the pitch. Therefore, it is suggested here notating these two articulations in the same manner. Thus the effect is depicted by presenting a drawing of the instruments (including its pins) in combination with a pitch-based notation system (cf. Figure 36 in the chapter on percussion instruments). Apparently, the graphic depiction of the instrument, as well as the possible extent of the *glissando* motions, is – as in the case of the strokes on the body and the *glissando* on the strings – dependent on the utilised models. However, since a listing of the framework of various piano models is available (cf. the »Appendix«), it is possible to depict *glissandi* in an exact manner and suggest models upon which these actions may be performed.

In the example presented in Figure 30, the pianist is supposed to perform two *glissandi* on the tuning pins. The first one is executed for the duration of a crotchet from the pins of »a/A3« to the pins of »c²/C5« and the second one for the same duration from the pins of »a♭¹/A♭4« to the pins of »a/A3«. These *glissandi* could, for instance, be performed on the *Bechstein B 212, L 167* and *M/P 192*, the *Boston GP-156 PE, GP-163, GP-163 PE* and *GP-178 PE*, the *Steinway C-227, D-274, O-180* and *S-155*, the *Wend & Lung 161* and the *Yamaha C3*. They could even be transferred to models with four crossbeams, such as the *Bechstein C 234, D 282* or the *Bösendorfer 225*. Further, more complex motions on the pins may clearly be notated with the help of the notation system. *Glissandi* on the tuning pins are, as *glissandi* on the strings, always chromatic.

---

[54] Cf. Lachenmann, Gefühle, no page named [foreword].

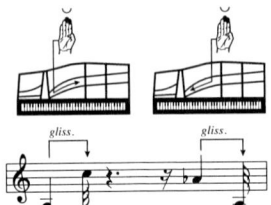

Fig. 30 *Glissandi* on the tuning pins.

Moreover, any kind of **attack on tuning pins** may be depicted in the same way as in Figure 26 with the difference that a graphic depiction of the frame and pins, as well as a pitch based notation system, is utilised in lieu of a graphic depiction of the keyboard lid and a single lined notation system. The pins that are supposed to be attacked can, in this case, also be exactly determined by means of the notation system. In the case of striking the pins of a string made of two or three wires, it is, as in the case of the *pizzicato* on the strings, at the player's discretion to determine the exact performance of the action. Further, *Lachenmann* in »Guero« requests *pizzicati* at the tip of a tuning peg[55]. However, such an attack is regarded here as a hit on a single tuning peg with the tip of the index finger.

5. 9 Preparing the instrument and its notation

The piano can, for instance, be prepared by muting a number of strings with adhesive tape, as it is requested by *Szalonek* in »Proporzioni II«[56]. Further, many examples of preparations can be found in *Cage's* works for prepared piano[57]. As in the case of the other instruments, there are numerous ways of preparing the piano. Similarly it is also, on the one hand, barely possible to list them all and subsequently develop a coherent method of depiction whilst, on the other hand, it is also not necessary to do so since most preparations are executed previously to a performance and may simply be described in the foreword to a work. Further, when preparations are supposed to be executed during a performance, they are suggested here always being notated by means of a sketch. This is because it is the simplest way of depicting these. Such a sketch should include the determination of the strings that are prepared, e. g. when only a certain range is muted with adhesive tape. When the sketch is not clear enough, it may be complemented by an explanation (cf. Chapter »1. 8 Preparing the instrument and its notation« and »2. 6. 2 Constructional modifications and their notation«). Nevertheless, preparations may lead to the introduction of new playing techniques that should then be notated in accordance with all other techniques presented in this work.

---

[55] Cf. Lachenmann, Guero, no page named [foreword].
[56] Cf. Szalonek, Proporzioni II, no page named [foreword].
[57] Cf. Cage, Prepared 1 and John Cage: Prepared piano music. Volume 2. 1940-47. New York et al. 1960.

6. VOCAL TECHNIQUES

The chapter on extended vocal techniques focuses on all voices, including bass, baritone, tenor, countertenor, contralto, mezzo-soprano and soprano. Many of the augmented techniques examined in this chapter are related to the playing techniques of wind instruments and can simply be transferred to voices. In such cases, a detailed discussion of the technique is dismissed and merely the already suggested method of notation presented. With regard to voices, the notation of the basic *vibrato* and *tremolo*, the *glissando* and the common articulations (*legato*, *staccato* etc.) are regarded as conventional[1]. Their notation can be adopted from the essential handbooks on instrumentation whilst most composers use the method of depiction that can be found there. Moreover, microtones may be produced by vocalists (cf. the introduction to the chapter on string instruments for their notation). Whereas, the main unconventional elements of sound production discussed in this chapter are extended *vibrato/tremolo* techniques, extended tongue techniques, extended singing and speaking techniques, »preparations«, whistling, muting, percussive effects and resonance effects. Concerning the dynamic level of these articulations, indications are – as far as possible – presented when the execution of the action is, in terms of the loudness, limited.

6. 1 *Smorzato* – The extended *vibrato/tremolo* and its notation

The ordinary *tremolo* is, in the case of voices, the guttural *tremolo* and notated in the conventional manner whilst a pronounced *vibrato* can also be requested in the common way[2]. However, *Berio*, in »Sequenza III«[3], makes use of a *tremolo* variant, referred to as dental *tremolo*:

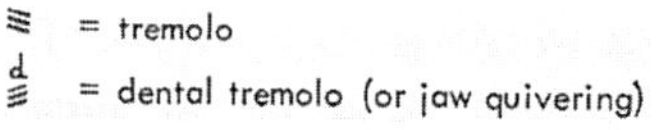

≋ ⦀ = tremolo

d ≋ = dental tremolo (or jaw quivering)

Fig. 1 Berio, Sequenza III, no page named [foreword].

As is apparent from Figure 1, the »dental *tremolo*« is supposed to be produced by jaw quivering and hence in the same way as the *smorzato* articulation on wind instruments, which can be described as a *tremolo* and *vibrato* hybrid. As shown in Chapter »2. 1 Extended *vibrato*, *tremolo* and trill techniques and their notation«, there are two types of *smorzati*, a regular and an irregular one. They can be notated by means of waved lines (derived from the *vibrato* notation) and the additional direction *smorzato* or *smorzato irregolare* (cf. Figure 3 in the chapter on wind instruments). Since the »dental *tremolo*« and the *smorzato* are strongly related, it is suggested here also requesting it in the described manner for voices.

6. 2 Extended tongue techniques and their notation

There are two extended tongue techniques that may be produced on wind instruments and – in a modified way – by all voices: the flutter tongue and the *pizzicato* effect. As shown in Chapters »2. 2. 1 The flutter tongue and its notation« and »2. 2. 2 The *pizzicato* effect and its notation«, these two techniques are winding techniques augmented by articulating certain phonemes. Hence the common production of a tone is complemented by a phoneme articulated through the respective instrument. However, when the phonemes are only produced with the mouth, the sound effect is not as strong as when they are produced on wind instruments. For instance, the clicks [!] and [⊙], still resemble the sound of a *pizzicato* when produced without an instrument, but actually only become *pizzicato* articulations when executed on wind instru-

---

[1] Cf. Stone, Notation, pp. 295, 301f. and 304.
[2] Cf. Stone, Notation, pp. 302 and 304.
[3] Luciano Berio: Sequenza III. For female voice. London 1968.

191

ments because they then complement the production of tones and are reinforced by being articulated through a tube. Therefore, these two techniques (as well as all other phonemes) are, in the case of voices, suggested being simply requested by notating the sound that is supposed to be produced by the player. Thus, in the case of the two »flutter tongue types«, the consonants [r] and [R] are suggested here being notated and, in the case of the two »pizzicato types«, the two displayed clicks. These phonemes should be placed above or below the notes that depict the singing or speaking technique the player utilises (cf. the following chapter for these techniques). Moreover, *Lachenmann*, in »temA«[4], requests a technique that resembles the flutter tongue and is referred to as flutter lip. This articulation may be depicted in the same manner and hence by either notating the consonant [p] (unvoiced flutter lip) or [b] (voiced flutter lip) and using longer durations. The International Phonetic Alphabet (IPA) is presented in Figure 3. However, an introduction into phonetics cannot be given here. Please refer for further insight to any standard phonetics compendium (e. g. *Pompino-Marschall*[5] or *Ashby and Maidment*[6]). Moreover, the other two extended tongue techniques, referred to as slap tongue and tongue ram, cannot be produced without additional instruments because, for instance, on the saxophone the slap tongue is executed by pressing the tongue against the reed and almost immediately pulling it off and, for instance, on the flutes the tongue ram is is performed by propelling the tongue into the embouchure hole with a strong thrust of air and then stopping it (cf. Chapters »2. 2. 3 The slap tongue« and »2. 2. 4 The tongue ram«). Hence both articulations require a tube and are coloured by the fingered pitch.

6. 3 Extended singing and speaking techniques

Four extended techniques are discussed in this chapter: the **highest/lowest possible tone**, the **singing and speaking modes**, **vocal effects** as well as **vocalisation**.

6. 3. 1 The highest/lowest possible tone and its notation

In Chapter »1. 4. 1 The highest possible tone and its notation« a method of notation for the highest possible tone on string instruments has been presented. Because this technique is strongly related to the production of the highest possible tone with the voice (and on wind instruments), it may be notated in the same manner. However, the method of notation can be simplified for voices since no additional explanation, such as *sul A* (cf. Figure 41 in the chapter on string instruments), needs to be employed. Hence the highest possible tone can, in the case of any vocal range, be depicted by means of a triangular note head pointing upwards, which is located above the five lines of the notation system. Moreover, the lowest possible tone may also be requested. Similarly, it can be notated by means of a triangular note head pointing downwards, which is located below the five lines of the notation system[7]:

Fig. 2 The highest/lowest possible tone.

---

4 Lachenmann, temA, p 15.
5 Pompino-Marschall, Phonetik.
6 Michael Ashby and John Maidment: Introducing phonetic science. Cambridge et al. 2005.
7 Cf. Stone, Notation, p. 294.

THE INTERNATIONAL PHONETIC ALPHABET (revised to 2005)

CONSONANTS (PULMONIC)

© 2005 IPA

	Bilabial	Labiodental	Dental	Alveolar	Postalveolar	Retroflex	Palatal	Velar	Uvular	Pharyngeal	Glottal
Plosive	p b			t d		ʈ ɖ	c ɟ	k ɡ	q ɢ		ʔ
Nasal	m	ɱ		n		ɳ	ɲ	ŋ	N		
Trill	B			r					R		
Tap or Flap		ⱱ		ɾ		ɽ					
Fricative	ɸ β	f v	θ ð	s z	ʃ ʒ	ʂ ʐ	ç ʝ	x ɣ	χ ʁ	ħ ʕ	h ɦ
Lateral fricative				ɬ ɮ							
Approximant		ʋ		ɹ		ɻ	j	ɰ			
Lateral approximant				l		ɭ	ʎ	L			

Where symbols appear in pairs, the one to the right represents a voiced consonant. Shaded areas denote articulations judged impossible.

CONSONANTS (NON-PULMONIC)

Clicks		Voiced implosives		Ejectives	
ʘ	Bilabial	ɓ	Bilabial	'	Examples:
ǀ	Dental	ɗ	Dental/alveolar	p'	Bilabial
ǃ	(Post)alveolar	ʄ	Palatal	t'	Dental/alveolar
ǂ	Palatoalveolar	ɠ	Velar	k'	Velar
ǁ	Alveolar lateral	ʛ	Uvular	s'	Alveolar fricative

OTHER SYMBOLS

ʍ Voiceless labial-velar fricative

w Voiced labial-velar approximant

ɥ Voiced labial-palatal approximant

H Voiceless epiglottal fricative

ʕ Voiced epiglottal fricative

ʡ Epiglottal plosive

ɕ ʑ Alveolo-palatal fricatives

ɺ Voiced alveolar lateral flap

ɧ Simultaneous ʃ and x

Affricates and double articulations can be represented by two symbols joined by a tie bar if necessary.

k͡p t͡s

VOWELS

Where symbols appear in pairs, the one to the right represents a rounded vowel.

SUPRASEGMENTALS

ˈ	Primary stress
ˌ	Secondary stress

ˌfoʊnəˈtɪʃən

ː	Long	eː
ˑ	Half-long	eˑ
˘	Extra-short	ĕ
ǀ	Minor (foot) group	
‖	Major (intonation) group	
.	Syllable break	ɹi.ækt
‿	Linking (absence of a break)	

DIACRITICS Diacritics may be placed above a symbol with a descender, e.g. ŋ̊

̥	Voiceless	n̥ d̥	̤	Breathy voiced	b̤ a̤	̪	Dental	t̪ d̪
̬	Voiced	s̬ t̬	̰	Creaky voiced	b̰ a̰	̺	Apical	t̺ d̺
ʰ	Aspirated	tʰ dʰ	̼	Linguolabial	t̼ d̼	̻	Laminal	t̻ d̻
̹	More rounded	ɔ̹	ʷ	Labialized	tʷ dʷ	̃	Nasalized	ẽ
̜	Less rounded	ɔ̜	ʲ	Palatalized	tʲ dʲ	ⁿ	Nasal release	dⁿ
̟	Advanced	u̟	ˠ	Velarized	tˠ dˠ	ˡ	Lateral release	dˡ
̠	Retracted	e̠	ˤ	Pharyngealized	tˤ dˤ	̚	No audible release	d̚
̈	Centralized	ë	̴	Velarized or pharyngealized	ɫ			
̽	Mid-centralized	e̽	̝	Raised	e̝	(ɹ̝ = voiced alveolar fricative)		
̩	Syllabic	n̩	̞	Lowered	e̞	(β̞ = voiced bilabial approximant)		
̯	Non-syllabic	e̯	̘	Advanced Tongue Root	e̘			
˞	Rhoticity	ɚ a˞	̙	Retracted Tongue Root	e̙			

TONES AND WORD ACCENTS

LEVEL			CONTOUR		
e̋ or	˥	Extra high	ě or	˩˥	Rising
é	˦	High	ê	˥˩	Falling
ē	˧	Mid	e᷄	˦˥	High rising
è	˨	Low	e᷅	˩˨	Low rising
ȅ	˩	Extra low	e᷈	˧˦˧	Rising-falling
↓		Downstep	↗		Global rise
↑		Upstep	↘		Global fall

Fig. 3 The International Phonetic Alphabet.

6. 3. 2 The singing and speaking modes

Besides normal singing, composers distinguish between a number of different singing and speaking modes. In his handbook on instrumentation *Stone* suggests three different modes: *Sprechgesang* or *Sprechton* (speech-song), *Sprechstimme* (spoken-voice) and speaking[8]. The term *Sprechton* was introduced by *Schönberg* in »Pierrot Lunaire«[9]. He defines that, in the case of **speech-song**, the pitch is adhered to, but only initially, after which the voice assumes speech with indefinite pitch[10]. Hence the pitch is only indicated[11]. Moreover, **spoken-voice** has speech »timbre«, but is depicted by means of the pitch-based notation system. However, the pitches are, in this case, always approximate. Speech-song is closer to singing than to speaking, whereas spoken-voice is closer to speaking than to singing. Further, **speaking** itself is ordinary speech in that voice inflections are notated[12]. *Stone* suggests three levels for this technique: high, medium and low[13]. By contrast, *Lachenmann*, in »temA«, determines the four levels high, medium high, medium low and low[14]. As is apparent from the IPA chart in Figure 3, there are, however, five standard brightness levels: extra high, high, mid, low and extra low. Another common element of singing is the *falsetto* voice, commonly applied by countertenors in order to reach the alto, mezzo-soprano or even soprano register. This technique can be used in normal singing or speech-song[15]. Finally, some composers additionally distinguish between normal singing and **half-sung**. For instance, *Haubenstock-Ramati*, makes use of this mode and explains that it is "considered as a middle stage between song and speech"[16]. *Boulez* further explains that this technique resembles the *flautando* (and hence *sul tasto*) articulation of string instruments[17]. The player is thus presumably supposed to produce less overtones.

6. 3. 2. 1 Previous methods of notation

The *Sprechgesang* articulation is often notated similarly to the way *Schönberg* notates it in »Pierrot lunaire« and hence by means of an x-shaped note head added to the tail:

Den Wein,den man mit   Au_gen trinkt,   gießt

Fig. 4 Schönberg, Pierrot, p. 5.

However, *Ligeti*, in »Nouvelles aventures«[18], requests speech-song by means of squared note heads (and spatial notation in the case of playing *senza tempo*):

---

8 Cf. ibid., pp. 297f.

9 Arnold Schönberg: Dreimal sieben Gedichte aus Albert Girauds Pierrot lunaire. For one Sprechstimme, piano, flute (also piccolo), clarinet (also bass clarinet), violin (also viola) and violincello. No city named 1914.

10 Schoenberg, Pierrot, p. 1 and Stone, Notation, p. 297.

11 Cf. Alban Berg: Wozzeck. Opera in 3 acts. Vienna 1931, p. 8.

12 Stone, Notation, pp. 297f.

13 Ibid., p. 198.

14 Lachenmann, temA, no page named [foreword].

15 Cf. Hans Werner Henze: Essay on pigs. For voice and orchestra. Mainz 1970, p. 6 (*Henze* further even requests the *falsetto* or a similar effect while speaking; however this effect is here, with reference to the IPA, described as the extra high speaking level).

16 Roman Haubenstock-Ramati: Credentials or «think, think lucky». For voice (Sprechgesang) and 8 players. Vienna 1963.

17 Cf. Pierre Boulez: Le visage nuptial. For soprano, contralto solos, women's choir and orchestra. Paris 1959.

18 György Ligeti: Nouvelles aventures. For three singers and seven instrumentalists. Frankfurt/M. et al. 1966.

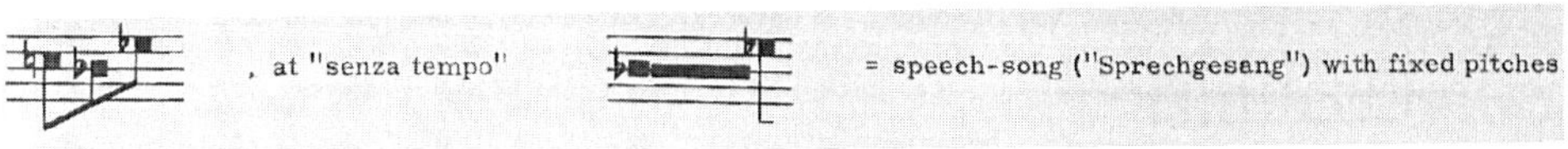

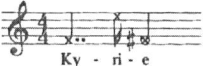 , at "senza tempo"   = speech-song ("Sprechgesang") with fixed pitches

Fig. 5 Ligeti, Nouvelles, p. 3 [comments].

As mentioned, spoken-voice is notated by means of the common notation system. *Stone* suggests depicting this technique by employing x-shaped note heads. This method of notation, which is presented in Figure 6, is most commonly employed[19].

Ky - ri - e

Fig. 6 Stone, Notation, p. 298.

By contrast, speaking is requested in various ways. *Lachenmann*, in »temA« for instance, makes use of note heads shaped like a plus sign (by him referred to as x) and a five lined notation system with no clef[20]. As mentioned, he further differentiates between four brightness levels:

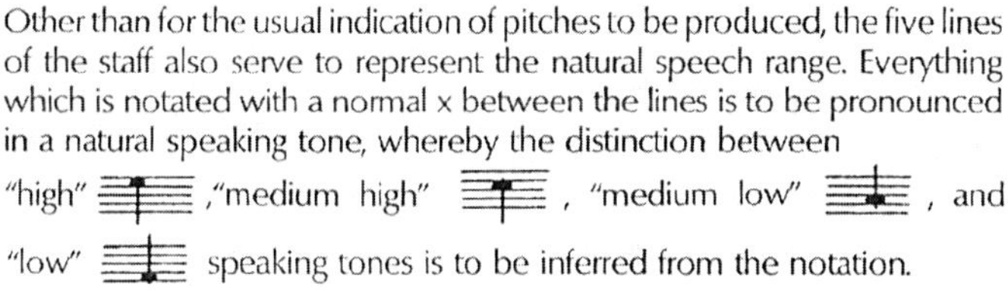

Other than for the usual indication of pitches to be produced, the five lines of the staff also serve to represent the natural speech range. Everything which is notated with a normal x between the lines is to be pronounced in a natural speaking tone, whereby the distinction between

"high" 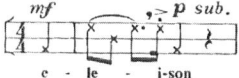 ,"medium high" ⊟ , "medium low" ⊟ , and

"low" ⊟ speaking tones is to be inferred from the notation.

Fig. 7 Lachenmann, temA, no page named [foreword].

Additionally, he requests further noises by notes which appear outside the five lines. Their brightness varies with the degree of distance from the staff lines[21]. Moreover, *Stone* suggests two methods of notation: 1. With voice inflections by means of a three lined notation system with no clef and x-shaped note heads. 2. With rhythmic indications only by means of a single lined notation system with no clef and x-shaped note heads:

1. WITH VOICE-INFLECTION GRID AND RHYTHMS (DURATIONS)

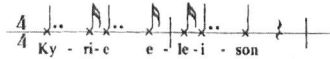

e - le - i-son

2. WITH RHYTHMIC INDICATIONS ONLY

Ky - ri- e   e - le-i - son

Fig. 8 Stone, Notation, p. 298.

---

[19] Cf., for instance, Boulez, Visage, p. 38, Krzysztof Penderecki: Passio et mors domini nostri iesu christi secundum lucam. Passion according to St Luke for solo soprano, baritone, and bass; speaker; boys choir; 3 mixed choirs; and orchestra. Celle 1967, p. 23 and Luciano Berio: Epifanie. [For orchestra and mezzo-soprano]. London 1969, p. 1 [a (M. Proust)] (here the spoken-voice is even introduced without a comment).

[20] Cf. Lachenmann, temA, pp. 1ff.

[21] Cf. ibid., no page named [foreword].

195

Another approach was to use the »method of notation« displayed in the IPA and hence additional accents added to a phoneme:

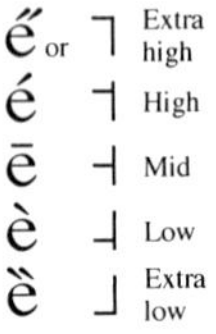

é̋ or ⌐ Extra high
é ˥ High
ē ˦ Mid
è ˧ Low
ḛ̀ ˩ Extra low

Fig. 9 Brightness levels (IPA).

Further, the *falsetto* is normally requested in the same way as harmonics. *Berg*, in »Wozzeck«, utilises a normal note head with a small circle above it and additionally explains that the falsetto [Falsett] voice is used:

Fig. 10 Berg, Wozzeck, p. 139.

The same method of notation is used by *Henze* in »Essay on pigs« as an augmentation of the singing voice and spoken-song[22]. However, *Stone* recommends using diamond-shaped note heads to indicate *falsetto* voice and the word *falsetto* at the first occurrence[23].

Finally, the half-sung articulation is in *Berg's* »Wozzeck« notated by means of adding a symbol to the note tail and giving the direction half-sung [halb gesungen]:

poco accel (ca 80 _ _ _ ca 100)
halb gesungen
selbst das Geld geht in Ver-wesung ü - ber;

Fig. 11 Berg, Wozzeck, p. 159.

In »Le visage nuptial«[24] *Boulez* notates this articulation in the same manner, whereas *Haubenstock-Ramati* simply gives the direction chanting, which – as he explains – means approximately *mezza voce*. The notation is similar to that for the normal singing voice[25].

6. 3. 2. 2 Discussion

The two methods of notation for *Sprechgesang* are simple and exact. However, the addition of symbols to the note tail (cf. Figure 4) might, as mentioned, lead to confusion when employing semibreves or additional *tremolo* symbols. Moreover, an additional note head suggests two sounds being produced simultaneously (cf., for instance, Chapter »2. 9. 1 Key/valve clicks«). Further, the pitch is actually, in the case of the spoken-song, adhered to and subsequently speech assumed. In order to depict this action correctly, a common grace note and a subsequent x-shaped note would have to be used. But such a method of notation would lead to a confusing appearance of the score. For these reasons, and because the *Sprechgesang* articula-

---

[22] Cf. Henze, Essay, p. 5.

[23] Cf. Stone, Notation, p. 293.

[24] Cf. Boulez, Visage, no page named [foreword].

[25] Cf. Haubenstock-Ramati, Credentials, no page named [foreword].

tion is closer to singing than speaking, it is preferred here to notate it by varying the normal voice notation. Thus *Ligeti's* approach (cf. Figure 5) is preferred over the one by *Schönberg*. The utilisation of squared note heads suggests that an alteration of the singing voice – and hence the spoken-song – be used. Further, the method of notation for the spoken-voice suggested by *Stone* (cf. Figure 6) is simple, exact and closely related to traditional notation. Moreover, it can even be regarded as nearly conventional. As mentioned, this technique is closer to speaking (which has an indefinite pitch) than singing, but assumes a certain pitch. Therefore, it is reasonable to notate such a transition between sounds with indefinite pitch – which are, in this work, commonly notated by means of x-shaped note heads in a single lined notation system (cf., for instance, the chapter on percussion instruments) – and sounds with definite pitch – which are conventionally depicted by means of a pitch-based notation system – in this way. Consequently, speaking should be notated by means of x-shaped note heads in a single lined notation system. Hence *Lachenmann's* approach needs to be dismissed because he makes use of special note heads instead of x-shaped ones (cf. Figure 7). As it is shown below, there is, moreover, no need to use a special method of notation in order to depict speaking noises because all kinds of sounds may be depicted by means of the IPA. Concerning the brightness levels of speaking, it can be said that the five degrees recommended by the IPA are also suggested here being utilised because it is the standard reference for phonetic sounds. However, it is preferred to notate the levels of brightness by »transposing« note heads rather than by employing accents to the text (cf. Figure 9). This is because – even though speaking may be defined as the production of sounds with indefinite pitch – the levels of brightness are related to pitch (the brighter, the higher the sound and the darker, the lower the sound) and all instrumentalists, including voices, are used to this method of notation. This »transposition« may be either depicted by using a five lined notation system with no clef or ledger lines in combination with a single lined notation system. However, as the single lined notation system is normally used in this work, the latter method of notation is preferred here. A natural-realistic conversation[26] could then be depicted by notating rhythmic indications only (cf. Figure 8). Furthermore, because the *falsetto* may be regarded as the production of harmonics with the voice, harmonic notation can be used to depict it. However, other than on string or wind instruments, harmonics are not produced here on a fundamental. Hence harmonic notation needs to be employed in another manner in the case of voices. Moreover, the *falsetto* may, as mentioned, be combined with spoken-song while this technique is requested here by means of squared note heads. If diamond-shaped note heads were, as suggested by *Stone*, applied to request the *falsetto*, another additional symbol or direction would have to be introduced in order to outline that this technique is combined with speech-song (because the squared note head was replaced by a diamond-shaped note head). An alternative was to utilise two note heads, a squared and a diamond-shaped one. However, this would suggest two sounds being produced simultaneously. Therefore, the simplest way of requesting *falsetto* is to notate a small circle above the common or squared note head that depicts – other than on string or wind instruments – the actual pitch that is produced (cf. Figure 10 for the ordinary *falsetto*). Finally, the half-sung articulation is a technique that strongly resembles *Sprechstimme* or *Sprechgesang*. In »Songs, drones and refrains of death«[27] *Crumb* states that halfsung actually means *Sprechstimme*[28], whereas *Haubenstock-Ramati*, in »Credentials«, mentions that a melodisation of speech-song boarders on half-sung[29]. Therefore, it is recommen-

---

[26] Cf. Berg, Wozzeck, p. 8.

[27] George Crumb: Songs, drones and refrains of death. Baritone, electric guitar, electric contrabass, electric piano (electric harpsichord), percussion (2 players). New York et al. 1971.

[28] Cf. ibid., p. 3.

[29] Cf. Haubenstock-Ramati, Credentials, no page named [foreword].

ded here only using this articulation very carefully. Concerning the notation of this technique, it may be said that *Berg's* approach (cf. Figure 11) could not be used without confusion in the case of employing semibreves or additional *tremolo* symbols (see above). However, it is also not necessary to add a symbol to the note tail because the technique could be adequately requested by giving a direction, such as half-sung or *mezza voce*. This method of notation complies with traditional notation because the equivalent *sul tasto* articulation is also conventionally requested by means of a direction.

6. 3. 2. 3 Suggestion for the notation of the singing and speaking modes

Hence speech-song and spoken-voice are suggested being notated by means of squared note heads and x-shaped note heads, respectively, in a pitch-based notation system whilst speaking is requested by utilising x-shaped note heads in a single lined notation system with optional ledger lines. These three modes are displayed in Figure 12. The player is supposed here to produce a »c/C3« in *Sprechgesang*, another »c/C3« in *Sprechstimme* and all five brightness levels of speaking. Alternatively, speaking may be requested by means of a five lined notation system with no clef. *Glissandi* between the brightness levels of speaking are also possible. In the case of not using these »transpositions«, the player may be directed to pronounce the text in a natural-realistic manner (see above).

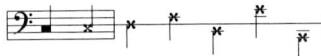

Fig. 12 Speech-song, spoken-voice and speaking

Further, *falsetto* is depicted here by means of a small circle above the note and the (optional) half-sung articulation by giving the direction *mezza voce*. In Figure 13, an »a¹/A4« is produced with *falsetto* voice and subsequently another »a¹/A4« with *falsetto* voice in *Sprechgesang*. Finally, a »c/C3« is half-sung.

Fig. 13 *Falsetto* and *mezza voce*.

As mentioned above, and in the chapter on wind instruments, text is, in this work, presented by means of the IPA. This has the advantage that it may be adequately pronounced by non-native speakers of the utilised language and the depicted phonemes can always be comprehended. As is apparent from the following chapter, this method of notation also enables the depiction of phonetic sounds that are, for example, inherent in foreign languages. Phonetic spelling can be used as the only presentation of text in the score or be complemented by the original text.

6. 3. 3 Vocal effects

There are numerous vocal effects that may be executed by voices. One group may be described as **changing the phoneme's sound value**. This means that a certain phoneme is, for instance, articulated in an unvoiced, breathy, nasal or pharyngealised manner. Another effect is the production of **simultaneous sounds**. This technique may be either executed whilst singing or speaking: an augmented singing technique is introduced by *Stockhausen* in

»Stimmung«[30] and can be described as the emphasis of certain overtones. *Stockhausen* makes use of a vowel chart in order to display it and explains that "each vowel has two numbers. They indicate the overtone that is heard as dominating while singing the vowel; the number below applies to low male voices (...), the number above the vowel applies to high male voices and low female voices"[31]:

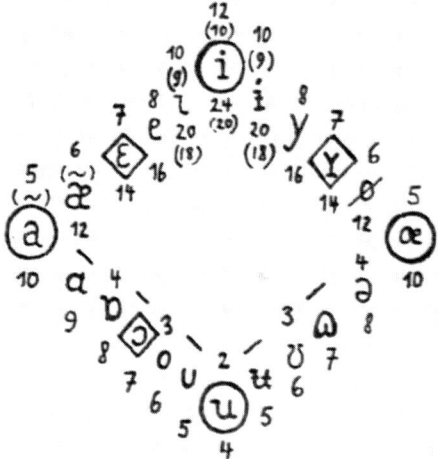

Fig. 14 Stockhausen, Stimmung, no page named [foreword].

He further elucidates that with "enough practice one can reach the point where the pitch one is singing is relatively soft and the dominating overtone relatively loud. (...) It is possible, depending on lip, mouth and tongue position, to intonate each overtone separately, from the 4th [low male voices] (or 2nd) [high male voices and low female voices] up to approximately the 24th [low male voices] (or 12th) [high male voices and low female voices]"[32]. However, in the case of requesting overtone *glissandi*, some harmonics may, for instance, fall away and the higher the register the fewer overtones can be articulated[33].

Another simultaneous technique is introduced by *Henze* in »Essay on pigs« and based on experience and vocal technique of the *Roy Hart School*, London. *Henze* distinguishes between two very high spoken sounds simultaneously, a high, medium and low spoken sound simultaneously, a high, medium and low spoken sound simultaneously in *falsetto* or similar effect as well as the *ad libitum* performance of two sounds at the same time[34]. Finally, **other effects**, such as laughing, coughing or snoring, are also discussed in this chapter.

6. 3. 3. 1 Previous methods of notation

A change in the sound value can be requested by means of the IPA. In phonetic science diacritics are used to depict unvoiced, breathy, nasalised, pharyngealised etc. articulations:

---

[30] Karlheinz Stockhausen: Stimmung. For six vocalists. Vienna 1969.

[31] Ibid., no page named [foreword].

[32] Ibid., no page named [foreword].

[33] Cf. ibid., no page named [foreword].

[34] Cf. Henze, Essay, p. 5.

DIACRITICS   Diacritics may be placed above a symbol with a descender, e.g. ŋ̊

̥	Voiceless	n̥ d̥	̈	Breathy voiced	b̤ a̤	̪	Dental	t̪ d̪
̬	Voiced	s̬ t̬	̰	Creaky voiced	b̰ a̰	̺	Apical	t̺ d̺
ʰ	Aspirated	tʰ dʰ	̼	Linguolabial	t̼ d̼	̻	Laminal	t̻ d̻
̹	More rounded	ɔ̹	ʷ	Labialized	tʷ dʷ	̃	Nasalized	ẽ
̜	Less rounded	ɔ̜	ʲ	Palatalized	tʲ dʲ	ⁿ	Nasal release	dⁿ
̟	Advanced	u̟	ˠ	Velarized	tˠ dˠ	ˡ	Lateral release	dˡ
̠	Retracted	e̠	ˤ	Pharyngealized	tˤ dˤ	̚	No audible release	d̚
̈	Centralized	ë	̴	Velarized or pharyngealized	ɫ			
̽	Mid-centralized	e̽	̝	Raised	e̝ (ɹ̝ = voiced alveolar fricative)			
̩	Syllabic	n̩	̞	Lowered	e̞ (β̞ = voiced bilabial approximant)			
̯	Non-syllabic	e̯	̘	Advanced Tongue Root	e̘			
˞	Rhoticity	ɚ a˞	̙	Retracted Tongue Root	e̙			

Fig. 15 Changing the phoneme's sound value (IPA).

Moreover, *Gaber*, in »Voce II« for instance, requests an unvoiced articulation by means of a spherical note head:

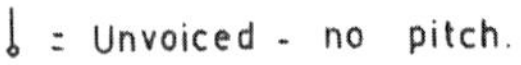

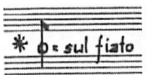 : Unvoiced - no pitch.

Fig. 16 Gaber, Voce II, p. VI.

By contrast, *Crumb*, in »Ancient voices of children«[35], simply gives the direction whispered (which refers to the unvoiced articulation). Further, in »Epifanie« *Berio* requests a breathy (*sul fiato*) articulation by means of adding a circle to the note tail:

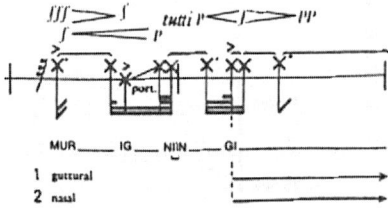

Fig. 17 Berio, Epifanie, p. 3 [a (M. Proust)].

Other changes in the phoneme's sound value, the nasal and a so-called guttural articulation are utilised by *Kagel* in »Anagrama«. He depicts these by means of directions[36] or – as can be seen in Figure 18 – directions and arrows placed underneath the notation system whilst the term guttural presumably refers to the pharyngealised articulation.

Fig. 18 Kagel, Anagrama, p. 2.

Additionally, *Lachenmann*, in »temA«, requests the pharyngealised articulation – referred to by him as pressed – by means of a special symbol placed above the note head:

= press

Fig. 19 Lachenmann, temA, no page named [foreword].

---

[35] Cf. Crumb, Ancient, p. 1.
[36] Cf. Kagel, Anagrama, p. 2.

Furthermore, *Stockhausen*, in »Stimmung«, notates the emphasis of overtones by means of the IPA and describes the produced overtone in numbers above and below the phonemes. As is apparent from Figure 20, the duration is indicated by note tails.

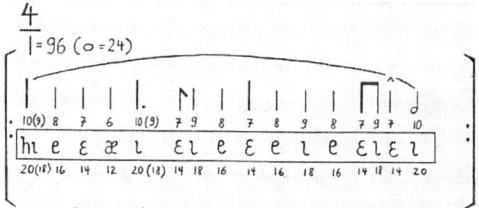

Fig. 20 Stockhausen, Stimmung, no page named [p. 10].

Henze, in »Essay on pigs«, depicts the production of simultaneous sounds while speaking by utilising special note heads (and tails) in a single lined notation system with no clef[37]:

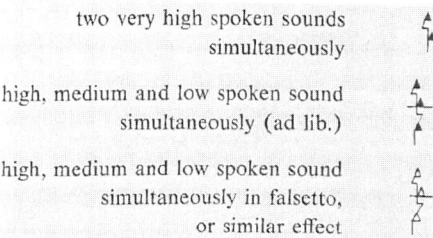

Fig. 21 Henze, Essay, p. 5.

Moreover, as is apparent from Figure 22, *Berio*, in »Sequenza III«, distinguishes between two types of laughter, a clearly articulated one – which is depicted by the letter L – and bursts of laughter – which are notated by means of a symbol resembling the phonetic sound [ʕ]. These symbols are placed below the notation system[38]. However, coughing is, in this piece, depicted by means of a special note head in a single lined notation system[39].

L.   Laughter must always be clearly articulated.

[ʔ]   = bursts of laughter to be used with any vowel freely chosen

Fig. 22 Berio, Sequenza III, no page named [foreword].

Further, snoring is described by *Lachenmann* in »NUN« as breathing through the nose on the consonants CH[40]. In »temA« he further explains that it can be regarded as a kind of *tremolo*. Therefore, the articulation is, in this piece, notated by means of an up-bow symbol, which requests inhaling, a *tremolo* symbol and the letters CH:

Snoring:

Fig. 23 Lachenmann, temA, no page named [foreword].

---

[37] Cf. Henze, Essay, p. 8.

[38] Cf. Berio, Sequenza III, p. 2.

[39] Cf. ibid., no page named [foreword] and p. 1.

[40] Cf. Lachenmann, NUN, p. XIV.

6. 3. 3. 2 Discussion

As is apparent from Figure 15, there are various ways of changing a phoneme's sound value. The introduction of special note heads (cf. Figure 16) or symbols added to the note tail (cf. Figure 17) for each one of these articulations is barely possible because it would result in a vast number of note heads or symbols that would have to be introduced. The same is valid for *Lachenmann's* approach of placing a symbol above the note head (cf. Figure 19). Further, there is no need to introduce symbols other than the standardised ones of the IPA. However, notating a change in the phoneme's sound value by means of a direction, as executed by *Crumb* (by the direction whispered) or in an extended manner by *Kagel* (cf. Figure 18), may be regarded as an alternative to adding diacritics. However, the IPA is, as mentioned, the standard reference for phonetic sounds and hence can be regarded as the simplest way of notating the described articulation. Moreover, opposed to the »transposition« of the speaking voice, there are no other common articulations in traditional notation that correspond to the changes of the phonemes' sound values. However, it may be helpful for vocal performers that are not used to the phonetic alphabet to additionally employ a (bracketed) direction, such as unvoiced or breathy at the first occurrence of a particular diacritic. Concerning the production of simultaneous sounds, it may be said that *Stockhausen's* method of notating the emphasis of certain overtones (cf. Figure 20) is not closely related to traditional notation. He rejects depicting the emphasised overtone by means of the traditional notation system because neither the performing vocalists nor the fundamentals are previously determined. However, when the vocal register and fundamental is constituted, the emphasised overtone can exactly be depicted by means of pitch-based notation. Such a method of notation would be more exact, easier to comprehend and closely related to traditional notation. Moreover, *Henze* derives the notation of simultaneous spoken sounds (cf. Figure 21) from his method of notating spoken sounds in general and the highest possible spoken sound (both are depicted by triangular note heads pointing upwards and the latter by means of an additional special note tail)[41]. However, as shown in the previous chapter, speaking is, in this work, depicted by means of x-shaped note heads in a single lined notation system with no clef. Therefore, simultaneous spoken sounds should be depicted in a similar manner and hence by depicting chords of x-shaped note heads. Further, the special effect of producing a high, medium and low spoken sound simultaneously in *falsetto* would consequently be notated by means of applying the *falsetto* notation (a small circle above the note) on the spoken voice. Even though the utilisation of this technique results in sounds that differ strongly from normal speaking, the method of notation for the spoken voice may be used. This is because, firstly, *Henze* defines these articulations as spoken sounds and, secondly – unless they differ strongly from normal speaking – simultaneous spoken sounds also have an indefinite pitch and, therefore, may not be notated by means of the traditional notation system. Further, in order to request simultaneous sounds that are produced at the vocalist's discretion, no special symbol needs to be introduced, but simply the approximate brightness level be notated and the traditional direction *ad libitum* be used. All other effects, such as laughing, coughing or snoring, can also be notated by means of the IPA. This is because these effects can be regarded as the articulation of certain consonants and/or vocals and hence as text. Therefore, all additional effects are – similarly to changing a phoneme's sound value and all other sorts of text – preferred here to be depicted by means of the IPA and not by letters, special symbols or notes (cf. Figure 22). Snoring can also be depicted in this way, but would need to be complemented by a symbol, which requests inhaling and the diacritic for nasalised. A symbol for inhaling has been introduced in Chapter »2. 5. 3 The air and tone technique«. In order to achieve the coherent notation of this technique, it is preferred here from *Lachenmann's* symbol (cf. Figure 23). Moreover, since the amplitude is not specifi-

---

[41] Cf. Henze, Essay, p. 5.

cally modulated in the case of this articulation, but simply the fricative [ʁ] (cf. Figure 3) nasalised and articulated in an inhaled manner, the *tremolo* symbol does not need to be employed. However, as in the case of the diacritics, it may, at the first occurrence of these sounds, be helpful to additionally explain that laughing, coughing, snoring etc. is depicted.

6. 3. 3. 3 Suggestion for the notation of vocal effects

Hence changes in the phonemes' sound value are suggested being requested by means of adding diacritics to the text. Optionally, an additional explanation (in brackets) may additionally be used. As is apparent from Figure 24, the phoneme [n] is articulated in four different ways in the order of unvoiced, breathy, nasalised and pharyngealised.

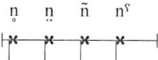

Fig. 24 Changing a phoneme's sound value.

The phonemes are placed here above the notation system, but may also be placed below it, especially when they are complemented by the original text. Moreover, for instance, the unvoiced articulation always has a low dynamic level and can only be used in combination with spoken-voice and speaking. Further, some composers specifically request shouting. This manner of articulation, however, cannot be regarded as a change in the phoneme's sound value, but may simply be requested by means of the highest dynamic levels in combination with speaking.

Further, the emphasis of overtones is depicted here by means of presenting the »chord« that is supposed to be produced and notating the vowel that is articulated. In Figure 25, the example of a low male voice (bass) is used. The vocalist is supposed to produce the overtones 4, 7, 10, 14 and 24 on the »c/C3«, which equals approximately 131 Hertz (Hz). The overtones are multiples of the fundamental frequency (f): first overtone or second partial = 2 × f, second overtone or third partial = 3 × f etc. Hence the pitches ~ 654 Hz ≈ »e²/E5«, ~ 1,047 Hz ≈ »c³/C6«, ~ 1,439 Hz ≈ »f♯³/F♯6«, ~ 1,962 Hz ≈ »h³/B6« (octave transposition) and ~ 3,270 Hz ≈ »a♭⁴/A♭7« (transposed by two octaves) are emphasised (cf. *Stockhausen's* vowel chart in Figure 14). Optionally, microtonal symbols could complement the notes in order to describe the produced pitches more exactly.

Fig. 25 Emphasising overtones.

A small circle above the note is not employed here because, firstly, the action could then be confused with the *falsetto* and, secondly, even though the overtone dominates the fundamental, both tones may be perceived (similarly to playing a chord). Further, as can be seen in the example, two notation systems might need to be used in order to depict the overtones and high pitches may be requested by means of octave transpositions (8va, 15ma, 22ma, 29ma etc.). Even frequencies that exceed the range of traditional instruments may be described in this way (cf. »Part II: Electroacoustic music – 1. 1. 1 Periodic wave generators and their envelopes«).

The production of spoken simultaneous sounds is requested in a similar manner. In Figure 26, three different »chords« are created on the vowel [a]: two very high spoken sounds simultaneously, high, medium and low spoken sounds simultaneously as well as high, medium and low spoken sounds simultaneously in *falsetto*. The *ad libitum* sounds could be depicted by using two transposed note heads in any combination and the direction *ad libitum*.

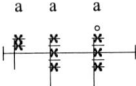

Fig. 26 Simultaneous spoken sounds.

Furthermore, other effects, such as laughing, coughing or snoring are suggested here being depicted by means of the IPA. As can be seen in Figure 27, these articulations are notated as spoken sounds. The first five semiquavers may be described as laughing, the two connected sounds after the semiquaver rest as coughing as well as the inhaled and nasalised articulation of the crotchet fricative as snoring. An arrow pointing downwards complements the last note because the phoneme is supposed to be articulated whilst inhaling and this symbol has been suggested for the depiction of this technique (cf. Chapter »2. 5. 3 The air and tone technique«). Optionally, additional explanations (in brackets) may be employed. Moreover, voiced effects, such as laughing, can also be sung and executed in *Sprechgesang* or *Sprechstimme*. However there is, for instance, only one way of performing the snoring effect and hence no brightness levels may be utilised. Additionally, the dynamic level can also barely be varied.

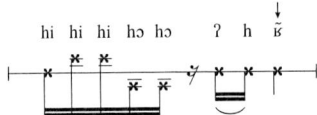

Fig. 27 Laughing, coughing and snoring.

Finally, besides singing and speaking modes as well as vocal effects, there is one factor that is especially important for voices: **expression**. Various examples for additional directions that further outline in which way notated phonemes may be articulated can, for instance, be found in *Ligeti's* »Aventures« and »Nouvelles aventures«. This factor is traditionally depicted above the notation system as a written direction.

6. 3. 4 Vocalisation and its notation

As explained in Chapter »2. 5. 4 Vocalisation and its notation«, vocalisation refers to an alteration of the mouth cavity's resonance. In the case of wind instruments, this action results in a change of the timbre. The technique may also be employed in order to change the timbre of sung voiced consonants or vowels and the brightness level of spoken fricatives. *Lachenmann*, in »NUN«, distinguishes between six vowel positions. In the score these bracketed vowels indicate the coloration of the brightness of the fricatives[42]:

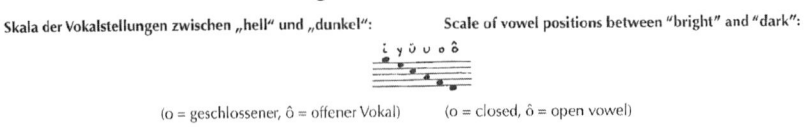

Skala der Vokalstellungen zwischen „hell" und „dunkel":   Scale of vowel positions between "bright" and "dark":

(ɔ = geschlossener, ô = offener Vokal)   (ɔ = closed, ô = open vowel)

Fig. 28 Lachenmann, NUN, p. XXIII.

---

[42] Cf. Lachenmann, NUN, pp. XXIIf.

As is apparent from Figure 28, *Lachenmann* does not make use of phonetic symbols to explain the vowel position. When comparing his explanation with the IPA chart (cf. Figure 3), it may nevertheless be concluded that the tongue position is presumably changed from close/front to open-mid/back and hence the vocals [i] to [ɔ] are supposed to be formed with the mouth whilst articulating fricatives. In order to notate this action in accordance with vocalised winding, two notation systems would have to be employed. The upper one would depict the articulated fricative, and the lower one would present the vowel that is formed with the mouth whilst the dynamic level of the vowel would be designated as »Ø« (cf. Figure 47 in the chapter on wind instruments). This method of notation can also be employed for voices when singing voiced fricatives. However, it is not necessary to make use of this method of notation when speaking because the articulation of spoken phonetic sounds is different from the production of tones on wind instruments: in the case of the fricatives, vocalists produce varying levels of brightness by means of vocalisation. However, the brightness level of other consonants is varied in another way. Moreover, as shown above, a change in the brightness level of spoken sounds can generally be requested by means of »transposing« x-shaped note heads (cf. Figure 12). Therefore, the introduction of varying methods of notation for the same effect would cause confusion and complicate the notation of spoken sounds. Concerning the number of brightness levels, the five stages recommended by the IPA are preferred here from *Lachenmann's* suggestion.

6. 4 »Preparations« and their notation

Apparently, voices cannot be prepared in the same way as the other instruments. Most commonly, the transformation of the original sound produced by the vocalists is achieved by making the performer sing through his hands or items. *Kagel*, in »..., den 24. xii. 1931«, for instance, makes the baritone cup his hands "in front of the mouth, like a newspaper vendor calling out his wares, but softly and supressed [sic]" [43]. This direction is employed above the baritone's notation system. Moreover, *Ligeti* makes a baritone take a speaking tube and sing through it[44]. The action is also requested by means of a direction. However, as can be seen in these scores, such directions may become quite long and hence lack instantaneous comprehension. Moreover, as mentioned above, the simplest method of notation is to present a sketch of the action. Therefore, it is suggested here requesting »preparations«, such as singing/speaking through cupped hands (or a single cupped hand) as well as through a speaking tube, by means of graphic depictions:

Fig. 29 Vocal »preparations«.

These symbols should be placed above the notation system while singing/speaking through other items than the described ones may be requested in a similar manner.

6. 5 Whistling and its notation

Whistling is a technique, which is mainly executed by voices. *Kagel*, for instance, frequently employs this manner of sound production. Generally, the whistling range is smaller than the vocal range. Therefore, *Kagel*, in »Hallelujah«[45], permits transposition if the pitches are diffi-

---

[43] Kagel, 1931, p. 153.

[44] Cf. Ligeti, Nouvelles, p. 5.

[45] Mauricio Kagel: Hallelujah. For voices. London 1970.

cult to perform[46]. Moreover, he depicts this articulation by giving the direction whistle [pfeifen][47] or – as in »Dressur« – by means of a distinct notation system and normal note heads:

Fig. 30 Kagel, Dressur, p. 15.

However, another method is employed in »..., den 24. xii. 1931«. As can be seen in Figure 31, a diamond-shaped note head is used to request whistling. Moreover, *Kagel* outlines that the baritone actually executes half-voice whistled pulses[48].

Fig. 31 Kagel, 1931, p. 91.

Further, in »Anagrama« he also makes the vocalist whistle whilst inhaling. This action is depicted by means of giving the direction inhaled whistling[49]. Concerning these methods of notation, it may be said that the approach of giving the direction whistling or using a distinct notation system can be preferred from employing diamond-shaped note heads. This is because diamond-shaped note heads are normally employed to depict the production of harmonics. However, when whistling, harmonics do not occur, but rather a special vocal technique is employed. In the case of voices, whistle tones are – as opposed to the production of such tones on wind instruments – not based on the overtone series and not created on a fundamental. Therefore, it is suggested here requesting this technique by employing an additional notation system or simply giving the direction whistled (or *fischiato*). However, the former method may be regarded as clearer especially when making instrumentalists other than voices whistle (because, for example, the notation of whistling in the system that normally depicts the fingered tones of wind instruments may cause confusion). Furthermore, half-voiced whistling is closely related to half-voiced singing. As shown above, this technique can be depicted by giving the direction *mezza voce* (cf. Figure 13). Therefore, this additional whistling technique may be requested in the same manner. As mentioned in Chapter »6. 3. 3 Vocal effects«, the inhaled performance of a technique may be requested by an arrow pointing downwards that complements the note (cf. Figure 27). Therefore, this method is also suggested being utilised for inhaled winding.

6. 6 Muting

The application of »mutes« refers to either muting the sound production by placing the hand over the mouth or closing the mouth. Moreover, when placing the hand over the mouth and removing it repetitively in a fast manner during the sound production, **the wah-wah effect** occurs. This effect may also be produced by means of closing and opening the mouth.

6. 6. 1 The application of »mutes« and its notation

As shown in Chapter »2. 8. 1 The application of mutes«, the attachment and removal of mutes can be requested by giving the direction *con/senza sordino* whilst the description of the mute

---

[46] Cf. ibid., p. IV.
[47] Cf. ibid., pp. 12f.
[48] Cf. Kagel, 1931, p. 91.
[49] Cf. Kagel, Anagrama, p. 39.

type may be given in brackets. In the case of applying the hand as a constant mute, this method of notation may also be used. However, the action of closing the mouth when singing/speaking is normally depicted by means of the direction mouth closed or *bocca chiusa*[50]. It is reasonable to use a special direction for this action because – even though it results in muting the produced sound (and veiling the text) – an exterior mute is not employed, but the sound producer itself closed and hence a different kind of muting executed. Moreover, the re-opening of the mouth can be requested by giving the direction mouth opened or *bocca aperta*[51] whilst some composers additionally distinguish an intermediate state, referred to as mouth half-closed or *bocca semichiusa*[52] (also cf. Figure 33).

6. 6. 2 The wah-wah effect and its notation

In Chapter »2. 8. 2 The wah-wah effect« the notation of the wah-wah effect (cf. for further details »Part II: Electroacoustic music – 2. 3. 1 High-pass, low-pass, band-pass and band-reject filters«) has been extensively discussed with regard to wind instruments. As this technique may be executed in a similar manner in the case of voices, it is suggested here notating the wah-wah effect in the same way and hence by means of the symbols »o« and »+« whilst the duration of the transition between these two states is depicted by using the symbols as note heads in combination with a single lined notation system with no clef. Moreover, articulation symbols, such as the *legato* slur or *staccato* dots, can be used to determine the character of the transition between the states whilst the muting technique used to create the effect needs to be described. Further, the additional state half-opened mouth needs to be depicted in the case of using the mouth itself to produce the wah-wah effect. As shown in Chapter »3. 4. 4 The wah-wah effect and its notation«, such an additional state may be notated by means of the symbol »(+)«.

In Figure 32, the wah-wah effect is produced by means of the mouth. The vocalist sings a semibreve »c¹/C4« [a] whilst opening and closing the mouth (cf. Figure 69 in the chapter on percussion instruments for a detailed description of the transitions). As mentioned in the chapter on wind and percussion instruments, an alternative method of notation was to use the two symbols as dots in a modified single lined »transposition« system (cf., for instance, Figure 23 in the chapter on wind instruments) because notes suggest sound being produced. However, the original sound is, in this case, actually transformed.

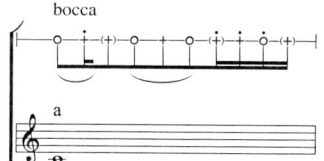

Fig. 32 The wah-wah effect with the mouth.

6. 7 Percussive effects and their notation

There are mainly two vocal percussive effects: in »NUN« *Lachenmann* employs one articulation, referred to as cheek attack. He explains that such strokes "are performed by loosely

---

[50] Cf. Pierre Boulez: Le soleil des eaux. For soprano, mixed choir and orchestra. Paris 1968, p. 16, Luigi Dallapiccola: Canti di prionia. For choir and several instruments. Milan 1971, p. 4 or Haubenstock-Ramati, Credentials, no page named [foreword].

[51] Cf. Haubenstock-Ramati, Credentials, no page named [foreword].

[52] Cf. Boulez, Soleil, p. 17 and Haubenstock-Ramati, Credentials, no page named [foreword].

»patting« the cheek while the mouth is open, using the three middle fingertips held stretched out together"[53]. He notates the articulation by giving the direction cheek attacks [Wangen-Schläge] in combination with special note heads[54]. However, as shown in the previous chapters on percussive effects, such strokes are, in this work, always depicted by means of presenting a sketch of the hand in combination with a graphic depiction of the spot that is hit. In this case, the point of impact is the cheek and hence a drawing of the head needs to be employed. Additionally, it needs to be determined whether the mouth is half-opened or opened (cf. the previous chapter). As is apparent from Figure 33, the vocalist is supposed to use the tip of the index, middle and ring finger in order to »pat« the left cheek. Four semiquaver strokes are executed here with *bocca semichiusa* and four semiquaver strokes with *bocca aperta*.

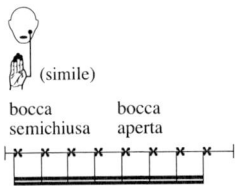

bocca   bocca
semichiusa   aperta

Fig. 33 Cheek attacks.

Cheek attacks cannot be performed in a loud manner. Moreover, this percussive effect may apparently also be produced by other instrumentalists and complement any singing or speaking mode. The other vocal percussive effect, which can be described as »patting« the vocal folds whilst singing/speaking, may be depicted in the same way. Further, all other percussive effects, such as clapping the hands, snapping the fingers or stomping the feet may be notated by presenting a sketch of the action (cf. Chapter »3. 2. 1 The extended utilisation of the agents of attack« for claps with drumsticks and the hands as well as »Part II: Electroacoustic music – 3. 3. 2 Non-instrumental sound sources«).

6. 8 Resonance effects and their notation

Like a wind instrument's bell, the mouth may be directed towards the strings of a grand piano with depressed pedal, a timpano or other percussion instruments. When the vocalist then sings, sympathetic vibrations are produced. The notation of this technique has been extensively discussed in Chapter »2. 10 Resonance effects« and may be executed in a similar manner in the case of voices. Therefore, the method of notation introduced in the chapter on wind instruments may also be used in the case of producing resonance effects with the voice. Hence a drawing of the instrument's body, dashed lines and arrows that depict the motion can be employed for its notation. However, because the air stream is not as directed as on wind instruments, it may also be sufficient to simply request the player to sing into the piano or onto a timpano by giving a direction (cf. Figure 72 in the chapter on wind instruments). As mentioned, an exact method of notation for the resonance effect makes use of a sketch, which presents the disposal of the instruments and the paths the players are supposed to walk. Additionally, such a sketch can be used in order to determine the distance between the bell and the resonating instrument. It may be presented in the foreword of the work or be a part of the score. An example of such a sketch is presented in the chapter on wind instruments (Figure 73).

---

[53] Lachenmann, NUN, p. XXIV.
[54] Cf. ibid., p. XXV.

6. 9 Other extended playing techniques and their notation

Another rare articulation is to move the head up and down or from left to right. When such motions are executed during normal singing/speaking, a similar (*Doppler*) effect as on wind instruments occurs. As shown in Chapter »2. 11 Other extended playing techniques and their notation«, an additional single lined notation system may be employed in order to notate the extent and duration of such motions in an exact manner. It can be used to depict the extent in degrees and the duration by means of the timeline. As can be seen in the chapter on wind instruments (Figure 78), the radius is depicted by a circle, which also contains the home position of the bell. However, in the case of voices, the home position is the middle of the radius. Any desired motion of the head can now be drawn into the circle.

PART II: ELECTROACOUSTIC MUSIC

The second part of the work presents the development of a coherent notation system for the processes in electroacoustic music. This field is divided into chapters on sound synthesis, audio processing and sound recording. The fundamental forms of sound production, transformation and modulation are explained with regard to these categories. Moreover, previous approaches towards their notation are analysed and suggestions for notation are presented. As mentioned in the introduction, there is a lack of notation in electroacoustic music. Therefore, previous examples of notation cannot always be presented. In such cases, a suggestion solely for the notation of the particular process is given. Further, whenever previous methods of notation could be found, they are, in the two following chapters, discussed with regard to the criteria defined in the introduction. The suggested methods of notation are supposed to fulfil these criteria in the best possible way. As a reminder, these criteria are exactness, simplicity and not contradicting traditional notation, but extending and being closely related to it, while consistency is achieved by the suggested methods being compatible with, and distinct from, all other signs of the system.

There have only been a few previous attempts to create a notation system for electroacoustic music. Notable among them is the approach by *Gariépy and Décarie*. Three systems are suggested here. The primary system corresponds to the production of sound materials. Basically, in this system each piece of equipment, module or manipulation is identified by a code. The audio signals are indicated by arrows and the electroacoustic devices are represented by specific symbols and links that clarify the relationship between the elements. The parameters frequency, duration and bandwidth are inscribed inside the symbols while the intensity is indicated on the output link of a specific symbol and described in Decibels, Volts or other predefined values[1]. The result is a complex system that makes use of code and various symbols. However, since the utilisation of code would require the performer to learn the meaning of many unrelated letters and numbers, it does not comply with the postulated requirement of simplicity. Moreover, this system is not closely related to traditional notation because the pitch and duration are not expressed by means of the traditional system and dynamic levels other than the traditional ones are preferred. Further, the secondary system corresponds to the steps of editing and mixing and mainly consists in the temporal organisation, the determination of the dynamic level and spatialisation. It is derived from *Stockhausen's* realisation score of »Telemusik«[2], which is used as an example in the paper[3]. However, as is shown in Chapter »1. 1 Basic elements«, this method of notation is inexact and can barely be combined with traditional notation. Moreover, because the secondary system is reliant on the primary system, the sound producers and transformation processes are not part of the score. Finally, the ternary system is used to organise the diffusion of an electroacoustic work, e. g. in concerts. It consists mainly of a graphic representation of the score, as used in the secondary system, and explains the emission device[4]. This matter is treated in Chapters »2. 2. 1 Basic loudspeaker types and their notation« and »2. 2. 2 Stereophonic and multichannel techniques«.

Furthermore, various compositions that involve electroacoustic means of sound production, transformation or modulation, require the utilisation of particular synthesisers, effects units or special audio software. However, due to the rapid evolution of technology, it is quite probable these will become obsolete. This development can be compared to the history of acoustic instruments. Performances that involve Renaissance instruments, such as soprano cromornes

---

[1] Cf. Louise Gariépy and Jean Décarie: A system of notation for electro-acoustic music. A proposition. In: Interface. Journal of New Music research, vol. 13. Lisse 1984, pp. 1-74, here: pp. 9-20.

[2] Karlheinz Stockhausen: Telemusik. Vienna 1969.

[3] Cf. ibid., pp. 9, 26 and 53f.

[4] Cf. ibid., pp. 9 and 30f.

or tenor shawms, are rare because these types of instruments are no longer part of the orchestral apparatus. With regard to electroacoustics, it is at present hard to determine whether a particular synthesiser will be part of the electroacoustic apparatus of the future. To give an example, it is possible that the *Yamaha* DX 7 II-FD, the *Roland* D-50 or the *Yamaha* effects unit SPX 900 *Stockhausen* employs in »Invasion-Explosion mit Abschied«[5] will still be available when this work is performed in a century or two. However, it is rather unrealistic since the manufacture of these devices has already ceased. The probable unavailability of the devices might have been the reason *Stockhausen* provided the synthetic timbres he used in the piece on an additional recording. *Pressing* further explains that many synthesiser types have already become extinct and adds that the usefulness of scores that involve these instruments is "compromised by their having been written specifically for equipment that is now obsolete"[6]. Therefore, the notation of electroacoustic music is not achieved here by the depiction of particular synthesisers, effects units or microphone models. Instead, the fundamental processes and parameters of electroacoustic sound production, transformation and modulation are examined and a notation system developed on this basis. By doing so, the developments rest upon accessible and sound knowledge that will most probably be preserved for the required period of time. Hence the processes they depict remain reproducible, can be realised without direct contact to the composer and are synthesiser-, device- and software-independent.

The processes described in this and the following chapters can be generally realised by means of a digital system. There are two fundamental parameters of digital audio, the **bit depth** and the **sampling rate**. The bit depth is related to the dynamic range (DR), which is the span between the softest and loudest sounds that can be handled by a system. The dynamic range of the human ear is 120 Decibels (dB) whilst the DR of a digital audio system is proportional to the quantisation of the system: 1 bit correlates to 6 dB. Hence a 16 bit system's DR is limited to 96 dB whilst an audio system that can handle 20 Bits has about the same dynamic range as the human hearing mechanism. Most digital mixers provide 24 to 64 bit resolution. This many bits are required when employing a large amount of channels simultaneously. Additionally, many digital filters require at least 24 bits to maintain high audio quality[7]. Analogue signals are, in opposition to digital signals, continuous. This means that every point of the waveform is smoothly connected to the rest of the signal. The digital signal is not continuous because it consists of a sequence of specific values sampled at discrete times. The amount of time between samples is known as the sampling interval or period. Its inverse, the number of times the signal is sampled in each segment, is called the sampling rate or frequency. It is measured in Hertz (Hz). The chosen sampling rate must be at least faster than twice the highest frequency contained in the analogue signal. Conversely, the highest frequency in the analogue signal must be less than half the sampling rate. This maximum is called the *Nyquist* **frequency**. It is always expressed by half the sampling rate and is the theoretical limit of the highest frequency that can be properly presented in a digital audio system. Compact discs use a rate of **44.1 kilohertz** (kHz) to store information. Another standard sampling rate is **48 kHz**. This properties are important for the conversion of an analogue to a digital signal. When analogue signals are converted, a low-pass filter (see Chapter »2. 3 Filters«) is usually employed. It is set at the *Nyquist* frequency. This is because if a signal that extends this frequency was transformed, **aliasing distortion or fold-over** would occur. Aliasing is caused by under-sampling. It is not limited to the conversion of analogue to digital signals,

[5] Karlheinz Stockhausen: Invasion-Explosion mit Abschied. II. Akt vom Dienstag aus Licht. For solo-soprano, tenor, bass, 3 trumpets, 3 trombones, 2 synthesiser players with 2 assistants, 2 percussionist with 2 assistants, 6 tutti-trumpets, 6 tutti-trombones (ad lib.), choir, 8-track tape and sound director. Kürten 1995.

[6] Jeff Pressing: Synthesizer performance and real-time techniques. Madison 1992, p. 183.

[7] Curtis Roads et al.: The Computer Music tutorial. Cambridge et al. 1996, p. 355.

but also occurs when, for instance, a tone above the *Nyquist* frequency is produced in digital synthesis. The consequence is that audible tones or signals below the *Nyquist* frequency are additionally produced. The aliased signal can be calculated by »the frequency of the sampling rate – the frequency of the signal«[8]. In order to avoid aliasing, higher sampling rates can be employed. High standard rates are **88.2 or 96 kHz**. Aliasing occurs on every multiple of the sampling rate. Frequencies higher than the sampling frequency will also result in signals below the *Nyquist* frequency. To calculate the aliased signal, the sampling frequency will have to be multiplied with a nonnegative integer n such that the result is below the *Nyquist* frequency whilst any negative value becomes positive[9]. However, there are composers that make use of fold-over to produce chordal structures and hence use aliasing distortion as a technique[10].

1. SOUND SYNTHESIS

The aim of the chapter on sound synthesis is to explain the substantial processes of synthetic sound production and present suggestions for their notation. Therefore, the basic elements of sound synthesis, oscillators and envelopes, are explained. Moreover, additive synthesis, subtractive synthesis, amplitude modulation, frequency modulation, waveshaping synthesis, physical modelling and granular synthesis are examined. The field of sound synthesis is vast. In order to limit the extent of this work, only the most important techniques are explained. Further, the topic is presented in such way that composers are able to employ a particular synthetic instrument in a score and give the realiser all the necessary information they need to implement this instrument. Therefore, only the fundamental information on the processes in sound synthesis is given, and technical or mathematical details are avoided whenever possible. Please refer for further insight to *Dodge and Jerse*[11], *Miranda*[12], *Moore*[13] or *Neukom*[14].

1. 1 Basic elements

The basic elements of sound synthesis are **periodic wave generators and their envelopes**, **noise generators** and **envelope detectors**.

1. 1. 1 Periodic wave generators and their envelopes

The basic materials an oscillator generates are audio frequency tones. There are four elementary types of periodic sounds that generators produce: **1. Sine wave** [⊘]. It does not contain any harmonics and thus consists of only one partial. **2. Sawtooth wave** [⊖]. It contains all

---

[8] When the sampling rate is, for example, 48 kHz, the *Nyquist* frequency is set at 24 kHz. A signal of 34 kHz would result in 48 kHz – 34 kHz = 14 kHz.

[9] When the sampling rate is, for example, 48 kHz and a signal of 100 kHz is produced, the nonnegative integer of n = 2 needs to be employed. The resulting frequency can be calculated by | 2 × 48 kHz – 100 kHz | = 4 kHz. The lines mean that a negative result (in this case –4 kHz) turns positive.

[10] Cf. Charles Dodge and Thomas A. Jerse: Computer Music. Synthesis, composition, and performance. 2nd edition. No city named [Australia et al.] 1997, pp. 63f.

[11] Dodge and Jerse, Computer.

[12] Eduardo Reck Miranda: Computer sound synthesis for the electronic musician. Oxford et al. 1998.

[13] F. Richard Moore: Elements of computer music. Englewood Cliffs 1990.

[14] Martin Neukom: Signale, Systeme und Klangsynthese [Signals, systems and sound synthesis]. Grundlagen der Computermusik [Foundations of Computer Music]. Zürcher Musikstudien [Zurich music studies], vol. 2. Bern 2003.

harmonics that are multiples of the fundamental frequency (2 × f, 3 × f, 4 × f etc.)[15]. They decrease by 6 Decibels per octave[16]. The symmetrical inverse of the original shape is often referred to as inverted sawtooth or ramp-down sawtooth. Both are legitimate sawtooth waves and, in spite of the reverse position of the leading edge, will sound the same. **3. Triangle wave** [⊘]. It contains only harmonics that are odd multiples of the fundamental frequency (3 × f, 5 × f, 7 × f etc.), decreasing by 12 dB per octave **4. Square wave** [⊕]. It contains only harmonics that are odd multiples of the fundamental frequency (3 × f, 5 × f, 7 × f etc.), decreasing by 6 dB per octave[17]. The square wave is one of a family of pulse waves, in this case with a 50% duty cycle. The duty cycle is defined by the ratio between the pulse duration and the period. As that proportion is changed, the spectrum also changes. This is the basis of the **pulse width modulation**, which many synthesisers provide with a square wave oscillator[18]. The larger the duty cycle, the larger the proportion of spectral energy at high frequencies and the smaller the duty cycle, the larger the proportion of spectral energy at low frequencies[19]. To avoid aliasing when using a sawtooth, triangle or square wave generator, shapes with band-limited spectra can be selected. This **anti-aliasing function** guarantees that the band-limited waveform contains harmonics only up to the *Nyquist* frequency[20]. There are, further, fixed and variable sampling rate oscillators. Please refer to Chapter »1. 7. 2 Waveshaping by phase distortion and its notation« for sound modifications by varying the sampling rate. Moreover, a **low frequency oscillator (LFO)** is an oscillator that creates frequencies below the absolute threshold of hearing. It normally works up to a limit of 20 Hz. The common outputs are the four periodic waveforms (1-4) mentioned above[21].

The **envelope** determines the shape of the amplitude variation during the course of a sound. It usually consists of four segments: **1. Attack** (A). This describes the time taken for the amplitude to rise during the onset of the tone up to its peak. **2. Decay** (D). This describes the time taken for the rundown from the peak to the steady state. **3. Sustain** (S). This describes the amplitude of the tone during its steady state. **4. Release** (R). This describes the time taken for the tone to die away[22]. There are two main shapes of the attack, decay and release portions: **1. Exponential** and **2. Linear**. A more constant change in loudness will be obtained by an exponential shape rather than by a linear one. A sound with a linear decay will appear to linger on after the beginning of the decay and then suddenly drop off, whilst a sound with an exponential decay will sound like a smooth diminution of amplitude. Almost all natural vibrations die away exponentially[23]. The envelope parameters can be combined in various ways and the envelope take any complex shape or only consist of an attack and release phase[24]. In addition to the ADSR envelope, *Pressing* determines five basic envelope shapes: 1. The tran-

---

[15] Whilst f = fundamental frequency (1st partial), 2 × f = 1st harmonic (2nd partial), 3 × f = 2nd harmonic (3rd partial) etc.

[16] 1st octave = 2 × f, 2nd octave = 4 × f, 3rd octave = 8 × f etc.

[17] Allen Strange: Electronic music. Systems, techniques, and controls. 2nd edition. Dubuque 1983, pp. 14-17 and Richard Dobson: A dictionary of electronic and Computer Music theory. Instruments, terms, techniques. Oxford and New York 1992, pp. 197-199.

[18] Dobson, Dictionary, pp. 199 and 201.

[19] Dodge and Jerse, Computer, pp. 169f.

[20] Ibid., p. 170.

[21] Cf. Martin Russ: Sound synthesis and sampling. 3rd edition. Oxford 2009, pp. 134-137.

[22] Cf. Dodge and Jerse, Computer, pp. 80f. and 84.

[23] Ibid., pp. 83-85.

[24] Cf. Russ, Sound, pp. 126-130.

sient, 2. The decaying, 3. The swelling. 4. The stabilising and 5. The evolving[25] (see below for their actual shape).

1. 1. 1. 1 Previous methods of notation

One method of depiction for periodic oscillators can be found in *Wehinger's* aural score of *Ligeti's* electroacoustic composition »Artikulation«[26]. In this work, sine waves are represented by yellow coloured shapes whilst a single notation system describes all events used in the piece. The (horizontal) x-axis represents the time in a spatial way whilst 1 second equals 2.7 cm. The size and surface extension correspond to the loudness of the signal. Moreover, the frequency of the tones is displayed by the (vertical) y-axis that represents the whole frequency range. However, the depiction is very approximate because this axis only holds the lowest and highest frequencies as a reference[27]. *Stockhausen* in the realisation score of »Telemusik« notates sine waves by means of a diagrammatic system. The x-axis depicts the time in seconds and the y-axis the approximate frequency. The dynamic level is described in Decibels. The system in Figure 1 ranges from 6 to 12 kilohertz and from 0 to 13 seconds. The sine wave oscillator starts generating at approximately 11 kHz. After 5 seconds, the frequency gradually drops to approximately 10 kHz and remains constant from 8 seconds on. After 10 seconds, the frequency drops again, this time to approximately 8 kHz, is raised and drops again. The lowest frequency of 6 kHz is reached after 13 seconds.

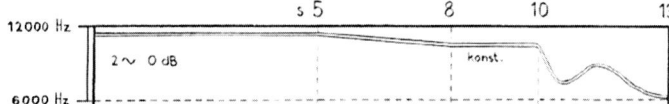

Fig. 1 Stockhausen, Telemusik, p. 2.

Finally, *Kagel*, in »Tremens«[28], notates a square wave generator by means of a single lined notation system with no clef, traditional durations and common note heads. The pitch is depicted in two ways: by determining the approximate frequency in Hertz (Hz) and a complementary traditional notation system, while the duration is depicted by the single lined notation system and additionally determined in seconds. The traditional system is, in Figure 2, in bass clef and depicts an »E/E2«, which equals approximately 82 Hz. In the example, no specific envelope is given, but it is determined that the dynamic level fluctuates between *pianissimo* and *piano*.

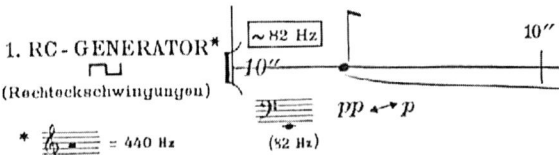

Fig. 2 Kagel, Tremens, p. 17.

---

[25] Cf. Pressing, Synthesizer, pp. 258f.

[26] György Ligeti: Artikulation. An aural score by Rainer Wehinger. Mainz 1970.

[27] Cf. ibid., pp. 24f. and 37.

[28] Mauricio Kagel: Tremens. Scenic montage of a test for two performers, electric instruments, percussion, tape and projections. London 1973.

1. 1. 1. 2 Discussion

Wehinger's approach, because it is an aural score, is very approximate. The frequency and the shape of the envelope could not be determined by means of the system he employs. Further, since the time axis of this system is spatial, it could not be combined with traditional durations. Moreover, *Stockhausen's* notation system also lacks an exact determination of the frequency. As is apparent from the description of Figure 1, it is not clear which frequency the oscillator is supposed to generate. Further, since he does not make use of traditional durations, it is difficult to combine this system with traditional notation. It could, however, be achieved by introducing a timeline that is based on common durations instead of the depiction of the time in seconds. Further, *Kagel's* method (cf. Figure 2) may be described as exact and closely related to traditional notation. However, the multiple depiction of the same information – e. g. determining the frequency in Hz and by pitch-based notation as well as explaining the duration in seconds and by note values – leads to a confusing appearance of the score. One reason for this redundancy might be that in electroacoustic music the frequency is normally determined in Hz and the time in seconds, while in traditional compositions these parameters are depicted by means of a pitch-based notation system and note values. In order to achieve a clearer appearance of the score, it would be useful only to employ one of the methods. The envelope of the square wave is, moreover, determined approximately. This is because it is difficult to describe a complex envelope by placing traditional dynamic symbols underneath the notation system. This method of notation works for traditional instruments because the envelope of, for instance, a tone produced by these is naturally complex. However, in the case of implementing *Kagel's* approach, the determination of the envelope would be very simplified.

1. 1. 1. 3 Suggestion for the notation of periodic wave generators and their envelopes

Since the approach by *Kagel* is exact and retains traditional notation, it is used here as a paradigm. The frequency and duration is, however, solely depicted in the traditional way. This is because the notation system is above all supposed to serve the needs of composers that are used to describing the pitch and duration in this way. Moreover, the whole spectrum from sub-audio frequencies above 0 Hz up to 20 kHz can theoretically be described by traditional notation's bass and treble clef, and periodic waves can be notated with regard to the common twelve tone equal temperament[29] because their structure is closely related to those of tones produced by traditional acoustic instruments. By employing **octave transpositions** (*8va*, *15ma*, *22ma*, *29ma* etc.) even frequencies that exceed the range of traditional instruments may be described. These frequencies can be calculated by means of the multiplication factor $^{12}\sqrt{2}$. If **microtones** are supposed to be produced, they are in traditional notation normally depicted by additional symbols. There is no convention for these symbols, but they vary from composer to composer. Three different symbols are introduced here: an **eighth tone** [↑↓] describes the transposition of ± 25 cents[30], a **sixth tone** [↕↓] of ± 33 cents and a **quarter tone** [↕↓] of ± 50 cents[31]. In the case of intending to make use of other transpositions than these, either more microtonal symbols could be introduced or the transposition could be determined by means of a direction, e. g. + 60 cents, – 25 cents or – 75 cents.

A suggestion for the notation of periodic waveform generators is presented in Figure 3. By employing the previously introduced symbols for the oscillator types, they may all be depic-

---

[29] The concert pitch of twelve tone equal temperament is »a¹/A4« = 440 Hz. Semitones are, in this system, derived by the factor $^{12}\sqrt{2}$, e. g. the frequency of »d¹/D4« can be calculated by »440 Hz ÷ $^{12}\sqrt{2^7}$« or »a♯2/A♯5« by »440 Hz × $^{12}\sqrt{2^{13}}$«.

[30] ±100 cents = a semitone and ±1200 cents = octave. Deviations of less than 5 cents cannot be perceived.

[31] Eight tones are derived by the factor $^{48}\sqrt{2}$, sixth tones by the factor $^{36}\sqrt{2}$, and quarter tones by the factor $^{48}\sqrt{2}$.

ted by a single notation system. The processes may be described as follows: a sine wave »ab¹/Ab4« (~ 415 Hz) is produced for the duration of a dotted crotchet and followed by a quaver rest. Subsequently, another sine wave »a↓b/A↓b3« (~ 204 Hz) is produced for the duration of a dotted crotchet. After this, a square wave generator is set at »a¹/A4« (440 Hz) with a duty cycle of 65%. This tone is produced for the duration of a minim and followed by a triangle wave »c¹/C4« (~ 262 Hz), which is produced for the duration of another minim. After a quaver rest, a sawtooth »e↑b²/E↑b5« (~ 631 Hz) is generated for the duration of dotted minim. Finally, a square wave generator is set at »b↓¹/B↓b4« (~ 453 Hz) with a duty cycle of 30%. This waveform is produced for the duration of a minim. If the utilised oscillators are supposed to be band-limited, it should be stated that the anti-aliasing function is applied by giving the direction of anti-aliasing.

Fig. 3 Periodic wave generators.

When an LFO is supposed to be depicted by a transposed bass clef, uncommon pitches need to be applied. A low frequency oscillator ranges from »₁₀A/A–8« (~ 0.1 Hz) to »₂D↑#/D↑#0« (~ 20 Hz). Examples for the depiction of an LFO can be found in Figures 23 and 29. In order to enable the notation of a complex envelope, an additional diagrammatic system with an independent timeline is used. The x-axis of this system represents, as usual, the time and the y-axis the dynamic level from »∅« (absence of sound) to *ffff*. This system has already been introduced in »Part I: Extended instrumental playing techniques – 2. 3. 1 The trumpet embouchure«. It is in the other part of the work referred to as the transposition system because it is only used to depict gliding changes in pitch. However, in this part of the work the diagram is used to notate all sorts of parameters that cannot be depicted by means of a pitch-based or single lined notation system. Rests are used in this system since no additional sound is produced (which would be suggested by notes). However, whenever utilising the diagrammatic system, the original sound is actually transformed.

The notation of different envelope types is presented in Figure 4. The oscillators from the previous example are now complemented by an envelope. Since this envelope determines the final dynamic level of the tone production, the system is designated as output level. The envelope shapes refer to the basic envelope types described in Chapter »1. 1. 1 Periodic wave generators and their envelopes«. The white dots (◇) depict the amplitude of the oscillator in time. The attack, decay and release can be, as explained, either exponential or linear. The normal shape here is exponential. In order to request a linear shape, the natural sign »♮« is used. This accidental applies only to the dot it directly precedes. To give some examples, the ADSR, transient and decaying envelope shapes can be described as follows: the sine wave »ab¹/Ab4« is shaped by a generic ADSR envelope: its dynamic level is increased from »∅« to *fortissimo* for the duration of a semiquaver (A), reduced to *mezzoforte* for the duration of another semiquaver (D), sustained for a dotted quaver and linearly released to »∅« for the duration of a semiquaver. After a quaver rest, the dotted crotched »a↓b/A↓b3« is shaped by a generic transient envelope. The dynamic level is increased here from »∅« to *mezzoforte* for the duration of a semiquaver, then further increased to *fortissimo* for another semiquaver, linearly reduced to *pianissimo* for the duration of a quaver, then further reduced to *piano pianissimo* for the duration of a demisemiquaver and released to »∅« for the duration of a dotted semiquaver. Subsequently, another oscillator produces a pulse at »a¹/A4«, which is shaped by a generic decaying envelope. Its dynamic level is increased from »∅« to *mezzopiano* for the duration of a semiquaver and then released to »∅« for the duration of a dotted crotchet and a semiquaver. The other envelopes may be described similarly. As is apparent from Figure 4, all related actions are connected by a line underneath the x-axis. This line ends after the release, in this case after the ADSR and the swelling envelope. When an envelope is directly followed by another envelope, these boundaries blur and the last dot of the previous envelope is at the same time the first dot of the following envelope.

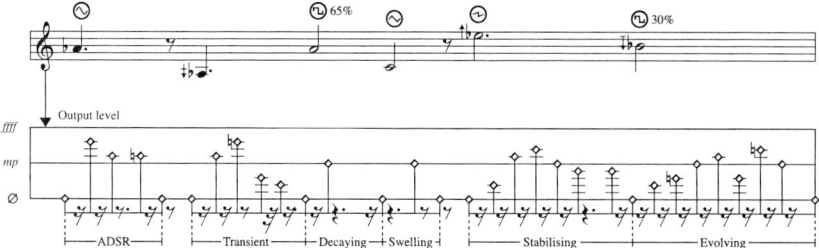

Fig. 4 Envelope types.

Moreover, it might be desirable to apply distinct envelopes to each tone of a chord. These envelopes can no longer be depicted by a single dot. Therefore, in Figure 5, two more symbols are introduced. The diamond-shaped white dot (◇) depicts always the envelope of the tone with the highest pitch and the diamond-shaped black dot (◆) the envelope of the tone with the lowest pitch. In the case of a third simultaneous event, the circular white dot (O) represents the tone in between these. In the example, the treble clef is transposed by three octaves (*22ma*). In the beginning, the three tones »g^5/G8« (~ 6,272 Hz), »d^5/D8« (~ 4,699 Hz) and »a^4/A7« (3,520 Hz) are generated by sawtooth oscillators for the duration of a dotted minim. The envelope shape of the »g^5/G8« is depicted by the diamond-shaped white dot, the envelope of the »d^5/D8« by the circular dot and the envelope of the »a^4/A7« by the diamond-shaped black dot. The processes in Figure 5 can be described as follows: the dynamic level of the »d^5/D8« is increased from »∅« to *mezzoforte* for the duration of a dotted quaver, decays to *mezzopiano* for the duration of another dotted quaver, is sustained for the duration of a crotchet and a semiquaver and released to »∅« for the duration of a semiquaver. At the same time, the envelope of the »d^5/D8« is increased from »∅« to *forte* for the duration of a crotchet and a semiquaver, decays to *piano* for the duration of a semiquaver, is sustained for the duration of a quaver and released for the duration of a crotchet. Finally, the amplitude of the »a^4/A7« is increased from »∅« to *forte* for the duration of a dotted quaver, decays to *mezzoforte* for the duration of a quaver, is sustained for the duration of a dotted quaver and released to »∅« for the duration of a crotchet. The minim rest is followed by a triangle oscillator producing an »f^4/F7« (~ 2,794 Hz) for the duration of a semibreve. After it has generated this tone for the duration of a dotted minim, another triangle waveform »b^5/B♭8« (~ 7,459 Hz) is produced. Since the latter sound has the higher pitch, its envelope shape is depicted by the white dot and the envelope of the previous tone by the black dot.

The shape of the envelopes in Figure 5 is constantly exponential because no natural sign is used. When different oscillator types are supposed to generate tones simultaneously, it is recommended that each oscillator is depicted here by a distinct system because the notation might otherwise become confusing. Further, if more than three simultaneous events are produced by a single oscillator, the appearance of the envelopes may become unclear. Therefore, additional notation systems should be applied if four or more synthetic tones with different envelope shapes are supposed to be created. However, if all these tone have the same envelope shape, they may be depicted by a single system. Alternatively, normal symbols for the dynamic level could be employed in order to depict the envelopes shape. In order to do so, the duration of the utilised *de-/crescendi* would have to be depicted in relation to the instrument's system or by means of an additional single lined notation system with no clef. However, complex simultaneous envelope shapes could only be depicted with difficulty in this way.

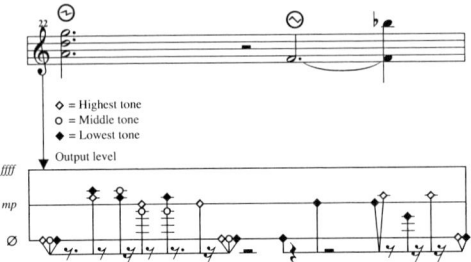

Fig. 5 Simultaneous events.

1. 1. 2 Noise generators and their notation

An oscillator is designed to produce a periodic waveform with well-defined spectral components. The spectrum is a discrete spectrum because the energy is found at harmonically related frequencies. The opposite of a discrete spectrum is a distributed spectrum. Here energy exists everywhere within a range of frequencies. Most of the natural noise sounds have distributed spectra. Therefore, algorithms designed to generate distributed spectra are called noise generators. Noise differs from all other waves by the fact that its wave form never repeats[32]. Three different types of noises can normally be synthetically created: **1. White noise** [⬤]. It is defined by each frequency being of the same amplitude. **2. Pink noise** [⬤]. The amplitude of its spectrum decreases by 3 dB per octave[33]. **3. Brown or Brownian noise** [⬤]. The amplitude of its spectrum decreases by 6 dB per octave[34].

Noise generators cannot be depicted by pitch-related notation systems since they have an indefinite pitch. They are, therefore, notated here by means of a system that is derived from the depiction of drum sounds with indefinite pitch (cf. »Part I: Extended instrumental playing techniques – 3. The techniques of percussion instruments«). Each spacing in between the lines refers to one of the three noise types. The upper one refers to white noise, the middle one to pink noise and the lower one to brown noise. Further, the envelope of each noise generator is depicted by a fixed symbol. The diamond-shaped white dot (◇) is related to white noise, the circular white dot (O) to pink noise and the diamond-shaped black dot (◆) to brown noise. The method of notation is presented in Figure 6 and can be described as follows: in the beginning white noise is created for the duration of a crotchet. Its envelope is increased from »∅« to *pianissimo* for the duration of a semiquaver, sustained for the duration of a dotted semiquaver and released to »∅« for the duration of another dotted semiquaver. Subsequently, brown noise is produced for the duration of a crotchet. Its dynamic level is as quickly as possible increased to *mezzopiano,* decays to *piano* for the duration of a quaver, is sustained for the duration a semiquaver and released to »∅« for the duration of another semiquaver. After this, pink noise is produced for the duration of a crotchet. The dynamic level is increased here from »∅« to *pianissimo* for the duration of a dotted semiquaver, further raised to *fortissimo* for the duration of another dotted semiquaver and linearly released to »∅« for the duration of a semiquaver. After a crotchet rest, white and brown noise is created simultaneously for the duration of a minim. Since their envelopes are, in the example, supposed to be equal, only one symbol needs to be applied. It is, therefore, stated that, with regard to this event, »◇ = ◆«.

---

[32] Dodge and Jerse, Computer, pp. 95f.

[33] Cf. Donald E. Hall: Musical acoustics. 3rd edition. No city named [Australia et al.] 2002, p. 136.

[34] Moore, Elements, p. 443.

After another crotchet rest, pink and brown noise is created simultaneously for the duration of a minim. In this case, the envelopes again differ.

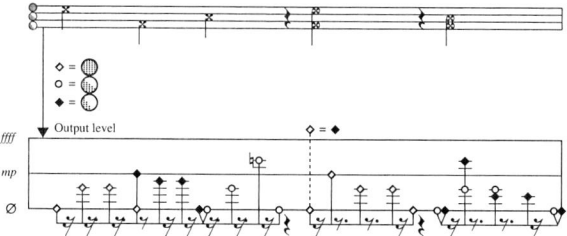

Fig. 6 Noise oscillators.

1. 1. 3 Envelope detectors and their notation

Envelope detectors or followers [ED] are devices that trace the amplitude envelope of an event[35]. This event can be, for instance, a recording of an acoustic instrument. The extracted time-varying envelope can then be imposed on another sound's amplitude or used to control other parameters, such as the cut-off frequency of a filter[36]. The notation of an envelope detector that is imposed on another's sound amplitude is presented in Figure 6. The envelope of a recorded instrument here is traced and applied to a simple sine wave. The recording technique and the instrument are not specified. A detailed explanation of recording techniques and an approach towards the notation of instrumental and non-instrumental sound sources can be found in Chapter »3. Sound recording«. Since the detection of the envelope and its subsequent imposition on the sine wave replaces the envelope notation (as presented in Figures 4-6), the instrument's notation system is designated as output level. The sonic events here are in brackets in order to determine that the sound is not supposed to be audible, but only serves as the envelope for the sine wave.

In the example presented in Figure 7, the instrumentalist performs a chromatic anabasis of semiquavers from »f¹/F4« to »c²/C5« with the dynamic level *mezzoforte*. The tones are played *staccato*. Subsequently, a minim »c#²/C#5« is played, which involves a *crescendo* from *pianissimo* to *mezzoforte*. The symbol for the envelope detector and the arrow request that the envelope of this complex is detected and subsequently imposed on the semibreve sine wave »c²/C5«. Further, when wishing to use the envelope detector in order to control, for instance, the cut-off frequency of a filter, the paradigm presented in Figure 7 needs to be combined with the notation of the respective filter (cf. Chapter »2. 3 Filters«).

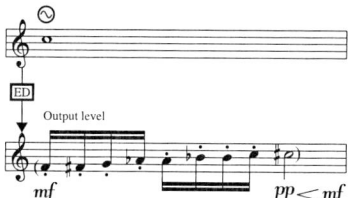

Fig. 7 Envelope detector.

---

[35] Roads, Tutorial, p. 623.
[36] Dodge and Jerse, Computer, p. 413.

1. 2 Additive synthesis

The model of additive synthesis [⊞] is the reversal of a *Fourier* analysis. The technique assumes that any periodic waveform can be modelled as a sum of sinusoids with various amplitude envelopes and time-varying frequencies. The components of the synthetic sound are produced by separate **sine wave oscillators**. The parameters of **frequency** and **envelope** need to be determined for every oscillator. Musical timbres contain several time-varying partials, including noise components. It requires dozens of oscillators and envelopes to obtain convincing acoustic simulations[37].

1. 2. 1 Previous methods of notation

Stockhausen's »Studie II«[38] is a simple example of additive synthesis. All generated timbres consist of five partials. Figure 8 shows a generic tone mixture. The fundamental is a sine wave of 100 Hz and the overtones are set at 107, 114, 121 and 129 Hz.

Beispiel: Tongemisch Nr. 1   Exemple: Complexe sonore No. 1   Example: Note mixture No. 1

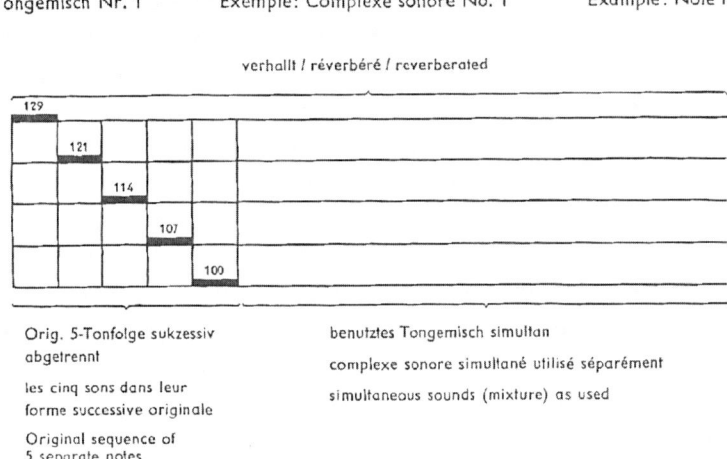

verhallt / réverbéré / reverberated

Orig. 5-Tonfolge sukzessiv   benutztes Tongemisch simultan
abgetrennt
                              complexe sonore simultané utilisé séparément
les cinq sons dans leur
forme successive originale   simultaneous sounds (mixture) as used

Original sequence of
5 separate notes

Fig. 8 Stockhausen, Studie II, p. VIII.

193 additions of a similar kind are created. Each timbre is obtained from one fundamental sine wave and four overtones. Their intervallic structure is calculated by means of a constant multiplication factor of $^{25}\sqrt{5}^{(1)}$, $^{25}\sqrt{5}^2$, $^{25}\sqrt{5}^3$, $^{25}\sqrt{5}^4$ or $^{25}\sqrt{5}^5$. There are thus, for instance, five different overtone combinations for the fundamental of 100 Hz[39]. The note mixtures are arranged in five groups (from top to bottom) and nine segments (from left to right). Except for the fifth group, each segment contains five note mixtures[40]. The first overtone of group 1

---

[37] Miranda, Synthesis, pp. 125f. and Martin Supper: Elektroakustische Musik und Computermusik [Electroacoustic music and Computer Music]. Geschichte – Ästhetik – Methoden – Systeme [History – aesthetics – methods – systems]. Darmstadt 1997, p. 38.

[38] Karlheinz Stockhausen: Elektronische Studien. Studie II. London 1956.

[39] In Stockhausen, Studie II, p. IV it is described wrongly that 1, 2, 3, 4 or 5 times $^{25}\sqrt{5}$ is used as a constant multiplication factor. However, this would lead to results other than the ones presented in Figure 9.

[40] For example, 1st group, 1st segment, 1st note mixture: 100 Hz = fundamental, $^{25}\sqrt{5}$ × 100 Hz = 1st harmonic, $^{25}\sqrt{5}^2$ × 100 Hz = 2nd harmonic, $^{25}\sqrt{5}^3$ × 100 Hz = 3rd harmonic, $^{25}\sqrt{5}^4$ × 100 Hz = 4th harmonic; 2nd group, 1st segment, 1st note mixture: 100 Hz, $^{25}\sqrt{5}^2$ × 100 Hz, $^{25}\sqrt{5}^4$ × 110 Hz, $^{25}\sqrt{5}^6$ × 100 Hz, $^{25}\sqrt{5}^8$ × 100 Hz; 3rd group, 1st segment, 1st note mixture: 100 Hz, $^{25}\sqrt{5}^3$ × 100 Hz, $^{25}\sqrt{5}^6$ × 100 Hz, $^{25}\sqrt{5}^9$ × 100 Hz, $^{25}\sqrt{5}^{12}$ × 100 Hz etc.

always becomes the fundamental for the following note mixture in each segment. But each segment of group 1-4 always begins with the same fundamental, determined by group 1 (previous segment, note mixture 1, overtone 4 multiplied with $^{25}\sqrt{5}$: 138 Hz = group 1, segment 1, note mixture 1, overtone $4 \times {}^{25}\sqrt{5}$, 190 Hz = group 1, segment 2, note mixture 1, overtone $4 \times {}^{25}\sqrt{5}$, 263 Hz = group 1, segment 3, note mixture 1, overtone $4 \times {}^{25}\sqrt{5}$ etc.). Only group 5 derives the first fundamental of every segment from overtone 2 of the previous note mixture:

Tabelle A

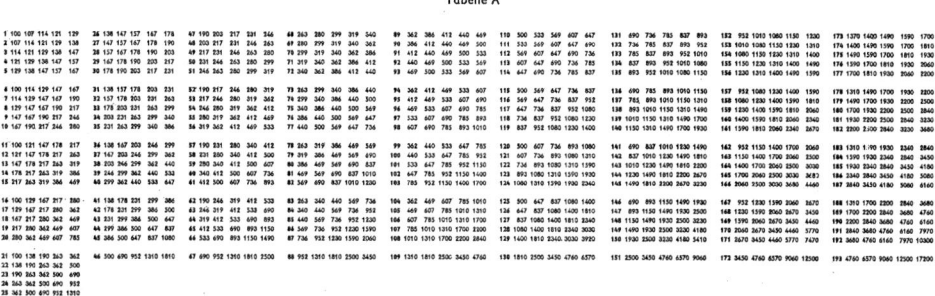

Fig. 9 Stockhausen, Studie II, p. IV.

The timbres are notated by means of a diagrammatic notation system. The y-axis of this system represents the frequency. It ranges from 100 to 17,200 Hz and corresponds to the interval $^{25}\sqrt{5}$:

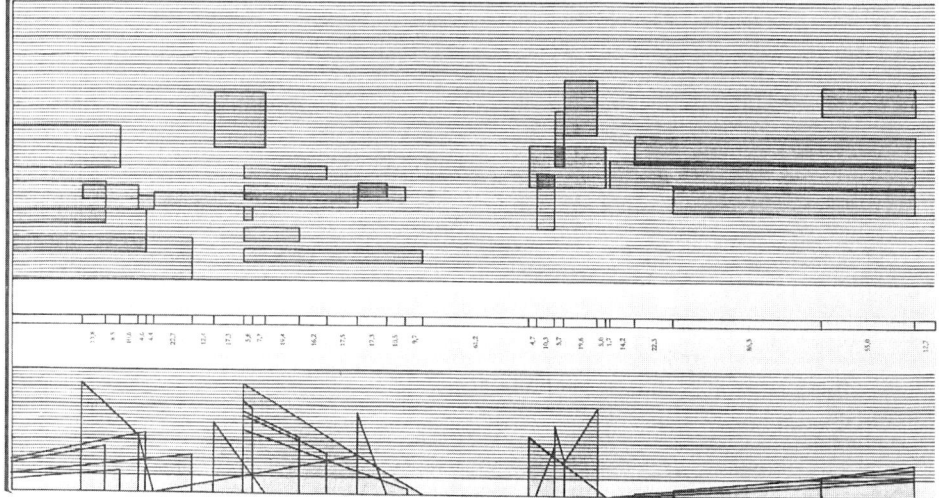

Fig. 10 Stockhausen, Studie II, p. 23.

In opposition to traditional notation – where the fundamental is depicted by the notation system and the overtones that determine the timbre are disregarded – another approach is adopted here: "[a]s each note mixture contains five frequencies with constant intervals, only the highest and lowest intervals are indicated by horizontal lines joined at the beginning and end by vertical lines, the enclosed space being shaded"[41]. The x-axis represents the time. In

---

[41] Stockhausen, Studie II, p. VI.

the score, it is indicated in cm and corresponds to the length of a tape played at 76.2 cm per second. The volume of the events is depicted by another system underneath the timeline. The y-axis here represents the loudness in dB. It ranges from 0 to –30 dB whilst each line embodies a 1 dB step. Additionally, there is a lower limit of –40 dB for the initial or final levels of rising or falling envelopes. The piece is supposed to be realised in a room with about 10 seconds reverberation time. This effect is, however, not depicted in the score, but explained in the foreword[42]. *Stockhausen's* method of notation enables the depiction of simultaneous events and their envelopes. As can be seen in Figure 10, the upper system describes the note mixtures and the lower system the corresponding dynamic level in time. The lowest line of the dynamic level's notation system is related to –40 dB and the next line to –30 dB. This is why the spacing differs from the other lines, which depict 1 dB steps.

1. 2. 2 Discussion

Stockhausen's approach may be described as exact. The frequency, duration and dynamic level of the events are quite clearly determined. However, his method of depiction cannot be utilised in combination with traditional notation. Moreover, the appearance of the notation system is – as is apparent from Figure 10 – confusing, especially when simultaneous events are depicted. If *Stockhausen's* diagrammatic notation was supposed to be combined with the notation of traditional instruments, the timeline would have to be modified. Such a modification would not cause difficulties, but could be executed by altering the timeline. The bigger problem is the confusing appearance of the sonic events and the dynamic level. The upper system needs to depict 81 frequencies (from 100 Hz to »$^{25}\sqrt{5}^{80} \times 100$ Hz«) and is, due to this, vast. It is, therefore, difficult to determine which shaded note mixture is related to which frequency. This lack of instantaneous comprehension even increases when simultaneous events with similar frequencies are depicted. The system for the dynamic level consists of 31 + 1 (–40 dB) lines. Due to that, it is also hard to comprehend quickly which exact volume is depicted. Further, all note mixtures in »Studie II« either start or end at another point in time. This is because, if they had the same duration and started at the same time, it could no longer be determined which dynamic level was related to which sonic event.

1. 2. 3 Suggestion for the notation of additive synthesis

Since *Stockhausen's* method lacks simplicity and instantaneous comprehension, another approach is adopted here. This approach is stronger related to traditional notation and developed with regard to the note mixtures utilised by *Stockhausen*. It may be described as a transformation of the note mixtures into traditional notation. By applying this approach, a clearer appearance of the score and greater degree of instantaneous comprehension is achieved because the pitch and duration can be quickly identified. The note mixtures may be transferred to pitch-based notation since their fundamental frequencies ascend and their spectrum is (more or less) discrete. However, it is not possible to depict all five groups by a single notation system. This is because in pitch-based notation only the fundamental is notated. If all five groups of »Studie II« were depicted by a single system, for instance, the tone with the fundamental of 100 Hz would be confused because every group contains it. Therefore, each group is regarded here as a distinct instrument and hence five different notation systems are employed, each representing one of the five interval ratios. In order to transfer *Stockhausen's* intervallic structure ($^{25}\sqrt{5}$) to twelve tone equal temperament ($^{12}\sqrt{2}$), each tone needs to be regarded as retuned while the timbre has to be additionally determined. This is executed here

---

[42] Cf. ibid., pp. VIf.

by relating the rounded integer frequencies of *Stockhausen's* note mixtures to the fundamental pitches of twelve-tone equal temperament[43].

The construction of a synthetic instrument, which is based on the frequencies of group 1, is presented in Figure 11. In order to balance the deviations, the lowest fundamental of 100 Hz is related to a »B/B♭2«. The original notation of the tones is preserved, meaning that even though a »B/B♭2« is depicted, the 100 Hz-timbre is heard. Concert notation would lead to a confusing appearance and require the introduction of additional microtonal symbols since it is impossible to express every frequency by means of eighth, sixth or quarter tones. To give an example, the »e/E3« is normally described by having a fundamental with the frequency of approximately 165 Hz and overtones of 330 Hz (octave), 494 Hz (octave and fifth), 659 Hz (double octave) etc., but now by having a fundamental of 147 Hz and overtones of 157, 167, 178 and 190 Hz. Hence when the »e/E3« is notated in the score, this exact timbre is supposed to be heard. The same is valid for all other tones.

Construction and *scordatura* of the synthetic instrument in Hz
Group 1

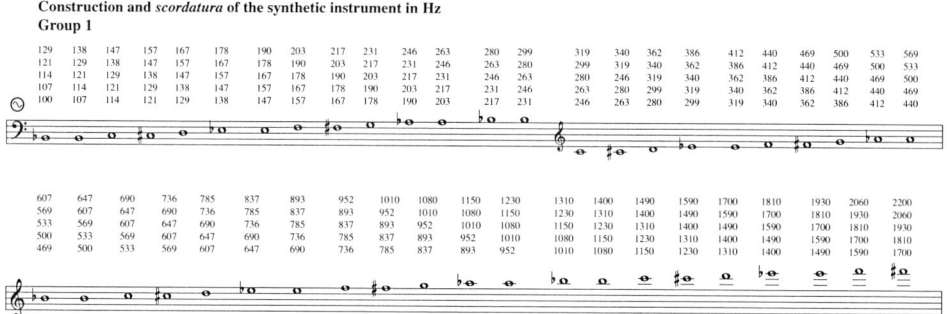

129	138	147	157	167	178	190	203	217	231	246	263	280	299		319	340	362	386	412	440	469	500	533	569
121	129	138	147	157	167	178	190	203	217	231	246	263	280		299	319	340	362	386	412	440	469	500	533
114	121	129	138	147	157	167	178	190	203	217	231	246	263		280	299	319	340	362	386	412	440	469	500
107	114	121	129	138	147	157	167	178	190	203	217	231	246		263	280	299	319	340	362	386	412	440	469
100	107	114	121	129	138	147	157	167	178	190	203	217	231		246	263	280	299	319	340	362	386	412	440

607	647	690	736	785	837	893	952	1010	1080	1150	1230		1310	1400	1490	1590	1700	1810	1930	2060	2200
569	607	647	690	736	785	837	893	952	1010	1080	1150		1230	1310	1400	1490	1590	1700	1810	1930	2060
533	569	607	647	690	736	785	837	893	952	1010	1080		1150	1230	1310	1400	1490	1590	1700	1810	1930
500	533	569	607	647	690	736	785	837	893	952	1010		1080	1150	1230	1310	1400	1490	1590	1700	1810
469	500	533	569	607	647	690	736	785	837	893	952		1010	1080	1150	1230	1310	1400	1490	1590	1700

Fig. 11 Transformation of group 1 to pitch-based notation.

Groups 2 to 5 need to be treated in the same way. After having done that, the complete sonic material of »Studie II« may be organised in time. Figure 12 shows how the application would look. In the example, the timbres of group 1, 2 and 4 are utilised. Three simultaneous events may be depicted per notation system because otherwise the envelope notation could, as mentioned, become confusing. Each of the note mixtures is shaped by a distinct envelope, depicted by the system designated as output level. In the case of group 1, the timbres related to »a♭/A♭3«, »e♭/E♭3« and »c/C3« are produced for the duration of a minim and followed by a minim rest. They all have different envelopes that are depicted with regard to the envelope notation, as suggested in Chapter »1. 1. 1 Periodic wave generators and their envelopes«. Further, since traditional notation is employed, traditional articulations can be used. The semibreve »f♯/F♯3« of group 2 is, for instance, complemented by a trill symbol. The trill is performed with the upper adjacent tone (»g/G3«). Since it is barely possible to depict the envelope of all tones that are involved in the trill, this action is regarded here as connected and a single continuous envelope applied. In the case of group 4, a constant *glissando* is employed. It starts at »a♭1/A♭4«, ends at »g1/G4« and involves the quavers »f♯1/F♯4«, »d1/D4«, »h1/B4« and »f/F3«. Since this action results in a single event with a constantly shifting pitch, the dynamic level may be depicted by a continuous envelope. It should be noted that such a *glissando* requires shifting the fundamental and the overtones of a note mixture to the fundamental and overtones of another note mixture. This might be easily realised when, as in the example, all timbres have the same number of overtones. However, if their number varies from note mixture to note mixture, the realisation becomes more complicated. Further, as

---

[43] The partial inexactness in *Stockhausen's* rounding is disregarded here.

223

mentioned above, the *glissando* is – in order to achieve a greater clarity and enable the depiction of *glissando* motions that do not involve changes in pitch – requested by means of an arrow and not in the traditional manner. Alternatively, the common method of notation may be restored.

Apparently, this approach requires more space than the one employed by *Stockhausen*. Further, the dynamic level is determined in a less exact way since only 10 + 1 instead of 31 + 1 dynamic levels are utilised. However, the new method is able to depict more complex actions. The events of Figure 12, for instance, could not be depicted by *Stockhausen's* system since they involve tones that simultaneously start and end. Moreover, traditional articulations – such as the trill or *glissando* – could not be used in combination with his diagrammatic system. Concerning the loudness, it is not necessary to employ as many dynamic levels as *Stockhausen* since the difference between, for example, –26 and –25 dB can be barely perceived. Finally, the new system may, as mentioned, be used in combination with the notation of acoustic instruments and offers a greater degree of instantaneous comprehension.

Fig. 12 The notation of note mixtures.

As mentioned, *Stockhausen* additionally employs natural reverberation. This effect is not discussed here, but approaches towards the notation of synthetic reverberation presented in Chapter »2. 4 Reverberation« and the depiction of natural reverberation described in Chapter »3. 3 Sound sources and the recording room«. Moreover, as explained in the beginning of this chapter, in additive synthesis the frequency and envelope need to be determined for each oscillator. However, *Stockhausen* does not define different amplitudes or envelopes for the partials. Hence whenever the amplitude changes, the amplitude of all partials changes in the same way. Since Figure 12 presents the transformation of *Stockhausen's* approach to traditional notation, the same is valid for the note mixtures depicted there. But the envelope of each partial may also be notated separately. Since only the fundamental is supposed to be depicted in the score, it needs to be defined before organising the timbres in time:

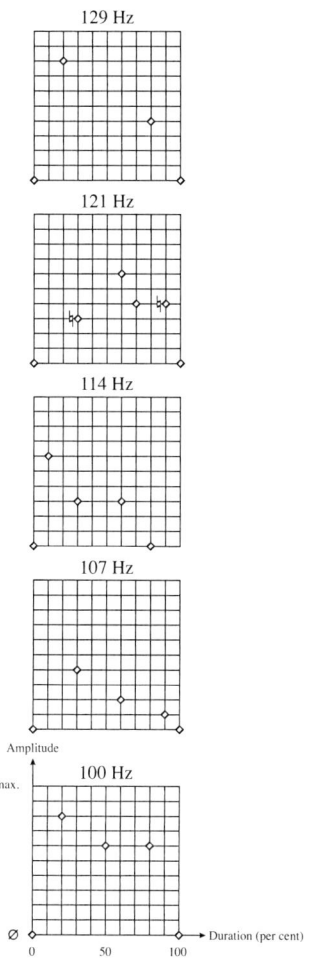

Fig. 13 Pre-determined envelopes for each partial.

Figure 13 shows how the envelope of a generic note mixture with five distinct oscillators may be determined. The envelope is notated here by means of a diagrammatic system that resembles the output level notation of the previous figure. The x-axis represents the duration whilst the y-axis depicts the amplitude in 10 + 1 steps (from minimum to maximum in 10 steps plus »∅«). This system is, in the example, applied to the first note mixture of group 1 (100, 107, 114, 121 and 129 Hz) and would have to be applied to all note mixtures that are supposed to be employed. With regard to »Studie II«, 965 envelopes (193 note mixtures each with five partials) would need to be determined. Since the duration of the envelope is described in per cent, it may adapt to any duration employed in the score, e. g. in the case of a semiquaver, 100 per cent equals the duration of a semiquaver and, in the case of a minim, 100 per cent equals the duration of a minim. Further, because the amplitude is described by a minimum and maximum level, it could also adapt to each output level employed in the score, e. g. if the output level is constantly *piano*, the maximum level equals *piano* and if it is constantly *forte*, the maximum level equals *forte*.

However, it needs to be noted in this context that the lower the output level, the more exact is the determination of the amplitude. This is because in the case of the output level being constantly *forte*, there are 10 steps from the minimum (quadruple *piano*) to the maximum (*forte*), whilst in the case of the output level being constantly *piano*, there are also 10 steps from the minimum (quadruple *piano*) to the maximum (*piano*). Thus a small extent is described by the same amount of steps as a large extent. The same is valid for short and long durations. But it is assumed here that this dissimilarity may be balanced by the interpreter. As is apparent, the preface of a work that makes use of a similar amount of such or even more complex note mixtures, will become extensive. A large list would have to precede the actual score. However, such a list is a necessity and related to the amount of work that the interpreter will have to execute in order to realise the piece. Anyway, it might be more desirable for a composer to employ techniques other than additive synthesis because they permit the creation of similarly interesting results and do not require such an extensive preparation. A number of these techniques are explained in the following chapters. Further, the utilisation of additive synthesis in combination with analysis and re-synthesis is presented in Chapter »1. 4. 1 Time/pitch changing and its notation«.

1. 3 Subtractive synthesis

Subtractive synthesis [⊟] creates musical material out of complex sources by sculpting away selected portions of the spectrum of the source. Normally, a source with a broad spectrum, such as white noise or a narrow pulse, serves as the raw material out of which **filters** shape new musical material. However, any sound can generally be used as a source for subtractive synthesis. The filters change the characteristics of a sound by rejecting unwanted components or by otherwise shaping the spectrum[44]. Examples for subtractive synthesis, as well as an explanation of the different types of filters and their employment, can be found in Chapter »1. 4. 1 Time/pitch changing and its notation« and »2. 3 Filters«.

1. 4 Analysis and re-synthesis

Many spectral modelling techniques work in two stages: analysis and re-synthesis. The re-synthesis stage uses parameters extracted from the analysis of a sampled sound in order to recreate it. The great advantage of this technique over plain sampling is that analysis data can be modified in a number of ways. There are two categories of spectrum analysis: harmonic and formant[45] analysis. The former is aimed at the identification of the frequencies and amplitudes of the spectrum components whilst the latter uses the estimation of the overall shape of the spectrum's amplitude envelope[46]. The fast *Fourier* transform (FFT) and wavelets analysis are typical examples of the harmonic analysis, whereas linear predictive coding (LPC) is a typical example of formant analysis[47]. The analysis techniques form the basis for the synthetic reproduction and further transformation of sound in the **time and pitch changing** technique

---

[44] Dodge and Jerse, Computer, pp. 169 and 171.

[45] A formant is a peaking in the spectral envelope of a tone, which can include both harmonic and enharmonic partials as well as noise. Formant peaks are characteristic of the vowels spoken by the human voice and the tones radiated by many musical instruments. A formant is caused by resonances, for instance, in the body of an instrument. The formant regions are, in such a case, related to the natural resonant frequencies of the instrument.

[46] Miranda, Synthesis, pp. 126f. and 133-135.

[47] Ibid., p. 127.

as well as in **harmonizer** and **phase vocoder** devices. Further, there are **other techniques** that cannot be presented in detail here in order to limit the extent of the work. They are, therefore, merely introduced.

1. 4. 1 Time/pitch changing and its notation

The so-called *Fourier* analysis can be used to determine the spectrum of a digital signal. Its most common implementation is the **fast *Fourier* transform**. The **short-term *Fourier* transform** (STFT) is a succession of FFTs, performed on small portions of the waveform. An FFT does not have the ability to directly measure the fundamental frequency of any arbitrary waveform. Instead, the algorithm can be thought of as a bank of band-pass filters (cf. Chapter »2. 3. 1 High-pass, low-pass, band-pass and band-reject filters«), ranging from the lowest to the highest frequency of the whole spectrum. These band-pass filters are called windows. Each of these windows reports the net amplitude of the spectral components passing through[48]. Moreover, each block of data generated by the FFT is called a frame[49]. The **window size** defines the frequency and time resolution of the analysis. It is determined in samples[50], normally specified as »2 to the power of x«, e. g. 256, 512, 1,024 etc. Longer windows have better frequency resolution than smaller ones, but smaller ones have better time resolution. If FFT is used to analyse tones, the size of the window should be related to the intervals of the partials. The frequency resolution, and thus the bandwidth of the windows, can be calculated by »the sampling rate ÷ window size« and the time resolution by the »window size ÷ sampling rate«[51]. There are, further, parameters that may be additionally determined, such as the window type or the overlap factor of the windows[52]. The size of the FFT window is constant. Hence all harmonic detectors have the same bandwidth and are placed linearly across the audio range. **Wavelets analysis** improves this situation by introducing a scaling mechanism whereby the size of the window varies according to the frequency being analysed[53]. The duration of each wavelet is dependent on its frequency content. The higher the frequency, the shorter the wavelet. This means that the temporal resolution of the wavelet is greater at high frequencies[54]. However, harmonic analysis methods are not entirely adequate for the analysis of sound with a high proportion of non-sinusoidal components and – to a certain extent – with non-harmonic combinations of partials. With regard to these kinds of sounds, formant analysis can be utilised[55] (cf. Chapter »1. 4. 4 Other techniques«). Further, **linear predictive coding** is a statistical method for predicting the future values of a waveform on the basis of its past values[56]. It involves computing a set of filter coefficients for each window and can be utilised to analyse all sorts of speech, but also as an analysis tool for other non-harmonic sound materials[57]. The result of the analysis stage is a series of frames, representing a greatly data-reduced version of the input signal. Each frame is described by a list of parameters, including the average amplitude of the residual and original sound, the ratio of the two amplitudes, the estimated pitch, the frame duration and the coefficients for the fil-

---

[48] Dodge and Jerse, Computer, p. 244.
[49] Roads, Tutorial, p. 552.
[50] Dodge and Jerse, Computer, p. 244.
[51] For instance, when the sample rate is 44,100 Hz and the size of the window is 1,024 samples, the frequency resolution is 43 Hz (rounded off) and the time resolution 0.023 seconds or 23 ms (rounded off).
[52] Cf. Miranda, Synthesis, pp. 129-132.
[53] Miranda, Synthesis, p. 132.
[54] Roads, Tutorial, p. 446.
[55] Miranda, Synthesis, pp. 132f.
[56] Dodge and Jerse, Computer, p. 226.
[57] Perry R. Cook: Real sound synthesis for interactive applications. 3rd edition. Wellesley 2007, pp. 90 and 93.

ter. As in the fast *Fourier* transform, the window size needs to be determined[58]. Time and pitch changing can be realised by means of FFT or STFT, wavelet transform or LPC. Before the re-synthesis, the duration of a sound can be stretched or shrunk whilst the pitch remains constant. Moreover, the pitch of a sound can also be shifted up or down whilst the duration remains constant. Additionally, these techniques can be employed in the classical way. In this case, changing the duration effects the pitch and vice versa[59]. The FFT results in a series of spectrum frames that capture the frequency-domain evolution of the sound over time. This data is used to re-synthesise the sound by **additive synthesis [⊞]** whilst each sine wave oscillator's frequency corresponds to an analysed frequency component. As in the FFT method, the wavelet transform splits a sampled sound into a collection of individual components, localised in time. These components are characterised by amplitude and phase values gained by the analysis. In order to modify the pitch or time, the analysis data must be altered before re-synthesis[60].

An approach towards the notation of time and pitch changing by means of STFT and wavelets is presented in Figure 14. The sound that is subject to this modification is produced by an unspecified instrument. It is supposed to be analysed, altered and finally re-synthesised by means of additive synthesis. STFT is applied in the first bar. The window size is estimated as 256 samples. Other parameters, such as the window type and overlap factor, are disregarded here. Subsequently, wavelets analysis is applied in the second bar. The transformation is depicted by the lower system. It is related to the upper system by making all corresponding sounds start at the same time. The processes can be described as follows: in the first bar the instrument produces at first a crotchet »eb1/Eb4«. It is followed by another crotchet »h1/B4«. After a crotchet rest, a crotchet »f1/F4« is finally produced. The »eb1/Eb4« is subject to a time and pitch change. Its duration is reduced to a quaver and it is transposed up to »e2/E5« before being re-synthesised. The duration of the »h1/B4« is increased to a minim. Since this minim is complemented by the direction classical, the change in duration results in a transposition downwards. The resulting pitch is, however, not depicted. Finally, the »f1/F4« is transposed upwards to »ab2/Ab5«. Since the direction *ordinario* is given, the transposition no longer affects the duration (and vice versa). Subsequently, the crotchets »a2/A5« and »ab1/Ab4« are both stretched to a dotted minim, which makes them overlap. The »a2/A5« is, moreover, transposed down to »ab1/Ab4« and the »ab1/Ab4« transposed up to »c2/C5«. Further, the original dynamic level *mezzoforte* is applied to the re-synthesised material since no additional output level is employed here.

Fig. 14 Time/pitch changing by STFT and wavelets.

---

[58] Roads, Tutorial, pp. 205-207.

[59] Time and pitch changing is achieved in the classical way by increasing or reducing the speed of a tape. When the tape speed changes, the material is transposed. A slower speed results in a transposition down, a higher speed in a transposition up.

[60] Roads, Tutorial, pp. 444-447.

Linear predictive coding is an analysis/re-synthesis method based on **subtractive synthesis** [⊟]. In LPC the analysis result is encoded as a sequence of short-duration frames, with each frame capturing the filter coefficients, pitch and voiced/unvoiced data for a given time slice of sound. To realise the time and pitch changing, the frame needs to be edited. The edited frame is then used to drive the re-synthesis[61]. LPC data is often utilised for speech synthesis. In such a case, a **variable-frequency pulse generator** [⊕] is employed to create voiced and **white noise** [⊛] to create unvoiced phonemes (cf. Chapter »1. 1 Basic elements«). Further, LPC can also be used to synthesise noisy sounds[62]. The re-synthesised sound created by linear predictive coding generally has an artificial character due to the details lost during the analysis[63].

An approach towards the notation of time and pitch changing by means of LPC is presented in Figure 15. The sound that is subject to the modification is an unspecified noise (for recording techniques and the notation of noisy sources please refer to Chapter »3. Sound recording«), which is notated by means of a single lined notation system with no clef and x-shaped note heads. Since the original sound is not notated by means of a pitch-based system, another approach towards the depiction of the »pitch« change needs to be adopted here. The »pitch« change refers, in this case, to a frequency change of the noisy material. The **LPC window size** is set at 2,048 samples. The sound is re-synthesised by means of subtractive synthesis in combination with a variable-frequency pulse generator and white noise. The original noisy sound has the duration of a crotchet. It is increased to a semibreve before being re-synthesised. Additionally, a frequency shift is performed. It is depicted here by simply giving the direction + 650 Hz, meaning that all the material is transposed 650 Hz up. Since no additional output level is employed, the original dynamic level *piano* is supposed to be applied to the re-synthesised sound.

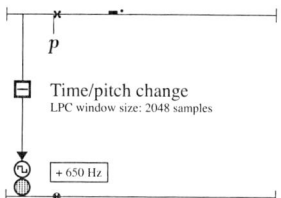

Fig. 15 Time/pitch changing by LPC.

The LPC synthesis system can be further modified to permit the use of a source other than noise or periodic pulse for the excitation of the filter. The new source may be any recorded or synthesised sound. The only factor that influences the choice of source is the necessity for a relatively broad spectrum. This technique is a type of cross-synthesis[64]. The notation of this modification is presented in Figure 16. The new source is an unspecified recorded noise. It is represented by the middle system in combination with the symbol for subtractive synthesis. The original sound is depicted by the highest and the transformed sound by the lowest system. The original sound »e♭1/E♭4« is produced by an unspecified instrument and has the duration of a crotchet. Its duration is increased to a semibreve and the tone simultaneously transposed up to »a1/A4«. The original sound is analysed by means of linear productive coding (window size: 2,048 samples), edited and then re-synthesised by means of subtractive synthesis and the noisy source.

[61] Ibid., p. 447.
[62] Cook, Sound, pp. 90-93.
[63] Roads, Tutorial, p. 447.
[64] Dodge and Jerse, Computer, p. 234.

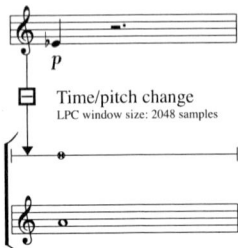

Fig. 16 A different source in time/pitch changing by LPC.

Furthermore, there is another time and pitch changing technique, which is based on a different approach. It is presented here because of being strongly related to the previously mentioned techniques. **Time-granulation** involves segmenting a stream of sound samples into short duration units called grains (cf. Chapter »1. 9 Granular synthesis«). In time granulation, the duration of each grain can vary from 1 to 200 milliseconds (ms). The time stretch is performed here by cloning (to stretch the duration) or deleting (to shrink the duration) grains whilst the frequency content of the grains is preserved. To transpose the signal upwards without changing its duration, the internal sampling rate is increased and grains are cloned to restore the original duration. To transpose the signal downwards without changing the duration, the internal sampling rate is conversely reduced and grains deleted to restore the original duration[65].

As is apparent from Figure 17, this time and pitch changing technique is notated similarly to time and pitch changing by means of STFT or wavelets. However, in this case, the sound is not re-synthesised by means of additive synthesis. Hence the symbol that depicts this type of synthesis is not employed. Further, stops here are subject to the transformation. When pitch shifts, the intervallic structure changes: the lowest tone of the original interval is »e♭¹/E♭4« (~ 311 Hz). A transposition up to »e²/E5« (~ 659 Hz) means that the tone is transposed by approximately 348 Hz or a major seventh. However, when the »a¹/A4« (440 Hz) is transposed up by 348 Hz, it is not transposed up by a major seventh and hence does not result in the complementary »a♭²/A♭5« (~ 831 Hz). Instead, the result is a tone with the fundamental frequency of approximately 788 Hz, which is depicted here by the »g²/G5« (~ 784 Hz). Hence the lowest tone determines the degree of transposition whilst the other tones of the chords are notated here as exact as possible. A similar effect also occurs when single tones are transposed. In such a case, the harmonic structure is stretched when transposed down or compressed when transposed up. Additionally, the stop is stretched to a semibreve.

Fig. 17 Time/pitch changing by time-granulation.

---

[65] Roads, Tutorial, pp. 441-444.

1. 4. 2 The harmonizer

A variant of pitch changing may be created by a harmonizer, which changes the pitch of an incoming signal without altering its duration. The function is based on changing the internal sampling rate of the signal. The pitch shift is determined by the ratio between the sampling rate of the original signal and the sampling rate of the resulting signal[66]. Additionally, the signal may be **fed back** to the harmonizer and hence the material may be repeatedly shifted[67].

1. 4. 2. 1 Previous methods of notation

Nono, in »A Pierre«[68], inter alia employs two harmonizers in order to transform the sound of a contrabass clarinet and a contrabass flute. In the piece, "the harmonizer must transpose a minor seventh down (Harmonizer 1) and a tritone down (Harmonizer 2)"[69]. The harmonizer and other effect units he employs are depicted in the foreword by means of a schematic circuit plan:

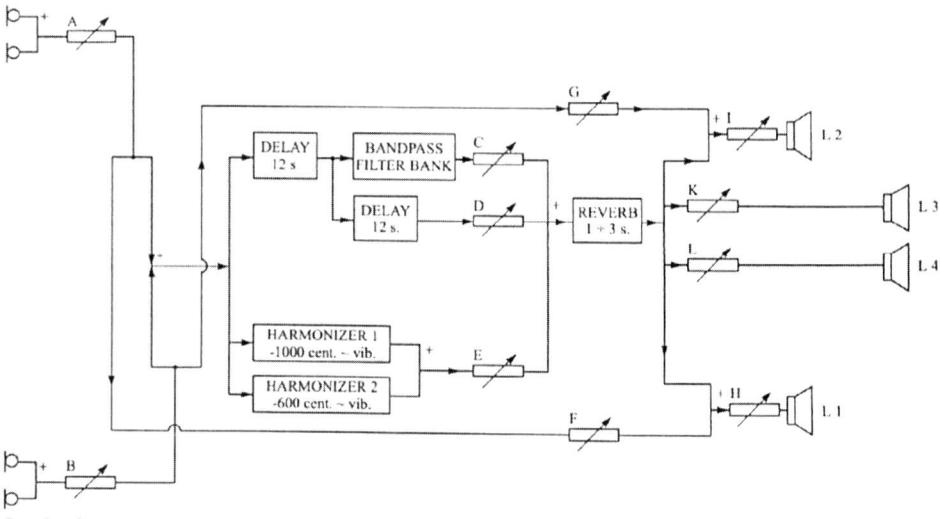

Fig. 18 Nono, A Pierre, p. XV.

In the score, the output level of the four loudspeakers (L 1-4) is, as is apparent from Figure 19, controlled by means of a diagrammatic depiction of the traditional dynamic levels. By doing so, the intensity of the chain of effects is controlled. The system ranges from »Ø« to *fortissimo* and does not have an independent timeline, but is always described in relation to the instrumental system.

---

[66] Ibid., p. 444.

[67] Hans-Joachim Maempel: Audiobearbeitung [Audio processing]. In: Stefan Weinzierl (ed.): Handbuch der Audiotechnik [Compendium of audio engineering]. Berlin et al. 2008, pp. 719-784, here: p. 755.

[68] Luigi Nono: A Pierre. Dell'azzurro silenzio, inquietum. For contrabass flute in G, contrabass flute in B flat and live-electronics. Final version. No city named [Italy] 1996.

[69] Nono, A Pierre, p. XIV.

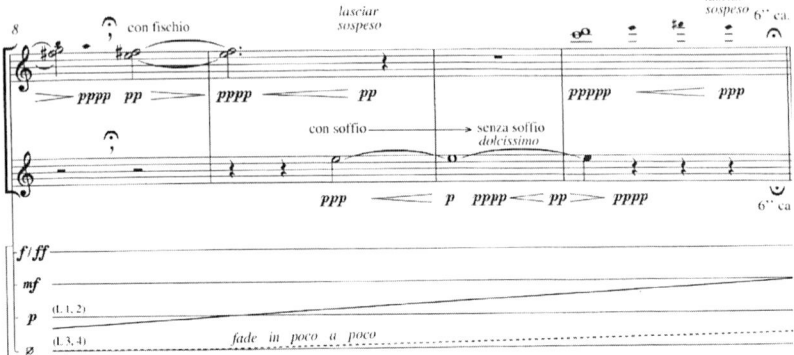

Fig. 19 Nono, A Pierre, p. 1.

1. 4. 2. 2 Discussion

Nono's approach can be described as simple. Only one additional notation system is necessary to depict a complex chain of effects. However, every parameter of each effects unit is fixed and only the speakers' output level may be controlled. The harmonizers, for instance, constantly transpose a minor seventh and a tritone down. In order to apply other combinations of effects or change parameters, another circuit plan would have to be employed. Hence when wanting to use a harmonizer in a more complex way, another method needs to be used. Otherwise, the foreword of the work would become very extensive and the simplicity of the approach would be compromised[70]. Further, since the utilisation of a harmonizer resembles the pitch changing technique, a similar method of notation as in Figure 14 may be employed.

1. 4. 2. 3 Suggestion for the notation of the harmonizer

The suggested method therefore resembles the one used for pitch changing. Unlike *Nono's* approach, this method permits the parameters to be changed during the course of the piece. Moreover, a feedback level in per cent is introduced in order to determine the intensity of the repeated pitch shift. Figure 20 presents the notation of the harmonizer. Several tones here are subject to the transposition. An »e♭¹/E♭4« is transposed here a tritone up to »a¹/A4« whilst the feedback rate is estimated as 30%. A »h¹/B4« is, further, transposed a tritone down to »f¹/F4« with a feedback rate of 55% and an »f¹/F4« transposed a major seventh up to »e²/E5« whilst the feedback rate is set at 15%. Since no additional output level is employed, the original dynamic level *mezzoforte* is applied to the transformed sounds.

Fig. 20 The harmonizer.

---

[70] Cf. Luigi Nono: Omaggio a György Kurtág. For contralto, flute, B♭ clarinet, bass tuba and live-electronics. No city named [Italy] 1996, p. X for more complex fixed chains of effects.

In the example, only one harmonizer is used at a time. When utilising – as *Nono* does – more than one harmonizer simultaneously, additional transposed notes could be added or, if the result becomes too complex, an additional notation system be employed.

1. 4. 3 The phase vocoder and its notation

Like the STFT, the phase vocoder is a channelised analysis tool that measures the amplitude of the spectral components of a signal in frequency bands before re-synthesising it by means of additive synthesis and imposing it on another signal. It also measures the frequency deviation of each component from the centre frequency of its window. As with the Fourier transform, the phase vocoder can be viewed as a bank of band-pass filters. The most common usage of the phase vocoder is to independently modify the frequency and duration of a sound[71]. Besides time and pitch changing, the sonic material may be transformed in various ways. *Miranda* mentions that software packages of this kind hold over 60 tools for tasks, such as blurring the spectrum or shuffling analysis windows[72]. There are, further, vocoders based on linear predictive coding[73]. The imposition of one signal on another signal is a type of cross-synthesis. The most common form uses the amplitude of the analysed sample to control the amplitude of a synthesiser. The phase vocoder handles harmonic, static or smoothly changing tones best. Noisy sounds, and any sound that is rapidly changing on a timescale of a few milliseconds or contains room noise, may result in echoes, flutter, unwanted resonances and undesirable coloured reverberation effects[74]. Since the phase vocoder works similarly to time/pitch changing by means of STFT (cf. Figure 14), it may be notated in the same way.

A suggestion for the notation of the channelised phase vocoder is presented in Figure 21. The original signal is depicted by the upper notation system, the transformed signal by the middle system and the synthesiser signal by the lower system. After the transformation, the sonic material is imposed on the synthesiser signal. This process can be described as follows: the quaver »e²/E5« is imposed on the quaver »c²/C5«. After a quaver rest, the classically shifted minim »h¹/B4« and the crotchet »ab²/Ab5« are imposed on the dotted minims »f¹ – a¹/ F4 – A4«. The synthesiser is depicted here in a simplified manner and also not specified. The device may make use of the synthesis processes explained in the following chapters, e. g. amplitude modulation or frequency modulation.

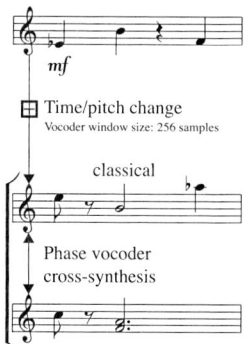

Fig. 21 The phase vocoder.

---

[71] Dodge and Jerse, Computer, pp. 251-253.

[72] Cf. Miranda, Synthesis, pp. 134-138.

[73] Cf. Richard V. Cox: Speech Coding. In: Vijay K. Madisetti and Douglas B. Williams (eds.): The digital signal processing handbook. Boca Raton 1998, pp. 45/1-45/19, here: p. 45/6.

[74] Cf. Roads, Tutorial, pp. 573-576.

As is apparent from the example, a simple phase vocoder is used while complex transformations are not discussed in order to limit the extent of the work. When wishing to further transform the spectrum, additional methods need to be introduced with reference to the essential handbooks. However, the new techniques should be notated in accordance with all other techniques presented in this work.

1. 4. 4 Other techniques

The previous chapter only examines the basic techniques and parameters of analysis and re-synthesis. However, the suggestions may be extended or elaborated when wishing to employ more sophisticated analyses or modifications: **re-synthesis by reintegration of discarded components** is an attempt to improve additive re-synthesis by adding a mechanism that reintegrates the information discarded during the STFT analysis. Each window is re-synthesised immediately after the analysis by additive synthesis. This signal is then subtracted from the original in order to obtain the residual part that has been discarded during the analysis process. The residual part is subsequently presented as an envelope for a filter that is used to shape white noise. The signal gathered from this kind of subtractive synthesis complements the existing signal gained from additive synthesis by adding noisy and other non-sinusoidal components. Re-synthesis by reintegration of discarded components takes advantage of harmonic and formant analysis[75]. For further information please refer to *Serra and Smith*[76]. **Formant synthesis** is another approach towards the re-synthesis of sound. It originated in research into human voice simulation. The mouth, nose and throat function in the production of speech as a resonating tube whereby formants are created. This resonating system can be simulated by a composition of parallel band-pass filters. One formant generator was developed by *Rodet* at the *Institut de Recherche et Coordination Acoustique/Musique*[77] (IRCAM). It is called *Fonction d'Onde Formantique*[78] and is the basis of the CHANT sound synthesis system. Please refer for an introduction to *Roads*[79] and for a description of CHANT to *Rodet*[80]. Further, *Kaegi* and *Tempellars* have developed a distinct voice simulator called **VOSIM**. The core idea is the generation of a repeating tone-burst signal, producing a strong formant component[81]. For an introduction please refer to *Roads*[82] and *Dodge and Jerse*[83] and for a detailed description of VOSIM to *Kaegi*[84]. Finally, **window function synthesis** is a multistage technique for formant synthesis using purely harmonic partials. The technique begins with the creation of a broadband harmonic signal, which is subsequently emphasised or attenuated in order to create time-varying formant regions that emulate the spectra of tradi-

---

[75] Miranda, Synthesis, pp. 140-145.

[76] Xavier Serra and Julius Smith: Spectral modeling synthesis. A sound analysis/synthesis system based on a deterministic plus stochastic decomposition. In: Computer Music Journal, vol. 14(4). Massachusetts 1990, pp. 12-24.

[77] Institute for Research and Coordination in Acoustics/Music.

[78] Function of formant waves.

[79] Roads, Tutorial, pp. 296-308.

[80] Xavier Rodet et al.: CHANT. De la synthèse de la voix chantée à la synthèse en général [From the synthesis of the singing voice to synthesis in general]. Rapports de recherche IRCAM [IRCAM research reports], vol. 35. Paris 1985.

[81] Roads, Tutorial, pp. 308f.

[82] Ibid., pp. 308-311.

[83] Dodge and Jerse, Computer, pp. 267-269.

[84] Werner Kaegi: VOSIM. A new sound synthesis system. In: Journal of the Audio Engineering Society, vol. 26. New York 1978, pp. 418-425.

tional instruments[85]. Please refer for an introduction to *Roads*[86] and for applications of the window function synthesis to *Bass and Goeddel*[87] or *Goeddel and Bass*[88].

1. 5 Amplitude modulation

Modulation is the alteration of the amplitude, phase or frequency of an oscillator in accordance with another signal. The oscillator that is being modulated is called the carrier oscillator. When modulation occurs, the carrier wave is changed[89]. In amplitude modulation (AM) [AM] there are various ways of changing the carrier wave. This chapter focuses on **classical amplitude modulation**, including the *tremolo*-effect and complex amplitude modulation, as well as on **ring modulation**.

1. 5. 1 Classical amplitude modulation and its notation

Amplitude modulation occurs when a modulator drives the amplitude of a carrier. The spectral components of a modulated signal are classified into carrier components and sidebands. The frequency of a carrier component is determined only by the frequency of the carrier oscillator, while the frequency of a sideband is determined by the **carrier** (C) [⬤] and the **modulator** (M) [Ⓜ]. In classical AM sine waves are employed for the carrier and modulator oscillator. The output from the modulating oscillator is added to a value that expresses the amplitude the carrier would have if there was no modulation. This proportion is described by the variable **modulation index** m. When m is higher than zero, the carrier wave will take an envelope with sinusoidal variation. When $m = 1$, the amplitude of the modulator equals the unmodulated amplitude of the carrier and 100 per cent of modulation is reached. In classical AM with two sine wave oscillators the spectrum of the resulting signal contains energy at three frequencies: the carrier frequency plus two sidebands, established by adding the modulator to the carrier frequency (sum tone) and by subtracting the modulator from the carrier frequency (difference tone)[90]. When partials occur in AM, which would be on the negative side of the y-axis (Hz), the modulation product is ignored[91].

A suggestion for the notation of amplitude modulation is presented in Figure 22. It is derived from the method of notation suggested for oscillators and their envelopes in Chapter »1. 1 Basic elements«. Both the modulator and carrier oscillator generate sine waves [◒]. The modulator is depicted by the upper and the carrier by the lower pitch-based notation system. In the example, the modulator oscillator generates a semibreve »f♯¹/F♯4« (~ 370 Hz). Simultaneously, the carrier oscillator produces a semibreve »c♯²/C♯5« (~ 554 Hz). Hence the carrier frequency, a sum tone of approximately 924 Hz (» 554 Hz + 370 Hz«) and a difference tone of approximately 184 Hz (» 554 Hz – 370 Hz«) can be perceived. The modulation index m is depicted by means of a diagrammatic notation system underneath the modulator's system. The x-axis of this system describes the time whilst the y-axis depicts the modulation index from »∅« to 1 in 10 + 1 steps. Hence the white dots (◇) depict m in time. In order to determine the modulation index more exactly, additions can be written over the system. During the

---

[85] Roads, Tutorial, p. 311.

[86] Ibid., pp. 311-314.

[87] Steven C. Bass and Thomas W. Goeddel: The efficient digital implementation of subtractive music synthesis. In: IEEE Micro, vol. 1(3). New York 1981, pp. 24-37.

[88] Thomas W. Goeddel and Steven C. Bass: High quality synthesis of musical voices in discrete time. In: IEEE transactions on acoustics, speech and signal processing, vol. 32(3). New York 1984, pp. 623-633.

[89] Dodge and Jerse, Computer, p. 90.

[90] Ibid., p. 90.

[91] Strange, Systems, p. 118.

described processes, *m* is reduced from an initial value of 0.5 to 0.35 for the duration of a dotted minim (the addition 0.35 refers to the dot that normally depicts a modulation index of 0.3). Subsequently, *m* is increased to 0.8 for the duration of a crotchet. The output level or envelope of the sounds is notated underneath the AM instrument. The x-axis describes here again the time and the y-axis the amplitude from »∅« to quadruple *forte* in 10 + 1 steps. In the example, an ADSR envelope (cf. Figure 4) is employed since the dynamic level is increased from »∅« to *fortissimo* for the duration of a quaver (attack), decreased to *mezzo-forte* for the duration of a crotchet (decay), then remains at this level for the duration of a minim (sustain) and is decreased to »∅« for the duration of a quaver (release).

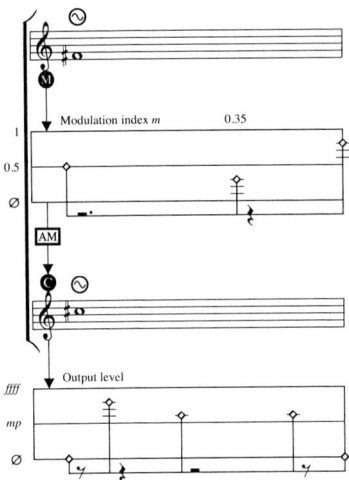

Fig. 22 Amplitude modulation.

Amplitude modulation can also be utilised to create the ***tremolo*-effect**. This is achieved by employing a **small modulation index *m*** and sub-audio frequencies produced by an **LFO**[92]:

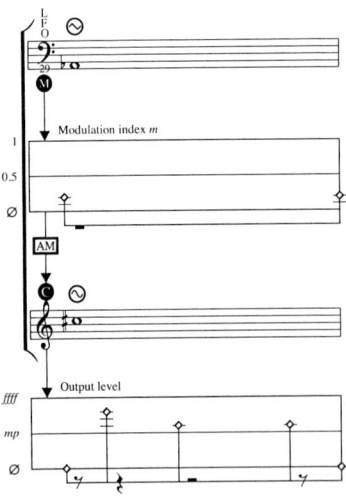

Fig. 23 The *tremolo*-effect.

---

[92] Dodge and Jerse, Computer, pp. 90-92.

Normally, sine or triangle waves are employed in this kind of AM[93]. Analogously, in Figure 23, the carrier oscillator generates the same material as in the previous example whilst the modulating LFO produces triangle waves [⊘]. The latter is depicted by a traditional system in bass clef, here transposed by four octaves (*29ma*). In the example, the LFO generates a semi-breve »₄A♭/A♭–2« (~ 6.5 Hz) while the modulation index *m* is constantly set at 0.2.

Further, **complex amplitude modulation** may involve more than two signals and amplitude modulated oscillators may modulate other oscillators. All wave generators – including noise – may be employed for carriers and modulators. But the more complex the signalling system, the harder it is to predict the outcome of the instrument[94]. When noise is used as a modulator, it might be useful to apply a low-pass filter beforehand (cf. Chapter »2. 3. 1 High-pass, low-pass, band-pass and band-reject filters«). If the noise is not filtered, the result may sound like a high-frequency noise component has been added to the carrier signal[95]. The notation of complex amplitude modulation can be derived from the paradigm presented in Figure 22. Moreover, symbols for all generator types are presented in Chapter »1. 1 Basic elements«. Please also refer to Chapter »1. 6. 2 Composite FM and its notation« for examples of complex modulation processes.

1. 5. 2 Ring modulation

Ring modulation (RM) [RM] is a variant of amplitude modulation. In ring modulation the amplitude of the carrier is entirely determined by the modulator signal and the resulting spectrum contains energy only at the sidebands. The difference and sum tone is created whilst the carrier is suppressed[96]. If the modulating signal is more complex and contains, for instance, several harmonics, the sidebands contain each harmonic of the modulator[97/98]. A ring modulator is normally supposed to process only one signal. This is why it contains, in most cases, only one oscillator which creates the carrier signal[99]. Either the **carrier** [●] or **modulator** [Ⓜ] is usually a sine wave[100]. Moreover, in RM the energy of the modulator signal is split between the two resulting sidebands[101]: when the modulator's amplitude is A, the amplitude of the sidebands is calculated by »A ÷ 2« whilst A is greater than zero. When A = 0, no sound at all is produced[102]. Further, when sidebands occur in RM, which would be on the negative side of the y-axis (Hz), they are reflected on the x-axis[103]. The change in sign of the frequency merely changes the sign of the phase. Components of identical frequency do – dependent on the phasing and amplitude – reinforce, attenuate or cancel each other[104]. Due to the fact that periodic tone signals are not destroyed as quickly as noisy signals, ring modulation is pre-

---

[93] Maempel, Audiobearbeitung, p. 758.

[94] Miranda, Synthesis, p. 59.

[95] Roads, Tutorial, pp. 336f.

[96] Miranda, Synthesis, p. 60.

[97] Dodge and Jerse, Computer, pp. 92f.

[98] When, for example, the carrier oscillator is a sine wave of 600 Hz and the modulator consists of three partials at 100 Hz (fundamental), 200 Hz (1st harmonic) and 300 Hz (2nd harmonic), the sum tones are set at 700 Hz (fundamental), 800 Hz (1st harmonic) and 900 Hz (2nd harmonic) and the difference tones at 500 Hz (fundamental), 400 Hz (1st harmonic) and 300 Hz (2nd harmonic).

[99] Maempel, Audiobearbeitung, p. 757.

[100] Roads, Tutorial, pp. 216f.

[101] Miranda, Synthesis, p. 60.

[102] Dodge and Jerse, Computer, p. 92.

[103] Thus a sideband of, for instance, –300 Hz flips to 300 Hz.

[104] Roads, Tutorial, pp. 217-220.

ferred to transform such sounds[105]. RM may also be realised without oscillators just by multiplying two recorded signals together. This kind of multiplication is called **general-purpose ring modulation**. The resulting spectrum will contain frequencies that are the sum of and difference between the frequencies of each component in the first sound (the carrier) and those of each component in the second sound (the modulator)[106]. Each amplitude in general-purpose RM is calculated by »the amplitude of the first signal × the amplitude of the second signal ÷ 2«[107].

1. 5. 2. 1 Previous methods of notation

Schafer, in »Music for the morning of the world«[108], employs a ring modulator in combination with a gong. The utilisation of the ring modulator is requested by simply giving the direction "ring modulated gong receding" [109]. Moreover, *Stockhausen,* in »Mikrophonie II«[110], uses four ring modulators. The modulators are applied to soprano and bass voices during a performance. Each ring modulator is notated by employing a symbol, which has the shape of a square. The ratio between the loudspeakers' output level and the voices is notated inside the square. In the case of the normal setting N, the loudspeaker level is slightly louder than the original sound. Further, *Stockhausen* inter alia introduces a symbol that requests continuously changing *crescendi* and *decrescendi* of the output level[111].

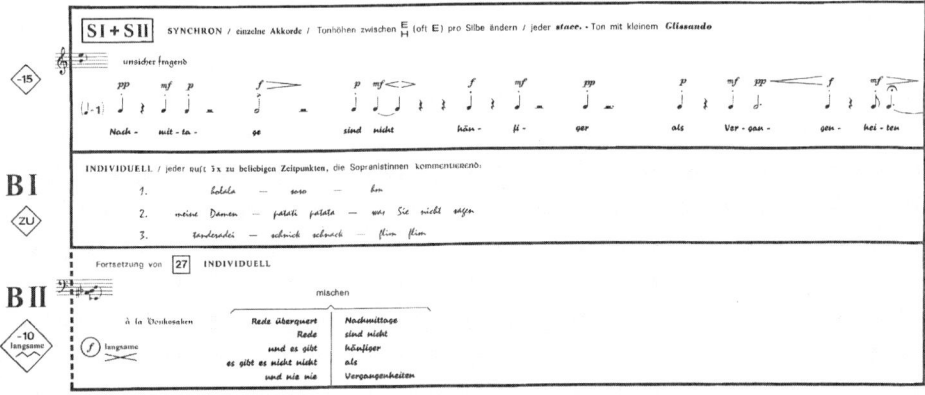

Fig. 24 Stockhausen, Mikrophonie II, p. 14.

Figure 24 presents an example of the notation of the ring modulator. Two groups of sopranos (S I + S II) are ring modulated in the same way. The number in the square (−15) indicates that the loudspeakers' output level is 15 dB lower compared to the normal setting N (and hence »N − 15 dB«). The first group of basses (B I) is not ring modulated, which is required by the direction *zu* (German for closed or off). However, the second group of basses (BII) is

---

[105]Maempel, Audiobearbeitung, p. 758.

[106]When the first signal contains, for instance, two frequencies at 500 Hz and 1,000 Hz and the second signal two frequencies at 100 Hz and 200 Hz, the resulting signal will contain 8 frequencies: 600 Hz, 400 Hz, 1,100 Hz, 900 Hz (the sum and difference tone of 100 Hz and the first signal) and 700 Hz, 300 Hz, 1200 Hz, 800 Hz (the sum and difference tone of 200 Hz and the first signal).

[107]Cf. Dodge and Jerse, Computer, pp. 93f.

[108]R. Murray Schafer: Music for the morning of the world. For soprano and tape. Toronto 1973.

[109]Ibid., p. 3.

[110]Karlheinz Stockhausen: Mikrophonie II. For choir, Hammond organ and 4 ring modulators. London 1974.

[111]Cf. Stockhausen, Mikrophonie II, no page named [foreword].

again ring modulated. Here the symbol for continuously changing *crescendi* and *decrescendi* is employed. The additions *langsame* (German for slow) and −10 request that they are supposed to be performed slowly and above the level of »N − 10 dB«[112]. The frequency of the ring modulator is not determined in »Mikrophonie II«. However, *Stockhausen* notates it in another composition called »Mixtur«[113]. The carrier wave is depicted here by means of a traditional notation system in treble clef and additionally writing down the exact frequency in Hz. *Glissandi* from one frequency to another are notated by means of a line that connects the frequencies. When very low frequencies are supposed to be employed, they are represented by a line, a determination of the frequency in Hz and dismissing the pitch-based notation system.

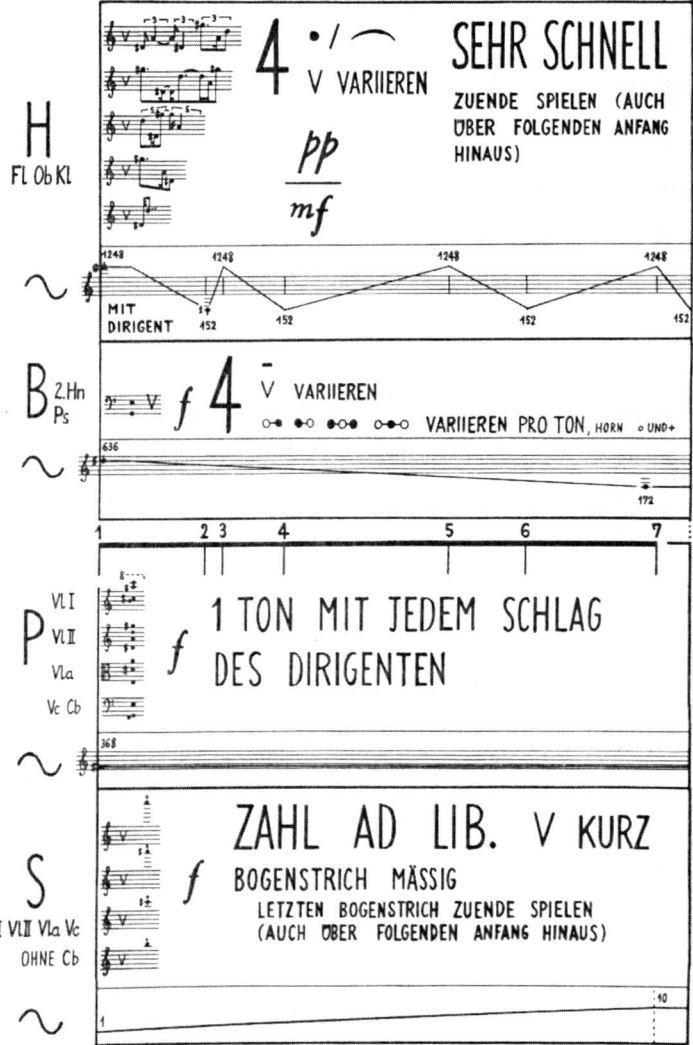

Fig. 25 Stockhausen, Mixtur, p. 1.

---

[112]Cf. ibid., no page named [foreword].

[113]Karlheinz Stockhausen: Mixtur. For orchestra, sine generators and ring modulators. Vienna 1968.

Both variants are presented in Figure 25. The duration of each modulator is determined in relation to the bars, which in the example are articulated by a conductor (beats 1 to 7). The control of the volume is free in »Mixtur«. However, the loudspeaker sound is generally supposed to be louder than the original sound[114]. To give some examples, the group of instruments designated as »H« consists of three flutes, three oboes, three clarinets and three bassoons[115]. The sine oscillator utilised to modulate these begins at 1,248 Hz (beat 1). After a short while, it is supposed to perform a *glissando* to 152 Hz (beat 2). The following *glissandi* describe a constant change between these two frequencies. At every beat the respective other frequency is reached. Moreover, the lowest five systems represent group S and its ring modulator. The oscillator here performs a *glissando* from 1 Hz (beat 1) to 10 Hz (beat 7).

1. 5. 2. 2 Discussion

The approach by *Schafer* can be described as very inexact since he does not provide any information about the ring modulator. Neither the frequency nor the output level of the speakers is determined. *Stockhausen* notates the ring modulator in a more exact way (cf. Figure 24). In »Mikrophonie II« the output level is clearly determined and varied, e. g. by requesting *crescendi* and *decrescendi*. However, the durations of the *de-/crescendi* are not depicted. *Stockhausen's* method of notating the loudspeakers' output level may also be described as confusing because he introduces several symbols and directions in order to notate a single parameter. Additionally, the frequency of the ring modulator is not determined. On the contrary, in »Mixtur« the frequency of the ring modulator is determined in an exact and simple manner. This method of notation can be well-combined with traditional notation. However, since the modulator system is deprived of a distinct timeline, its duration needs to be related to the instruments or else it remains approximate. Exact durations are only occasionally employed in the piece since *Stockhausen* consciously utilises approximate notation. However, a distinct timeline for the ring modulator could easily be implemented by utilising traditional note values instead of a line. When employing notes, they could additionally be used to depict the frequency of the oscillator. As shown above, the complementary description of the frequency in Hertz would then become redundant since it is possible to notate virtually all frequencies by means of pitch-based notation. Moreover, because the control of the volume is free, this parameter is not determined in »Mixtur«. In order to depict it in an exact manner, the method of notation for the output level, introduced in Chapter »1. 1 Basic elements« could be used. When applying these changes, ring modulation is notated in the same way as amplitude modulation.

1. 5. 2. 3 Suggestion for the notation of ring modulation

Hence the suggested method of notation is an elaboration of the method employed by *Stockhausen* in »Mixtur«. Figure 26 shows how ring modulation may be notated. The upper system depicts the modulator, in this case an unspecified instrument, and the lower system represents the ring modulator's carrier sine wave. Moreover, the symbol for ring modulation [RM] requests that this specific technique is applied. It needs to be noted here that the instrument has to be picked up by a microphone in order to apply ring modulation. The notation of microphone techniques and the treatment of instrumental sound sources are explained in Chapter »3. Sound recording«. In the example, the instrumentalist plays a semibreve »f♯¹/F♯4« with the dynamic level *forte*. This signal modulates the carrier sine wave, which performs a *glissando*. The output level of the ring modulated signal is depicted under-

---

[114]Cf. ibid., p. 12 [foreword].
[115]Cf. ibid., p. 11 [foreword].

neath the RM instrument. In the case of a performance, the original instrumental sound source would apparently be audible. However, if the example presented pre-recorded music, only the sidebands could be perceived.

Fig. 26 Ring modulation.

As mentioned, in this work the *glissando* – in order to achieve a greater clarity and enable the depiction of *glissando* motions that do not involve changes in pitch – is requested by means of an arrow and not in the traditional manner. Alternatively, the common method of notation could be restored. Further, general-purpose ring modulation can be notated in the same way as RM. Its notation is presented in Figure 27. Both modulator and carrier are produced by instruments, while the output level can be derived from the applied dynamic levels. As mentioned, it can be described by »the amplitude of the first signal (C) × the amplitude of the second signal (M) ÷ 2«. If the sound was supposed to be amplified with another dynamic level, an additional system for the loudspeaker's output level could be employed underneath the general-purpose RM instrument.

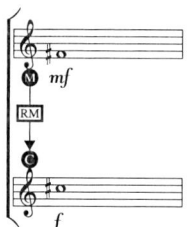

Fig. 27 General-purpose ring modulation.

1. 6 Frequency modulation

Frequency modulation (FM) [FM] was originated in the late 1960's by *John Chowning*[116]. It can be thought of as the alteration or distortion of the frequency of an oscillator in accordance with the amplitude of a modulating signal[117]. There are various ways of designing FM instruments. In this chapter **simple FM**, including the *vibrato*-effect, **composite FM** and **asymmetrical FM** are explained.

---

[116]Miranda, Synthesis, p. 61.

[117]Dodge and Jerse, Computer, p. 115.

1.6.1 Simple FM and its notation

The most basic FM instrument is composed of two sine wave oscillators. A constant carrier frequency is added to the output of the **modulator** [◉] oscillator and the result is applied to the frequency input of the **carrier** [◉] oscillator. When modulation occurs, the signal from the modulating oscillator drives the frequency of the carrier oscillator both above and below the carrier frequency and sidebands on either side of the carrier are created. The sidebands are at a distance equal to the modulator frequency while the frequency of the sideband pairs in FM is theory normally calculated by means of the factor k, an integer greater than zero, which corresponds to the order of partial counting[118]. Moreover, the amplitude is described as the frequency deviation, referred to as d and expressed in Hz. The number of partials on each side of the carrier is dependent on the deviation. The greater the value of d, the greater their number. FM theory, further, provides a useful tool for the control of the number of audible sidebands, expressed by the **modulation index** i. It is calculated by »the deviation ÷ the modulator's frequency«. As the modulation index increases, the number of audible sidebands also increases and the energy of the carrier is distributed among them. The number of sideband pairs with significant amplitudes can generally be predicted as »the modulation index $i + 1$«. Thus if, for instance, the modulation index $i = 3$, there are four audible sidebands on each side of the carrier. The carrier frequency is often the most prominent partial in an FM sound and the amplitude of sidebands decreases with their order. Moreover, the value of the modulation index must be large to obtain significant amplitudes in high-order sidebands[119]. The exact amplitudes of the partials in FM can be calculated by non-linear *Bessel* functions. The calculation of the amplitudes is quite complex and cannot be explained in detail here. However, some general aspects should be mentioned: *Bessel* functions determine the amplitude scaling factors for pairs of sidebands in relation to their position to the carrier's frequency[120]. Each order of *Bessel* functions starts up more gradually, indicating that high-order sidebands enter gently as the modulation index is increased. Further, as the modulation index increases, amplitudes of all components oscillate between their extreme values, passing through zero in between. This implies that it is possible for virtually any component of a frequency modulation waveform to have a small amplitude while adjacent sidebands have amplitudes that are quite significant[121]. When partials occur in FM, which would be on the negative side of the y-axis (Hz), they are reflected on the x-axis and phase shifted 180°. As a result, they either become part of the sidebands on the positive side – and, depending on the phase and amplitude, reinforce, attenuate or cancel each other – or emerge as new sidebands in between these. In any case, the reflection has a great impact on the resulting sound[122].

Due to the fact that both these techniques strongly resemble each other, simple frequency modulation can be notated similarly to classical amplitude modulation (cf. Figure 22): both the modulator and carrier oscillator generate sine waves [◌]. The modulator is depicted by the upper system and the carrier by the lower system. In the example, the modulator oscillator generates a semibreve »f♯1/F♯4« (~ 370 Hz). Simultaneously, the carrier oscillator produces a semibreve »c♯2/C♯5« (~ 554 Hz). The modulation index i is depicted by means of a diagram-

---

[118]Each sideband frequency is calculated by »the carrier's frequency $\pm k \times$ the modulator's frequency«, whilst for the first sideband $k = 1$, for the second sideband $k = 2$, for the third sideband $k = 3$ etc. The first sideband pair is set at »the carrier's frequency $\pm 1 \times$ the modulator's frequency«, the second sideband pair at »the carrier's frequency $\pm 2 \times$ the modulator's frequency«, the third sideband pair at »the carrier's frequency $\pm 3 \times$ the modulator's frequency« etc.

[119]Dodge and Jerse, Computer, pp. 115f. and Miranda, Synthesis, pp. 60-64.

[120]Miranda, Synthesis, p. 65.

[121]Moore, Elements, p. 322.

[122]Supper, Musik, p. 43 and Cook, Tutorial, pp. 230f.

matic notation system underneath the modulator's system. The x-axis of this system describes the time whilst the y-axis depicts the modulation index from »Ø« to 20 in increments of one. Hence the white dots (◇) depict i in time. In Figure 28, the modulation index i is constantly set at 2. Therefore, three sidebands with significant amplitudes are produced on each side of the carrier. Actually, sidebands at approximately 924 Hz, 1,294 Hz, 1,664 Hz (»554 Hz + k × 370 Hz«), 184 Hz, 186 Hz and 556 Hz (»554 Hz − k × 370 Hz«) are created[123]. The output level of the frequency modulated signal is depicted underneath the FM instrument. As in the case of classical AM, an ADSR envelope is employed here (cf. Chapter »1. 1. 1 Periodic wave generators and their envelopes«). Further, please refer for basic applications of simple FM to *Chowning*[124] and applications like the simulation of acoustic instruments and the description of C : M ratios to *Roads and Strawn*[125]. Moreover, an approach towards natural-sounding spectra is presented by *Lazzarina et al.*[126].

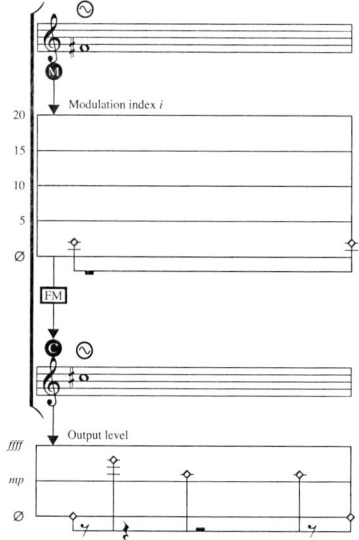

Fig. 28 Frequency modulation.

FM can be also used to simulate the ***vibrato*-effect** by utilising a sub-audio rate, realised by an **LFO** and a ***vibrato* width** of typically less than a semitone. During the *vibrato*, the instantaneous frequency of the carrier oscillator changes on every sample, varying between the frequency of the carrier oscillator ± the *vibrato* width[127]. A sinusoidal LFO creates a very natural *vibrato*. Sounds that resemble trills and rapid fluctuations of pitch can be obtained by means of a square wave LFO[128]. Figure 29 presents the notation of the *vibrato*-effect. It is depicted similarly to the *tremolo*-effect (cf. Figure 23). Both the modulating low frequency oscillator

---

[123]The sidebands that would be on the negative side of the y-axis (−186 Hz and −556 Hz) are reflected on the x-axis and phase shifted 180°.

[124]John Chowning and David Bristow: FM theory and applications. Tokyo 1986.

[125]Curtis Roads and John Strawn (eds.): Foundations of computer music. Cambridge and London 1985.

[126]Victor Lazzarini et al.: The generation of natural-synthetic spectra by means of adaptive frequency modulation. In: Computer Music Journal, vol. 32(2). Massachusetts 2008, pp. 9-22.

[127]Dodge and Jerse, Computer, pp. 94f. and Neukom, Signale, p. 414.

[128]Gianpolo Evangelista: Time and frequency warping musical signals. In: Udo Zoelzer (ed.): DAFX. Digital audio effects. Chichester 2002, pp. 439-463, here: p. 460.

and the carrier oscillator produce sine waves. The LFO is depicted by a traditional system in bass clef, here transposed by four octaves (*29ma*). The vibrato width is depicted by a diagrammatic system in cent[129], ranging from »∅« to 100 in increments of ten. When more exact values are required, they can be written over the system (cf. Figure 22). In the example, the width is constantly set at 20 cents.

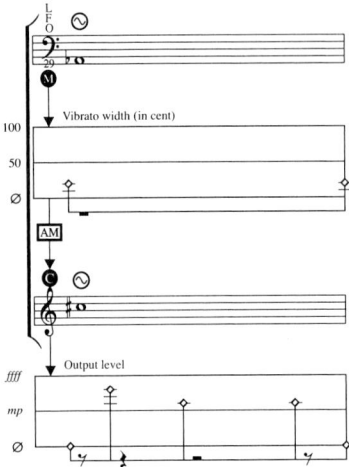

Fig. 29 The *vibrato*-effect.

In frequency modulation, waveforms other than sinusoids are not necessarily needed for modulator and carrier in order to create interesting material[130]. However, any other periodic oscillator can theoretically be employed[131]. If a sawtooth, triangle or rectangular waveform oscillator which produces the carrier and the modulator is a sinusoid, all partials of the complex waveform forge a carrier for the modulation signal[132]. However, if a sinusoid is employed as a carrier and a sawtooth, triangle or square wave oscillator produces the modulator, the fundamental of the complex waveform acts as the main modulator and the harmonics affect the resulting spectrum as the modulation index increases. But the influence of the harmonics only becomes significant in combination with a high modulation index and the resulting spectra resemble – due to the dominance of the fundamental – those of simple FM with two sine wave oscillators[133]. Further, when a waveform with a large number of spectral components frequency modulates another, the resulting spectrum can be so dense that it sounds harsh and undefined[134]. Moreover, noise can also be utilised as a modulator. When a noise generator is employed, it might be – as in amplitude modulation – useful to apply a low-pass filter (see Chapter »2. 3. 1 High-pass, low-pass, band-pass and band-reject filters«) before using the signal to modulate the carrier. When the noise has a wider bandwidth, the result of modulation is a type of coloured noise, i. e. a noise band centred around the carrier

[129]As mentioned, ±100 cents = a semitone and ±1200 cents = octave.

[130]Miranda, Synthesis, p. 63.

[131]Cf. Neukom, Signale, p. 425.

[132]When the carrier is, for example, a sawtooth wave with partials of 500 Hz, 1,000 Hz, 1,500 Hz etc. and the modulator a sine wave at 100 Hz, the first sidebands are: 500 Hz ± 100 Hz, 1000 Hz ± 100 Hz, 1,500 Hz ± 100 Hz etc., the second sidebands are 500 Hz ± 200 Hz, 1000 Hz ± 200 Hz etc.

[133]This behaviour of timbral spectre and sine waves was examined in several experiments.

[134]Dodge and Jerse, Computer, p. 117.

frequency of the oscillator[135]. The notation of this kind of complex frequency modulation can be derived from Figure 28 while methods of depiction for all generator types are presented in Chapter »1. 1 Basic elements«.

1. 6. 2 Composite FM and its notation

Compared to the utilisation of waveforms other than sinusoid for either carrier or modulator, separate modulator or carrier oscillators allow independent control of modulation indices and give more precise control over the spectra produced[136]. More complex FM instruments may employ various modulators and carriers. There are at least five basic combinatory schemes for building composite FM: **1. Additive carriers with independent modulators.** Two or more independent instruments are constructed. Their sound is often combined to achieve certain timbres[137]. The notation of this scheme can be achieved by extending the paradigm presented in Figure 28. **2. Additive carriers with one modulator.** One oscillator modulates two or more carrier oscillators. The spectra that result are positioned as in simple FM[138].

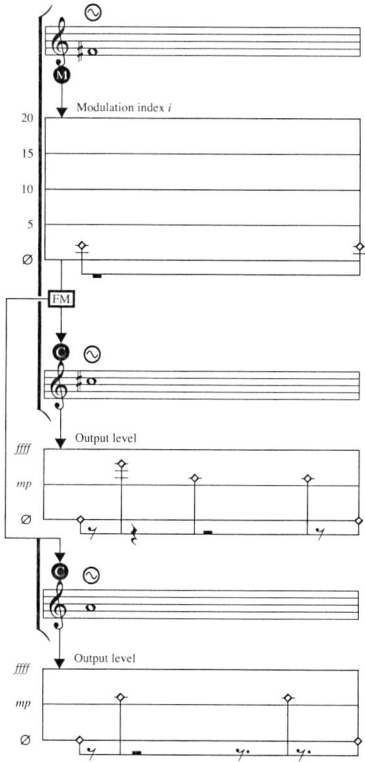

Fig. 30 Additive carriers with one oscillator.

---

[135]Roads, Tutorial, pp. 336f.

[136]Cf. Bill Schottstaedt: The simulation of natural instrument tones using frequency modulation with a complex modulating wave. In: Curtis Roads and John Strawn (eds.): Foundations of Computer Music. Cambridge and London 1985, pp. 54-64, here: p. 54.

[137]Cf. Dexter Morrill: Trumpet algorithms for computer composition. In: Curtis Roads and John Strawn (eds.): Foundations of computer music. Cambridge and London 1985, pp. 30-44, here: pp. 39-43.

[138]Cf. Miranda, Synthesis, p. 70.

A suggestion for the notation of this kind of composite FM is presented in Figure 30. The simple FM instrument from Figure 28 is extended here by another carrier, which is connected to the modulator. The additive carrier is also generated by a sine wave oscillator, which produces a semibreve »a¹/A4« (440 Hz). The arrows request that the modulator is utilised to transform both carrier oscillators independently. By doing so, two FM instruments are created whilst the dynamic level of each instrument may be controlled distinctly. Therefore, two systems for the output level are employed.

3. Single carrier with parallel modulators. In this type of modulation two oscillators simultaneously modulate a single carrier wave[139]. With regard to Figure 31, the spectrum that results is as though the partials produced by oscillator 1 (M1) and oscillator 3 (C) are modulated (as carriers) by oscillator 2 (M2). Hence each of the partials produced by M1 and C becomes a carrier for M2[140]. The sidebands can be calculated by means of the modulation index i and the factor k: »the frequency of C $\pm$ i of M1 $\times$ the frequency of M1 $\pm$ k of M2 $\times$ the frequency of M2«[141].

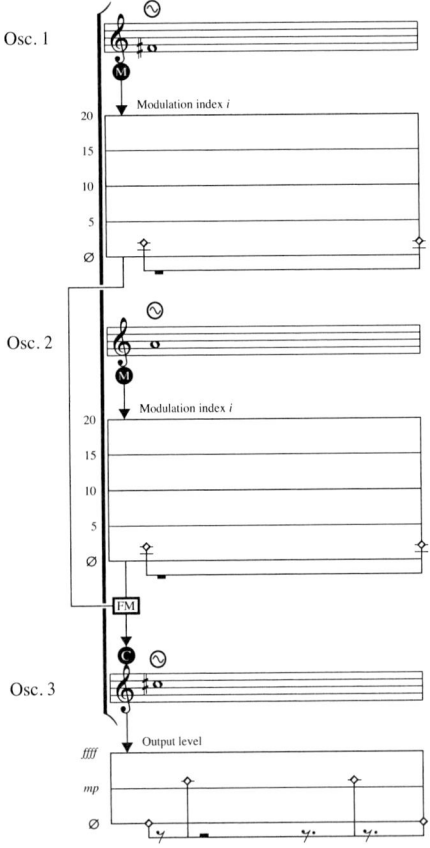

Fig. 31 Single carrier with parallel modulators.

---

[139]Cf. Miranda, Synthesis, p. 71.

[140]Thomas J. Mitchell et al.: Frequency modulation tone matching using a fuzzy clustering evolution strategy. Audio Engineering Society convention paper, 118th convention. Barcelona 2005, p. 3.

[141]Cf. Dodge and Jerse, Computer, p. 133 and Roads, Tutorial, p. 239.

The simple FM instrument from Figure 28 is, in the example presented in Figure 31, extended by another modulator, which generates a semibreve sine wave »a¹/A4« (440 Hz). The modulation indices of M1 and M2 are independent from each other and depicted by the two diagrammatic systems underneath oscillator 1 and 2. The output level of the sound produced is notated underneath this complex FM instrument.

4. Single carrier with serial modulators. In this scheme a frequency modulated oscillator modulates a carrier. In Figure 32, it can be seen that oscillator 1 (M1) at first modulates oscillator 2 (C/M2). This oscillator is then used to modulate oscillator 3 (C). Each sideband produced by oscillators 2 and 3 has its own sidebands that were produced in the first modulation (by oscillators 1 and 2). The sideband frequencies can be calculated using the same method as in the previous scheme[142]. The main differences from the third type of composite FM are that the former tends to have sidebands with higher amplitude values and that no sideband components from M2 are generated around the carrier's centre frequency[143].

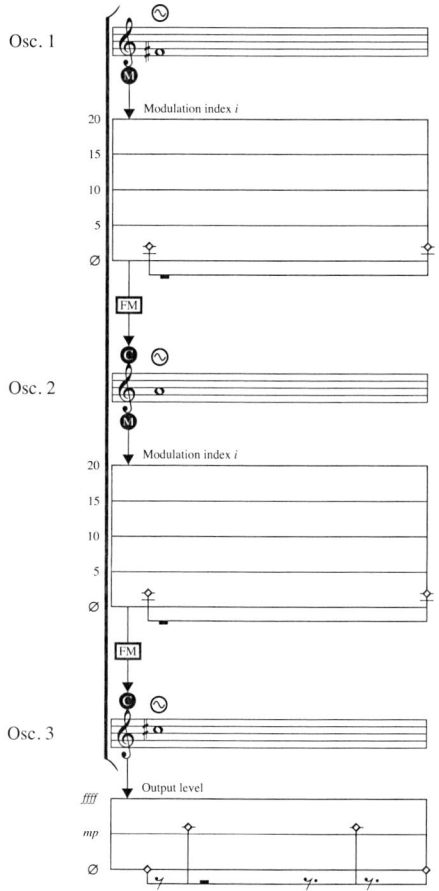

Fig. 32 Single carrier with serial modulators.

[142]Miranda, Synthesis, pp. 72f.

[143]Ibid., pp. 70-74.

As is apparent from Figure 32, this type of composite FM can be depicted similarly to the third scheme. However, oscillator 2 is designated here as carrier and modulator because the complex modulation is serial and not simultaneous. The arrows clearly outline that oscillator 1 modulates oscillator 2 and the frequency modulated oscillator 2 is then used to modulate oscillator 3. The output level of the sounds produced by the serial FM method are notated underneath the instrument. Further, it is also possible to use more than two serial modulators. There have been, for instance, attempts to simulate string-like tones using three serial modulators[144]. The notation of this type of FM may be derived from the paradigm presented in Figure 32. C/M3 and its modulation index would, in such a case, be notated underneath C/M2.

5. Self-modulating carrier. In this type of modulation the output of a single oscillator is employed to modulate its own frequency. The oscillator output signal is multiplied by a **feedback** factor. When doing so, a waveform similar to a sawtooth wave is created. This is because it works with a 1:1 frequency ratio. When the carrier and modulator frequency are the same, the first lower sideband is always 0 Hz. The second sideband is set at the negative carrier frequency. It is reflected on the x-axis and becomes the carrier frequency. The third lower sideband is then set at twice the carrier frequency. For instance, when C and M = 500 Hz, the lower sidebands are set at 0 Hz, 500 Hz (reflected from −500 Hz), 1,000 Hz (reflected from −1,000 Hz) etc. and the upper sidebands at 1,000 Hz, 1,500 Hz, 2,000 Hz etc. Hence the timbre of a sawtooth wave is produced (cf. Chapter »1. 1 Basic elements«). However, sidebands of the same frequency may, depending on the phasing and amplitude, reinforce, attenuate or cancel each other. The feedback factor is very sensitive. Harsh white noise is created by its full extent[145]. The number of sidebands is in this scheme increased by augmenting the feedback factor[146]. The notation of self-modulating carrier FM is presented in Figure 33. A carrier and a modulator symbol are utilised in combination with a single sine wave oscillator. The arrow requests that the oscillator is used to modulate itself. The feedback factor is determined in per cent and, in the beginning, set at 35%. It is from this point on increased and reaches 50% at the end of the example. This process is depicted by means of a *crescendo* symbol.

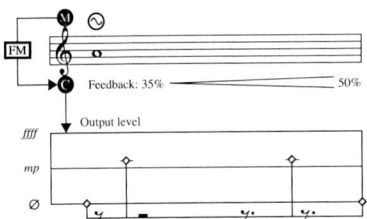

Fig. 33 Self-modulating carrier.

It is, further, possible to employ a **two-oscillator feedback**, meaning that a self-modulated carrier modulates another carrier[147]. The notation of this instrument is achieved by extending the self-modulating oscillator by an additional modulation index and a carrier. An additional modulator symbol is, in Figure 34, used to express that the oscillator modulates itself and is subsequently used to modulate another oscillator with the modulation index depicted underneath it.

---

[144]Roads, Tutorial, p. 242.

[145]There are two types of feedback. Negative feedback has the tendency to bring a system to an idle or balanced state, whereas positive feedback escalates, destabilises and may even destroy the system.

[146]Cf. Miranda, Synthesis, pp. 73f.

[147]Roads, Tutorial, pp. 246 and 248.

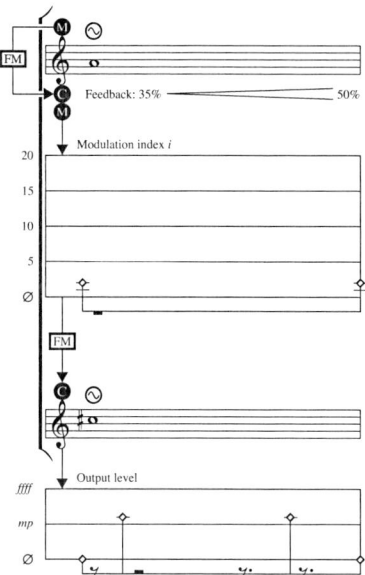

Fig. 34 Two-oscillator feedback.

Finally, a **three-oscillator feedback** technique with indirect feedback may also be constructed. In this scheme one oscillator modulates a carrier, which in turn modulates a third oscillator. The result of this series of modulation is then again used to modulate the first oscillator by means of a feedback factor[148]. A suggestion for the notation of this instrument is presented in Figure 35. It resembles the serial FM instrument depicted in Figure 32. Oscillator 1 here modulates oscillator 2. The result of the first modulation is then used to modulate oscillator 3. Subsequently, the result of this series of modulation is again utilised to modulate oscillator 1 with the feedback factor depicted above the highest system. The output level of sound produced by the three-oscillator feedback instrument is then notated underneath the instrument.

1. 6. 3 Asymmetrical FM and its notation

FM synthesis is able to create a broad variety of sounds. However, the symmetry limits the dynamic spectral envelopes that can be synthesised by frequency modulation. Asymmetrical FM provides an advanced synthesis algorithm that generates waveforms with an asymmetric spectral envelope controlled by a **symmetry index r** and the **index of modulation i**. The upper sidebands have larger amplitudes than the corresponding lower ones for values of $r > 1$. Conversely, values of $0 < r < 1$ emphasise the lower sidebands at the expense of the upper ones. Further, the spectrum is symmetrical when $r = 1$[149]. Asymmetrical FM is notated here by means of additional symbols. They can, for instance, be used to complement simple FM (cf. Figure 28).

---

[148]Roads, Tutorial, p. 250.
[149]Dodge and Jerse, Computer, pp. 164f.

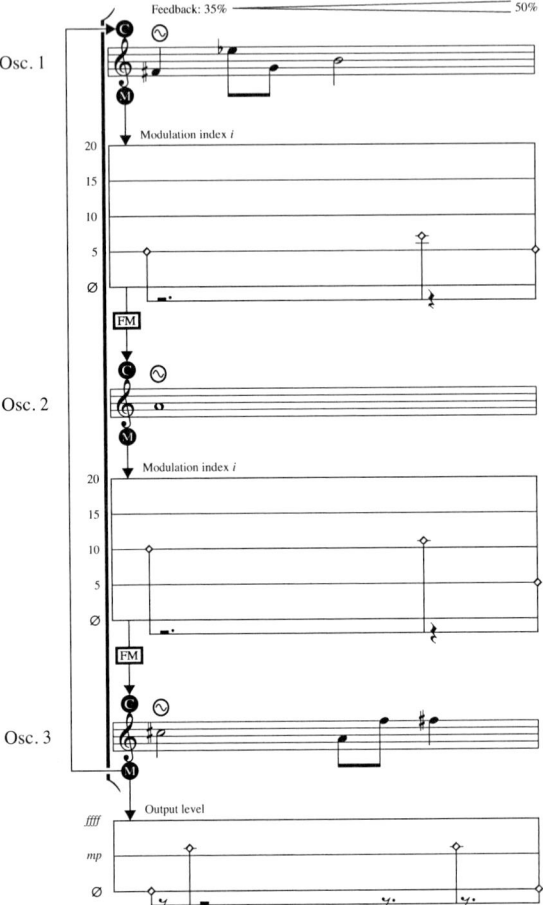

Fig. 35 Three-oscillator feedback.

In Figure 36, three symbols are applied to the carrier wave's notation system. The symbol that is employed in the beginning requests that the upper sidebands are emphasised. After a minim, it is followed by the symbol for the emphasis of the lower sidebands ($0 < r < 1$). The last adjustment is reached at the end of the example and describes that at this point the spectrum is symmetrical. Arrows are used to depict the transition from one state to another instead of *de-/crescendi* symbols because, for instance, a transition from the emphasis of the upper sidebands to the emphasis of the lower sidebands is not regarded as an increase or decrease of a value. Even though, in this case, the symmetry index r is actually decreased from $r > 1$ to $0 < r < 1$, the utilisation of a *decrescendo* sign in combination with the three symbols would be confusing. A variant of notation could be to employ the symmetry index in a less illustrative way, e. g. by stating that $r > 1$. In such a case, it would be useful to apply a *decrescendo* symbol when a transition to $0 < r < 1$ is supposed to be performed. Moreover, it might be desirable to describe the intensity of emphasis. This can, for instance, be achieved by complementary directions, such as *molto*, *poco* and *normale*.

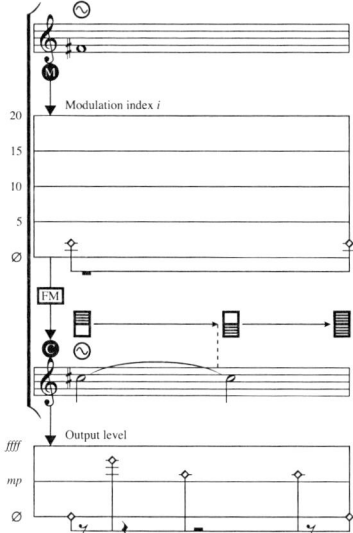

Fig. 36 Asymmetrical FM.

1. 7 Waveshaping synthesis

Waveshaping synthesis creates composite spectra by applying distortion to a simple sound. The technique functions by passing a sound through a unit that distorts its waveform. The central element of a waveshaping instrument is a waveshaper, or non-linear processor, that alters the shape of the waveform. A simple example of this type of distortion is the clipping[150] that occurs when an audio amplifier is overdriven[151]. Like frequency modulation, it is more efficient than additive synthesis for the realisation of complex timbres. Unlike FM, waveshaping provides the capability of generating a band-limited spectrum with a specifiable maximum harmonic number. The spectrum produced by a waveshaping instrument is altered with the amplitude of the sound. Because this change in timbre corresponds to the characteristic sound of acoustic instruments, waveshaping synthesis has proven to produce tones that resemble the ones created by traditional instruments[152]. In a linear processor, such as an ideal amplifier, a change in the amplitude of the input signal produces a similar change in the output signal whilst the shape of the waveform is preserved. For instance, doubling the amplitude of the input signal results in the amplitude of the output signal being doubled as well. However, in a non-linear processor, the relationship between input and output depends on the amplitude of the input signal and the nature of the non-linearity. In most cases, increasing the amplitude of the input will cause the output waveform to change shape. When the shape is modified, its spectrum changes. This generally causes an increase in the number and intensity of harmonics[153]. There are various ways of creating waveshaping synthesis. This chapter focuses on **classical waveshaping** by means of *Chebyshev* polynomials and **waveshaping by phase distortion**.

---

[150]When the amplitude is larger than the processing system can handle, clipping is created. The peaks of the amplitude are chopped off, producing a distortion.

[151]Miranda, Synthesis, pp. 76-78.

[152]Dodge and Jerse, Computer, pp. 139f.

[153]Miranda, Synthesis, p. 78.

1.7.1 Classical waveshaping and its notation

A waveshaper is characterised by its transfer function, which relates the amplitude of the signal at the output to the input. The success of a waveshaping instrument depends on the choice of transfer function[154]. The classical waveshaping technique is achieved by sending a sine wave through a shaping function called **Chebyshev polynomials**[155] [W⟨⟩]. When a sine wave with an amplitude equal to one is sent through a function of the kth order, the kth partial is created[156/157]. Further, applying this function to sinusoid material results in band-limited spectra. Thus aliasing can be avoided[158]. Moreover, the input to the waveshaper can be any sound, even a concrete recording. The effect is not unlike phasing since the harmonics of the input undulate in a time-varying way[159] (cf. Chapter »2.6.3 The phasing-effect and its notation«). However, when the waveform applied to the waveshaper is non-sinusoidal, the resulting spectrum is more difficult to predict and often not band-limited. The shape of the waveform, and hence its spectrum, changes with the amplitude of the input signal, which in waveshaping synthesis is expressed by **distortion index α**. It is analogous to the modulation index i in frequency modulation (cf. Chapter »1.6 Frequency modulation«). The spectrum becomes richer as the value of distortion index α increases. When α = 1, the maximum input amplitude a waveshaper is able to manage is reached[160].

A suggestion for the notation of a classical waveshaper is presented in Figure 37. The instrument is depicted by employing the symbol for waveshaping by *Chebyshev* polynomials, a diagrammatic system, which represents the distortion index α from »∅« to 1 in increments of 0.1 and determining the order of the function. The x-axis of the diagrammatic system describes the duration whilst the y-axis depicts the distortion index. Hence the white dots (◇) determine the distortion index in time whilst the order of the polynomials is written underneath the system. In the example, a sine wave is fed to the waveshaper. The oscillator generates a semibreve »c♯2/C♯5« (~ 554 Hz) while the distortion index is constantly set at 1. Since the amplitude of the input signal is therefore equal to one, a function of the kth order creates the kth partial: the »c♯2/C♯5« is in the beginning transformed by means of an 8th-order *Chebyshev* polynomial and the harmonic at approximately 4,432 Hz (»554 Hz × 8«) is produced. After a minim, a function of the 3rd order is applied, followed by a function of the 5th order after a quaver and finally a function of the 2nd order after another quaver. Hence the partials at approximately 1,662 Hz, 2,770 Hz and 1,108 Hz are created. The output level is depicted underneath the waveshaping synthesis instrument (cf. Chapter »1.1 Basic elements« for an explanation).

---

[154]Dodge and Jerse, Computer, pp. 141 and 146.

[155]Roads, Tutorial, p. 258.

[156]1st order = fundamental, 2nd order = one octave (2 × fundamental), 3rd order = one octave and a fifth (3 × fundamental), 4th order = two octaves (4 × fundamental), 5th order ≈ two octaves and a major third (5 × fundamental), 6th order ≈ two octaves and a fifth (6 × fundamental), 7th order ≈ two octaves and a minor seventh (7 × fundamental), 8th order = three octaves (8 × fundamental), 9th order ≈ three octaves and a major second (9 × fundamental) and 10th order ≈ three octaves and a major third (10 × fundamental). Please note that some of the harmonics slightly deviate from the tempered system (from the 5th order on only the third octave is a really exact value).

[157]Miranda, Synthesis, pp. 79f. and Dodge and Jerse, Computer, pp. 146f.

[158]Roads, Tutorial, p. 259.

[159]Ibid., pp. 258f.

[160]Dodge and Jerse, Computer, p. 146.

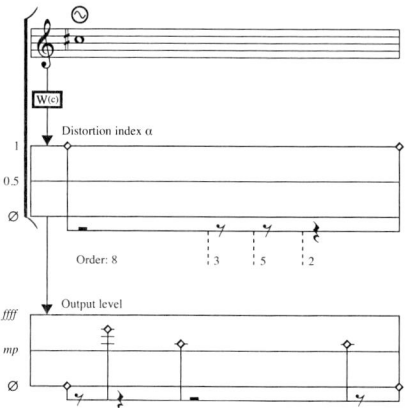

Fig. 37 Classical waveshaping synthesis.

Chebyshev polynomials are widely used for specifying transfer functions for waveshaping synthesis[161]. However, there are variations of this classical waveshaping technique. Please refer for further insight to *Roads*[162] and for more examples of employing non-linear processors to Chapter »2. 7 Distortion«.

1. 7. 2 Waveshaping by phase distortion and its notation

Most digital oscillators use stored waveforms for the sake of efficiency. This waveform is evaluated prior to the generation of any sound. The computer calculates the value of many uniformly spaced points on a cycle of the waveform and stores them in its memory as a block called wavetable or lookup table. A wavetable consists of a long sequence of numbers, each corresponding to the sampled value of successive points on the waveform. Once the waveform has been stored, the oscillator can generate sample values by simply retrieving values from the wavetable. The two varieties of a digital oscillator are fixed and variable sampling rate oscillators. Variable sampling rates can be used for sound modifications[163]. The distortion of a sine wave can be achieved by speeding up the **scanning interval** from 0 to π and then slowing it down from π to 2π. The frequency is constant, but as the amount of speeding up and slowing down increases, the original sine turns into a kind of triangle wave and finally into a quasi-sawtooth waveform[164]. This technique of changing the rate of reading is called **phase distortion** (PD)[165] [PD].

A suggestion for the notation of phase distortion is presented in Figure 38. The sound source is the same as in the previous example, but here transformed by means of PD. The scanning interval is depicted by a diagrammatic notation system whilst the x-axis describes the time and the y-axis the interval from »∅« over π to 2π in 10 plus 1 steps. Hence there are four degrees of transition between »∅« and π as well as another four degrees of transition between π and 2π. In the example, the scanning interval is increased from »∅« to degree 1 between π and 2π for the duration of a quaver. After this level is reached, it is further increased to 2π (and hence at this point virtually turned into a sawtooth waveform) for the

[161]Cf. Miranda, Synthesis, p. 79.
[162]Roads, Tutorial, pp. 252-260.
[163]Dodge and Jerse, Computer, pp. 76f.
[164]Roads, Tutorial, pp. 250 and 252.
[165]Russ, Sound, p. 278.

duration of a crotchet before being decreased to »∅« for the duration of a minim and a quaver. The output level is again notated underneath the waveshaping synthesis instrument.

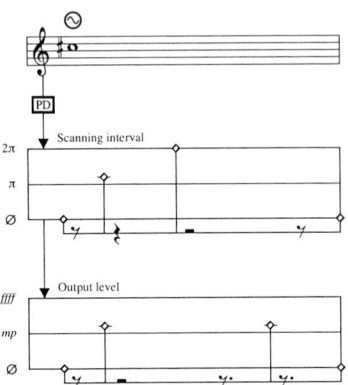

Fig. 38 Phase distortion.

1.8 Physical modelling

Physical modelling (PM) is a class of different techniques that share some fundamental principles. PM works by emulating the functioning of acoustic instruments. The key issue is the emulation of acoustic sound generators rather than the sounds themselves. Emulations of acoustic instruments, including the production of expressive sound attributes, such as the noise of fingers sliding over strings and the breathing of a clarinettist, can be achieved by using physical modelling techniques. Additionally, instruments that cannot be created in reality may be simulated by means of PM[166]. In this chapter two different approaches towards physical modelling are presented: **modal synthesis** and **functional PM by waveguide filtering**. However, since the latter requires techniques that are explained in Chapter »2. Audio processing«, its notation is demonstrated there. In order to limit the extent of the work, various **other techniques** and applications of physical modelling cannot be described in detail here, but are merely introduced.

1.8.1 Modal PM and its notation

There are many ways of modelling the action of the resonator: the classical approach emulates the behaviour of vibrating media using a network of interconnected mechanical units called mass and spring. It has the ability to capture two essential physical properties of vibrating media: **mass density**[167] and **elasticity**. For example, a string can be modelled as a series of masses connected by springs. The density of the string model is determined by the amount of mass units and its elasticity by the strength of the springs. The compromise between the mass density and the elasticity of the model defines the speed of the propagation, the amount of resistance of the model to disturbance and the time it takes to restore its equilibrium[168]. The modal synthesis technique is inspired by the mass-spring paradigm. The idea is that a sound-producing object can be represented as a collection of vibrating substructures. These substructures are taken from acoustic instruments. Tools that implement modal synthesis normally provide **ready-made substructures**, such as strings, air columns or membranes, as well as **substructures for the simulation of stimulation**, such as bowing, hammering or plucking.

---

[166]Miranda, Synthesis, pp. 90f.
[167]Mass density = mass ÷ volume. It describes the mass per unit amount.
[168]Miranda, Synthesis, pp. 92f.

This technique enables **time-varying synthesis effects** (e. g. expanding or shrinking the instrument) and the creation of timbral hybrids by combining substructures of different instruments[169]. Moreover, modal synthesis is able to highlight the resonant frequencies of the system[170]. The notation of modal PM can be achieved by transferring the common way of depicting instrumental articulations. This is because, as mentioned, physical modelling aims at simulating the functions of acoustic instruments. However, if the utilised instrument is not supposed to be a 1:1 imitation of a real instrument, the sound source's properties (e. g. the size and weight of the instrument or the material it is made of) need to be described. Such a description may be presented in the foreword of the score. When doing so, the mass density and elasticity may be derived. After the determination of the instrument type, common and extended playing techniques may be utilised and notated similarly to the way they are notated when applying a particular acoustic instruments.

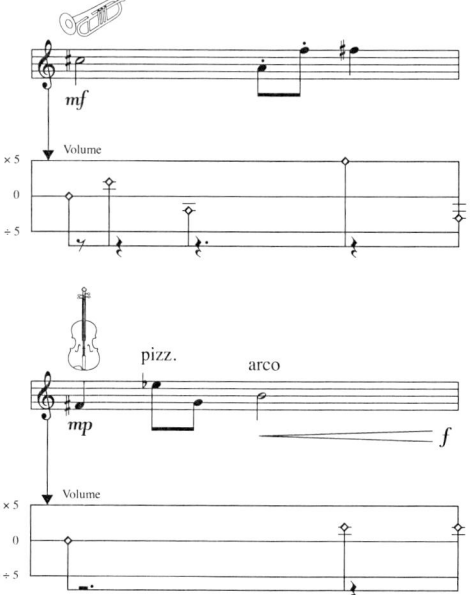

Fig. 39 Modal PM.

Figure 39 presents the notation of two modelled instruments. The template for the synthesised instruments is a trumpet and a violin, respectively. They are, as is apparent, introduced by means of symbols, but could also be introduced in the same way as acoustic instruments. The output level of these instruments can be depicted by means of common dynamic levels because their envelope is naturally complex. Further, a diagrammatic system determines the volume of the instrument. The x-axis of this diagram represents the time whilst the y-axis describes the volume from »the original volume ÷ 5« to »the original volume × 5« in 10 plus 1 steps. In the example, common articulations of these instruments are employed, such as *staccati* in the case of the trumpet and *pizzicati* in the case of the violin. Additionally, the volume of the instruments is changed during the performance. In the beginning, the volume of the trumpet is set at its original amount. It is then increased to »the original volume × 2« for the duration of a quaver, decreased to »the original volume ÷ 2« for the duration of a crotchet,

---

[169]Ibid., pp. 95f.
[170]Dodge and Jerse, Computer, p. 286.

increased to »the original volume × 5« for the duration of a dotted crotchet and finally decreased to »the original volume ÷ 3« for the duration of a crotchet. The volume of the violin is also set at the original amount in the beginning and increased to »the original volume × 2« for the duration of a dotted minim. This volume then remains unchanged until the end of the example. The playing techniques applied here are basic articulations. When utilising unconventional ways of instrumental sound production, it might be reasonable to present an alternative in case a particular technique cannot be realised (cf. »Part I: Extended instrumental playing techniques« for the notation of unconventional instrumental techniques). Additionally, the mass density and/or elasticity may be changed during the sound production. These procedures may be depicted in the same way as the change of volume.

1. 8. 2 Functional PM by waveguide filtering

The functional approach towards PM is based upon the principle that the behaviour of an instrument is determined by the two main components **excitation source** and **resonator** whilst the resonator works as a filter. The two categories of **feed-forward** and **feedback** explain the interaction between the source and the resonator. The term feed-forward expresses that a signal is fed into a resonator while feedback means that the resulting signal from the resonator is fed back to the source. The latter category often produces more convincing results because it is the interaction between the source and the resonator that creates the characteristic sound of most acoustic instruments[171]. The most common partition is based on subtractive synthesis, while analysis and re-synthesis by means of LPC (cf. Chapter »1. 4. 1 Time/pitch changing and its notation«) can be regarded as an example of a source or excitation signal being injected into a resonant filter[172]. The excitation source used for a physical model is generally derived from an analysis of the instrument to be modelled[173]. The sound synthesis techniques presented in the previous chapters can be used to create this kind of source. A type of functional approach towards PM is the waveguide filtering technique. A waveguide filter comprises a variety of signal processing units, mostly delays and low-pass filters. In contrast to subtractive synthesis, waveguide filtering is based on the feedback interaction between the sound source and the filter[174]. Since the notation of a waveguide filter is achieved by means of utilising filters and delays, it cannot be presented at this point. Please refer to Chapters »2. 3. Filters« and »2. 5 Delay« for an explanation of these audio processing techniques and to Chapter »2. 5. 2 The waveguide filter and its notation« for an example of notation. Further, please refer concerning the excitation produced in traditional acoustic instruments to *Fletcher and Rossing*[175]. The physics of most acoustic instruments is explained in this work. Moreover, an introduction to synthetic excitation modelling is presented by *Dodge and Jerse*[176].

1. 8. 3 Other techniques

There are numerous techniques and applications of physical modelling that cannot be explained in detail here, e. g. several instrument designs based on **frequency modulation** or **waveshaping synthesis**. Many examples of application can, however, be found in the *Computer Music Journal*[177]. There is, further, a program that enables the composer to access high-

---

[171]Miranda, Synthesis, pp. 93f.

[172]Roads, Tutorial, pp. 268f.

[173]Dodge and Jerse, Computer, pp. 277-279.

[174]Miranda, Synthesis, p. 100.

[175]Neville H. Fletcher and Thomas D. Rossing: The physics of musical instruments. 2nd edition. New York 1998.

[176]Dodge and Jerse, Computer, pp. 278f.

[177]Computer Music Journal, vol. 16(4). Massachusetts 1992.

quality synthetic vocal sounds, called **Singing Physical Articulatory Synthesis Model**. The vocal tract is modelled here by a waveguide filter with nine sections[178]. Please refer to *Cook*[179] for the presentation of this model. Another approach that should be mentioned is the simulation of plucked-string and drum sounds by means of an algorithm developed by *Kevin Karplus* and *Alex Strong*, known as the **Karplus-Strong technique**[180]. The algorithm involves a noise source, a delay line and a low-pass filter. Initially, the delay line is filled with a burst of noise. When the delay line is full, the noise generator is disconnected and the output fed through a low-pass filter and back into the delay line. The low-pass filter is given a cut-off frequency of one-half the *Nyquist* frequency. Every time the waveform passes around the loop, the low-pass filter causes the higher harmonics to lose more energy than the lower ones. This makes the higher harmonics decay more rapidly[181]. Although these techniques are not discussed in detail here, they may be notated by using the methods presented for the synthesis or audio processing techniques they make use of (cf., for instance, Chapters »1. 6 Frequency modulation«, »1. 7 Waveshaping synthesis«, »2. 3 Filters« and »2. 5 Delay«)

1. 9 Granular Synthesis

In this technique the fundamental compositional elements that are used to create a continuous sound are grains. They can be described as small bursts of sound energy encased in an envelope[182]. Granular synthesis works by generating a rapid succession of them[183]. There are many different approaches towards granular synthesis. Here only **manual granular synthesis** and **grain loops** will be considered. Please refer for grain generator instruments and high-level granular organisations to *Roads*[184].

1. 9. 1 Manual granular synthesis and its notation

The duration of a grain is generally set in the range of **5 to 50 ms** to preclude a single grain from inducing a pitched response in the listener. An envelope generator is necessary because abruptly turning the waveform on and off without a transition region results in audible clicks[185]. In order to notate a succession of sounds with very short durations, the sounds that are supposed to be used, are pre-constructed here. As can be seen in Figure 40, four steps are necessary for the construction of a granular sound. **Step 1**: sound »④« with the duration of two seconds is recorded (for the notation of recording techniques and non-instrumental sound sources refer to Chapter »3. Sound recording«). Alternatively, it could be created synthetically. At the very high tempo ♩ = 600, 2 seconds equal five semibreves. **Step 2**: sound »④« is cut into 40 quaver fragments. At the designated tempo, a quaver equals 50 ms. **Step 3**: the fragments are now recombined in the order of 22, 4, 8, 26 etc. Since some grains, e. g. grains 6 and 7, are repeatedly used, not all of the forty fragments are utilised. Further, envelopes should be applied to these fragments. However, since no envelopes are depicted here, it is at

[178]Dodge and Jerse, Computer, pp. 282f.

[179]Perry R. Cook: SPASM, a real time vocal tract physical controller; and Singer, the companion software system. In: Computer Music Journal, vol. 17(1). Massachusetts 1993, pp. 30-44.

[180]Cf. Kevin Karplus and Alex Strong: Digital Synthesis of plucked-string and drum timbres. In: Computer Music Journal, vol. 7(2). Massachusetts 1983, pp. 43-55 and David A. Jaffe and Julius O. Smith: Extensions of the Karplus-Strong plucked string algorithm. In: Computer Music Journal, vol. 7(2). Massachusetts 1983, pp. 56-69.

[181]Dodge and Jerse, Computer, pp. 305f.

[182]Dodge and Jerse, Computer, p. 262.

[183]Miranda, Synthesis, p. 107.

[184]Roads, Tutorial, pp. 171-184.

[185]Dodge and Jerse, Computer, p. 262.

the interpreter's discretion to employ them and determine their shapes. **Step 4**: the tempo is reduced to ♩ = 60 and the recombined fragments condensed to a single note called granular sound »ⓐ1«. At the given tempo, two seconds equal a minim.

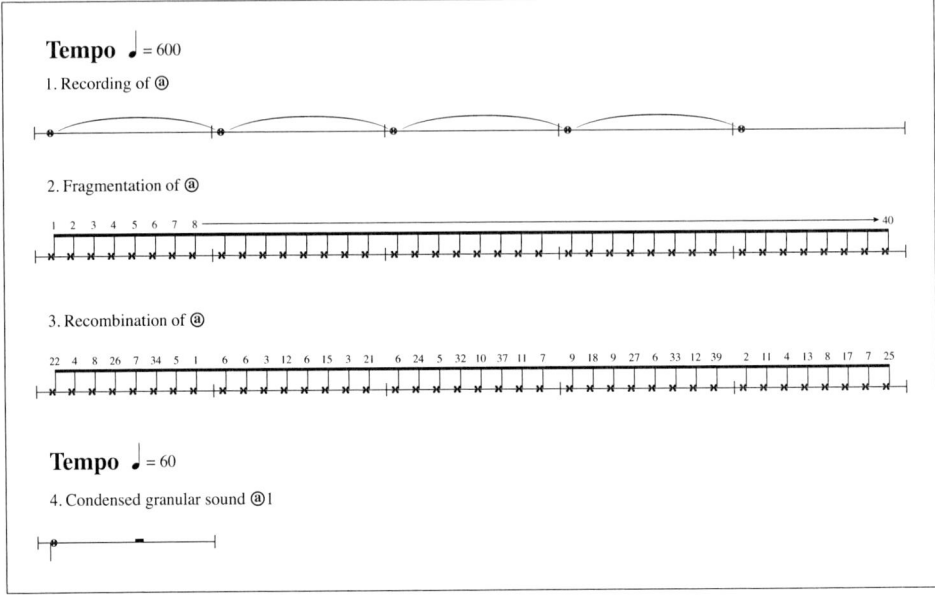

Fig. 40 Construction of granular sounds.

The manually constructed granular sound »ⓐ1« can now be organised in time. An example of the employment of pre-constructed granular sounds is presented in Figure 41. They are all assumed to be constructed in the same way. When utilising durations that are shorter than the original granular sound, only a part of the whole sound is supposed to be played. For instance, in Figure 41 sound »ⓐ1« has the duration of a dotted quaver. This means that only the first 0.75 seconds of this sound can be heard. Moreover, when the duration of the applied sound is longer than the original duration, the recombined fragments will need to be played repeatedly.

Tempo ♩ = 60

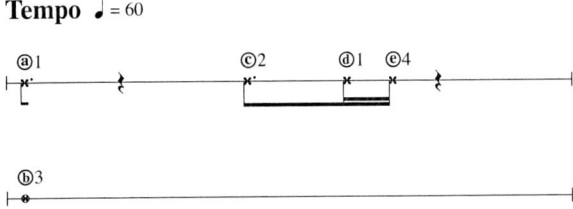

Fig. 41 Notation of granular sounds.

1.9.2 Grain loops and their notation

If a grain is played in a loop, periodic oscillation occurs and a kind of tone can be heard. The fundamental frequency of this sound is equivalent to the reciprocal of the period and the envelope of the loop is equivalent to the envelope of the single grain. When the same grain is repeated at half the rate – meaning that only every second grain is part of the loop – the fundamental frequency is one octave lower while the envelope remains. Moreover, when the grains are repeated in such a way that they overlap at half their duration, their fundamental

258

frequency is one octave higher while the envelope remains[186]. Hence in order to modulate the pitch of a grain loop, the repetition rate merely needs to be changed. The timbre is controlled by the spectrum of the grain whilst the amplitude is dependent on the frequency. The lower the frequency, the lower the amplitude. Conversely, the higher the frequency, the higher the amplitude. If the grains overlap, the amplitude is dependent on their nature and cannot be determined generically[187]. Grain loops may be created in the same way as other granular sounds. An example of pre-constructing the described types of grain loops is presented in Figure 42. A single grain is utilised here to produce three sounds with definite pitch. Sound »④1« is created by playing semiquaver grain 4 in a loop, sound »④2« by repeating grain 4 at half the rate and sound »④3« by repeating grain 4 in such a way that it overlaps at half its duration. Since, in the case of sound »④1«, the period amounts to 0.025 seconds, the frequency of the loop is 40 Hz. Further, the frequency of sound »④2« is set at 20 Hz and the frequency of sound »④3« amounts to 80 Hz. Grain loops may adapt to each duration at any given tempo and do not need to be specifically condensed. Therefore, step 4 is not employed here. Theoretically, an instrument can be constructed on the basis of grain loops and, consequently, depicted by a pitch-based notation system. This could be achieved by relating different grain loops to particular tones (cf. Chapter »1. 2 Additive synthesis« and specifically Figure 11 for an approach towards the construction of a synthetic instrument).

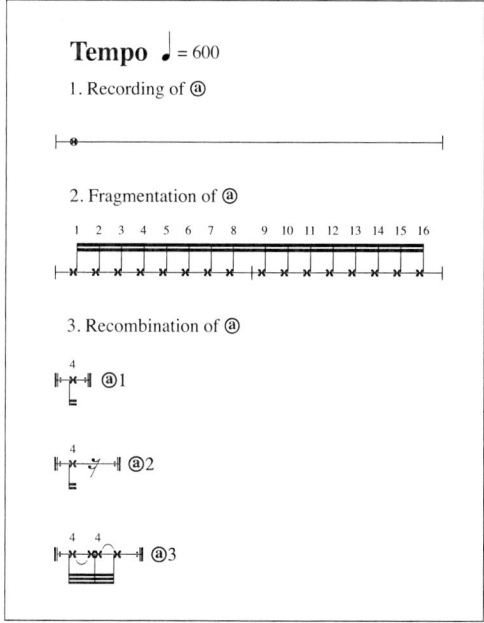

Fig. 42 Grain loops.

---

[186]The reciprocal of a number x is calculated by »$1 \div x$« while, for example, the fundamental of a period of 0.01 seconds is 100 Hz. When only every second grain is part of the loop, the fundamental frequency is set at 50 Hz and hence one octave lower. Moreover, when the grains overlap at half their duration, the fundamental is set at 200 Hz.

[187]Neukom, Signale, pp. 480f.

2. AUDIO PROCESSING

The chapter on audio processing aims at explaining the main processes of sound transformation by means of electroacoustic devices and presenting suggestions for their notation. Therefore, the basic elements of audio processing, spatialisation, filters, reverberation, the delay, chorus-, flanging- and phasing-effects as well as distortion are discussed. Other effects units which are mainly used for the mastering process cannot be explained in detail here, but are merely introduced. There are numerous methods of shaping and transforming sound. The effects units described are regarded as the most important means of audio processing. The topic is presented in such a way that composers are able to employ a particular electroacoustic device in a score and give the realisers all the necessary information they need to implement it. This is why the essential characteristics of these units are outlined in this chapter, but the technical details disregarded. The notation of these units is achieved by depicting their standard parameters, as they are presented in compendiums and handbooks. By doing so, they may be realised by means of any software or electroacoustic device. Further, the sound sources in this chapter are generally not explained in detail. All the information concerning synthetic sound sources is presented in Chapter »1. Sound synthesis« while all relevant aspects of non-instrumental sound sources are explained in Chapter »3. Sound recording«. For instrumental sound sources please refer to »Part I: Extended instrumental playing techniques«.

2. 1 Basic elements

The basic elements of audio processing explained in this chapter are **fragmentation and recombination** as well as the **retrograde technique**.

2. 1. 1 Fragmentation and recombination and its notation

Fragmentation is a fundamental audio processing technique. When employed, an extract of an audio signal is cut out and isolated from its context. As shown, granular synthesis (cf. Chapter »1. 9 Granular synthesis«) makes use of it by dealing with very small fragments called grains. This technique can, for instance, be used to cut a single tone into different parts and combine it in another way. When a fragment is isolated, audible clicks are normally perceived or, in the case of overlapping or adjacent signals, discontinuities (and clicks). This problem can be solved by either creating fade in/out envelopes or – in order to merge two audio signals – by employing a crossfader tool[1]. The notation of this technique can be achieved similarly to the notation of manual granular synthesis. However, the fragments do not, in this case, need to be pre-constructed and condensed. Figure 1 shows how fragmentation and recombination may be notated. The first three steps of manual granular synthesis are applied here. As a reminder, these steps are, firstly, the recording or synthetic creation of a sound, secondly, the fragmentation of this sound and, thirdly, the recombination of the fragments. Two sounds are utilised in the example: an unspecified instrumental sound »ⓐ« and an unspecified noise »ⓑ«. In opposition to granular synthesis, step 1 and 2 are combined here. The instrumental sound »a¹/A4« is cut into six fragments, in the order of two semiquavers (1 and 2), a crotchet (3), two semiquavers (4 and 5) and a minim (6). The noisy sound is also cut into six fragments in the order of two semiquavers (1 and 2), a minim (3), a crotchet (4) and two semiquavers (5 and 6). The two original sounds here are in brackets in order to outline that they are not supposed to be audible. The recombination is depicted by the two lower notation systems. The instrumental sound is recombined in the order of 3, 2, 1, 5, 4, 6 and the noise in the order of 4, 2, 1, 6, 5, 3.

---

[1] Cf. Miranda, Synthesis, pp. 114-116.

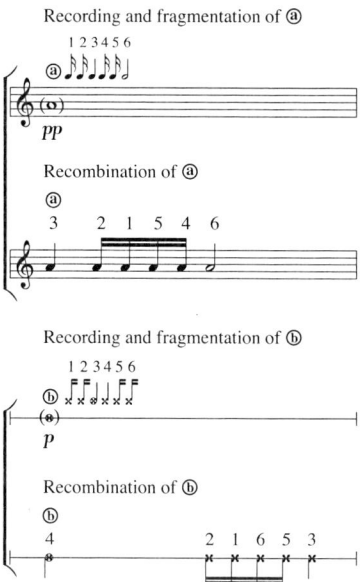

Fig. 1 Fragmentation and recombination.

In order to prevent clicks, a fade in/out envelope or a crossfader tool, respectively, needs to be applied to the recombined material. These processing tools are not depicted here and are assumed to be implemented at the interpreter's discretion. A variant of notation would be to depict a normal fade in/out envelope by means of a *staccato* symbol, a strong fade in/out envelope by a *staccatissimo* symbol and the crossfader tool by a *legato* symbol. However, notating these techniques in this way would lead to subsequent problems because it had not yet been defined how to notate the combination of, for instance, a strong fade in and a normal fade out envelope or the combination of no fade in envelope and a normal fade out envelope. Since the depiction of these events would either lead to a confusing appearance of the score or an insufficient method of notation, the fade in/out envelope and the crossfader tool are completely subjected to interpretation here.

2. 1. 2 The retrograde technique and its notation

The other basic element of audio processing resembles a traditional composition technique called the retrograde. However, a transformation of this kind could not be realised without technical equipment. In audio processing, this is achieved by playing the material backwards. The notation of the retrograde technique is presented in Figure 2. Two unspecified instrumental sounds are subjected here to this transformation: a semibreve »a¹/A4« and a sequence of the same tone. An additional system is used to show that the sound is supposed to be played backwards. Since the semibreve is a continuous sound, the retrograde cannot be illustrated. However, when a sequence is transferred, the retrograde can be notated as if this technique was employed in the traditional way.

Fig. 2 The retrograde technique.

The complement to the retrograde technique is called inversion. Its application in audio processing results in the inversion of amplitudes[2]. This method can be used in the case of phase cancellations. However, it is regarded here as a tool of interpretation.

2. 2 Spatialisation

The spatialisation of sound can serve as an important structural element in an electroacoustic composition. It can be achieved in a physical or virtual way. Physically by projecting the sound over a multichannel sound system in a concert hall from a variety of positions and virtually by imposing effects, such as filters, reverberation, delays or panning in order to create an imaginary environment[3]. When sound is supposed to be played back in a concert, the loudspeaker disposal may be determined. In this context the utilised loudspeaker type is of importance. However, in order to limit the extent of the work, this factor will not be discussed in detail here. Even though the choice of loudspeakers does have a great influence on the material reproduced, it is subjected to interpretation. This is because loudspeakers always have to be adjusted to the particular space they are placed in and concert houses often make use of a default system for sound reinforcement. Hence a complete control over the loud-speaker set-up cannot be achieved and might sometimes be compromised by the circumstan-ces. Therefore, this chapter only presents an introduction to the employment of loudspeakers in concerts and explains the **basic loudspeaker types** as well as the main **stereophonic and multichannel techniques**. The most advanced concept for spatial sound field reproductions is called wave field synthesis. Due to its importance, it is introduced here, but cannot be dis-cussed in detail. Further, most of the virtual ways of creating spatialisation, such as filters, reverberation or delays, are presented in their respective chapter (cf. Chapters »2. 3 Filters«, »2. 4 Reverberation« and »2. 5 Delay«) while in this chapter only **panning** and the *Doppler* **effect** simulation are explained. These effects are solely related to the motion of sound and hence differ from the other effects. Moreover, they may be depicted with relatively low effort and do not need to be dealt with separately. Finally, there are numerous **special construction types**. An overview of all important loudspeaker varieties is beyond the scope of this work. However, two examples that deal with the spatialisation of sound are presented in this chap-ter: *Stockhausen's* rotating loudspeaker and the Leslie speaker.

---

[2] Cf. Roads, Tutorial, pp. 18f.
[3] Roads, Tutorial, p. 451.

2. 2. 1 Basic loudspeaker types and their notation

According to *Goertz*, there are five basic loudspeaker types[4]: **1. Recording monitor loudspeakers**. Monitor loudspeakers meet the highest technical and sound-wise requirements, including an extended bandwidth, a linear frequency response and low distortion at normally required operating levels. **2. Systems for sound reinforcement**. Sound reinforcement can range from a subtle reinforcement of an instrumentalist or speaker to the reinforcement of live events in very large auditoria. The requirements for these systems are also a linear frequency response, a high sound quality and a correct directivity. **3. Public address systems**. Public address systems are normally focused on the reinforcement of speech. The general requirements for intelligible speech reinforcement are inter alia system stability and an adequate signal to reverberant level at each listener. **4. Systems for film**. Cinema sound systems commonly make use of the surround-sound technique, employ huge subwoofers and are especially designed for movie theatres. **5. Consumer loudspeakers**. This category ranges from computer loudspeakers to high fidelity systems and includes 5.1 home cinema sound systems. Like monitor loudspeakers, high quality home systems may meet the highest technical and sound-wise standards[5].

In concert houses, systems for sound reinforcement are normally utilised. They can consist of **single loudspeakers**, **arrays of loudspeakers**, **subwoofers** or **horn loudspeakers**. A subwoofer is designed to reproduce low frequencies only and may be part of a wider range system. A single subwoofer is often used to carry a mono-based signal working with two-channel, stereo, upper range systems[6]. However, it can also be combined with a multichannel setup. There are numerous concepts for the enclosure of subwoofers whilst horn loudspeakers and open dipole speakers may also be used for low frequency reproduction[7]. Moreover, a horn is basically an acoustic transformer. It transforms a small area diaphragm into an effective large area diaphragm. The basic parameters for designing a horn are maximum acoustic power, frequency range and tolerable distortion. When these are given, the driving unit can be specified and the throat and mouth diameters, as well as the shape and length of the horn, be calculated[8]. Loudspeaker arrays can be described as a combination of single loudspeaker systems of the same or different type. They are used for sound reinforcement in large halls to achieve an equally high sound pressure for the whole space[9]. Figure 3 presents a suggestion for the notation of these basic loudspeaker types used in concert halls. The symbols represent from left to right a common single loudspeaker, a subwoofer, a horn speaker and a horn subwoofer. Loudspeaker arrays are not specifically depicted here because they are used for the reproduction of sound in large halls and hence are mainly utilised for the amplification of popular music.

Fig. 3 The basic loudspeaker types.

[4] Cf. Anselm Goertz: Lautsprecher [Loudspeakers]. In: Stefan Weinzierl (ed.): Handbuch der Audiotechnik [Handbook of audio engineering]. Berlin et al. 2008, pp. 421-490, here: pp. 421f.

[5] Goertz. Lautsprecher, pp. 421f., John Eargle: Loudspeaker handbook. London et al. 1997, pp. 200 and 219 and Peter Mapp: Sound reinforcement and public address. In: John Borwick (ed.): Loudspeaker and headphone handbook. 3rd edition Oxford et al. 2001, pp. 411-470, here: pp. 411 and 463f.

[6] Cf. Martin Colloms: High performance loudspeakers. 5th edition. Chichester et al. 1997, p. 168.

[7] Cf. Goertz, Lautsprecher, pp. 431-434.

[8] Stan Kelly: Loudspeaker enclosures. In: Ian Sinclair (ed.): Audio and hi-fi handbook. 3rd edition. Oxford et al. 1998, pp. 290-309, here: p. 300.

[9] Goertz, Lautsprecher, pp. 441f.

2. 2. 2 Stereophonic and multichannel techniques

There are many examples of spatial projection in electroacoustic music. *Roads* inter alia mentions *Varèse's* »Poème electronique« or *Xenakis'* »Concret PH«, which were projected over 425 loudspeakers at the Brussels World Fair in 1958, or the loudspeaker system used by *Stockhausen* at the EXPO 70 in Osaka. In the case of the latter, the loudspeakers were distributed on the interior surface of a geodesic dome[10]. Many different sound spatialisation systems have been developed. However, here only the basic techniques of creating a spatial impression can be explained. **Stereophonic** systems attempt to reproduce spatial attributes to the sound. Stereophony is based on two simultaneous audio channels feeding two spaced loudspeakers and works by creating differences of phase, amplitude and time of arrival. However, when the listener is not in the concentric monitoring position, which is referred to as the sweet spot, the localisation of the sound source is affected[11]. Moreover, **quadraphonic** disposals are commonly used to create the illusion of surround sound. The loudspeakers are placed at the corners of a square, either in the standard configuration, by using two front and two back speakers, or in the dynaquad array, by using a front, back, left and right speaker. **Octophonic** disposals are also frequently employed. In such a case, eight loudspeakers are commonly arranged in a circular pattern[12]. Further, the most advanced concept for creating a spatial sound field reproduction is called **wave field synthesis** (WFS). This technique aims at creating authentic reproductions of auditory scenes. Wave field synthesis utilises a high number of loudspeakers to produce a virtual auditory scene over a large listening area. It overcomes some of the limitations of stereophonic reproduction techniques, e. g. the sweet spot. The loudspeakers are usually distributed in a linear way (two-dimensional WFS), but arbitrarily shaped distributions of loudspeakers and three-dimensional reproductions are also possible[13]. However, due to the enormous effort to install a system of several hundreds of loudspeakers that make use of this technology and the relative novelty of this approach, WFS is disregarded here as a fundamental technique of expression. Anyway, it holds a lot of potential for composers interested in spatial audio. For further insight please refer to *Rabenstein et al.*[14] or *Spors*[15].

2. 2. 2. 1 Previous methods of notation

Whenever loudspeakers are used in performances, set-ups are commonly depicted in the foreword of the work. An example of the utilisation of a quadraphonic disposal in standard configuration can be found in *Nono's* »A Pierre«. He sketches a generic concert hall in order to display it:

---

[10] Cf. Roads, Tutorial, pp. 452-454.

[11] John Watkinson: The art of sound reproduction. Oxford et al. 1998, p. 202 and Karl Slavik and Stefan Weinzierl: Wiedergabeverfahren [Reproduction techniques]. In: Stefan Weinzierl (ed.): Handbuch der Audiotechnik [Handbook of audio engineering]. Berlin et al. 2008, pp. 609-685, here: pp. 611f.

[12] Cf. Slavik and Weinzierl, Wiedergabeverfahren, pp. 612f.

[13] Sascha Spors et al.: The theory of wave field synthesis revisited. Audio Engineering Society convention paper, 124th convention. Amsterdam 2008, pp. 1f.

[14] Rudolf Rabenstein et al.: Wave field synthesis techniques for spatial sound reproduction. In: Eberhard Hänsler and Gerhard Schmidt (eds.): Topics in acoustic echo and noise control. Selected methods for the cancellation of acoustic echoes, the reduction of background noise, and speech processing. Berlin et al. 2006, pp. 517-545.

[15] Spors, Revisited.

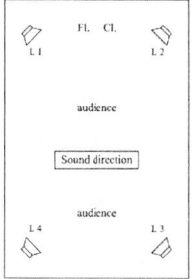

Fig. 4 Nono, A Pierre, p. IV.

Further, *Nono* makes use of an additional sketch, among other things to outline which sound is amplified by which loudspeaker (cf. Figure 18 in the chapter on sound synthesis). Moreover, in »Sirius«[16] *Stockhausen* employs a common octophonic set-up: "[t]he 8 tracks of the 8-track tape recorder are indicated by roman [sic] numerals. They are transmitted over 8 loudspeakers arranged in a circle"[17]. The disposal of the loudspeakers is shown in a sketch:

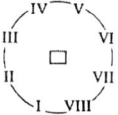

Fig. 5 Stockhausen, Sirius, p. 38 [foreword].

In *Stockhausen's* »Geburtstags-Formel«[18] one can find another example of such a method of depiction. Here the uncommon octophonic disposal is also explained by sketching a generic concert hall. The eight speakers are placed on towers of at least 3.5 m height. It is quite precisely displayed in which direction they are supposed to point, and the loudspeaker set-up is complemented by a circuit plan:

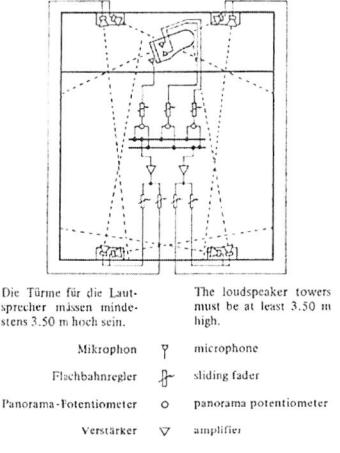

Die Türme für die Laut-sprecher müssen minde-stens 3.50 m hoch sein.		The loudspeaker towers must be at least 3.50 m high.
Mikrophon	ϙ	microphone
Flachbahnregler	ȷ̵	sliding fader
Panorama-Potentiometer	o	panorama potentiometer
Verstärker	▽	amplifier

Fig. 6 Stockhausen, Geburtstags-Formel, p. I.

---

[16] Karlheinz Stockhausen: Sirius. For electronic music, trumpet, soprano, bass clarinet and bass. Kürten 1981.

[17] Stockhausen, Sirius, p. 38 [foreword].

[18] Karlheinz Stockhausen: Geburtstags-Formel (Klavierstück XIV) vom Montag aus Licht. Kürten 1985.

2. 2. 2. 2 Discussion

All the examples presented explain the disposal of loudspeakers in a concert hall sufficiently. They can be used as a reference by the sound engineers that arrange the speakers with regard to the acoustic conditions of a particular space. Since the examples only function as indications, they do not need to be exact, but may only approximately depict the disposal. Further, since the loudspeaker set-up is normally not changed during the performance, it can be described in the foreword to the work. Moreover, it needs to be determined which sound source is sent to which speakers. This necessity is depicted in *Nono's* »A Pierre« or *Stockhausen's* »Geburtstags-Formel« by means of a circuit plan. However, circuit plans like these are not able to describe complex interactions between the sound source and the speakers, but are limited to a fixed system. This is because when employing a circuit plan in order to describe the interaction between the sound sources and the loudspeakers, it can, as mentioned above, only be altered by introducing another plan. Hence this method of notation does not enable complex interactions and becomes unclear when a large number of sound sources is utilised. In such cases, another method of notation needs to be introduced. Further, in none of these examples is the loudspeaker type specified, while a more exact method of notation would at least determine if normal or horn loudspeakers are used and if a subwoofer is employed.

2. 2. 2. 3 Suggestion for the notation of stereophonic and multichannel techniques

Since they adequately depict stereophonic and multichannel techniques, the examples by *Nono* and *Stockhausen* here serve as a template for the suggested method of depiction. They are, however, further elaborated by utilising the three loudspeaker types displayed in Figure 3. Figure 7 presents, from left to right, a stereophonic disposal, a quadraphonic disposal in the standard configuration, a quadraphonic disposal in the dynaquad array and an octophonic disposal. The standard quadraphonic configuration is complemented by a subwoofer placed in the back of the room and the octophonic set-up consists of four common and four horn speakers.

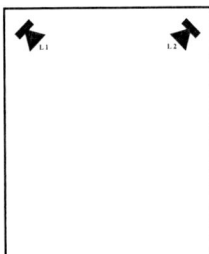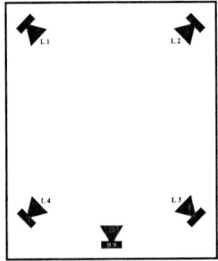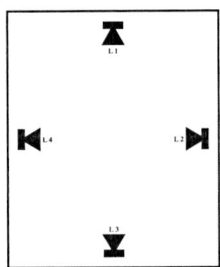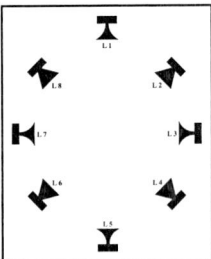

Fig. 7 Loudspeaker disposals.

By giving each loudspeaker a name, it can be determined which sound source is sending to which loudspeaker. In Figure 8 a method of notation that enables the depiction of complex interactions between the sound sources and the loudspeakers is presented. The example refers to the standard quadraphonic disposal from the previous figure. The sounds are produced by unspecified instruments while the determination of the loudspeakers they are sending to is depicted by extending the method presented in Chapter »1. 1. 1 Periodic wave generators and their envelopes«. This approach can be used when wanting to change the connection between the sound sources and the loudspeakers. The output level of the sound is notated by means of a diagrammatic system. The x-axis of this system represents the time and the y-axis the dynamic level from »∅« to quadruple *forte*. Hence the white dots (◇) depict the output level in time. In the example, the upper instrument produces a semibreve »d/D3«. Its output level is increased from »Ø« to *mezzoforte* for the whole duration of this tone. The tone is sent to loudspeakers 2, 3 and 4. The other tone is a »H/B2« with a varying output level. It is increased from »Ø« to *forte* for the duration of a dotted crotchet, decreased to *pianissimo* for the duration of a crotchet and released to »Ø« for the duration of a dotted crotchet. This instrumental sound is sent to loudspeakers 1 and 3 as well as to the subwoofer.

Fig. 8 Advanced spatialisation.

2. 2. 3 Panning and its notation

A more subtle spatialisation may be achieved by means of **panning a stereo** or **multichannel signal**. The panoramic potentiometer or pan control determines the localisation of a sound in a stereo panorama created by loudspeakers. Every track that is sent to the two loudspeakers can be localised further to the left or right side, creating a stereophonic impression. The notation of stereo panning is achieved here by depicting five different adjustments for each side plus the centre position, reaching from the hard left to the hard right position[19]:

Fig. 9 Panning symbols.

It should be noted that, in the case of the hard left/right position, the other loudspeaker is normally not completely muted. Moreover, the law of sound intensity[20] is, with respect to the notation of panning, regarded as subject to interpretation. Transitions from one position to another are depicted by means of arrows and relating the transition to a duration. *Crescendo* or *decrescendo* symbols should not be used in this context because they are related to an increase or decrease of a certain value, which is not given here. In Figure 10 a stereo signal is panned. This is here notated by means of the system that depicts the output level. In the example, an instrumental sound »d/D3« is sent to loudspeakers 1 and 2. The panoramic potentiometer is, in the beginning, adjusted to the right (position 2) and gradually changes to the left (position 1) for the duration of a minim. After it has reached this position, the potentio-

---

[19] Cf. Roey Izhaki: Mixing audio. Concepts, practices and tools. Amsterdam et al. 2008, p. 188.

[20] When a stereophonic sound is, for instance, moved from the hard left to the centre position, the perceived velocity level increases. There are four pan laws that deal with this effect, the 0 dB, −3 dB, −4.5 dB and −6 dB pan law. The −3 dB law, for example, compensates the centre boost for stereophonic signals so that all positions have the same level.

meter is gradually adjusted to the right (position 3) for the duration of another minim. During these events, the output level is additionally increased from »∅« to *mezzoforte* for the duration of a semibreve.

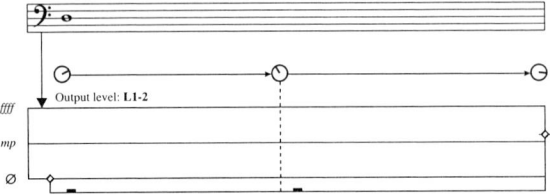

Fig. 10 Stereo panning.

Further, the surround-panorama of quadraphonic, octophonic or other disposals of loudspeakers determines the localisation of sound in a multichannel set-up. However, it needs to be noted that it can only be perfectly perceived in the sweet spot[21]. In Figure 11 a quadrophonic surround-panorama is panned. The panning is depicted here by means of a dot that represents the localisation. The motions are drawn onto an illustration of the loudspeaker disposal. This method of notation permits the depiction of complex motions of the sound source by employing arrows and relating them to a duration as well as the depiction of a constant setting by using a dot. The »d/D3« is in this example sent to loudspeakers 1 to 4. The first motion of the sound source starts in the beginning of the example and is performed for the duration of a minim. The arrow describes how the source should be moved. The second motion is performed for the duration of another minim. The circular arrow depicts a repetitive rotation of the sound source. Because the starting point and endpoint are undetermined, the drawing needs to be complemented by a speed level. Therefore, the parameter tempo is introduced. It ranges from 1 to 6 and is increased here from levels 1 to 5 for the duration of a minim (also cf. »Part I: Extended instrumental playing techniques – 2. 10 Resonance effects« and »3. 2. 4 Rubbing and bowing motions«). In the case of the second motion, no dots are used in order to retain a clear appearance. In order to request a subsequent constant setting, another illustration should be employed.

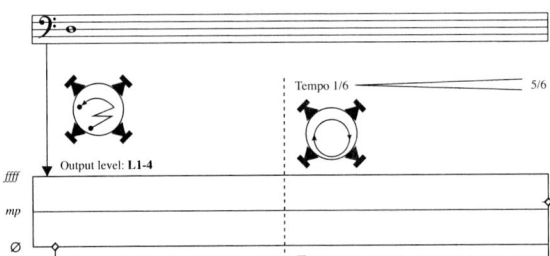

Fig. 11 Surround panning.

2. 2. 4 The *Doppler* effect and its notation

When the sound source or the listener is moving, the frequency created by the source and the frequency the listener perceives do not coincide. The perceived frequency is higher when source and listener approach each other and lower when they recede. It can be simulated in an advanced way mainly by means of the delay effect and a pan potentiometer. The simulation becomes more complex when both, the sound source and the listener, are moving. Audio

---

[21] Cf. Maempel, Audiobearbeitung, pp. 728f.

software is able to compute and realise these movements when the **speed** of the sound source and listener, as well as the **distance** between them, is given. Further, the change in pitch may be calculated on the basis of the sound source's frequency[22]. Please refer for further insight to *Neukom*[23], *Roads*[24] or *Rocchesso*[25].

Any recorded or synthetic sound can be subject to the *Doppler* effect simulation while the speed can be calculated when depicting the distance the sound source and listener travel and the time it takes. Figure 12 presents the notation of the Doppler effect. The sound source here is an unspecified instrument, and the *Doppler* effect is notated by determining the distance the sound and listener travel, the time it takes as well as the distance between the sound and listener by means of two single lined notation systems. The sound source travels 500 metres in total. After it has travelled 240 metres for the duration of a semibreve and a dotted quaver, the listener starts travelling 180 metres. By determining at which point in time the sound source and listener have travelled a certain distance, the speed may be varied. The sound source, for instance, needs a semibreve and a dotted quaver to travel from 0 to 240 metres, a dotted crotchet and a semiquaver to travel from 240 metres to 360 metres, a dotted quaver from 360 to 420 metres and a dotted crotchet and a semiquaver from 420 to 500 metres. A variant of notation would be to employ agogic designations. Moreover, in the beginning the distance between the sound source and the listener amounts to 250 metres. When the listener starts moving, the distance is set at 10 metres, and when the *Doppler* effect comes to an end, the distance amounts to 320 metres. The change in pitch is not depicted here in order to retain simplicity. It is also not necessary to do so because all relevant parameters are already given.

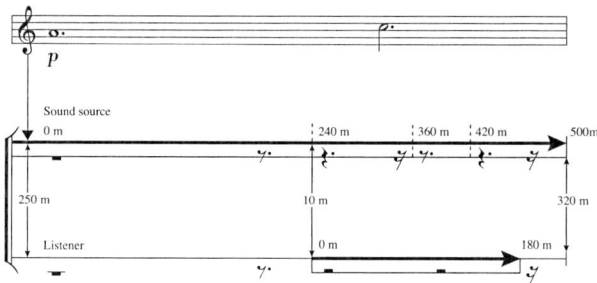

Fig. 12 The *Doppler* effect.

2. 2. 5 Special construction types and their notation

There are numerous loudspeaker designs. It is beyond the scope of this work to give an overview of all types. However, two of the most common construction types, the **rotating loudspeaker**, as invented by *Stockhausen*, and the **Leslie speaker** are explained here. In the case of intending to focus on the transformation of sound by means of loudspeakers, please refer for further insight to *Borwick*[26], *Eargle*[27], *Goertz*[28], *Slavik and Weinzierl*[29] or *Watkin-*

[22] Neukom, Signale, pp. 67f. and 624-627.

[23] Ibid., pp. 67f. and 624-627.

[24] Roads, Tutorial, pp. 463-466.

[25] Davide Rocchesso: Spatial effects. In: Udo Zoelzer (ed.): DAFX. Digital audio effects. Chichester 2002, pp. 137-200, here: pp. 145-147.

[26] Borwick; Loudspeaker.

[27] Eargle, Loudspeaker.

[28] Goertz, Lautsprecher.

[29] Slavik and Weinzierl, Wiedergabeverfahren.

son[30]. A special method of creating sound movements has been realised by the electronic music studio of the *Westdeutscher Rundfunk*[31]. The device, a rotation table with a loudspeaker mounted onto the centre of it, was built for *Stockhausen* who employed it inter alia in his work »Sirius«. This rotating loudspeaker could perform a maximum speed of approximately 12 revolutions per second, clockwise or counter-clockwise[32]. The rotation is requested by a direction in the score: "[n]oise of the rotating loudspeaker, which turns at the speed of approximately 10 revolutions per second"[33]. However, this method of depiction apparently lacks instantaneous comprehension and hence does not agree with the third criterion. A more illustrative method is, therefore, suggested here. As is apparent from Figure 13, a symbol is used to depict the rotating loudspeaker. The main parameters, **activation** or **deactivation** of the rotation and **six stages of rotation speed**, are notated above the system for the output level (for the notation of the output level cf. Chapter »1. 1. 1 Periodic wave generators and their envelopes«). The symbol that represents this loudspeaker is similar to the one for the rotation of the surround-panorama. In the example, it is complemented by the direction on while the deactivation of the rotation would correspondingly be requested by the direction off. The loudspeaker is activated in the beginning while an instrumental sound »d/D3« is sent to it. The rotation speed here is not determined in revolutions per second, but by the speed level 1 to 6. The tempo is, in the beginning, set at 2 and increased after a minim from 2 to 6. The highest rotation speed is reached at the end of the example. In the example, the speaker is rotating clockwise. A change in the running direction may be requested by making the arrows point in the opposite direction.

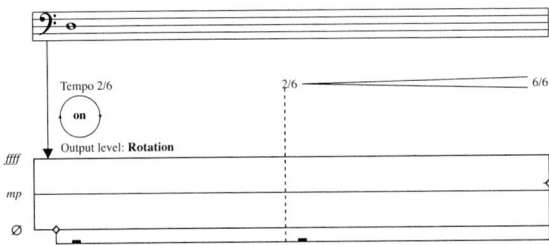

Fig. 13 The rotating loudspeaker.

The *Leslie* speaker[34] also makes use of rotation. The rotating loudspeaker mechanism routes an incoming signal into two separate rotating mechanisms, a spinning horn for high frequencies and a rotating baffle[35]. The periodical deviations in the distance between the sound source and the listeners, as well as between the sound source and the reflecting surfaces, cause changes in pitch (by the *Doppler* effect), loudness, timbre, the impression of spaciousness and, marginally, localisation. The parameters that can be controlled are **activation** or **deactivation** of the rotation and commonly **two stages of rotation speed** called chorale and *tremolo*[36]. The *Leslie* speaker may be depicted similarly to *Stockhausen's* rotating loudspeaker. This is because both loudspeakers' transformation of the sound are based on rotation. Even though the same symbol is applied, it can be clearly determined whether the sound

[30] Watkinson, Art.

[31] West-German Radio.

[32] Stockhausen, Sirius, p. 37 [foreword].

[33] Ibid., p. 1 [Vorstellung/presentation].

[34] Developed by *Donald James Leslie*.

[35] Roads, Tutorial, p. 470.

[36] Cf. Maempel, Audiobearbeitung, pp. 758f.

source is sent to a *Leslie* or a rotating loudspeaker because the rotating loudspeaker's six stages of rotation speed can be clearly distinguished from the *Leslie* speaker's two stages of rotation speed. In Figure 14 the *Leslie* speaker starts rotating in the beginning of the example and is set at the chorale stage. After the duration of a minim, the rotation speed changes to *tremolo*. In the case of employing a software version of the loudspeaker, it needs to be noted that digital reconstructions mainly use *Doppler* and *tremolo* effects to simulate the rotation. However, the enormously important all-round sound propagation cannot be transferred[37].

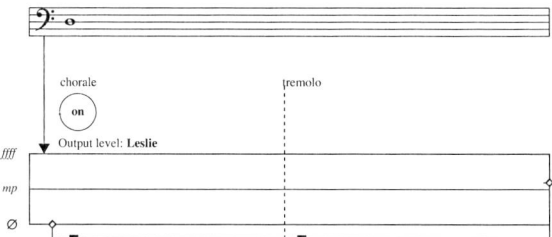

Fig. 14 The *Leslie* speaker.

2. 3 Filters

Filters are employed in order to influence the spectrum of the audio signal and hence produce a modification of the sound[38]. This chapter focuses on **high-pass, low-pass, band-pass filters and band-reject filters** and examines the wah-wah effect. Further, **high-shelf, low-shelf and parametric filters** are discussed. An **equaliser** makes use of these filters types and is, therefore, also introduced here while another type of filter, called the all-pass filter, is explained in Chapter »2. 6. 3 The phasing-effect«.

2. 3. 1 High-pass, low-pass, band-pass and band-reject filters

The most important simple filters are **high-pass** [▣] and **low-pass** [▣] filters[39]. The former attenuates the spectrum of an audio signal below the adjusted **cut-off frequency** and the latter conversely above. There is always a smooth transition between pass-through and cut-off and the signal already attenuated by −3 dB at the cut-off frequency. The edge steepness/slope of the filter is normally described in dB per octave and technically by an **ordinal number** n. The higher the order, the higher the edge steepness, which can be calculated by »$n \times 6$ dB« per octave[40/41]. Further, high-pass and low-pass filters can have different response curves depending on the parameter called **quality** (Q). This can be used to create a resonance at the cut-off frequency[42], e. g. by altering an attenuation of 3 dB to a boost of 6

[37] Ibid., p. 759.

[38] Udo Zoelzer: Signalverarbeitung, Filter und Effekte [Signal processing, filters and effects]. In: Stefan Weinzierl (ed.): Handbuch der Audiotechnik [Handbook of audio engineering]. Berlin et al. 2008, pp. 813-848, here: p. 831

[39] Ibid., p. 831.

[40] Maempel, Audiobearbeitung, pp. 744f. and Miranda, Synthesis, p. 98.

[41] For example, when the ordinal number is $n = 4$ and the cut-off frequency of a high-pass filter is 400 Hz, the signal is attenuated by −3 dB at 400 Hz and the edge steepness set at 24 dB per octave (4 × 6 dB). Thus the signal is attenuated by »−3 dB − 24 dB = −27 dB« at 200 Hz (octave), by »−27 dB − 24 dB = −51 dB« at 100 Hz (second octave) etc. When full attenuation is reached, all lower frequencies are from that point on completely muted. The higher the edge steepness, the closer is the complete attenuation to the cut-off frequency of the filter. Low-pass filters work conversely.

[42] Russ, Sound, p. 118.

dB. Such an alteration results in an automatic increase of the edge steepness[43]. When Q = 0, the attenuation at the cut-off frequency is –3 dB. In Figure 15 a low-pass filter is sketched. It can be seen how the increase of the ordinal number n and the quality affects the shape of the filter.

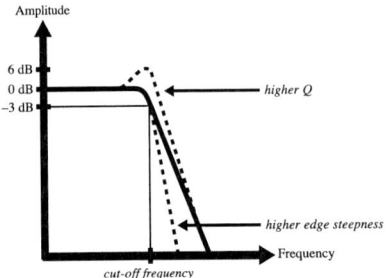

Fig. 15 Sketch of a low-pass filter.

A **band-pass** filter [▢] rejects both high and low frequencies with a pass band in between. Conversely, a **band-reject filter** [▢] attenuates a band of frequencies whilst all others pass. The **width of the band** is calculated by subtracting the higher cut-off frequency from the lower cut-off frequency. A band-pass filter attenuates the spectrum of an audio signal above the higher cut-off and below the lower cut-off frequency whilst a band-reject filter conversely attenuates the signal below the higher cut-off and above the lower cut-off frequency. Another reference for these kinds of filters is the **centre frequency** of the band[44]. There is only one **ordinal number n** applied to each band-pass or band-reject filter and the edge steepness is therefore symmetrical. The quality is defined by »Q = centre frequency ÷ (higher cut-off frequency – lower cut-off frequency)«[45]. Thus adjusting the Q is the same as adjusting the bandwidth[46]. In opposition to low-pass and high-pass filters, no resonance is created at the cut-off frequency[47]. Figure 16 presents the sketch of a band-pass and a band-reject filter. It can be seen how these filters are shaped by increasing the edge steepness.

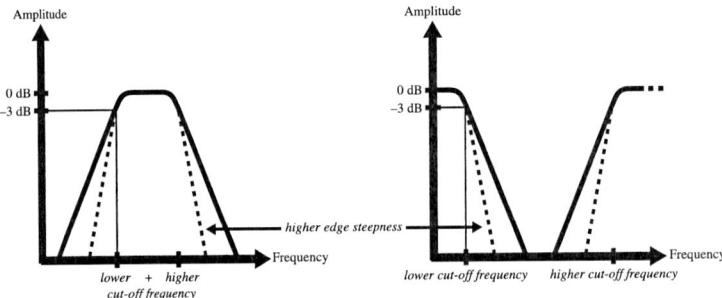

Fig. 16 Sketches of a band-pass and a band-reject filter.

---

[43] Cf. Pierre Dutilleux and Udo Zoelzer: Filters. In: Udo Zoelzer (ed.): DAFX. Digital audio effects. Chichester 2002, pp. 31-62, here: p. 33.

[44] When the higher cut-off frequency of the band is, for instance, set at 600 Hz and the lower cut-off frequency at 400 Hz, the width of the band that passes/is rejected amounts to 200 Hz and the centre frequency to 500 Hz.

[45] When using the values of the previous footnote, the quality is »500 Hz ÷ (600 Hz – 400 Hz) = 2.5«.

[46] Roads, Tutorial, pp. 189f.

[47] Cf. Russ, Sound, pp. 118f.

The **wah-wah effect** is produced when varying the centre frequency of a **band-pass filter** with a small bandwidth. The variation is often controlled by a pedal. Moving the pedal changes the centre frequency. However, the variation can also be controlled by software. In order to employ the wah-wah effect, **the ordinal number *n*,** as well as the ratio between the direct original audio signal and the modulated signal, need to be determined. The latter is defined by the parameters **dry and wet**[48].

2. 3. 1. 1 Previous methods of notation

There have been a number of attempts to notate filters. *Schafer*, in »Music for the morning of the world«, depicts them by simply giving directions like "highish filtered cymbal"[49] or "low filtered gong"[50]. Moreover, *Wehinger* introduces four different graphic representations for four different filter types in his aural score for *Ligeti's* »Artikulation«[51]:

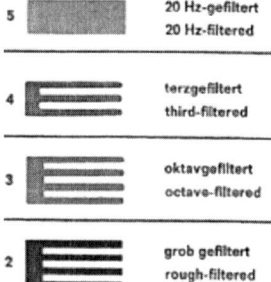

Fig. 17 Ligeti, Artikulation, p. 37.

These filters are subsequently employed in a special notation system. As mentioned in Chapter »1. 1 Basic elements«, the x-axis of this system represents the time in a spatial way whilst 1 second equals 2.7 cm. Moreover, the frequency is displayed by the y-axis which represents the whole frequency range:

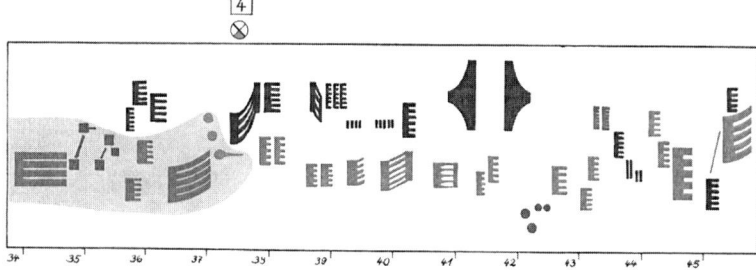

Fig. 18 Ligeti, Artikulation, p. 47.

Moreover, *Schnebel*, in »Für Stimmen (... missa est)«[52], employs a filter in a graphic way and by means of a distinct notation system designated as »F«. The filter is supposed to shape

---

[48] Maempel, Audiobearbeitung, pp. 759f.

[49] Schafer, Morning, p. 2.

[50] Ibid., p. 3.

[51] The symbols are coloured in the original score.

[52] Dieter Schnebel: Für Stimmen (... missa est). Choralvorspiele I/II. For organ, auxiliary instruments and tape. Mainz 1971.

the sound of an organ in a concert[53]. There is no explanation given concerning the filter type or cut-off frequency. The shape of the graphic only seems to suggest either a high-pass filter, which cuts off the fundamental tone and probably a number of harmonics, or a low-cut filter, which cuts off a number of harmonics, being employed.

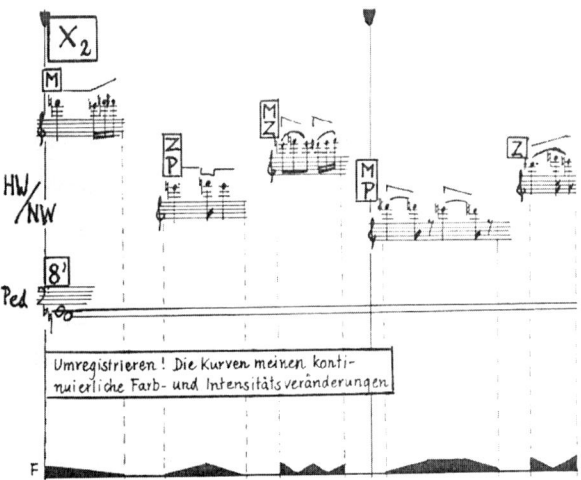

Fig. 19 Schnebel, Stimmen, p. 21.

Further, in »Mikrophonie I« *Stockhausen* utilises band-pass filters. The notation is derived from the characteristics of the model he used, the analogue filter W 49 produced by *Maihak*. The greatest bandwidth of the filter is 30 to 10,000 Hz and the narrowest corresponds to the distance between two adjacent frequency numbers. The possible frequency settings are subdivided into three ranges by dashed lines – 1. Low, from 30 to 450 Hz. 2. Middle, from 450 Hz to 1,000 Hz. 3. High, from 1,000 to 10,000 Hz. Each range is, further, subdivided into three steps, e. g. the middle range into 450 to 600 Hz (step 1), 600 to 800 Hz (step 2) and 800 to 1,000 Hz (step 3). Hence 450 and 600 Hz are, for example, two adjacent frequency numbers. In order to perform »Mikrophonie I« a filter with at least nine band settings is needed. Moreover, the edge steepness is always set at the maximum level[54]. Figure 20 shows how the filter is notated. The three ranges and nine steps can be clearly identified. To give some examples, the bandwidth of the filter in the beginning of Figure 20 is set at step 2 of the high range, followed by step 1, step 2, step 3 and step 1. The higher cut-off frequency is then as quickly as possible changed to the highest frequency (10,000 Hz) and the lower cut-off frequency gradually changed to the lowest frequency (30 Hz). When the lowest frequency is reached, the filter is set at its greatest bandwidth. The duration of the described events is determined in relation to the system of the sound producer by means of vertical lines.

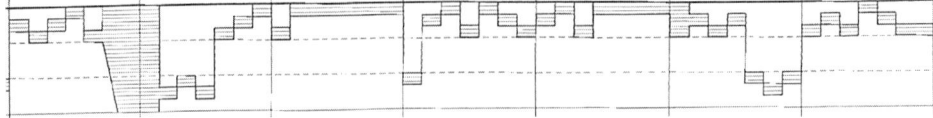

Fig. 20 Stockhausen, Mikrophonie I, Moment "RASCHELND (RATTELND) MURMELND".

---

[53] Cf. Schnebel, Stimmen, pp. 20-23.

[54] Stockhausen, Mikrophonie I, pp. 10 and 14.

2. 3. 1. 2 Discussion

The notation of high-pass and low-pass filters by *Schafer* is very approximate. He neither determines a cut-off frequency nor the edge steepness and quality. Further, if these parameters were notated by means of directions, it would lead to very long sentences which could not fulfil the requirement of instantaneous comprehension. However, *Wehinger's* approach (cf. Figures 17 and 18) is very illustrative and contains a higher degree of instantaneous comprehension. However, as can be seen in Figure 18, his method is very approximate because the y-axis only holds the lowest and highest frequency as a reference[55]. Hence the cut-off frequency can only be assumed. Moreover, since the grid is not very detailed, the depiction of the duration is also inexact. Additionally, neither the edge steepness nor the quality is determined while the system could only be combined with traditional notation if the timeline was altered. *Schnebel's* approach (cf. Figure 19) resembles the depiction of filters in *Wehinger's* aural score. It may be described as illustrative, but lacks at the same time the depiction of the exact cut-off frequency, edge steepness and Q. Finally, *Stockhausen's* approach towards the notation of filters (cf. Figure 20) is the most exact one. His method of depiction also contains a high degree of instantaneous comprehension since the alteration of the cut-off frequency can be quickly understood. If the cut-off frequency was supposed to be controlled independently, this system could be easily extended by introducing a distinct timeline. However, even though *Stockhausen's* method of depiction is the most exact one, it is still quite approximate. This is because only nine cut-off frequencies may be depicted by this system and the edge steepness cannot be controlled. Further, as mentioned in Chapter »1. 1. 1 Periodic wave generators and their envelopes«, the whole spectrum from sub-audio frequencies above 0 Hz up to 20 kHz can theoretically be described by the traditional notation's bass and treble clef. Since pitch-based notation may also be used to depict the cut-off frequency, it is preferred here over any graphic representation of filters. This method can be described as simple, exact and strongly related to traditional notation. Additionally, the Q and n would need to be described, if necessary.

2. 3. 1. 3 Suggestion for the notation of high-pass, low-pass, band-pass and band-reject filters

Hence the suggested method of notation depicts the basic filters by means of pitch-based notation. In Figure 21 an unspecified recorded noise is filtered by means of a high-pass and a low-pass filter. The two filter types are depicted by two systems, one in treble and one in bass clef, whilst the triangular note heads pointing upwards represent the high-pass filter and the triangular note heads pointing downwards the low-pass filter. They are, further, complemented by the high-pass filter [▣] and the low-pass filter symbol [▣], respectively. These symbols do not, however, necessarily have to be employed. The ordinal number n here is an integer number theoretically ranging from 1 to 12 while the Q may range from 0 to 25 in increments of 0.5. In the example, the source has the duration of a semibreve. It is at first filtered by a high-pass filter with a cut-off frequency of »c#²/C#5« (~ 554 Hz), an initial ordinal number n of 10 and a Q of 8.5. The cut-off frequency and the Q remain constant whilst n is decreased to 6. This edge steepness is reached at the end of the example. The signal is also filtered by a low-pass filter, which is represented by the lowest system. A *glissando* of the cut-off frequency is performed here. It is initially set at »a/A3« (220 Hz), changed to »c#/C3« (~ 139 Hz) for the duration of a crotchet, then increased to »f/F3« (~ 175 Hz) for the duration of another crotchet and finally decreased to »e♭/E♭3« (~ 156 Hz) for the duration of another crotchet. This is the end of the *glissando* and the cut-off frequency then remains »e♭/E♭3« for the duration of a crotchet. Moreover, the ordinal number n is set at 4 whilst the Q is, from the begin-

---

[55] Cf. Ligeti, Artikulation, pp. 24f and 37.

275

ning onwards, increased from 12.5 to 20. This high quality is reached at the end of the example. As mentioned above, in this work the *glissando* – in order to achieve a greater clarity and enable the depiction of *glissando* motions that do not involve changes in pitch – is requested by means of an arrow and not in the traditional manner. Alternatively, the common method of depiction may be restored.

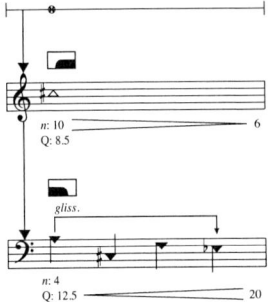

Fig. 21 High-pass and low-pass filters.

Band-pass and band-reject filters may be notated similarly. However, these filter types are depicted here by means of the centre frequency and the bandwidth instead of by the cut-off frequencies, in order to facilitate the notation of a stable bandwidth. As mentioned, the parameter quality does not need to be determined. The band-pass filter is represented here by squared note heads and the band-reject filter by x-shaped note heads. They are, further, complemented by the band-pass filter symbol [▢] and the band-reject filter symbol [▢], respectively. The source is at first filtered by a band-reject filter with a centre frequency of »c♯2/C♯5« (~ 554 Hz), a bandwidth of 250 Hz and an initial ordinal number n of 10. The centre frequency and the bandwidth remain constant whilst n is decreased to 6. This edge steepness is reached at the end of the example. The signal is subsequently filtered by a band-pass filter, depicted by the lowest system. A *glissando* of the centre frequency is performed here. It is initially set at »a/A3« (220 Hz), changed to »c♯/C♯3« (~ 139 Hz) for the duration of a crotchet, then raised to »f/F3« (~ 175 Hz) for the duration of another crotchet and finally changed to »e♭/E♭3« (~ 156 Hz), also for the duration of a crotchet. At this point the *glissando* ends and the centre frequency remains »e♭/E♭3« for the duration of a crotchet. Simultaneously, the ordinal number n is set at 4 whilst the bandwidth is increased from 70 to 120 Hz. This larger bandwidth is reached at the end of the example.

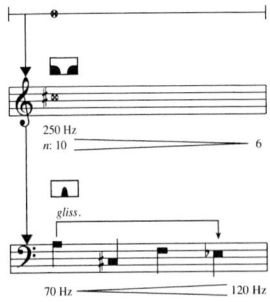

Fig. 22 Band-pass and band-reject filters.

Further, a suggestion for the notation of the wah-wah effect is presented in Figure 23. As mentioned, the effect is achieved by varying the centre frequency of a band-pass filter with a

276

small bandwidth. The wah-wah effect is, in the example, produced by employing a bandwidth of 35 Hz while the variation of the centre frequency is depicted by means of notating a *glissando*. Additionally, the dry and wet ratio needs to be determined. It is described here in per cent and set at 40% to 60%. This means that the loudness of the original signal here amounts to 40% of the overall output level whilst the loudness of the transformed signal amounts to 60% of the overall output level.

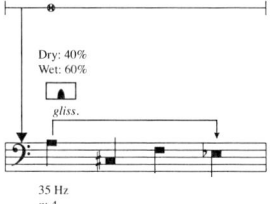

Fig. 23 The wah-wah effect.

Theoretically, more than one, as well as different, filter types may be depicted by a single notation system. However, when the appearance of the score becomes unclear, additional systems should be utilised. Further, the ordinal number n and/or the quality Q may alternatively be depicted by means of a diagrammatic notation system in order to control these parameters independently.

2. 3. 2 High-shelf, low-shelf and parametric filters and their notation

Shelving filters may be described as a parallel connection of an unfiltered signal and a high-pass or low-pass filter. The output signal of the respective filter is added to the unfiltered signal with respect to a positive or negative **gain factor**. Low or high frequencies can therefore be either reinforced or attenuated[56]. There are two types of shelving filters: the high-shelf filter [▱◀] – which derives from the high-pass filter – and the low-shelf filter [▶▱] – which derives from the low-pass filter. For both filter types the **cut-off frequency**, the **ordinal number** n and the **quality** need to be defined. Further, **parametric filters** [▱●] consist of a parallel connection of an unfiltered signal and a band-pass filter. The output signal of the band-pass filter is added to the unfiltered signal with respect to a positive or negative **gain factor**. Hence a particular bandwidth can be either reinforced or attenuated. For this filter type the **centre frequency**, the **bandwidth** and the **ordinal number** n need to be determined[57].

The notation of high-shelf, low-shelf and parametric filters is presented in Figure 24. The high-shelf filter is depicted by means of note heads with the shape of a half-circle pointing upwards whilst the low-shelf filter is depicted by note heads with the shape of a half-circle pointing downwards. The note heads of the parametric filter are spherical. In order to retain clarity, the gain factor is depicted by a diagrammatic notation system. The x-axis of this system represents the time whilst the y-axis describes the gain factor in dB, ranging from −15 to +15 dB in increments of three. Hence the white dots (◇) depict the gain factor in time. In the example, the cut-off frequency of the high-shelf filter is constantly set at »c♯²/C♯5« (~ 554 Hz), and a Q of 8.5 is employed. The ordinal number n is decreased from initially 10 to 6. The high-shelf filter's gain factor is in the beginning set at +9 dB. It is decreased to −6 dB for the duration of a dotted crotchet and remains on this level until the end of the example. Moreover, the low-shelf filter's cut-off frequency performs a *glissando* from »a/A3« (220 Hz) to »e♭/ E♭3« (~ 156 Hz). Its ordinal number n is constantly set at 4 whilst the Q is increased from

---

[56] Zoelzer, Signalverarbeitung, p. 835.

[57] Ibid., p. 835.

12.5 to 20, and the low-shelf filter's gain factor amounts to +6 dB. Further, the centre frequency of the parametric filter is set at »f¹/F4« (~ 349 Hz), the bandwidth at 250 Hz and the ordinal number n at 4. The gain factor of initially »Ø« is decreased to –9 dB for the duration of a dotted minim and subsequently increased to –3 dB for the duration of a crotchet.

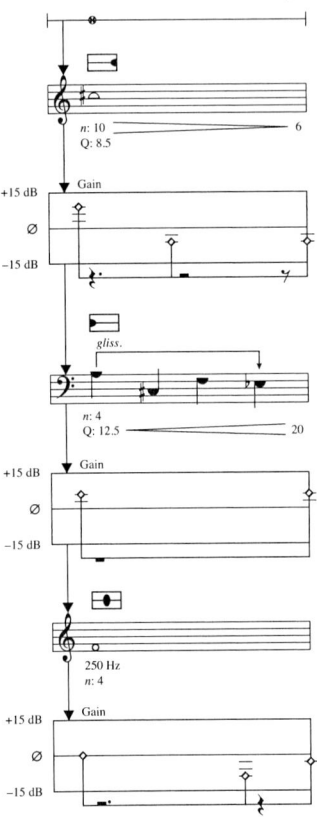

Fig. 24 High-shelf, low-shelf and parametric filters.

2. 3. 3 The equaliser and its notation

An equaliser is a combination of different filter types that shape the whole spectrum. It could, for instance, consist of a high-pass, low-shelf, parametric, high-shelf and low-pass filter. Its notation can be achieved by combining the paradigms presented in the previous chapters. An equaliser is often employed as a tool in the mastering process, which is regarded here as subject to interpretation (cf. Chapter »2. 8 Other audio processing techniques«). Further, graphic equalisers are commonly used in live performances to prevent microphone feedback. They consist of many adjacent mini faders and normally a fixed ordinal number and Q[58]. The utilisation of such devices, for instance, in a concert is also regarded here as subject to interpretation.

---

[58] Cf. Izhaki, Audio, p. 231.

2. 4 Reverberation

A digital reverb is able to simulate the acoustic properties of a certain space or to create spaces that could in reality never be constructed[59]. In this chapter two different types of reverberation are presented, the **convolution reverb** and **classical reverberation**.

2. 4. 1 The convolution reverb and its notation

Artificial reverberation may be generated by various algorithms. The most exact way of simulating a space can be achieved by convolving an audio signal with the impulse response of an artificial or real space. An impulse response is either produced by measuring a real room or by model based computation[60]. Many kinds of softwares additionally offer a library of impulse responses. When employing a convolution reverb, the **type of space** and the **reverb time** need to be described. If a **pre-delay time** is defined, the reverb enters after the audio signal. The **envelope** controls the dynamic level of the reverb and is related to the initial reverb time, but may also reduce it[61]. Reverberation by impulse response is able to imitate any room's reverberation in a very exact way. The only lack is that a movement of the sound source or listener cannot be simulated[62].

In Figure 25 the notation of the convolution reverb is presented. Two spaces – a mosque and a church – are employed here. The reverb time of the mosque is approximately four seconds and the reverb time of the church three seconds. At a tempo of ♩ = 60, four seconds equal a semibreve and three seconds equal a dotted minim. The duration and intensity of each reverb is depicted by means of an envelope diagram (cf. Chapter »1. 1. 1 Periodic wave generators and their envelopes«). The x-axis of this system represents the time whilst the y-axis depicts the dynamic level from »∅« to quadruple *forte* in 10 + 1 steps. Opposed to the notation of a simple envelope, two dots are employed in order to depict the complex reverberation envelope. The envelope of a reverb is more complex because it is constantly triggered during the sound production. In order to display the full extent of the envelope, the white dots (◇) represent the envelope in relation to the first triggering and the black dots (◆) the envelope in relation to the last triggering. The pre-delay time here ranges from 0 to 200 ms and is written above the diagrammatic system. In the example, an unspecified instrument is subject to the convolution reverb. At first, an »a¹/A4« is produced for the duration of a minim. The dynamic level of this sound is *forte*. It is virtually placed into a mosque with 4 seconds reverb time and a pre-delay time of 35 ms. Both depicted envelopes can be described in the same way since they resemble each other. The intensity of the reverb is increased from »∅« to *forte* for the duration of semiquaver, reduced to *mezzopiano* for the duration a quaver, sustained for the duration of a minim and a semiquaver and released for the duration of a crotchet. The second arrow that is employed (*senza*), requests that this reverb is supposed to be switched off after the last triggering. The second sound, a semiquaver »g¹/G4«, is therefore only transformed by the church reverberation with a pre-delay time of 120 ms. The arrow employed in combination with this reverb, requires that this effects unit is switched on when the second sound is produced. The envelopes of the church reverb are increased from »∅« to *mezzoforte* for the duration of a semiquaver, decreased to *piano* for the duration of another semiquaver, sustained for the duration of a dotted crotchet and released for the duration of a crotchet.

Both envelopes are depicted in a slightly inexact way. This is because the pre-delay time is not considered and the last envelope starts off right after the sound production has ended, but

---

[59] Supper, Musik, p. 16.
[60] Zoelzer, Signalverarbeitung, p. 846.
[61] Cf. Maempel, Audiobearbeitung, pp. 754f.
[62] Ibid., p. 755.

is actually triggered by the very last sound wave and also delayed if the pre-delay time $\neq 0$. Further, it is possible that the envelope – dependent on the tempo and reverb time – cannot always be depicted exactly by means of traditional durations. Another difficulty is that when the interpreter is supposed to create an impulse response, a space with the required reverberation time and envelope may not be available. A solution to this problem might be to use an impulse response with a larger reverb time and adapt it to the required setting of the reverb or to utilise a computed impulse response. Further, the space may be described in a more detailed way than it is by simply mentioning that the reverb is created in a mosque or church. Such a description may be presented in the foreword of the score and be related to the symbol used for the representation of the particular convolution reverb.

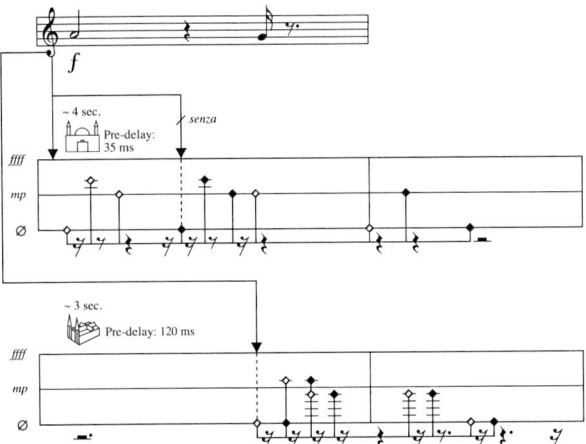

Fig. 25 Convolution reverb.

2. 4. 2 Classical reverberation and its notation

Most other types of reverberation are based on the reconstruction or approximation of an impulse response[63]. When it is not intended to simulate a space, but to add specific characteristics of this place to an audio signal, they can be a vital tool for sound processing. There are a lot more parameters that need to be controlled by an effect unit that employs this kind of reverberation. At first, the **type of space** (commonly church, hall, chamber or room) is chosen. Normally, simulations of **plate**[64] or **spring**[65] reverberators are also available. Moreover, the **size of the room** needs to be determined. In most cases, it is linked to the decay time and the early reflections pattern[66]. Sometimes it is also possible to choose the **shape of the room** (commonly from triangular to octagonal). Other parameters are the **reverb and bass**

---

[63] Zoelzer, Signalverarbeitung, p. 846.

[64] This kind of reverb was originally created by suspending a large steel plate in a tensioning frame. Activated by a transducer, waves travel to the boundaries of the plate and are reflected back to be detected by strategically placed transducers and converted into an electrical signal.

[65] The signal to be treated is applied to the end of a long metal coil spring by a transducer and detected at the other end by a second transducer. The sound is reflected by the ends of the spring and will travel back and forth several times before decaying. The decay time is determined by the length of the spring.

[66] Shortly after the direct sound, bounced reflections start arriving at the listener. Most of the early reflections only bounce from one or two surfaces. The early reflections provide information about the characteristics of the space and the distance between source and listener. The pre-delay of early reflections is normally lower than the pre-delay of the reverb. Neither plate nor spring reverbs have distinct early reflections due to their small size.

reverb time[67]. Further, the **pre-delay time**, the **envelope**, the **density** of reflections and the **diffusion** need to be set. The term diffusion is used to describe the scattering of a sound. It is determined by many factors, such as the material that reflects the sound or the shape of the room. When diffusion occurs, the reflection pattern becomes more complex in terms of spacing and levels[68].

There are only a few approaches towards the notation of classical reverberation. *Schnebel* makes use of a simple reverb in his work »Für Stimmen (... missa est)«. The reverb is notated by means of giving directions like "very reverberant"[69], "modify (...) reverb constantly"[70] or "+ a lot of reverb"[71]. He also utilises a line in order to depict the modification of the reverb's envelope and requests the player to modify the loudness (reverb and sound) in a more discontinuous way [stärker diskontinuierliche Veränderung von Lautstärke (Hall und Klang)]. The line is connected to the sound producer by means of vertical lines while the y-axis of this diagrammatic notation system does not have any reference points.

Fig. 26 Schnebel, Stimmen, p. 41.

Schnebel's approach may be described as simple. However, as is apparent from the example, the directions and the representation of the envelope are very approximate. Most of the parameters of classical reverberation are not depicted at all and the intensity of this effect is only described in a very vague way. Therefore, another method needs to be introduced. The method used here is based on the notation of the convolution reverb (cf. Figure 25). It is more exact because it includes all standard parameters of classical reverberation, but may be described as more complex when compared to *Schnebel's* approach. However, a simpler method of notation could be produced by reducing the amount of parameters.

A suggestion for the notation of classical reverberation is presented in Figure 27. The type of space here is »chamber«, the size of the room is 80 square metres and the shape pentagonal. The reverb time is set at four seconds and the bass reverb time at two seconds. The predelay time is determined as 35 ms. The envelopes of the reverb and the bass reverb time are depicted by means of a diagrammatic system. The x-axis of this system represents the time whilst the y-axis depicts the dynamic level from »∅« to quadruple *forte* in 10 + 1 steps. The white dots (◇) represent the reverberation envelope in relation to the first triggering and the black dots (◆) the envelope in relation to the last triggering. The bass reverb time is notated in the same system. Therefore, the dots need to be shaped differently: the squared white dots (□) represent the envelope of the bass reverb time in relation to the first triggering and the squared black dots (■) the envelope of the bass reverb time in relation to the last triggering. Further, the density and diffusion are depicted by another diagrammatic system. The x-axis of this system represents the time whilst the y-axis describes the intensity of these parameters in per cent and increments of ten. The white dots (◇) represent the parameter density and the black dots (◆) the parameter diffusion in time. In Figure 27 a minim »F/F2« is transformed. The envelopes of the reverb time equal the first two envelopes presented in Figure 25. They are complemented by the envelopes of the bass reverb time, which are increased from »∅« to *mezzoforte* for the duration of a semiquaver, sustained for the duration of a dotted crotchet

[67] Also referred to as bass multiply and, in such a case, described as the factor for the lowest frequencies' reverb time alteration.

[68] Cf. Maempel, Audiobearbeitung, p. 754 and Izhaki, Audio, pp. 421-440.

[69] Schnebel, Stimmen, p. 35.

[70] Ibid., p. 37.

[71] Ibid., p. 32.

and released for the duration of semiquaver. The density is initially set at 30%, increased to 60% for the duration of a dotted minim and a semiquaver, decreased to 40% for the duration of a dotted crotchet and a semiquaver and then it remains on this level until the end of the reverberation. The diffusion is initially set at 20%, increased to 40% for the duration of a semibreve, decreased to 20% for the duration of a crotchet and a semiquaver and sustained until the reverberation ends.

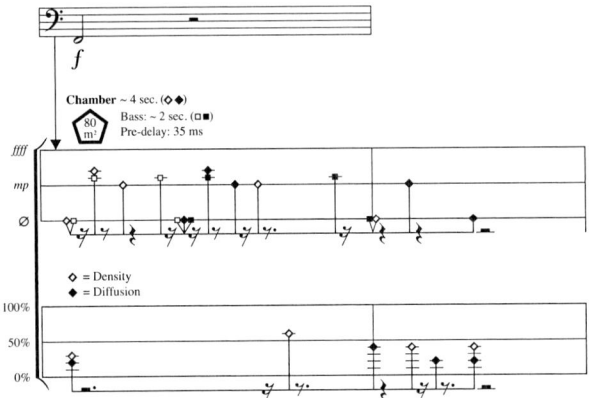

Fig. 27 Classical reverberation.

When more exact values are required with regard to the density and diffusion, they can be notated above the system (cf. Figure 22 in the chapter on sound synthesis). Further, the range of the bass reverb may be defined. Otherwise, it would have to be determined by the interpreter. The method of notation used here is quite complex, but also depicts numerous parameters and two types of reverberation. It could be simplified by depicting the bass reverb's envelopes by means of a distinct system or, as mentioned, by reducing parameters. Furthermore, the plate and spring reverb may be notated in the same way as classical reverberation. However, the parameter room size does not need to be determined. Two symbols, which could represent these reverberation types, are presented in Figure 28.

Fig. 28 Symbols for the plate and spring reverb.

2. 5 Delay

Many effects units are based on delaying audio signals[72]. This chapter presents the **mono and stereo delay** effect. Further, a suggestion for the notation of a **waveguide filter** is given. This approach towards physical modelling makes use of filters and the delay effect.

2. 5. 1 The mono and stereo delay and its notation

The delay of audio signals can be easily achieved digitally. The most basic requirement is to set the amount of **delay time**. Further, a **feedback** is often applied. As mentioned, the term feedback means that the resulting signal is fed back to the source. A mono delay can be, and a stereo delay is always, controlled by **panoramic potentiometers**. The ratio between the direct

---

[72] Maempel, Audiobearbeitung, p. 748.

original audio signal and the modulated signal is determined by the parameters **dry and wet**[73].

There are only a few valid examples of notation. In »Time and motion study II«[74] *Ferneyhough* utilises, for example, two analogue tape delays in order to transform the sound of a cello. There are two fixed delay times of 9 (tape 1) and 14 seconds (tape 2). Both delays are controlled by means of a pedal: "[t]he position of the performer's footpedal is given in approximate (graphic) notation in the systems situated above and below the instrumental stave(s), whereby the upper indicates always the pedal controlling the 9" delay tape and the contact microphone located under the fingerboard (F. B.), the lower, meanwhile, the contact microphone attached to the body of the instrument (B.) and the 14" tape loop"[75]. Moreover, the upper boundary of each system represents the maximum and the lower boundary the minimum dynamic level. The continuous line depicts all intermediate levels and the transition from one level to another. Moreover, the dotted vertical lines connect these two systems to the instrumental notation system. *Ferneyhough's* approach towards the notation of the delay effect is presented in Figure 29.

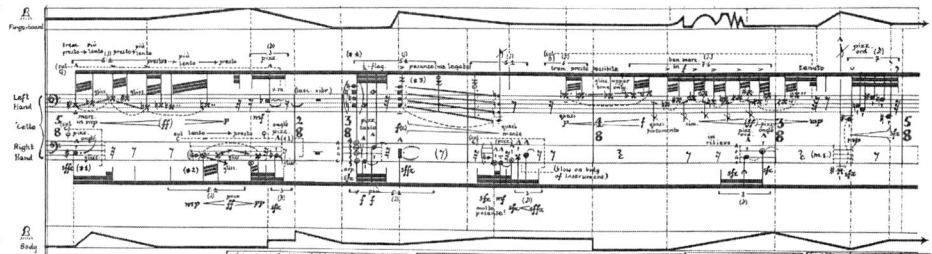

Fig. 29 Ferneyhough, Time, p. 1.

As is apparent, this method resembles *Nono's* approach towards the notation of a harmonizer (cf. Chapter »1. 4. 2 The harmonizer«) and may also be described as simple. However, the depiction of the dynamic level is inexact since only two reference points, the maximum and minimum volume, are given. Further, the parameter delay time cannot be controlled and no feedback or pan potentiometer is applied. Therefore, another approach needs to be adopted here. It resembles the notation of the reverberation envelope (cf. Figure 25) and is presented in Figure 30. The sound source, a minim »a¹/A4«, is produced by an unspecified instrument. The delay time is depicted by means of a single lined notation system with no clef whilst the white dots (◇) describe the delay time in relation to the first triggering and the black dots (◆) the delay time in relation to the last triggering. The first dot of a kind shows when the delay is triggered and the second dot displays the delay time with regard to this triggering. Additionally, the panoramic potentiometer is notated by means of symbols introduced in Chapter »2. 2. 3 Panning and its notation«. Two notation systems are employed here in order to depict a stereo delay. The upper system makes use of three different delay times: a crotchet (delay 1), a dotted quaver (delay 2) and a semiquaver (delay 3). These delay times are initially determined by the first and second white dot. Since the delay times are, in the example, not altered, the respective black dots depict the same delay times with regard to the last triggering. The panoramic potentiometer is initially set at the left (position 3) and gradually adjusted to the right (position 2) for the duration of dotted minim. Finally, the feedback is set at 20%. The signal is at the same time fed to another delay depicted by the lower system. Here only a sin-

---

[73] Cf. Maempel, Audiobearbeitung, pp. 748-751 and Izhaki, Audio, pp. 383-395.

[74] Brian Ferneyhough: Time and motion study II. For solo 'cello and electronics. London 1978.

[75] Ferneyhough, Time, no page named [foreword].

gle delay time is used, which is in the beginning determined as a dotted quaver. However, in this case, the delay time is supposed to be constantly changed. The transition from one delay time to another is, similarly to the transition of the panning, depicted by means of an arrow. In the example, the new delay time of a semiquaver is reached simultaneously with the last triggering. The pan potentiometer here is constantly set at the right (position 4) while the feedback is initially set at 35% and decreased to 20% for the duration of a minim. The intensity of the dry signal constantly amounts to 35% while the intensities of the wet signals are set at 35% (delay 1) and 45% (delay 2) of the overall output level.

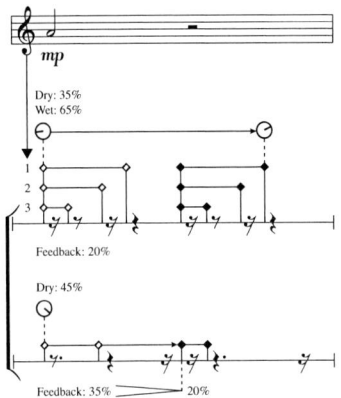

Fig. 30 The stereo delay.

The delay of the last triggering starts right after the sound production has ended, but is actually triggered by the very last sound wave. It therefore needs to be understood as slightly shifted in time. Furthermore, the approach presented in Figure 30 needs to be elaborated when the delay time is supposed to be changed, for instance, after a continuous sound production has begun. Such an event is presented in Figure 31. The sound subject to the delay here is a semibreve »a¹/A4« and the initial delay time of a mono delay set at a dotted quaver. The last triggering of the first delay time is reached after a crotchet. It is from this point on changed to the delay time of a crotchet. The first triggering of the new delay time is reached after a minim and a semiquaver. It is last triggered when the sound ends.

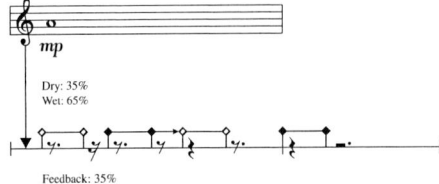

Fig. 31 Complex alteration of the delay time.

When the delay time is supposed to be changed before the last triggering of the previous delay time has faded, the method of depiction does even have to be further elaborated. In Figure 32 such an elaboration is presented. The last triggering of the first delay time is again reached after a crotchet. However, in this case, the first triggering of the new delay is already reached after a dotted crotchet while the new delay time amounts to a dotted crotchet and a semiquaver.

284

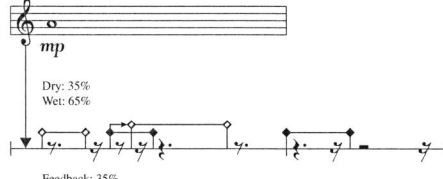

Fig. 32 Altering the delay time directly after the last triggering.

Another special case would occur if the delay time was larger than the duration of the delayed sound. In such a case, the first black dot would have to be placed before the second white dot. Further, when wishing to employ very small delay times, it might be inadequate to depict these by means of traditional durations. In such cases, the method of depiction needs to be altered. Figure 33 presents the notation of small delay times. Only two dots are used her to describe the duration of the delay. The white dots (◊) represent the first triggering and the black dots (◆) the last triggering of the delay. Three mono delays are employed in the example. The delay time of the first delay is constantly set at 80 ms. The delay time of the second delay is initially set at 55 ms and increased to 90 ms for the duration of a dotted crotchet and a semiquaver. The third delay time is initially set at 30 ms. It is decreased to 10 ms for the duration of a dotted minim and a semiquaver.

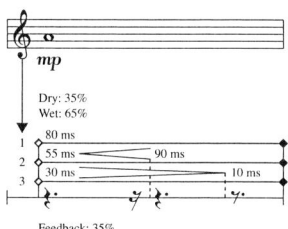

Fig. 33 Small delay times.

Theoretically, any delay time may be depicted by the method introduced in Figure 33. It may also be described as simpler than the notation of the delay solely by means of the time axis. Nevertheless, the notation of the delay time by means of traditional durations is also presented here since it is more illustrative than simply writing the delay time down. Either the two methods may be used in combination or else the second method may be utilised alone.

2. 5. 2 The waveguide filter and its notation

The function of the waveguide filter is explained in Chapter »1. 8. 2 Functional PM by waveguide filtering«. A generic waveguide filter instrument consists of a delay and two filters. A **source** signal is fed into a **bidirectional delay line** and reaches **filter A**. The filtered signal is then **fed back** to the delay and at the same time passed through **filter B**. This line models the effect of a so-called scattering junction, such as a hole in a cylindrical tube or a finger pressed on a string[76]. A waveguide filter is often used to model the action of the resonator in a physical model. The body of a wind instrument, such as the tube of a clarinet, can be analysed as a waveguide to predict the filtering that it imparts to the waveform produced at the mouth-

---

[76] Miranda, Synthesis, pp. 100f.

piece[77]. For further insight into waveguide filtering please refer to *Miranda*[78] and *Dodge and Jerse*[79]. For further applications of waveguide filtering please refer to *Smith*[80].

The waveguide filter presented in Figure 34 is a very simple example of the application of such a chain of effects. The sound source is an unspecified noise. It is at first sent to a delay with a delay time of a semiquaver and a dry and wet ratio of 40% to 60%. The delayed sound is then sent to a low-pass filter (cf. Chapter »2. 3. 1 High-pass, low-pass, band-pass and band-reject filters«). The cut-off frequency of the filter is »eb3/Eb6« (~ 1,245 Hz), the ordinal number *n* amounts to 4 and the quality is set at 8. The delayed and filtered signal is subsequently fed back to the delay with a feedback factor of 30% and passed through a second low-pass filter. The cut-off frequency of this filter is set at »a2/A5« (880 Hz), the ordinal number at 2 and the Q at 12.

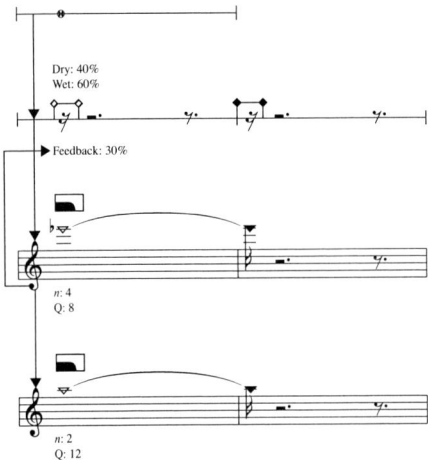

Fig. 34 The waveguide filter.

The noisy sound source is applied here in order to give a simple example of a generic waveguide filter. In physical modelling the sources are normally synthetic sounds produced by means of sound synthesis techniques and derived from the analysis of the instrument to be modelled. References concerning the production of the sources are presented in the chapter on waveguide filtering.

2. 6 The chorus-, flanging- and phasing-effects

The modulation of delay lines results in the effects called **chorus**, **flanging** and **phasing**. These three effects are discussed in this chapter.

2. 6. 1 The chorus-effect and its notation

The chorus-effect simulates the slight differences in pitch and loudness as they occur when, for instance, a choir sings the same tone with the same dynamic level. Similar deviations in amplitude and pitch can be achieved by layering several phase and amplitude modulated sig-

[77] Dodge and Jerse, Computer, p. 280.

[78] Miranda, Synthesis, pp. 100-102.

[79] Dodge and Jerse, Computer, pp. 280-283.

[80] Julius O. Smith: Physical modeling using digital waveguides. In: Computer Music Journal, vol. 16(4). Massachusetts 1992, pp. 74-91.

nals[81]. The **delay time** is set here between 10 and 50 ms[82]. Moreover, the technique entails the use of several variable delay lines connected in parallel[83]. A **low frequency oscillator** (LFO) is applied to each delayed signal. It is utilised to create the ***tremolo*-effect** by employing a **small modulation index *m*** and sine or triangle waves. The ratio between the direct original signal and the modulated signal is expressed by the parameters **dry and wet**. Additionally, a **feedback** may be employed[84]. The notation of the chorus effect can be achieved by combining the method of depiction for small delay times (cf. Figure 33) and a variation of the method used to notate the *tremolo*-effect (cf. Figure 23 in the chapter on sound synthesis).

A suggestion for the notation of the chorus-effect is presented in Figure 35. The sound source is an unspecified instrument. It is passed through a line of delays. The delay time of the first delay is constantly set at 10 ms, the delay time of the second delay is increased from initially 25 ms to 40 ms for the duration of a dotted crotchet and a semiquaver while the delay time of the third delay is decreased from initially 30 ms to 10 ms for the duration of a dotted minim and a semiquaver. These delayed signals are then amplitude modulated by means of a sine wave LFO. The frequency of the oscillator is »4A/A–2« (~ 6.9 Hz) and the modulation index *m* is constantly set at 0.2. The modulator here is, in opposition to the method of notation used for amplitude modulation, depicted by the lower system because the signal is at first delayed and then modulated. Additionally, a feedback is applied. It is written underneath the effect and amounts to 35%. The dry and wet ratio is written above the effect and set at 35% to 65%. Hence the loudness of the original signal here amounts to 35% of the overall output level whilst the loudness of the transformed signal amounts to 65% of the overall output level.

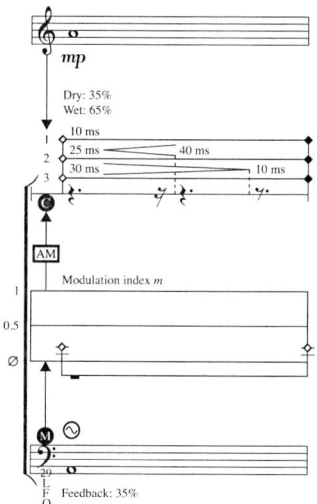

Fig. 35 The chorus-effect.

2. 6. 2 The flanging-effect and its notation

The flanging-effect was first discovered when playing two copies of the same audio signal on two tape recorders and reducing the speed of one tape with the thumb. By the slower play-

---

[81] Cf. Zoelzer, Signalverarbeitung, p. 840.

[82] Or, alternatively, 10 and 25 ms, as in Pierre Dutilleux and Udo Zoelzer: Delays. In: Udo Zoelzer (ed.): DAFX. Digital audio effects. Chichester 2002, pp. 63-74, here: p. 70.

[83] Dodge and Jerse, Computer, p. 304.

[84] Cf. Izhaki, Audio, p. 401.

back, the pitch of the tape decreased, which created the flanging-effect. Generally speaking, in this kind of modulation a reflection is superimposed on a direct signal whilst the reflection's period is slowly altered[85]. The **delay time** is set here between 1 and 15 ms[86]. A typical use of this configuration is to apply a function of time to the delay input that sweeps the amount of delay[87]. In place of manual pressure on a tape reel, the delay time of an electronic flanger is varied by an **LFO**, usually emitting a sine or triangle wave. The intensity of the delay time modulation is determined by the **amount of variation**[88] while the parameters **dry and wet** control the ratio between the direct original signal and the delayed signal, determining the prominence of the flanging effect[89]. Additionally, a **feedback** may be applied[90].

A suggestion for the notation of the flanging-effect is presented in Figure 36. It resembles the notation of the chorus-effect (cf. Figure 35). The delay time is again notated by the method of depiction for small delay times (cf. Figure 33) and set at 7 ms. The LFO is emitting a sine wave at »$_4$A/A–2« (~ 6.9 Hz), which is modulating the delay time. The amount of variation is described here in per cent by a diagrammatic notation system. The x-axis of this system represents the time whilst the y-axis depicts the amount of variation from »∅« to 100 percent in 10 + 1 steps. Hence the white dots (◇) depict the amount of variation in time. In the example, it is set at 30%. When more exact values are required, they can be notated above the system (cf. Figure 22 in the chapter on sound synthesis). The feedback is written underneath the lowest system and set at 35% whilst the dry and wet ratio is written above the highest system and set at 35% to 65%.

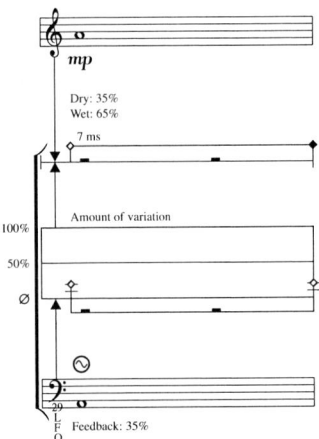

Fig. 36 The flanging-effect.

2. 6. 3 The phasing-effect and its notation

The phasing-effect is similar to the effect a flanger creates. However, the time variable delay is realised here by a line of **all-pass filters** [▨]. These filters, instead of altering the amplitude of specific frequencies, shift their phase. The delayed signal is then superimposed on the original signal. First order all-pass filters are normally used for the phasing-effect. The **phase**

---

[85] Zoelzer, Signalverarbeitung, pp. 840f.

[86] Dutilleux, Delays, p. 70.

[87] Dodge and Jerse, Computer, pp. 303f.

[88] Cf. Roads, Tutorial, pp. 437f.

[89] Dodge and Jerse, Computer, p. 304.

[90] Cf. Izhaki, Audio, p. 403.

shift of each filter reaches from 0° to −180°[91] while the parameters **dry and wet** control the ratio between the direct original signal and the phased signal. The phasing effect is the greatest when both signals are at equal gain[92]. Additionally, a **feedback** may be employed[93]. The notation of the phasing-effect suggested here resembles the notation of small delay times (cf. Figure 33). However, in this case, the delay is expressed by means of the phase shift in increments of ten. Further, the symbol for all-pass filters is employed. In the example, six filters with a constant phase shift of −50°, −70°, −90°, −110°, −130° and −150° are utilised. Further, the dry and wet signals are at equal gain and the feedback is set at 35%.

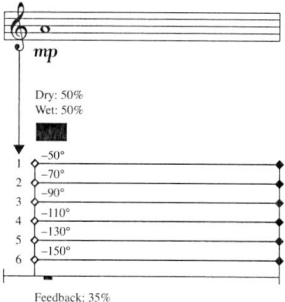

Fig. 37 The phasing-effect.

2. 7 Distortion

Every distortion is non-linear, meaning that input and output are disproportional. It is normally created by overdriving amplifier stages in preamplifiers, power amplifiers or effects units[94]. This chapter focuses on **digital and analogue distortion** as well as on an artefact of digital audio: **distortion by bit depth and sampling rate reduction**.

2. 7. 1 Digital and analogue distortion and its notation

When an audio signal is distorted, it is – according to the **gain** – heavily deformed or subject to clipping[95]. In the case of the input signal being a single frequency, harmonic distortion occurs. When the input waveform consists of signals at two or more distinct frequencies, a further type of distortion will occur, in which the amplitudes of each of the signals will be modulated to some extent by the frequency of the others. This type of distortion is called intermodulation distortion[96]. Distortion produced within a digital system may differ from distortion produced within an analogue system. This is because the highest frequency a digital system can accommodate is the *Nyquist* frequency, which is always half the sampling rate. Any content produced within the system that exceeds the *Nyquist* frequency is mirrored around it and creates aliasing frequencies below it. This effect can be avoided by using higher sampling rates. Some digital distortion-effects are also able to cope with this problem by internal up-sampling and the employment of an **anti-aliasing** filter. On an analogue system aliasing does not occur, but frequencies above 20 kHz are simply inaudible[97]. The various

---

[91] Zoelzer, Signalverarbeitung, pp. 841f.

[92] Strange, Systems, p. 205.

[93] Cf. Maempel, Audiobearbeitung, p. 756.

[94] Maempel, Audiobearbeitung, p. 747.

[95] Ibid., p. 747.

[96] John Linsey Hood: Audio electronics. 2nd edition. Oxford et al. 1997, pp. 284f.

[97] Cf. Izhaki, Audio, pp. 456f.

amplifiers or effects units differ mainly by their characteristic curve, which is responsible for the shaping of distinct series of overtones[98]. The properties of two large groups of operational amplifiers are determined by the choice of the input amplifying device, called **bipolar transistor** or **field-effect transistor**[99]. In a bipolar transistor the current flows through two types of semiconductor material, whereas in field-effect transistors the current flows only in one type of semiconductor material[100]. Digital and analogue distortion may be notated similarly. In the case of employing a digital device, it needs to be outlined whether anti-aliasing is employed or not.

In Figure 38 the sound produced by an unspecified instrument is subject to distortion. It produces an »a¹/A4« with the dynamic level *mezzopiano*. A bipolar transistor is used to create the distortion. The gain is depicted by means of a diagrammatic notation system. The x-axis of this system represents the time whilst the y-axis depicts the gain from »∅« to 48 dB in increments of three. Hence the white dots (◊) depict the gain factor in time. It is increased from »∅« to 33 dB for the duration of a dotted minim and subsequently decreased to 12 db for the duration of a crotchet. Additionally, in the case of utilising a digital effects unit, the direction (no) anti-aliasing should be written over the diagrammatic system.

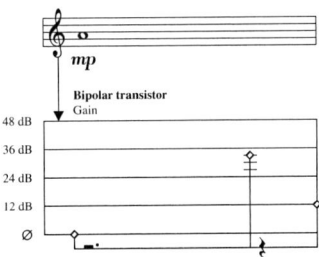

Fig. 38 Digital and analogue distortion.

2.7.2 Distortion by bit depth and sampling rate reduction and its notation

There are distortion-effects that employ artefacts of digital audio. In the case of the distortion by bit reduction and sampling rate reduction, the audio signal is transformed by reducing the **bit depth** and/or the **sampling rate**[101]. The bit depth and sampling rate are fundamentals of digital audio (cf. Chapter »2. Audio processing«). A suggestion for the notation of distortion by bit depth and sampling rate reduction is presented in Figure 39. An unspecified instrument is again subject to the transformation. The bit depth is depicted by means of a diagrammatic system. The x-axis of this system represents the time whilst the y-axis depicts the bit depth from »∅« to 20 in increments of one. Hence the white dots (◊) depict the bit depth in time. In the case of the bit depth reduction being »∅«, the original bit depth is supposed to be employed. The sampling rate reduction is described by means of the ratio between the original sampling rate and the reduced sampling rate. In the example, the original sampling rate is defined as 48 kHz. In the beginning, the bit depth is set at 15. It is decreased for the duration of a dotted minim to 8 and subsequently increased to 12 for the duration of a crotchet. The reduced sampling rate initially amounts to 10:1 (4,800 Hz). It is changed to 15:1 (3,200 Hz) for the duration of a dotted minim. A *crescendo* symbol is utilised to depict this change of the

---

[98] Maempel, Audiobearbeitung, p. 747.

[99] Jiří Dostál: Operational amplifiers. 2nd edition. Boston et al. 1993, p. 27.

[100] N. F. Thornhill: An introduction to analogue electronics with practical demonstrations. London et al. 1997, pp. 112 and 114.

[101] Cf. Izhaki, Audio, p. 461 and Maempel, Audiobearbeitung, pp. 749f.

sampling rate. This is because by lowering the sampling rate, the intensity of the distortion is increased.

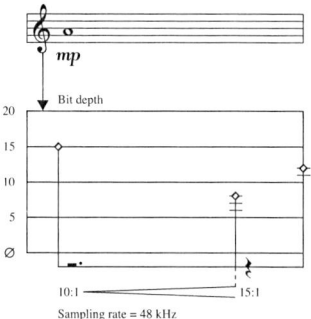

Fig. 39 Distortion by bit depth and sampling rate reduction.

2. 8 Other audio processing techniques

There are some effects units that are mainly used in the field of mastering, which is regarded here as part of the interpretation process when producing electroacoustic music for fixed media. The most important tools are the **enhancer**, the **compressor and limiter**, the **expander** and the **noise gate**. These units are merely introduced in this chapter. When wishing to notate them, the basic parameters mentioned here should be depicted in accordance with all other techniques presented in this work.

2. 8. 1 The enhancer

Enhancers or exciters are, similarly to distortion effects, used for the creation of harmonics. In this case, an enrichment of the timbre is, however, perceived instead of a distinct artefact. An enhancer creates harmonics from filtered parts of the original audio signal. Normally, **high-pass or band-pass filters** are employed (cf. Chapter » 2. 3. 1 High-pass, low-pass, band-pass and band-reject filters«). The parameters of such a unit are the **cut-off frequency**, the **ordinal number** n, the **quality**, the **intensity** of the harmonic production as well as the **dry and wet** ratio[102].

2. 8. 2 The compressor and limiter

A compressor is an amplifier whose **gain** is controlled by its input signal. One use of a compressor is to keep the output relatively constant. When the input signal rises above a specified upper bound, the compressor attenuates the gain[103]. The **threshold** defines the level above which the gain reduction starts[104] while the **compression ratio** describes the ratio of the input signal's change versus the output signal's change when the input signal overshoots the threshold. A linear amplifier has a compression ratio of 1:1. A ratio of, for instance, 4:1 means that a 4 dB change in the input signal causes only a 1 dB change in the output signal. Increasing the parameter called the **knee** smoothes the transition from the performance below to the performance above the threshold. Inside the compressor, a detector circuit monitors the amplitude of the input signal. It can either respond to the **peak** or **the root mean square** amplitude of the input. The **attack** describes the time the compressor needs for the gain reduction once the sig-

---

[102]Maempel, Audiobearbeitung, p. 748.
[103]Roads, Tutorial, p. 391.
[104]Izhaki, Audio, p. 279.

nal has overshot the threshold whilst the **release** describes the time the compressor needs for returning the original gain factor when the threshold is undershot again[105].

2.8.3 The expander

An expander is the opposite of a compressor. The **gain** is controlled by its input signal. When the input signal rises above the **threshold**, the expander increases the gain. An **expander ratio** of, for instance, 1:4 means that a 1 dB change in the input signal causes a 4 dB change in the output when the input signal overshoots the threshold. The **knee** smoothes the transition from the performance below the threshold. The **peak** or **root mean square** button, as well as the **attack** and **decay** time, are normally part of an expander[106].

2.8.4 The noise gate

Finally, noise gates work with **two thresholds** called the **opening threshold** and the **closing threshold**. The signal below the closing threshold is attenuated by the parameter **gain** whilst the signal above the opening threshold is not changed at all. Two thresholds need to be introduced because fluctuations in level would cross the threshold in both directions many times over a short period of time. This would cause rapid opening and closing of the gate, which would produce a type of distortion called chattering. To allow quick opening once the signal exceeds the threshold, the level detection on most gates is based on **peak-sensing**. The **attack** controls how quickly the gate opens and the **release** how quickly the gate closes while the parameter **hold** determines how long the gate's gain reduction is held unaltered. Once the hold period is completed, the release phase starts[107].

---

[105]Roads, Tutorial, pp. 392-394 and Maempel, Audiobearbeitung, pp. 731f.
[106]Cf. Maempel, Audiobearbeitung, pp. 739-741 and Roads, Tutorial, p. 394.
[107]Cf. Izhaki, Audio, pp. 340-349.

3. SOUND RECORDING

Whenever audio processing techniques are applied to non-synthetic material, the sound needs to be recorded before it can be transformed. Moreover, instruments are often picked up in concerts in order to amplify their sound or store the performance on fixed media and field recordings used as musical material in a composition. Whenever employing microphones, the type of microphone, the recording technique and the recording room have a great influence on the quality of the recording. The chapter on sound recording focuses on these factors and presents suggestions for the notation of recording sound. With regard to microphones, the essential transducer types and polar patterns as well as various construction types are examined. Further, monophonic/stereophonic/multichannel recording techniques and their disposal in concerts are discussed, the application of the recording techniques is explained with regard to instrumental and non-instrumental sound sources and the impact of the recording room is examined. There are also elements that are not explained in this chapter, but must be considered when creating a recording. These are, for instance, the utilisation of wind shields, pop screens or noise reduction as well as the influence of the power supply or choice of cable. These elements are regarded here as subject to interpretation. Furthermore, no detailed introduction to orchestral recording is given in order to limit the extent of the work. For insight into these topics please refer to *Bartlett*[1], *Borwick*[2], *Gayford*[3] or *Schneider*[4].

3. 1 Microphones

In order to understand how sound may be recorded, it is necessary to be aware of the different **transducer types and polar patterns** a microphone can have. The behaviour of a microphone may mainly be defined by means of these two factors. Further, there are various **construction types** that effect the standard microphones.

3. 1. 1 Transducer types and polar patterns

The transmission characteristics of microphones result from the complex behaviour of the acoustic-mechanic-electric conversion. There are five main operating principles: **1. Condenser** or **capacitor microphones**. The transducer of a condenser microphone operates as a variable capacitor formed by the diaphragm and the back electrode. The distance between both electrodes varies as the diaphragm is excited by sound signals. The conversion of acoustic information via mechanical vibrations into electrical signals requires additional electrical biasing. A signal has to be applied to the transducer, acting as a carrier that is modulated by variations of the transducer's capacitance. Two alternative operating principles are used to achieve this: the low-frequency method and the radio-frequency method. Low-frequency condenser microphones use DC biasing and a carrier with frequency zero whilst radio-frequency condenser microphones apply a high-frequency signal[5]. The condenser microphone is the preferred type for stereo recording because it generally has a wide smooth frequency response, a detailed sound quality and high sensitivity[6]. Moreover, high-frequency signals and high dyna-

---

[1] Bruce Bartlett: Stereo microphone techniques. Stoneham 1991.

[2] John Borwick: Microphones. Technology and technique. London and Boston 1990.

[3] Michael Gayford (ed.): Microphone engineering handbook. Oxford et al. 1994.

[4] Martin Schneider: Mikrofone [Microphones]. In: Stefan Weinzierl (ed.): Handbuch der Audiotechnik [Handbook of audio engineering]. Berlin et al. 2008, pp. 315-419.

[5] Manfred Hibbing: High-quality RF condenser microphones. In: Michael Gayford (ed.): Microphone engineering handbook. Oxford et al. 1994, pp. 158-186, here: p. 158.

[6] Bartlett, Stereo, p. 4.

mic levels (up to ca. 130 dB) may be transmitted by this type of microphone[7]. **2. Electro-dynamic microphones**. In an electrodynamic microphone a conductor is suspended in the magnetic field of a permanent magnet. The conductor is moved by sound waves exciting it and induces a voltage. Two different types have been established, the moving coil and the ribbon microphone[8]. In a moving coil microphone a voice coil attached to a diaphragm is suspended in a magnetic field[9]. Units normally have near-cylindrical cases with a diaphragm close to the front face behind protective grilles or openings, with bass equalising tube/barometric leak and connectors at the far ends. The resonance of the moving-coil system in free air is 200-500 Hz, but the overall response is substantially flat[10]. In a ribbon microphone a flat moving conductor is suspended in a transverse magnetic field. The ribbon can be made from very thin light metal foil and meets one of the basic criteria for a microphone, which is that the moving system should be of low mass, so as to allow a good transient response, and to be as near as possible a match to the air load[11]. A ribbon microphone can linearly transmit frequencies up to ca. 10-15 kHz[12]. **3. Piezoelectric, crystal** or **ceramic microphones**. In a piezoelectric microphone certain crystalline elements generate an electrical potential between the opposing sides of their structure when mechanically deformed. Typically, crystal rods are agglutinated and on both sides furnished with conductive foil. A diaphragm transmits the sound waves to the crystal that is as a result bent. This bending leads to a voltage variation in an amplifier. Piezoelectric elements are, for instance, used in hydrophones and as pick-ups for plate reverberators or instruments[13]. They are used in hydrophones because the material is a better match to the medium than other transducer types. Further, they have the advantage that they can be completely sealed[14]. Piezoelectric microphones normally have a frequency response from 80 to 6,500 Hz, but can be made to have a flat response up to 16 kHz[15]. **4. Electromagnetic microphones**. These microphones make use of a horseshoe magnet that is wound with a coil. The vibrations of the diaphragm influence the magnetic flux and induce an AC voltage. The electromagnetic principle cannot be used for high-quality transducers, but is particularly employed in pick-ups for electric string instruments[16]. **5. Contact micro-phones**. Contact microphones are designed to sense, for instance, the vibrations of the body of a musical instrument to produce an electrical signal[17]. In a contact microphone a diaphragm is moved by sound waves and actuates a contact. Carbon microphones make use of this principle[18]. They consist of several hundred small carbon granules that are held in close contact in a brass cup called a button, which is attached to the centre of a metallic diaphragm. Sound waves striking the surface of the diaphragm disturb the carbon granules, changing the

---

[7] Schneider, Mikrofone, p. 323.

[8] Ibid., p. 320.

[9] Bartlett, Stereo, p. 5.

[10] Michael Gayford: Microphone techniques. In: Michael Gayford (ed.): Microphone engineering handbook. Oxford et al. 1994, pp. 1-61, here: pp. 38f.

[11] Ibid., p. 42.

[12] Schneider, Mikrofone, pp. 320f.

[13] Schneider, Mikrofone, p. 139 and David Huber: Microphone manual. Design and application. Boston and London 1988, p. 22.

[14] Torben Nielsen: Precision microphones for measurements and sound reproduction. In: Michael Gayford (ed.): Microphone engineering handbook. Oxford et al. 1994, pp. 62-139, here: p. 63.

[15] Glen Ballou et al.: Microphones. In: Glen Ballou (ed.): Handbook for sound engineers. Amsterdam et al. 2008, pp. 489-594, here: p. 503.

[16] Schneider, Mikrofone, p. 328.

[17] Watkinson, Art, p. 145.

[18] Schneider, Mikrofone, p. 318.

contact resistance between their surfaces. A battery or DC power source is connected in series with the button and an audio impedance-matching transformer. The change in contact resistance makes the current from the power supply vary in amplitude. The result is a current waveform similar to the acoustic waveform striking the diaphragm. The signal quality of these types of microphones is low and the frequency range restricted. Carbon microphones have very limited frequency response, are very noisy and have high distortion[19]. They are primarily used in communications since carbon microphones match the required frequency range of telephones, which is 300 to 3,400 Hz[20]. There are, further, other transducer types – such as thermophones, gas microphones, optical microphones and digital microphones – that are either only of historical significance or not commonly used[21]. They are, therefore, not discussed here. Please refer for further insight to *Gayford*[22] or *Schneider*[23].

Furthermore, microphones differ in the way they respond to sounds coming from different directions. Some respond the same to sounds from all directions, others have different output levels for sources at different angles around the microphone. This varying sensitivity versus angle can be graphed as polar pattern. There are three major polar patterns: **1. Omnidirectional**. An omnidirectional microphone is equally sensitive to sounds arriving from all directions. **2. Unidirectional**. A unidirectional microphone is most sensitive to sounds arriving from one direction, in front of the microphone, and discriminates all sounds entering the sides or rear. It can be further divided into four patterns: **A. Wide cardioid**. A microphone with a wide cardioid pattern is sensitive to sounds arriving from a broad angle in front of the microphone. It is 3 dB less sensitive at ±90°, 6 dB less sensitive at ±132° and has a null[24] at 180° off axis[25]. The wide cardioid pattern is 8 dB down at this point. **B. Cardioid**. It is 3dB less sensitive at ±65°, 6 dB less sensitive at ±90° and has a null at 180° off axis. This pattern is the only one that completely rejects sounds entering the rear. **C. Supercardioid**. The supercardioid pattern is 3 dB down at ±57°, 6 dB down at ±78° and 8.6 dB down at ±90° off axis. It has two nulls at ±126° and is 11.7 dB down at 180° off axis. **D. Hypercardioid**. The hypercardioid pattern is 3 dB down at ±52°, 6 dB down at ±70° and 12 dB down at ±90° off axis. It has two nulls at ±110° and is 6 dB less sensitive at 180° off axis. **3. Bidirectional or figure-of-eight**. A bidirectional microphone is most sensitive to sounds arriving from two directions, in front of and behind the microphone. It is 3 dB down at ±45°, 6 dB down at ±60° and has two nulls at ±90° off axis. Sounds entering the front and the rear are treated equally. This pattern is the only one that completely rejects sounds entering the side[26].

The polar pattern is related to two different microphone types: 1. The pressure transducer. This is a capsule system in which only one side of the diaphragm is exposed to the sound field. The diaphragm is sensitive to pressure variations on its surface regardless of the sound source's direction. The resultant pick-up pattern is omnidirectional. 2. The pressure-gradient transducer. This is similar to the pressure transducer, except for a difference between the front and back of the diaphragm which is created by admitting acoustic energy to the rear of the diaphragm. This enables directionality. The time difference between the sound entering the front and the rear is the criterion for the angle of entry. Pressure-gradient transducers are

---

[19] Ballou, Microphones, pp. 502f.

[20] Schneider, Mikrofone, p. 319.

[21] Cf. ibid., pp. 328f.

[22] Gayford, Techniques, pp. 140-157 (optical microphones).

[23] Schneider, Mikrofone, pp. 328-330.

[24] Point of least pick-up.

[25] Away from the front.

[26] Schneider, Mikrofone, pp. 330-332 and Bartlett, Stereo, pp. 1-4.

microphones with a unidirectional or bidirectional polar pattern[27]. Most hydrophones are constructed as pressure transducers with an omnidirectional polar response[28]. However, there are attachments that can give omnidirectional hydrophones a directivity close to a supercardioid[29]. Condenser and moving-coil microphones may be designed to be either a pressure or pressure-gradient pick-up device[30]. The ribbon microphone is in principle a pressure-gradient transducer with a bidirectional polar response. However, special constructions allow the realisation of other polar patterns[31]. Additionally, there are microphones with selectable polar patterns. The polar pattern of a transducer may be varied either mechanically, by opening or closing the capsule, or electrically, by combining two or more transducers. The construction of a mechanically varying microphone involves, however, a higher effort than the combination of transducers, and the proximity effect[32] is less intense when using double diaphragm microphones[33].

3. 1. 1. 1 Previous methods of notation

The utilisation of microphones is normally explained by means of a circuit plan, displayed in the foreword of a work. However, in most cases, the microphone type is not determined[34]. An example of a circuit diagram with determined microphone types can, however, be found in *Stockhausen's* »Mikrophonie I«. As is apparent from Figure 1, a condenser microphone is employed in this work. This condenser microphone is supposed to have a high directional sensitivity[35].

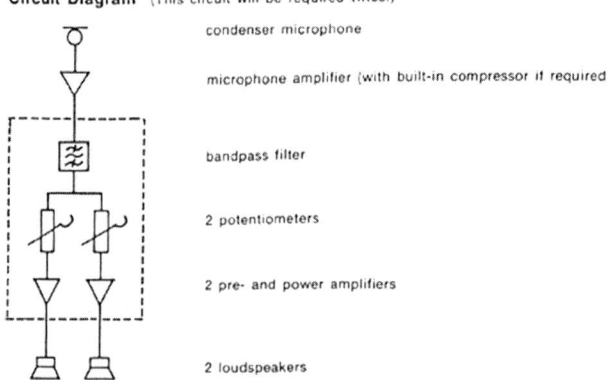

Circuit Diagram (This circuit will be required twice.)

condenser microphone

microphone amplifier (with built-in compressor if required)

bandpass filter

2 potentiometers

2 pre- and power amplifiers

2 loudspeakers

Fig. 1 Stockhausen, Mikrophonie I, p. 10.

---

[27] Huber, Manual, p. 20 and Jörg Wuttke: Mikrofonaufsätze [Microphone essays]. 2nd, extended edition. Karlsruhe 2000, pp. 12-14.

[28] Cf. *Brüel and Kjær* hydrophones 8103, 8104, 8105 and 8106, *Sonar Surround* hydrophones Ambient TC4013, TC4032 and TC4042 or *Aquarian Audio Products* hydrophones H1a-3, H1b, H2a-3 and H2b.

[29] For example, the *Sonar Surround* directivity sphere.

[30] Huber, Manual, pp. 9 and 20.

[31] Schneider, Mikrofone, p. 321.

[32] Many directional microphones show an increase in their bass response as the signal source is brought closer to the microphone capsule. This phenomenon starts to become noticeable when the source is brought within 30 cm of the microphone and increases as the distance decreases.

[33] Schneider, Mikrofone, pp. 336-339.

[34] Cf. Halffter, Noche, no page named [foreword], Schnebel, Stimmen, p. 6 or Kagel, Tremens, pp. II and IV.

[35] Stockhausen, Mikrophonie I, p. 10.

Further, in »Time and motion study« *Ferneyhough* inter alia employs contact microphones. They are depicted by means of an illustration of a cello. By doing so, it can be quite exactly defined where the microphone is supposed to be attached. As is apparent from Figure 2, two contact microphones are attached to the body of the instrument, one below the right F hole and one on or below the fingerboard:

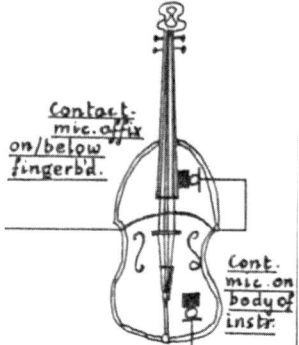

Fig. 2 Ferneyhough, Time, no page named [foreword].

3. 1. 1. 2 Discussion

Stockhausen's explanation of the microphone (cf. Figure 1) is quite exact since he determines the transducer type and approximately defines the polar pattern. Moreover, the depiction of the microphone type in the foreword is adequate when the circuit remains unchanged during a piece, meaning that, for instance, each instrument is only picked up by a single microphone in the course of a piece. However, when, for instance an instrument is supposed to be picked up by one microphone in the first movement and another microphone in the second movement, it may become necessary to depict the microphones in the score. In such cases, *Stockhausen's* method of notation would result in a lack of instantaneous comprehension. Further, *Ferneyhough's* approach towards the employment of contact microphones (cf. Figure 2) may be regarded as simple and exact. He clearly indicates what type of microphone is supposed to be used and where it should be attached. Further, the illustration of the contact microphone could also serve as a symbolic representation of the microphone type in the score.

3. 1. 1. 3 Suggestion for the notation of transducer types and polar patterns

Since *Stockhausen's* method lacks a high degree of instantaneous comprehension and, to some extent, exactness, it needs to be elaborated. This elaboration is presented in Figure 3. It is, on the one hand, more exact concerning the directivity of the microphones because each polar pattern – including all cardioid types – is depicted and, on the other hand, contains a greater degree of instantaneous comprehension since these patterns can be quickly identified by means of their directional response characteristic, which is drawn into the microphone symbol[36]. The polar pattern of the microphones is, from left to right, omnidirectional, wide cardioid, cardioid, supercardioid, hypercardioid and bidirectional. They are further specified by means of two transducer types: condenser (C) and electrodynamic (ED).

C/ED C/ED C/ED C/ED C/ED C/ED

Fig. 3 Standard microphone types.

---

[36] For the polar patterns cf. Ballou, Microphones, p. 493, Bartlett, Stereo, p. 4 and Schneider, Mikrofone, p. 332.

As mentioned, most hydrophones contain a piezoelectric transducer and have an omnidirectional polar pattern. This type of microphone may be depicted similarly to an omnidirectional (or, in the case of employing an attachment, to a supercardioid) microphone while the transducer type should be additionally specified as »PE«. When microphones with selectable polar patterns are supposed to be utilised, it should be noted in the foreword of the work and the switch be requested by using the symbols presented in Figure 3 as well as, optionally, a direction, such as switch. The electromagnetic principle, as mentioned, cannot be used for high-quality transducers. However, it is discussed in the following chapter with regard to pick ups. Further, since *Ferneyhough's* depiction of contact microphones is simple and exact, it serves here as a paradigm for the notation of these microphones. The two microphones in Figure 4 are used in the same way as in »Time and motion study« and hence attached to the body of a cello. They can be distinguished by their index number and can be employed in a score by means of their symbolic representation presented on the right side of the example.

Fig. 4 Contact microphones and their symbolic representations.

3. 1. 2 Construction types and their notation

There are several construction types that influence the behaviour of the standard microphone types. Condenser microphones with a capsule diameter of ca. 25-45 mm are commonly called **large-diaphragm microphones**. They are often constructed as a double diaphragm system by positioning two transducers with a cardioid directivity offset to one another. The larger capsule influences the entering sound waves more than smaller microphones, which results in a less linear frequency response. These kinds of microphones are often used for voice recordings since they are, due to the larger capsule, less sensitive to wind or popping noise[37]. Large-diaphragm microphones are, moreover, either constructed as condenser or electrodynamic microphones and are depicted here by means of a larger polar pattern:

C/ED

Fig. 5 Large-diaphragm microphone.

Lapel microphones cover a wide class of units that are mounted on a neck cord/tie or are otherwise attached to the person in the vicinity of the chest. They are mainly used for voice

---

[37] Schneider, Mikrofone, p. 343.

recordings because they guarantee a constant microphone distance and that the speaker can move freely. Lapel microphones that are attached directly in front of the chest are called **lava-lier microphones**. Pressure transducers are the preferred type of lapel microphones[38]. Hence the polar pattern is normally omnidirectional. Lapel microphones may be notated similarly to contact microphones since they also need to be attached to a surface. They can be distinguished from contact microphones because their omnidirectional polar pattern is part of the depiction. In Figure 6 a lapel microphone is attached to a tie. Since it is placed directly in front of the chest, this type of lapel is referred to as a lavalier microphone.

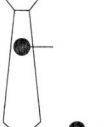

Fig. 6 Lapel/lavalier microphone and its symbolic representation.

Noise-cancelling microphones pick up close-proximity signals while effectively cancelling out high-level background noise[39]. They are often used for picking up vocals in performances. Electrodynamic moving-coil or condenser transducer types can be used for these constructions. A noise-cancelling microphone with an omnidirectional polar pattern is less sensitive to wind or popping noise. Further, no proximity effect occurs. However, it is sensitive to noise from all directions. Therefore, pressure-gradient transducers with a cardioid, supercardioid or hypercardioid polar pattern can be utilised if the noise-cancellation of the pressure transducer is insufficient. In order to equalise the proximity effect of this microphone type, the bass frequency response needs to be lowered. Moreover, an additional external wind shield needs to be attached to vocal microphones. Noise-cancelling microphones are often used in conjunction with a hands-free headset-microphone combination[40]. Figure 7 presents the notation of these kinds of microphones. An additional symbol for the default sound source picked up by these microphones complements the polar pattern. The headset-microphone is depicted by augmenting the symbol for the vocal sound. In the example, it has an omnidirectional directivity.

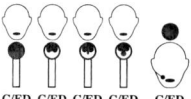

C/ED   C/ED   C/ED   C/ED   C/ED

Fig. 7 Noise-cancelling microphones.

When a pressure transducer is mounted on a big even surface, the sound pressure is doubled for the whole frequency range, effectively increasing the microphone sensitivity or output. Further, comb filter effects, which may occur when the reflected sound is imposed on the direct sound, can be avoided by employing special construction types called **pressure zone microphones** (PZM). In order to achieve a linear frequency response, pressure zone microphones need to be mounted on large surfaces, e. g. floors, walls, big tabletops or the lid of a piano. The sensitivity of the microphone is increased by 6 dB when mounted on such surfaces. It can be further increased by 6 dB when placed close to another boundary, e. g. a wall, or by 12 dB when two boundaries are added, e. g. the corner of a room. Even though the

---

[38] Gayford, Techniques, pp. 53f. and Schneider, Mikrofone, pp. 345f.

[39] Huber, Manual, p. 37.

[40] Cf. Schneider, Mikrofone, pp. 346-349 and John Eargle: The microphone book. Boston et al. 2001, pp. 301f.

acoustic sensitivity rises, the electronic noise of the microphone stays constant. Hence the effective signal-to-noise ratio of the microphone improves 6 dB each time a boundary is added at right angles. The polar pattern of a PZM on a large surface is **hemispherical**, meaning that the microphone picks up equally well in any direction above the surface plane (from ±90° degrees off axis to 0°) at all frequencies[41]. Figure 8 presents the depiction of two PZMs. The first one is mounted on the floor and placed in the corner of a room. Hence its sensitivity is increased by 18 dB. The second microphone is mounted on a piano lid. The installation of these kinds of microphones is explained here, respectively, by means of an illustration of the room and piano. It may be presented in the foreword of a score. Subsequently, pressure zone microphones can be depicted in a score by means of the symbol that represents their hemispherical polar pattern (and, as in Figure 4, by additional numbers, if necessary).

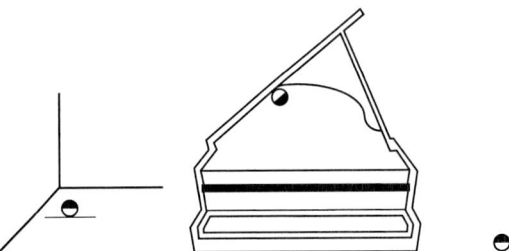

Fig. 8 Pressure zone microphones and their symbolic representation.

Tubular microphones make use of a single or several tubes to increase the directivity. The most common type is a **shotgun** or **rifle microphone**. It consists of a single tube with holes spaced along the length that is mounted in front of the diaphragm. All sound waves impinging at an oblique angle of incidence change their direction of propagation after entering the opening. The sound component at any one opening is out of phase with the sound components entering at any other opening and either attenuated or cancelled[42]. Only waves that incident at angles near the 0° axis will arrive at the diaphragm in phase and not be attenuated. The polar pattern of a shotgun microphone is of lobe-shaped directional characteristic. For the polar diagram to be of similar shape at all frequencies with the response range, the effective tube length must grow shorter with increasingly higher frequencies. For this reason, the side slits are covered with layers of acoustically semitransparent material. However, at frequencies below 500 Hz, the polar diagram becomes broader[43]. The most common transducer type is condenser. The shotgun microphone is, along with the other microphone types, depicted here by means of its directional response characteristic:

c

Fig. 9 Shotgun microphone.

---

[41] Schneider, Mikrofone, pp. 349f. and Bruce Bartlett: The PZM boundary booklet. A basic primer and experimenter's guide. In: David Huber: Microphone manual. Design and application. Boston and London 1988, pp. 239-255, here: pp. 239-242.

[42] As mentioned, phase describes the time relationship between two or more waveforms. It is measured in degrees. One cycle of, for instance, a sine wave signifies 360°, half a cycle 180° etc. Two sine waves of the same frequency, amplitude and phasing cancel each other because the negative and positive amplitude are equal.

[43] Huber, Manual, pp. 34-36, Schneider, Mikrofone, p. 351 and Gayford, Techniques, pp. 54f.

Parabolic or **dish microphones** function as highly directional units that work most effectively within the middle- and high frequency range. They operate by placing an omnidirectional microphone at the focal point of a parabola. The parabola, which is often constructed of clear plexiglass, serves to collect on axis audio signals at this focal point while off axis signals are rejected. The larger the dish, the better the directionality at low frequencies[44]. Parabolic microphones overemphasise high frequencies. This behaviour can be reduced by placing the microphone slightly outside the focal point. However, due to the frequency-dependent overemphasis, parabolic microphones are solely used for far distance sound recordings[45]. In Figure 9 the parabolic microphone is depicted by means of its directional response characteristic and an illustration of the parabola.

Fig. 10 Parabolic microphone.

Pick-ups for instruments are constructed as structure-borne sound microphones according to the electrodynamic or piezoelectric principle. However, when they are supposed to pick up metallic strings, they are constructed according to the electromagnetic principle. Because they are not sensitive to feedback, pick-ups are particularly used for sound sources with a low dynamic level, e. g. contrabasses or acoustic guitars[46]. These kinds of microphones can be depicted by means of the paradigm for contact microphones (cf. Figure 4) and the additions electrodynamic (ED), piezoelectric (PE) or electromagnetic (EM), which distinguish them from the normal contact microphone.

3. 2 Recording techniques

When recording, acoustic signals are – with the help of electroacoustic transducers – converted into electrical signals[47]. Signals can be recorded by using monophonic, stereophonic or multi-channel recording techniques. Besides the type of microphone that is used, the distance between the microphone and the sound source, as well as the angle at which the sound waves incident, influence the sound of the recording. These factors are the **basic elements** of recording sound and here explained by means of monophonic recordings. Further, **stereophonic techniques**, including intensity stereophony, time-of-arrival stereophony, the near-coincident principle, the binaural technique and baffle-derived stereophony are discussed here. Finally, various **multi-microphone arrangements**, such as the soundfield microphone, double MS, the ABC technique and the ICA 3 technique are examined. Other multi-channel techniques cannot be discussed here in detail in order to limit the extent of the work and are, therefore, only introduced. Further, when recording sound during a performance, the **disposal of the microphones** needs to be determined. This matter is discussed in the final chapter.

3. 2. 1 Basic elements (monophonic recordings)

The distance between the microphone and the sound source has great influence on the recording[48]. According to *Huber* there are two categories for the spacing between a microphone

---

[44] Huber, Manual, p. 37.

[45] Schneider, Mikrofone, p. 353.

[46] Ibid., p. 354.

[47] Stefan Weinzierl: Aufnahmeverfahren [Recording techniques]. In: Stefan Weinzierl (ed.): Handbuch der Audiotechnik [Handbook of audio engineering]. Berlin et al. 2008, pp. 551-607, here: p. 551.

[48] Cf. Weinzierl, Aufnahmeverfahren, p. 569.

and its respective source: **1. Distant microphone placement**. This refers to the positioning of a microphone at one or more metres from the source signal. Distant miking is often used in order to record large instrumental ensembles. Microphones that are placed at a large distance from the source strongly transmit the characteristics of the room[49]. This is because when the microphone is placed far from the source, the time difference between direct and reflected sound decreases and the reflections become predominant on the recording[50]. **2. Close microphone placement**. It refers to the positioning of a microphone from about 25 mm to 1 metre from the source[51]. The direct sound is dominant when recording in this way[52]. Close miking serves the need to create a tight, present sound quality and effectively excludes the acoustical environment from being picked up. Moreover, moving a microphone at close working distances can have great influence on the recording and affect the tonal balance[53]. The adjustment of the microphone also has an influence on the spectrum of the recorded signal. Generally, the more the **angle of incidence** deviates from the major axis (0°-direction), the stronger is the roll-off at high frequencies. This behaviour is independent from the polar pattern and the stronger the larger the diaphragm is[54].

3. 2. 1. 1 Previous methods of notation

As can be seen in Figure 11, *Stockhausen*, in »Mikrophonie I«, employs two (highly directional) condenser microphones. He also makes suggestions for the microphone placement and angle of incidence. *Stockhausen* determines three different spacings between the microphone and sound source: 1. Very close. 2. More distant. 3. Far away. A line is used to depict these degrees. The thicker the line, the closer is the microphone to the sound source. The player holding the microphone in his hand is also supposed to perform transitions between the positions, e. g. from very close to more distant. The performers can, within defined limits, determine which spacing is connected to the three positions and perform the piece in that way. Further, *Stockhausen* determines three angles of incidence: 1. Direct. 2. More distant. 3. Indirect. They are depicted by means of the position in the notation system whilst the highest position is related to the first angle of incidence[55]. The articulations are depicted by a special notation system, which is connected to the system that depicts the sound production.

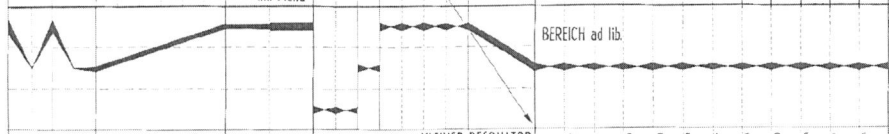

Fig. 11 Stockhausen, Mikrophonie I, Moment "TUTTI 157", p. 2.

The notation of the spacing and angle can be understood from Figure 11. To give an example, the notation starts with a very close microphone placement (thick line) and direct angle (upper system). This is followed by a transition to far away (thin line) and a simultaneous shift to a more distant angle of incidence (middle system). The player is subsequently supposed to move the microphone back to the initial position and angle and then again to the second configuration, before placing the microphone more distant from the sound source

[49] Huber, Manual, pp. 86-89.

[50] Cf. Wuttke, Mikrofonaufsätze, p. 4.

[51] Huber, Manual, p. 89.

[52] Wuttke, Mikrofonaufsätze, p. 4.

[53] Huber, Manual, pp. 89f.

[54] Cf. Weinzierl, Aufnahmeverfahren, pp. 570f.

[55] Cf. Stockhausen, Mikrophonie I, p. 14.

(thicker line) and subsequently performing a slower transition from the more distant angle (middle system) to the direct angle (upper system). The following actions can be described in the same way.

3. 2. 1. 2 Discussion

The notation of the microphone placement and angle of incidence meets the requirement of simplicity and can be used in combination with traditional notation. The relative inexactness with regard to the microphone placement and angle of incidence is a necessity since it is hard to predict how close the spacing of the microphone to the sound source needs to be and how indirect the sound may incident in order to achieve a satisfying result. However, *Stockhausen* does not determine whether all degrees of spacing are related to a close microphone placement or if the third position may be described as distant miking. But since the player holds the microphone in his hand and is supposed to perform fast transitions from very close to far away, it can be assumed that all positions are within the range of 25 mm to 1 m. Further, the notation of the microphone placement by means of lines that vary in thickness may lead to ambiguity, e. g. when only a single microphone placement is employed on a page of the score. In some cases, it might be difficult to determine whether the microphone is, for instance, supposed to be placed far away or more distant from the source. However, even though the spacing and angle of incidence cannot be determined in an exact way, it may be desirable to determine it in a more exact way than *Stockhausen*, e. g. by defining the approximate spacing and depicting the angle in degrees.

3. 2. 1. 3 Suggestion for the notation of the basic elements

In order to depict *Stockhausen's* three spacings, symbols are introduced and the spacings further specified: **1. Very close** *(25 mm to 20 cm)* is represented by the signs »+++«. **2. More distant** (20 to 60 cm) is represented by the signs »++«. **3. Far away** (60 cm to 1m) is represented by the sign »+«. Additionally, a **distant microphone placement** (1 m and further) is notated here by the sign »–«. The spacings may be determined differently and should be regarded as one possible suggestion. Transitions can be depicted by means of a *crescendo* or *decrescendo* symbol. A specific distance for the distant microphone placement is not defined here because it is strongly related to the characteristics of the particular space and needs to be determined by an experienced audio engineer. The depiction of the angle of incidence can be achieved by determining the deviation from the major axis in degrees, e. g. 20° would mean that the angle of incidence amounts to 20 degrees. The **four angles** 0, 20, 40 and 60 degrees are employed here. However, they should be understood as approximate suggestions. Transitions from one position to another can also be depicted by *de-/crescendo* symbols. A suggestion for the notation of the microphone placement and angle of incidence is presented in Figure 12. In the example, a supercardioid electrodynamic microphone is supposed to record unspecified noise for the duration of a breve (for the notation of noise see Chapter »3. 3. 2 Non-instrumental sound sources«). In the beginning, the spacing between the microphone and the sound source is set at 60 cm to 1 m (+). It is then changed to 20 to 60 cm (++) for the duration of a semibreve. The angle of incidence initially amounts to 0 degrees. It is increased for the duration of a breve to approximately 40°.

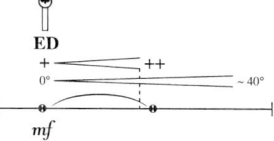

Fig. 12 Microphone placement and angle of incidence.

303

Optionally, these parameters may be controlled by means of an additional single lined notation system or a diagrammatic system. This may be desirable when many changes or an independent control of the parameters are required as well as when wishing to reduce the number of parameters depicted by the system of the sound source. In Figure 13 an example of the independent control of the parameters spacing and angle of incidence is given. The spacing is, in the example, changed from 60 cm to 1 m (+) to 20 cm to 60 cm (++) for the duration of a semibreve and a dotted crotchet. The angle of incidence is changed from 0° to approximately 40° for the duration of a dotted minim and a quaver. Subsequently, the angle of incidence is reduced to approximately 20° for the duration of another dotted minim and a quaver.

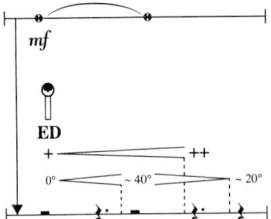

Fig. 13 Variant of notation for the microphone placement and angle of incidence.

3. 2. 2 Stereophonic techniques and their notation

In stereophonic recordings the signals are coded during the recording in such a way that a certain sound and room characteristic is already inherent in the converted signal[56]. The goal of any stereophonic pick-up is to create the illusion of directionality in a recording[57]. This chapter focuses on the notation techniques that are able to create such an effect. For an introduction to the directional perception of human hearing please refer to *Rumsey*[58] and *Huber*[59]. Stereo microphones are microphones that are capable of providing outputs that include directional information about the sound source. This is achieved by the position of the source being coded by the time-of-arrival difference or dynamic level difference. There are three basic ways to produce a stereophonic recording with two microphones: **intensity stereophony** or **the coincident pair principle** (only dynamic level differences), **time-of-arrival stereophony** or **the spaced pair principle** (only time differences), **the near-coincident principle** (level and time differences). Further, two special cases of stereophonic recording can be named, the **binaural principle** (frequency dependent dynamic level differences, specifically for playback via headphones) and **baffle-derived stereophony** (frequency dependent dynamic level differences)[60].

All stereophonic recording techniques in which the left and right channels differ only by dynamic level are called **intensity stereophony**. Since the coincident pick-up is closely spaced, there is no time or phase difference, respectively. For example, a sound source that is louder on the right than on the left channel is localised on the right side. The coincident pair principle can be achieved by means of the XY technique or the MS technique[61]. **The XY technique** utilises a pair of directional microphones, vertically aligned on a common axis and

[56] Cf. Weinzierl, Aufnahmeverfahren, p. 551.

[57] Francis Rumsey: Microphones in stereophonic applications. In: Michael Gayford (ed.): Microphone engineering handbook. Oxford et al. 1994, pp. 349-420, here: p. 349.

[58] Rumsey, Stereophonic, pp. 349-359.

[59] Huber, Manual, pp. 107-110.

[60] Huber, Manual, p. 111 and Weinzierl, Aufnahmeverfahren, p. 572.

[61] Weinzierl, Aufnahmeverfahren, p. 574 and Huber, Manual, p. 114.

set at a specific angle along the horizontal plane[62]. The choice of microphone polar pattern is limited to cardioid, supercardioid, hypercardioid and bidirectional[63]. The microphones are normally set at an included angle reaching from 90° to 135°. Moreover, they should be placed close to the sound source. When a distant pick-up with a large reverberant component is intended, angles up to 180° may be employed[64]. In the case of utilising two bidirectional microphones at an angle of 90°, the technique is referred to as the *Blumlein* or stereosonic technique[65]. Figure 14 presents the notation of the XY technique. Four configurations are depicted: cardioid microphones at an included angle of 100°, supercardioid microphones at an angle of 135°, hypercardioid microphones at an angle of 100° and the *Blumlein* technique, which makes use of bidirectional microphones at an angle of 90° (from the left to the right). They are notated by means of their polar pattern, the included angle and a symbolic representation of the XY technique (cf. Chapter »3. 1. 1 Transducer types and polar patterns«.

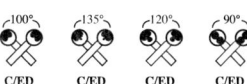

Fig. 14 The XY technique.

In the **MS technique**, one microphone is directed towards the sound source whilst the other one records the spatial information. The microphone for the middle component (M) may have any directivity, including omnidirectional. It faces to the centre front. The side component (S) always consists of a sideways-facing bidirectional microphone with its positive lobe facing left[66]. The two microphones are, as in the XY technique, aligned vertically[67]. This technique is often used to record the sound produced by an orchestra[68]. It needs to be noted that MS signals cannot be monitored directly. They are sum and difference components and must be converted to XY format[69]. However, an MS-directional mixer can be applied in order to convert the components already during the recording[70]. In figure 15 the microphone for the M component has the polar pattern of a cardioid. It is, moreover, depicted with the positive lobe of the bidirectional microphone for the S component facing left.

Fig. 15 The MS technique.

All stereophonic recording techniques in which the left and right channel only differ by time and not (or only slightly) by dynamic level are designated as **time-of-arrival stereophony**. For example, a sound source that arrives earlier on the right than on the left microphone is localised on the right side. The spaced pair principle can be achieved by means of the AB technique with two microphones or by techniques that utilise several microphones[71]. For the latter techniques consult Chapter »3. 2. 3 Multi-microphone arrangements and their nota-

---

[62] Huber, Manual, p. 114.

[63] Wuttke, Mikrofonaufsätze, p. 7.

[64] Huber, Manual, pp. 114f.

[65] Wuttke, Mikrofonaufsätze, p. 7.

[66] Wuttke, Mikrofonaufsätze, pp. 7f. and Rumsey, Stereophonic, p. 384.

[67] Weinzierl, Aufnahmeverfahren, p. 576.

[68] Cf. Wuttke, Mikrofonaufsätze, pp. 7f.

[69] Rumsey, Stereophonic, p. 384.

[70] Cf. Weinzierl, Aufnahmeverfahren, pp. 577f.

[71] Ibid., pp. 578f.

tion«. In the **AB technique**, two capsules with the same polar pattern are set symmetrically along a centre line perpendicular to the front plane of the sound source. The polar pattern of this stereo pair and their spacing is variable[72]. The most common set-up is to use microphones with omnidirectional directivity[73]. Spacings normally reach from 40-80 cm (small-AB) to 6 m (big-AB). 50 cm is a spacing that often produces satisfying results[74]. The spacing can even be smaller than 40 cm, but may then lead to unsatisfying results. A special technique, the symmetrical setting of two bidirectional microphones with a spacing of 20 cm, is called the *Faulkner* configuration[75]. In the case of recording an orchestra, the spacing between the pairs is dependent on the distance from the sound source. Generally, the further from the orchestra the microphones are placed, the bigger their spacing needs to be because the time difference decreases with the distance[76]. Two different set-ups are presented in Figure 16, a small-AB spacing of 50 cm with omnidirectional microphones and the *Faulkner* configuration, which makes use of two bidirectional microphones and a spacing of 20 cm.

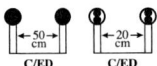

Fig. 16 The AB technique.

The class of techniques in which the left and right channel differ by dynamic level and time are designated as the **near-coincident principle**[77]. There are two main configurations. The first is the **ORTF technique**, which is named after the *Office de Radiodiffusion-Télévision Française*[78]. Two cardioid capsules are set symmetrically, oriented outward from the centre line of the sound source with an included angle of 110° and a spacing of 17 cm[79]. The other main configuration is the **NOS technique**, which is named after the *Nederlande Omroep Stichting*[80]. Two cardioid capsules are spaced apart by 30 cm and angled at 90°[81]. However, the ORTF technique is often preferred. Even the NOS itself have stopped using their own configuration in favour of the ORTF technique[82]. Depictions of the ORTF (110° and 17 cm) and NOS (90° and 30 cm) configuration are presented in Figure 17. Since both techniques make use only of cardioid capsules and one particular angle and spacing, the example presents the only possible ways of employing these techniques.

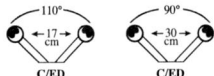

Fig. 17 The ORTF and NOS technique.

There are other special configurations that also belong to the class of techniques designated as the near-coincident principle. In the **binaural technique**, normal hearing is imitated. It is commonly configured by using two omnidirectional microphones that are placed in the

[72] Huber, Manual, p. 111.

[73] Weinzierl, Aufnahmeverfahren, p. 579.

[74] Wuttke, Mikrofonaufsätze, p. 9 and Huber, Manual, pp. 112f.

[75] Weinzierl, Aufnahmeverfahren, pp. 579f.

[76] Wuttke, Mikrofonaufsätze, pp. 24f.

[77] Weinzierl, Aufnahmeverfahren, p. 582.

[78] Office of the French Radio and Television.

[79] Wuttke, Mikrofonaufsätze, p. 9 and Huber, Manual, p. 120.

[80] Dutch Broadcasting Company.

[81] Rumsey, Stereophonic, p. 397.

[82] Wuttke, Mikrofonaufsätze, p. 9.

ears of a dummy head. This technique can be very realistic, providing a good illusion in both the horizontal and vertical planes[83]. Some manufacturers even provide dummies that can move their head, controlled by software. Further, the two microphones can also be placed in a person's ear canal[84]. Binaural recordings are intended for headphone reproduction and normally do not translate well in direct stereo playback. However, it is possible to convert a binaural recording into stereo by using a crosstalk cancelling method[85] (for an introduction to this method please refer to *Eargle*[86]). Another disadvantage of the binaural technique is the phenomenon that sound waves that arrive from the front and those that arrive from the back cannot be distinguished in the recording[87]. Figure 18 presents the notation of the binaural technique. Whenever the artificial head is supposed to be moved by means of software, the angle of incidence changes. Hence the paradigms presented in Figures 12 and 13 may be used to depict such actions.

Fig. 18 The binaural technique.

In **baffle-derived stereophony**, differences in the dynamic levels of the left and right channel are not created by means of polar patterns, but by the baffle[88]. Spherical baffles are similar to artificial heads. They can be used for stereo recordings with no requisite crosstalk cancellation. An example of baffle-derived stereophony is the *Jecklin* **disc**. Here a disc of approximately 30 cm in diameter[89] is placed between two omnidirectional microphones, spaced apart by 20 cm[90]. Another example is the **sphere microphone**. This recording technique makes use of two omnidirectional microphones mounted into a spherical baffle of 20 cm in diameter. There are many competing stereo systems embodying baffles. Other construction types are, for instance, the *SASS* microphone or a type, which makes use of a parabolic baffle, called *Clara*[91]. Figure 19 presents the depiction of a *Jecklin* disc and spherical baffle. Both techniques make use of omnidirectional polar patterns. Other techniques may be depicted similarly.

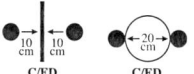

Fig. 19 The *Jecklin* disc and the spherical baffle.

3. 2. 3 Multi-microphone arrangements and their notation

In multichannel recordings level and time differences are coded for more than two channels to provide a strong spatial impression when playing the signal back over a multichannel loud-

---

[83] Huber, Manual, pp. 121f.

[84] Weinzierl, Aufnahmeverfahren, pp. 586-589.

[85] Eargle, Book, p. 213.

[86] Ibid., pp. 213f.

[87] Weinzierl, Aufnahmeverfahren, p. 589.

[88] Ibid., p. 584.

[89] 30 cm in Weinzierl, Aufnahmeverfahren, p. 584 and 28 cm in Eargle, Book, p. 213.

[90] Eargle, Book, pp. 213-215 and Weinzierl, Aufnahmeverfahren, p. 584.

[91] Cf. Weinzierl, Aufnahmeverfahren, pp. 584f.

speaker setup. However, in contrast to stereophonic techniques, the level and time differences may not vary very much[92].

The **soundfield microphone** was developed by *Calrec Audio Ltd.* and utilises four microphones that are fitted into a single housing[93]. It may be regarded as an extension of the MS technique to three spatial dimensions. However, in opposition to the MS microphone, the middle and side components are not created by means of omnidirectional and bidirectional microphones. Instead, four microphones with a wide cardioid pattern are arranged in a near-coincident tetrahedron[94]. Either a four-channel recording can be made in this way or the signal immediately processed for resolution into quadraphonic or stereo signals[95]. MS decoding may also be accomplished by a dual-transformer arrangement[96]. Two cardioids facing the front and back (M), as well as a bidirectional microphone for a combined side component (S), are used in this technique. These two MS signals can be utilised for the playback on, for instance, a 5.1 surround sound system. When doing so, the front MS signal is fed to the front speakers and the back MS signal to the back speakers whilst the front M component can be used for the centre channel[97]. This technique is called **double MS**. In Figure 20 the suggested methods of notation for these two techniques are presented. The soundfield microphone is depicted by means of the wide cardioid polar pattern and a pyramid symbol that refers to their arrangement in a near-coincident tetrahedron. The double MS technique is notated similarly to the common MS technique with the difference that a second cardioid capsule is added (cf. figure 15).

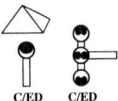

C/ED   C/ED

Fig. 20 The soundfield microphone and double MS.

When utilising omnidirectional microphones and the AB technique, the localisation of the sound sources can be imprecise[98]. Therefore, a third centre microphone may be employed and mixed with the two outer pairs. This technique is called the **ABC technique**. One possible application is the *Decca Tree*, named after the British *Decca* label. The ABC technique is used to record large sound sources, such as an orchestra. In this configuration, three omnidirectional microphones are positioned in an equilateral triangle whilst the centre microphone is placed in front. The spacing between the microphones is dependent on the recording angle, and hence the extent of the sound source, with regard to the microphone position. In the case of the recording angle being 100°, spacing a (A to C and B to C) is supposed to be 87.5 cm and spacing b (A to B) 158.5 cm. At 120° $a = 74$ cm and $b = 128$ cm, at 140° $a = 64.5$ cm and $b = 104.5$ cm and at 160° $a = 57.5$ cm and $b = 88$ cm[99]. Figure 21 presents the notation of the ABC technique. Since the recording angle is hard to predict, the spacings are disregarded here and their determination subjected to interpretation.

---

[92] Ibid., p. 589.

[93] Huber, Manual, p. 123.

[94] Weinzierl, Aufnahmeverfahren, pp. 591-593.

[95] Huber, Manual, pp. 123f.

[96] Ibid., p. 118.

[97] Cf. Weinzierl, Aufnahmeverfahren, pp. 593f.

[98] Wuttke, Mikrofonaufsätze, p. 9.

[99] Weinzierl, Aufnahmeverfahren, pp. 580f. and 594f.

Fig. 21 The ABC technique.

Techniques that make use of four or five omnidirectional microphones are called ABCD or ABCDE. They are utilised for recording very large sound sources. However, the addition of that many signals with time differences may lead to an imprecise localisation[100]. In the case of employing these uncommon techniques, the notation can be achieved analogously to the ABC technique.

Further, the **ICA 3 technique**[101] makes use of three microphones L, C and R with the polar pattern of a cardioid, arranged in such a way that LC and RC do not overlap. When doing so, a large sound source may be recorded. The result is a complete reproduction of the source. Three front loudspeakers are used for the playback. The spacing between the microphones here is also dependent on the recording angle. At 100° spacing a (L to C and R to C) = 69 cm and spacing b (L to R) = 126 cm, at 120° a = 53 cm and b = 92 cm, at 140° a = 42 cm and b = 68 cm and at 160° a = 32 cm and b = 49 cm. This technique can be even further extended to five microphones (ICA 5). However, the ICA 5 technique is mainly used for recording the atmosphere in film or television productions[102]. For this reason, it is disregarded here. The ICA 3 technique is depicted here similarly to the ABC technique. As is apparent from Figure 22, the spacings are also not notated, but supposed to be determined by the interpreter.

Fig. 22 The ICA 3 technique.

There are various other multi-microphone arrangements that cannot be discussed here in detail in order to limit the scope of the work. However, the most important multichannel techniques may be introduced briefly: the OCT[103] technique resembles the ICA 3 technique. However, L and R here consist of two microphones with a supercardioid polar pattern. The *Fukada* tree makes use of a similar concept. Five cardioid microphones and two additional omnidirectional microphones are utilised here. The bidirectional spherical baffle is an extension of the stereophonic variant (cf. Figure 19), two additional front-facing microphones with a bidirectional polar pattern are used to create a multichannel signal. Another elaborated technique makes use of four cardioid microphones disposed in a square. The spacing between the microphones is normally set at 20-25cm. This technique is called IRT-cross and especially used for recording atmospheric signals[104]. A similar technique called the *Hamasaki* square, makes use of bidirectional and supercardioid microphones spaced at 3 m intervals[105]. For fur-

---

[100]Ibid., p. 581.

[101]Ideal Cardioid Arrangement.

[102]Weinzierl, Aufnahmeverfahren, pp. 595f.

[103]Optimised Cardioid Triangle.

[104]Weinzierl, Aufnahmeverfahren, pp. 596-599.

[105]Kimio Hamasaki et al.: Approach and mixing technique for natural sound recording of multichannel audio. In: Proceedings of the AES 19th international conference. Surround sound. Techniques, technology, and perception. No city named [United States of America] 2001, pp. 176-181, here: p. 180.

ther insight please refer to *Weinzierl*[106] or for the OCT technique to *Theile*[107], for the *Fukada* tree to *Fukada*[108], for the IRT-cross to *Wuttke*[109] and for the *Hamasaki* square to *Hamasaki*[110].

3. 2. 4 The disposal of the microphones and its notation

When microphones are utilised in performances, it becomes necessary to depict their disposal. The microphone set-up is similarly to the loudspeaker set-up commonly depicted in the fore-word of a work by means of a sketch of a generic concert hall. Examples can, for instance, be found in *Ferneyhough's* »Time and motion study«[111] or *Halffter's* »Noche pasiva del sentido«[112] (also cf. Chapter »2. 2. 2 Stereophonic and multichannel techniques« and specifically Figure 6 in this chapter). However, microphones, construction types, stereophonic and multi-channel techniques are normally not explained in as much detail as in the previous chapter. When wanting to employ microphones in a concert, their disposal can be displayed by means of the methods of notation suggested for the microphone types and the recording techniques as well as by employing a sketch of the concert hall or stage explaining which instruments are picked up by which microphone(s).

3. 3 Sound sources and the recording room

In order to employ the previously described microphone techniques in a score, the sound that is supposed to be recorded needs to be notated. Here two main groups of sounds are defined: **instrumental** and **non-instrumental sound sources**. Apparently, it is easier to depict sounds that are created by traditional instruments than all other sounds. Therefore, the basic elements of notating the recording of acoustic sound sources are explained with regard to instruments. Moreover, the field of non-instrumental sounds is so vast that a complete systematic notation cannot be developed. Anyway, an initial approach is presented in this chapter. It is supposed to give the composer, who aims at using such sonic material, an idea of how the notation can be achieved. Moreover, whenever making a recording, the **recording room** has a great influence on the shape of the recorded material. Therefore, it is discussed how this impact can be adequately represented in a score.

3. 3. 1 Basic elements (instrumental sound sources)

Instruments are picked up in order to make a recording, to amplify the sound sources or to transform their sound. Recordings of instruments can be manipulated or complemented by the techniques described in Chapter »1. Sound synthesis« and/or Chapter »2. Audio processing«, stored on fixed media and, subsequently, played to an audience. Further, these processes can also be performed in realtime (live-electronics). Here the amplification of instruments, the manipulation of pre-recorded sounds and the transformation of the sonic material in realtime is of interest. Simple recordings of performances are normally produced by experienced audio

---

[106]Weinzierl, Aufnahmeverfahren, pp. 596-599.

[107]Günther Theile: Natural 5.1 music recording based on psychoacoustic principles. In: Proceedings of the AES 19th international conference. Surround sound. Techniques, technology, and perception. No city named [United States of America] 2001, pp. 201-229.

[108]Akira Fukada: A challenge in multichannel music recording. Surround sound. Techniques, technology, and perception. In: The proceedings of the AES 19th international conference. Surround sound. Techniques, technology, and perception. No city named [United States of America] 2001, pp. 439-447.

[109]Wuttke, Mikrofonaufsätze.

[110]Hamasaki, Multichannel.

[111]Ferneyhough, Time, no page named [foreword].

[112]Halffter, Noche, no page named [foreword].

engineers. Hence there is no need to specifically notate them. However, suggestions of recording techniques could be given in the foreword of a work. When notating recordings, the **output level** of the recorded sound, as well as its **original dynamic level,** need to be determined. As mentioned, it needs to be further outlined which **microphone types** and **recording techniques,** including the **microphone placement** and **angle of incidence,** are utilised. In the case of employing microphones in a live performance, it needs to be additionally explained when they are switched on or off.

3. 3. 1. 1 Previous methods of notation

There are various works that deal with the recording of instruments. As mentioned, most composers make use of a circuit plan that describes which microphone is supposed to pick up which instrument. By doing so, the instruments may be notated as usual and audio effects that manipulate their sound be added. As shown in the chapter on sound synthesis (cf. Figure 19), *Nono* makes use of a diagrammatic system that refers to traditional dynamic levels in order to depict the amplified sound: "[t]he (..) diagrams sum up the control of dynamic levels of general outputs on loudspeakers L1, 2, 3, 4" [113]. He further adds that the "linear representation is of course to be interpreted in a musical sense" [114]. The x-axis of this diagram represents the time whilst the y-axis represents the dynamic level *from »Ø« to forte/fortissimo.* These diagrams are related to another notation system that depicts the actions of the instrumentalists. The absence of the system, or the line that represents the volume, means the output level of the speakers is equal to zero.

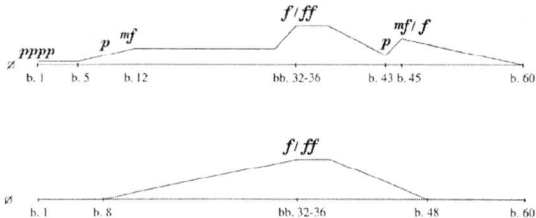

Fig. 23 Nono, A Pierre, p. XIV.

Further, *Kagel* employs pre-recorded instrumental material in his work »Tremens«. The dynamic level of the loudspeaker's output (L) is supposed to be adjusted according to the dramaturgic situation and divided into seven levels, ranging from 0 (minimum, equal to non audible) over 1/4, 1/3, 1/2, 2/3 and 3/4 to 1 (maximum). Additionally, the high (treble clef) and low (bass clef) frequency range of the amplifier can be adjusted independently [115]. A symbolic representation of a tape recorder determines that the instrumental part is not performed live, but actually pre-recorded [116]:

Fig. 24 Kagel, Tremens, p. 34.

---

[113]Nono, A Pierre, p. XIV.
[114]Ibid., p. XIV.
[115]Kagel, Tremens, p. IIIf.
[116] Cf. ibid., p. II.

Figure 25 shows how the recording is depicted. The instrument is, in this example, a contra-bass, picked up by a contact microphone[117]. The dynamic level underneath the system is a direction for the instrumentalist while the output level of the amplifier [Verstärker] is notated over the system.

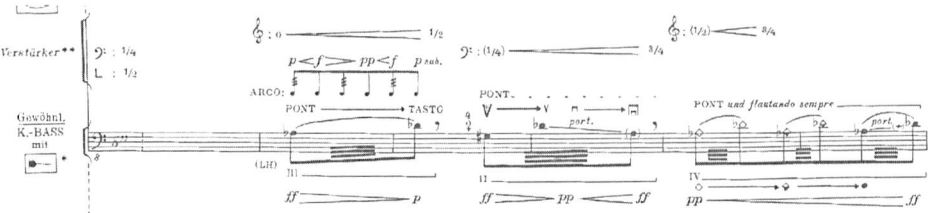

Fig. 25 Kagel, Tremens, p. 34.

In *Halffter's* »Noche pasiva del sentido« the volume of the loudspeakers is always the same as that of the performers[118]. Therefore, he needs to only employ symbols that describe when a particular microphone is turned on or off:

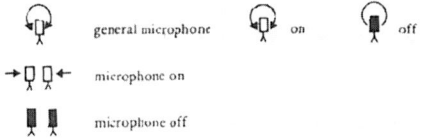

Fig. 26 Halffter, Noche, no page named [foreword].

3. 3. 1. 2 Discussion

Concerning the notation of the output level, *Nono's* approach (cf. Figure 23) can be described as simple and exact. It is, further, strongly related to traditional notation because common dynamic levels are utilised. By doing so, the loudspeaker's volume can be compared to the original dynamic level of the instrument(s). This is important in live performances and sim-plifies the interaction between instrumentalists and sound engineers. *Nono's* method also strongly resembles the method used to depict the dynamic level (or envelope) of a synthetic instruments (cf. Chapter »1. 1. 1 Periodic wave generators and their envelopes«). It can actually be regarded as a variant of notation. In order to coherently depict the output level, one would solely have to introduce a distinct timeline for the independent control of the vol-ume and replace the lines by dots (or constantly use *Nono's* method). Further, concerning *Kagel's* approach of depicting pre-recorded sound material (cf. Figure 24), it may be said that whenever instruments are recorded, they can be notated as usual. However, it needs to be outlined that the sounds are played back. The symbol *Kagel* utilises can be quickly identified as a tape recorder and, therefore, fulfils the requirements of simplicity and instantaneous com-prehension. Even though this device is no longer commonly used, it may – due to its historical importance for electroacoustic music – still be employed as a symbolic representation of pre-recorded material. However, the seven dynamic levels that depict the loudspeakers' output levels (cf. Figure 25) do not fulfil the requirements of simplicity and close relation to traditio-nal notation. In contrast, *Nono's* approach, as mentioned, fulfils these requirements. It is, therefore, preferred to the one by *Kagel*. Moreover, the treble and bass boost can be regarded as a simplified high-shelf and low-shelf filter. In order to depict it in a more exact manner, the

---

[117]Cf. ibid., p. 34.
[118]Halffter, Noche, no page named [foreword].

frequency range of the bass and the treble boost, the ordinal number *n* and the quality would need to be determined. Please refer for these filter types to Chapter »2. 3. 2 High-shelf, low-shelf and parametric filters and their notation«. Further, whenever the volume of the speakers is not changed during the course of a piece, there is no need to employ a special notation system for the output control. In such a case, *Halffter's* approach of introducing two symbols that explain when the microphone is switched on or off is sufficient and simpler than, for example, constantly depicting an output level that equals the instrumental dynamic level. However, *Halffter's* symbolic language becomes insufficient when several different microphone types or recording techniques are employed and would then have to be extended by the methods introduced in Chapters »3. 1 Microphones« and »3. 2 Recording techniques«.

3. 3. 1. 3 Suggestion for the notation of instrumental sound sources

Hence the suggested method of notation is an elaborated hybrid of *Nono's* and *Halffter's* approaches. The paradigm displayed in Figure 26 combines and augments their methods by depicting the microphone types and recording techniques as suggested in the previous chapters. Whenever the volume of the loudspeakers equals the dynamic level of the instrument, it is sufficient solely to use a microphone symbol that explains which kind of microphone picks up the instrument and which recording technique is used. The additions on and off determine whether the instrumental sound is picked up or not. This method of notation is an extended variant of *Halffter's* approach that now enables the depiction of various microphone types and recording techniques. When no additional output level is used, the instrumental dynamic level = output level. However, it could, for instance, also be determined that the output level is always slightly louder than the dynamic level of the instrument.

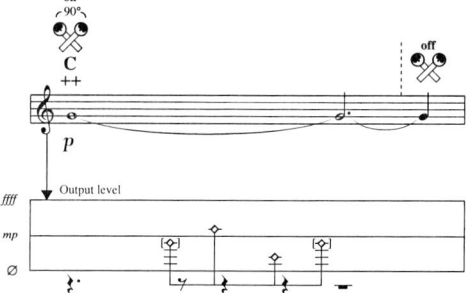

Fig. 27 Instrumental sound recording.

In the example, two condenser supercardioid capsules in XY configuration with an included angle of 90° pick up the instrument (cf. Figure 14). The spacing between the microphones and the sound source is set at 20 to 60 cm (++). Since no microphone angle is determined, the default position (0°) is employed. Moreover, in order to depict a variation between the output level of the loudspeakers and the dynamic level of the instrumental sound, a diagrammatic system is employed. The x-axis of this system describes the time while the y-axis includes all traditional dynamic levels, ranging from »∅« to quadruple *forte*. Hence the white dots (◇) depict the loudspeakers' output level in time. When this system is employed, the instrumental dynamic level ≠ output level. The sound source employed in Figure 27 is produced by an unspecified instrument. The instrumentalist plays a breve »g¹/G4« with the dynamic level *piano*. The sound is, from the beginning on, picked up. This is depicted by employing a microphone symbol in combination with the direction on. Since no additional output level is determined, the dynamic level of the instrument equals the volume of the loudspeakers. After a dotted crotchet, the output variation starts. Because it is a variation from the initial output level *piano*, the starting point is in squared brackets. From this point on, the output level is increased to *mezzoforte* for the duration of a quaver, decreased to *piano pianissimo* for the duration of a crotchet – meaning that the loudspeakers' output level is lower than the dynamic level of the instrumental sound – and finally increased to *piano* for the duration of another crotchet. At this point, the output level is again equal to the dynamic level of the instrumental sound. The amplification ends after a semibreve and a dotted minim, which is depicted by the microphone symbol in combination with the direction off.

Further, in a live performance it needs to be determined at any time to which loudspeakers the microphones are sending. The notation of this requirement has been examined in Chapter »2. 2. 2 Stereophonic and multichannel techniques«. The circuit plan displayed in the chapter on audio processing (Figure 7) could be complemented by a depiction of the sound producers, the microphones used to pick them up and a determination of which loudspeakers they are sending to. If the connection between the speakers is supposed to be changed during the course of a piece, the configuration could be depicted above the notation system for the output level (cf. Figures 8, 10 and 11 in the chapter on audio processing). Concerning the playback of pre-recorded sounds during a performance, *Kagel's* approach is adopted here. In order to point out that sonic material of this kind is used, the symbol presented in Figure 28 may be employed in the score (for examples of application please refer to Figures 38-41).

Fig. 28 Symbol for pre-recorded material.

3. 3. 2 Non-instrumental sound sources

Non-instrumental sounds are regarded here as sonic events not created by means of an instrument (including acoustic, electric and synthetic instruments). Instrumental sounds cannot be clearly categorised as tones because on instruments noise may also be created, e. g. string instruments are able to produce a huge number of sounds with indefinite pitch, and non-instrumental sounds cannot be categorised as noises because they may also have quasi-harmonic spectra, e. g. sounds created by animals, such as the buzzing of a bee swarm or a bird's chirping, as well as sounds that are transformed by means of acoustic filters, such as tubes[119]. Moreover, the two subcategories **reproducible** and **extractable sounds** are utilised here to further classify non-instrumental sounds. Reproducible sounds can be repeatedly created by a person and hence, for instance, become part of a performance. Thus these kinds of sounds do not necessarily need to be recorded in order to be utilised as the sonic material of a musical work, whereas extractable sounds cannot be removed from their environment, but need to be recorded in order to become part of a musical work.

3. 3. 2. 1 Previous methods of notation

Stockhausen's »Herbstmusik«[120] is a piece that makes use of various reproducible sounds. For instance, in the first movement a roof is supposed to be nailed. *Stockhausen* gives detailed instructions concerning the sizes of the nails, the type of hammer and how the sounds are supposed to be created[121]. The manner of performance is explained by means of descriptive nota-

---

[119]Resonating tubes are able create an overtone series by sympathetic resonance when placed at a select spot within an urban sound environment. This principle is called »tuning tube« and was employed by soundscape composers *Sam Auinger* and *Bruce Odland*.

[120]Karlheinz Stockhausen: Herbstmusik. For four players. Kürten 1977.

[121]Cf. ibid., pp. 33f. and 37f.

tion, which means that directions, such as "a) Make a transition from initially nailing to ever more finely differentiated timbres and rhythms" [122] or "d) The hammering is now at its most intense, and a whole series of nails – especially larger ones – is hammered into the wood" [123], are not depicted by means of a notation system. In some cases, these directions are complemented by an illustration. For instance, the instruction "[r]apid quivering of the hammer (long tapered point) between two nails or two rows of nails" [124] is illustrated by the image displayed in Figure 29.

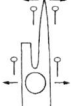

Fig. 29 Stockhausen, Herbstmusik, p. 37.

Cage, in »Water walk« [125], also employs many reproducible sounds. He requests the performer to place ice cubes in a glass or to release steam from a pressure cooker [126]. The set-up is displayed in the foreword of the work:

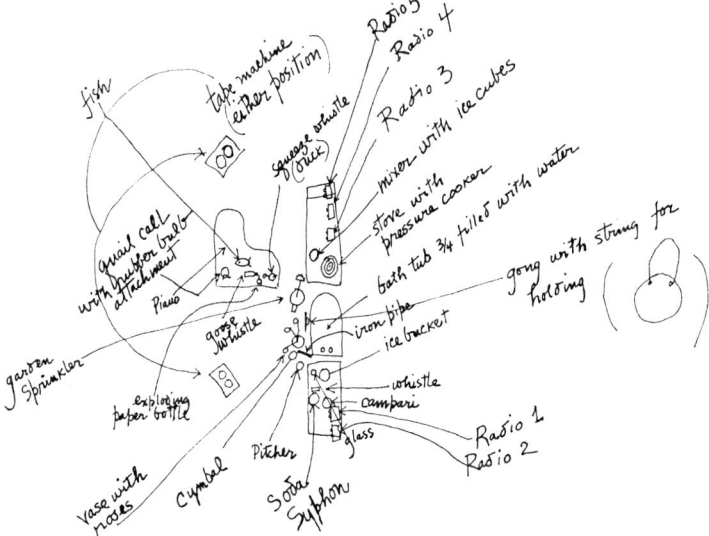

Fig. 30 Cage, Water, no page named [foreword].

The performance is structured by employing an approximate timeline in seconds and giving directions that are sometimes complemented by an illustration of the sound producer. The action that refers to the direction or symbol is explained in the foreword of the work. For example, steam refers to "[p]roduce steam by opening cap-valve of pressure cooker. Reclose" [127].

---

[122]Ibid., p. 38.

[123]Ibid., p. 39.

[124]Ibid., p. 37.

[125]John Cage: Water walk. For solo television performer. New York 1961.

[126] Cf. ibid., no page named [foreword].

[127]Ibid., no page named [foreword].

315

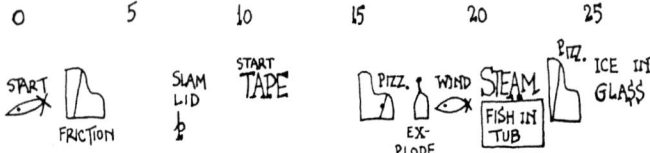

Fig. 31 Cage, Water, p. 0.

Cage also makes use of radios. They can be slapped, pushed off the table or switched on during the performance. In the case of the latter, they are supposed to be tuned to different "stations or static or both" [128]. The method of notation resembles the one presented in Figure 31 [129]. Radios are also utilised by *Stockhausen* in his cycle »Spiral« [130], »Pole« and »Expo« [131]. In »Spiral«, for instance, the "events received by a soloist on a short-wave radio are imitated, transformed and transcended" [132]. The sounds created by the radio are not completely arbitrary, but structured by means of four parameters and a plus, minus or equal sign. The "DURATION (..), REGISTER (..), DYNAMICS (...) and RHYTHMIC SEGMENTA-TION (...)" [133] are defined "according to the sequence of signs in the score" [134]. A plus sign means that the event is longer, higher, louder or has more segments than the previous one, a minus sign means that it is shorter, lower, softer or has less segments than the previous one, and an equal sign means that all four parameters remain the same [135]. "To choose a short-wave event one searches quietly from station to station until one has found something that approximately corresponds" [136] to the parameters. The segmentation is achieved either by controlling the volume or switching through the stations [137]. Furthermore, *Holliger* also makes use of transistor radios in his work »Pneuma«. However, the current radio programme is not used as musical material, but virtually white noise, created by VHF transistor radios when adjusted to intermediate frequencies. The radios may be switched on or off and the dynamic level (supported by adjusting the treble and bass level) can be controlled. Every radio *Holliger* employs is depicted by means of a distinct single lined notation system with no clef whilst common notes are utilised to display the duration [138]. Further, *Kagel* often employs reproducible sounds in order to extend the percussive apparatus. In »Norden« from the cycle »Die Stücke der Windrose« he utilises inter alia a branch, a sleigh bell and a fan in combination. The "branch with (dried?) leaves" [139] is "at least 50 cm long. When shaken, a rustling sound should be clearly perceptible" [140]. Further, "ca. 15 white thin strips of light-weight paper, cloth or satin at least 50 cm long, are fastened to the grille" [141] of the fan. In the excerpt presented in Figure 32,

[128] Ibid., no page named [foreword].

[129] Cf. ibid., p. 1.

[130] Karlheinz Stockhausen: Spiral. For a solo player. Vienna 1973.

[131] Karlheinz Stockhausen: Pole. For two. Expo. For three. Kürten 1974.

[132] Stockhausen, Spiral, p. 11.

[133] Ibid., p. 11.

[134] Ibid., p. 11.

[135] Cf. Ibid., p. 11.

[136] Ibid., p. 12.

[137] Ibid., p. 12.

[138] Cf. Holliger, Pneuma, pp. 9-27.

[139] Kagel, Norden, no page named [foreword].

[140] Ibid., no page named [foreword].

[141] Ibid., no page named [foreword].

the "fan is further resting on the bass drum with the blades facing upwards"[142]. The branch can be shaken and the dynamic level of this sound can be controlled. The fan can be switched on or off. These actions are depicted by a single lined notation system which refers to the particular item by means of an illustration. In the case of the branch, common note heads are used in combination with a *tremolo* symbol, depicting the way the branch is supposed to be shaken. In the case of the fan, diamond-shaped note heads are employed.

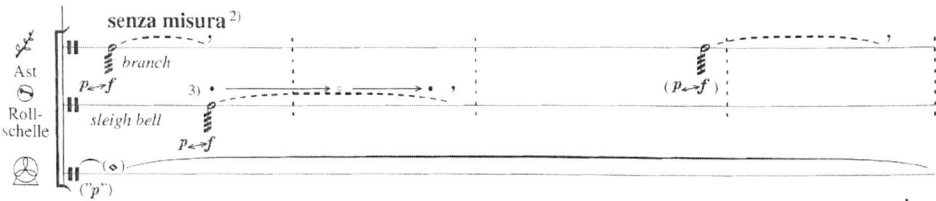

Fig. 32 Kagel, Norden, p. 120.

More examples can be found in »Südwesten«[143], another work from the cycle. Here inter alia "3 cushions of different sizes – roughly 25 × 25 cm, 30 × 30 cm, and 35 × 35 cm – well stuffed, lying loose or tied to a table"[144] and "1 container filled with water, small enough to be hand-held"[145] are utilised. The cushions may be struck. Since he employs three different sizes that create slightly varying sounds, a notation system with three lines is used to notate this action in combination with common note heads:

Fig. 33 Kagel, Südwesten, p. 1.

The container is used to "[d]rip water into a large, almost empty metal pail on the floor"[146]. The player is supposed to either drip water from a distance, which he has previously determined by experiment[147], or to release a continuous jet of water and, while doing so, sometimes also change the height of the container. All actions are, as displayed in Figure 34, depicted by means of a single lined notation system (in drum clef). Further, the continuous jet is notated in a spatial way. The quavers are positioned closer to each other in order to request a continuous jet of water (or a fast series of single drips).

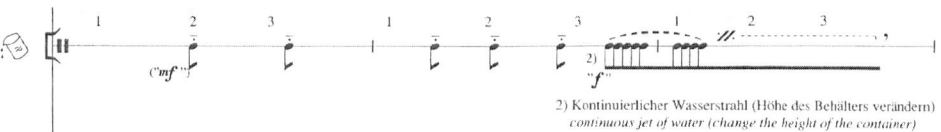

2) Kontinuierlicher Wasserstrahl (Höhe des Behälters verändern)
continuous jet of water (change the height of the container)

Fig. 34 Kagel, Südwesten, p. 89.

---

[142]Ibid., p. 118.

[143]Mauricio Kagel: Die Stücke der Windrose. Südwesten. Frankfurt/M. et al. 1994.

[144]Ibid., no page named [foreword].

[145]Ibid., no page named [foreword].

[146]Ibid., no page named [foreword].

[147]Cf. ibid., no page named [foreword].

Moreover, in »Mitternachtsstük«[148] *Kagel* makes use of leaves, which are placed loosely in a container[149]. The player is supposed to perform an irregular rustling of the leaves or try to produce two distinct noises. A single lined notation system is employed to depict these articulations. The rustling is notated on the line and in combination with a *tremolo* symbol[150] (similarly to shaking the branch in »Norden«) whilst the two distinct noises are depicted by »transposing« the notes[151]:

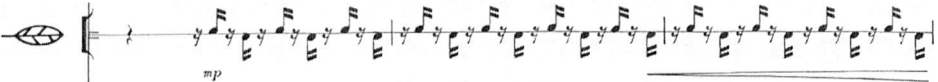

Fig. 35 Kagel, Mitternachtsstük, p. 8.

Kagel further employs various unconventional methods of sound production in »Staatstheater«. The actions are not, most of the times, explained in the foreword, but in the score itself. One example is the construction of a simple instrument by combining the bridge of a contrabass, a polystyrene hemisphere, a leather buckle and elastic band. This instrument is able to produce sounds with definite pitch (that can only be determined approximately) whilst the pitch is changed by bending the lower arm[152]:

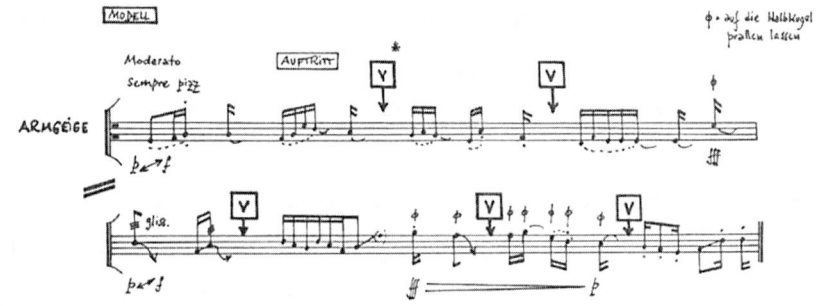

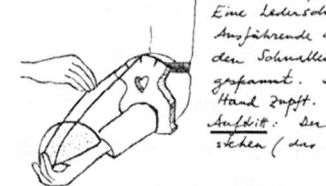

Fig. 36 Kagel, Staatstheater, p. 11 [Repertoire].

---

[148]Mauricio Kagel: Mitternachtsstük über vier Fragmente aus dem Tagebuch von Robert Schumann. For voices and instruments. Frankfurt/M. 1989.

[149]Cf. ibid., no page named [foreword].

[150]Cf. ibid., p. 1.

[151]Cf. ibid., p. 8.

[152]Cf. Kagel, Staatstheater, p. 11 [Repertoire].

As is apparent from Figure 36, the depiction of the sonic events is strongly related to traditional notation: *Kagel* determines nine different pitches for the instrument, which are depicted by a common notation system with no clef. The standard articulation is *pizzicato*. Further, even a technique resembling the *Bartók pizzicato*, which is created by pulling the band upwards and making it snap sharply against the hemisphere [auf die Halbkugel prallen lassen], is employed. In order to notate it, *Kagel* makes use of a symbol, which resembles the symbol used for the depiction of the traditional articulation (ᵩ). Additionally, approximate *glissandi* are also supposed to be produced and the dynamic level controlled. The *glissandi* are depicted by giving the direction *glissando* (at the first occurrence) and using an arrow, which determines the approximate pitch shift.

As shown, there are many attempts that grapple with the notation of reproducible sounds. However, there are only a few works that deal with the depiction of extractable non-instrumental sounds. *Kagel*, in »Phantasie«[153], employs a single lined notation system and action notation in order to depict pre-recorded extractable and reproducible sounds. He utilises expressions, such as "RAIN: on window-panes"[154], "UNDERGROUND TRAIN: moving train (record inside)"[155], or "TAP: direct the stream of water onto dishes in the basin; move the hose. Alter the water-pressure"[156]. Apparently, the material of the first two recordings may only be extracted since natural rain cannot be controlled and an underground train can hardly move through a concert hall. The third recording may, however, be defined as a reproducible sound that is pre-recorded instead of being created during a performance. The directions are normally complemented by an approximate specification of their duration and related to the instrumental stave(s) by means of dotted lines:

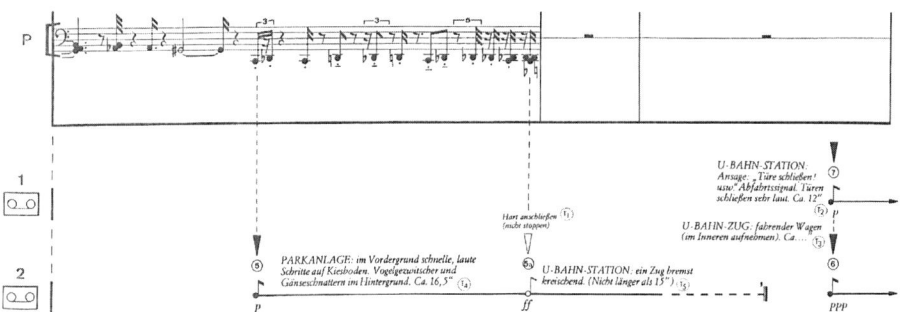

Fig. 37 Kagel, Phantasie, p. 13.

Kagel again employs the tape symbol (cf. Figures 24 and 28) to point out that the sonic material is pre-recorded. Further, the "dynamic markings (...) are only intended for the playback of the tapes. When recording, the volume-control should be on normal level"[157] while the performer himself is supposed to record all events prior to the concert[158].

3. 3. 2. 2 Discussion

The method of notation used by *Stockhausen* in »Herbstmusik« (cf. Figure 29) is purely descriptive. Therefore, it cannot be brought into accordance with traditional notation. Even

[153]Mauricio Kagel: Phantasie. For organ with obligati. London 1977.
[154]Ibid., pp. 6 [score] and 19 [translation].
[155]Ibid., pp. 13 [score] and 20 [translation].
[156]Ibid., pp. 8 [score] and 19 [translation].
[157]Ibid., p. IV [foreword].
[158]Ibid., p. IV [foreword].

though the actions are described in an exact way, they do not fulfil the requirement of exactness with regard to the determination of the duration. Further, the directions are so long that they could also not be instantaneously comprehended if applied as directions in a score. Moreover, *Cage's* approach towards the notation of non-instrumental sounds (cf. Figures 30 and 31) may be described as simple. It fulfils the requirement of instantaneous comprehension. However, it is at the same time – with regard to the duration and dynamic level of the events – very approximate. Even though the production of the sounds is related to a timeline, *Cage* does not exactly determine how long a particular event lasts and when it starts. Additionally, dynamic levels are not employed at all. This approach would become especially confusing if more than one performer was involved and could not be combined with traditional notation. Further, the illustration of the set-up is very unclear and could be easily realised in a simpler and more comprehensive manner.

The utilisation of radios in performances is a special problem. As shown above, these kinds of sound producers have been widely employed by composers. *Cage's* approach is, as stated above, very inexact since it is missing the determination of the exact duration and the control of the dynamic level. However, *Stockhausen* equips the sound that is created by the radios with a set of parameters. In addition to the duration and dynamics, the register and rhythmic segmentation are used to control the unpredictable. But all the parameters *Stockhausen* introduces are only determined approximately and in reference to the preceding acoustic event. It is obvious that the register needs to be determined in this way since the characteristics of the sonic material can barely be anticipated. However, the control of the duration, dynamic level and rhythmic segmentation could be determined exactly. It may be defined when the radio is switched on or off, how loud it is going to play and – with regard to the rhythmic segmentation – at which point in time the performer is supposed to switch stations[159]. A special case is the utilisation of radios in *Holliger's* »Pneuma«. The sonic material here is more predictable and the dynamic level and duration exactly controlled. However, the static noise he employs is produced by an analogue device that will probably become obsolete whilst in digital communication these kinds of noises are not created. In order to guarantee that the sounds remain reproducible, it might be more suitable to use noise oscillators and filters for the simulation of static (cf. Chapters »1. 1. 2 Noise generators and their notation« and »2. 3 Filters«).

Furthermore, *Kagel's* approach towards the notation of reproducible sounds is very exact and simple. In the first example from »Norden« (cf. Figure 32), it can be clearly comprehended which item is supposed to be used since it is introduced by means of an illustration, accompanied by its name. It does, further, make sense to use the *tremolo* symbol to describe the shaking of the branch because it resembles the motion that is performed when playing *tremolo* on a string instrument. Whenever there is only one articulation (plus a dynamic level) applied to an item, it is sufficient to utilise a single lined notation system since this method is commonly used to depict sounds with indefinite pitch (cf., for instance, »Part I: Extended instrumental playing techniques – 3. The techniques of percussion instruments«). However, since common note heads normally depict sounds with definite pitch and x-shaped note heads normally depict sounds with indefinite pitch, x-shaped note heads are preferred here. In the case of employing three items that resemble each other, the utilisation of one system with three lines (cf. Figure 33) further simplifies the depiction. Moreover, in the case of dripping water or releasing a jet of water (cf. Figure 34), two parameters may be controlled. The first is the release of water. A drip equals a short time event and the continuous release of a jet of water a long time event. The water jet is, as mentioned, notated in a spatial way. The duration of the sonic events no longer equals quavers, but can be understood as fast successions of

---

[159]The radio's volume is regarded here as equal to the parameter dynamic level and not – as in »Spiral« – as part of the rhythmic segmentation.

drips. However, this kind of spatial notation is irritating since the utilisation of quavers in a spatial way contradicts their common employment. The second parameter that may be controlled is the change in height. *Kagel* determines this action in an approximate way by simply giving the direction of performing a change in height. A more exact notation would try to control this parameter. An example of an augmented control of sounds can be found in *Kagel's* »Mitternachtsstük« (cf. Figure 35). The »transposition« of the note heads clearly depicts that two distinct sounds are supposed to be created.

Further, a valid method of notation for non-instrumental sounds with various articulations is presented in *Kagel's* »Staatstheater« (cf. Figure 36). The item that is supposed to be used can be quickly identified because it is depicted by an illustration. However, when the description of a particular item becomes too long, it might be more suitable to present it in the foreword of the work. Since the produced sounds are related to pitch, a system that resembles traditional notation may be employed. It is useful to depict the articulations in a traditional way since they are clearly referring to conventional articulations. Finally, *Kagel's* approach of notating pre-recorded reproducible and extractable sounds in »Phantasie« (cf. Figure 37) may be described as simple. However, it lacks instantaneous comprehension and exactness. This is because the descriptions are, in some cases, quite long and the duration of the sound is only determined in an approximate way.

3. 3. 2. 3 Suggestion for the notation of non-instrumental sound sources

As shown, *Kagel's* approaches towards the notation of reproducible sounds presented in Figures 32-36 are the simplest and most exact ones. He retains instantaneous comprehension and the method of depiction does not interfere with traditional notation because common durations are used. Therefore, *Kagel's* method here serves as the main paradigm for the depiction of reproducible non-instrumental sounds and is also applied to extractable sounds. However, all sounds with indefinite pitch are depicted here by x-shaped note heads. Further, it is, as mentioned, impossible to present an approach towards the notation of all non-instrumental sounds since there are innumerable sounds of this kind. This is why various examples, from which the notation of other sounds of this kind may be derived, are presented in the following examples. Additionally, the methods introduced in Chapters »3. 1 Microphones« and »3. 2 Recording techniques« are employed.

Figure 38 presents the notation of three sound producers utilised by *Cage* and *Stockhausen* (cf. Figures 29-31). The first sound is created by the rapid quivering (*tremolo*) of a hammer between two rows of nails. The sound is, in this case, played from tape and recorded by means of the AB technique, using two electrodynamic omnidirectional microphones with a spacing of 50 cm[160]. The spacing between the microphones and the sound source is set at 20 to 60 cm (++) while the angle of incidence is altered from approximately 40° to the centre position (0°) for the duration of a semibreve. The articulation is depicted by means of an illustration and an additional *tremolo* symbol. Further, a *crescendo* from *piano pianissimo* to *mezzopiano* is performed. After this repetitive action, three short strokes (left, right, right) are supposed to be executed. No additional notation system is applied, and hence a previously determined output level is employed, e. g. the dynamic level of the sound production = output level (cf. Chapter »3. 3. 1 Basic elements (instrumental sound sources)«). The second system presents the notation of putting ice cubes into a glass, a sound utilised by *Cage*. The frozen water is depicted here by the common frost symbol in combination with the chemical sign »H_2O«. The sound is created live and recorded by means of the XY technique, using two condenser hypercardioid microphones at an included angle of 90°. The spacing between the microphone and the sound source is set at 25 mm to 20 cm (+++). Since no information on the angle of

---

[160]Since the sound is played back from tape and not recorded live, it is not necessary to give the direction on/off.

incidence is given, the default angle (0°) is employed. Moreover, the original dynamic level is determined as *pianissimo* and the output level as *mezzoforte*. The last sound is produced by a radio. Its volume is controlled by traditional dynamic levels and the articulation of switching the stations is depicted here by »transposing« the note. Whenever the position is changed, the programme of a new (arbitrary) station is supposed to be played back. The switch might be complemented by attributes, such as news, speech or contemporary pop, given that the performer may silently switch through the stations before playing the material back. Further, it might be suitable to give directions, such as previous station, or to group the sounds into station 1, station 2 etc. and make the player tune back into one of these. These stations could also be related to more than two »pitches«.

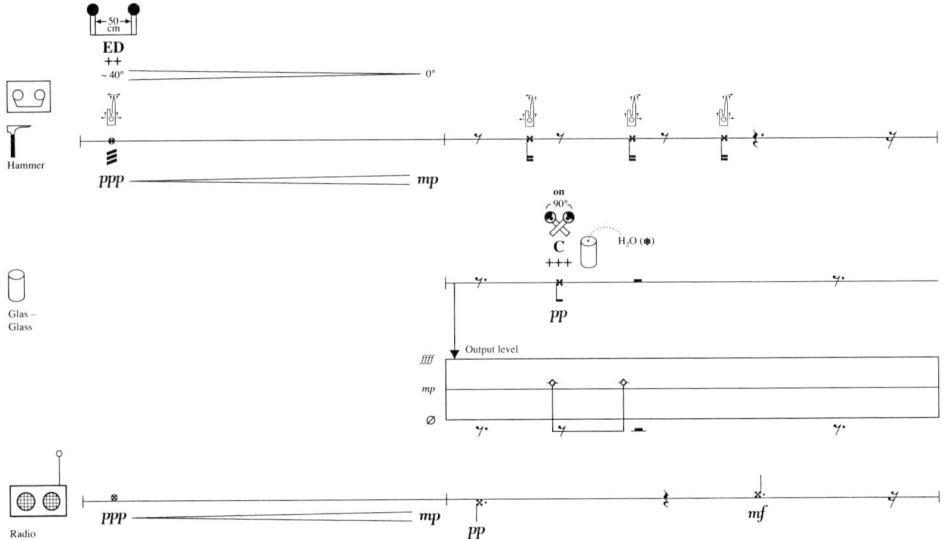

Fig. 38 Reproducible sounds by *Cage* and *Stockhausen*.

Further, in Figure 39 sounds similar to those used by *Kagel* in Figures 32-35 are notated in a uniform way. The upper system depicts the sound that is produced by shaking the branch. As in »Norden«, a *tremolo* symbol underlines the character of this motion. Moreover, the player is supposed to perform a *decrescendo* from *mezzopiano* to *pianissimo* for the duration of a semibreve. The second sound starts after a dotted minim by switching on a fan, which is placed on a tom-tom drum. Since it is difficult to previously determine the actual dynamic level, it is designated here as approximately *piano*. No microphone symbol complements these actions, which means that they are not amplified. The third sound is produced by hitting three different cushions. As in »Südwesten«, a notation system with three lines is used to depict the three percussive-like sound producers. The cushions are supposed to be struck with the index, middle, ring and little finger, which is determined by means of an illustration of the hand and colouring these fingers black (cf. »Part I: Extended instrumental playing techniques – 1. 7 Percussive effects« for this articulation). Two condenser cardioid microphones in ORTF configuration are utilised to record the sounds. All sounds are produced with the dynamic level *piano* whilst the output level is *forte*. In the fourth system, the dripping of water from a container into a metal pail is depicted. The dripping action is notated by means of an arrow and the water designated as »H₂O«. The player is supposed to start the sound production by releasing a continuous stream of water for the duration of a semibreve. While doing so, the height of the container is changed from high to low for the duration of a dotted crotchet and

322

from low to very low for the duration of a minim and a quaver. At the same time, a *decrescendo* from *mezzoforte* to *pianissimo* is executed (by releasing less water and lowering the container). The subsequent transition of a demisemiquaver into a quaver depicts that even less water is released and the continuous sound blends into distinct acoustic events. Since the exact duration of this transition cannot be exactly depicted by the notes, it is additionally determined by the dotted crotchet in brackets. Hence the transition is notated in a spatial way whilst the overall duration of this blending is described. Finally, a single drip from a high position is performed. The dynamic level is again *mezzoforte*. The last sound is created by rustling leaves, which are loosely placed in a container. The sound is recorded by means of an electrodynamic microphone with wide cardioid polar pattern and played back from tape. The spacing between the microphones and the sound source is set at 25 mm to 20 cm (+++). The notation is similar to the one by *Kagel*. Two distinct noises are supposed to be created. As two different recordings may be combined, they can also be produced simultaneously.

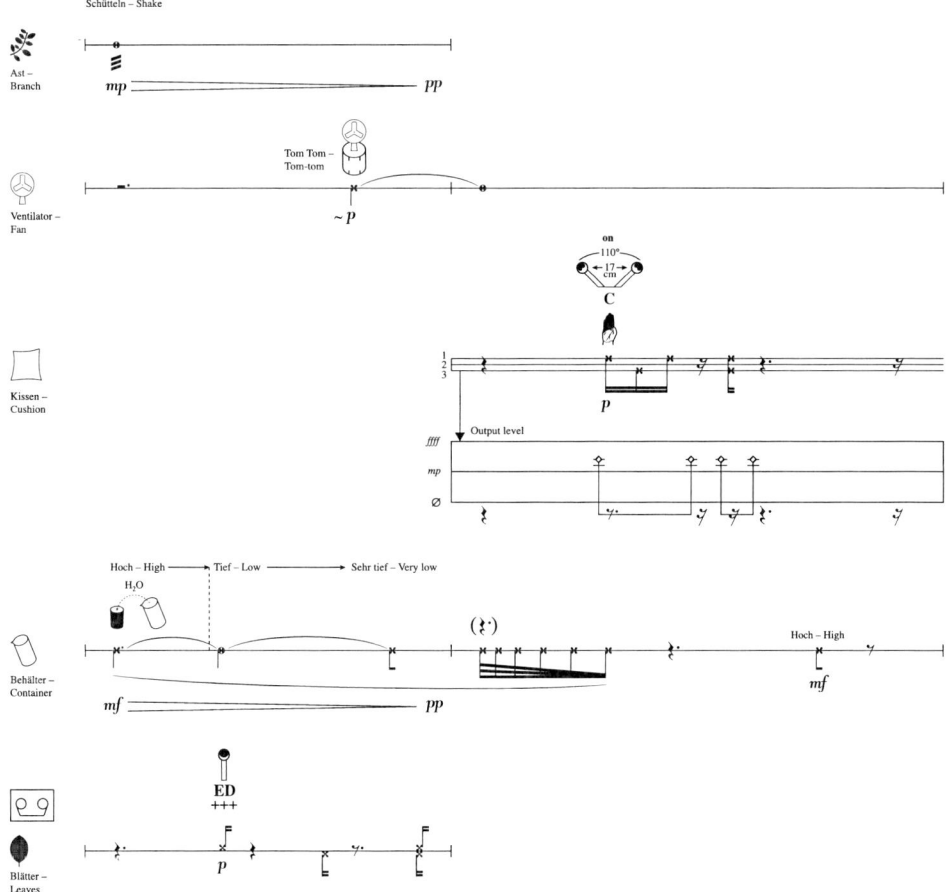

Fig. 39 Reproducible sounds by *Kagel*.

Further, in the case of utilising reproducible non-instrumental sounds that resemble the sound production of instrumental sounds, *Kagel's* approach, as presented in »Staatstheater« (cf. Figure 36), serves as a paradigm. Since it is simple, exact and retains traditional notation, an elaborated method does not need to be presented here. However, it needs to be

323

noted that *Kagel* uses the *Bartók pizzicato* symbol in a slightly varying way while the *glissando is* notated differently from the way it is notated in this work. Generally, when reproducible non-instrumental sounds resemble the production of instrumental sounds they should be notated in accordance with all other techniques presented in this work (cf. »Part I: Extended instrumental playing techniques« and specifically Chapter »1. 8 Preparing the instrument and its notation«).

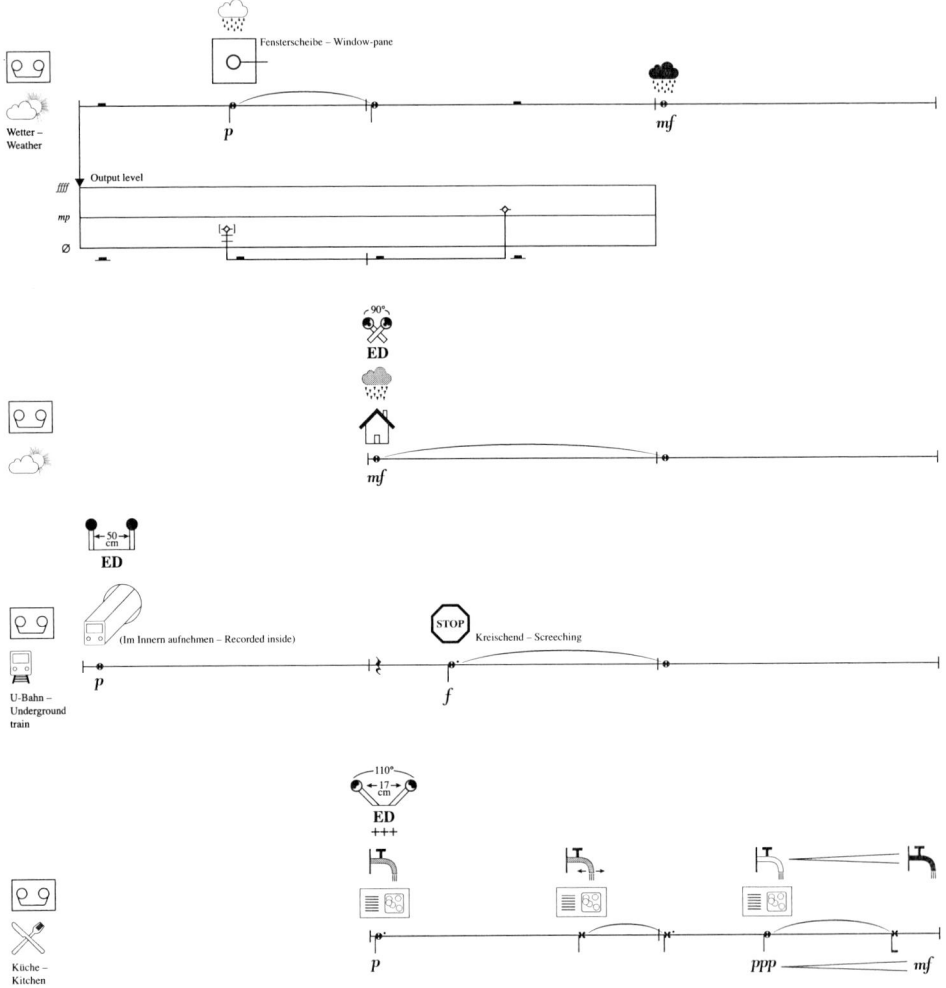

Fig. 40 Extractable and reproducible sounds by *Kagel*.

As shown, reproducible sounds can, in most cases, be clearly notated. However, it is more difficult to depict extractable sounds. An approach, which is based on *Kagel's* methods and deals with the sonic events used in »Phantasie« (cf. Figure 37), is presented in Figure 40. In order to achieve a clear depiction, it may be useful to group the sounds that are used. *Kagel*, for instance, employs different weather-related sounds (rain, hail, wind)[161], sounds related to underground trains (the moving train recorded from the inside, the stopping train, the signal

---

[161]Cf. Kagel, Phantasie, pp. 6f.

for closing the doors)[162] and sounds that can be produced in a kitchen (a tap directed onto dishes). In Figure 40 these three groups are represented by symbols and all related sounds notated in the group's notation system. The sounds represented by the upper system (designated as weather) are recorded by means of a contact microphone placed on a window-pane. Soft rain and strong rain, which is falling on this window, is supposed to be recorded. Soft rain is depicted by a white cloud and strong rain by a black cloud. In the example, the original dynamic level of soft rain is estimated as *piano* and of strong rain as *mezzoforte*. Moreover, the output level of the first sound is subsequently changed since a *crescendo* from *piano* to *mezzoforte* is supposed to be executed. The second system depicts another weather-related sound. Hail, which is falling on roofs, is supposed to be recorded here by means of two electrodynamic hypercardioid microphones in XY configuration at an included angle of 90°. The hail itself is depicted by triangular shapes. Since the colour of the cloud is grey, hail of medium strength is supposed to be recorded. In this case, the spacing between the microphone and the sound source cannot be determined. Therefore, it is disregarded and subject to interpretation. The next notation system depicts sounds created by an underground train. They are recorded by means of the AB technique, using two omnidirectional microphones with a spacing of 50 cm. The first recording is made inside a moving train. The second sound is created by a train stopping in a loud manner. The last sound is theoretically reproducible. Water from a tap is directed onto dishes, the hose moved and the water pressure altered from low to strong. A low water pressure is depicted here by a white tap, water pressure of medium strength by a grey tap and strong water pressure by a black tap. These articulations are in »Phantasie« not related to distinct durations, but regarded as a single continuous event[163]. By determining their duration, the recording becomes more exact. Moreover, the last event of altering the water pressure is complemented by a change in dynamic level, which is related to the continuous increase of the pressure. All sounds are recorded by means of the ORTF technique, using two electrodynamic cardioid microphones.

3. 3. 3 The recording room and its notation

The space in which a particular sound is recorded has great influence on the sound because it is shaped by the characteristics of the space. *Alvin Lucier*, in »I am sitting in a room«[164], has illustrated this impact: he records his own voice, plays it back into a room and records it again. He repeats this action "until the resonant frequencies of the room reinforce themselves so that any semblance of my speech (...) is destroyed"[165]. After several repetitions, only "the natural resonant frequencies of the room articulated by speech"[166] are audible. Normally, only one recording is made and the impact of the room's characteristic is not as strong as in this piece. Nevertheless, depending on the size and nature of the room, this factor may still be clearly perceived. To give an example, the difference between a recording that was made in a cathedral or a small living room is huge. When extractable sounds are recorded, these recordings are often made outside a room and referred to as field recordings. In such cases, the sound may still be reflected, e. g. from buildings or big rocks. However, if recorded in free field, only the direct sound is audible. There are only a few works that explicitly deal with the influence of the room. One example is *Stockhausen's* »Studie II«. In the foreword of the work, he mentions that the synthetic material is "played and recorded at 0 dB in a room with about

---

[162]Cf. ibid., p. 13.

[163]Cf. ibid., p. 8.

[164]Alvin Lucier: I am sitting in a room. For voice on tape. New York 1990.

[165]Ibid., no page named [on the recording].

[166]Ibid., no page named [on the recording].

10 seconds reverberation time and regular frequency response"[167]. *Kagel* is also aware of the impact of the room and requires the pre-recordings in »Phantasie« to be very dry: "[w]ith most of the recordings the fullest possible presence of the sound is desirable. Tape-recordings made where there is an echo [Verräumlichung] are to be avoided, as the place where the performance takes place probably has more than average reverberation anyway"[168]. However, even though *Stockhausen's* and *Kagel's* approaches deal with the recording room, neither of them explicitly presents a method of notation. A simple statement concerning the recording room may be sufficient when all recordings are made in the same room or as dry as possible, but it is insufficient when different recording rooms are involved. Hence in order to enable the depiction of the recording room in a score, another method needs to be developed.

The impact of the recording room on a sound can be compared to processing audio data by means of a convolution reverb. As explained in Chapter »2. 4. 1 The convolution reverb and its notation«, an effects unit of this kind is able to create an authentic simulation of the properties of a space. Therefore, the approach towards its depiction presented in this chapter here serves as a paradigm for the notation of a real room's impact on a recording. However, in this case, the notation needs to be far more indeterminate because the pre-delay time and the envelope cannot be predicted. But nevertheless, the recording room may be described as exactly as possible and represented by a symbol that complements the sound source's notation system. It is depicted here by means of a single lined notation system with no clef and two dots (◇◆), which describe the overall duration of the reverberation. In Figure 41, the sound that evolves when shaking a branch (cf. Figure 39) is now pre-recorded and played back from tape. It is supposed to be recorded by means of two electrodynamic microphones with a hypercardioid polar pattern in XY configuration at an included angle of 90°. The spacing between the microphone and the sound source is set at 60 cm to 1 m (+). The recording is supposed to be made in a mosque with approximately 8 seconds reverberation time. At an assumed tempo of ♩ = 60, a crotchet equals 1 second. Therefore, the reverb here lasts a semibreve longer than the action that excites it. Further, whenever the recording is supposed to be as dry as possible, or the sound is produced in free field or recorded during a concert, it does not need to be to be complemented by a notation of the recording room. This is because there is either a minimum influence of the »room« or the reverberation unpredictable.

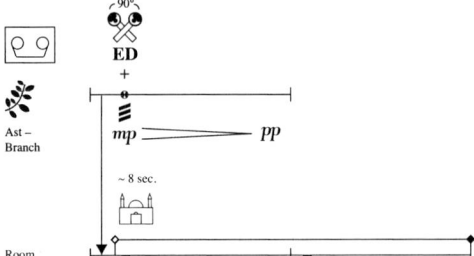

Fig. 41 A generic recording room.

---

[167]Stockhausen, Studie II, p. VII.

[168]Kagel, Phantasie, p. IV.

CONCLUSION

In this work, coherent and consistent methods of notation for most of the unconventional elements in music, including extended playing techniques of the common orchestral instruments and electroacoustic music, were developed. In order to fulfil this task, a set of criteria was defined and used to judge previous methods of notation. On the basis of these analyses a system of methods that agrees with the criteria was then developed while it was considered that the additions are compatible with, and distinct from, all other signs of the system. This procedure was executed with regard to the unconventional playing techniques of string instruments, wind instruments, percussion instruments, plucked instruments, keyboard instruments and vocal techniques as well as sound synthesis, audio processing and sound recording when previous methods of notation were available. Otherwise, a method that complies with the criteria was developed without prior discussion. The developments made within this work were subsequently applied in compositional works in order to test their practicability. However, these applications could not be reflected in the work in order to limit its size.

The developments made within this work are coherent because they all agree with the criteria postulated in the introduction. All previous methods of notation were discussed with regard to these criteria. Hence it was examined if they are simple, exact and closely related to traditional notation. As a result, either one of the already existing methods was suggested or, if they all failed to agree with the criteria, a simpler, more exact and/or more traditional method was suggested. However, in some cases, one of the criteria was emphasised and the others were set aside. An example of this is the discussion of the *saltando*, *balzando* and *toccato*. As explained in »Part I: Extended instrumental playing techniques – 1. 3. 3 The *saltando*, *balzando* and *toccato* and its notation«, these techniques are related to the traditional articulations *col arco/legno gettato* and *col arco/legno battuto*. Consequently, they are notated in the same fashion and hence by means of directions. However, this means that the third criterion (close relation to traditional notation) is emphasised and the second criterion (simplicity) neglected. This is because the described articulations may theoretically be notated in a simpler manner than by utilising directions, e. g. by means of an illustration. Nevertheless, the emphasis of the third criterion is consequently applied in the work because any unconventional articulation that is strongly related to a conventional articulation is depicted similarly to the conventional one. Examples for this are the *pizzicato* effect on wind instruments, which is notated in the same way as the *pizzicato* on string instruments (cf. »Part I: Extended instrumental playing techniques – 2. 2. 2 The *pizzicato* effect and its notation«), the slap tongue articulation, which is notated in the same way as the *Bartók pizzicato* because the character of both sounds is similar (cf. »Part I: Extended instrumental playing techniques – 2. 2. 3 The slap tongue«), or the playing techniques of plucked instruments that may also be produced on string instruments and, therefore, are always notated in the same way (cf. the chapter on plucked instruments). Similarly, since many extended techniques that may be executed on the strings of a piano strongly resemble the techniques of the harp, they are also notated in the same way (cf. the chapter on keyboard instruments). The third criterion is, in such cases, indeed emphasised. However, the performance of these techniques is also facilitated because it is easier for instrumentalists to comprehend a particular unconventional playing technique when it is depicted in the same way as its conventional counterpart.

Further, the developments made within this work are consistent because, as mentioned, they are compatible with, and distinct from, all other signs of the system. Hence no extension suggested in this work compromises any of the conventional methods and the other developments. An example of such a consistent extension is the so-called transposition system (cf., for instance, Figure 23 in the chapter on wind instruments). It is used to depict an unconventional technique, but is compatible with the conventional depiction of tones. All methods introduced in this work are also distinct from each other. This means that the same method is not used to depict two distinct articulations of the same instrument, e. g. the *Bartók pizzicato* symbol is not used to request the *Bartók pizzicato* and the *saltando*. However, the *Bartók pizzicato* symbol may also be used to request the slap tongue articulation on wind instruments because the player cannot confuse it with the original articulation. This is because a common *Bartók pizzicato* can only be produced on string or plucked instruments. However, even though the developments are therefore coherent and consistent, it has to be acknowledged that the approach towards the notation of unconventional musical elements presented in this treatise is ambitious and has its flaws. Some of these limitations have already been hinted in the introduction and are discussed in more detail below.

1. On the practicability of the extensions: the practicability of the developed methods was not yet adequately observed. This is because various compositions that make use of the developments exist, but most of them have not yet been realised. A final estimate of the usability can only be given after the realisation of an adequate number of pieces, including works for solo instruments, small/large chamber ensemble, orchestra (all with and without live-electronics), for live-electronics only and for fixed media. But the composition and realisation of such works is a long process, which could not be completed before finishing this treatise. This is because, for instance, realising of the works composed and revised during the writing process of the treatise requires a large number of performers. Moreover, the performers need to rehearse the work adequately. Hence they have to spend a lot of time on studying the utilised methods of notation, practicing the playing techniques and interacting with each other. Therefore, great effort has to be expended for a single performance of each piece. Moreover, the practicability can only be adequately observed after a number of performances because each interpreter may react differently to the methods of notation. Thus an even larger effort needs to be expended in order to gain a final estimate concerning the practicability of the developed methods. Additionally, so far only eight works that make use of the developments have been composed. In order to further test the applicability of the methods in scores, more pieces need to be produced. This is a long process because it takes a lot of time to compose, for example, a work for orchestra while the subsequent realisation of the piece further prolongs the observation process. However, it could be shortened if other composers made use of the methods in their works. **2. On the limitation of the exactness criterion**: the criterion of exactness is limited. This is because the factor of interpretation may lead to an uncertainty between the depiction and the realisation. Additionally, when human performers are involved in the realisation of a musical work, a requested technique might be executed in an inaccurate manner. Furthermore, during the writing of the treatise, it had to be acknowledged that it is also not possible to control every little detail of every instrumental or electroacoustic technique, but rather it is necessary to transfer the responsibility for some of the parameters to the interpreter. One example is the pitch bending articulation. This *glissando* technique may, in the case of woodwinds, be performed in different ways. However, the introduction of a special method of notation for each bending technique would have resulted in a more complex notation system. Therefore, a diagrammatic (transposition) system was used to depict the technique and the exact performance left to the player's discretion (cf. »Part I: Extended instrumental playing techniques – 2. 4 Pitch bending – the extended *glissando*«). Another example is the *pizzicato* on the strings. When requesting the player to pluck a string, which is made of two or three wires, it is not determined if he is supposed to pluck only one or all wires. This is because it would also lead to a very complex method of notation, which is at the same time dependent on the utilised piano model. Instead, the decision whether to pluck one, two or three wires is also transferred to the player (cf. »Part I: Extended instrumental playing techniques – 5. 1. 2 The *pizzicato* on the strings and its notation«). Likewise, it is in »Part II: Electroacoustic music – 2. 1. 1 Fragmentation and recombination and its notation« determined that the fade in/out envelope and the crossfader tool should be subjected to interpretation because the depiction of these events would either lead to a confusing appearance of the score or an insufficient notation. **3. On the preferences of composers**: this problem is especially related to the preparation of instruments and electroacoustic music in general. It is owed to the fact that composers might want to use other techniques than the ones described in the work. In order to limit the extent of the work, some of the unconventional means of sound production, however, had to be neglected. As mentioned above, there are numerous ways of preparing orchestral instruments while these preparations may lead to the introduction of new playing techniques that are not discussed in the work. Some instruments, such as the organ, harpsichord or plucked idiophones, were also not discussed while it is impossible to present a complete notation system for the innumerable non-instrumental sounds. Moreover, in order to limit the extent of the work, not every electroacoustic technique was discussed and – since electroacoustic sound production is still a new field – more techniques might still be identified. It would especially be helpful to further extend the work by discussing instrumental preparations and the resulting playing techniques as well as the unconventional techniques of the organ and harpsichord. Further, it needs to be admitted that even though there are, as shown in the introduction, good reasons for the utilisation of the criteria, they might not be accepted by all composers and, even if accepted, they might lead to results other than the ones presented in this treatise. Concerning these possible limitations, it may be replied that the developments should – as mentioned – be regarded as initial suggestions that may be adapted to the needs of the composer who makes use of it. Hence the system may be changed, revised or augmented. If changed, the analyses and suggestions may serve as a source of inspiration. If revised, methods that agree better with the criteria may be developed on the basis of the already existing suggestions and replace the methods suggested in work, whereas if augmented, the new techniques may simply be notated in accordance with all other techniques presented in this work. Generally, this treatise should be considered as a starting point and work in progress. In any case, it will hopefully contribute to the process of conventional methods of notation coming into existence for most articulations in the (distant) future. **4. On the constraints of paper size**: this problem is inherent to notated music in general and might limit the utilisation of the unconventional playing techniques and electroacoustic music. It is owed to the fact that the vertical space[1] of a score is limited. This problem is especially important for this work because most of the developed methods of notation require a larger amount of vertical space than the methods used to notate the conventional elements of music. Such a limitation will become most notable in compositions for large ensemble or orchestra as well as in electroacoustic works. However, there have been various attempts to overcome it. Many composers have extended the vertical space by producing large-format scores. Famous examples that enable the depiction of a huge number of simultaneous events are *Ligeti's* »Apparitions«, *Stockhausen's* »Punkte«[2] or *Boulez'* »Notation I-IV«[3]. Nevertheless, it needs to be acknowledged that the number of concurrent events has to be limited. This is because when a score is very large, it becomes – either due to its sheer size or the number of simultaneous events unreadable – which would in turn violate the third requirement because instantaneous comprehension would then be compromised.

In conclusion, I can say that I hope the treatise will prove useful for other composers[4] and that the utilisation of extended means of sound production will be facilitated by the existence of a conventional extended system. This treatise is regarded as a small contribution to the emergence of such conventions.

---

[1] The available space from the top to the bottom of a page.

[2] Karlheinz Stockhausen: Punkte. For orchestra. London 1966.

[3] Pierre Boulez: Notation I-IV. For orchestra. London 1978.

[4] Composers may download the symbols on http://christiandimpker.de and import them in notation software.

APPENDIX

In the following chart the beam positions and the covered strings of various piano models are listed. On some piano models two types of crossbeams can be found. The ordinary cross-beams are located in between the strings and restrict for instance the execution of certain *glissandi* on the strings while additional crossbeams that connect the ordinary crossbeams, moreover, restrict, for instance, the performance of certain vertical *glissandi*. Two ranges of covered strings are used here. The first range refers to strings that are completely covered by the bass strings and cannot be plucked at all. On some models these covered strings may alternatively be plucked in the rear end of the piano (*Steinway B-211*, *C-227*, *D-274* and *O-180*, all *Bechstein* models, *Yamaha C 3* and *Wendt & Lung 161*). The second range refers to the strings that are partially covered by the bass strings. They can be plucked *sul smorzatore*, but for instance certain harmonics cannot be fingered on them. All other strings are completely open (for the described techniques cf. the chapter on keyboard instruments). This list was produced with the friendly assistance of the *Bechstein* centre Berlin, the piano house *Goecke und Farenholtz* and the *Steinway* house Berlin. It mainly consists of recent piano models. The frames of historic piano models might vary.

❙ = crossbeam [CB] = additional crossbeam

Model	Bechstein B 212
Beam positions	^{2}A – F♯ [CB] ❙ G – c^2 ❙ c♯^{2} – f♯^{3} ❙ g^3 – c^5 A0 – F♯2 [CB] ❙ G2 – C5 ❙ C♯5 – F♯6 ❙ G6 – C8
Covered strings	G – G♯/A (completely covered) A/A♯ – c^1 (partially covered) G2 – G♯2/A2 (completely covered) A2/A♯2 – C4 (partially covered)

Model	Bechstein C 234
Beam positions	^{2}A – E [CB] ❙ F – g♯ ❙ a – c^2 ❙ c♯^{2} – f♯^{3} ❙ g^3 – c^5 A0 – E2 [CB] ❙ F2 – G♯3 ❙ A3 – C5 ❙ C♯5 – F♯6 ❙ G6 – C8
Covered strings	F – F♯/G (completely covered) G/G♯ – e (partially covered) F2 – F♯2/G2 (completely covered) G2/G♯2 – E3 (partially covered)

Model	Bechstein D 282
Beam positions	^{2}A – C♯ [CB] ❙ D – f♯ ❙ g – c^2 ❙ c♯^{2} – f♯^{3} ❙ f♯^{3} – c^5 A0 – C♯2 [CB] ❙ D2 – F♯3 ❙ G3 – C5 ❙ C♯5 – F♯6 ❙ F♯6 – C8
Covered strings	D – D♯/E (completely covered) E/F♯ – e (partially covered) D2 – D2♯/E2 (completely covered) E2/F♯2 – E3 (partially covered)

Model	Bechstein L167 and M/P 192
Beam positions	^{2}A – A [CB] ❙ A♯ – c^2 ❙ c♯^{2} – f♯^{3} ❙ g^3 – c^5 A0 – A2 [CB] ❙ A♯2 – C5 ❙ C♯5 – F♯6 ❙ G6 – C8
Covered strings	A♯ – H/c (completely covered) c/c♯ – d^1 (partially covered) A♯2 – B2/C3 (completely covered) C3/C♯3 – D4 (partially covered)

Model	Bösendorfer 170
Beam positions	^{2}A – H [CB] I c – a^1 I a#^{1} – e^3 I f^3 – c^5 A0 – B2 [CB] I C3 – A4 I A#4 – E6 I F6 – C8
Covered strings	c/c – c# (completely covered) c#/d – d#^{1} (partially covered) C3/C3 – C#3 (completely covered) C#3/D3 – D#4 (partially covered)

Model	Bösendorfer 200
Beam positions	^{2}A – A# [CB] I H – g#^{1} [CB] I a^1 – d#^{3} I e^3 – c^5 A0 – A#2 [CB] I B2 – G#4 [CB] I A4 – D#6 I E6 – C8
Covered strings	H (completely covered) c – c#^{1} (partially covered) B2 (completely covered) C3 – C#4 (partially covered)

Model	Bösendorfer 225
Beam positions	^{2}A – D# [CB] I E – g [CB] I g# – d^2 [CB] I d#^{2} – f^3 I f#^{3} – c^5 A0 – D#2 [CB] I E2 – G3 [CB] I G#3 – D5 [CB] I D#5 – F6 I F#6 – C8
Covered strings	E/E – F (completely covered) F/F# – g (partially covered) E2/E2 – F2 (completely covered) F2/F#2 – G3 (partially covered)

Model	Boston GP-156 PE
Beam positions	^{2}A – A# I H – d^2 I d#^{2} – g#^{3} I a^3 – c^5 A0 – A#2 I B2 – D5 I D#5 – G#6 I A6 – C8
Covered strings	H – c/c# (completely covered) c#/d – e^1 (partially covered) B – C3/C#3 (completely covered) C#3/D3 – E4 (partially covered)

Model	Boston GP-163 and GP-163 PE
Beam positions	^{2}A – A# I H – d^2 I d#^{2} – g#^{3} I a^3 – c^5 A0 – A#2 I B2 – D5 I D#5 – G#6 I A6 – C8
Covered strings	H – c/c# (completely covered) c#/d – d#^{1} (partially covered) B – C3/C#3 (completely covered) C#3/D3 – D#4 (partially covered)

Model	Boston GP-178 PE
Beam positions	^{2}A – A# I H – d^2 I d#^{2} – g#^{3} I a^3 – c^5 A0 – A#2 I B2 – D5 I D#5 – G#6 I A6 – C8
Covered strings	H – c/c# (completely covered) c#/d – d^1 (partially covered) B – C3/C#3 (completely covered) C#3/D3 – D4 (partially covered)

331

Model	Steinway B-211
Beam positions	^{2}A – E [CB] I F – h^1 [CB] I c^2 – e^3 I f^3 – c^5 A0 – E2 [CB] I F2 – B4 [CB] I C5 – E6 I F6 – C8
Covered strings	F – F#/G (completely covered) G/G# – a# (partially covered) F2 – F#2/G2 (completely covered) G2/G#2 – A#3 (partially covered)

Model	Steinway C-227
Beam positions	^{2}A – E [CB] I F – c^2 [CB] I c#^{2} – f#^{3} I g^3 – c^5 A0 – E2 [CB] I F2 – C5 [CB] I C#5 – F#6 I G6 – C8
Covered strings	F – F#/G (completely covered) G/G# – a (partially covered) F2 – F#2/G2 (completely covered) G2/G#2 – A3 (partially covered)

Model	Steinway D-274
Beam positions	^{2}A – E [CB] I F – c#^{2} [CB] I d^2 – g^3 I g#^{3} – c^5 A0 – E2 [CB] I F2 – C#5 [CB] I D5 – G6 I G#6 – C8
Covered strings	F – F#/G (completely covered) G/G# – g (partially covered) F2 – F#2/G2 (completely covered) G2/G#2 – G3 (partially covered)

Model	Steinway O-180 and S-155
Beam positions	^{2}A – A# I H – c^2 I c#^{2} – f#^{3} I g^3 – c^5 A0 – A#2 I B2 – C5 I C#5 – F#6 I G6 – C8
Covered strings	H – c/c# (completely covered) c#/d – c^1 (partially covered) B2 – C3/C#3 (completely covered) C#3/D3 – C4 (partially covered)

Model	Wendt & Lung 161
Beam positions	^{2}A – A# [CB] I H – c#^{2} I d^2 – g^3 I g#^{3} – c^5 A0 – A#2 [CB] I B2 – C#5 I D5 – G6 I G#6 – C8
Covered strings	H – c/c# (completely covered) c#/d – g#^{1} (partially covered) B2 – C3/C#3 (completely covered) C#3/D3 – G#4 (partially covered)

Model	Yamaha C3
Beam positions	^{2}A – A# I H – d^2 I d#^{2} – g^3 I g#^{3} – c^5 A0 – A#2 I B2 – D5 I D#5 – G6 I G#6 – C8
Covered strings	H – c/c# (completely covered) c#/d – d#^{1} (partially covered) B2 – C3/C#3 (completely covered) C#3/D3 – D#4 (partially covered)

Further, the listing by *Vaes*[1] is also presented here (except for the *Bösendorfer 200* and the *Steinway B* and *D* model because they are described in the previous chart). However, it does not contain information about the covered strings. Further, in the case of the *Fazioli 278*, the listing contains a mistake[2]. Therefore, this model is disregarded here.

Model	Bechstein B-88 (208 cm)
Beam positions	^{2}A – A [CB]	A♯ – c²	c♯² – f♯³	g³ – c⁵ A0 – A2 [CB]	A♯2 – C5	C♯5 – F♯6	G6 – C8

Model	Fazioli 183
Beam positions	^{2}A – c♯ [CB]	d – g♯¹ [CB]	a¹ – d♯³	e³ – c⁵ A0 – C♯3 [CB]	D3 – G♯4 [CB]	A4 – D♯6	E6 – C8

Model	Fazioli 212
Beam positions	^{2}A – F♯ [CB]	G♯ – g♯¹	a¹ – d♯³	e³ – c⁵ A0 – F♯2 [CB]	G♯2 – G♯4	A4 – D♯6	E6 – C8

Model	Fazioli 228
Beam positions	^{2}A – F♯ [CB]	G – f♯¹	g¹ – d♯³	e³ – c⁵ A0 – F♯2 [CB]	G2 – F♯4	G4 – D♯6	E6 – C8

Model	Fazioli 308
Beam positions	^{2}A – D♯ [CB]	E – h¹ [CB]	c² – f³	f♯³ – c⁵ A0 – D♯2 [CB]	E2 – B4 [CB]	C5 – F6	F♯6 – C8

Model	Kawai RX-3
Beam positions	^{2}A – E [CB]	F – e¹	f¹ – d³	d♯³ – c⁵ A0 – E2 [CB]	F2 – E4	F4 – D6	D♯6 – C8

Model	Kawai RX-5
Beam positions	^{2}A – E [CB]	F – e¹	f¹ – d³	d♯³ – c⁵ A0 – E2 [CB]	F2 – E4	F4 – D6	D♯6 – C8

Model	Seiler 242
Beam positions	^{2}A – F♯ [CB]	G – a♯¹	h¹ – f♯³	g³ – c⁵ A0 – F♯2 [CB]	G2 – A♯4	B4 – F♯6	G6 – C8

---

[1] Vaes, Extended, pp. 1032-1048.

[2] The strings »c♯¹ – d²/C♯4 – D5« are in Vaes, Extended, p. 1035 described as being adjacent to each other.

Model	Yamaha C2
Beam positions	^{2}A – A$\sharp$ [CB] I H – d^2 I d$\sharp^2$ – g^3 I g$\sharp^3$ – c^5 A0 – A$\sharp$2 [CB] I B2 – D5 I D$\sharp$5 – G6 I G$\sharp$6 – C8

Model	Yamaha C6 and S6
Beam positions	^{2}A – G [CB] I G$\sharp$ – a$\sharp^1$ I h^1 – f$\sharp^3$ I g^3 – c^5 A0 – G2 [CB] I G$\sharp$2 – A$\sharp$4 I B4 – F$\sharp$6 I G6 – C8

Model	Yamaha C7
Beam positions	^{2}A – E [CB] I F – a$\sharp^1$ I h^1 – f$\sharp^3$ I g^3 – c^5 A0 – E2 [CB] I F2 – A$\sharp$4 I B4 – F$\sharp$6 I G6 – C8

Model	Yamaha CFIIIS
Beam positions	^{2}A – E [CB] I F – g I g$\sharp$ – c$\sharp^2$ I d^2 – g^3 I g$\sharp^3$ – c^5 A0 – E2 [CB] I F2 – G3 I G$\sharp$3 – C$\sharp$5 I D5 – G5 I G$\sharp$6 – C8

LIST OF REFERENCES

1. Books

Adler, Samuel: The study of orchestration. 3rd edition. New York and London 2002.

Ashby, Michael and **Maidment**, John: Introducing phonetic science. Cambridge et al. 2005.

Ballou, Glen (ed.): Handbook for sound engineers. Amsterdam et al. 2008.

Ballou, Glen et al.: Microphones. In: Glen Ballou (ed.): Handbook for sound engineers. Amsterdam et al. 2008, pp. 489-594.

Bartlett, Bruce: Stereo microphone techniques. Stoneham 1991.

Bartlett, Bruce: The PZM boundary booklet. A basic primer and experimenter's guide. In: David Huber: Microphone manual. Design and application. Boston and London 1988, pp. 239-255.

Bartolozzi, Bruno: Neue Klänge für Holzblasinstrumente [New sounds for woodwinds]. Mainz 1971.

Borwick, John (ed.): Loudspeaker and headphone handbook. 3rd edition. Oxford et al. 2001.

Borwick, John: Microphones. Technology and technique. London and Boston 1990.

Brasseur, Lee: Visualizing technical information. A cultural critique. New York 2003.

Chowning, John and **Bristow**, David: FM theory and applications. Tokyo 1986.

Colloms, Martin: High performance loudspeakers. 5th edition. Chichester et al. 1997.

Cook, Perry R.: Real sound synthesis for interactive applications. 3rd edition. Wellesley 2007.

Cox, Richard V.: Speech Coding. In: Vijay K. Madisetti and Douglas B. Williams (eds.): The digital signal processing handbook. Boca Raton 1998, pp. 45/1-45/19.

Dahlhaus, Carl: Notenschrift heute [Notation today]. In: Ernst Thomas (ed.): Notation Neuer Musik [Notation of New Music]. Darmstädter Beiträge zur Neuen Musik IX [Darmstadt's contributions to New Music IX]. Mainz 1965, pp. 9-34.

Dick, Robert: Neuer Klang durch neue Technik [Tone development through extended techniques]. Frankfurt/M. 1992.

Dobson, Richard: A dictionary of electronic and Computer Music theory. Instruments, terms, techniques. Oxford and New York 1992.

Dodge, Charles and **Jerse**, Thomas A.: Computer Music. Synthesis, composition, and performance. 2nd edition. No city named [Australia et al.] 1997.

Dostál, Jiří: Operational amplifiers. 2nd edition. Boston et al. 1993.

Dutilleux, Pierre and **Zoelzer**, Udo: Delays. In: Udo Zoelzer (ed.): DAFX. Digital audio effects. Chichester 2002, pp. 63-74.

Dutilleux, Pierre and **Zoelzer**, Udo: Filters. In: Udo Zoelzer (ed.): DAFX. Digital audio effects. Chichester 2002, pp. 31-62.

Eargle, John: Loudspeaker handbook. London et al. 1997.

Eargle, John: The microphone book. Boston et al. 2001.

Evangelista, Gianpolo: Time and frequency warping musical signals. In: Udo Zoelzer (ed.): DAFX. Digital audio effects. Chichester 2002, pp. 439-463.

Fletcher, Neville H. and **Rossing**, Thomas D.: The physics of musical instruments. 2nd edition. New York 1998.

Gallois, Pascal. The techniques of bassoon playing. Kassel et al. 2009.

Gayford, Michael: Microphone techniques. In: Michael Gayford (ed.): Microphone engineering handbook. Oxford et al. 1994, pp. 1-61.

Gayford, Michael (ed.): Microphone engineering handbook. Oxford et al. 1994.

Goertz, Anselm: Lautsprecher [Loudspeakers]. In: Stefan Weinzierl (ed.): Handbuch der Audiotechnik [Handbook of audio engineering]. Berlin et al. 2008, pp. 421-490.

Hänsler, Eberhard and **Schmidt**, Gerhard (eds.): Topics in acoustic echo and noise control. Selected methods for the cancellation of acoustic echoes, the reduction of background noise, and speech processing. Berlin et al. 2006.

Hall, Donald E.: Musical acoustics. 3rd edition. No city named [Australia et al.] 2002.

Haubenstock-Ramati, Roman: Notation – Material und Form [Notation – material and form]. In: Ernst Thomas (ed.): Notation Neuer Musik [Notation of New Music]. Darmstädter Beiträge zur Neuen Musik IX [Darmstadt's contributions to New Music IX]. Mainz 1965, pp. 51-54.

Hibbing, Manfred: High-quality RF condenser microphones. In: Michael Gayford (ed.): Microphone engineering handbook. Oxford et al. 1994, pp. 158-186.

Hood, John Linsey: Audio electronics. 2nd edition. Oxford et al. 1997.

Huber, David: Microphone manual. Design and application. Boston and London 1988.

Izhaki, Roey: Mixing audio. Concepts, practices and tools. Amsterdam et al. 2008.

Karkoschka, Erhard: Notation in New Music. A critical guide to interpretation and realisation. Translation by Ruth Koenig. 1st published in german 1966. New York and Washington 1972.

Kelly, Stan: Loudspeaker enclosures. In: Ian Sinclair (ed.): Audio and hi-fi handbook. 3rd edition. Oxford et al. 1998, pp. 290-309.

Kientzy, Daniel: Les sons multiples aux saxophones [Multiphonics on saxophones]. For sopranino, soprano, alto, tenor and baritone saxophones. Paris 1982.

Krassnitzer, Gerhard: Multiphonics für Klarinette mit deutschem System und andere erweiterte Spieltechniken [Multiphonics for clarinets with german system and other contemporary playing techniques]. Aachen 2002.

Levine, Carin and **Mitropoulos-Bott**, Christina: The techniques of flute playing. Kassel et al. 2002.

Levine, Carin and **Mitropoulos-Bott**, Christina: The techniques of flute playing II. Piccolo, alto and bass flute. Kassel et al. 2004.

Ligeti, Gyoergi: Neue Notation – Kommunikationsmittel oder Selbstzweck? [New notation – medium of communication or self purpose?]. In: Ernst Thomas (ed.): Notation Neuer Musik [Notation of New Music]. Darmstädter Beiträge zur Neuen Musik IX [Darmstadt's contributions to New Music IX]. Mainz 1965, pp. 35-50.

Madisetti, Vijay K. and **Wiliams**, Douglas B. (eds.): The digital signal processing handbook. Boca Raton 1998.

Maempel, Hans-Joachim et al.: Audiobearbeitung [Audio processing]. In: Stefan Weinzierl (ed.): Handbuch der Audiotechnik [Handbook of audio engineering]. Berlin et al. 2008, pp. 719-784.

Mapp, Peter: Sound reinforcement and public address. In: John Borwick (ed.): Loudspeaker and headphone handbook. 3rd edition. Oxford et al. 2001

Miranda, Eduardo Reck: Computer sound synthesis for the electronic musician. Oxford et al. 1998.

Moore, F. Richard: Elements of computer music. Englewood Cliffs 1990.

Morrill, Dexter: Trumpet algorithms for computer composition. In: Curtis Roads and John Strawn (eds.): Foundations of computer music. Cambridge and London 1985, pp. 30-44.

Neukom, Martin: Signale, Systeme und Klangsynthese [Signals, systems and sound synthesis]. Grundlagen der Computermusik [Foundations of Computer Music]. Zürcher Musikstudien [Zurich music studies], vol. 2. Bern 2003.

Nielsen, Torben: Precision microphones for measurements and sound reproduction. In: Michael Gayford (ed.): Microphone engineering handbook. Oxford et al. 1994, pp. 62-139.

Pompino-Marschall, Bernd: Einführung in die Phonetik [Introduction to phonetics]. 2nd revised and extended edition. Berlin and New York 2003.

Pressing, Jeff: Synthesizer performance and real-time techniques. Madison 1992.

Rabenstein, Rudolf et al.: Wave field synthesis techniques for spatial sound reproduction. In: Eberhard Hänsler and Schmidt, Gerhard Schmidt (eds.): Topics in acoustic echo and noise control. Selected methods for the cancellation of acoustic echoes, the reduction of background noise, and speech processing. Berlin et al. 2006, pp. 517-545.

Read, Gardner: Contemporary instrumental techniques New York and London 1976.

Rehfeldt, Phillip: New directions for clarinet. Los Angeles and London 1977.

Risatti, Howard: New music vocabulary. A guide to notational signs for contemporary music. Chicago and London 1975.

Roads, Curtis et al.: The Computer Music tutorial. Cambridge et al. 1996.

Roads, Curtis and **Strawn**, John (eds.): Foundations of Computer Music. Cambridge and London 1985.

Rocchesso, Davide: Spatial effects. In: Udo Zoelzer (ed.): DAFX. Digital audio effects. Chichester 2002, pp. 137-200.

Roggenkamp, Peter: Schriftbild und Interpretation in neuer Klaviermusik [Type face and interpretation in new piano music]. Vienna 1996.

Rumsey, Francis: Microphones in stereophonic applications. In: Michael Gayford (ed.): Microphone engineering handbook. Oxford et al. 1994, pp. 349-420.

Russ, Martin: Sound synthesis and sampling. 3rd edition. Oxford 2009.

Schneider, Martin: Mikrofone [Microphones]. In: Stefan Weinzierl (ed.): Handbuch der Audiotechnik [Handbook of audio engineering]. Berlin et al. 2008, pp. 315-419.

Schottstaedt, Bill: The simulation of natural instrument tones using frequency modulation with a complex modulating wave. In: Curtis Roads and John Strawn (eds.): Foundations of Computer Music. Cambridge and London 1985, pp. 54-64.

Sevsay, Ertuğrul: Handbuch der Instrumentationspraxis [Handbook of instrumentation practice]. Kassel et al. 2005.

Sinclair, Ian R. (ed.): Audio and hi-fi handbook. 3rd edition. Oxford et al. 1998.

Slavik, Karl and **Weinzierl**, Stefan: Wiedergabeverfahren [Reproduction techniques]. In: Stefan Weinzierl (ed.): Handbuch der Audiotechnik [Handbook of audio engineering]. Berlin et al. 2008, pp. 609-685.

Stone, Kurt: Music notation in the twentieth century. New York and London 1980.

Strange, Allen: Electronic music. Systems, techniques, and controls. 2nd edition. Dubuque 1983.

Supper, Martin: Elektroakustische Musik und Computermusik [Electroacoustic music and Computer Music]. Geschichte – Ästhetik – Methoden – Systeme [History – aesthetics – methods – systems]. Darmstadt 1997.

Thomas, Ernst (ed.): Notation Neuer Musik [Notation of New Music]. Darmstädter Beiträge zur Neuen Musik IX [Darmstadt's contributions to New Music IX]. Mainz 1965.

Thornhill, N. F.: An introduction to analogue electronics with practical demonstrations. London et al. 1997.

Vaes, Luk: Extended piano techniques. In theory, history and performance practice. No city named 2009.

Veale, Peter et al.: The techniques of oboe playing. Kassel et al. 1994.

Watkinson, John: The art of sound reproduction. Oxford et al. 1998.

Weinzierl, Stefan: Aufnahmeverfahren [Recording techniques]. In: Stefan Weinzierl (ed.): Handbuch der Audiotechnik [Handbook of audio engineering]. Berlin et al. 2008, pp. 551-607.

Weinzierl, Stefan (ed.): Handbuch der Audiotechnik [Handbook of audio engineering]. Berlin et al. 2008.

Weiss, Marcus and **Netti**, Giorgio: The techniques of saxophone playing. Kassel et al. 2010.

Wittgenstein, Ludwig: Tractatus logico-philosophicus. Translated by D. F. Pears and B. F. McGuinness. Reprinted with corrections. London et al. 1972.

Wuttke, Jörg: Mikrofonaufsätze [Microphone essays]. 2nd, extended edition. Karlsruhe 2000.

Zoelzer, Udo (ed.): DAFX. Digital audio effects. Chichester 2002.

Zoelzer, Udo: Signalverarbeitung, Filter und Effekte [Signal processing, filters and effects]. In: Stefan Weinzierl (ed.): Handbuch der Audiotechnik [Handbook of audio engineering]. Berlin et al. 2008, pp. 813-848.

2. Journals and articles

Bass, Steven C. and **Goeddel**, Thomas W.: The efficient digital implementation of subtractive music synthesis. In: IEEE Micro, vol. 1(3). New York 1981, pp. 24-37.

Chen, Jer-Ming et al.: Pitch bending and glissandi on the clarinet. Roles of the vocal tract and partial tone hole closure. In: Journal of the Acoustic Society of America, vol. 126(3). No city named 2009, pp. 1511-1520.

Computer Music Journal, vol. 7(2). Massachusetts 1983.

Computer Music Journal, vol. 14(4). Massachusetts 1990.

Computer Music Journal, vol. 16(4). Massachusetts 1992.

Computer Music Journal, vol. 17(1). Massachusetts 1993.

Computer Music Journal, vol. 32(2). Massachusetts 2008.

Cook, Perry R.: SPASM, a real time vocal tract physical controller; and Singer, the companion software system. In: Computer Music Journal, vol. 17(1). Massachusetts 1993, pp. 30-44.

Fukada, Akira: A challenge in multichannel music recording. Surround sound. Techniques, technology, and perception. In: The proceedings of the AES 19th international conference. Surround sound. Techniques, technology, and perception. No city named [United States of America] 2001, pp. 439-447.

Gariépy, Louise and **Décarie**, Jean: A system of notation for electro-acoustic music. A proposition. In: Interface. Journal of New Music research, vol. 13. Lisse 1984, pp. 1-74.

Goebels, Franzpeter: Gestalt und Gestaltung musikalischer Grafik [Shape and design of musical graphics]. In: Melos. Zeitschrift für Neue Musik [Journal for New Music]. Mainz 1972, pp. 23-34.

Goeddel, Thomas W. and **Bass**, Steven C.: High quality synthesis of musical voices in discrete time. In: IEEE transactions on acoustics, speech and signal processing, vol. 32(3). New York 1984, pp. 623-633.

Hamasaki, Kimio et al.: Approach and mixing technique for natural sound recording of multichannel audio. In: The proceedings of the AES 19th international conference. Surround sound. Techniques, technology, and perception. No city named [United States of America] 2001, pp. 176-181.

IEEE Micro, vol. 1(3). New York 1981.

IEEE transactions on acoustics, speech and signal processing, vol. 32(3). New York 1984.

Interface. Journal of New Music research, vol. 13. Lisse 1984

Jaffe, David A. and **Smith**, Julius O.: Extensions of the Karplus-Strong plucked string algorithm. In: Computer Music Journal, vol. 7(2). Massachusetts 1983, pp. 56-69.

Journal of the Acoustic Society of America, vol. 126(3). No city named 2009.

Journal of the Audio Engineering Society, vol. 26. New York 1978.

Kaegi, Werner: VOSIM. A new sound synthesis system. In: Journal of the Audio Engineering Society, vol. 26. New York 1978, pp. 418-425.

Karplus, Kevin and **Strong**, Alex: Digital Synthesis of plucked-string and drum timbres. In: Computer Music Journal, vol. 7(2). Massachusetts 1983, pp. 43-55.

Lazzarini, Victor et al.: The generation of natural-synthetic spectra by means of adaptive frequency modulation. In: Computer Music Journal, vol. 32(2). Massachusetts 2008, pp. 9-22.

Melos. Zeitschrift für Neue Musik [Journal for New Music]. Mainz 1972.

Mitchell, Thomas J. et al.: Frequency modulation tone matching using a fuzzy clustering evolution strategy. Audio Engineering Society convention paper, 118th convention. Barcelona 2005.

Proceedings of the AES 19th international conference. Surround sound. Techniques, technology, and perception. No city named [United States of America] 2001.

Rodet, Xavier et al.: CHANT. De la synthèse de la voix chantée à la synthèse en général [From the synthesis of the singing voice to synthesis in general]. Rapports de recherche IRCAM [IRCAM research reports], vol. 35. Paris 1985.

Serra, Xavier and **Smith**, Julius: Spectral modeling synthesis. A sound amalysis/synthesis system based on a deterministic plus stochastic decomposition. In: Computer Music Journal, vol. 14(4). Massachusetts 1990, pp. 12-24.

Smith, Julius O.: Physical modeling using digital waveguides. In: Computer Music Journal, vol. 16(4). Massachusetts 1992, pp. 74-91.

Spors, Sascha et al.: The theory of wave field synthesis revisited. Audio Engineering Society convention paper, 124th convention. Amsterdam 2008.

Theile, Günther: Natural 5.1 music recording based on psychoacoustic principles. In: Proceedings of the AES 19th international conference. Surround sound. Techniques, technology, and perception. No city named [United States of America] 2001, pp. 201-229.

3. Scores and musical works

Alsina, Carlos Roqué: Consecuenza. Trombone solo. Berlin and Wiesbaden 1969.

Berg, Alban: Wozzeck. Opera in 3 acts. Vienna 1931.

Berio, Luciano: Epifanie. [For orchestra and mezzo-soprano]. London 1969.

Berio, Luciano: Gesti. For alto recorder. London 1970.

Berio, Luciano: Sequenza II. For harp alone. London 1965.

Berio, Luciano: Sequenza III. For female voice. London 1968.

Boulez, Pierre: Le soleil des eaux. For soprano, mixed choir and orchestra. Paris 1968.

Boulez, Pierre: Le visage nuptial. For soprano, contralto solos, women's choir and orchestra. Paris 1959.

Boulez, Pierre: Notation I-IV. For orchestra. London 1978.

Brahms, Johannes: Hungarian dances I and II. For piano four hands. Mainz and Leipzig no year named [ca. 1920].

Braun, Gerhard: Tuba - Tabu. For tuba solo. Bad Schwalbach 2004.

Brown, Earle: December 1952. For one or more instruments and/or sound-producing media. In: Earle Brown: Folio and 4 systems. New York 1961, no page named.

Brown, Earle: Folio and 4 Systems. New York 1961.

Cage, John: First construction (in metal). Percussion sextet with assistant. New York 1962.

Cage, John: In the name of the holocaust. Music for the dance by Merce Cunningham. In: John Cage: Prepared piano music. Volume 1. 1940-47. New York et al. 1960, pp. 25-29.

Cage, John: Music of changes II. New York 1961.

Cage, John: Music of changes III. For piano. New York et al. 1961.

Cage, John: Prepared piano music. Volume 1. 1940-47. New York et al. 1960.

Cage, John: Prepared piano music. Volume 2. 1940-47. New York et al. 1960.

Cage, John: Water walk. For solo television performer. New York 1961.

Cerha, Friedrich: Enjambement. [For flute, violin, percussion, trumpet, trombone and double-bass]. Vienna 1963.

Cervetti, Sergio: Zinctum. For string quartet. Celle 1969.

Cowell, Henry: The piano music of Henry Cowell. Volume two. New York and London 1982.

Cowell, Henry: Vestiges. In: Henry Cowell: The piano music of Henry Cowell. Volume two. New York and London 1982, pp. 3-6.

Crumb, George: Ancient voices of children. Soprano, boy soprano, oboe, mandolin, harp, electric piano, percussion. New York et al. 1970.

Crumb, George: Echoes of time and the river. Four processionals for orchestra. New York 1986.

Crumb, George: Mundus canis ("A dog's world"). Guitar and percussion. New York et al. 2000.

Crumb, George: Songs, drones and refrains of death. Baritone, electric guitar, electric contrabass, electric piano (electric harpsichord), percussion (2 players). New York et al. 1971.

Dallapiccola, Luigi: Canti di prionia. For choir and several instruments. Milan 1971.

Delás, José Luis: Outremer clair et foncé. In: Alfons Kontarsky (ed.): Pro musica nova. Studies for playing avant-garde music. For piano. Cologne 1972, pp. 30-33.

Dittrich, Paul-Heinz: – the – m –. For bassoon solo and live-electronics based on an epigram by e. e. cummings. In: Dieter Hähnchen (ed.): Zeitgenössische Musik für Fagott solo [Contemporary music for bassoon alone]. Leipzig 1986, pp. 19-33.

Dittrich, Paul-Heinz: Streichquartett III. Nacht-Musik. Wiesbaden et al. 1995.

Eloy, Jean-Claude: Equivalences. For 18 instrumentalists. Paris 1965.

Essl, Karlheinz: Sequitur XII. For harpsichord and live-electronics. No city named 2009.

Ferneyhough, Brian: Incipits. Solo viola, percussion and six instruments. London et al. 2002.

Ferneyhough, Brian: Mnemosyne. Bass flute and pre-recorded tape. London et al. 1996.

Ferneyhough, Brian: Third string quartet. London et al. 1988.

Ferneyhough, Brian: Time and motion study II. For solo 'cello and electronics. London 1978.

Foss, Lukas: Echoi. For four soloists. Clarinet, cello, percussion, and piano. New York and Mainz 1964.

Furrer, Beat: Spur. For string quartet and piano. Kassel 1998.

Gaber, Harley: Voce II. Female voice, alto flute, and percussion. Cincinnati 1967.

Gubaidulina, Sofia: Dots, lines and zigzag. For bass clarinet and piano. Hamburg 1995.

Hähnchen, Dieter (ed.): Zeitgenössische Musik für Fagott solo [Contemporary music for bassoon alone]. Leipzig 1986.

Halffter, Cristobal: Lineas y puntos. For 20 instruments, 2 loudspeakers and tape. London 1967.

Halffter, Cristobal: Noche pasiva del sentido (San Juan de la Cruz). For soprano, percussion and electronics. London 1973.

Haubenstock-Ramati, Roman: Credentials or «think, think lucky». For voice (Sprechgesang) and 8 players. Vienna 1963.

Haubenstock-Ramati, Roman: Séquences. Music for violin and orchestra. London 1961.

Henze, Hans Werner: 4th string quartet. Mainz 1976.

Henze, Hans Werner: Essay on pigs. For voice and orchestra. Mainz 1970.

Henze, Hans Werner: Sinfonia N. 6. For two chamber orchestras. Mainz 1970.

Holliger, Heinz: Duo II. For violin and violincello. Mainz et al. 2005.

Holliger, Heinz: Elis. Three nocturnal pieces for piano. Mainz 1964.

Holliger, Heinz: Partita. For piano. Mainz et al. 2003.

Holliger, Heinz: Partita (II). For harp. Mainz 2004.

Holliger, Heinz: Pneuma. For wind, percussion, organ and radios. Mainz 1972.

Holliger, Heinz: Siebengesang. For oboe, orchestra, singing voices and loudspeaker. Mainz 1969.

Holliger, Heinz: Sonate (in)solit(air)e. For flute solo. Mainz et al. 1998.

Holliger, Heinz: Three pieces: For bassoon solo. Mainz 2002.

Holliger, Heinz: Vier Lieder ohne Worte. Mainz 1987.

Hosokawa, Toshio: Sen I. For flute. Mainz et al. 1993.

Kagel, Mauricio: ..., den 24. xii. 1931. Garbled messages for baritone and instruments. Frankfurt/M. et al. 1995.

Kagel, Mauricio: Anagrama. For four solo singers, speaking choir and chamber ensemble. London 1965.

Kagel, Mauricio: Atem. For a wind instrumentalist. London 1976.

Kagel, Mauricio: Die Stücke der Windrose. Norden. For salon orchestra. Frankfurt/M. et al. 1966.

Kagel, Mauricio: Die Stücke der Windrose. Südwesten. Frankfurt/M. et al. 1994.

Kagel, Mauricio: Dressur. Drum trio for wood instruments. Frankfurt/M. et al. 1983.

Kagel, Mauricio: Fürst Igor, Strawinsky. For bass voice and instruments. Frankfurt/M. et al. 1988.

Kagel, Mauricio: Hallelujah. For voices. London 1970.

Kagel, Mauricio: Heterophonie. For orchestra. Frankfurt/M. et al. 1969.

Kagel, Mauricio: L'art bruit. Solo for two. Frankfurt/M. et al. 1998.

Kagel, Mauricio: Match. For three players. London 1967.

Kagel, Mauricio: Mitternachtsstük über vier Fragmente aus dem Tagebuch von Robert Schumann. For voices and instruments. Frankfurt/M. 1989.

Kagel, Mauricio: Passé composé. Frankfurt/M. et al. 1996.

Kagel, Mauricio: Phantasie. For organ with obbligati. London 1977.

Kagel, Mauricio: Schattenklänge. Three pieces for bass clarinet. Frankfurt/M. et al. 1997.

Kagel, Mauricio: Sonant (1969/....). For guitar, harp, double bass and membranophones. Frankfurt/M. et al. 1964.

Kagel, Mauricio: Staatstheater. Scenic composition. London 1971.

Kagel, Mauricio: Streichquartett I/II. London 1974.

Kagel, Mauricio: Transición II. For piano, percussion and two magnetic tapes. London 1963.

Kagel, Mauricio: Tremens. Scenic montage of a test for two performers, electric instruments, percussion, tape and projections. London 1973.

Katzer, Georg: Dialog imaginär. For flute and tape. In: Werner Tast (ed.): Zeitgenössische Musik für Flöte solo [Contemporary music for flute alone]. Leipzig 1987, piece no. 8.

Kelemen, Milko: Changeant. For violincello and orchestra. Frankfurt/M. et al. 1969.

Koch-Raphael, Erwin: Spuren. Tenor trombone solo with optional percussion. Berlin and Wiesbaden 1980.

König, Gottfried Michael: Essay. Composition for electronic sounds. Vienna 1960.

Köszeghy, Pèter: Mortualium (coins for Charon). For ensemble. No city named [Berlin] 2008.

Kontarsky, Alfons (ed.): Pro musica nova. Studies for playing avant-garde music. For piano. Cologne 1972.

Kotoński, Włodozmierz: A battere. For percussion, guitar, harpsichord, viola and violincello. Celle 1963.

Lachenmann, Helmut: „.... zwei Gefühle ...", Musik mit Leonardo. For speakers and ensemble. Wiesbaden et al. 2002.

Lachenmann, Helmut: Accanto. Music for a clarinetist with orchestra. Wiesbaden 1984.

Lachenmann, Helmut: Air. Music for large orchestra and percussion-solo. Revised edition. Wiesbaden et al. 1994.

Lachenmann, Helmut: Allegro sostenuto. For clarinet, bass clarinet in B, violincello and piano. Wiesbaden et al. 2003.

Lachenmann, Helmut: Dal niente (Interieur III). For a solo clarinet-player. Cologne 1974.

Lachenmann, Helmut: Gran torso. Music for string quartet. Wiesbaden 1972.

Lachenmann, Helmut: Guero. For piano. Wiesbaden 1972.

Lachenmann, Helmut: Klangschatten – mein Saitenspiel. For 48 strings and 3 grand pianos. Cologne 1978.

Lachenmann, Helmut: Mouvement (– vor der Erstarrung). For ensemble. Wiesbaden 1985.

Lachenmann, Helmut: NUN. Music for flute, trombone, male voices and orchestra. Wiesbaden 2002.

Lachenmann, Helmut: Pression. For one cellist. Cologne 1972.

Lachenmann, Helmut: Salut für Caudwell. For two guitarists. Wiesbaden 1985.

Lachenmann, Helmut: Staub. For orchestra. Wiesbaden et al. 1997.

Lachenmann, Helmut: temA. For flute, voice (mezzo-soprano) and violincello. Cologne 1971.

Lachenmann, Helmut: Toccatina. Study for violin alone. Wiesbaden et al. 2006.

Lehmann, Hans Ulrich: Arco. In: Eckart Schloifer (ed.): Pro musica nova. Studies for playing contemporary music. For violin. Wiesbaden 1986, pp. 27-31.

Leidel, Wolf-G.: Drei Aperçus. For bassoon. In: Dieter Hähnchen (ed.): Zeitgenössische Musik für Fagott solo [Contemporary music for bassoon alone]. Leipzig 1986, p. 54a.

Ligeti, György: Apparitions. For orchestra. 2nd revised edition. Vienna 1971.

Ligeti, György: Artikulation. An aural score by Rainer Wehinger. Mainz 1970.

Ligeti, György: Aventures. For three singers and seven instrumentalists. Frankfurt/M. et al. 1964.

Ligeti, György: Nouvelles aventures. For three singers and seven instrumentalists. Frankfurt/M. et al. 1966.

Logothetis, Anestis: Styx. Composition for any combination of instruments. Cologne 1972.

Lucier, Alvin: I am sitting in a room. For voice on tape. 1st published 1970. New York 1990.

Maderna, Bruno: Widmung. For violin alone. Milan 1976.

Matsuoka, Takashi: Pietà. For flute alone. Tokyo 1989.

Michael, Frank: Epigramme. For trombone alone. Berlin 1982.

Michael, Frank: Invocationes. For flute alone. Berlin and Wiesbaden 1979.

Moran, Robert: Four visions. For flute, harp and string quartet. London 1974.

Nono, Luigi: A Pierre. Dell'azzurro silenzio, inquietum. For contrabass flute in G, contrabass flute in B flat and live-electronics. Final version. No city named [Italy] 1996.

Nono, Luigi: Composizione per orchestra nr. 2. Diario polacco '58. Mainz 1959.

Nono, Luigi: Omaggio a György Kurtág. For contralto, flute, B♭ clarinet, bass tuba and live-electronics.

Pagh-Paan, Younghi: Dreisam-Nore. For flute alone. Munich et al. 1980.

Penderecki, Krzysztof: Capriccio. For oboe and 11 strings. Celle and Kraków 1968.

Penderecki, Krzysztof: Fluorescences. For orchestra. Celle 1962.

Penderecki, Krzysztof: Passio et mors domini nostri iesu christi secundum lucam. Passion according to St Luke for solo soprano, baritone, and bass; speaker; boys choir; 3 mixed choirs; and orchestra. Celle 1967.

Penderecki, Krzysztof: Threnody. To the victims of Hiroshima. For 52 strings. London et al. 1961.

Pousseur, Henri: Caractères 1a, 1b. Piano solo. Vienna 1962.

Pröve, Bernfried: Firebird. For violin alone. Celle 1993.

Redel, Martin: Musik für Klavier und Schlaginstrumente. Berlin and Wiesbaden 1970.

Redel, Martin: Rounds. For percussion solo. Berlin and Wiesbaden 1979.

Saariaho, Kaija: Laconisme de l'aile. For flute solo with optional electronics. No city and year named [Helsinki 2002].

Schafer, R. Murray: Music for the morning of the world. For soprano and tape. Toronto 1973.

Schloifer, Eckart (ed.): Pro musica nova. Studies for playing contemporary music. For violin. Wiesbaden 1986.

Schnebel, Dieter: Für Stimmen (... missa est). Choralvorspiele I/II. For organ, auxiliary instruments and tape. Mainz 1971.

Schönberg, Arnold: Drei Klavierstücke [Three piano pieces]. Los Angeles 1910.

Schönberg, Arnold: Dreimal sieben Gedichte aus Albert Girauds Pierrot lunaire. For one Sprechstimme, piano, flute (also piccolo), clarinet (also bass clarinet), violin (also viola) and violincello. No city named 1914.

Schönberg, Arnold: Two songs for voice and piano. I. Gedenken. II. Am Strande. Los Angeles 1966.

Sciarrino, Salvatore: All'aure in una lontanza. For G flute (or C flute or bass flute). In: Salvatore Sciarrino: L'opera per flauto. Milan 1990, pp. 3-6.

Sciarrino, Salvatore: L'opera per flauto. Milan 1990.

Serocki, Kazimierz: Segmenti. For chamber orchestra. Celle 1962.

Serocki, Kazimierz: Swinging music. For clarinet, trombone, cello (or double bass), and piano. Celle 1971.

Sotelo, Mauricio: Del aura al suspira. For contrabass flute (or alto flute) and sound carrier. Vienna 2001.

Stockhausen, Karlheinz: Elektronische Studien. Studie II. London 1956.

Stockhausen, Karlheinz: Geburtstags-Formel (Klavierstück XIV) vom Montag aus Licht. Kürten 1985.

Stockhausen, Karlheinz: Herbstmusik. For four players. Kürten 1977.

Stockhausen, Karlheinz: Invasion-Explosion mit Abschied. II. Akt vom Dienstag aus Licht. For Solo-soprano, tenor, bass, 3 trumpets, 3 trombones, 2 synthesizer-players with 2 assistants, 2 percussionists with two assistants, 6 tutti-trumpets, 6 tutti-trombones (ad lib.), choir, 8-track tape and sound director. Kürten 1995.

Stockhausen, Karlheinz: Klavierstück VI. London 1965.

Stockhausen, Karlheinz: Klavierstück XII. Examen von Donnerstag aus Licht. As a piano solo. Kürten 1983.

Stockhausen, Karlheinz: Kontakte. For electronic sounds, piano and percussion. London 1966.

Stockhausen, Karlheinz: Kontra-Punkte. For ten instruments. London 1953.

Stockhausen, Karlheinz: Luzifers Traum oder Klavierstück XIII. As a piano solo. Kürten 1982.

Stockhausen, Karlheinz: Mikrophonie I. For tamtam, 2 microphones, 2 filters and controller. London 1964.

Stockhausen, Karlheinz: Mikrophonie II. For choir, Hammond organ and 4 ring modulators. London 1974.

Stockhausen, Karlheinz: Mixtur. For orchestra, sine generators and ring modulators. Vienna 1968.

Stockhausen, Karlheinz: Pole. For two. Expo. For three. Kürten 1974.

Stockhausen, Karlheinz: Punkte. For orchestra. London 1966.

Stockhausen, Karlheinz: Spiral. For a solo player. Vienna 1973.

Stockhausen, Karlheinz: Sirius. For electronic music, trumpet, soprano, bass clarinet and bass. Kürten 1981.

Stockhausen, Karlheinz: Stimmung. For six vocalists. Vienna 1969.

Stockhausen, Karlheinz: Telemusik. Vienna 1969.

Szalonek, Witold: Concertino. For flute and chamber orchestra. Warsaw 1965.

Szalonek, Witold: Piernikiana. For tube solo. Kraków and Munich 1978.

Szalonek, Witold: Proporzioni II. For flute, violincello and grand piano (or harp). Kraków 1971.

Tast, Werner (ed.): Zeitgenössische Musik für Flöte solo [Contemporary music for flute alone]. Leipzig 1987.

Varèse, Edgard: Amériques. Performance edition prepared form the original manuscript by Chou Wen-chung. San Giuliano Milanese 1997.

Varèse, Edgard: Intégrales. For small orchestra and percussion. No city named 1926.

Varèse, Edgard: Offrandes. For soprano and chamber orchestra. New York 1927.

Xenakis, Iannis: Linaia – Agon. For horn, trombone and tuba. Paris 1972.

Zimmermann, Bernd Alois: Canto di speranza. Mainz 1958.